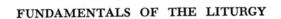

FUNDAMENTALS OF THE LITURGY

FUNDAMENTALS
OF THE LITURGY

Rev. John H. Miller, C.S.C., S.T.D.

FIDES PUBLISHERS ASSOCIATION
NOTRE DAME, INDIANA

NIHIL OBSTAT: Rev. Charles J. Corcoran, C.S.C.
Censor deputatus
March 22, 1959

IMPRIMI POTEST: Rev. Theodore J. Mehling, C.S.C.
Provincial Superior
March 25, 1959

IMPRIMATUR: Most Rev. Leo A. Pursley, D.D.
Bishop of Fort Wayne, Indiana
March 25, 1959

Library of Congress Catalog Card Number: 60-8444

Dedication

Dedicated with profound admiration and gratitude to the Reverend Louis M. Kelley, C.S.C., S.T.D., former Professor of Theology, Holy Cross College, Washington, D.C.; President of the University of Portland in Oregon; Pastor of Sacred Heart of Jesus Church, New Orleans, Louisiana; Head of the Department of Religion at the University of Notre Dame; Assistant General of the Congregation of Holy Cross. It was in him, as Pastor of Sacred Heart Church, that the present author discovered the priestly learning, devotion and zeal which attracted him so forcefully to become a brother priest of Holy Cross.

Preface

More than fifty years after the promulgation of *Motu Proprio* [1] by St. Pius X and twelve years after *Mediator Dei* [2] there is much evidence that the liturgical movement is growing both in extent and in depth. In the beginning the usual obstacles were encountered: criticism on the part of those who were unwilling to look at the movement objectively; the mistakes of zealous and pious people who, improperly informed but full of enthusiasm, tended to confound Liturgy with antiquarianism; false starts and mistakes almost inevitable when any worth-while project is launched. But now, encouraged steadily by the Church and particularly by the liturgical reforms of Pius XII, the movement is gradually coming into its own, and its effects are being felt in the very heart of Catholic life.

This does not mean, however, that, overnight, Catholics have become liturgically-minded. By no means. But they are beginning to see that Liturgy is something quite distinct from rubrics; that the great prayerbook of the Church is the Psalms; that the Eucharist is at the center of the Liturgy, and that the sacraments, particularly Baptism, are not passing events, but are daily operative in their lives. On the other hand, much more indoctrination is needed to impress Catholics with the idea that the Liturgy is also meant to mold and fashion their lives; that the Mass, even in dialogue or when sung, is not merely an act of devotion but the corporate worship of the Mystical Body and that its effects are meant to be felt throughout the day; that the Liturgy is not merely a commemoration of what once existed, but that it is living and real. [3]

The liturgical movement, and the reforms which have followed in its wake, should lead, of course, to a living of the liturgical life. To really live in the spirit of the Liturgy our piety must become less subjective, less egocentric and more objective and theocentric. [4] This means, in practice, that we throw our souls open to the divine life within us which we have received through Baptism and which is constantly renewed and developed through the Eucharist. The Eucharist is at once the sacrifice offered by the Mystical Body of Christ and the nourishment of each member of the Body. Likewise the

[1] *ASS*, 1903, p. 329.
[2] *AAS*, 1947, pp. 521-595.
[3] R. Guardini, *The Spirit of the Liturgy* (New York, 1940), p. 158.
[4] Cf. Pius Parsch, *Le guide dans l'Année Liturgique*, translated from the German by Abbé Marcel Gautier (Mulhouse, Haut-Rhin, 1935), I, p. 10.

liturgical life implies a knowledge and appreciation of our role as members of the Church which is the Mystical Body. It is only after we have grasped these basic realities that we can really appreciate what is called the liturgical year and live in its spirit.

All of this requires formation, and it is to that important task that Father Miller devotes himself. First of all there is the question of historical and theoretical information. The Liturgy as it is today can neither be fully understood nor appreciated without some knowledge of its historical development. But history is studied in this case, not with a view to reviving the past as such,[5] but to help recapture the spirit of the Liturgy as it existed before excessive individualism and subjectivism began to exercise an influence on Christian piety. At the same time this historical study, embracing as it does not only the Latin Liturgy but also the great Liturgies of the Orient, helps immensely towards acquiring a more accurate and sympathetic understanding of the Oriental Church in general — of which too little is known in the Western world. Likewise, a good knowledge of the development of the Liturgy will dissipate many objections which are raised, simply because those who raise them are not properly informed. A typical instance of this is the question of celebrating Mass facing the congregation.[6]

Once we are on solid historical ground, the various elements of the theory of Liturgy can be more safely discussed, particularly in the light of the teaching of the Church and the latest liturgical reforms initiated by the late Holy Father, Pope Pius XII. In this respect, the science of liturgiology proceeds in the same fashion as the other theological sciences. And it is important that it be kept on that plane; otherwise it will occupy second rank in theological training and will not have the effect the Church wishes it to have. Too long have we been accustomed to equating the study of Liturgy with the study of rubrics and ceremonies.[7] In his treatment of the subject Father Miller, guided not only by long research culminating in a Doctor's degree from the University of Trier, but also by several years of teaching, has succeeded admirably in justifying the position which the scientific study of Liturgy should occupy in any theological curriculum. A careful and reflective study of this volume, therefore, should give everyone who is interested in the subject, particularly priests, seminarians and religious, well-rounded notions of the general structure of the Liturgy, together with all the component parts which go to form it, with the Eucharist as center from which all else radiates. In this respect the study of Liturgy can serve as a kind of synthesis or meeting-point for all the branches of theology.

[5] *Mediator Dei*, par. 61-64.
[6] Cf. John H. Miller, C.S.C., "Altar Facing the People: Fact or Fable?" *Worship*, Jan. 1959, pp. 83 ff.
[7] Cf. *Mediator Dei*, par. 25.

But in order to understand the Liturgy completely, historical and theoretical formation will not suffice. This must be supplemented by what we may call ascetical formation in the Liturgy. Because liturgiology is not only a speculative but also a practical science, it lends itself readily to this second type of formation. Liturgy is not merely something to be known; it is a life that is to be lived. *Gustate et videte quod suavis est Dominus.* It is only when the theory of the Liturgy is understood in function of our daily lives that the formative influence of what is called the liturgical year (or perhaps more properly the Christian year) will be exercised. Thus our theoretical understanding of the Liturgy will be deepened by our living of the Liturgy. St. Thomas has said that our knowledge of God is not complete unless love be joined to it. We may apply the same notion to our knowledge of the Liturgy. With a genuine love for the Liturgy and stimulated by knowledge, new vistas of appreciation will be opened to us. We will then see more clearly the great plan of Redemption as it is operative among us through the Liturgy. We will understand better our place in the Mystical Body as it daily worships God, particularly through the Mass and the Divine Office, and, in return, is purified, strengthened and enlightened by the supernatural gifts that God gives so generously.

It is scarcely necessary to indicate how important a study such as Father Miller's is for the seminarian and the priest because it is to them particularly that will be confided the task of instructing the faithful in their charge. They must know what they are about lest they unwittingly preach, not Christ crucified, but their own personal version of the Christian life. As Father Miller has wisely remarked, it is a knowledge of the Liturgy that will enable the priest to form the Christian conscience and life as the Church wishes them to be formed. Throughout this volume the teachings of the Church are most conscientiously followed so that whoever reads it may be sure of guidance that is theologically correct, ascetically sound and, at the same time, stimulating and inspiring.

Christopher J. O'Toole, c.s.c.
Superior General

Congregazione di Santa Croce
Curia Generalizia
Via Aurelia Antica, 19
Roma

March 7, 1959
Feast of St. Thomas Aquinas

Acknowledgments

So many and so varied have been the helps and encouragement coming from so many quarters, Sisters, priests, seminarians and devoted friends in the laity — particularly the inestimable assistance of prayer — that it would be impossible for the author to acquit himself of the pleasant duty of fittingly speaking his gratitude to all. This he leaves confidently in the hands of the all-seeing and rewarding God, from whom come all good gifts, not least among them loving friends.

In particular the author feels obligated to the Very Reverend Christopher J. O'Toole, C.S.C., Superior General, for his enduring, enthusiastic support, evidenced above all in his writing the preface to this book. Sincere thanks are also due to the Reverend Theodore J. Mehling, C.S.C., Provincial Superior, and Reverend Bernard McAvoy, C.S.C., Superior of Holy Cross College, Washington, D.C., for their encouragement and generosity in allowing the author the time and facilities needed to complete this work; to Mr. Thomas H. Locraft, R.I.P., late Head of the Department of Architecture, The Catholic University of America, Washington, D.C., and Reverend S. Youree Watson, S.J., Professor of Aesthetics, Spring Hill University, Mobile, Alabama, the author's former high school instructor, for invaluable suggestions concerning Chapter 4: "Liturgical Places"; to Reverend Charles J. Corcoran, C.S.C., Professor of Dogmatic and Ascetical Theology, Holy Cross College, Washington, D.C., for patiently reading the manuscript and for his treasured advice.

Acknowledgment is herewith made to the following publishers for the permission to quote extensively from works bearing their copyright. Princeton University Press: T. Greene's *The Arts and the Art of Criticism;* The Bloch Publishing Company: *The Haggadah of Passover,* edited by Rabbi and Mrs. David de Sola Pool; Sheed and Ward, Inc.: R. Guardini's *The Church and the Catholic and the Spirit of the Liturgy,* translated by Ada Lane; P. J. Kenedy and Sons: the diagram of the Canon of the Mass taken from *The Meaning of the Mass* by P. Bussard and F. Kirsch, O.F.M., illustrated by Adé de Bethune; The Newman Press: F. Cabrol's *Liturgical Prayer;* the B. Herder Book Company of St. Louis and Sands and Company of London: G. Lefèbvre, *Catholic Liturgy* and C. Marmion, *Christ the Ideal of the Monk;* Dover Publications, Inc.: H. Wölfflin's *Principles of Art History.*

John H. Miller, C.S.C.
Washington, D.C.

Abbreviations

AAS: Acta Apostolicae Sedis.

ALW: Archiv für Liturgiewissenschaft.

AER: American Ecclesiastical Review.

ASS: Acta Sanctae Sedis.

CCSL: Cours et Conférences des Semaines Liturgiques.

CIC: Codex Iuris Canonici.

DACL: Dictionnaire d'Archéologie Chrétienne et de Liturgie.

Denz: Denzinger, Enchiridion Symbolorum. Freiburg, 1957.

DTC: Dictionnaire de Théologie Catholique.

EL: Ephemerides Liturgicae.

Etudes: Etudes des Pères Jésuites.

GCS: Griechischen christlichen Schriftsteller der ersten drei Jahrhunderte.

JLW: Jahrbuch für Liturgiewissenschaft.

LJ: Liturgisches Jahrbuch.

MPG: Migne, Patrologia Graeca.

MPL: Migne, Patrologia Latina.

OF: Orate Fratres.

Periodica: Periodica de re morali, canonica, liturgica.

QLP: Questions Liturgiques et Paroissiales.

SCR: Sacred Congregation of Rites.

Contents

The Study of Liturgy

Liturgy itself is not a science; it is the prayer and sacramental action of the Church. The science dealing with Liturgy is properly called liturgiology. Nor is the student of Liturgy called a liturgist, though very often this term is used to designate him. A liturgist is the minister of Liturgy. It is not an exaggeration, therefore, to say that we want to make every priest a fervent and meaningful liturgist. The student of Liturgy is called a liturgiologist. While it would be an exaggeration to say that every priest must be a liturgiologist, in itself it is greatly to be desired that more and more liturgists become dedicated liturgiologists: i.e., students of a scientific study of the sacred Liturgy.

With all the misunderstanding that envelops the popular mind today regarding the Liturgy, and the prejudice against men who devote their lives to its study and promotion, at first sight it might seem unlikely that we can truly call its study a science. Yet such it is. Liturgiology is a *science which treats of the ceremonies, texts, symbols and actions which the Church, continuing the priesthood of Christ through persons especially deputed for this, uses in her public and official worship in order to glorify God and redeem and sanctify mankind.*

This definition means that:

1. Liturgiology is a speculative science, since it explains the texts and rites of the Liturgy and thus arrives at the dogmatic and ascetical doctrine of the Church contained in them. But it is also a practical science, for as it explains such prayers and actions, it teaches the soul the proper dispositions with which to engage in liturgical worship. Hence, it is not concerned merely, nor primarily or principally with rubrics, or what might be better characterized as "liturgical casuistry," for it does not consider the external arrangement of worship alone. As Pius XII says, "The chief element of divine worship must be interior." [1] If this is so, then the interior element is the object which primarily comes under consideration in our science. And that means that we are seeking above all a genuine understanding of the Liturgy.

2. Nor is our science merely an historical one, since it does not limit itself to a consideration of the historical evolution of worship.

[1] *Mediator Dei* (America Press Edition), par. 24.

Rather does it turn its attention to historical matters only for the sake of arriving at the true meaning of the Church's present system of worship.

3. It is a genuine *theological* science, not only because of its material object: the Mass, the sacraments, the Divine Office, etc., but precisely because of its formal object: these very sacred actions as revealed by God or at least as developed by the Church with the authority committed to her by God and under His guidance. It fully measures up to St. Anselm's definition of theology: *fides quaerens intellectum,* which St. Thomas himself accepts and teaches, if not in so many words.[2] We do not study the Liturgy as a purely human institution, no matter how beautiful, esoteric or interesting it may be. We cannot for a moment allow ourselves to forget that the object that stands before us is a God-given means of salvation. And it is in this light that we study it.

Relationship to other theological disciplines

According to St. Thomas, theology is *one* science; what we might call branches of theology are only parts, special fields, areas of the one and only theological science. As such they all bear some relationship to each other and the whole. This is certainly true of liturgiology.

To *Dogma.* Liturgiology presupposes much that is proved as revealed in Dogma and there explained: e.g., our relationship to God as creature to the Creator; the foundation and intimate constitution of the Church as Christ's Mystical Body, dependent, therefore, on Christ's Act of Redemption; the nature of sacrifice and sacrament; etc. Indeed, Liturgy is Dogma in practice. Repeatedly have popes called the Liturgy the ordinary teaching organ of the Church. And it teaches, not only directly by word, but also indirectly (and perhaps more pedagogically) through action. We act out our belief in the above-mentioned truths; we live that belief in liturgical action. Liturgiology, therefore, cannot prescind from these considerations. Though it must presuppose them as revealed and already explained, it must neverthe-less bring them clearly into sight and use them in certain sections of its study of divine worship.

To *Moral.* In Moral theology we study the divine life in us and how we exercise that life. We find that sanctifying grace enables our soul to live the Christian life and that the virtues elevate our intellect and will and empower them to act in a Christian way. Now both these types of *habitus,* or supernatural power (entitative and operative), we receive in one way or another from the Liturgy.

To *Canon Law.* This gives us rules for the correct celebration of the sacred Liturgy. We know that the Liturgy depends on the vicarious authority and power entrusted by Christ to His Church. It

---

[2] *Summa Theologica,* I, q. 1, arts. 2, 6, and 8.

is left to the Church, therefore, to regulate the expressions of liturgical life. We find such regulation in Canon Law.

To *History.* If the science of liturgiology is going to achieve its aim of explaining the rites, prayers, and symbols of the Liturgy, history will be of the utmost importance. The ritual of the Liturgy cannot be fully understood unless we go back to history and find out when, how, and why it originated. To discover what a particular rite means we must ask the man or men who started it what they intended by it. Only they, or at least the times and practices of the periods in which they lived, can tell us — unless the Church has since intentionally changed the meaning of the rite. Only with such sound historical investigation behind us can we truthfully say: The Church means *this* when she says this prayer or performs this action.

To *Scripture.* Somewhat close to 90 per cent of the Liturgy is Scripture. Indeed, much of it is obviously intended to be a forthright proclamation of the word of God. How can we understand this divine manifestation of God's will to His People if we lack the rules for exegesis and the historical perspective against which it was made and which forms its human context?

Importance of this study

Theologically speaking, Liturgy is a theological *locus,* or source. According to the age-old adage, *legem credendi lex statuit supplicandi,*[3] the Liturgy is the normal teacher of divine truth. Since it is composed of the inspired writings of the Prophets, Apostles, the commentaries on these written by the Fathers of the Church, and has developed under the strict supervision of the Vicars of Jesus Christ, the Liturgy cannot teach falsehood. As Pius XII has said, "The entire Liturgy has the Catholic faith for its content, inasmuch as it bears public witness to the faith of the Church." [4]

From the point of view of the practical everyday living of the spiritual life, the Liturgy must be regarded as source and guide.

The Messias was foretold to be a	*Prophet*	*Priest* and	*King.*
Christ Himself said that He was the	*Truth*	*Life* and	*Way.*
In fact, He gave us a	*Creed*	*Cult* and	*Code.*
And these are concretized in our	*Dogma*	*Liturgy* and	*Moral.*

Which is the most important of the three? The question is badly put. They are all important. *Fides ex auditu,* St. Paul tells us.[5] We acquire faith in revealed truth through the teaching and preaching of Christ's Church. Without it we know neither where we are going nor what we

---

[3] Prosper of Aquitaine, *De gratia Dei "Indiculus,"* cap. 8. Denz., 139. This phrase was re-emphasized again and authoritatively explained by Pius XII in *Mediator Dei,* par. 45-48.

[4] *Mediator Dei,* par. 47.

[5] Rom. 10:17.

must do in order to be saved. But faith without charity and the works of charity is dead; faith must be put into practice — hence, morality. And both of these aspects of the spiritual life find their source and *raison d'être* in the *life* Christ gives us, a life begun and consummated in the sacred Liturgy. In other words, faith leads us to the source of life, and this source produces virtue. Hence, without an appreciation of the Liturgy the faithful run the risk of divorcing their spiritual life from its proper source and thus living a denatured, unbalanced life. If they do not base their spiritual life on the objective truth and reality which is the sacramental Christ, that life may become nothing more nor less than a pure projection of their subjective imagination.

Pastorally speaking, the priest is the teacher, guide, and sanctifier of God's People. If his life does not spring from the Liturgy, if it is not the center of his life, he will not be a priest first but only second, and even then not the priest who is supposed to guide the people to Christ. His apostolate is in danger of being anything but supernatural. Instead of preaching Christ and Him crucified, he will very probably offer the people nothing but himself and impose upon the minds of his precious charges, not the objective Christ of Christianity, but again the product of his own imagination. Certainly God's omnipotence can produce good even through an unworthy and faulty instrument. But the normal course of sanctification implies that the priest *lead* his people. *Verba docent, exempla trahunt!* The priest may teach his people what is objectively true and good, but if he lacks this liturgical orientation, he will lead them in making the most sacred things into an empty formalism.

No textbook can do everything for the student. It can only lay a solid foundation for the seminarian, the religious and the lay apostle who is learning the tools of his sacred trade. Neither textbook nor teacher can relieve the student of his role in absorbing what is presented. Furthermore, a textbook of necessity is a brief summary of the subject a student starts out to master. Basically, a textbook will always be an *introduction.* We have endeavored to offer both teacher and student the essential historical and theological arguments, complete with bibliographical references, for the principal truths and procedures that must guide intelligent liturgical action, and more particularly that must underlie an enlightened leadership on the part of priest and apostle in matters pertaining to the liturgical aspects of the spiritual life. But this is still only an introduction; it provides merely the foundation. The student must build the rest through study, prayer, and meditation; and in the application of the principles we will hope to impart, he must exercise a truly supernatural prudence and zeal. The important thing is, however, that he mold his life and priestly practice and apostolate around the sacred realities which claim his first and best attention. In the words of the Roman Pontifical: *Imitamini quod tractatis!*

CHAPTER ONE

The Nature of the Liturgy

The first problem that confronts the student of Liturgy is not how the Liturgy is performed, or what the Liturgy says, or how it has developed, but precisely what is this thing called Liturgy. Before we can appreciate, from a genuinely theological point of view, all the manifold ways in which Liturgy is expressed, we must have an adequate understanding of the nature of Liturgy, of the reality and essence of the thing which can and has taken on such varied external dress. We often hear it said that the habit does not make the monk; it would be a sad mistake to confuse the monastic tonsure or the color and shape of the monk's garb with the essence of monasticism. Such externals are pure nonsense to the non-believer precisely because he is unable to look behind the veil of appearances to see the reality they clothe. Likewise in matters liturgical: We will be incapable of evaluating the norms and ceremonies of liturgical life unless we pierce through them and discover the nature that operates and works in these ways.

This is not a light matter. If we look back into history,[1] we are forced to admit that much of the difficulty encountered by the liturgical apostolate was due to confusion on this very score. At the beginning of this century the French Jesuit Jean Navatel became the unwitting spokesman for that particular brand of opposition to the liturgical revival which rests squarely on a complete misunderstanding of the Liturgy and which remains solidly entrenched even to the present day:

> The Liturgy will always have but an occasional and, in general, a very secondary role in the mysterious operation which opens a heart blind to the light of the Gospel. Were we to include in this term the Holy Mass, the sacraments, and the Divine Office, the whole of religion would come into play. In that case, let us no longer speak of the Liturgy but rather of the influence of religion. For then it is evident that all souls

[1] For an exposé of the history of this question and the various solutions proposed see our article: "The Nature and Definition of the Liturgy," *Theological Studies,* 18 (1957), 325-356.

will be subject to the Liturgy, since, as sacrificial, laudatory
and sacramental, it seizes and brings every Christian under
its sway.[2]

Even liturgiologists, it must be admitted, have displayed quite a bit
of disagreement on the definition of the Liturgy and its correct interpretation, because they often have not gone deep enough and have
been enmeshed in its external appearances.

But if we are to arrive at an authentic concept of the Liturgy and
its role in the Christian life, we cannot be satisfied with accidentals.
The question must unfold in a realm far above prejudice, local usage,
temporary expedience, or the practices and outlook peculiar to different
religious orders or nationalities. We must discover that ultimate, essential, and intimate property of the Liturgy which definitely sets it off
from everything else and makes it what it is.

A. The Term

The word liturgy comes from the Greek *leitourgia,* which is a
combination of *leitos,* an adjective which means pertaining to the
people *(laos),* and *ergon,* a noun which means work. Hence, etymologically, the word means any service done for the common welfare.

Since the term originated among the Greeks, it is only natural to
look into their history to see what they meant by it. For them it designated any service rendered to the community at personal expense
or at least without remuneration; e.g., preparation of war matériel,
help rendered for public entertainment or education, etc. When generosity cooled and the state used pressure to force its citizens to perform such services, the word liturgy was broadened to include such
forced-labor. From there on the concept grew consistently larger to
embrace any number of actions which might have repercussions in
the social and political sphere.[3]

With the Hellenization of other parts of the Mediterranean world
this word found its way into Egypt. It was there that Hebrew and
Hellenic culture met; there the Septuagint translation of the Hebrew
text of the Old Testament was made. Hence it was there that the
term "liturgy" made its way into the terminology of revealed literature.
What did it mean for the translators? They used it almost exclusively
for the great work of the people, the worship of Yahweh.[4] Nevertheless
they used it, though less frequently, when referring to something done
for the people or its leaders, since the Jewish state was a theocracy:
the Jews were God's chosen people, their rulers His representatives.[5]

[2] J. Navatel, "L' Apostolat liturgique et la piété personnelle," *Etudes,* 137
(1913), 452-453.
[3] E. Raitz von Frentz, "Der Weg des Wortes *Liturgie* in der Geschichte,"
Ephemerides Liturgicae, 55 (1941), 75.
[4] E.g., Ex. 28:43, 29:30; 2 Chr. 13:10.
[5] E.g., 3 Kings 19:21; 2 Chr. 17:19, 22:8.

The New Testament followed suit. Luke speaks of Zachary's liturgy.[6] Paul speaks of himself in his role of Apostle as the "liturgist of Christ Jesus to the Gentiles."[7] But he also uses the word in reference to the collection taken up for the poor Christians in Jerusalem [8] and for the services rendered to his own person.[9] Finally, in his Epistle to the Hebrews, he uses the word liturgy in its specifically Christian sense, the priestly work of Jesus Christ, so different from the worship of the Jews, which was mere copy and shadow: "We have such a high priest . . . a minister (*leitourgos,* liturgist) of the Holies, and of the true tabernacle which the Lord has erected and not man. . . . But now He has obtained a superior ministry (*leitourgias,* liturgy), in proportion as He is the mediator of a superior covenant, enacted on the basis of superior promises"[10] This is the work *par excellence* of the Christian people, since through it they are able to render to God acceptable worship and receive from Him the fruits of the Christian dispensation, grace and virtue.

In Christian antiquity the term liturgy was used both in the general sense of service as well as in the more spiritual sense of prayer and sacrifice — in the latter case more frequently as denoting an official or community service as opposed to the works of purely private piety; e.g., in the *Didache,*[11] Clement of Rome,[12] the Synods of Ancyra [13] and Antioch.[14] In the East, however, a tendency gradually showed itself to limit the word to the Eucharistic sacrifice, and even today one speaks of the Liturgy of St. James, the Liturgy of St. Basil and the Liturgy of St. John Chrysostom, all the while meaning the Mass.

According to Odo Casel [15] a mere transliteration of the Greek word was not entirely accepted in the West. In profane use (e.g., by the jurists) as well as sacred (e.g., in the sacramentaries) the Latin equivalent was not *liturgia* but *munus. Ministerium, servitus, officium* were also used. But according to the evidence that Casel uncovers we are led to conclude that *munus* had right of place. *Munus* means, therefore, not only "gift" but also "service." Even in the Middle Ages *liturgia* was unknown to the language of Western ecclesiastical literature.

---

[6] Luke 1:23 (text of A. Merk, *Novum testamentum graece et latine,* Rome, 1944).

[7] Rom. 15:16.

[8] 2 Cor. 9:12.

[9] Phil. 2:30.

[10] Heb. 8:1-6.

[11] *Didache* 15, 1. M. J. Rouët de Journel, *Enchiridion Patristicum* (Barcelona, 1946), 4.

[12] *Epistola ad Corinthios* 40, 2-5; 41, 1. *MPG,* 1:288-289.

[13] Canon 1. Hefele-Leclerq, *Histoire des Conciles* 1:302.

[14] Canon 4. C. Kirch, *Enchiridion fontium historiae ecclesiasticae antiquae* (Barcelona, 1947), 490.

[15] "Leitourgia-Munus," *Oriens Christianus,* 29 (1932), 289-302.

It was left to humanism, busy with the liturgical books of the Greeks, to rediscover the word and give it a place of honor in the literature of the West. There appeared in 1558 a book of Cassander's, using for the first time the title *Liturgica*. Pamelius followed him in 1571 with his *Liturgica latinorum*. Thereafter the word appears over and over again until finally in the Code of Canon Law it is used to designate the officially ordered worship of the Church.

B. Definition of the Liturgy

From the past half-century three authors stand out in that their attempts to define the Liturgy exemplify a basic misunderstanding which is still widespread today. We have already seen that Jean Navatel looked upon the Liturgy as nothing but externalism. In his own words, "Liturgy is but the purely sensible, ceremonial, and decorative part of Catholic worship." [16] He saw in it nothing more than an empty symbolism [17] and therefore could attribute to it no inherent sanctifying power.[18] C. Callewaert defines Liturgy as "the ecclesiastical regulation of the exercise of public worship." [19] The definition as worded would indicate that Liturgy is nothing more than rubrics, simply a list of laws and prescriptions. Though this is a common opinion today, actually Callewaert did not share it, for he treats the Liturgy in his textbook in such a manner that it becomes clear he regards the Liturgy as an *act* of worship, not simply its regulation. The third author whose ideas we wish to call attention to is Emile Mersch. He calls the Liturgy "the sacred context given to the Savior's sacrifice." [20] In other words, the Liturgy is but the ritual prolongation or surrounding of the Consecration; the latter is not a liturgical act.

The majority of liturgiologists define the Liturgy as the public worship of the Church;[21] they carefully note that "public" or "exterior" does not exclude the interior or sanctifying element, but that all the elements coalesce to form one, sole, concrete liturgical act which is both external, because public, and interior both as regards the min-

[16] Art. cit., (supra n. 2), p. 452.
[17] *Ibid.*, p. 455.
[18] *Ibid.*, p. 456.
[19] *Liturgicae Institutiones* 1: *De sacra liturgia universim* (3rd ed.; Bruges, 1933), 6.
[20] "Prière de chrétiens, prière de membres," *Nouvelle revue théologique*, 58 (1931), 100.
[21] Thus: M. Festugière, "La liturgie catholique," *Revue thomiste*, 22 (1914), 44, 45; L. Beauduin, "Mise au point nécessaire," *QLP*, 4 (1913), 86; F. Cabrol, "Liturgie," *DTC*, 9,787; J. Braun, *Liturgisches Handlexikon* (Regensburg, 1924), p. 196; J. Hanssens, "De natura liturgiae ad mentem s. Thomae," *Periodica*, 24 (1935), p. 159; K. Stapper, *Catholic Liturgics* (Paterson, N. J., 1935), pp. 20-21; Lechner-Eisenhofer, *Liturgik des römischen Ritus* (Freiburg, 1953), p. 3; P. Oppenheim, *Institutiones systematico-historicae in s. liturgiam* 6: *Notiones liturgiae fundamentales* (Turin, 1941), 20, 21 ff.; M. Righetti, *Manuale di storia liturgica* 1: *Introduzione generale* (2nd ed.; Milan, 1950), p. 6; J. Jungmann, "Was ist Liturgie?", in *Gewordene Liturgie* (Innsbruck, 1941), pp. 1-2; *idem, Der Gottesdienst der Kirche* (Innsbruck, 1955), p. 1.

ister and the recipient and the intrinsic power of sanctification of the act itself.

The definition proposed by Odo Casel and his so-called *Mysterium* school of thought does not differ essentially from that of the greater number of liturgiologists; it simply seeks to put the internal content of the Liturgy more in relief. He says: "The Liturgy is the ritual accomplishment of the redemptive work of Christ in and through the Church." [22] He calls this the *Mysterium* and further defines it as "a holy ritual action in which a salvific act is made present and brings salvation for the worshipping community which participates in it." [23] Such a definition decisively removes liturgical worship from the sphere of pure ceremonial.

1. Papal teaching

In his encyclical *Mediator Dei* Pius XII spoke of set purpose on the nature of the Liturgy. What did he have to say about the definitions thus far proposed?

Is the Liturgy simply externals? The Pope says: "It is an error, consequently, and a mistake to think of the sacred Liturgy as merely the outward or visible part of divine worship or as an ornamental ceremonial." [24] The definition, therefore, of J. Navatel can no longer be seriously sustained. [25] For that matter, neither can that of Callewaert, [26] for the Pope goes on to say: "No less erroneous is the notion that it consists solely in a list of laws and prescriptions according to which the ecclesiastical hierarchy orders the sacred rites to be performed." [27] And he explains the reason for this:

> The worship rendered by the Church to God must be, in its entirety, interior as well as exterior. It is exterior because the nature of man as a composite of body and soul requires it to be so. Likewise because Divine Providence has disposed that while we recognize God visibly, we may be drawn by Him to love things unseen. Every impulse of the human heart, besides, expresses itself naturally through the senses. [28]
>
> But the chief element of divine worship must be interior . . . Otherwise religion clearly amounts to mere formalism, without meaning and without content. [29]

[22] "Mysteriengegenwart," *JLW*, 8 (1928), p. 145.
[23] "Mysterienfrömmigkeit," *Bonner Zeitschrift für Theologie und Seelsorge*, 4 (1927), p. 104.
[24] Par. 25.
[25] Navatel was immediately criticized for his false conception by Festugière, *art. cit.*, (supra n. 21), pp. 39-64, and by Beauduin, pp. 83-104.
[26] Cf. J. Hanssens, "La définition de la liturgie," *Gregorianum*, 8 (1927), 204-228, for a refutation of Callewaert's position.
[27] *Mediator Dei*, par. 25.
[28] *Ibid.*, 23.
[29] *Ibid.*, 24.

It should be clear to all, then, that God cannot be honored worthily unless the mind and heart turn to Him in quest of the perfect life.[30]

Nor is the Liturgy simply the sacred context given to the sacrifice of Christ, as suggested by E. Mersch. Very soon after Mersch published his ideas on this subject, the renowned Abbot Bernard Capelle took issue with him and said, "The traditional use of the word liturgy ranks the sacrifice among the major acts of the Liturgy — the very first act." [31] And the teaching of Pius XII fully supports this stand. At the very beginning of *Mediator Dei*, when writing of how the Church continues the priestly mission of Jesus Christ, he says: "She does this in the first place at the altar, where constantly the sacrifice of the cross is represented and, with a single difference in the manner of its offering, renewed." [32] And later, when he speaks of "the mystery of the Holy Eucharist which Christ, the High Priest, instituted, and which He commands to be continually renewed in the Church by His ministers," he calls it "the crowning act of the sacred Liturgy." [33]

The definition, however, which has become practically universal among liturgiologists is now, we can say, the official teaching of the Church, since the Pope proposed it in his encyclical — in much more detailed and explicit form than given here, of course. "The sacred Liturgy is the public worship which our Redeemer as Head of the Church renders to the Father, as well as the worship which the community of the faithful renders to its Founder, and through Him to the heavenly Father. In short, it is the public worship rendered by the Mystical Body of Christ in the entirety of its Head and members." [34] Thus, the Liturgy is the public worship of the Church, but the Church adequately understood as the Mystical Body of Christ, the worship of both Head and members together: Christ worshiping the Father in and with His members, the members worshiping God in and through their Head, Christ.

2. Papal definition explained

Worship is the acknowledgment of God's supreme excellence and the expression of man's submission to His absolute dominion resulting therefrom. As such it pertains to the virtue of religion, the virtue, therefore, which inclines us to render to Almighty God the honor and service due to His supreme majesty. The three words, "worship," "cult" and "latria," are very frequently used to designate the same action, though etymologically they denote aspects of the one action. "Cult" comes from *colere*, to cultivate or honor; "latria" is a Greek word

---

[30] *Ibid.*, 26.
[31] "L'Idée liturgique," *QLP*, 19 (1934), 162.
[32] Par. 3.
[33] *Ibid.*, 66.
[34] *Ibid.*, 20.

whose Latin equivalent is *servitus*, service, submission, obedience; "worship" comes from the Anglo-Saxon word composed of *woerth*, worth, and *scipe*, render acknowledgment. Note that St. Thomas in his treatment of the virtue of religion speaks of the latter sometimes as the action by which we pay honor to God, sometimes as the *habitus* or virtue which inclines us to do so.[35] And he says that worship of God is based on our relationship to Him as creature to Creator.[36] We render to Him the honor and submission due to Him because of His supreme excellence as our Creator on whom we depend for our being as well as for everything we have.

Cult or worship can be considered in two ways: *what* is done to honor God (concrete acts, therefore), and *how,* or the manner in which He is honored, or in which these acts are performed. The first is worship considered from the material aspect; the second is worship considered from the formal aspect.

The following is St. Thomas' classification of the acts of religion according to their material and formal aspects:

1. *According to the material aspect:* [37]

INTERNAL { devotion (q. 82)
            prayer (q. 83)

EXTERNAL
- adoration (q. 84)
- offering (external object)
  - giving
    - sacrifice (q. 85)
    - oblations (q. 86, aa. 1-3)
    - first fruits (q. 86, a. 4)
    - tithes (q. 87)
  - promising: vow (q. 88)
- accepting (external object)
  - sacraments (q. 89, praef.)
  - Divine Name
    - oath (q. 89)
    - adjuration (q. 90)
    - invocation
      - prayer (q. 83, a. 12)
      - praise (q. 91) [38]

---

[35] *Summa Theol.*, II-II, q. 81.
[36] *Ibid.*, a. 1.
[37] All references are to *Summa Theol.*, II-II.
[38] Under this heading would also come the *readings* and *instructions*: *Summa Theol.*, III, q. 83, a. 4.

2. *According to the formal aspect:* [39]

NATURAL

SUPERNATURAL $\begin{cases} \text{interior} \\ \text{\textit{exterior}} \end{cases}$ $\begin{cases} \text{of the Old Testament} \\ \text{\textit{of the New Testament}} \end{cases}$ $\begin{cases} \text{private} \\ \text{\textit{common}} \end{cases}$

Worship *in general* is concerned with all of these acts and all of the modes of performing them. But the question arises: which of the acts enumerated in the first outline pertain to the sacred Liturgy? All those in italicized print in the first outline are or can be liturgical if they are performed in the manner indicated by the italicized print in the second outline.[40] Worship becomes Liturgy when those certain acts are performed in the supernatural, exterior, common manner which Christ bequeathed to us. This we believe to be the mind of St. Thomas. But note that he uses the word "common"; the papal definition contains the word "public." Are they one and the same?

Public is a broad term; it can mean several things. Many actions are done in public in the sense of being done together with others and in the sight of all. Is this what the word "public" means in the papal definition? We do not believe this to be the intention of the Holy Father, for he clearly states: "Though they [the methods of popular participation] show also in an outward manner that the very nature of the sacrifice, as offered by the Mediator between God and men, must be regarded as the act of the whole Mystical Body of Christ, still they are by no means necessary to constitute it a public act or to give it a social character." [41] And in another place in the same encyclical he insists on this intrinsically public character of the Mass apart from any consideration of externals, assigning as the reason for this the fact that "he who offers it acts in the name of Christ and of the faithful" whether the latter "are present—as we desire and commend them to be in great numbers and with devotion—or are not present . . ." [42]

Hence the Pope's insistence in his definition on "the *entirety* of its Head and members," on the worship which the "*community* of the faithful renders." [43] "Public" here does not mean the number of the faithful who attend divine services or the external quality of these services. "Public" rather refers to the fact that what is done or said expresses and affects the whole body of the faithful—even when none

---

[39] For the distinction between natural and supernatural, cf. *Summa Theol.*, I-II, q. 99, a. 3; between interior and exterior, and of the Old and New Testaments: *ibid.*, I-II, q. 101, a. 2; and between private and common: *ibid.*, II-II, q. 83, a. 12; q. 93, a. 1.

[40] *Summa Theol.*, II-II, q. 83, a. 12; q. 93, a. 1.

[41] *Mediator Dei,* 106.

[42] *Ibid.,* 96.

[43] *Ibid.,* 20.

of the faithful are physically present. Now St. Thomas, as we have seen, employs the word "common." And he seems to mean the same thing as the Pope, for he defines common worship as that "which is offered to God by ministers in the person of the entire Church." [44] In another place he defines common prayer as that "which is offered to God by ministers of the Church in the person of all the faithful." [45] Hence, according to St. Thomas, common prayer or worship is what is offered in the name of the whole Church as opposed to what the individual does all alone.[46]

Furthermore, the Code of Canon Law defines public worship in the same strain: "Worship is called public if it is offered in the name of the Church by persons legitimately deputed for this by means of acts instituted by the Church to be presented to God, the saints and the blessed only; otherwise it is called private." [47] The Code, therefore, also understands the word "public" in the same way: what is done in the name of the entire Church. And the *Instruction on Sacred Music and Liturgy,* promulgated by Pius XII on September 3, 1958, makes this definition of the Code more precise: "Liturgical functions are those sacred rites which have been instituted by Jesus Christ or the Church and are performed by legitimately appointed persons according to the liturgical books approved by the Holy See, in order to give due worship to God, the Saints and the Blessed. Other sacred acts performed inside or outside of the church, even if performed by a priest or in his presence, are called 'pious exercises.' " [47a]

Thus, the Pope, St. Thomas, and canon law are all in accord in this matter. The Liturgy is public worship in the sense that the *whole* Church offers it: i.e., not just its priests—they are only its instruments, its *ministri,* through which the whole Church acts, offers, prays. From what we have seen, the mere external appearance of any particular act of worship is definitely excluded from constituting that act as public; such exterior qualities as number present, degree of solemnity, etc., are only expressions of an invisible quality that, even without them, can and must be present if the act is to be public and liturgical.

Hence, even if a priest should recite his Breviary all alone without any outward manifestation except the movement of his lips, all the members of the Church would pray through him. Or if the Mass were to be celebrated in the darkest corner of a concentration camp with

[44] *Summa Theol.,* II-II, q. 93, a. 1: "qui per ministros exhibetur in persona totius ecclesiae."

[45] *Ibid.,* II-II, q. 83, a. 12: "quae per ministros ecclesiae in persona totius fidelium populi Deo offertur."

[46] *Ibid.,* "oratio singularis est quae offertur a singulari persona cuiuscumque."

[47] CIC, can. 1256.

[47a] N. 1. AAS, 50 (1958), 632. It is noteworthy that paragraph 40 of the *Instruction* clearly insists that regardless of the manner in which the Divine Office is recited, whether in choir, in common, or alone, "it must always be considered an act of *public* worship rendered to God in the name of the Church, if it is said by those persons who are deputed by ecclesiastical laws for its recitation. (Emphasis added.)

no one else present but the sacrificing priest himself, every Catholic throughout the world would be offering through him what he consecrated. What a tremendous thing! Whether you advert to it or not, you are acting in and affected by every single liturgical act performed no matter where in the world. No other action of man can lay claim to such an awe-inspiring breadth: A liturgical act is truly the common act of the Mystical Body,[48] held and shared, done and enjoyed by every man made child of God through Baptism. That is what "public" or "common" means when used in reference to the worship of the Church.

Of the Church. The concept of the Church has already entered our discussion of the word "public," but we must consider it in its own right. One obvious meaning of the expression "worship of the Church" is that of worship regulated by the Church, ordered and arranged by her authority. But this is true only because it is the worship which the Church herself renders, worship in which the Church herself is the agent using ministers as her deputed instruments, worship performed in her name. But even then what exactly do we mean by "the Church"? Is she only a juridical organization, a more or less perfect human society, which organizes and regulates its worship, which deputes certain men as its instruments and is only *reputed* to act when they act? Is her worship said to be performed in her name only because many individual members *intentionally* unite themselves to her ministers as they pray according to the commission she has given them? None of these solutions seem adequate to us.

Pius XII says: "The divine Redeemer has so willed it that the priestly life begun with the supplication and sacrifice of His mortal body should continue without interruption down the ages in His Mystical Body which is the Church."[49] He continues: "That is why He established a visible priesthood to offer everywhere the clean oblation."[50] Already the Pope introduces the idea of the Mystical Body and the priesthood in his concept of Liturgy. We have also heard him speak of the Church as the Mystical Body of Christ in the definition of Liturgy quoted above. The Church in his definition, then, is not simply the Church considered as a perfect human society or as a juridical organization. It must be understood as the Mystical Body of Christ adequately taken. And what is that?

We know that the Mystical Body is some sort of union of the faithful with Christ resulting from the endeavor of the former to find their way towards their eternal and supernatural destiny. Their union with Christ is based on the fact that the success of this endeavor depends on holiness or "godliness." But "holiness begins from Christ; by Christ it is effected. For no act conducive to salvation can be per-

[48] Cf. T. Wesseling, *Liturgy and Life* (London, 1938), p. 33.
[49] *Mediator Dei*, 2.
[50] *Ibid.*

formed unless it proceeds from Him as its supernatural cause. 'Without me,' He says, 'you can do nothing.' " [51] The society of salvation which He started we call His Body in some sense, for He founded it, He is its Head. But "as Bellarmine notes with acumen and accuracy, this naming of the Body of Christ is not to be explained solely by the fact that Christ must be called the Head of His Mystical Body, but also by the fact that He so sustains the Church, and so in a certain sense lives in the Church that it is, as it were, another Christ." [52] And He sustains the Church by sharing with it "His most personal prerogatives in such a way that she may portray in her whole life, both external and interior, a most faithful image of Christ." [53]

How does He do this and what type of union arises thereby between Him and His members? The union that results is not such that the human person becomes identified with Christ: "In a natural body the principle of unity so unites the parts that each lacks its own individual subsistence; on the contrary in the Mystical Body that mutual union, though intrinsic, links the members by a bond which leaves to each intact his own personality." [54] And yet it is not just a moral union of members: "In the moral body, the principle of union is nothing more than the common end and the common cooperation of all under authority for the attainment of that end; whereas in the Mystical Body this collaboration is supplemented by a distinct internal principle which exists effectively in the whole and in each of its parts." [55] Therefore the union between Christ and His members is more than simply juridical or moral: "What lifts the society of Christians far, far above the whole natural order is the Spirit of our Redeemer, who until the end of time penetrates every part of the Church's being and is active within it. He is the source of every grace and every gift and every miraculous power." [56]

The internal principle of unity in the Mystical Body, therefore, is the Holy Spirit who operates through grace and the infused virtues. And these are physical realities, physical bonds (not material, however, but physical in the sense of real, though spiritual, qualities). Hence our union is not simply moral; and though not a bodily union, it is truly physical, i.e., real but spiritual.

This physical union is further expressed by the fact that His Mystical Body can perform certain of Christ's very own actions: "In virtue of the juridical mission by which our divine Redeemer sent His Apostles into the world, as He had been sent by the Father, it is He who through the Church baptizes, teaches, rules, looses, binds, offers, sacrifices." [57] And what is it that enables a human being to perform certain

[51] *Mystici Corporis* (America Press Edition), 63.
[52] *Ibid.*, 66.
[53] *Ibid.*, 67.
[54] *Ibid.*, 74
[55] *Ibid.*, 75.
[56] *Ibid.*, 77.
[57] *Ibid.*, 67.

of Christ's own actions? Theology teaches us that it is the character imprinted on the soul in Baptism, Confirmation and Holy Orders. And St. Thomas tells us that the character is a participation in the priesthood of Christ.[58] He says further that this character is a spiritual power which enables a person to receive something or to be an instrument—in this case an instrument of Christ to perform certain acts of divine worship, in other words, of ritual or liturgical worship.[59] As a spiritual power which resides in the powers of the soul,[60] the character is also an *ens physicum,* a physical or real being, just as sanctifying grace is. Thus we have another bond which unites us physically to Christ and to each other.

The consequence? In the sacraments "the ministers act in the person not only of our Savior but of the whole Mystical Body and of everyone of the faithful." [61] "When the sacraments of the Church are administered by external rite, it is He who produces their effect in the soul." [62] "In virtue of that higher, interior and wholly sublime communication . . . Christ our Lord brings the Church to live His own supernatural life, by His divine power He permeates His whole Body and nourishes and sustains each of the members according to the place which they occupy in the Body, very much as the vine nourishes and makes fruitful the branches which are joined to it. " [63]

Through sanctifying grace we are enabled to live Christ's life; through the sacramental character we enjoy Christ's priestly power of praising and sacrificing to Almighty God in such a way that He is infinitely pleased. There we have two physical (spiritual but real) powers which unite us to Christ and to each other. That is what we mean by the Church: a supernatural organism each of whose members is empowered to live the divine life (sanctifying grace and the infused virtues) and further enjoys divine power to posit divine acts of worship (the character which enables us to perform Christ's own acts of praise, sacrifice, and sacramental sanctification).

From this it follows that Liturgy is not the worship of the Church acting independently of Christ her Head. Everything the Church does in Liturgy is done precisely as the act of Christ. Such acts require a priesthood. And that priestly power (power to act as Christ's agent or instrument in some ritual action) is imparted by means of the characters. Every Catholic possesses at least one of them. Therefore every single sanctifying action or word of praise of the Liturgy, whether it be an *Amen* on the part of the layman, or the most sublime

---

[58] *Summa theologica,* III, q. 63, a. 3.
[59] *Ibid.,* a. 2. The words "divini cultus" used by St. Thomas throughout this question are explained by the words "secundum ritum Christianae religionis." Therefore the character is neither intended for nor employed in purely private prayer.
[60] *Ibid.,* a. 4.
[61] *Mystici corporis,* 97.
[62] *Ibid.,* 63.
[63] *Ibid.,* 67.

act of all, the renewal of Christ's sacrifice on the cross on the part of the priest, is Christ's act—not a human act but a divine-human one: divine in its power and efficacy, human in its expression. The participation of the laity as well as the action of the ordained priest is Liturgy because that participation is an act of Christ done through the power of priesthood.[64]

If we wish to be theologically exact, of course, we must recognize different levels among the various acts of the Liturgy. When we say that all the acts of the Liturgy are divine, are Christ's, we must make a distinction between those which were instituted by Him and in which He is the *immediate* principal minister, and those which the Church institutes, using the authority committed to her by Him, and in which He is the *mediate* principal minister. The latter, however, are more than His acts imputatively, i.e., acts in which He is *considered* to act because He authorizes the Church to act for Him. In all her acts of worship the Church acts, not only in virtue of the commission given to her by Christ, but "in closest union with Him her Head" [65] and through His mediation—*per Christum Dominum nostrum,* who is the one and universal mediator standing before the Father to intercede for us.[66] And she acts by means of His priestly power, a real physical power, not a mere intentional or juridical deputation. Thus the character empowers us to act for Christ not simply imputatively, but as His mouthpiece or instrument in joining His members to His eternal mediation before the Father.

C. Ultimate Distinctive Quality of Liturgy

Even though the papal definition of Liturgy should of itself provide us with an adequate understanding of its nature, the meaning of the Liturgy is still widely misinterpreted. Therefore we need to go deeper into the question and try to discover that inner quality which definitively characterizes a particular act or prayer as Liturgy and thus sets it off adequately from every other exercise of the virtue of religion. We must find that formality which makes a liturgical act to be what it is.

Though most liturgiologists have always maintained a definite distinction between the Liturgy, on the one hand, and the so-called public popular devotions and private prayer, on the other, they have not always been in agreement as to what ultimately constitutes this distinction. One school of thought holds that the juridical element is the final, decisive factor: ecclesiastical regulation and deputation are

---

[64] The juridical act on the part of the Church necessary to raise something to the dignity of Christ's act, therefore to Liturgy, will be treated later on.

[65] *Mediator Dei,* 27, 144.

[66] *Ibid.,* 146. Cf. also: P. Oppenheim, *op. cit.,* 118-32; Lechner-Eisenhofer, *op. cit.,* 3; C. Callewaert, *op. cit.,* 19, 22; L. Beaudin, "La Liturgie: définition, hiérarchie, tradition," *CCSL,* 15 (1948), 131-134; in the same publication, J. Hild, "L'Encyclique *Mediator* et la sacramentalité des actes liturgiques," 186-203.

the distinctive marks.[67] Close to this school, in fact dependent on it, is the opinion of those who qualify as liturgical only what the official liturgical books of the Church contain or what we have thus inherited from the ancient and medieval Church. We might call this the archeological school of thought.[68] Still others emphasize the external communal character of a rite as the quality which makes it liturgical.[69] Finally, there is a group which insists that for an act to be liturgical it must be produced by the priesthood of Christ.[70]

Which school of thought is right? To decide this we cannot be satisfied with the limited viewpoint evident in some of them. The question can never be solved by judging the Liturgy by its appearances.

Actually the first two opinions do not even touch the question of the intimate constitution of the liturgical act. They simply attempt to indicate how something becomes liturgical. The third position, while addressing itself to the real matter at hand, unfortunately restricts itself to a consideration of the externals of Liturgy. It understands the word "public" as meaning a togetherness in time and place. It equates public with exterior, before the public eye.[71] But that, as we have seen, is not the meaning of the term in St. Thomas, Pius XII, or the Code. And in these sources, let us repeat, the term does

---

[67] Thus: C. Callewaert, *op. cit.*, 4-8; Lechner-Eisenhofer, *op. cit.*, 4; J. Braun, *op. cit.*, 196; F. Cabrol, *op. cit.*, 9, 787; J. Hanssens, "La définition de la liturgie," *Gregorianum*, 8 (1927), 206; B. Capelle, *art. cit.*, 12; J. Jungmann, *Gewordene Liturgie*, 9, 16; H. Keller, "Liturgie und Kirchenrecht," *Scholastik*, 17 (1942), 342-384.

[68] Thus: A. Wilmart, "Pour les prières de dévotion," *La vie et les arts liturgiques*, 9 (1923), 486; J. Kramp, "Liturgische Bestrebungen der Gegenwart," *Stimmen der Zeit*, 99 (1920-21), 316.

[69] Thus: J. Umberg, "Gemeinschaftsgebet und Liturgie," *Zeitschrift für Aszese und Mystik*, 3 (1928), 240-252; J. Bütler, "Die Mysterienlehre der Laacher Schule im Zusammenhang scholastischer Theologie," *Zeitschrift für katholische Theologie*, 59 (1935), 569.

[70] P. Parsch, *Volksliturgie* (2nd edit.; Klosterneuburg, 1952), 123; *idem*, *Liturgische Erneuerung* (Klosterneuburg, 1931), 8-10; A. Schmid, "Unterschied zwischen liturgischer und ausserliturgischer Handlung," *Linzer Quartalschrift*, 63 (1910), 308-311; C. Panfoeder, *Christus unser Liturge* (Mainz, 1924), 17-18; Schüch-Polz, *Handbuch der Pastoraltheologie* (Innsbruck, 1925), 319; R. Guardini, "Der Gesamtzusammenhang des christlichen Gebetslebens," in *Volksliturgie und Seelsorge* (Kolmar-im-Elsass, 1942), 19; G. Lefèbvre, *Catholic Liturgy* (rev. ed.; St. Louis, 1954), 255-256; A. Vonier, "Liturgie," *Liturgische Zeitschrift*, 3 (1930-31), 341-347; P. Oppenheim, *op. cit.*, 20; J. Pinsk, "Alles Liturgie?", *Liturgische Zeitschrift*, 3 (1930-31), 327-328; H. Elfers, "Was ist Liturgie?", *Theologie und Glaube*, 34 (1942), 122-132; L. Beauduin, "La liturgie: définition, hiérarchie, tradition," *CCSL*, 15 (1948), 123-144; A. Stenzel, "Cultus publicus: Ein Beitrag zum Begriff und ekklesiologischen Ort der Liturgie," *Zeitschrift für katholische Theologie*, 75 (1953), 174-214.

[71] An indication that even Jungmann made this mistake is evident in his original essay, where, speaking of what is included in Liturgy, he says: "but the sacraments also are not excluded from the concept of Liturgy, although they are directed to man, for in the solemnity (note: this means something external and done by a group, if only two or three) and reverence which surround them, they breathe a spirit of adoration and presuppose the same in the recipients." Cf. "Was ist Liturgie?", *Zeitschrift für katholische Theologie*, 55 (1931), 84.

not imply a purely juridical type of public quality that is neither a *de facto* communal character (many people worshiping actively together, though this is much to be desired), nor a *de iure* sort (when the Church's ministers do this or that in Liturgy, and therefore all are *reputed* to act). No, the public or common quality is based on the inner nature of the Mystical Body, namely, on the sacramental characters of Baptism, Confirmation, and Holy Orders.

We cannot overrate the work of Odo Casel for the role it played in deepening discussion on the nature of the liturgy. His Mysterium theory raised a storm of criticism, it is true; but it served to draw minds once again to the core of the liturgical question—its priestly-sacramental content and all that that content implies. After all the smoke of controversy lifted, liturgiologists began to realize that Casel had hit upon something of prime importance both to the liturgical movement and to the Liturgy itself: the inner realities upon which the whole structure of liturgical life depends and revolves. The core of his theory remains undeniable, for it is simply a fuller statement of what St. Thomas [72] and the whole of Christian tradition has always taught: Christ redeems and sanctifies us through sacramental actions: *sacramenta efficiunt id quod significant.*

Any complete solution to the liturgical problem cannot afford to overlook the profound insight into the essence of the Liturgy gained by theology through Casel's work.[73] Indeed, it is precisely the more theological side of the Liturgy—as opposed to the purely juridical conception of it—which must come into its own, if we are to attain a genuine appreciation of the reality at hand. We must be guided by a deeper respect for the content of Liturgy and the demands which that content places on whatever aspires to be Liturgy.

Not every prayer is Liturgy without further ado, not even if it is officially commanded for the entire Church and offered by a community.[74] Two things seem to be required in order that any prayer or devotional act can become Liturgy formally speaking. And these must constitute its formality, must be intrinsic to the act or prayer as liturgical. First, the act or prayer in question must be performed by the power of priesthood, or in other words it must be the act of Christ as the principal minister. Secondly, it must express in sensible signs (symbolical actions) the exchange of divine life and human homage. In short, a liturgical act, in its intimate formality, is an act in which the minister is the instrument of Christ continuing His sacramental glorification of the Father and sanctification of man. It is, therefore, a *priestly-sacramental* action.

Let us first consider the priestly element.

[72] *Summa Theol.*, III, q. 79, a. 1.
[73] Later we will discuss exactly what is made present in the liturgical rites and the manner of such presence, when we treat the various parts of the Liturgy.
[74] J. Pinsk, *op. cit.*, 328.

Previously, we said that what the Church means in the papal definition of the Liturgy is a priestly society continuing the work of Christ. From the very first moment of His Incarnation Christ was essentially a priest, a Mediator between God and man, bringing to God the submission of mankind and to man the rich blessings of supernatural grace. The precise purpose of His Mystical Body is to continue this work of Christ, His priestly mission. And the Liturgy, according to Pius XII, "is nothing more nor less than the exercise of this priestly function." [75] And thus the priesthood of Jesus Christ becomes a "continuous and living reality through all the ages till the end of time." [76]

Christ conferred His priesthood on the Apostles and their successors and others upon whom such successors have imposed hands. "By virtue of this priesthood," the Pope continues, such men "represent the person of Jesus Christ before their people, acting at the same time as representatives of the people before God." [77] In Holy Orders, the Pope goes on to say, an indelible character is printed on their souls, "indicating the sacred ministers' conformity to Jesus Christ the Priest and qualifying them to perform official acts of religion by which men are sanctified and God is duly glorified in keeping with the divine laws and regulations."[78] Thus, by means of this indelible mark or sign, these ministers have become conformed to Christ the Priest and are made instruments which God uses to communicate supernatural life from on high to the Mystical Body of Jesus Christ; they are so empowered that whatever they bless may be blessed, whatever they consecrate may become holy and sacred.[79]

The conclusion that the Pope draws from these considerations is that in the Liturgy the Church "acts always in closest union with her Head," [80] and "along with the Church her Divine Founder is present at every liturgical celebration or action. Christ is present at the august sacrifice of the altar both in the person of His minister and above all under the Eucharistic species. He is present in the sacraments, infusing into them the power which makes them ready instruments of sanctification. He is present, finally, in the prayer of praise and petition we direct to God." [81]

The Church, then, in the sense of a holy cult-community or priestly society, is not involved when just any group of our modern Church organization assembles to pray, but only "where the community engrafted onto Christ the Priest through Baptism, Confirmation and Holy Orders, represents a living symbol, a permanent sacrament, as

[75] *Mediator Dei*, 22.
[76] *Ibid.*
[77] *Ibid.*, 40.
[78] *Ibid.*, 42.
[79] *Ibid.*, 43.
[80] *Ibid.*, 27.
[81] *Ibid.*, 20.

it were, of the High Priest. Through the character imprinted on the soul in these sacraments, which gives a share in Christ's priesthood, the cult-community becomes the image of Christ's priestly life and continues His priestly mediation." [82]

✠ In other words, as A. Stenzel so rightly insists, "Only that worship is Liturgy in which the 'people of God as a people' acts in its proper condition of holy cult-community." [83] And when is that? "When someone appointed through the sacrament of Holy Orders and hierarchically chosen from among the people [which itself is already hierarchically constituted through the power of orders, i.e., the three characters of Baptism, Confirmation, and Holy Orders, and through the power of jurisdiction] acts as the minister of Christ." [84] For the minister in this case leads the people precisely as the Body of Christ and he bears the image of Christ the Head of the Body, as St. Thomas says: "minister gerit typum Christi, Christum repraesentat." [85] It is precisely because of this union of the entire Church in its strictly priestly activity that Pius XII could say in his address to the participants in the Congress of Pastoral Liturgy held at Assisi in September of 1956: "The contribution of the Hierarchy as well as that made by the faithful in the Liturgy are not to each other as two separate quantities, but they represent the collaboration of the members of the same organism which acts as a single living being." [86]

It may be concluded here that for a person to be able to perform a liturgical act as liturgical he must possess some spiritual qualification or power. This, of course, is the power of priesthood. But it would be a mistake to think that only ordained priests possess priestly power. True, only ordained priests possess the priesthood in its most perfect sense: the power to consecrate the Holy Eucharist. In addition to this they also have the power to confect most of the sacraments. But laymen too are empowered with a lesser kind of priesthood to perform certain liturgical acts implied in their participation in the Mass (in the offering of what the ordained priest has consecrated [87]), in the sacraments, and in the other liturgical prayers of the Church. And they receive this spiritual qualification to do so through the character of Baptism. This is forcefully brought out again in the Instruction on Sacred Music and Liturgy: "The laity also exercise an active liturgical participation by virtue of their baptismal character, because of which

---

[82] H. Elfers, art. cit., 124.
[83] Art. cit., 190.
[84] Ibid., 202.
[85] Summa Theol., Suppl., q. 40, a. 4, ad 3m.
[86] AAS, 48 (1956), p. 714: "La contribution que la Hiérarchie et celle que les fidèles apportent à la liturgie ne s'additionnent pas comme deux quantités séparées, mais représentent la collaboration des membres d'un même organisme, qui agit comme un seul être vivant."
[87] Mediator Dei, 92, 93.

in the Holy Sacrifice of the Mass they offer in their own way, along
with the priest, the divine victim to God the Father." [87a]

The reality [88] of this priestly power is so great that, no matter
how energetically a non-baptized person may take part in the Mass or
any other liturgical function, he cannot be said to offer or perform such
liturgical acts in any sense whatsoever, though it is true that he may
benefit from them, since the Church prays for him in her Liturgy.
However, it is equally true that the exercise of this priestly power on
the part of the layman is essentially dependent on the exercise on the
part of the ordained priest of his character of Holy Orders—except in
the case of Baptism of Necessity and Matrimony. So the layman, too,
can represent Christ the Priest in some liturgical acts; through him,
too, is the priestly activity of Christ continued.

A second element that is an essential part of the intrinsic formal
make-up of a liturgical act is its sacramental quality. A liturgical act
must give symbolic expression to the conferring of divine life by
Christ on His Church and the offering to the Father through Christ
of the worship of His holy people. It must represent, therefore, in

[87a] N. 93b: *Laici autem participationem liturgicam actuosam praestant.* . . .
Note also that in part "c" of this same paragraph the Congregation of Rites speaks
of the "direct but delegated ministerial service" which young men exercise when
singing in the liturgical choir or serving at the altar. *AAS,* 50 (1958), 656.

[88] Though the reality of the layman's priesthood cannot be denied, because
the priestly character imprinted on his soul in Baptism is very real ("he participates, according to his condition, in the priesthood of Christ," *Mediator Dei,* 88),
nevertheless we must surely recognize that the term priesthood is here used in an
analogical sense. Exactly what sense? Since Pius XII says that the proper and chief
function of the priesthood is to sacrifice, we cannot claim that the application of
the term "priest" to the layman is according to what philosophers call an analogy
of proper proportion. "Sacerdotis munus proprium et praecipuum semper fuit et
est 'sacrificare', ita ut, ubi nulla sit proprie vereque dicenda potestas
sacrificandi, nec inveniatur proprie vereque appellandum sacerdotium." (*Magnificate Dominum, AAS,* 46 [1954,] 667). It is an analogy of proportionality,
however, because, since the power is attributed to the layman by intrinsic denomination, it is more than just metaphorical, that is, simply an extrinsic likeness.
Hence, we would call the use of this term in the case of the layman an analogy
of imperfect proportionality: He possesses *a* real priestly power, but not the
supreme and chief priestly power to sacrifice. Some interesting studies on this
subject are: P. Palmer, "Lay Priesthood — Real or Metaphorical," *Theological
Studies,* 8 (1947), 574-613; *idem,* "The Lay Priesthood — towards a Terminology,"
ibid., 10 (1949), 235-250; J. Rea, *The Common Priesthood of the Members of the
Mystical Body* (Washington, D. C.: 1947); J. Lécuyer, "Essai sur le sacerdoce
des fidèles chez les pères," *La Maison-Dieu,* n. 27 (1951), 7-50; Y. Congar,
"Structure du sacerdoce chrétien," *ibid.,* 51-85; "L'Idée du sacerdoce des fidèles
dans la tradition," *CCSL,* 11 (1933): I. B. Botte, "L'Antiquité chrétienne," 21-28;
II, P. Charlier, "Les grands docteurs scolastiques," 29-39; III. A. Robeyns, "Le
Concile de Trente et la théologie moderne," 41-67; IV. B. Capelle, "Synthèse et
conclusion," 69-74; E. Mersch, "Tous prêtres dans l'unique Prêtre," *ibid.,* 95-117;
J. Brinktrine, "Das Amtspriestertum und das allgemeine Priestertum der Gläubig-
en," *Divus Thomas,* 22 (1944), 291-308; B. Durst, *Dreifaches Priestertum*
(Neresheim, 1947); J. Jungmann, "Christus — Gemeinde — Priester," *Volksliturgie
und Seelsorge* (Kolmar im Elsass, 1942), 25-30; E. Walter, "Weihe-und Laien-
priestertum, das eine Priestertum der Kirche," *ibid.,* 31-47.

sensible signs this *sacrum commercium,* this holy exchange of divine
life and divine-human homage.[89]

There was in the priesthood of Christ a twofold movement: one
directly towards God, another directly towards man. Each movement
implies the other, for through His priesthood Christ not only ap-
peased God's wrath by offering to the Father the submission and
homage of man which were His due, but thereby also brought man
God's gift of grace, divine life. And man, for his part, in accepting
God's gifts (sacraments), submits himself to God and gives Him honor.
We must not think that this manward tendency is any less liturgical
than the Godward tendency, for St. Thomas says that by the submission implied in accepting God's gifts we declare and make manifest
His supreme dominion over us.[90]

Thus, these two things are necessary for Liturgy: It must give
God glory and bring man God's life. In some actions of the Liturgy
one aspect may be more apparent, but the other is always implied and
in some way realized. In the praises of the Divine Office it is more
apparent that we give glory to God, while in the sacraments our
reception of God's grace is more apparent. Nevertheless, in the former
by praising God we submit ourselves more efficaciously to Him and
receive grace, and in the latter by receiving God's grace we submit
ourselves to His dominion and thus give Him glory.

This is clearly the teaching of Pius XII. He says that "it is an
unquestionable fact that the work of our redemption is continued and
that its fruits are imparted to us during the celebration of the Liturgy." [91] In other words, "the worship rendered to God by the Church
in union with her divine Head is the most efficacious means of achieving sanctity." [92] This efficacy, as the Pope points out, when it is a question of the Mass and the sacraments, derives from the act itself (*ex
opere operato*), that is it possesses some real inner power to sanctify
the soul. However, when it is a question of the Church's prayer said
through the power of Christ's priesthood, this efficacy is derived from
her power of impetration (*ex opere operantis Ecclesiae*), precisely
because she is holy and acts through Christ. [93] In either instance God
is infinitely pleased and His life is offered to man; thus the work of
redemption is continued, is made present either as sacrament or as
sacramental.

---

[89] Cf. J. Pinsk, *art. cit.,* 329; H. Elfers, *art. cit.,* 128-29.

[90] *Summa theol.,* II-II, q. 81, a. 3, ad 2m: "Dicendum quod eodem actu
homo servit Deo et colit ipsum: nam cultus respicit Dei excellentiam, cui reverentia
debetur; servitus autem respicit subiectionem hominis, qui ex sua conditione
obligatur ad exhibendum reverentiam Deo. Et ad haec duo pertinent omnes actus
qui religioni attribuuntur: quia per omnes homo protestatur divinam excellentiam
et subiectionem sui ad Deum, vel exhibendo aliquid ei, vel iterum assumendo
aliquid divinum."

[91] *Mediator Dei,* 29.

[92] *Ibid.,* 26: "cultum . . . sanctitudinis adipiscendae habere efficacitatem quam
maximam."

[93] *Ibid.,* 27.

Pius XII sums up this doctrine when he says that "through the Liturgy is distributed the treasures of the *depositum gratiae,* which our Lord transmitted to His Apostles: sanctifying grace, the virtues, the gifts [of the Holy Spirit], the power to baptize, to confer the Holy Spirit, to remit sins in the sacrament of Penance and to consecrate priests. At the heart of the Liturgy unfolds the celebration of the Eucharist, sacrifice and banquet; there too the sacraments are conferred, and by means of the sacramentals the Church abundantly multiplies the benefits of grace for the most diverse circumstances." [94]

Having answered the question of *what* a liturgical act is, i.e., what its intimate constitution is, we must now address ourselves to an equally important matter: *How* does something *become* liturgical?

Certainly we must not think that there is an *absolutely* essential connection between the priesthood of Christ and all those acts and prayers which today concretely make up the Liturgy; Christ could have chosen other religious acts as expressions of His priesthood. The fact is that He actually did decide to accomplish the salvation of mankind through certain actions and to continue to distribute salvific grace to men of future ages through definite, specific means. This decision on the part of Christ provides us with what is essential in the liturgical functions.

The Church, by virtue of the juridical commission given to her by her Founder and Head, has not hesitated to use her divine authority to develop a system of sacramentals, holy signs, symbols and prayers, which ritually prepare for, accompany, enlarge, and prolong the essentials of the sacraments instituted by Christ. In other words, through her juridical decision the Church makes a part of Christ's mediation of God's grace and man's homage whatever actions of the virtue of religion which she has deemed worthy and suitable to aid in His priestly mediation.

The ecclesiastical hierarchy, says Pius XII, "has organized and regulated divine worship, enriching it constantly with new splendor and beauty, to the glory of God and the spiritual profit of Christians. What is more, it has not been slow—keeping carefully intact the substance of the Mass and sacraments—to modify what it deemed not altogether fitting and to add what appeared more likely to increase the honor paid to Jesus Christ and the august Trinity, and to instruct and stimulate the Christian people to greater advantage." [95] While those elements instituted by Christ cannot be changed in any way, "the human components admit of various modifications, as the need of the age, circumstance and the good of souls may require, and as the ecclesiastical hierarchy, under the guidance of the Holy Spirit, may have authorized." [96] Hence, for any religious act to enjoy the priestly-

---

[94] Allocution to the participants of the Assisi Congress for Pastoral Liturgy, *AAS,* 48 (1956), 713.
[95] *Mediator Dei,* 49.
[96] *Ibid.,* 50.

sacramental quality of the Liturgy, it must have been established as liturgical either by Christ or His Church.

The question naturally arises: Who within the Church has the authority to recognize something as liturgical? While it is true that in former ages all bishops and even pastors were empowered to begin new liturgical rites or alter those already in existence, the Code of Canon Law, promulgated in 1917, definitely reserved to the Holy See alone the exercise of the authority to regulate liturgical rites. Canon 1257 states: "It belongs to the Apostolic See alone both to order the sacred Liturgy as well as to approve liturgical books." [97] Though the language of this Canon seems quite clear to us, some have still maintained, since the promulgation of the Code, that only final supervision was reserved to the Holy See and that bishops and pastors still retained the right to regulate concrete expressions of Liturgy within their respective dioceses and parishes.[98] Hence, it is understandable that, in his encyclical *Mediator Dei*, Pius XII felt obliged to state "that the Sovereign Pontiff alone enjoys the right to recognize and establish any practice touching the worship of God, to introduce and approve new rites, as also to modify those he judges to require modification." [99]

What, then is left to the bishops? The Pope goes on to say that "Bishops, for their part, have the right and duty carefully to watch over the exact observance of the prescriptions of the sacred canons respecting divine worship. Private individuals, even though they be clerics, may not be left to decide for themselves in these holy and venerable matters, involving as they do the religious life of Christian society along with the exercise of the priesthood of Jesus Christ and worship of God." [100] In other words, the Pope determines what is or shall be Liturgy, the bishops carry out such liturgical legislation emanating from Rome, and other clerics and the laity must receive such decisions in a spirit of obedience. Although the bishops no longer possess true legislative power regarding the Liturgy, properly speaking, they do possess legislative power when it is a question of any other prayer or exercise of piety performed in a church.[101] The first legislative power is the Pope's alone and is the prerogative to reserve something to the power of priesthood, thereby involving the name and

[97] "Unius apostolicae Sedis est tum sacram ordinare liturgiam, tum liturgicos approbare libros."

[98] E.g., J. Jungmann, *Gewordene Liturgie*, 10-18. Thus Jungmann arrives at the position that all the evening devotions observed in the diocese or parish church are truly liturgical: ibid., 15, 18.

[99] Par. 58. This he says by way of commentary on canon 1257, as can be seen from footnote 50 in the same encyclical. Cf. also *Magnificate Dominum, AAS,* 46 (1954), 670; Allocution to Assisi Congress, *AAS,* 48 (1956), 714-715.

[100] *Mediator Dei*, 58. *Instruction on Sacred Music and Liturgy*, n. 1: for an action to be liturgical it must be performed "according to liturgical books approved by the Holy See."

[101] CIC, cc. 1259, 1261.

power of the entire Mystical Body; the second, proper to bishops, is that authority which must safeguard both obedience to prescriptions of the Holy See as well as the faith and morals of the local flock when devotions not approved by Rome are at issue.

We must conclude that only the Supreme Pontiff has the authority to make something liturgical; whatever is not explicitly established as liturgical by Rome simply is not part of the Church's Liturgy.

One more element is required for an act or prayer to be liturgical. Since there are within the Church different kinds of priesthood as well as a variety of liturgical acts, it remains to the Church to determine, if Christ Himself has not already done so, to which kind of priesthood shall pertain the ministration of any given liturgical act. Such determination as to the minister of a liturgical act we call deputation.[102] For instance, Christ Himself has decided that only the bishop shall be the ordinary minister of Holy Orders, only the priest shall be the minister of the sacramental action whereby bread and wine become the Body and Blood of Christ and of the other sacramental actions except, of necessity, Matrimony and Baptism.

For her part, the Church has decided that only certain persons may give blessings in her name or lead in the recitation of the Divine Office.[103] Even though one may reasonably claim that all baptized persons have the basic priestly power to perform many of the liturgical actions instituted by the Church, for a person to use such power and actually make his activity truly liturgical, he must either possess a special deputation for this act or prayer, or pray together or act with someone who does enjoy such deputation by the Church. Deputation, therefore, is of strict necessity. Without it, even if a person recites a prayer from a liturgical book, even if he should pray the entire Divine Office, his prayer will never be a liturgical prayer; it will never be the prayer of the entire Mystical Body of Christ.

Of the four elements necessary for Liturgy the first two form the intrinsic constitution of the liturgical act, while the second two indicate the way in which an act of the virtue of religion acquires such a new, higher formality. A juridical act of the Church—of the Holy See, to be more exact—is necessary for any particular action or prayer to *become* Liturgy. This authoritative act on the part of the Church

---

[102] *Ibid.*, can. 1256. *Instr. on Sacred Music and Liturgy*, nn. 1 and 40. AAS, 50 (1958), 632, 645.

[103] Even though some authors maintain that even when a lay person recites the Breviary he is performing the prayer of the Church: e.g., L. Bouyer, "The Breviary and the Spiritual Life," *Orate Fratres*, 21 (1947), p. 147, note 2, Pius XII takes a clearly contrary stand in *Mediator Dei*. In paragraph 142 he says: "The divine Office is the prayer of the Mystical Body of Jesus Christ, offered to God in the name and on behalf of all Christians, when recited by priests and other ministers of the Church and by religious deputed by the Church for this." The *Instruction on Sacred Music and Liturgy*, par. 40, explicitly states that the Divine Office is to be considered an act of public worship "if it is said by those persons who are *deputed* by ecclesiastical laws for its recitation." (Emphasis added.)

places a latreutic act among her own priestly acts; she thereby re-
serves it to her power of priesthood. In other words, through her
juridical decision the Church elevates this act or prayer to the dignity of being performed by her priestly power, thus involving the
name and power of the entire Mystical Body, the priesthood of Jesus
Christ, and hence invests the act with a sacramental quality, gives it
a sacramental efficacy (whether *ex opere operato* or *ex opere operantis
Ecclesiae*). But notice that this juridical act does not enter into the
intimate, intrinsic essence of the liturgical act; it remains extrinsic to
it. The priestly-sacramental element, however, does enter into the
liturgical act's formal constitution; this is *what* a liturgical act is: the
sacramental exercise of Christ's priesthood. The juridical decision of
the Church is *how* some latreutic act acquires such a relationship to
the priesthood of Christ. Whatever has not been invested by Christ
or His Church with this connection with the priestly and sacramental
mediation of Christ, the priestly and sacramental worship of God
and dispensation of divine grace, cannot be considered Liturgy in the
strict sense of the word.

D. What Forms of Worship Are Liturgical?

Having discussed the exact understanding of the Papal definition
of Liturgy and having discovered the Liturgy's essential constitutive
property, let us now ask what concrete acts of the virtue of religion
are to be considered liturgical.

Since the answer to this question obviously depends on a juridical
decision of the Church for those things which have not been determined by Christ Himself, we have but to turn to the official pronouncements of the Holy See. In his encyclical *Mediator Dei*, Pius XII very
clearly states that the Liturgy includes "the Mass, the sacraments, the
Divine Office." [104] Although the sacramentals are not explicitly mentioned in this part of the encyclical, the Pope does speak of them in
another place in such a way that it is clear he intends to include them
in the Liturgy. When describing the efficacy of the worship which the
Church renders to God in union with her divine Head, he says this
efficacy is derived *ex opere operato* when one speaks of the Mass or
the sacraments, but *ex opere operantis Ecclesiae* when one speaks of
the sacramentals.[105] In his allocution to the Congress of Pastoral Liturgy held at Assisi in September of 1956, Pius XII is even more explicit regarding the liturgical quality of the sacramentals. He states:
"At the heart of the Liturgy unfolds the celebration of the Eucharist,
sacrifice and banquet; there too the sacraments are conferred, and by
means of the sacramentals the Church abundantly multiplies the benefits of grace for the most diverse circumstances." [106] Lastly, in the

[104] Par. 171.
[105] *Mediator Dei*, 10, 27.
[106] AAS, 48 (1956), 713.

Instruction on Sacred Music and Liturgy, September 3, 1958, the Congregation of Rites declares Benediction of the Blessed Sacrament to be a true liturgical action.[106a]

By sacramentals, of course, we do not mean blessed *objects*, but rather all those prayers, exorcisms, anointings, and ceremonies with which she surrounds the matter and form of the sacraments as well as all the blessings and consecrations which she uses to bring her assistance and the benefits of grace to our private prayer and even to the material world about us. Blessed objects would better be called *effects* of sacramental action; their private use certainly is not Liturgy. Through them the power of the Church's prayer helps us in our private devotions. Sacramentals, understood as Liturgy, must necessarily, we believe, be limited to combinations of the prayer and action of the Church and should not be extended to include the purely private prayer and action of an individual. Hence, for instance, the blessing of a Rosary is liturgical; the recitation of the Rosary, even though the beads may have been blessed, still remains private prayer.

Among the many ceremonies and rites instituted by Holy Mother Church to embellish the Holy Sacrifice and the sacraments and to prolong Christ's mediation of grace, there are certainly many acts which could be exercises either of private or public prayer. The Church, "acting always in closest union with her Head," [107] has decided that such acts in certain circumstances, i.e., when performed in a certain manner and by her lawfully deputed ministers, shall be her own prayer. As Stenzel remarks,[108] there are four categories of acts of worship: (1) acts which belong to the individual as such, which can be characterized by our Lord's words: "Go into thy chamber, close the door, and pray to thy Father in secret" (Matt. 6:6); (2) acts which by their very nature can be made part of the liturgical order but which *without a positive acceptance on the part of the Church* cannot be called her own prayer: e.g., the breviary prayed by the priest in private, or the Pater, the Creed; (3) acts which by their very nature can be and *are* recognized by the Church as her prayer: again, the breviary prayed in private, the Pater and the Creed in the Mass; (4) acts which necessarily belong to the liturgical order: e.g., the Mass and the sacraments, which were instituted by Christ Himself. Needless to say, acts falling in the second category must be suitable to the liturgical order. Should the Church wish to use something belonging to the first category, it should be fairly obvious that she must adapt it, reshape it to a degree, and make it compatible with the exigencies of prayer in common. In such cases, let us repeat, the Church, by a positive act of her juridical power, removes something from the realm

[106a] N. 47. AAS, 50 (1958), 646.
[107] *Mediator Dei*, 27.
[108] A. Stenzel, *art. cit.*, 210-211.

of private prayer and connects it with the exercise of her priestly power, thus making it Christ's own prayer.

We should also recognize in the various acts which the Church has established as liturgical a certain unity. Some authors divide the acts into essential, integral, and accidental. While this may be justifiable, all of them are related to the sacrifice of the Mass; in it they find their *raison d'être*. On Calvary Christ achieved His great redemptive work. His sacrifice is the source and fount of all grace. Since in the Mass we renew that sacrifice, the Mass is the center and source of all liturgical worship, as well as all sanctity. Whatever else is done in the Liturgy is meant either to prepare us for the Mass in which the saving sacrifice is renewed and represented, or to channel off the graces gained in that sacrifice. In the beginning the Mass was the germ from which the entire edifice of liturgical worship sprung and the point towards which everything converged. For example, the hour of Matins in the Divine Office seems to find its ultimate roots in the primitive nocturnal synaxes which prepared for the celebration of Mass. In fact, the Mass and the Divine Office constitute one *officium diei*; the Office prepares for or continues the action of the Mass. The sacraments offer the same prospect: Baptism, Confirmation, Penance, Holy Orders prepare us and qualify us for participation in the Mass, while the other sacraments increase and preserve for us the grace we have received through the Mass. The entire liturgical year finds its origin in assembling to celebrate the Lord's Supper on the day of the Lord's resurrection, Sunday, which gradually overflowed into a system of sanctification for the entire week and year. Many of the consecrations and blessings of the Church are given during the Mass, and still, when not thus conferred, they retain their meaning as a preparation for or as an extension of the Mass; yes, as a channeling off of the power of the Mass into even the material world about us. Thus, indeed the Eucharistic Sacrifice is the "end and consummation of all the sacraments," [109] the summary of the mysteries of the Incarnation and redemption, the synthesis of Christianity, the very reason for our priesthood.[110]

E. Are Modern Devotions Liturgical?

While saying that there are other exercises of piety "which do not strictly belong to the sacred Liturgy," Pius XII states that "they enjoy such importance and dignity that they may be considered to be somehow inserted into the liturgical order." [111] What does this mean? They are not Liturgy; still they may somehow be considered liturgical. The Pope gives us some clues as to how they enjoy this dignity:

[109] Attributed to Dionysius by St. Thomas: *Summa Theol.*, III, q. 63, a. 6.
[110] Cf. C. Callewaert, *op. cit.*, pp. 8, 166; P. Oppenheim, *op. cit.*, 420-425.
[111] *Mediator Dei*, 182. The Latin version according to Bugnini, par. 180, reads thus: "Alia praeterea pietatis exercitia habentur, quae, quamvis ad sacram Liturgiam districto iure non pertineant, peculiari tamen momento dignitateque pollent, ita ut in liturgicum ordinem quodammodo inserta censeantur."

> They have been approved and praised over and over
> again by the Apostolic See and by the bishops . . . they make
> us partakers in a salutary manner of the liturgical cult,
> because they urge the faithful to go frequently to the sacra-
> ment of penance, to attend Mass and receive Holy Com-
> munion with devotion, and encourage them to meditate on
> the mysteries of our redemption and imitate the example of
> the saints.[112]

Among such exercises of piety the Pope enumerates the prayers
said during the month of Mary and those said during the month of
the Sacred Heart, also triduums, novenas, the stations of the cross—in
other words, popular devotions performed in common.

Judging from the reasons given by the Pope for the dignity of
such devotions, we may conclude that popular devotions are liturgical
only in a metaphorical sense,[113] for they have never been specifically
established by Rome as liturgical. They are not Liturgy; they merely
resemble Liturgy in some way, for they lack that priestly-sacramental
quality that would make them truly liturgical. They may resemble
the Liturgy because (1) they are approved, or even commanded, by
some Church authority; (2) they are performed by people gathered
together in a public sacred place; (3) they are led by a priest, though
this is not necessary, for they have not been reserved to priestly power
in the sense we have already explained (the local bishop might *de
facto* reserve them to the priest by reason of the fact that they are performed in a church and under ecclesiastical auspices); (4) they imitate liturgical style.

Such devotions are not really Liturgy because (1) they are not
instituted by the Church, i.e., they have not been authoritatively made
part of her prayer; (2) they are not public in the sacramental sense
upon which we have insisted; (3) the presence of the priest or anyone possessing some priestly power is not really necessary for their
validity or liceity; (4) they might even lack that basic suitability
which is necessary before a prayer or action is accepted by the Church
as her own liturgical prayer. It follows that even though these exercises may resemble liturgical forms of worship, they are not Liturgy,
but rather pious exercises performed together by a group of individuals. And the *Instruction on Sacred Music and Liturgy* of September
3, 1958, confirms this view, when it says that sacred actions which
lack any one of the qualities mentioned in its definition of Liturgy
should be called "pious exercises." [113a]

❉   ❉   ❉

This, then, is the wholly supernatural world of liturgical prayer.
It is a prayer that is permeated through and through with Christ's

[112] *Ibid.*, (America Press Edition) 182-183.
[113] By extrinsic denomination.
[113a] N. 1. *AAS*, 50 (1958), 632.

power; it is Christ's priestly prayer, it is a divine prayer. By way of summary, we might enlarge on the definition of Liturgy given by Pius XII: Liturgy is the public worship of the Mystical Body in the entirety of its Head and members; a worship common to all the members of the Mystical Body, because it is the prayer and action of their Head, Christ; a divinely efficacious worship which brings about a holy exchange of God's life and human homage by means of sacramental actions done by a person spiritually qualified as well as juridically deputed to be the instrument of Christ the Priest; worship ultimately organized and constituted by the Holy See exercising the divine authority committed to it by Jesus Christ, invisible Head of the Mystical Body; worship which is concretized in the Mass, the sacraments, the Divine Office, and the sacramentals; worship, finally, which inserts Christ's members into the heavenly current of adoration, propitiation, thanksgiving, and petition carried on by our glorified Head before the throne of God the Father for all eternity.

F. Properties of the Liturgy

1. Christian

As we have already seen, the Liturgy is eminently Christian; it is based throughout on the work and priestly power of Christ. The whole of Christian worship is derived from Christ's work of redemption. Christ Himself is the Supreme Pontiff of the entirety of liturgical worship. We have seen that whatever the Church has done to enrich the primitive Liturgy as it came to her from the hands of her Founder, she has done only by reason of the divine authority and mission given her by Christ. And, furthermore, whenever she exercises her power of priesthood, she does so in closest union with her Head [114] and through His mediation: *per Christum Dominum nostrum.* Thus, ultimately all the Church's prayer has its efficacy from Christ who acts universally as the "minister of holy things,"[115] as the unique and universal mediator between God and men.

Through the marvellous sacramental system which Christ instituted, His great salvific actions are applied to mankind today. As St. Leo the Great says, "That which was visible in our Redeemer has now passed into the sacraments!"[116] And in *Mediator Dei* we see this same idea expressed in the sound theological terms of Pius XII:

> In the Mass "the High Priest . . . does the same as He already did upon the cross, offering Himself as most acceptable victim to the Eternal Father."[117] "It is an unquestionable

---

[114] *Mediator Dei,* 27.
[115] Hebr. 7:2.
[116] "Quod itaque redemptoris nostri conspicuum fuit, in sacramenta transivit." *MPL,* 54:398.
[117] *Mediator Dei,* 68.

fact that the work of our redemption is continued, and that its fruits are imparted to us, during the celebration of the Liturgy, notably in the august sacrifice of the altar. Christ acts each day to save us in the sacraments and in His holy sacrifice." [118] As for the Divine Office, "by assuming human nature, the Divine Word introduced into this earthly exile a hymn which is sung in heaven for all eternity. He united to Himself the whole human race and with it sings this hymn to the praise of God . . . Christ prays for us as our priest." [119] "As our Mediator with God He shows to the heavenly Father His glorified wounds, always living to make intercession for us." [120]

And the liturgical year "is not a cold and lifeless representation of the events of the past . . . it is rather Christ Himself who is ever living in His Church. Here He continues that journey of immense mercy which He lovingly began in His mortal life, going about doing good, with the design of bringing men to know His mysteries and in a way to live by them. . . . These mysteries are ever present and active" in the sense that they are "shining examples of Christian perfection, as well as sources of divine grace, due to the merits and prayers of Christ; they still influence us because each mystery brings its own special grace for our salvation." [121]

We see that in the Liturgy Christ is made present as well as His redemptive work—either in its substance (i.e., the central redemptive act of Christ offering Himself as victim: *Christus passus* [122]), or in its power, as this comes directly from the Passion of Christ,[123] or as it is channelled and applied by the Church in her solemn prayer [124] in which she acts in closest union with her Head.

The Liturgy, therefore, is the Mystery of Christ operative in our midst. It brings "Christ and His own life, the life that He won for His whole mystical body on the cross, into contact with the daily life of each one of us. And in so doing, it shows how the whole sacramental order is nothing else than the realization of that Christ-mysticism which is the heart of St. Paul's teaching." [125]

2. Hierarchical

"The Divine Redeemer," says Pius XII, "has so willed it that the priestly life begun with the supplication and sacrifice of His mortal

[118] *Ibid.*, 29.
[119] *Ibid.*, 144.
[120] *Ibid.*, 146.
[121] *Ibid.*, 165.
[122] *Summa Theol.*, III, q. 75, a. 1.
[123] "Sacramenta Ecclesiae specialiter habent virtutem ex passione Christi, cuius virtus quodammodo nobis copulatur per eorum susceptionem." *Ibid.*, III. q. 62, a. 5.
[124] *Ibid.*, III, q. 64, a. 1, ad 2m.
[125] L. Bouyer, *Liturgical Piety* (Notre Dame, Indiana, 1955), 89.

body should continue without intermission down the ages in His Mystical Body which is the Church. That is why He established a visible priesthood to offer everywhere the clean oblation which would enable men from East to West, freed from the shackles of sin, to offer God that unconstrained and voluntary homage which their conscience dictates." [126]

The Church, then, is entrusted with the continuance of Christ's priestly prayer. There is no such thing as liturgical worship except in the Church. Christ is the principal minister of the entire Liturgy, but in this He has joined to Himself the Church as His fullness, His Mystical Body. Hence, the Church, founded by Christ and under His constant guidance and action, orders, arranges, and continues His worship of the Father. And she does this precisely by reason of that charismatic power which Christ gave her, that of His priesthood. This in no way detracts from the unique and personal character of Christ's mediation. It simply means that God has seen fit to use human instruments to continue that entirely sublime role of interceding for mankind before the Father.

But note that Christ does not accept any man indiscriminately as His instrument. Nor does this power of priesthood emanate from the Christian community.[127] It is conferred by Christ on designated men through what may be called "the spiritual generation of Holy Orders."[128] Elevated to such a supernatural power, certain men become the "ambassadors of the divine Redeemer . . . God's vice-gerents in the midst of His flock."[129] And it is only because the priest is the representative of Christ the Head of the Mystical Body that he is also the representative of the Head's members. Thus Christ established and founded His Church on a holy order, a sacred hierarchy, through which the stream of sanctification gradually penetrates all the members of His Mystical Body.[130]

Since it is to the priesthood that this sacramental sanctification of mankind is entrusted, it is obvious that the organization, regulation, and settlement of details of the Liturgy are the prerogatives of the same sacred hierarchy.[131] In any well ordered society the coordination of the efforts of all its members toward their common end rests with some authority. The determining of means for the end cannot be left to private initiative. As Pius XII rightly insists, "private individuals, even though they be clerics, may not be left to decide for themselves in these holy and venerable matters, involving as they do the religious life of Christian society along with the exercise of the priesthood of

[126] *Mediator Dei*, 2.
[127] *Ibid.*, 40.
[128] *Ibid.*, 41.
[129] *Ibid.*, 40.
[130] Cf. *ibid.*, 39, 40, 43.
[131] *Ibid.*, 44.

Christ and the worship of God." [132] And the supreme authority in the Church has seen fit to reserve to itself alone "the right to recognize and establish any practice touching divine worship, to introduce and approve new rites, as also to modify those he judges to require modification." [133]

3. Social

All liturgical acts, by reason of the Church's participation in Christ's priesthood, possess a truly communal, social, public character. By virtue of the bond arising from the baptismal character all the faithful are intimately united to Christ their Head. Thus they share in His priestly power according to their condition.[134] This fact makes all liturgical acts eminently common to all members of the Mystical Body since, united to their Head, Christians are represented by Him in all the acts of worship done in His name and power. Liturgy, therefore, is *essentially* social in that it involves and affects all the members of the Church.

However, since the Church is a visible society, this social character of liturgical acts must be expressed through visible, exterior actions. If the Liturgy is to achieve its purpose of actually uniting people, in common prayer, it is necessary that they externally act and pray together. "A common rite is good," says H. Schmidt, "when all those assisting perform it together, but if only a small part of the congregation gives its active cooperation, then there is a certain deficiency in the rite. The genuine atmosphere is lacking to a feast when the congregation does not take its proper part. For any society the community is indispensable. The community of the faithful is required for the ecclesiastical society. And the social life of the Church needs to be social in its very living and realized in the actual concurrence of many persons." [135] Pope Pius X considered this active participation so important that he did not hesitate to call it the "primary and indispensable source of the true Christian spirit." [136]

As we have seen, all members of the Church are spiritually equipped and empowered for this active participation through the character imprinted on their souls in Baptism. It obviously remains to the authority in the Church to determine which liturgical acts belong to the laity, and that authority has spoken on many occasions: In Matrimony the contracting parties are the proper ministers; in Baptism of necessity the layman is the extraordinary minister; in the Mass the laity takes its legitimate part in offering through and with

---

[132] *Ibid.*, 58.
[133] *Ibid., loc. cit.*
[134] *Ibid.*, 88.
[135] H. Schmidt, "Grandeur et misère du rite," *La Maison-Dieu*, n. 35 (1953), 114-115.
[136] *Tra le sollecitudini*, Bugnini, 12-13.

the priest what he has consecrated and in responding to the prayers
and in singing certain parts of the Ordinary; in the sacraments the
lay role is again to receive them and to respond to the prayers said
by the minister; and in the Divine Office the laity may make the
responses and may alternate with the celebrant and choir in singing
the psalms and hymns.

The participation of the laity in the manner prescribed by the
Church is, therefore, liturgical in every respect; its role should not be
brushed off as something entirely accidental. In all these actions the
layman exercises his basic power of priesthood. The Church, to be
sure, can change the determination as to how he shall exercise his
power, for such exercise is essentially dependent on her authority.
But such determination pertains to the highest authority in the
Church; never should any cleric presume to take away from the layman what the Church allows him. The priest exists as a priest precisely for the layman, for his sanctification, to join his prayer to the
prayer of Christ. Let him not defeat the whole purpose of his existence
by dismissing the lay person as unimportant or as a member of a
group which must be treated as beneath the priest. Let the priest not
rob the layman of that activity which is the "primary and indispensable source of the true Christian spirit."

To be the source of the true Christian spirit, however, participation in the Liturgy in an active way must really and truly be an
expression of the inner man. The whole purpose of the exterior act
is to express what is interior to man and, in turn, to intensify his
interior dispositions. If a man were to lose himself in externals, to allow himself to become "collectivized," for want of interior attention
and devotion, he would be engaging in an empty formalism which is
the death of all genuine religion. God cannot be honored with the
lips alone. However, the remedy against this danger is not to run
away from the necessary externals of the Liturgy, but rather to inform
them with flesh and blood, the soul of interior attention and devotion.

4. Holy

That the Liturgy is both sacred and sanctifying follows from all
that we have thus far said. It is sacred because all its acts proceed
from the virtue of religion and have as their object the glory of God.
This sacredness is enhanced by reason of the peculiar character of
these acts of worship, namely, their priestly and sacramental quality
which makes them acts of Christ's virtue of religion, thus rendering
them infinitely pleasing and acceptable to the Father.[137]

But the Liturgy is also sanctifying. And this sanctification of man
is not to be understood as though it were a secondary end of Liturgy.

---

[137] I. Mennessier, *La Religion*. I (*Somme Théologique*, Paris: Editions du
Cerf, 1953), 332.

Since God cannot be honored without the sanctification of man, the latter forms part of the primary end of the Liturgy.[138] By its very nature Liturgy is ordained by God as the primary instrument for the sanctification of mankind. The sacrifice of the Mass renews the sacrifice of the cross and thus applies the merits of the latter to mankind. The sacraments are all actions instituted by Christ to confer grace. The Divine Office carries the power of grace into all the hours of the day. And the sacramentals bring the uplifting power of the prayer of the Mystical Body into even the material universe about us. No wonder then that St. Thomas calls the sacraments the *instrumenta separata* of God to cause grace just as the sacred Humanity of the Word was the *instrumentum coniunctum*.[139] Since all the actions of the Liturgy participate to a greater or lesser degree in this same sacramental quality, they too must all be considered as integral parts of the primary means of our sanctification. As such they possess great intrinsic sanctifying power.[140] Except for a few rare instances,[141] theologians have been in complete agreement on this point.[142]

Though "the worship rendered to God by the Church in union with her Head is the most efficacious means of achieving sanctity," [143] if it is "to produce its proper effect, it is absolutely necessary that our hearts be properly disposed." [144] Hence, the members of Christ's body "are strictly required to put their own lips to the fountain, imbibe and absorb for themselves the life-giving water, and rid themselves personally of anything that might hinder its nutritive effect in their souls." [145] Liturgy, private prayer, and personal asceticism must cooperate in order to achieve their common end: "that Christ be formed in us." [146] There is no opposition between "the action of God . . . and the collaboration of man." [147] The two must merge harmoniously into one concrete spiritual life. Just as the Liturgy needs personal effort, so that same personal effort needs the Liturgy.

As Pope Pius XII said, "if the private and interior devotion of individuals were to neglect the august sacrifice of the altar and the sacraments, and to withdraw them from the stream of vital energy

---

[138] P. Oppenheim, *op. cit.*, 81.

[139] *Summa Theol.*, III, q. 62, a. 5.

[140] *Mediator Dei*, 26.

[141] E.g., those who completely misunderstood the nature of the Liturgy and attributed absolutely no sanctifying force to it: J. Navatel, *art. cit.*, 456.

[142] Some representative authors are: C. Callewaert, *op. cit.*, 20, 26; P. Oppenheim, *op. cit.*, 44-49; M. Righetti, *op. cit.*, 18; L. Kerkhofs, "Prière liturgique et prière privée," *CCSL*, (Louvain, 1932), 135; I. Mennessier, *op. cit.*, 332; E. Raitz von Frentz, "Liturgisches und mystisches Beten," *Zeitschrift für Aszese und Mystik*, 14 (1939), 52, 56; R. Garrigou-Lagrange, *The Three Ages of the Interior Life*. I (St. Louis, 1951), 410.

[143] *Mediator Dei*, 26.

[144] *Ibid.*, 31.

[145] *Ibid.*

[146] *Ibid.*, 37.

[147] *Ibid.*, 36.

that flows from Head to members, it would indeed be sterile." [147a]
Why? Because "Liturgy is something objective. It is a higher world
which raises us up to God especially through the sacraments. In this
it is a gift of God's goodness, as grace itself, and *precedes* all our
human action." [148] The Liturgy, according to the teaching of Pius XII
and theologians, is the objective source and cause of our spiritual life—
the instrument of Christ who is the vital, efficient and exemplary
cause of that life—while private prayer and the other personal efforts
towards asceticism are the subjective collaboration with Christ's
divine action as well as the continuation and prolongation of the
supernatural life initiated in the Liturgy. All spiritual life, therefore,
must build on the common supernatural ground which is Liturgy,
but really build upon it; we must absorb and translate into our proper
needs the nutritive effect of God's action in the Liturgy.[149]

5. Traditional yet pastoral

The slightest acquaintance with the Liturgy will convince us
that one of the basic laws upon which it thrives is faithfulness to the
traditions of the Church. At the very core of the Liturgy—the Canon
of the Mass—we find a form of prayer that goes back, even in its present form, at least as far as Pope St. Gelasius I (494-496).[150] Indeed,
there is some evidence for the conjecture that the Roman Canon as
we have it today was the creation (or translation) of St. Ambrose
(374-397).[151] Yet more, an examination of all the available preceding
texts shows that the Roman Canon is in the direct line of development
and elaboration of the Eucharistic Passover prayer used by our Lord
at the Last Supper. This fact alone would be sufficient to convince us
of the supra-temporal quality of liturgical prayer, a quality which but
heightens the communal character of the Church's prayer and empha-
sizes our oneness with the Apostolic and Patristic Church in its prayer.

The Church has always manifested a preference for any rite which
has behind it the force of long tradition. She naturally regards as
more holy and deserving of respect those forms which have been hal-
lowed by age and have proved their efficacy in producing fruits of
sanctity. The wisdom of experience constitutes for the Liturgy a genuine *lex orandi*, a real order of religious expression which demands
observance and fulfillment if the Liturgy is to ring true to its nature.
If in questions of dogma and morality the Church is so meticulous in

[147a] *Ibid.*, 32.
[148] J. A. Jungmann, "Unsere liturgische Bewegung im Lichte des Rund-
schreibens Mediator Dei," *Geist und Leben*, 21 (1948), 254. Emphasis added.
[149] For a fuller treatment of the sanctifying role of the Liturgy in the spiritual
life, as well as for complete bibliography on the question, cf. J. Miller, *The
Relationship between Liturgical and Private Prayer* (Trier, 1955), esp. chapters
IV and V.
[150] J. A. Jungmann, *The Mass of the Roman Rite*. I (New York, 1951), 55.
[151] T. Klauser, *The Western Liturgy and its History* (London, 1952), 21.

preserving tradition, lest she dilute her precious deposit of revelation, her *lex credendi*, it is not less important for her to remain faithful to her sacred traditions of prayer for fear of diluting the objectivity and universality of her Liturgy and of foisting upon the faithful something purely subjective, something which corresponds to the dispositions of one individual alone instead of to the basic laws of the Christian at prayer. Change, if it is to be healthy, must be an organic development, not a deformation. Growth is good when it is an harmonious unfolding of the potential characteristics of any given thing in response to changing conditions and circumstances; it is bad when it produces a monster.[152]

In this respect the Patristic Age is of utmost importance to the Liturgy. Indeed, it is the latter's "golden age," for it was during this period that the Liturgy was molded by men who were the direct heirs of the Apostolic tradition. It was they who made an immediate application of the divine elements of the Liturgy to the needs of the communities they served. Insofar as this was true, the Liturgy of the Patristic Age was a perfect expression of the spiritual exigencies and aspirations of the worshipping community and in this respect serves as a model for all subsequent ages in all that purports to be a *living* Liturgy.[153]

Just as every truth can be exaggerated, so the principles we have just explained can be pushed to an extreme. In his encyclical *Mediator Dei* Pope Pius XII condemns what he calls "antiquarianism," [154] a false love of antiquity which manifests a preference for ancient practices simply, as the Pope says, because they "carry the savor and aroma of antiquity." [155] He does not mean to disapprove of a sane and wholesome respect for the traditions of ecclesiastical prayer, for he also says, "Assuredly it is a wise and most laudable thing to return in spirit and affection to the sources of the sacred Liturgy. For research in this field of study, by tracing it back to its origins, contributes valuable assistance towards a more thorough and careful examination of the significance of feast-days, and of the meaning of the texts and sacred ceremonies employed on their occasion." [156]

What the Pope is against is a senseless copying of the past. The Liturgy is traditional in the sense that it must be faithful to the traditional lines of its development, but it must "adapt and accommodate itself to temporal needs and circumstances." [157] It must take into account the pastoral needs of the Church in any given period of its history. The quality which makes the Patristic period stand out in liturgical practice is precisely the manner in which the Liturgy of that

---

[152] Cf. R. Guardini, *Ein Wort zur liturgischen Frage* (Mainz, 1940), 14-15.
[153] Cf. L. Bouyer, *Liturgical Piety*, 21.
[154] Par. 61-64.
[155] *Ibid.*, 61.
[156] *Ibid.*, 62.
[157] *Ibid.*, 59.

period corresponded to the needs and modes of expression of the early Christians. Pius XII devotes a long passage of *Mediator Dei* to this point in an endeavor to show how and why the Liturgy developed the way it did.[158]

If the Liturgy is the chief source of sanctification, to fulfill its role in the spiritual life it must be adapted to the receiving capacity of the faithful; it must speak to them in terms they understand, it must suit the psychological and social conditions of those who use it. It is precisely because the Liturgy has failed to evolve along with the needs of the people that we find today such a plethora of definitely second-rate devotions.[159] When we cease to practice the Liturgy in a living fashion, our spiritual life must seek out other sources of self-expression and nourishment.[160]

Many examples from the past could be marshalled to show how the Church, keenly aware of the need for adaptation, has tried to bring the Liturgy into closer harmony with the mentality of the people. Some of the hours of the Divine Office were originally pious practices of the people: prayer at the third, sixth, and ninth hours gradually became the official prayer hours of Tierce, Sext, and None.[161] Church legislation requiring the burial of martyrs' relics in the altar stone grew out of popular veneration of the martyrs.[162] And the modern marks of special reverence to the Blessed Sacrament, the practice of Benediction, the feast of Corpus Christi and its procession—all these had their ultimate root in the pious popular belief that the very sight of the consecrated species brought with it a special power of benediction.[163]

Perhaps the best example, because it is a statement of principle, comes from Pope St. Gregory the Great. After sending Augustine to Britain to evangelize the heathens there, Gregory offered him many counsels by letter. In one letter he advises him to give heed to the traditions of the Church by selecting from the Roman, Gallican, or other churches whatever appropriate practices he could find, using them as the basis of English liturgical practice: "Choose whatever is pious, religious and correct in the individual churches, make a collection of it, and establish it as the custom among the English." [164] In still another letter Gregory cautions Augustine to have consideration

---

[158] *Ibid.,* 49-56.

[159] E. g.: J. A. Jungmann, *Die Frohbotschaft und unsere Glaubensverkündigung* (Regensburg, 1936), 96-97; P. Doncoeur, "Conditions d'une renaissance de l'Office Canonial," *Etudes,* 245 (1945), 262; *idem,* "Exercices de piété non strictement liturgiques," *CCSL,* 15 (1948), 210-212; C. Howell, *Of Sacraments and Sacrifice* (Collegeville, 1952), 155-156; L. Bouyer, *Liturgical Piety,* 244.

[160] P. Doncoeur, "Exercices de piété non strictement liturgiques," 211.

[161] Cf. J. A. Jungmann, "The Liturgical Movement in the Discipline of the Ancient Church and the Church of Today," *The American Ecclesiastical Review,* 94 (1936), 5.

[162] *Ibid.,* 13.

[163] Cf. E. Dumoutet, *Le Désir de voir l'hostie.* (Paris, 1926).

[164] *Epistularum lib.* XI, 64. *MPL,* 77:1187.

for the customs of the heathen English which can be turned to good:

> One should not destroy the temples of the demons
> among this people, but only the idols in them. Let the temples
> be sprinkled with holy water and altars built and relics set
> into them. As long as they (the temples) are well built, one
> should transfer them from the service of the idols to the
> worship of the true God, so that the people, seeing that their
> places of worship are preserved, will more willingly gather
> in those places to which they are accustomed in order to
> acknowledge and adore the true God and thus lay aside their
> error. And since the Anglo-Saxons were in the habit of slaying
> many oxen in their sacrifices to idols, one should use some of
> these things in Christian celebrations: for instance, on the
> days of dedication of churches or on feast-days of the martyrs
> whose relics are buried in them let them build huts of tree
> branches around the outside of the church, converted over
> from a pagan temple, and celebrate the feast with religious
> meals. However, let them no longer immolate animals in
> honor of the devil, but rather for the glory of God let them
> slaughter the animals for food and thank the Giver of all gifts
> for their fullness, so that as they retain some of their external
> rejoicings they may the more easily experience interior joys.
> For doubtless it is impossible to take away from hardened
> hearts all that is old at once, since after all he who wishes to
> ascend the heights must do so step for step, not all in one
> jump.[165]

While being true to its essential characteristics as found in its
past history, the Liturgy must truly grow and develop along with
the evolution of society in order to be the genuine and sincere expression of society's spiritual life.

6. Infallible

Since faith is the principle of religion, it follows naturally that
there will be a close connection between the doctrine of the Church
and her Liturgy. Liturgy is always an external manifestation or
protestation of some doctrine in which we believe. Since the truth
of our faith is insured by an infallible teaching authority, our Liturgy
will be pure of error by reason of the vigilance of that same authority.
So careful has the Church been in exercising this authority, so insistent has she been, in other words, on the traditional, that Pope
Celestine I could say that the Church's prayer constituted a veritable
law of belief.[166] This means that once the Church has decided what is
proper for the worship of God the texts of the Liturgy, thus approved,
serve in turn as a source of doctrine and for the instruction of the

---

[165] *Ibid.,* 76. *MPL, 77:*1215-1216.
[166] ". . . ut legem credendi lex statuat supplicandi." *De gratia Dei* "Indiculus,"
cap. 8. Denz. 139.

faithful in subsequent ages. The Liturgy is both a *locus theologicus* and, as Pius XI stated, the ordinary and most efficacious manner in which the Church teaches the people.[167]

This teaching function should be already evident from the nature of the first part of the Mass, which is intended to serve as a period of instruction, a service of the word, for the faithful as well as for catechumens. It is also true of the rest of the Liturgy, depending as it does on the infallible teaching of the Church. Pius XI did not hesitate to call the Liturgy the teaching method of the Church [168] and Pius XII has repeated the idea:

> The entire Liturgy has the Catholic faith for its content, inasmuch as it bears public witness to the faith of the Church. For this reason, whenever there was question of defining a truth revealed by God, the Sovereign Pontiff and the Councils in their recourse to the theological sources, as they are called, have not seldom drawn many an argument from this sacred science of the Liturgy. For an example in point, Our predecessor of immortal memory, Pius IX, so argued when he proclaimed the Immaculate Conception of the Virgin Mary. Similarly during the discussion of a doubtful or controversial truth, the Church and the Holy Fathers have not failed to look to the age-old and time-honored sacred rites for enlightenment. Hence the well known and venerable maxim, *Legem credendi lex statuat supplicandi.*[169]

In his Allocution to the Assisi Congress of Pastoral Liturgy the same Pontiff said: "It would be very difficult to find one truth of the Christian faith which is not expressed in some way in the Liturgy. . . . In the Liturgy the Church communicates abundantly the treasures of the deposit of faith, of the truth of Christ." [170] Certainly this is not to imply that Christian education ends with Liturgy. In the same address Pius XII insists that "the Liturgy does not exhaust the Church's activities, especially her teaching role and her care of souls. . . ." [171] The latter two concerns extend far beyond the Liturgy: There are dogmatic and disciplinary matters which the Liturgy alone cannot definitively settle; there is also the question of training the Christian mind in an ever more scientific understanding of revealed truth.

Appendix
The Meaning and Use of Certain Terms

Ceremony. The word comes from the Sanskrit *Karmon,* meaning a thing done.[172] In the broad sense, the term means the externals

---

[167] *Quas Primas,* encyclical on the Kingship of Christ: Bugnini, 57.
[168] "Liturgia, Didascalia Ecclesiae," Bugnini, 70.
[169] *Mediator Dei,* 47-48.
[170] *AAS,* 48 (1956), 713.
[171] *Ibid.,* 714-715.
[172] Cf. J. Baudot, "Cérémonies," *DACL,* II: 3297-3298; A. Schulte, "Ceremony," *Catholic Encyclopedia,* III:538.

involved in the worship of the Church; in the strict sense, it means movements and actions accompanying but accidental to the sacramental forms; the individual actions, therefore, of a rite.

Rite. This word comes from the Latin word *recte*; it is a *mos* or *approbata consuetudo.*[173] It means the ensemble of formulas, actions, and practical norms to be followed in the accomplishment of a determined liturgical function: e.g., the rite of Baptism, the rite of the consecration of a bishop, etc. Nevertheless, the term is also used in a broader sense to designate the liturgical functions of one of the great liturgical families: Roman Rite, Byzantine Rite, etc. Ritual is also used in the narrow sense, to mean a particular book of rites.

Rubrics. Comes from the Latin word *rubrica,* a sort of reddish earth used for painting or writing. Red color was first used to print the titles of books, then later came to be used for the remarks made on a given text. As used to mean the norms of ceremonial, the word first appears in the fourteenth century.[174] Thus rubrics are the rules indicating which ceremonies are to be performed and the manner in which they are to be performed. Hence the saying: *Lege rubrum si vis intelligere nigrum.*

Liturgical. Liturgy, as already defined, is the entirety of public worship of the Mystical Body. Hence liturgical can be applied to whatever pertains strictly to this domain: liturgical art, liturgical vestments, liturgical chant, etc. In a broader sense the word liturgical is used to qualify any action or prayer which is in keeping with the spirit of the Liturgy: liturgical spirituality, liturgical meditation, liturgical philosophy of life. One ought to be careful, however, when using this term not to apply it in such a way so as to leave the liturgical apostolate open to ridicule.

As for the spirit of the Liturgy, Pius XII offers us some help in making this concept more precise. He says, "It is necessary that the spirit of the sacred Liturgy and its directives should exercise such a salutary influence on [exercises of piety not strictly liturgical] that nothing improper be introduced nor anything unworthy of the house of God or detrimental to the sacred functions or opposed to solid piety." [175] He also states that the criterion for deciding whether inspirations to follow extraordinary paths in the spiritual life come from the Father of Lights will be "their effectiveness in making the divine cult loved and spread daily more widely, and in making the faithful approach the sacraments with more longing desire, and in obtaining for all holy things due respect and honor. If on the contrary they are an obstacle to the principles and norms of divine worship, or if they oppose or hinder them, one must surely conclude

---

[173] Cf. A. Forcellini, *Totius Latinitatis Lexicon.* II (London, 1828), 437.
[174] Cf. M. Righetti, *op. cit.,* 19; A. Forcellini, *op. cit.,* II, 446; F. Cabrol, "Rubrics," *Catholic Encyclopedia,* XIII: 1216.
[175] *Mediator Dei,* 184.

that they are not in keeping with prudence and enlightened zeal." [176]

From these statements we may conclude that the spirit of the Liturgy means: (1) a willingness to follow the Liturgy as norm and guide for our private spiritual lives; (2) a concern with the discretion and sense of proportion as well as the theological content of the Liturgy, and an application of these qualities to our spiritual life; (3) an appreciation of the Liturgy as the primary and indispensable source of the true Christian spirit; (4) a refusal to let anything hinder our living of the liturgical life; (5) an avoidance of the overly emotional and sentimental, the bizarre and novel, in our practice of asceticism; (6) a freeing of ourselves from any individualistic attitudes and an orientation of our lives and our activity towards the beautiful doctrines of the Mystical Body of Christ and the Communion of Saints.

We gain an added insight into Pius XII's understanding and appreciation of the liturgical spirit from a letter which Archbishop Montini, then Pro-Secretary of State, wrote at the Pope's behest to the *Centro di Azione Liturgica* during the Marian Year. There we read: "It cannot be repeated often enough what precious treasures in the Church would be opened to each individual and to all, if the powerful stream of love for Mary, which affords our troubled times the brightest note of hope, were informed and regulated by the spirit of the Liturgy. For then our relationship to Mary would not be spent and exhausted in superficial feeling or in an anxious, self-interested plea for help in the hour of need, but rather would gain that quality of maturity and depth on which depend the constancy and fruitfulness of the spiritual life." [177]

[176] *Ibid.,* 181.
[177] *Liturgisches Jahrbuch,* 4 (1954), 246.

CHAPTER TWO

Liturgical Families of Christendom [1]

The prototype of all Christian Liturgies is the Last Supper. Within the setting of a Jewish meal—the great meal of the entire Jewish year, commemorative of the passing of the Angel of Death and the exodus of the Chosen People from the land of the Pharaohs through the Red Sea—our Savior instituted the Eucharistic sacrifice. It was essentially from this simple rite that the whole Christian Liturgy was born.

After our Lord's Ascension His followers "continued steadfastly in the teaching of the Apostles and in the communion of the breaking of the bread and in the prayers." [2] In other words, the Apostles began to instruct converts in the teachings of Jesus of Nazareth, to initiate them into a sharing in our Lord's sacrifice, and to teach them prayers with which they might prepare themselves for and continue the effects of the Lord's Supper; a Liturgy was already developing under the divinely guided hands of the Apostles. But notice that the Christian Liturgy was not a sudden break with Judaism; the Christians continued daily with one accord in the *temple* and broke bread in their *houses*.[3] They went to the temple or synagogue for the service of the Word, for the reading of the Scriptures, and joined in the hymns and psalms sung by the Jews on such occasions. But then they retired to the home of a Christian to "break bread," to celebrate the Eucharistic Sacrifice.[4] Here we have the obvious origin of the arrangement of our Mass into its two principal parts: service of the Word and service of sacrifice.

---

[1] For a more extensive treatment of this question, cf.: L. Duchesne, *Christian Worship* (London, 1949), 1-55; J. A. Jungmann, *The Mass of the Roman Rite*, I (New York, 1951), 7-49; M. Righetti, *Manuale di Storia Liturgica*. I: *Introduzione Generale* (Milan, 1950), 86-154.

[2] Acts 2:42.

[3] *Ibid.*, 46.

[4] This is not to imply that the early Christians of the first century did not, at least on occasion, hold their own private gatherings in which both these elements were united. Acts 20:7-11 certainly offers us proof that such was the case. Before midnight the faithful had assembled to "break bread," but before doing so they listened to an address made by Paul. This "address" was indeed a normal part of the service of the Word; today we speak of it as a homily. Only after he had finished did the community finally "break bread." Cf. Oscar Cullman, *Early Christian Worship* (London, 1954), 27-31.

This same schema of divine worship is described more in detail by St. Justin Martyr in the middle of the second century. His report is the oldest piece of Christian evidence we have concerning the Mass. He is well qualified to describe the practices of the early Church, for he was thoroughly acquainted with worship throughout the Christian world. He lived in Rome for a long time, was born and reared in Palestine, converted in Asia Minor, and had wandered as a philosopher through many other provinces of the Roman Empire. Hence his description should be representative of all these areas. He says:

> On the day which is called the day of the sun we have a common assembly of all who live in the cities or outlying districts. The memoirs of the Apostles or the writings of the Prophets are read as long as there is time. Then, when the reader has finished, the president of the assembly verbally admonishes and invites all to imitate such examples of virtue. Then we all stand and offer up our prayers (in common for ourselves, for the newly baptized, for all other persons wherever they may be, in order that, since we have found the truth, we may be found worthy through our actions to be esteemed as good citizens and observers of the law, and thus attain eternal salvation. At the conclusion of the prayers we greet one another with a kiss). And as we said before, after we finish our prayers, bread and wine are presented. He who presides likewise offers up prayers and thanksgivings to the best of his ability, and the people express their approval by saying "Amen." The Eucharistic elements are distributed and consumed by those present, and to those who are absent they are sent through the deacons. The wealthy, if they wish, contribute whatever they desire, and the collection is placed in the custody of the president. . . .[5]

What do we have here? A series of readings, prayers for different categories of the faithful, the anaphora or sacrificial action, with communion, finally a collection taken up for those in need.

In general, says Jungmann, we can speak of a uniform development of the Liturgy throughout Christendom all the way up until the fourth century.[6] But Duchesne insists that there was never a complete identity of the details of worship among the various Churches, not even in the ones founded by the Apostles, for it was not in accordance with the practice of early days to attach to things of this nature an importance that would sanction and fix them.[7] Uniformity, therefore, was only approximate.

There were too many factors militating against this situation for it to continue. True, there were many ties among the various localities. In the beginning there was a perpetual intercourse of apostles,

[5] I Apology 67. J. Quasten, Monumenta eucharistica et liturgica vetustissima (Florilegium Patristicum, VII, Bonn, 1935), 19. Parenthesis is taken from Ch. 65., Quasten, 16.
[6] Der Gottesdienst der Kirche (Innsbruck, 1955), 24.
[7] Op. cit., 54.

missionaries, prophets and catechists who were not attached to any
fixed locality in the exercise of their ministry. They went from one
Christian body to another, moving in all directions, either to carry
the Gospel into regions as yet unevangelized, or to encourage, instruct and defend struggling infant communities.[8] But this soon ceased
to be the case. And when this itinerant ministry disappeared, there
remained nothing more than the local ecclesiastical organization. The
tendency toward local differentiation then asserted itself, for at least
three good reasons:

1. The liturgical formulas themselves were uncertain. We saw
that Justin said the presiding official at Mass offered "prayers and
thanksgivings" *as best he could.* That is to say, the formulas for Mass
were very seldom fixed or written; the president of the liturgical assembly simply improvised. Even as late as 215 Hippolytus could
write: "Let the bishop give thanks according to the models we have
given above. It is not, however, at all necessary that he recite the
same words as we have given, as though he must say them by heart
in his thanksgiving to God; but let each one pray according to his
ability." [9] In other words, though written models had already appeared, there was not as yet any obligation to remain faithful to them.
On this head alone there was a large margin of difference.

2. There was a great variety of circumstances, needs, and ethnic
traits to which the Liturgy had to adapt itself. Where the Church was
persecuted, rites had to be modest and secret. Elsewhere it was possible to build spacious churches in which elaborate ceremonies could
take place. One group of people was speculatively inclined, another
more emotional, etc.

3. At this early age it was extremely difficult to maintain stable
and constant communications between various Churches. On the contrary, due to the spasmodic and irregular character of their contacts,
Churches developed differently. It is even probable, at this time, that
daughter foundations could not maintain strict adhesion to the liturgical practices of their mother-Churches.

At the beginning of the fifth century, St. Augustine could say
that, while as far as essentials went there was unity within the Church,
other things varied according to different regions. Some received the
Body and Blood of our Lord every day, others only on certain days.
In some places never a day went by without offering the Holy Sacrifice; in other places it was offered only on Saturdays and Sundays,
still in others only on Sundays.[10]

A. Evolution of Liturgical Types

A tendency, common in the days of Charlemagne, already showed
itself very powerful in the early centuries of Christianity. Churches

---

[8] *Ibid.,* 13-14.
[9] *La Tradition Apostolique* (Ed. B. Botte, Paris, 1946), p. 14.
[10] *Epistola 54. MPL,* 33:200.

of lesser importance, from the point of view of prestige, government, and tradition, liked to copy the usages of other Churches which enjoyed the leadership of gifted men, or a longer tradition—even going back, sometimes, to apostolic foundation—or which possessed some sort of political or moral hegemony, as with an episcopal city which was at the same time the seat of provincial political power.

History shows that certain cities, both in East and West, enjoyed such a prestige. With the destruction of Jerusalem under Titus, the eyes of all turned to *Rome*, where the supreme Head of the Church had set up the central seat of Church government. Yet there were other great cities which exercised a notable influence in ecclesiastical affairs. *Carthage*, though bound closely to Rome by reason of its nearness, was the center of activity for African Christianity. The same was true of *Alexandria* and *Antioch*; the bishops of these Sees were constantly intervening in the affairs of neighboring dioceses. *Caesaria* in Cappadocia extended its influence over Pontus and Armenia. But from the time the Imperial residence was located at *Constantinople*, this See began to take precedence over all the cities of the East; its bishop came gradually to be regarded as an Eastern quasi-pope. North of Rome, *Milan* enjoyed extraordinary authority over dioceses in Spain and France and even as far north as Germany and the British Isles. Only under Pope Zosimus (417-418) did the See of *Arles* attain any pre-eminence in Gaul. Yet due to their extreme remoteness and infrequent contacts with the rest of Christianity, the Anglo-Saxons, Celts, and even the Spaniards, to a degree, developed somewhat independently.

"In proportion as these great metropolitan Churches widened the area of their mission," Duchesne remarks, "they extended also the circle of their special uses, for it is altogether natural that the use of the Mother Church should become a law to the daughter Churches." [11] Other Churches too, not directly founded by the metropolitan ones, came under the sway of the latter for one reason or another. Thus the ecclesiastical provinces became quite naturally the lines of demarcation for liturgical evolution; they became "liturgical provinces."

These considerations provide the background for our division of the various liturgies into what we call "types." All existing Rites within the Church can more or less perfectly be traced back to certain chief groups or types that basically took their origin from the above-mentioned ecclesiastical areas of influence. Therefore we feel that to classify the various Liturgies according to their historical origin has more logic behind it than to use a variety of criteria such as those proposed by A. Raes: i.e., the Churches which use these Liturgies, the doctrine proposed in them, the language used, and, finally, the ceremonies proper to them.[12] It is true, of course, that all such characteris-

---

[11] *Op. cit.*, 54-55.
[12] *Introductio in Liturgiam Orientalem* (Rome, 1947), 7-8.

tics may serve to distinguish the Rites within Christendom. It seems more important, however, to lay stress on the common family stock to be found in the liturgical types.

The fundamental types, therefore, are four: Antiochian, Alexandrian, Gallican, and Roman. These, in turn, may be subdivided into the following:

Antiochian
    East Syrian (Nestorian, Chaldean and Malabar Rites)
    West Syrian (Syrian Jacobite and Uniate, Maronite,
               Armenian and Byzantine Rites)
Alexandrian
    Coptic (Egypt)
    Abyssinian (Ethiopia)
Gallican
    Gallican properly so-called (Gaul)
    Celtic (Irish and Scots)
    Mozarabic (Spain)
    Ambrosian (Milan)
Roman

B. Classification of Types

1. Antiochian Liturgies

Though the regions east of Antioch are known to have been evangelized by missionaries from this city and therefore most certainly received their primitive Liturgy from their hands, difference in language and nationality soon resulted in liturgical particularism. These eastern provinces remained faithful to the Church until the condemnation of Nestorius at the Council of Ephesus (431). During the long period of schism which followed, substantial differences were introduced into the original Liturgy. In the fifteenth century some of these Nestorians returned to the Church and are known today as the Chaldean Uniates. Today the Liturgy of Sts. Addai and Mari,[13] dating from the beginning of the seventh century, is followed by both Nestorians and Chaldean Uniates as well as by the schismatic and uniate Malabar Christians, though the latter adhere to a more Romanized form. The early historical development of this Liturgy can be best appreciated by having reference to such sources as the homilies of St. Aphraates (d.367),[14] the compositions of St. Ephrem (d.373),[15] and the homilies of Narsai of Edessa (d.503).[16] The East Syrian Liturgy uses only three anaphoras, that is, variable formulas comparable

---

[13] See translation in F. E. Brightman, *Liturgies Eastern and Western* (Oxford, 1896), I, 247-305.
[14] *Patrologia Syriaca*, I, 1-2 (Ed. Parisot; Paris, 1894-1907).
[15] Th. Lamy, *S. Ephrem Syri hymni et sermones*. 4 vols. Mecheln, 1882-1902.
[16] H. Connolly, *The Liturgical Homilies of Narsai*. Cambridge, 1909.

to our Roman Mass-Canon. A characteristic feature of these East Syrian Rites is the occurrence of the great prayer of intercession immediately before the Anamnesis and Epiclesis, as opposed to its occurrence after these in the West Syrian Rites.[17]

Emanating from Antioch, which in turn received much of its liturgical usage from Jerusalem, the West Syrian Liturgies predominate over all other Oriental Rites. Their evolution begins with the fourth century *Apostolic Constitutions* [18] which contains materials from a much earlier time. This Liturgy is also attested to by other fourth and fifth century documents; e.g., The *Mystagogical Catechesis* of St. Cyril of Jerusalem,[19] the diary of the nun Etheria's pilgrimage to the Holy Places,[20] *The Testament of our Lord Jesus Christ*,[21] and the homilies of St. John Chrysostom.[22]

The oldest complete formulary for the West Syrian Rite is the Greek Liturgy of St. James, dating certainly from before the seventh century.[23] Since the twelfth century, however, it has fallen into almost complete disuse; it is employed by the Greek Orthodox once a year, on the feast of St. James, in Jerusalem and on the islands of Cyprus and Zante. This same Liturgy of St. James was translated into Syriac [24] by the schismatic monophysite Jacobites (named after their organizer, Jacobus Baradaeus) some time after the Council of Chalcedon (451). Though the Jacobites have more than sixty anaphoras, only a few of them are in use today. This Syriac Liturgy of St. James is followed, not only by the Jacobite Syrians, but also by the Syrians who returned to the Church in 1781 and by the Maronites, the latter having Romanized it to a degree.

The Greek Liturgy of St. James was subsequently transformed by Sts. Basil [25] and John Chrysostom [26] and is known today as the Byzantine Rite. Due to the predominant influence of Constantinople, this Rite has succeeded in either transplanting other Liturgies of the East or at least in impregnating them with some of its characteristics. It is the most widely used of all the Oriental Liturgies. While the Liturgy of St. Basil is now limited to but a few days in the year—Sundays of Lent, Thursday and Saturday of Holy Week, the Vigils of Christmas and Epiphany, New Year's Day and the feast of St. Basil—the Liturgy of St. John Chrysostom is practically of daily use. A special form of Mass of the Presanctified is followed for the fast days of Lent, since

---

[17] Cf. Raes, *op. cit.*, 92-93.
[18] Esp. Book II, ch. 57 and Book VIII, ch. 5-15, reproduced in Brightman, I, 3-30.
[19] Contained in *MPG*, vol. 33.
[20] Ethérie, *Journal de Voyage*. Ed Hélène Pétré, Paris, 1948.
[21] Discovered and edited by I. E. Rahmani, *Testamentum Domini Nostri Jesu Christi*. Mainz, 1899. It is reproduced in part in J. Quasten, *op. cit.*, 237-273.
[22] Contained in *MPG*, vols. 49-50.
[23] Reproduced in Brightman, I, 31-68.
[24] Reproduced in Brightman, I, 69-110.
[25] See Brightman, I, 309-344.
[26] *Ibid.*, I, 353-399. See also more ancient forms of this Rite: 527-552.

the celebration of Mass on such days is still forbidden according to ancient discipline.[27]

One last representative of this branch of Liturgies is the Armenian Rite.[28] It may be said to be an early stage of development of the Byzantine Liturgy, inasmuch as it combines the earlier forms of the Syrian Rite with many Byzantine modifications. And those Armenians who have returned to the Church have introduced further alterations stemming from Roman influence.

2. Alexandrian Liturgies

Contrary to the tendency manifested among the Churches in the East, Alexandria always resisted the allure of Antioch and consequently developed an independent Liturgy. It was only after the condemnation of Dioscorus by the Council of Chalcedon (451) that the small group which kept its ties with the Church (who today are called the Melchites) began to modify their Liturgy until it became identical with the Byzantine Rite of Constantinople.

The earliest known document pertaining to the Alexandrian Rite is the so-called *Papyrus Dêr-Balyzeh* [29] dating from the third century. From the fourth century we have the *Euchologion* of Serapion, Bishop of Thmuis (d.362).[30] The Rite is also represented, though with many Byzantine modifications, in the Greek Liturgy of St. Mark [31] which may go back as far as the fourth century. The heretical group in Egypt, and even those returned to the Church, follow the Liturgy of Sts. Cyril and Basil, using Coptic as the liturgical language,[32] while the schismatics and uniates in Abyssinia follow the Liturgy of the Twelve Apostles [33] and use Ethiopic or Ge'ez for their liturgical language.

The characteristic of the Alexandrian type as opposed to the Antiochian is the occurrence of the great prayer of intercession within the Preface instead of after the Consecration. Thus the Sanctus, the words of institution, and the Epiclesis come a little later than in the Antiochian Liturgies.[34]

3. Gallican Liturgies

The term "Gallican" as used here must not be confused with the trend in the last few centuries of some ecclesiastics in France to form

[27] *Ibid.*, I, 345-352.
[28] *Ibid.*, I, 412-457.
[29] Reproduced in J. Quasten, *op. cit.*, 37-44.
[30] The Mass prayers of this manuscript are reproduced by J. Quasten, 48-67: cf. also L. Duchesne, *op. cit.*, 76-78.
[31] Brightman, I, 113-143. Fragments of a papyrus from the fourth century are reproduced in Quasten, 44-48.
[32] See translation in Brightman, I, 144-188.
[33] This is fundamentally an Ethiopian version of the Coptic Liturgy of St. Cyril; see translation in Brightman, I, 194-244.
[34] See comparative tables in A. Raes, *op. cit.*, 92-93.

themselves into a national church. Rather the word is here used in a general sense to refer to all those Liturgies of the West different from that of Rome. This liturgical type comprises those rites peculiar to the north of Italy, Spain, France, Germany and the British Isles, and it is subdivided into four chief forms: the Gallican Liturgy properly so-called, the Celtic, Mozarabic and Ambrosian.

The problem of the origin of these diverse western Rites is a difficult one, and a variety of theses have been proposed to explain it. L. Duchesne [35] and H. Leclercq,[36] with support from many other authors, claim that the Gallican Liturgies are basically of Oriental origin, coming to the West via Milan and radiating thence to the other centers of Western culture. Whether Milan was actually this center of diffusion of Oriental influence or not has certainly not been proven to the satisfaction of all.[37] However, there are indeed noteworthy features of the Gallican Liturgies in general which serve to bring out their Oriental inspiration: the preparation of the matter of sacrifice at the very beginning of Mass, the singing of the Trisagium before the reading of the lessons, the solemn Offertory procession and incensation of the oblation, the placing of the kiss of peace at this point and, in the Ambrosian Rite, the recitation of the Credo (in the Mozarabic Rite it is sung as an accompanying chant for the Confraction), the presence of an Epiclesis after the words of institution, and many other interesting formulas and ceremonies of definitely Eastern flavor.

Against this thesis G. Dix argues that the Gallican Liturgies are but adaptations of the early Liturgy of Rome.[38] F. Probst goes even further and states that they were the original Liturgy of the West later abandoned by Rome.[39] But this latter opinion runs up against the major difficulty that the Gallican type already represents a late stage of development.[40]

The facts seem to warrant our adoption of a compromise position. Certainly the major portions of Western civilization received the Gospel from Rome and together with it Rome's Liturgy. Gallican lands, in turn, later accepted various rites and ceremonies imported from Oriental areas by Oriental bishops and clerics who took up residence in the West.

The *Gallican Liturgy* strictly so-called is that used in the regions of Gaul during the early part of the Middle Ages up until approximately the eighth century when, in an attempt to obtain some uniformity of observances, both rulers and bishops turned once again to Roman sources. As we shall see more in detail, what actually hap-

---

[35] *Op. cit.,* 90-95.
[36] "Gallicane (Liturgie)", *DACL,* VI, 474.
[37] Cf. G. Dix, *The Shape of the Liturgy* (Westminster, England, 1952), 460; M. Righetti, *op. cit.,* I, 126.
[38] *Op. cit.* 460-469, esp. 469.
[39] *Die abendländische Messe vom 5 bis 8 Jahrhundert* (Münster, 1896), 264-268, cited in Jungmann, *Mass of the Roman Rite,* I, 47.
[40] Jungmann, I, 47.

pened was the gradual evolution of a hybrid rite accepted later even by Rome. The Gallican Rite was preserved more faithfully by the clerics of the diocese of Lyons and by certain religious Orders such as the Dominicans and Carthusians.

The chief documents of the old Gallican Liturgy that have come down to us are: the *Missale Gothicum*,[41] believed to be a Sacramentary of the Church of Autun from the seventh century and containing elements from Rome, the south of France, and Spain; the so-called *Masses of Mone,* probably dating from the seventh century region of Burgundy; [42] the *Vetus Missale Gallicanum*,[43] written probably for the Church of Auxerre towards the end of the seventh century; the *Sacramentarium Gallicanum*,[44] often called the *Bobbio Missal* after the place where it was discovered, dating probably from the seventh century and compiled from Roman elements with a Gallican substratum and many traces of Spanish and Celtic influence; the *Lectionary of Luxeuil*, from the seventh century and destined for the Church of Paris; [45] and finally the description of the Gallican Mass contained in the *Expositio brevis antiquae liturgiaè gallicanae*,[46] coming from the seventh century, possibly from Autun, though falsely attributed to St. Germain of Paris (d.576).

The *Celtic Liturgies* [47] were in use in Brittany until the ninth century, in Scotland until the eleventh, and in England and Ireland until the twelfth. We cannot really speak of one Celtic Liturgy, but rather of many, for during the Middle Ages these peoples enjoyed no liturgical uniformity. Their Liturgies were really woven from many patterns and elements—Roman, Gallican, Mozarabic and Oriental, for the monks who evangelized these Isles paid many a visit and spent long sojourns on the continent whence they brought back with them liturgical customs and notions of varied origin. Missionaries from these Isles went, in turn, all over the continent and brought with them their own Celtic observances. We find their liturgical books in Frankish territory, Gaul and Germany, as well as in north Italy. The two most important documents belonging to these rites of the Celts are the *Stowe Missal* [48] and the *Antiphonary of Bangor*,[49] the first being substantially from the eighth and ninth centuries, the second from the seventh century.

[41] Reproduced in *MPL*, 72: 225-318.
[42] Reproduced in *MPL*, 138: 863-882.
[43] Reproduced in *MPL*, 72: 339-382.
[44] Reproduced in *MPL*, 72: 451-578.
[45] Reproduced in *MPL*, 72: 171-216; cf. a critical edition by P. Salmon, *Le Lectionnaire de Luxeuil, édition et étude comparative*, Rome, 1944.
[46] Reproduced in *MPL*, 72: 89-98.
[47] Cf. L. Gougaud, "Celtiques (Liturgies)," *DACL*, II, 2969-2971; H. Jenner, "Celtic Rite," *The Catholic Encyclopedia*, III, 492-504.
[48] For reproductions see: G. F. Warner, *The Stowe Missal*, 2 vols., London, 1906 and 1915.
[49] E. Warren, *The Antiphonary of Bangor*, 2 vols., London, 1893 and 1895.

The *Mozarabic Liturgy*,[50] receiving its name from the time when Spain came under the rule of the Arabs (*musta rab*, or *mos arabica*), is simply the ancient Spanish Rite. Spain most certainly received its primitive Liturgy from Rome but then evolved it with much help from the Greeks, the Milanese, and the Churches of Aquitaine and Arles. This liturgy flourished already in the third and fourth centuries and reached its zenith in the seventh century under such men of sanctity as Sts. Leander, Isidore, Eugene and Ildephonse. It was long suspected of heretical tendencies, though nothing has been conclusively proved. And from the eleventh century on, various Popes, especially Gregory VII (1073-1085), tried to substitute for it the genuine Roman Rite. Today it is limited to a few churches in Toledo. The principal liturgical books of this Rite are: the *Missale Mixtum* edited by Cardinal Ximenes in 1500,[51] the *Breviarium Gothicum* published by the same Cardinal in 1502,[52] the Ritual and Pontifical called the *Liber Ordinum*,[53] and a Sacramentary.[54]

The *Ambrosian Rite*,[55] still followed today in Milan and in a few parishes of other neighboring dioceses, takes its name from the famous bishop of Milan, St. Ambrose (374-397). But did St. Ambrose author it? There are so many similarities in style between the writings of St. Ambrose and the Rite of Milan, that many think that he had a definitive hand in its formation.[56] Duchesne, as we have already remarked, thinks that, because of word-for-word likenesses in both the Ambrosian and Syro-Byzantine Rites, the former in its peculiarities was imported from the East by Auxentius, an Arian bishop coming from Cappadocia and occupying the See of Milan from 355-374.[57] Some maintain, however, that the Ambrosian Rite is fundamentally Roman but that St. Ambrose's writings themselves show certain non-Roman elements and that later even more Eastern peculiarities were introduced into the Rite.[58] Although St. Ambrose himself attests to his desire to follow the Roman usage, he nevertheless insists that it is reasonable to adopt practices from other Churches.[59] One proof that is

---

[50] Cf. F. Cabrol, "Mozarabe (La Liturgie)," *DACL*, XII, 392; H. Jenner, "Mozarabic Rite," *The Catholic Encyclopedia*, X, 611-623; A. King, *Liturgies of the Primatial Sees* (London, 1957), pp. 457-631.

[51] Reproduced in *MPL*, vol. 85.

[52] Reproduced in *MPL*, vol. 86.

[53] Republished by M. Férotin, *Le Liber Ordinum*, Paris, 1904.

[54] Republished by M. Férotin, *Le Liber mozarabicus sacramentorum*, Paris, 1912.

[55] Cf. P. Lejay, "Ambrosien (rit)," *DACL*, I, 1373-1442; H. Jenner, "Ambrosian Liturgy and Rite," *The Catholic Encyclopedia*, I, 394-403; P. Borella, "La Messa Ambrosiana," excursus in M. Righetti, *op. cit.*, III, 508-568; A. King, *op. cit.*, 286-456.

[56] P. Lejay, *art. cit.*, 1373-1374.

[57] *Op. cit.*, 93-94.

[58] M. Righetti, *op. cit.*, I, 144-146.

[59] "In omnibus cupio sequi ecclesiam Romanam; sed tamen et nos homines sensum habemus; ideo, quod alibi rectius servatur, et nos rectius custodimus." Ambrose, *De sacramentis* III, 1, 5. J. Quasten, 152.

often proffered in support of the claim that the Milanese Rite is basically Roman is the fact that Milan at some time or other, perhaps
during the episcopate of Ambrose,[60] introduced the use of the Roman
Mass-Canon.[61]

For texts, besides the works of St. Ambrose and other Fathers of
the fifth century, there is the *Expositio Missae Canonicae*, a literal
commentary on the Ambrosian Mass of the first part of the ninth century; [62] the two oldest Sacramentaries that have been preserved for
us are those of Biasca [63] and Bergamo,[64] both dating from the tenth
century.

4. Roman Liturgy

By the Roman Rite we mean specifically that type of Mass and
sacramental ritual belonging to the city of Rome itself which gradually
succeeded in gaining the ascendancy over all other types in the West—
albeit with many a Gallican addition. The oldest books of this Rite
are the Leonine, Gelasian and Gregorian Sacramentaries.[65] Still another work, recently discovered, offers us the Liturgy of Rome in a
more ancient form, namely, the *Apostolic Tradition* of Hippolytus
(d.235). The Roman Rite succeeded in supplanting the liturgical
forms of the North, not simply by abolishing them, but rather by assimilating them to a degree. Both Pepin and Charlemagne attempted
to introduce authoritatively the Liturgy of Rome into their realms. To
do this, Charlemagne requested of Pope Hadrian a copy of the Roman
service book and had his "minister in charge of Liturgy," Alcuin,
oversee its observance. But opposition was too great, and while Charlemagne had started out to bring the Gallican usage in line with the
pure Roman forms, what he actually achieved was quite the opposite:
There resulted a mixed form in which the Gelasian, Gregorian, and
old Gallican elements were combined into a single unit. Moreover,
due to the expeditions of the Ottos to Rome, this mixture found its
way into Italy, and finally Rome, and is now the official Roman Liturgy.

The opposition of the Frankish clergy and people was understandable, for the pure Roman Rite, if we are to accept the description of
E. Bishop,[66] was of almost puritanical sobriety and brevity. The Galli-

---

[60] He cites whole sections of the Roman Canon: cf. *ibid.*, V-VI. Quasten,
160-162.

[61] Christine Mohrmann inclines to this opinion — *Liturgical Latin* (Washington, 1957), 64-65 — against those who hold that Rome borrowed the Canon from
Ambrose: cf. O. Casel, "Oblatio rationabilis," *Theologische Quartalschrift*, 99
(1917-1918), 429-438; T. Klauser, *The Western Liturgy and its History*, 20-21.

[62] Edited by A. Wilmart in *JLW*, 2 (1922), 47-67.

[63] Cf. A. Ebner, *Quellen und Forschungen zur Geschichte und Kunstges-
chichte des Missale Romanum im Mittelalter. Iter Italicum* (Freiburg 1896), 75.

[64] Cf. *Auctarium Solesmense*. I. Solesmes, 1900.

[65] They will be discussed in detail in the following chapter.

[66] See Ch. 1 "The Genius of the Roman Rite," *Liturgica Historica* (Oxford,
1918), 1-19.

can lands were accustomed to greater richness and symbolic play. In fact, the Roman form was really incomplete as far as the development of many of the sacraments and sacramentals (Baptism aside). This development as well as a greater richness in word and symbol in the Mass were added to the Roman Liturgy by the clerics of the Frankish realm. And, as we have seen, the native Liturgies (Gallican, Celtic, etc,) from which they drew were greatly influenced by Oriental usage. So to understand our present Roman Liturgy, it is necessary, not only to study the Gallican Rites, but also to obtain some notion of the ceremonies and spirit of worship in the Eastern Church.

While a great deal of consideration will be paid to elements from Frankish territory when the occasion presents itself, we take this opportunity to afford, before turning to the study of our Roman Rite, some basic descriptions of the Oriental Mass and Church furnishings which will give us a sound background for future reference.

Appendix

A. General Order of Mass in the Eastern Rites

Because of its wider use in the East and greater importance for Western developments, the outline of the *Byzantine* Mass will be presented here. Divergencies among the various Oriental Rites will be noted by means of footnotes. The modern Byzantine Mass may be divided into five parts: 1. Preparatory rite, 2. Mass of the catechumens, 3. Offertory, 4. Anaphora, or Canon, 5. Communion.

1. Preparatory rite:
    a. Vesting and lavabo in sanctuary. [67]
    b. Preparation and incensation of bread and wine.[68]
    c. Incensation of the altar, sanctuary, and people.
2. Mass of the catechumens
    a. Opening rite: Ektenes surrounding antiphonal chanting of psalms with silent prayers said by the celebrant.
    b. Little entry of the Gospel.
    c. Troparia [69] and Trisagion.[70]

[67] The Armenians vest in the sacristy, but the celebrant washes his hands before the altar.

[68] This is an involved ceremonial among the Byzantines. The preparation of the gift at this moment is certainly of later introduction; the whole introductory service did not become stable in the Byzantine Rite until after the sixteenth century. Today most of the Oriental Rites place the preparation of gifts at this point; the Chaldeans and Malabarese still remain faithful to the ancient practice of preparing the gifts at the regular Offertory.

[69] The Tropes are hymns of ecclesiastical composition proper to the occasion. During the Tropes the celebrant recites an apology silently.

[70] The *Hagios ho Theos*, etc., corresponding to our *Improperia* sung during the Mass of the Presanctified on Good Friday. In the Armenian Rite the Ektenes usually follow the Trisagion; in other Oriental Rites the position of the Trisagion varies from before the readings to a position between them.

    d. Reading of the lessons, generally two: one from the Epistles and another from the Gospels,[71] the Epistle is preceded by the chanting of the Prokimen, or psalm of the day, while the Gospel is preceded by the singing of the Alleluia.

    e. Ektenes [72] and dismissal of catechumens followed by a shorter Ektene with two silent prayers said by the celebrant for the faithful.

3. Offertory

    a. The Great Entry, or procession with the gifts, preceded by a hymn and an apology prayed silently by the celebrant, and accompanied by another hymn.

    b. Arranging and incensation of gifts on altar.

    c. Ektenes, during which celebrant prays silently an apology.

    d. Kiss of peace.

    e. The Creed.[73]

4. Anaphora (Canon)

    a. Preface.[74]

    b. Sanctus.

    c. Consecration containing the words of Institution.[75]

    d. Anamnesis with elevation of offering.

    e. Epiclesis.

    f. The Great Intercession, or commemoration of the saints and memento for the living and dead, concluding with the Doxology.[76]

5. Communion

    a. Blessing and Ektenes.

    b. Pater Noster.[77]

[71] The ancient use, still followed by the Chaldeans, Copts and Ethiopians, was to read four lessons: two from the Law and the Prophets and two from the New Testament. Though the Copts and Ethiopians retain four lessons, they are usually taken from the New Testament. The Armenians have three: Old Testament, Epistles, and Gospel. The Syrian Rite has six: two from the Old Testament and four from the New.

[72] This is the original place of the long list of prayers said for all the catechumens and various categories of the faithful; cf. *The Apostolic Constitutions*, VII, 6-11. *MPG*, 1: 1075-1091.

[73] The Armenians and Malabarese recite the Creed immediately after the reading of the Gospel, while the Syrians, Maronites, Copts and Ethiopians recite it before the kiss of peace and before the washing of the celebrant's hands. The latter is totally missing at this point in the Byzantine Rite.

[74] Immediately between the introductory dialogue with the people and the Preface proper the Chaldeans and Malabarese insert an apology for the priest; still another is found after the Sanctus. These two apologies are called *Cusapa*. The Alexandrian Rites, let us recall, place the Great Intercession, similar to our Mementoes in the Canon, within the Preface itself and before the Sanctus.

[75] In the Nestorian East Syrian Rite the words of Institution are lacking; the Catholic Chaldeans, of course, have reinserted them. The Malabarese, on the other hand, place the words of Institution after what we would normally call the Canon of the Mass just before the Fraction of the consecrated bread.

[76] It is just at this point after the Doxology, that the Malabarese recite the words of Institution.

[77] The Pater comes after the Fraction in the West Syrian, Chaldean, Malabar, and Alexandrian Rites.

c. Prayer of inclination.
d. Washing of celebrant's hands.
e. Elevation for adoration with exclamation: *Sancta Sanctis!*
f. Fraction and Commingling.
g. Communion hymn.
h. Confession of faith and guilt.
i. Distribution of Communion.
j. Blessing of people with remaining sacred species.
k. Ablutions at the table of oblation (Prothesis).
l. Ektenes and thanksgiving prayers.[78]
m. Blessing and dismissal.

Obviously such a Mass-order differs greatly from the simple form described by Justin in the second century and even from that of the fourth century *Apostolic Constitutions*. The various additions, especially the preparation of the matter of sacrifice before the real beginning of Mass (the specially developed ceremony called the *Prothesis*), and the numerous instances of Ektenes, are attested to already in the Byzantine *Codex Barberianus* of the eighth century.[79] Their use in other Eastern Liturgies is due, in great part, to the influence of the Byzantine Rite.[80]

B. Oriental Church Furnishings

1. The church

Eastern churches, especially of the Byzantine Rite, have ordinarily retained the plan of the Constantinian basilica. This was basically in the form of a parallelogram three times as long as its breadth and divided into three naves or aisles by a double row of columns. At the extreme end of the building from the main entrance is normally to be found an apse or *concha*, so called because of its vaulted ceiling and round, shell-like form. In this apse is located the throne of the bishop and seats for the rest of the clergy. Immediately in front of these seats is found the altar. On either side of the altar towards the side walls of the church are places for the vestments and furnishings called the *diakonikon* and a receptacle for the offerings, the *gazophylakion*, with a table for the preparation of the matter of sacrifice called the *prothesis*. This whole section of the church is called the sanctuary.

The sanctuary is separated from the rest of the church by the *iconostasis* upon which are hung statues or paintings of Christ and the

---

[78] The Chaldeans, Malabarese Copts, and Ethiopians include the Pater Noster as a thanksgiving prayer, while the Armenians recite the Prologue of St. John's Gospel.
[79] See tables in Raes, 55, 59.
[80] Cf. S. Salaville, *An Introduction to the Study of Eastern Liturgies* (Trans. J. Barton; London 1938), p. 23.

saints called *icons*. The section in front of the *iconostasis* is the *solea* or
step to the sanctuary. At either end of this area near the walls of the
building are located choirs, each having an *analogion* or lectern for
the reading of lessons. The main section of the church in which the
people congregate is called the *naos*. Here near the *solea* are to be
found two structures used for carrying *icons* proper to the occasion
and bear the name *proskynêtarion* from the low bow made before
them. In monastic churches stalls are arranged against the walls for
the monks. The rear end of the nave is walled off and called the narthex of *pronaos*; it was formerly intended for the catechumens and
penitents. Outside the main entrance of the church runs a portico
called the *esonarthex*.

Plan of the Byzantine Church

I. Sanctuary
II. Solea
III. Naos
IV. Pronaos
V. Portico

a. Altar
b. Prothesis
c. Diakonikon
d. Thronos
e. Iconostasis
f. Holy Door
g. North and south doors
h. Icon of Christ
i. Icon of Mary
j. Choir
k. Analogion
l. Ambo
m. Proskynêtarion
n. Stalls
o. Superior's stall (in monasteries)
p. Baptismal font
q. Royal Door (also applied
   to Holy Door)

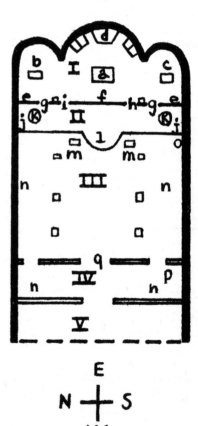

Along with this regular basilica type church, some churches are built on a circular plan with a dome. A combination of this circular plan and the basilica type (with transepts) produced churches in the shape of a Greek cross,[81] of which *Hagia Sophia* in Constantinople is a perfect example. Despite the circular structure and domes, the interior arrangement remains basically that of the basilica.

It is also worthy of note that normally Eastern Churches were *orientated*, i.e., were made to face the East. The facade of the church faced the West, while the apse was directed toward the East and the rising sun, which is conceived of as a figure of Christ.

2. Furnishings

The *iconostasis* is a wall separating the sanctuary from the rest of the church. Upon it are hung icons, or they are painted or sculptured. At first it was a low chancel intended to mark off the beginning of the sanctuary, as is common in most Latin churches. The origin of the high, altar-concealing barrier is to be traced to Russia, more precisely to the vicinity of Novgorod, according to authorities in this matter.[82] Its development was due to the over-abundance of icons and to the Russian practice of building and painting on wood. And it is a rather late development beginning with the appearance of the first wooden icons, i.e., the end of the fourteenth and beginning of the fifteenth centuries.[83] Hence we must not think that the iconostasis has an essential connection with the celebration of the sacred mysteries in Eastern worship, or that it was destined to *hide* the "mysterious" action of the Mass.

The *altar* is very similar to those formerly used in churches of the West: either a simple wooden table, or a stone slab supported by stone columns, over which a ciborium or canopy of stone rests on four or more columns. Upon the altar are placed two altar cloths which are attached to the altar immediately after its consecration. During Mass still another cloth is spread over these and contains the *antimension* (frequently called a Greek corporal), into which are sewn the relics of saints. Above the altar but below the ciborium hangs what is called the *peristera*, a dove-shaped vessel containing the reserved Eucharistic species (as is done in some Western churches even today; e.g., the abbey Church of Solesme). There is normally only one altar in every church.

The sacred vessels used at Mass are: the chalice, the paten (*diskos*); the lance used by the priest to detach from the large altar-bread the central portion then known as the "Lamb," which serves as

---

[81] The original plan of St. Peter's was projected by Michelangelo along these lines.

[82] Cf. Paul Mouratoff, *L'Ancienne peinture russe* (Prague and Rome, 1925), 100-107 cited in S. Salaville, *op. cit.*, 107-110.

[83] Mouratoff, 105. Salaville, 110.

the principal host; the star (*asteriskos*), a sort of cross of precious metal, made of two strips crossed one upon the other, from the middle of which is suspended a small star symbolizing the star of Bethlehem; a veil placed over the entire *asteriskos* in order to cover the sacred species; a spoon (*labis*) used for the distribution of Holy Communion under both species.

Other vessels and objects used at Mass but not blessed are: a holy water bowl, a *bikion* containing holy chrism, the *aleiptron*, a sort of brush used for anointing, the *thermarion* for holding the warm water poured into the chalice just before communion, the *thymiatêrion* or thurible, with shorter chains than the Latin one, to which are attached small bells, the *katzion* or incense pan sometimes used instead of the thurible, the *rhipidion* or *hexapterigon*, a sort of metal fan originally used to drive away flies or mosquitoes and now used as an ornament in processions. Besides the candles used on the altar during Mass, there are the *Dikêrion* and *Trikêrion*, two little candelabra having two and three crossed candles respectively (symbolizing the two natures in Christ and the three persons in the Trinity); these are used to bless the people.

3. Vestments

The clerical and choir dress consist of: the cassock, similar to that worn by Jesuits and Redemptorists, black being obligatory for religious, any dark color being sufficient for secular priests; the cincture, a small band of black material used to gather the cassock in around the waist (sometimes different colors are used by certain dignitaries); the *Konton*, a short coat with broad sleeves and no buttons, worn over the cassock; the *Rason*, a full cloak comparable to our academic gowns; the *Kamelaukion*, originally a head-covering made of camel skin to cover the nape of the neck, now a stiff cylindrical hat about six inches in height and, at least among the Greeks, having a brim at the top of it; the *Epanôkamelaukion*, a black veil attached to the hat, covering the nape of the neck and falling down upon the shoulders and back.

The sacred vestments and insignia are principally the following: the *stikharion*, similar to our alb except that the ends of the sleeves are fastened by a string drawn through the hem; the *Epitrakhêlion*, like our stole but worn by the bishop and priest, the deacon's stole being called the *ôrarion*; the *epimanikia*, two sleevelets ornamented with a cross which cover the ends of the *stikharion's* sleeves (they were originally gloves); the *epigonation*, a square piece of stiff material hanging by a band from the cincture and reaching to the right knee, originally a kind of napkin but now a mark of distinction; the *phailonion*, the Oriental equivalent of our chasuble and worn by priests; the *polystaurion*, the chasuble embroidered with many crosses worn by bishops; the *sakkos*, a shorter tunic slit at the sides from top to bottom but joined together by means of ribbons or bells, having half sleeves, worn by Patriarchs; the *Omophorion*, analogous to our Latin pallium, of the same color as the other vestments and worn by bishops; the *Encolpion*, an oval shaped medallion of the Blessed Mother or our Lord worn by bishops in addition to their pectoral cross; the *Mitra*, similar to our western mitre in use, but shaped like a round or quadrilobate crown, ornamented with jewels and surmounted by a cross; the *dikanikion*, the Oriental crozier, a staff ending in two branches which curve and are ornamented with serpents' heads.

4. Books

The Oriental books are chiefly: the *Typikon*, corresponding to our Latin *Ordo*, or even better to the *Ordines Romani* of the medieval Church, therefore a book of rubrics; *Leitourgikon*, originally containing only the Ordinary of the Mass and the rites of some of the sacraments, but now the equivalent of our Latin Missal, since it contains also the Propers for the chief feasts of the year; *Euchologion* which is similar to our Roman Ritual; *Apostolos*, containing extracts from the Epistles and Acts of the Apostles for the entire year; *Evangelion*, containing the four Gospels arranged in sections or pericopes following the order in which they are read during the year; *Psalterion*, containing the psalms divided into *kathismata* or session, meaning groups of psalms sung together; the *Hôrologion* with the Common of Saints and Seasons for use in the Divine Office; the *Octoêkhos*, in reality two distinct books, a smaller one with eight Sunday offices, one for each tone, the larger having, in addition, the office of the eight tones for every day of the week; the *Triôdion*, containing the proper offices for the ten weeks which precede Easter; the *Pentekostarion*, with the proper offices for the Sundays from Easter to the Sunday after Pentecost; the *Menaia* with the proper offices for the Saints; and lastly, the *Heirmologion*, which is a collection of tropes, or model clauses of Odes sung during Mass and office.

CHAPTER THREE

Liturgical Books of the Roman Rite

In our treatment of the liturgical families of Christendom, we saw that, in general, the development of the Liturgy was a transition, gradual but inevitable, from improvisation to codified liturgical texts of obligation for all Churches falling within given liturgical provinces. The successive phases in this development for the Roman liturgical province can be schematized as follows: (1) the period of charismatic improvisation, (2) the period of primitive model-formulas, (3) the period of free composition, (4) the period of the first collections.

1. We have already considered the testimony of St. Justin that in his day the celebrant improvised for those parts of the Mass which belonged to him: "He who presides likewise offers up prayers and thanksgivings to the best of his ability." [1] We find a similar statement in the *Didache.* "Let the prophets render thanks as much as they desire." [2] Thus in the first two centuries we have a situation in which the celebrant prays his parts of the Mass without the help of a book or written formula; he prays *ex abundantia cordis.*

2. In the third century an official Church Order awaits examination; it is the *Apostolic Tradition* of Hippolytus. Here he offers priests model-formulas which he recommends while stating explicitly that their use is not obligatory: "Nevertheless, it is not necessary that he recite the same words that we have given . . . only let them be orthodox." [3] Thus in this period there is apparent a tendency to circulate already composed formulas, in order to provide for all a schema of ideas and expressions of proven orthodoxy for the priestly prayers of the Mass.

3. The fourth and fifth centuries witnessed a flowering of liturgical composition. Following the time-honored general order of thought

---

[1] I *Apology* 67. J. Quasten, *op. cit.,* 20.

[2] *Didache* 10, 7. J. Quasten, *op. cit.,* 12. The fact that throughout this book the "prophets" are put on a level with the bishops and deacons and that in ch. 13, 3, it is said "they are your high priests" leads Quasten to conclude that they were entitled to celebrate Mass. Cf. Quasten's *Patrology* I (Westminster, Maryland, 1951), 34.

[3] Ch. 10. B. Botte, *La Tradition Apostolique,* Sources Chrétiennes (Paris, 1946), pp. 41-42.

for the prayers of the priest at Mass, local men would, with a touch of originality, weave their own Eucharistic prayers, commit them to writing, and then read them or recite them from memory at Mass. This was, of course, not without its inconveniences. With such liberty, men of doubtful religious tenets were bound to insert their false ideas into the Liturgy. Consequently many a voice [4] was to be heard bemoaning the freedom with which heretical and incompetent men circulated their *libelli missarum*, in which unorthodox doctrines could be found.

4. To stem the tide of such arbitrary and doubtful composition of liturgical texts, men of responsibility in the fifth, sixth, and seventh centuries turned to making compilations of the best compositions they could find. Binding them together, they thus provided the clergy with a choice variety of sound and usable formulas. Some of the more famous compilers were Pope St. Leo I, Pope St. Gelasius I, Pope Vigilius, Sidonius Apollinaris, St. Paulinus of Nola, St. Gregory of Tours, Pope St. Gregory I, Museus (a priest of Marseilles), and the famous bishop of Ravenna, Maximianus.

A. Sacramentaries

The oldest and most famous of these compilations which have come down to us are the three Sacramentaries named after Leo, Gelasius and Gregory the Great. The title for collections like these was *Liber Sacramentorum*. They did not, however, contain all the prayers and ceremonies of the Church's sacramental activity, but only the prayers said by bishop or priest during the celebration of Mass: the Collects, Secret, Preface (and Canon) and Postcommunion. Also to be found in them are the sacerdotal prayers peculiar to certain sacraments as Baptism, Confirmation, and Holy Orders, as well as some occasional prayers. Prayers and readings from the Mass recited by other ministers were placed in other collections. The three Sacramentaries which we have mentioned are the most important, for in the course of history they influenced the development of our Roman Rite more than any other compilations, due allowance being made for the eventual role played by the Gallican formularies.

1. The Leonine Sacramentary

This is the name given, rather arbitrarily, by Giuseppe Bianchini to the manuscript found in the Capitular Library of the Cathedral of Verona.[5] While some of the formulas contained in this Sacramentary

---

[4] Cf. for example, St. Augustine's criticism in *De Baptismo* 6, 25. *MPL*, 43: 213.

[5] *Codex Bibl. Capit. Veron.* no. 85 (formerly 80). This has recently been republished by K. Mohlberg, *Sacramentarium Veronense.* Rerum Ecclesiasticarum Documenta, Series Maior, I. Rome, 1956.

were certainly composed by Pope St. Leo I (440-461),[6] the compilation itself was not made by him, for it also contains formulas composed by Pope Gelasius (492-496) [7] and Pope Vigilius (537-555).[8] From these simple facts it is seen that this compilation cannot date any earlier than the end of Vigilius' pontificate, or at least the latter part of it.[9] Because of its faulty ordering and copious marginal notes, scholars are agreed that this collection was certainly never intended as an official liturgical book, that is, one to be used at the altar during liturgical services. It was only a privately collected group of loose Mass sheets which had been gathered during the fifth and sixth centuries in the papal archives. While not using the collection itself during Mass, a priest might find inspiration and directions in it to aid him in preparing for a forthcoming Mass or other liturgical function. Though the influence of foreign elements on this book is not of itself excluded,[10] its prayers are regarded almost universally as of Roman origin.

2. The Gelasian Sacramentary

Tradition tells us that another compilation of prayers bears witness to fifth and sixth century Roman liturgical practice.[11] It has often been attributed to Pope St. Gelasius. Such attribution is based on several medieval witnesses. Two ninth century writers, John the Deacon,[12] biographer of Gregory the Great, and Walafrid Strabo,[13] speak of a Gelasian collection of liturgical prayers. Both of these

[6] Though C. Callewaert started out by claiming a very large part of the Leonine Sacramentary for Leo's authorship, "Saint Léon le Grand et les textes du Léonien," *Sacris Erudiri*, 1 (1948), 36-164, Artur Lang has recently investigated in detailed fashion the various formulas of alleged Leonine origin in both the Leonine and Gelasian Sacramentaries and recognizes serious objections against such an extensive attribution: *Leo der Grosse und die Texte des Altgelasianums* (Steyl, 1957), pp. 4-6, 460-475, 503-511. And, in general, Leo's authorship is restricted by the attribution of certain formulas to Gelasius and Vigilius (see following two footnotes).
[7] Some eighteen Masses have been attributed to Pope Gelasius: B. Capelle, "Messes du pape S. Gélase dans le sacramentaire léonien," *Revue Bénédictine*, 56 (1945-46), 12-41; "L'oeuvre liturgique de S. Gélase," *Journal of Theological Studies*, 2 (1951), 132; A. Chavasse, "Messes du pape Vigile dans le sacramentaire léonien," *Ephemerides Liturgicae*, 64 (1950), pp. 177-179, 187, 206, 212.
[8] A. Chavasse, "Messes du pape Vigile dans le sacramentaire léonien," *Ephemerides Liturgicae*, 64 (1950), 161-213; 66 (1952), 145-219.
[9] *Ibid.*, 66 (1952), 151-154, 167-215. Chavasse even admits the possibility of the collection being made under Pelagius I (556-561) or in the first years of John III's pontificate (561-574): *ibid.*, 64 (1950), 213. Capelle prefers to place the assembly of this collection under Vigilius, from whom, he says, it has received at least sixty-eight Masses: "L'oeuvre liturgique de S. Gélase," *Journal of Theological Studies*, 2 (1951), 135.
[10] For indications of possible foreign elements see K. Mohlberg, *Sacramentarium Veronense*, p. LXII-LXIII.
[11] *Cod. Vat. Regin. lat.* 316. A handy edition of this Sacramentary was published by H. A. Wilson, *The Gelasian Sacramentary*. Oxford, 1894. A new and more critical edition is being prepared in Rome under the direction of K. Mohlberg.
[12] *Vita S. Gregorii* II, 17. *MPL*, 75: 94.
[13] *De rebus ecclesiasticis* 22. *MPL*, 114: 946.

authors may have based their statements on a note added by a later [14]
hand to a work of Gennadius of Marseilles regarding the liturgical
activity of Gelasius. But Gennadius did not say that Gelasius had
compiled a Sacramentary, rather that he wrote tracts pertaining to,
or to be used in, the sacred mysteries.[15] We find a similar assertion in
the Liber Pontificalis,[16] this time much more explicit: Gelasius composed Prefaces and Orations for the sacred mysteries. This does not
necessarily mean that he compiled a Sacramentary.[17]

In fact, no one today seriously believes that the Sacramentary
that has come down to us under the name of Pope Gelasius was really
put together by him or in his time, since it contains many Masses composed by one of his successors, Vigilius.[18] Indeed, since the hand of
Pope Pelagius (556-561) is also apparent in the collection, Chavasse
thinks that it cannot date before 560; nor should its compilation be
placed after 600, for it does not yet identify the March Ember Saturday with the Saturday of the first week of Lent.[19] Furthermore, the
Gregorian Sacramentary certainly depends on it.[20] All this serves to
prove that the so-called Gelasian Sacramentary was composed in
Rome of purely Roman material, which is further borne out by the
fact that it remains faithful to an exclusively Roman sanctoral calendar [21] and is in essential accord with the temporal cycle observed
in other Roman books of the sixth century.[22] This is not to say, of
course, that the codex which we presently possess has not suffered
later interpolations at Gallican hands.[23] For this reason its contents

[14] Gennadius wrote about 480; Gelasius' pontificate extended from 492 to 496.
[15] "Scripsit et tractatus diversarum scripturarum, et sacramentorum, elimato
sermone," De viris illustribus 94. MPL, 58: 1115-1116.
[16] Ed. Louis Duchesne (Paris, 1955), I, 255: "fecit etiam et sacramentorum
praefationes et orationes cauto sermone."
[17] See B. Capelle's exegesis of this text in "L'oeuvre liturgique de S. Gélase,"
Journal of Theological Studies, 2 (1951), 129; also Duchesne's commentary on
the Liber Pontificalis, I, 257.
[18] Cf. A. Chavasse, "Messes du pape Vigile dans le léonien," Ephemerides
Liturgicae, 66 (1952), 156-161; "Les messes quadragésimales du sacramentaire
Gélasien," Ibid., 63 (1949), 267-270.
[19] "Les messes quadragésimales," Ephemerides Liturgicae, 63 (1949), 260-
267, 270-275.
[20] Ibid., 259.
[21] B. Capelle, "Le sacramentaire romain avant S. Grégoire," Revue Bénédictine, 64 (1954), 161.
[22] Ibid., 162. These facts stand in direct opposition to the opinion recently
proposed by H. Schmidt, "De sacramentariis romanis," Gregorianum, 34 (1953),
742, that our Codex Vat. Regin. lat. 316 is a Gallican compilation of both Roman
and Gallican materials. Such a position would suppose that all Gallican saints
had been dropped from the calendar in Gaul in order to introduce the use of
a purely Roman sanctoral calendar, which is unthinkable. What is more, when
the Roman clerics after Gregory the Great's time went about furnishing the
Thursdays of Lent with proper Masses, they took such formulas from our Gelasian
book. That Romans would knowingly have recourse to Gallican materials to
compose their Masses is absurd: cf. M. Andrieu, "Les messes des jeudis de carême
et les anciens sacramentaires," Revue des Sciences Religieuses, 9 (1929), 343-375.
[23] E. Bourque, Etude sur les Sacramentaires Romains. Les Textes Primitifs,
Studi di Antichità Christiana, XX (Rome, 1949), 233-261.

must be carefully scrutinized and compared with other contemporary Roman evidence before they can be used as witnesses to sixth century Roman liturgical practice.

This so-called Gelasian Sacramentary found its way into Frankish territory sometime in the seventh century. From it arose a new type of service book with a definitely syncretistic character, combining many Frankish elements with a Gelasian substratum. And this has been called the Eighth Century Gelasian.[24]

3. The Gregorian Sacramentary

An eighth century bishop of York, Egbert, speaks of a missal which his predecessor, Augustine, had received from Gregory the Great.[25] A century later, John the Deacon says that Gregory had compiled a Sacramentary by transforming the Gelasian book, deleting much of it, changing some of its prayers, and adding quite a few more.[26] Gregory did, then, compile a service book, and by comparing representative copies of this book with the known calendar of Gregory's day, Dom Mohlberg has been able to point to the year 595 as the time of its composition.[27] Unfortunately none of the manuscripts still extant contains the Sacramentary exactly as it was compiled by Gregory; they have all been added to by subsequent popes and retouched, here and there, by Gallican hands. The very oldest form available, however, is seen to be that of the Paduan Codex.[28] Arguing from its contents and the liturgical offices known to have been introduced during the seventh century, E. Bourque claims that the prototype of this codex must have left Rome for Frankish territory in 683.[29] While this representative of Gregory's original Sacramentary contains a complete arrangement of Masses for the Sundays after Epiphany and Pentecost, the other Sundays and important ferias of the temporal cycle, as well as the Canon of the Mass, it lacks the formulas of ordination, the blessing of Holy Oils on Holy Thursday, the blessing of the font on Holy Saturday and many other elements pertaining to the Ritual and Pontifical.[30]

Gregory's Sacramentary is also represented by the volume sent to Charlemagne in 785-786 by Pope Hadrian. The latter considered it to

[24] There are two major examples: the Sacramentary of St. Gall edited by K. Mohlberg, *Das fränkische Sacramentarium Gelasianum in alamanischer Überlieferung*. Liturgiegeschichtliche Quellen, 1-2. Münster, 2nd edition, 1939; and the Sacramentary of Gellone edited by P. de Puniet, *Le Sacramentaire Romain de Gellone*. Bibliotheca "Ephemerides Liturgicae." Rome, 1938.
[25] *De institutione catholica dialogus* 16, 1-2. *MPL*, 89: 441.
[26] *Vita Gregorii* II, 17. *MPL*, 75: 94: "Sed et Gelasianum codicem de missarum solemniis, multa subtrahens, pauca convertens, nonnulla super-adjiciens . . . in unius volumine coarctavit."
[27] *Die älteste erreichbare Gestalt des Liber Sacramentorum anni circuli der römischen Kirche*, Liturgiegeschichtliche Quellen, 11-12 (Münster, 1927), xxxix.
[28] Published by Dom Mohlberg, see note 27, the 9th century *Cod. Pad. D 47*.
[29] *Op. cit.*, 318-320.
[30] Cf. E. Bourque, *op. cit.*, 321 and notes 1 and 2.

Evolution of Sacramentaries

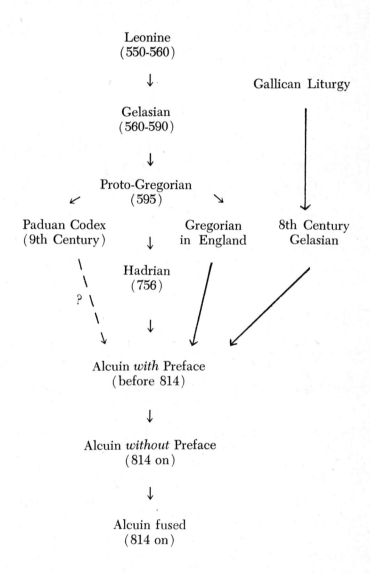

Leonine
(550-560)

↓

Gallican Liturgy

Gelasian
(560-590)

↓

Proto-Gregorian
(595)

Paduan Codex   Gregorian   8th Century
(9th Century)   in England   Gelasian

Hadrian
(756)

?

↓

Alcuin *with* Preface
(before 814)

↓

Alcuin *without* Preface
(814 on)

↓

Alcuin fused
(814 on)

be the authentic work of Gregory.[31] Once in Charlemagne's hands this Sacramentary began a fateful adventure. Wanting to unify liturgical practice in his domain, the Emperor charged Alcuin,[32] an English monk serving him at court, with the preparation of a service book based on the Gregorian Sacramentary yet preserving the good Frankish customs dear to the people of his realm. Alcuin, presumably already familiar with the pure Gregorian tradition of his homeland, needed little time to see that the book sent to his lord by Pope Hadrian was anything but pure Gregorian: it had been added to by subsequent Popes, and, furthermore, it was incomplete, for the Mass formularies for the Sundays after Epiphany, Easter,[33] and Pentecost[34] were missing. Alcuin tried to make up for these deficiencies by including material from other liturgical books. In this he clearly depended on what is commonly called the Eighth Century Gelasian, or the Gallicanized version of the Gelasian Sacramentary. It also seems certain that for his new service book Alcuin transcribed the Mass formularies for the Sundays after Epiphany, Easter, and Pentecost from some book representing the pure Gregorian tradition (perhaps he used the Sacramentary which Gregory gave to Augustine for the Anglo-Saxon Church), for these formularies are practically identical with those which appear in the Paduan Codex.[35] All told, in his work of compiling, Alcuin trebled the original size of the Hadrian book, all the while respecting the integrity of the latter. He clearly distinguished between what belonged to the Hadrian book and what he himself added to it by placing a preface entitled "Hucusque" at the end of the newly arrived Roman document and before the additions which he felt obliged to make.[36]

This was indeed thoughtful of Master Alcuin, for this arrangement has permitted modern scholars to ascertain fairly well the original Liturgy of Rome before it suffered Gallican interpolations. However, not all medieval copyists manifested the same reserve when faced with the papal manuscript. Alcuin's compilation met the fate of all such volumes in those days. His book was placed on display, so to speak, in the royal library. All other service books of the realm

---

[31] *Epist. ad Carolum. MPL,* 98: 436: "De sacramentario vero a sancto praedecessore nostro, Deifluo Gregorio papa, disposito . . . "

[32] See the excellent treatments of Alcuin's work in: Eleanor S. Duckett, *Alcuin, Friend of Charlemagne* (New York, 1950), 190-200; Gerald Ellard, *Master Alcuin, Liturgist.* Chicago, 1956.

[33] Except for Low Sunday: H. A. Wilson, *The Gregorian Sacramentary* (London, 1915), 65-66; same as in Paduan Codex, Mohlberg, p. 28.

[34] Except for the first Sunday and two others in September preceding the feast of Sts. Cosmas and Damian: Wilson, *The Gregorian Sacramentary,* 81-82, 103, 105; same as in Paduan Codex, Mohlberg, pp. 39, 55, 56.

[35] Compare the formularies of Alcuin's appendix, Wilson, *The Gregorian Sacramentary,* pp. 164-177, with those in Mohlberg's edition of the Paduan Codex, *Die älteste erreichbare Gestalt,* pp. 7, 9, 10, 11, 30-33, 35, 40-42, 44-47, 49-53, 57-60.

[36] See the text of this preface in Wilson, *The Gregorian Sacramentary,* p. 145-146.

were to be brought into conformity with it, according to royal decree. That meant that the bishops had to have copies made of it. Even the slightest acquaintance with the methods of medieval copyists would serve to indicate what was in store for the original, and subsequent events only serve to confirm our preconceived suspicions. Some copyists faithfully adhered to Alcuin's division: the Roman book, the preface, then the supplement. But others didn't bother to reproduce the preface "Hucusque," and thus no trace was left of the end of the Roman book and the beginning of the supplement. And still a third group of copyists felt justified in inserting portions of the supplement into their logical places within the text of the original Roman Sacramentary.

Thus the Gregorian Sacramentary is to be found today in at least four different arrangements, none of which are absolutely faithful reproductions of Gregory's original collection:
a) the pre-Hadrian type which represents the oldest form, still not complete, of the Gregorian Sacramentary: the Paduan Codex,[37]
b) the Hadrian form which, though lacking many Sundays of the year, contains much of Gregory's reform plus the additions made by subsequent Popes and is pure Roman,[38]
c) the compilation made by Alcuin containing the Hadrian book separated from the supplement by the preface "Hucusque," [39]
d) a form in which the Roman book and Alcuin's supplement are completely fused.[40] It is this last form which, after being added to in the course of the ninth and tenth centuries, found its way back to Rome and was subsequently adopted by Rome itself.

B. Other Old Roman Books

As we noted, the Sacramentaries alone were not sufficient for the celebration of the Liturgy; other books were needed. In the early concept of liturgical worship, there was, we might say, a strict division of labor. In the very celebration of the Mass, the hierarchical nature of the Mystical Body found striking expression. Order, if it means anything, denotes an harmonious arrangement of parts to the whole as well as to each other. The sacrament of Holy Orders puts order into the Mystical Body by arranging the various members of the clergy according to gradated priestly power. And so, to use the words of Pope St. Clement I, "special functions are assigned to the high priest, a special office is imposed upon the priests, and special ministrations

[37] K. Mohlberg, *Die älteste erreichbare Gestalt des Liber Sacramentorum anni circuli der römischen Kirche*, Münster, 1927.
[38] Hans Lietzmann, *Das Sacramentarium Gregorianum nach dem Aachener Urexemplar*. Liturgiegeschichtliche Quellen, 3. Münster, 1921.
[39] H. A. Wilson, *The Gregorian Sacramentary under Charles the Great*. Henry Bradshaw Society, 49. London, 1915.
[40] A fairly close example of this type would be the *Sancti Gregorii Magni Liber Sacramentorum. MPL,* 78: 25-264.

fall to the levites. The layman is bound by rules laid down for the laity." [41] And hence, he adds, "Take care not to deviate from the established rule of service [liturgy]." [42] This, then, is the fundamental reason why many books were needed for the Liturgy: each minister had his own particular role to play in the Mass, and each part was to be found in a special book. The celebrant of the Mass had his Sacramentary, the deacon his Gospel book and Diptychs, the subdeacon his book of Epistles, the Master of Ceremonies his rubrics book, and the *schola cantorum* its Antiphonary, Graduale, and Cantatorium. Let us examine briefly each type of book which the medieval Church employed in her Liturgy.

1. The Lectionaries

In the beginning the one who presided over the liturgical assembly simply indicated to the lector which passage he should read from Holy Scripture, and it was customary to read the various books of the Bible straight through (*lectio continua*) at successive services. Hence, no other book but the Bible was necessary. Gradually a special system of Biblical excerpts was developed in order to make the reading fit the feast. This was done first of all for the principal feasts of the year: Easter, Ascension, Pentecost, Christmas; later it became customary to attach particular passages of Scripture to the various Sundays throughout the year. This was called the pericope system. The collections of homilies given by great men like Sts. Leo I., Augustine, Peter Chrysologus, John Chrysostom, and others show that already in the fifth century the various Churches followed some such system of readings. The specified passages from Scripture, however, had not yet been transcribed from the Bible into special reading books; it was found sufficient to indicate the proper texts by means of either marginal notes in the Bible or lists containing only the opening and concluding phrases of the Biblical texts. These last were called *capitularia*, that is, lists indicating chapters and verses. Such a list might also be called in the seventh century *capitulare lectionum* or *capitulare evangeliorum*.[43] The lists did not always constitute independent books; they have been found simply appended to a codex of Scripture or to a book of the Gospels or Epistles.

Another stage in the development of the Lectionary is the actual transcribing of pericopes from their Biblical context into special books. Sometimes the Epistle pericopes were assembled in books called variously *Apostolus, Epistolium, Comes* or, simply, Lectionary. The Gospel

---

[41] I *Epistola ad Corinthios* 40, 5. *MPG*, 1: 290.
[42] *Ibid.*, 41, 1. *MPG*, 1: 290.
[43] Cf. T. Klauser, *Das römische Capitulare evangeliorum. Texte und Untersuchungen zu seiner ältesten Geschichte.* I. *Typen.* Liturgiegeschichtliche Quellen und Forschungen, 28. Münster, 1935; W. H. Frere, *Studies in Early Roman Liturgy.* II: *The Roman Gospel-Lectionary.* III: *The Roman Epistle-Lectionary.* Alcuin Club Collections, 30, 32. Oxford, 1934, 1935.

pericopes were also collected in special books called *Evangelarium,*
Liber evangeliorum, etc. And sometimes both Epistle and Gospel
pericopes were placed together in the same volume, which might be
called simply the Lectionary or the *Liber Comicus.*[44] The oldest list
of Roman pericopes for both Epistles and Gospels is to be found in
the *Comes* of Würzburg which goes back to the seventh century.[45]
Also of Roman character is a *Comes* worked on by Alcuin.[46] But most
important of all for our present Roman system of pericopes, is the
eighth century *Comes* of Murbach, containing both Epistles and Gospels; its readings are based on the liturgical calendar followed by the
Gelasian-Gregorian Sacramentaries of the same century and were,
with that type of Sacramentary, finally adopted by Rome.[47]

2. Books for the Divine Office

The Breviary is a relatively modern invention; it is indeed an
abbreviation of the numerous books which used to be employed for
the chanting of the Office: Psalter, Homiliary, Passional, Hymnal,
Antiphonary, and Martyrology.

The *Psalter.* After the Church decided to use the psalms instead
of hymns for the body of her canonical hours,[48] the former were lifted
from the Bible to form a book of their own. At least four different types
of Psalter were used by the Church: a) a simple text of the psalms in
the numerical order in which they appear in the Bible, b) the psalms
according to the same numerical order but with marginal notes indicating the day of the week on which they were to be recited, c) the
psalms still in the Biblical numerical order but with the *Ordinarium*
de tempore (a complex of hymns, antiphons, versicles and little chapters), d) the psalms in the order in which they are recited during the
week.

There are three versions of the psalms currently in use for the
Divine Office. The oldest, called the Roman, is that which resulted
from St. Jerome's correction of the *Vetus Latina* or *Itala* version; it

[44] It is to be noted that many of these titles were used for books of different
character; *Comes* or *Lectionarium* might refer on occasion to either a book of
Epistles or Gospels or to a book combining both.

[45] G. Morin, "Le plus ancien comes ou lectionnaire de l'église romaine,"
Revue Bénédictine, 27 (1910), 41-74; 28 (1911), 297-317. This has also been
reproduced in the *DACL:* the Epistles by H. Leclercq, "Lectionnaire," 8: 2285-
2300; the Gospels by G. Godu, "Evangiles," 5: 901-908.

[46] Reproduced by G. Godu, "Epîtres," *DACL,* 5: 300-310. A critical edition
was published by A. Wilmart, "Le lectionnaire d'Alcuin," *Ephemerides Liturgicae,*
51 (1937), 136-197.

[47] Edited by A. Wilmart, "Le comes de Murbach," *Revue Bénédictine,* 30
(1913), 25-69; also by G. Godu, "Epîtres," *DACL,* 5: 316-320; "Evangiles,"
DACL, 5: 908-914. A very interesting comparative table of Epistles from
several medieval manuscripts was prepared by G. Godu in the above article,
"Epîtres," 335-342.

[48] Cf. Balt. Fischer, "Christ in the Psalms," *Theology Digest,* 1 (1953), 53; *Die*
Psalmenfrömmigkeit der Märtyrerkirche (Freiburg, 1949), 2-3.

was used in Rome until the time of Pius V. Jerome made another version of the Psalter from the Septuagint; this is the one contained in the Vulgate and is called the Gallican Psalter because it was used in Frankish territory, though later it was imposed by Pius V on all following the Roman Rite. Recently Pius XII authorized the use of a new version of the Psalter made from the original Hebrew.

The *Homiliary* was a collection of Patristic homilies for use as commentaries on the Scripture readings of Matins. Though the Middle Ages saw many such collections, that made by Paul Warnefried (d.797) [49] succeeded in becoming almost universal in the West.

The *Passional* was a volume from which the lives and sufferings of the martyrs were read at Matins. Sometimes a different book was used for the lives of confessors, the *Legendary*. Such books multiplied incredibly, and, as time went on, the lives increased in length, all the while incorporating items which were not always authentic.[50]

The *Martyrology*. In the early Church at least the principal communities were accustomed to note down the days on which their martyrs suffered in order to observe these dates each year. Such names of martyrs, and later other saints, would be read on the anniversary day from the *Diptychs* (two tablets, connected by a hinge, containing the names of persons to be specially commemorated at liturgical services). It was from such documents that later generations made up their Calendars (lists of feasts ordinarily celebrated each year) and Martyrologies (lists of saints' names to be read to the public on the day of their death).[51] Almost every Church and city had its own Calendar and Martyrology. In addition to a bare mention of the saint or martyr, sometimes these Martyrologies would give further pertinent items concerning the lives of these persons. Somewhere between 336 and 354 Furius Dionysius Philocalus made a single Calendar out of two earlier ones, the *Depositio episcoporum* and the *Depositio martyrum*.[52] One of the earliest Martyrologies for the entire Church is the so-called Martyrology of St. Jerome, which originated between 592 and 600.[53] On the other hand the Venerable Bede (d.735) was the first to compile an historical Martyrology, one, in other words, containing a few facts from the lives of the saints in addition to the mere mention of their names.[54] However, the most influential of all medieval Martyrologies was that composed by the monk Usuardus

[49] Reproduced in *MPL*, 95: 1159 ff.

[50] Cf. H. Delehaye, *Les Légendes Hagiographiques*. Subsidia Hagiographica, 18. Bruxelles, 4th edition, 1955; *Les Passions des Martyrs et les Genres Littéraires*. Subsidia Hagiographica, 13b. Bruxelles, 1921; *Sanctus, Essai sur le Culte des Saints dans l'Antiquité*. Subsidia Hagiographica 17. Bruxelles, 1927.

[51] Cf. H. Kellner's treatment of the ancient Calendars and Martyrologies in *Heortology, A History of the Christian Festivals from their Origin to the Present Day* (London, 1908), 347-418; also H. Delehaye, *Sanctus*, 189-191.

[52] Both reproduced by L. Duchesne, *Liber Pontificalis*, I, 10-12.

[53] Cf. Kellner, 366-369. The document is reproduced in *MPL*, 30: 449-502.

[54] Reproduced in *MPL*, 94: 799-1148.

(d.877). He increased the number of saints reported and abbreviated the historical notices concerning them, thus bringing the book to the form which it kept during the rest of the Middle Ages.[55] It was his volume that Pope Gregory XIII entrusted for revision to several learned men, among them Baronius and Agelius, and subsequently imposed on the Latin Church.

The *Hymnal* contained the many metrical compositions intended to be sung during the Divine Office. Such volumes flourished in the Middle Ages. C. Blume has already collected some 30,000 hymns.[56]

3. Books of chant

The musical parts of the Mass sung by the *schola cantorum* (Introit, Offertory, Communion) were gathered together in a book called the Antiphonary, while those sung by a soloist (Gradual, Tract, or Alleluia verse) were contained in the Cantatorium.[57] We know that Gregory the Great compiled an Antiphonary, but unfortunately it survives only in manuscripts dating from the Carolingian period.[58] In time both these books were combined and from the ninth century on began to be called *Gradualia*. Originally these chant books did not contain notation, only the text. The music apparently was sung from memory. Since this presented an obvious difficulty for the choirs, from the eighth century on musical signs, or neums, of one sort or another, began to appear in the manuscripts.[59] The neums at first were not for the choir as a whole but only for the director, who would attempt to describe them in the air with gestures of the hand (whence the name "cheironomy": law of the hand). More and more attempts were made to describe these musical intervals graphically by printing neums higher or lower, now above a single line, now below it, until finally Guido d'Arezzo (c.1027) developed a four-line system with which he was able to express every interval perfectly.

Another book, the *Troparius*, contained the tropes, or phrases, which were inserted into certain sung parts of the Mass (Kyrie, Sanctus, Alleluia, Gloria, Agnus Dei). We still see a remnant of this practice in the titles given to the Gregorian Masses contained in the Kyriale: *Lux et origo*, *Fons bonitatis*, etc. These were the tropes inserted into the Kyrie.

[55] Reproduced in *MPL*, 123: 601- 124:858.

[56] C. Blume and G. Dreves, *Analecta Hymnica Medii Aevi*. Leipzig, 1886 —. It comprises more than 58 volumes.

[57] This is the term used for the book used by the cantor at the Gradual and Allelulia verse in the oldest Roman Ordo: *Ordo Romanus* I, n. 57. M. Andrieu, *Les Ordines Romani du Haut Moyen Age* (Louvain, 1948), p. 86.

[58] One such tenth century manuscript is reproduced in *MPL*, 78: 725-850.

[59] See examples of such manuscripts in G. Sunol, *Introduction à la Paléographie musicale grégorienne* (Paris, 1935), 33.

4. Rubric books

Thus far we have described books which contained texts to be read or sung during divine services. Still another type of book was needed to organize and harmonize all the texts and actions of the Liturgy. This was the *Ordo* or Ordinal, the manual of rubrics for the Master of Ceremonies. These Ordinals were subsequently broken down into the *Caeremoniale Episcoporum,* for those sacramental rites pertaining to bishops, and the *Rituale* and *Missale,* for those rites administered by priests. M. Andrieu has edited a series of Ordinal manuscripts, the earliest of which date from the ninth century but which undoubtedly describe liturgical ceremonies of previous centuries.[60] The *Ordo Romanus Primus* even portrays the papal Liturgy of the seventh century.[61] Such documents are of the greatest importance for the history of the Roman Rite, for they alone will yield the details of liturgical ceremonial. The other books rarely contain rubrical directions.

C. Condensation into Modern Books

In general it seems due to the growing practice of private celebration of Mass that a rearrangement of the liturgical books occurred. While it is true that the books we have thus far considered were primarily intended for use in the cathedrals and churches of large cities, as well as monasteries, where it was possible to assemble enough clergy for the offices of deacon, subdeacon, and lector, the country parishes also endeavored to remain faithful to the principle of a hierarchy of ministers. Only where it was impossible to find a good reader, cantor, or choir, would the priest execute some of the parts belonging to other ministers. This seems to be borne out by the fact that the earliest missals we can find originated in monasteries where, we know, the practice of private Masses also gained momentum.[62] This practice of the *missa lecta* offered by the priest alone had, as we shall see, very unfortunate consequences for the development of the Roman Rite.

In keeping with this growing desire to celebrate privately, even daily, the monks and priests who traveled (at one time the *clerici vagabundi* became somewhat of a menace!) found it inconvenient to have to carry along with them so many different manuals. A compendium in which could be found all the essential texts of the Mass combined into one volume was a welcome luxury. The Missal of Bobbio from its very smallness was probably intended for such a purpose.[63]

---

[60] M. Andrieu, *Les Ordines Romani du Haut Moyen Age.* 4 vols. Louvain, 1931, 1948, 1951, 1956. A fifth volume is now being prepared.

[61] *Ibid.,* II, 51.

[62] J. A. Jungmann, *The Mass of the Roman Rite,* I, 106.

[63] It contained, in addition to the Ordinary parts of the Mass, the antiphons and lessons for the Proper.

Once the movement got under way to assemble all the Mass texts in one book, it was only a small step to bring together the formulas and ceremonies of the administration of the sacraments into another book, the elements necessary for the recitation of the Divine Office into still another and so on.

1. The Missal

In general the historical evolution of our modern Missal can be said to have gone through four periods. Until approximately the seventh century, the hierarchical celebration of the Liturgy by a plurality of ministers was more or less strictly adhered to; a plurality of liturgical books was then the normal thing. With the seventh century, however, we enter upon the second period, wherein the private Mass begins to intrude. Here there are found isolated instances where the priest's Mass book contains not only his own part, but also other parts of the Mass which, until this time, had been reserved to the minor ministers. In this second period, where the Bobbio Missal is the earliest example, the manuscripts range from those including the lessons to those that even insist on the sung texts being recited by the celebrant. The twelfth century was the culmination of this period, for by that time the Missal was a book which contained everything said or done at Mass. A third period opens with the thirteenth century, in which the Franciscans propagated the Missal of the Roman Curia in their missionary journeys throughout Europe. The utility of the Missal was easily seen by the clergy they visited; it was quickly adopted and its use became almost universal.

A fourth and final period followed, that in which pontifical authority entered into the regulation of the Missal. Even after the Curial Missal became universal, local bishops and abbots did not hesitate to modify it to suit their tastes. The Council of Trent, seeing the disorder which reigned in the celebration of Mass, nominated a commission to see to the unification of texts and ceremonies. The commission's reform was brought to an end when its work was promulgated by Pius V in 1570. According to his Bull of promulgation, *Quo primum*, every diocese and order of the Latin Rite was obliged to adopt the reformed Missal, the only exceptions being those regions and orders whose Liturgies enjoyed a tradition of at least two hundred years. Although the Missal underwent later changes under Clement VIII (1604), Urban VIII (1634), and Benedict XV (1920), these were merely of a minor rubrical nature. Hence, our present Missal is substantially the same as that imposed by Pius V.

2. The Pontifical

A relatively modern volume, the Pontifical as a separate book took its origin outside of Rome. Just as in the case of the Missal, the more ancient contents of the Pontifical were originally to be found either in the Sacramentaries (the formulas) or in the Ordinals (the rubrical directions). When it became the practice to codify different rites into separate books, it was only natural that those functions proper to the bishop were placed in a special volume called *Liber Pontificalis*.[64] Some of the earliest attempts at compiling such books took place in England, France and Germany. There was the Pontifical of Egbert of York (732-766),[65] the Pontifical of Poitiers (c.800) [66] and the Romano-Germanic Pontifical of the tenth century from Mainz.[67] Hittorp called the latter the *Ordo Romanus Antiquus*,[68] but its contents show that, as a whole, it is neither Roman nor ancient. It is, rather, a compilation of Roman and Gallican sources.

This *Romano-Germanic Pontifical* is of the greatest importance for the development of our present Roman Pontifical, for it was precisely this book that was brought to Rome, probably by one of the Ottos in the course of the tenth century, and adopted there.[69] The book, of course, had to be adapted to local exigencies, and thus arose the Roman Pontifical of the twelfth century, the first *Ordo* of papal ceremonies executed under Papal auspices.[70] During the thirteenth century this Pontifical was revised—probably under Innocent III (1198-1216)—and is known as the *Pontifical of the Roman Curia of the XIII Century*.[71]

Another work that exercised great influence upon the ultimate formation of our Pontifical was that of William Durand (d.1296), long-time canonist of the papal Curia and finally Bishop of Mende.[72] His reputation was such that it gave his Pontifical great authority and it was widely adopted. Actually it combined most of the rites until then observed in Rome with many other elements from Gallican sources. Innocent VIII (1484-1492) adopted it for Rome itself and charged Patricius Piccolomini (the future Pius II) and John Burchard to make a revision of it. This the Pope offered to the bishops of the Latin Rite as authentic Roman practice. Piccolomini's Pontifical underwent revision after revision: in 1496 by James de Luciis, in 1511 by Julius II

[64] Not to be confused with the medieval record of the popes also called *Liber Pontificalis*.

[65] Edited by W. Greenwell, *The Pontifical of Egbert Archbishop of York*. Publications of the Surtees Society, 27. Durham, 1853.

[66] Described by A. Wilmart, "Notice du Pontifical de Poitiers," *Jahrbuch für Liturgiewissenschaft*, 4 (1924), 48-81.

[67] For the name, date and place of origin of this Pontifical, cf. M. Andrieu, *Les Ordines Romani*, I, 495-499.

[68] M. Hittorp, *De divinis catholicae Ecclesiae officiis* (Paris, 1610), col. 21-180. Andrieu restricts the name *Ordo Romanus Antiquus* to col. 21-94 which concerns the Liturgical Year, cf. *op. cit.*, I, 496, note 1.

[69] Andrieu, I, 511-519.

[70] Reproduced in a critical edition as the first volume in Andrieu's monumental work, *Le Pontifical Romain au Moyen Age*. Studi e Testi, 86, 87, 88, 89. Vatican City, 1938-1941.

[71] Critical edition, *ibid.*, II.

[72] Critical edition, *ibid.*, III.

(who was the first to use the title *Pontificale*), in 1520 by the Dominican Albert Castellani and in 1561 by Pius V. Before this, the popes had seen to it that the formulas of the Pontifical were orthodox and an authentic reproduction of Roman practice; they did not, however, impose the book generally. Following out the wishes of the Council of Trent, that the received and approved rites for the administration of the sacraments should not be departed from, Clement VIII in 1595 promulgated a new edition of the *Pontificale Romanum* and obliged all churches of the Latin Rite to use it.

3. The Ritual

Similar to the manual containing episcopal ceremonies was another collection of formulas needed by the priest in his sacramental ministrations. At a relatively early date we have evidence of a special priest's manual. The Council of Toledo (633), for example, orders bishops to provide their pastors with a *libellus officialis* for the rites proper to them.[73] Unfortunately none of these *libelli* are extant. The earliest example of a monastic Ritual is that of St. Florian of the twelfth century,[74] while the first attempt at an official diocesan Ritual would be the fourteenth century manual of Bishop Heinrich I of Breslau.[75] From this time on we often find such manuals for the use of the secular clergy called *Agenda, Liber Ritualis, Sacerdotalia, Pastorale, Manuale,* or *Obsequiale*. Of particular importance for the ultimate form of our present Roman Ritual were the two *Sacerdotale*, of Albert Castellani (1537) and of Francesco Samarini (1579), and the *Rituale Sacramentorum Romanum* compiled by Cardinal Santorio in 1584 by order of Gregory XIII.[76] The latter book was the basis for the *Rituale Romanum* published as the official Ritual of the Roman Rite by Pope Paul V in 1614.

Prudently the Pope did not impose the use of this Ritual but only warmly recommended it; there was such a variety of regional differences that he feared it would disturb the faithful too much were he to suppress the differences. The collection was well received and was modified and added to by subsequent popes.[77] Though the editions published by recent popes were called *typical*, the Roman Ritual still has never been officially imposed on the Latin Church. Nevertheless, the *de facto* universality of its own use gives its formulas and rubrics the force of law. The practice of Pius XII of approv-

[73] Can. 26. Hefele-Leclercq, *Histoire des Conciles*, III, 271.

[74] Published by Adolf Franz, *Das Rituale von St. Florian*. Freiburg, 1904.

[75] Published by Adolf Franz, *Das Rituale des Bischofs Heinrich I von Breslau*. Freiburg, 1912.

[76] Cf. B. Löwenberg, *Das Rituale des Kardinals Julius Antonius Sanctorius, Ein Beitrag zur Entstehungsgeschichte des Rituale Romanum*. Munich, 1937.

[77] Benedict XIV in 1752, Pius IX in 1872, Leo XIII in 1884, Pius XI in 1925, and Pius XII in 1952.

ing national Rituals as appendices of the *Rituale Romanum* seems to confirm this view.

4. The Breviary

The constant practice of the Church up until the eleventh century was to insist on maintaining the choral recitation of the Divine Office for both monks and secular clergy. This does not mean that private recitation was unknown or disapproved. The normal manner of reciting the Office, however, was in choir. After the eleventh century this practice began to yield more and more to private recitation. To make the latter easier, all the pertinent texts and rubrics were gathered from the various books in use up until that time, and an abbreviation (*breviarium*) or contraction of them was made. This consisted mainly in the elimination of the musical notation and a radical shortening of the readings.

Such abbreviations became frequent in the thirteenth century. Innocent III approved one of these Breviaries for his Curia.[78] The Franciscans adopted the abbreviations approved by Innocent III and added to them the Gallican Psalter. This revised Breviary was then prescribed for the churches of Rome by Pope Nicholas III (1277-1280).[79] A second time the Friars Minor hastened the spread of the Roman Liturgy, this time by carrying their Breviaries all over Europe. Notwithstanding the efforts of Cardinal Quignonez to establish the use of another form of Breviary in 1536, the type propagated by the Franciscans became the basis of the Breviary made obligatory on the Latin Rite by Pius V in 1568 (again the retention of all Breviaries having at least a two hundred year tradition behind them was allowed).

Many reforms took place after this. To note only a few: Clement VIII brought the scriptural readings into conformity with the Vulgate, while Urban VIII revised some of the rubrics and "corrected" the latinity of the metrical hymns. Leo XIII retouched many of the historical lessons, and Pius X restored the Psalter to its early arrangement, thus making allowance for a weekly recitation of practically all 150 psalms. Finally, Pius XII permitted the use of the new translation of the psalms from the original Hebrew text and sanctioned the simplification of rubrics and reduction in rank of many feasts.

D. Liturgical Law

Before the time of St. Pius V there existed a much greater liberty in liturgical matters. We have already noted the slow progression from localized liturgical legislative power to a strictly centralized authority. The institution of feasts and rites, as well as their alteration

---

[78] S. Bäumer — R. Biron, *Histoire du Bréviaire* (Paris, 1905), II, 22.
[79] *Ibid.*, 24.

and suppression, rested with the local Ordinaries—sometimes even with pastors. There were, of course, frequent abuses. This is why the popes have tried from time to time to restrict this right. Pius V succeeded in doing just this, but only for the contents of certain liturgical books. The Code of Canon Law definitively reserved to the Holy See all power regarding the institution of feasts, the editing of liturgical books, as well as for any changes in the rites.[80] In his encyclical, *Mediator Dei*, Pius XII explains this legislation as meaning that "the Sovereign Pontiff alone enjoys the right to recognize and establish any practice touching the worship of God, to introduce new rites, as also to modify those he judges to require modification."[81]

The obligation to accept whatever changes the Holy See deems fit to make regarding the books and rites of the Latin Church is in itself a grave one, the gravity of the obligation always depending on the tenor of the pontifical documents. When it is certain that the Roman Pontiffs wish to oblige all to a certain manner of executing the Sacred Liturgy, all are obliged *sub gravi* (allowance being made for light matter) to conform to such prescribed ritual unless a sufficient reason excuses. In one of its canons on the sacraments, the Council of Trent condemns anyone who would hold that the approved rites of the Church may be treated with contempt, omitted without sin by ministers whenever they so desire, or changed for new ones by any pastor whatsoever.[82] By way of explanation of such a stand on the part of the Church, Pius XII states: "Private individuals, even though they be clerics, may not be left to decide for themselves in these holy and venerable matters, *involving as they do the religious life of Christian society along with the exercise of the priesthood of Jesus Christ and worship of God.*"[83]

[80] Can. 1257.
[81] *Mediator Dei*, 58.
[82] Sess. VII, can. 13 *de sacramentis in genere*. Denz. 856: "Si quis dixerit receptos et approbatos Ecclesiae catholicae ritus in solemni sacramentorum administratione adhiberi consuetos aut contemni, aut sine peccato a ministris pro libito omitti, aut in novos alios per quemcumque ecclesiarum pastorem mutari posse, A. S."
[83] *Mediator Dei*, 58. Emphasis added.

CHAPTER FOUR

Liturgical Places

A. The Church and its Furnishings

The Christian church is not an ordinary building. One cannot simply throw up four walls, cover them with a roof, and call such a structure a church. The Christian church must have a special meaning which is ultimately based on its purpose. In other words, it must be different from those structures used by anti-sacramental sects; it is not simply a meeting-house or auditorium. It is even less a museum or theatre.

Early Christians gave a name to their place of worship which expresses well its true meaning. They called it the *domus Dei*, or House of God.[1] Christian writers also used combinations or derivatives of the same expression: *dominicum* (the Lord's), *domus dominica* (the Lord's house) and *domus ecclesiae* (the Church's house).[2] Our English word church comes from the German *Kirche* which, in turn, is derived from the Greek *Kuriakon*, meaning "the Lord's." The common Latin term *ecclesia* means the assembly, a calling together. The Romance languages retained this root in their *chiesa*, *église*, and *iglesia*. The ancient Church also used another word, *basilica*, or house of the King, for the principal churches.

The Church, then, looks upon her place of worship as the House of God, something belonging to the Lord, the place where the faithful assemble, the House of the King. Let us recall that it was not the Eucharistic presence which gave the name House of God to the church; the reservation of the Blessed Sacrament is a much later development. The church was called the House of God because His sacred mysteries, His sacraments, were enacted there, because His children assembled there and broke with their heavenly Father the bread of life, and because there they gathered to hear His word as He spoke to them in the Sacred Scriptures.

[1] Tertullian, *De idololatria* 7. *MPL*, 1: 745; Hippolytus, *Comm. in Daniel* I, 20. *GCS*, 1: 34.
[2] Cyprian, *De opere et eleemosyna* 15. *MPL*, 4: 646; Clement of Alexandria, *Stromata* 3, 18. *MPG*, 8: 1212; Eusebius, *Historia Ecclesiastica* 7, 30, 19. *GCS*, 9(2), 714, 4.

This sacred building, therefore, must, in some way, reflect in its very structure the holiness of what takes place within its walls.[3] Its construction is not an occasion for the artist or architect to erect a monument to his own personality, nor for any given people to express its national character to such a degree as to obscure the essential nature and primary purpose of the church building.

Let us trace the development of the church structure throughout history and see what success the Church has met with in adapting this principle to concrete circumstances and particular ages.

1. Origin and development of the church building

Primitive churches were nothing else than the private homes of early Christians who were financially well off.[4] Perhaps the early appellation *domus ecclesiae* referred to houses held in common by the Church (a house belonging to the Church). Though it was not always possible in the beginning, because of lack of legal security for the Christians in those years, common ownership did become a reality later.[5] But the expression *domus ecclesiae* also indicated that the exterior (and very likely the interior) of the primitive church remained faithful to the appearance and plan of the Roman house:

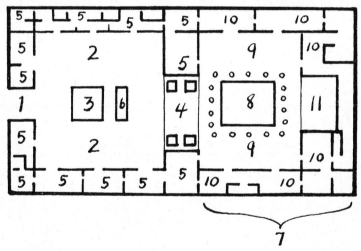

The Roman house was essentially made up as follows: (1) *ostium* or entrance, (2) *atrium,* a large central hall with no win-

---

[3] Cf. Theodore Greene, *The Arts and the Art of Criticism* (Princeton, 1947), 322.

[4] Even the present titular churches in Rome still indicate through their title the original ownership. Often the title was shifted, however, from the owner's private house, where Mass had been habitually celebrated, to the larger adjacent basilicas built much later: cf. J. Kirsch, *Die römischen Titelkirchen im Altertum* (Paderborn, 1918), 118-126.

[5] Cf. the decree of the Emperor Aurelian concerning the controverted question of Church property between the Christians of Antioch and their deposed

dows but an opening in the roof to permit light to enter, (3) *impluvium*, a small pond in the center of the floor directly under the hole in the roof for the purpose of catching the rain, (4) *tablinum*, a room at the far end of the *atrium* raised by several steps, one side of which was completely open to the *atrium*; it was used as a combination home shrine, reception room and general family sitting room. (5) Surrounding the *atrium* were other common and private rooms, such as a dining room, *triclinium*, and a kitchen, as well as bedrooms and servants' quarters. (6) A *cartibulum*, or table, often stood in the *atrium* near the *tablinum*. (7) In imitation of Greek architecture, another section was added to the rich noble's house. It consisted of: (8) the open garden or *peristylium*, (9) surrounded by a covered walk, and (10) the private rooms for the family. (11) At the far end was to be found the *oecus*, or family sitting room; the *tablinum* and other rooms in the *atrium* section were given over to the servants.

For Christian worship the *atrium* became the place where the body of the faithful stood (our present nave); the *impluvium* was very convenient for the administration of Baptism. The *cartibulum* was used as an altar; it was also possible that it was carried into the *tablinum*, where the bishop's throne was normally placed, so that all might be able to see the sacred action. But in the Greco-Roman houses, the *atrium* was reserved for the catechumens and penitents, while the faithful occupied the *peristylium* and the altar and bishop's throne were placed in the *oecus*.

The Latin Basilica

Even in pre-Constantinian times [6] special halls had been built for Christian worship. These were made necessary by the ever increasing

---

bishop, Paul of Samosata: Eusebius, *Historia Ecclesiastica* 7,30,19. *GCS*, 9(2), 714, 4-7; cf. also the decree of the Emperor Gallienus to Dionysius of Alexandria: *ibid.*, 7,13. *GCS*, 9(2), 666, 14-23.

[6] Religious services in the Catacombs need not detain us here. They exercised no influence over the development of the Christian church, except in so far as they heightened devotion to the martyrs. It is a general but erroneous opinion that, during the persecutions at least, Mass was held regularly in the Catacombs. This is based on a popular misconception of these cemeteries and on the more romantic than realistic belief that early Christians could hide in them. The Catacombs were public places and well known to the pagan authorities and people: cf. L. Hertling — E. Kirschbaum, *The Roman Catacombs and their Martyrs* (Milwaukee, 1956), 133. They would not serve as a hiding place or a safe locale for celebrating the Mass any better than the private homes of Roman citizens. The narrowness of the passages would certainly not suit them for an assembly place. And the humidity and presence of decaying corpses would not recommend them from a hygienic point of view. It is hardly thinkable, therefore, that these circumstances would encourage a frequent and regular religious service. Whatever services were held in the Catacombs had a strictly exceptional character: a funeral or anniversary celebration. And these latter were customarily held above ground in a little chapel, *cella memoriae* or *cella martyris* (cf. H. Leclercq, "Cella," *DACL*, 2: 2885), built directly above the place where the martyr was buried. These were so small that only the celebrant, or at most the ministers, could enter. The rest of the faithful had to remain outside.

number of faithful. With the coming of peace under Constantine, this problem grew to enormous proportions and necessitated ever larger buildings. The architectural type chosen for these churches was what we call today the Latin basilica.

Soon after his victory over Maxentius (312) Constantine had a sumptuous basilica erected over what was once a military encampment near the house of the Lateran family. This basilica, originally called the Basilica of the Savior but renamed in the twelfth century by Pope Lucius II as St. John Lateran, was the first cathedral of Rome and still is the city's cathedral; it is often referred to as the mother of Christian churches. To show his devotion to St. Peter, Constantine also built the first martyr's shrine over the tomb of St. Peter in the Vatican cemetery. By 345 the two building projects of Constantine had set the pace for years to come; we have the beginning of the Christian basilica and the Christian monument,[7] styles which were to be copied until the late Middle Ages.

Since it was during the era after the persecutions that the Roman Liturgy developed its classical lines, and did this within the walls of these Latin basilicas, this architectural type has a special claim on our attention and respect. We will see later how this form, more than any other, suits the liturgical ceremonial of the Latin West both for the interpretation of ideas and in actual practice.

Though St. John Lateran and St. Peter's were the original basilicas, the latter has been completely rebuilt in another style, and the former has been thoroughly modified. The churches in Rome which best represent the pure basilica type are San Clemente, Santa Maria in Cosmedin, and Santa Sabina. An analysis of these churches provides the following floor plan:

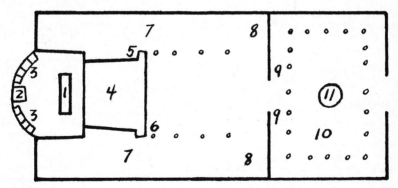

1. Altar. 2. Bishop's throne. 3. Seats for the clergy. 4. Area for the *Schola Cantorum*. 5. Gospel ambo. 6. Epistle ambo. 7. Congregation. 8. Catechumens. 9. Penitents. 10. Atrium. 11. Fountain.

[7] Though employing the same structural type as St. John Lateran, St. Peter's basilica differed from it in *idea* because of the connection with a martyr's tomb.

The atrium was a rectangular yard in front of the basilica. It contained a fountain for ablutions and was surrounded by a colonnaded walk. The part of the colonnade against the facade of the basilica was called the narthex (our modern vestibule). The nave was a large hall divided by two rows of columns into three sections. Men and women were usually separated and occupied the two smaller sections of the nave or side naves, while in the middle near the sanctuary was located a fenced-off area reserved for the *Schola Cantorum*. The sanctuary, at the opposite end of the nave from the atrium, was slightly elevated and rounded out in a shell-like form or apse. Some of the Latin basilicas had transepts which enlarged the width of the building just before the apse.

Since the bishop's throne was located against the back wall of the apse, it was only natural that the altar was placed between him and the people. This was the arrangement in the Roman house-church, and it seems rather obvious that the basilica floor plan simply followed the example of its forerunner. Hence, the original reason for the altar facing the people was the hierarchical set-up of the church.[8] The bishop's throne was the center of activity and attraction, and thus it stood at a point facing all. When the bishop approached the altar, he did the natural thing and went directly to the side facing him. At the altar, as at the throne, he continued his role as a representative

[8] Veneration of the martyrs' relics buried beneath or within the altar and the alleged near-universal principle of orientation are put forth by some as reasons for the altar being built facing the people: P. Anson, "Mass Facing the People," *Liturgical Arts*, 24 (1955), 3; J. A. Jungmann, *"The Mass of the Roman Rite*, I, 255; J. Braun, *Der christliche Altar in seiner geschichtlichen Entwicklung* (Munich, 1924), I, 412-413.

The principle of orientation, that is of facing the East at prayer, in no wise affected the Roman Liturgy. Not only do we not find any trace of an official practice of this kind in Rome itself, but Leo I was definitely opposed to it as a remnant of paganism: cf. F-J. Dölger, *Sol Salutis* (Münster, 1925), 3-5. It was only in the Oriental and Gallican Rites that this idea found acceptance: cf. J. Quasten, *Monumenta*, p. 35, note 1; M. Andrieu, "Note sur une ancienne rédaction de l'*Ordo Romanus Primus*," *Revue des Sciences Religieuses*, 1 (1921), 394-395; *idem, Les Ordines Romani*, II, 55. The idea certainly, therefore, had nothing to do with the altar facing the people in Rome. Rather it contributed to the discontinuance of this practice elsewhere: cf. H. Leclercq, "Orientation," *DACL*, 12: 2666. For the principle of orientation, when rightly carried out, meant that the apse was at the east end of the church, the facade at the west: cf. *Didascalia Apostolorum* II, 57, 2-5. J. Quasten, *Monumenta*, 34-35. Hence, the normal position of the priest at Mass in orientated churches was on the people's side of the altar.

The other reason alleged for this type of altar, namely, that it was to permit the people to approach the altar and venerate the relics of the martyrs buried there, or because of the presence of the confession, or sunken pit, immediately before the altar, is not at all convincing. Such confessions were not built on the people's side of the altar until the sixteenth century: cf. F. Grossi Gondi, *I Monumenti Cristiani* (Rome, 1923), 431, note 2. Before this era confessions did exist, but they were crypts built *behind* the altar and *beneath* the floor of the sanctuary. The people were allowed access to them by means of stairways on either side of the apse. But even these crypts date only from the sixth century: *ibid.*, 429. Hence, the altar *versus populum* arrangement antedates the construction of confessions of either type.

from God to the people, breaking bread with the children of God's household.

What is the origin of the basilica type church? This is a question that has been disputed for some time. Though archeologists have concerned themselves with the problem for more than seventy years, none of the solutions proposed have so far met with general acceptance.

There are those [9] who consider the Christian basilica to have been derived from the Roman forensic basilicas. In general the Christian basilica does resemble the public imperial ones, but there are dissimilarities. The side naves of the Christian basilica are lower than the central one, and the latter is pierced with windows. In the civil basilica all the naves are of the same height. The atrium and transept often found in Christian basilicas are never part of the civil ones.[10]

The very items which serve to differentiate the Christian from the public basilica tend at the same time to identify it with the plan of the Roman house. In private Roman mansions the peristyle was clearly the biggest section of the house. Were this roofed over against the weather in such a way as to allow space for windows, a clerestory would be produced. This would explain how the side naves of the Christian basilica come to be lower than the central nave. The apse is easily seen as a transformation of the *oecus*, or family reception room. The atrium of Christian basilicas also finds an obvious precedent in the same feature of the Roman house. This explanation of the origin of the Christian basilica is, according to Grisar,[11] the simplest and most probable.

Still a third theory considers the Christian church to be a combination of various elements, principally the Roman house and forensic basilica.[12] This is the opinion most widespread among archeologists. They see the influence of the Roman house in the higher elevation of the central nave over the side ones and the frequent use of the atrium and apse; the influence of the public basilicas is seen in the length and general height of the Christian church. Certainly, if the early Christians adopted the general plan of the larger quarters of the Roman house for their churches, they did not do so slavishly, but rather adapted appropriate elements from other already existing buildings and attempted a fusion of all the elements.

Romanesque

From the eighth to the tenth century the West saw the rise of a new type of church, the romanesque. This is the term for those phases of European architecture which were based on Roman art. Roman-

---

[9] F. Grossi Gondi, *op. cit.*, 416-417.

[10] Cf. M. Righetti, *Manuale di Storia Liturgica*, I, 356.

[11] Hartmann Grisar, *History of Rome and the Pope in the Middle Ages*, II (St. Louis, 1912), 88.

[12] H. Leclercq, "Basilique," *DACL*, 2: 536.

esque arose from the ruins of Europe after the barbarian invasions. Thus the old Roman art was the quarry for the new architecture; to that degree it necessarily determined the latter's character.[13] It must also be admitted that Byzantine art exercised some influence on the birth of this new style, for it had traveled its way to the West through the great trade centers, Venice, Ravenna, Marseilles. In addition to these two basic influences, we find that regional differences in climate and geological resources determined many of the peculiarities of the romanesque style throughout Europe.

The principal characteristics of this form of architecture may be summed up in the following points:

1. *Plan:* Transepts, generally of the same breadth as the nave, were added to the latter, and the sanctuary was extended, thus making the floor-plan a well defined cross; the sanctuary was usually raised above the level of the nave and rested on piers over a vaulted crypt; later churches often carried aisles all the way round the sanctuary to form a deambulatory, thus allowing people to visit votive chapels behind the sanctuary; towers begin to appear at the east and west ends and above the spot where nave and transepts meet; the altar is deep in the sanctuary, far away from the nave.

2. *Ceiling:* All three naves (or more, depending on the immensity of the church) usually had vaulted ceilings which were formed as a half cylinder or semicircle. In some places these vaults were stilted, that is, lifted slightly higher than a regular semicircle would warrant. Molded ribs were often employed here and there to reinforce these vaults. Frequently, crossed vaults are to be seen, that is, a ceiling formed by a series of intersecting vaults. Some architects also used a system of internal flying buttresses to support the vaulted ceiling of the middle nave; these they would hide between the ceiling and roof of the side naves.

3. *Walls:* The exterior walls were thick and heavy, often reinforced with buttresses formed of pilaster strips connected at the top by a band of horizontal molding or by a series of semicircular arches. The thickness of the walls was necessitated by the heavy downward thrust of the vaulted ceilings.

4. *Openings:* Doors and windows were characteristically arched in semicircular fashion, while their jambs or sides formed a series of receding concentric rings. Due to the thick walls, windows were usually few and small.

Some of the more important examples of this type of architecture are: St. Sernin in Toulouse (11-12 cent.), Notre Dame la Grande in Poitiers (12 cent.), St. Ambrose in Milan (12 cent.), the Cathedral of Modena (12 cent.), the Cathedral of Parma (11-12 cent.), San Miniato of Florence (12 cent.), the Pisa Cathedral and its Baptistery (11-12 cent.), the Benedictine Abbey Church of Maria Laach (12 cent.),

[13] B. Fletcher, *A History of Architecture* (London, 1928), 247.

the Cathedral of Speyer (11-12 cent.), and the Cathedral of Mainz
(12-13 cent.).

Gothic

The evolution of romanesque into gothic came almost insensibly,
for the skeleton that was hidden in the former only gradually lost its
skin and flesh: the stresses became more and more obvious. Flying
buttresses were devised to carry away the thrust of the pointed arches
of the vaults. This, of course, relieved the weight on the walls which
then could be pierced with more and larger windows.

But "gothic" is a misnomer; it is synonymous with "barbaric."
Christopher Wren first used it as a term of reproach for this departure
from the classical lines of architecture.[14] A more exact descriptive
name would be *ogival* architecture, for this refers to the distinctive
pointed arch used in the vaults of this type of church. Born in the
north of France, ogival architecture began to appear in the twelfth
century, reached its apogee in the thirteenth and fourteenth centuries,
and in the fifteenth began its decline, scorned by the rising Renaissance.

The essential characteristics of ogival architecture are:

1. *The flying buttress.* The vault thrusts are both downward, by
reason of gravitation, and outward, by reason of the action of the
voussoirs (wedge-shaped stones in the arch). Both stresses are collected by the meeting of the ribs at the angles of the vaulting com-
partments. The resulting pressure is oblique or slanting, and this is
counteracted and transmitted to the ground by the flying buttresses,
these, in turn, being weighted down by the pinnacles.

2. *The pointed arch and rib.* The pointed arch helps to direct the
stress downward rather than outward, so that the weight of the pin-
nacle can more easily prevent the buttress from overturning. And the
ribs play an even more important role in gothic than they did in romanesque, for now the network of ribs actually support the panels of
the vaults. In other words, the arches of the gothic church are formed
of strong ribs upon which are laid very thin stone panels. It is these
arched ribs which gather the pressure from above, carry it to the angles
of the vaults and there pass it on to the flying buttresses.

3. With such a highly developed system for disposing of the stresses and strains, the walls are no longer necessary as supports; they are
now nothing more than enclosures. This enables the gothic architect
to pierce the side of the church with huge and delicately designed
windows. In some instances, we find churches whose walls are mostly
glass, suffering only occasional interruptions for a buttress (La Sainte
Chapelle in Paris).

[14] *Ibid.,* 300.

4. Thus the architect is now permitted to add greater emphasis on height and slenderness. The gothic church seems to reach to heaven.

These qualities of the gothic church are indeed great feats of engineering. But sometimes the emphasis on height and slenderness produced untoward effects, as far as liturgical worship is concerned; often the naves and aisles were endlessly long, the altar far away. This had tragic consequences for active participation in the sacred mysteries.

Also to be deplored is a piece of furniture (quite incidental to gothic) often found in gothic churches, the so-called Rood Screen. This is a wall, sometimes of marble, sometimes of glass and columns, sometimes only a grill with or without curtains, located between the sanctuary or choir and the nave; above it is placed a cross (Rood) or Calvary group. Beautiful though it may be in some instances, it admirably succeeds in cutting off the people's view of the altar and reducing considerably their participation in the Mass. Its origin is somewhat obscure. It might have begun as a support, pure and simple, for the Calvary group above, or it might have been an exaggerated development of the chancel, or communion rail.[15] It may have been designed originally for the comfort of the choir, to reduce the draft so frequent in the huge cathedrals. Or, finally, it may have started as an unreasonable bringing back of the old basilical enclosure for the *schola cantorum*. Historians have not come to a definite conclusion.

Some of the best examples of gothic architecture are: Notre Dame of Paris (12-13 cent.), Notre Dame of Chartres (12-13 cent.), Notre Dame of Amiens (13 cent.), Notre Dame of Rheims (13 cent.), the Liebfrauenkirche of Trier, Germany (13 cent.), the Cathedral of Cologne (13-14 cent.), the Cathedral of Ulm (14-15 cent.), St. George of Windsor (15 cent.), the Cathedral of Toledo (13 cent.), the Cathedral of Burgos (13 cent.).

Renaissance and baroque

We naturally look to Italy as the birthplace of Renaissance art and architecture. Gothic had never taken firm root there; older traditions were too strong: Italy was rich in the lore of ancient Roman civilization. Furthermore, fifteenth century Christians, partly in reaction to a decadent scholasticism, were busy discovering the riches of the past; spurred on by the new findings in science and the exploration of the New World, they were constructing a new, man-centered humanism. The cultural inheritance of Greece and Rome became the symbols of the new era. In architecture and art this meant a return to the forms of classical times.

[15] There is a parallel instance in the Byzantine Iconostasis originating around the same time in Russia.

Strangely enough, however, this movement was never a complete return. Although the outward form and decoration were classical—the ancient Roman columns, arches, cornices and mythological themes— gothic methods of construction almost always prevailed. Baroque, even in using such forms and themes, came actually as a revolt against the formality and restraint of the almost blind conformity to rules laid down by the earlier Renaissance classicists.

Yet, some call baroque purely pagan in essence.[16] It is naively confused with its predecessor because of outward appearances. Just because baroque employs classical forms and pagan mythological themes, this does not make it pagan. In the Renaissance, the "horizontal architecture of antiquity was revived in conformity with the horizontal outlook of humanism." [17] Themes from classical mythology are treated for their own sake all too often, not, like the mythological representations in Dante's Purgatory, to illustrate Christian teaching. Even where the subjects of Renaissance art are sacred, the suspicion looms large that they are mere cloaks for the secular.[18] The impression seems inescapable that, at times, it is but an attempt to glorify man.

Baroque, on the contrary, endeavors to make God incarnate and to spur man on to an ascent to God. It may use the same media of expression as the Renaissance, but it infuses into them a new spirit: Christ and Christianity as a fulfillment of human aspirations; the infinite in the context of the finite; the vertical as a completion of the horizontal.[19] Watkin defines baroque as the employment of classical forms by gothic feeling; though the matter of baroque is classical, its "form" or spirit is gothic.[20] It may deal with the things of sense, but it does this to arrive at the spirit behind them, for when baroque achieves its aim, it uses the sensible, we may even say sensuous, "to signify the spiritualisation of sense, the sublimation of man's passionate energy in an ecstatic love of God." [21] For baroque everything below is the symbol of something above, every object of sense the symbol of a spiritual reality.[22]

This fundamental distinction between Renaissance and baroque can be clearly brought out by principles of art criticism. Heinrich Wölfflin, whose masterful *Principles of Art History* appeared in its first German edition in 1915, has taught us, once and for all, how to appreciate baroque and to distinguish it from Renaissance. He gives five principles according to which these two styles are clearly distinguished:

16 L. Bouyer, *Liturgical Piety*, 5, 52.
17 Cf. E. I. Watkin, *Catholic Art and Culture* (New York, 1944), 109.
18 *Ibid.*, 109-110.
19 *Ibid.*, 126-127.
20 *Ibid.*, 121.
21 *Ibid.*, 134, 146-147.
22 *Ibid.*, 150.

(a) Renaissance art is primarily linear and tactile, baroque primarily what he calls "painterly" (*malerisch*) and visual. The emphasis in the former falls upon clearly defined outlines and edges, and therefore things seem limited, isolated, solid and tangible. In the latter, however, stress is laid upon mass and space, and therefore the attention is withdrawn from the edges; things seem limitless, they shift, they merge.[23]

(b) Renaissance art lays stress on the plane, baroque on the visual third dimension, depth. "Plane is the element of line, extension in one plane the form of the greatest explicitness: with the discounting of the contour comes the discounting of the plane, and the eye relates objects essentially in the direction of forwards and backwards." [24]

(c) In Renaissance art the closed form is emphasized, in baroque the open. Wölfflin explains: "Every work of art must be a finite whole, and it is a defect if we do not feel that it is self-contained, but the interpretation of this demand in the sixteenth and seventeenth centuries is so different that, in comparison with the loose form of the baroque, classic design may be taken as *the* form of closed composition." [25]

(d) The Renaissance stresses multiplicity, baroque unity of the whole. In the former, though the single parts are rooted in the whole and conditioned by the whole, they still maintain their own life and independence; in baroque, unity is achieved by a union of parts in a single theme, subordination to one unconditioned dominant.[26]

(e) *Absolute* clarity is the aim of Renaissance art, only *relative* clarity that of baroque. "Composition, light and color [in baroque] no longer merely serve to define form, but have their own life." This is a difference between "the representation of things as they are, taken singly and accessible to plastic feeling, and the representation of things as they look, seen as a whole by their non-plastic qualities." [27]

Thus in baroque "a movement (purely visual) is set going over the sum of forms, independently of the particular viewpoint. The wall vibrates, the space quivers in every corner. . . . Even in tectonic art, nothing is to settle into tangible lines and surfaces; even in tectonic art, the impression of permanence is to be supplanted by the impression of change; even in tectonic art, form must breathe. That is, apart from all expressional differences, the basic notion of baroque" [28]—the impression of movement, the infinite.[29] As T. Greene remarks so well, "It is because the baroque artist saw the world and interpreted life

---

[23] H. Wölfflin, *Principles of Art History* (New York, 1932), 14, 18-72.
[24] *Ibid.*, 15; cf. also pp. 73-122.
[25] *Ibid.*, 15; cf. also pp. 124-154.
[26] *Ibid.*, 15; cf. also pp. 155-195.
[27] *Ibid.*, 15-16; cf. also pp. 196-225.
[28] *Ibid.*, 65.
[29] Cf. Sigfried Giedion, *Space, Time and Architecture* (Cambridge, 1954), 109-111.

as he did that he gradually evolved those stylistic forms which would most effectively enable him to express what he wished to express: the forms were dictated by the artist's intent. What he wished to express was an emotionally vivid sense of human finitude in the face of cosmic infinity." [30] Baroque was the expression of the Counter-reformation and its spirit, man's vivid sense of his spiritual relation to God and his dependence on Him; the infinite God who had revealed Himself to man in Christ, who became incarnate to bring finite man to know and possess the Infinite. All baroque art, whether religious or secular, is curiously expressive of the spirit which permeated the latter sixteenth and seventeenth centuries.

However, in certain examples of baroque, often characterized by the term rococo, we see the danger incurred by a too lavish or otherwise injudicious use of architectural decoration. What Greene has to say is quite to the point. "Decoration is injurious to the architectural effect if it obscures or otherwise renders visually ineffective the main structural forms upon which the building must depend primarily for its architectural expressiveness." [31] When this happens we have a corresponding loss of architectural integrity. But the danger lies, not so much in the amount of decoration, as in its stylistic quality and, above all, in its relation to the main architectural structure. In this connection, Greene points out, the rococo style in southern Germany of the eighteenth century was prone to overdecoration that failed to exploit the expressive potentialities of the visible architectonic structure and the building materials.[32]

If, therefore, we say that baroque architecture is not, in all its exemplifications, completely adapted to the needs and exigencies of the Church's Liturgy, we do not thereby mean that it is not good art. Its tendency to overdecorate by that very fact distracts from and interferes with the liturgical action. Although the baroque church essentially draws one directly to the altar, it is not the altar of sacrifice or the table of the sacrificial meal, but rather the throne of the Real Presence. The former should be the primary liturgical focus, not the latter. In the baroque church, the meaning of the altar is all too often obscured by its mountainous rear-structure. Baroque has indeed sought, by and large, to erect a monstrous monstrance, a sumptuous setting for the Blessed Sacrament. We do not wish to criticize this historical fact; it was perhaps necessary for its time, for the Real Presence was under fire from the "reformers" of the north. But it would certainly be a mistake to continue in this vein today.

This detailed explanation of the art principles upon which baroque is based has been necessary to dispel the misunderstanding that has arisen in its regard. As a matter of fact, as we pass from the gothic

[30] *The Arts and the Art of Criticism* (Princeton, 1947), 379.
[31] *Ibid.*, 328.
[32] *Ibid.*, 417-418.

into the Renaissance and baroque periods, we become less conscious of architectural functionalism than of style, perhaps for the very simple reason that now the chief architects were sculptors and painters as well. Man had perfected his art to such a degree, had acquired the ability to manipulate matter and infuse such expressiveness into a building, that the eye of future generations would *first* be drawn altogether naturally to the artistic style of baroque rather than to its architectural and liturgical functionalism. As far as its architectural functionalism is concerned, we have mentioned the fact that good baroque enjoys a high degree of it and that its inner structural method is that of gothic. But now let us turn to the more detailed items of plan and structure.

Though circular churches in this period of the Renaissance and the baroque are not unknown, the plan of the baroque church is habitually rectangular. When transepts are present, they often form side chapels. The church is generally shorter than in the gothic period. And the altar stands at the far end of the sanctuary, against the back wall, and is often dwarfed by elaborately painted or sculptured backgrounds.

While the ceiling is usually delicately painted or sculptured, now barrel-shaped, now somewhat flattened, walls are thicker than in gothic, bearing hidden within them the methods of construction inherited from gothic. Pediments are of low pitch, due to classical influence, or semi-circular, often filled with sculpture. Openings in the wall are greatly restricted. Light is no longer *absolutely* free to stream through the building; it is controlled, particularly in baroque, and exploited to emphasize artistic detail. And domes are frequently used precisely to serve this contrived illumination, again especially in baroque.

Summary

All the styles of church architecture developed throughout the past nineteen hundred years have at least this in common: they have endeavored, more or less perfectly, to bring out the idea that the church building is the dwelling place of God among men. Though this aim remains constant in all styles, what changes is man's idea of God and of His relationship to mankind. This change, however, is more in emphasis than in fundamental beliefs.

In the basilica, God's house takes the appearance of the house of the Emperor, the *Pantocrator* or Ruler of all men. Christ is the new universal king. His victory over the enemy—the devil and paganism—is emphasized. And hence, His mediatorship more than His divinity is the focal point of devotion.

With the romanesque church, God's house becomes a castle of the victorious warrior Lord, with the faithful as His vassals. Just as the vassals of the earthly lord clustered about his castle to form a society, so the Church and its members form a society—the *civitas Dei,* the Kingdom of God on earth. And the mediatorship of Christ is still the point of emphasis.

In the gothic cathedral we see the castle of the divine Lord, although the castle idea is now more refined and points directly towards heaven and God's infinity and divinity by means of the cathedral's stark vertical lines. God is far away here, though still present as the object of man's inquisitiveness, analysis, and contemplation. This is also the age of passion-mysticism; it stresses Christ as the suffering God. And art depicts Him displaying the trophies of His passion, His wounds, in the company of His heavenly followers, the saints and martyrs.

Although the Renaissance church embodies the idea of the "house of God" it may appear more like a monument of human fulfillment through natural means; Christ is depicted in its art more as a humanist hero, the great athlete. Baroque portrays God's hall of state on earth. The church is the hall of the Real Presence; the altar is His throne. Human fulfillment is certainly stressed, but fulfillment through God's power, and this is brought out in painting and sculpture: man is glorified through Christ triumphant in heaven, who is the sensible, tangible, beautiful joy of the saints.

When the religion-culture of baroque times fell, art echoed the spirit of those times: It became commercialized and fell into the snare of utopian romanticism, copying the past to cover up for its present hopeless lack of spark and initiative. It was the age of Catholic repository art, which, we are tempted to think, did not want to face the chaos of society, or the challenge to Christianity; it was conservative art, afraid to step into the future. This, we feel, was a degradation of true art and a betrayal of genuine Catholic culture, which has as its mission to bring redemption to the world in which it finds itself, not to hide the mistakes and woes of mankind behind plaster and glass-eyed statuary.

With modern times a genuine art-religion culture seems to be emerging from the "sweetness," and "life-likeness" of the sentimental conservative romanticist. Art and architecture are using the materials of their times to express the needs of their times. As man looks about him and sees the devastation that pock-marked his world during two terrible wars and foresees little security in the future, his confidence is shaken despite all his advances in technology. Having become a wanderer (e.g., the refugees) and insecure, he is more aware than ever before of the utter transitoriness of this earth and life. He cries for redemption, salvation. He sees God's earthly abode as a symbol of man's *passing* to better things. The church more and more today is coming to resemble the "tent" [33] of God our Redeemer, with whom we are *en voyage* to the heavenly Jerusalem. Today, we are an *ecclesia peregrinans*.

Modern trends

The Church has never made any particular architectural style her own. She leaves the matter of style an open question for those who are responsible for the construction of a new church, so long as the creative talent of artist and architect truly serve the purpose of worship. Church law simply states that the local Ordinary, after seeking the advice of experts, should take care that the *forms* handed down by Christian tradition and the laws of sacred art be observed in the construction and restoration of churches.[34] But traditional forms are not the same as styles of the past. As long as the church structure expresses the idea that it is the "house of God and the house of prayer" and respects and promotes the liturgical worship of the Church, it may be said to be faithful to tradition.

The purposes of the church structure, arranged in order of importance, are: (1) the celebration of Mass, (2) the partaking of the fruits of Christ's redeeming sacrifice by means of the sacraments, (3) the preaching of the Word of God, (4) the adoration of the presence of our Lord in the Blessed Sacrament, (5) the accomplishment of various public, nonliturgical devotions, (6) the exercise of purely private devotion on the part of individual Catholics. An architect has as his primary duty to find material solutions which will satisfy these ends according to their respective importance.

If we are to be faithful to this hierarchy of purposes, the ground plan of the interior of a church should be determined chiefly by the requirements of the Eucharistic sacrifice and not, as so often happens, primarily for the sake of devotion to the Real Presence—a purpose which requires spatial arrangements to be made chiefly to serve adoration and contemplation.

Some may think that the ideal form of church is circular, with the altar in the very middle of the congregation. This is a mistake. The Holy Sacrifice, for which the edifice is primarily intended, is, according to the *rationale* of the Roman Liturgy, an action, the action of Christ, through His representative the priest, evoking a response on the part of the faithful. This mutual collaboration is expressed during the Mass by the responses of the people to the greetings and prayers of the priest as well as by the processions for the Offertory and Communion. This supposes a spatial arrangement directed toward the altar, so that there is an exchange of address and response between sanctuary and nave, between priest and people, and processional

[33] Cf. the interesting remarks apropos this idea in A. Henze — Th. Filthaut, *Contemporary Church Art* (New York, 1956), 32-33, 41-43.
[34] Canon 1164.

movement to and from the altar. An altar placed right in the midst of the congregation does not fit this purpose well, for when the priest addresses the congregation, there will always be some members of it behind him. Two distinct poles of activity are much more preferable. However, this does not mean that the altar should be placed at the far end of the sanctuary, a position which discourages active participation. To encourage participation and yet preserve the expression of hierarchical ordering supposed by the Mass, it would be well to place the altar at the point where sanctuary and nave meet.

Since the altar is the sacrificial banquet table of the people of God, it is incorrect to make it a mere wall-appendage, as though its purpose were merely to serve as a pedestal for tabernacle, crucifix, candelabra, and reliquaries or elaborate backgrounds. The altar should stand out as a *table* and should have the greatest prominence as the most sacred object in the Church, for it is the bearer of Christ's sacrifice. It should be the center and heart of the whole environment. To be this, it must be situated in an isolated, but not distant, spot; it must be relatively elevated; it must be well-proportioned and well-made in the given material; it must be monumental in relation to the size of the entire edifice; it must be situated in the right perspective at the point where there is the most light; and it must be surmounted by a baldachin or canopy.

While canon law and recent decrees demand that the tabernacle as a rule be placed on the main altar, it also allows for exceptions to this rule.[35] It is clearly in keeping with tradition that the altar *versus populum* of the basilica style be continued in our times. Pontifical documents recognize that there are sound reasons of pastoral import for this practice of celebrating Mass facing the people. Pius XII, though commanding respect for the canons which concern union of tabernacle and altar, expressed hope that specialists would devise some way of arranging the tabernacle so that *it will not hinder* such a practice.[36] Bugnini, a consultor of the Congregation of Rites, declares that this practice is a good reason for allowing an exception to the rule that the tabernacle must be regularly kept on the main altar, as mentioned in canon 1268.[37] Of course, where there is only one altar, it cannot be built *versus populum*, for the tabernacle must be in the center of it.[38] Hence, when this practice is desired, and is approved by the local Ordinary, it is recommended that a fitting altar be prepared, either behind the main altar or in a side chapel, to receive the tabernacle.

[35] Can. 1268, #2 and 3.

[36] Allocution to the Assisi Congress for Pastoral Liturgy, AAS, 48 (1956), 722.

[37] "Commentarium super decretum de forma et usu tabernaculi," *Ephemerides Liturgicae,* 71 (1957), 443.

[38] Decree of the Sacred Congregation of Rites, June 1, 1957: "De forma et usu tabernaculi," *Ephemerides Liturgicae,* 71 (1957), 441.

Windows piercing the wall behind the altar, especially when the rays of the sun will stream through them during Mass, and paintings on this same wall which have no relation to the Eucharistic action are to be discouraged, for they will serve only to distract those who assist at Mass. The architecture and decoration of the sanctuary should be so designed as to draw the eye to the altar. When paintings adorn the sanctuary walls, they should represent ideas taken from the Canon of the Mass; they should be, not historical events, but timeless motifs. And since the altar and sanctuary constitute the primary liturgical focus, the primary architectural focus should also be there. All the lines of the church should converge upon the altar. Whatever is secondary ought to be subordinated to it: side altars, confessionals, Stations of the Cross, light fixtures, benches, and chairs. Indispensable items could be placed in a lower or side chapel especially designed for private devotion, perhaps in a side chapel of the Blessed Sacrament if one is available.

The sacristy ought to be located near the sanctuary in such a way as to permit a festive approach to the altar on feast days and to make it possible once again to execute the Introit as a genuine entrance hymn.

According to the Liturgy, preaching which is in organic relation to the Eucharistic Sacrifice should be primarily an extension and explanation of the word of God proclaimed in the Mass of the Catechumens—preaching centered on the Epistle and Gospel, therefore. Like the Epistle and Gospel, the sermon should normally issue forth from the sanctuary and not from a pulpit located in the middle of the church. Thus the sermon's intimate connection with the liturgical action would be brought out.

The function of the choir or *schola cantorum* is to lead the congregation in prayers and hymns and the regular liturgical acclamations, to alternate with the congregation in the responsorial chants, and to represent the congregation now and then. In accordance with its function, it should be located at the forward end of the congregation and next to the sanctuary, possibly in a slightly sunken section immediately before the altar. It is unfortunate when the choir is located in a high gallery in the rear of the church, for then it loses contact with the congregation, and its chances of leading it are lessened. The organ console might also be better placed towards the front of the congregation near the *schola*, for its function is to sustain both choir and people in their singing—not to furnish solo pieces during the misnamed "pauses" of the Mass. The liturgical office of the choir members is often enhanced by their use of cassock and surplice.

A second liturgical focus is the place for the administration of the sacraments of Baptism and Penance. To bring out their role as a gateway to the Eucharist, as a purification before entering the Church, a special structure or room for administering them might stand at the opposite end of the edifice from the sanctuary. In the early Church circular or octagonal baptisteries were preferred. The baptismal font itself could be sunken below the level of the floor, so that the candidate would have to descend a short flight of steps to reach it. This would bring out the Pauline theology of Baptism as a burial with Christ and a rising to new life through His grace. Since Penance also plays the role of a second Baptism, confessionals would appropriately fit into the theme of this baptismal "chapel." [39]

Finally, it is a mistake to entrust the building and decoration of a church to one man alone, the pastor, or to the whims of a generous donor. The sacred edifice, by its very nature, must suit the needs of the community as a whole, reflect its character, but, most important of all, it must meet strictly and perfectly the laws and spirit of the sacred Liturgy. Hence, a diocesan commission, made up of experts both in art and liturgiology, men genuinely competent in their fields,[40] ought to be entrusted with such a sacred and serious responsibility; the responsibility for producing for the Christian community an edifice intended as its heavenly home here below, a home to be loved and cherished, a home wherein the minds and hearts of its members shall be fed the solid meat of the supernatural life, wherein precious souls shall be born unto God, warmed with His love, inspired towards perfection, led to the maturity of likeness to the image of Christ.

Church law

It would be well if, at this point, we summarize the official legislation of the Church contained in canons 1162 to 1178.

No church may be built without the written consent of the local Ordinary, and such permission should not be granted unless he prudently foresees that the material means necessary for its construction will not be wanting.[41] An obligation also rests with the Ordinary to see to it, after having heard the advice of experts if need be, that Christian tradition and the rules of sacred art be faithfully observed in the construction of the edifice.[42]

No opening may be made from the church to the homes of laymen. If there are any rooms above or below the church, they must not be used for merely profane purposes.[43] Respected canonists hold

[39] For other suggestions indicative of modern trends one might profitably consult the German Liturgical Commission's *Directives for the Building of a Church*. Collegeville, Minnesota, 1949.
[40] It is difficult to staff such a commission; its very existence demands preparation, thorough study, and genuine Christian living from its members. It also postulates that its members have qualities necessary for its task: education, genuine and not pseudo-appreciation of art, prudence, honesty and loyalty towards Mother Church and a sincere preoccupation with the spiritual life of the faithful. Without such qualities, a commission would be more of a menace than a help towards furthering a holy union between religion and culture.
[41] Can. 1162.
[42] Can. 1164, 1.
[43] Can. 1164, 2.

that this clearly forbids the holding of dances, banquets, dramatic performances (except of a religious nature), or secular meetings in such areas, and that the space above a church must not be used as a bedroom.[44] However, authors permit the use of such areas for religious libraries, lecture classes, and meetings of parochial societies.

Divine services may not be conducted in a new church until it has been dedicated either through solemn consecration or at least through blessing.[45] However, the needs of the faithful cannot always wait, and the bishop may permit the celebration of Mass in an uncompleted church or in some other provisional hall, as long as it is a fitting and clean place. This can be done only for a limited time; should the emergency perdure, the Ordinary should request a special indult.[46] If, once the Ordinary has given his consent for the construction of a church, it becomes evident that the building will have to be given over to profane uses, he should neither consecrate it nor bless it.[47]

Cathedral churches are to be solemnly consecrated and, as far as possible, collegiate, conventual, and parochial churches also.[48] While churches built of wood or metal may not be consecrated but only blessed,[49] those built of stone, brick, or reinforced concrete may be consecrated, provided that in the latter case the places for the twelve crosses and the door posts of the main entrance be of stone.[50] Though an altar may be consecrated at any time apart from the consecration of the church, no church may be consecrated unless at least one altar be also so dedicated at the same time.[51]

Every consecrated or blessed church must have its proper title which cannot be changed after the dedication; a church may not be dedicated to the Blessed, that is those not yet canonized, without a special Apostolic indult.[52]

It is fitting that every church be equipped with bells with which to summon the faithful to liturgical worship and other religious exercises. They must be consecrated or at least blessed, and they may not be used for profane purposes without necessity, nor without the permission of the Ordinary or the allowance of legitimate custom.[53]

The church and its contents are to be kept clean as befits the house of God. Furthermore, business transactions and public sales must not take place in church, even though the sales are for a pious purpose. Anything that is not in harmony with the sacredness of the place is to be avoided.[54]

[44] Cf. J. Abbo — J. Hannan, *The Sacred Canons* (St. Louis, 1952), II, 438.
[45] Can. 1165, 1.
[46] Cf. can. 822.
[47] Can. 1165, 2.
[48] Can. 1165, 3.
[49] Can. 1165, 4.
[50] SCR, 4240.
[51] Can. 1165, 5.
[52] Can. 1168, 1 and 2.
[53] Can. 1169.
[54] Can. 1178.

2. The altar

The most sacred object in the church is the altar, for it is the point where heaven and earth meet, the "holy of holies" in which the manifestation of God takes place, a second Calvary where the Son of God renews His salvific sacrifice and, in so doing, becomes present and offers Himself to man as nourishment for his soul. The altar from earliest times came to be regarded as a symbol of Christ. Even now the same honors are paid to it as to Christ; it is kissed, incensed, bowed to—and all this apart from any consideration of the tabernacle.

Historical development of the altar

At first the Christian sacrifice was offered at a common supper table; it was in the context of the Passover meal that our Lord instituted the sacrifice. The same held true of the apostolic and subapostolic era, for there were no churches but only the homes of Christians in which the Mass could be offered.[55] In fact, to the celebration of the Mass proper was added the meal of holy fellowship, the Agape, at which the same table was used. Little wonder, then, that the early Christians called the altar "the table of the Lord," *mensa dominica*.[56] It is in this context that we must understand the accusation often made by pagans against the Christians that the latter had no altars. Minucius Felix openly admitted this.[57] He, of course, uses the word *ara*, which in antiquity referred to the altars used in the cult of the dead and, in general, of the pagan gods.[58] Because of this connection, Christians refused to use the term for divine worship, but gradually accepted the word *altare*, for even in the pagan mind such an object was reserved for the worship of the superior gods.

And so, in the primitive Church, since Christians used the homes of private citizens for the Mass and often united the Eucharist with the Agape, the form of altar used was an ordinary table. In the Roman house, as we saw, there was always available a table or *cartibulum*; a *tribadion*, or three-legged table, was also used. Hence, the altar was a simple portable table, usually of wood, moved into place only for the sacrificial part of the Mass.[59]

Stone and metal altars began to appear in the time of Constantine, more quickly in the East (fourth century) than in the West (sixth century). Once the fear of persecution passed, and the Church enjoyed a legal existence, regular houses of worship specially built for the purpose became more common, and with them altars of heavy material fixed to the ground. But even in this period, when stone and

---

[55] Acts 2: 46; 20: 8.
[56] Thus St. Paul in 1 Cor. 10:21
[57] *Octavius* 32. MPL, 3: 339.
[58] Cf. H. Leclercq, "Autel," *DACL*, I: 3155.
[59] Deacons carried it into place: cf. *Quaestiones ex vetere et novo testamento* 101. MPL, 35: 2301; also *Acta Thomae* 49. J. Quasten, *Monumenta*, 343.

metal began to be used, altars remained faithful to the table-like form.[60]

From the time of Constantine, at the very latest,[61] we find the altar surmounted by a baldachin or ciborium on four columns. Authors interpret this phenomenon differently. Edmund Bishop sees here an example of the tendency of the ancients to veil sacred objects,[62] and Noële Boulet concurs in this opinion.[63] Lechner and Eisenhofer say that the custom may have been taken over from the Byzantine court where the throne of the Emperor was sheltered by such a structure.[64] However, they refer to the opinion of A. Heisenberg as also probable. According to him, the Christian world followed as a model the superstructure built over the Lord's sepulchre in the Church of the Resurrection at Jerusalem. As a matter of fact, the word ciborium comes from the semitic term for grave (Syriac: *kebôrâ*, Hebrew: *keber*, and even Greek: *kibourin*). And as late as the sixth century we find given to this structure in St. Peter's Basilica the name *ciborium sepulcri*.[65] But P. Anson seems to prefer the opinion that the ciborium comes from the Byzantine court arrangement, since it resembles so closely the *tegurium* which stood over both the chief magistrate's seat in the civil basilicas and those structures which enshrined the statues of the Roman deities.[66] However, since the word *tegurium* is simply a corrupted form of *ciborium*, there does not seem to be much difference between these opinions.

Until this time the altar in Rome, and to a large extent in the remainder of the West, was always arranged so that the celebrant faced the people during Mass.[67] Due to Eastern influence, the principle of orientation at prayer came into vogue during the sixth and seventh centuries, particularly in Gaul (Africa vacillated between Roman and Oriental practice). Thus churches were built with the apse at the east end. And the celebrant, in order to face the East during Mass, assumed his place on the people's side of the altar with his back to them.[68]

The cult of the martyrs also greatly added to the evolution of the Christian altar. Our present practice of burying the relics of martyrs in the altar table goes back, not to the imagined necessity during the times of persecution of celebrating the Eucharist in the catacombs

---

[60] Even today canon law defines the altar as *mensa et stipes*: can. 1197.

[61] N. Boulet, "L'autel dans l'antiquité chrétienne," *La Maison-Dieu*, 29 (1952), 45.

[62] *Liturgica Historica* (Oxford, 1918), 22.

[63] *Art. cit.*, cf. note 61.

[64] *Liturgik des Römischen Ritus* (Freiburg, 6th edit., 1953), 100.

[65] A. Heisenberg, *Grabeskirche und Apostelkirche* (Leipzig, 1908), I, 215, ff. cited in Lechner-Eisenhofer, op. cit., 100. Cf. also J. Braun, *Der christliche Altar*, II, 190.

[66] *Churches, their Plan and Furnishing* (Milwaukee, 1948), 100; cf. also I. Schuster, *The Sacramentary* (New York, 1924), I, 162 ff.

[67] See our treatment of the basilica style, especially note 8.

[68] Cf. Noële Boulet, *art. cit.*, 51.

over the graves of martyrs, but rather to the post-Constantinian effort to honor the martyrs by building churches near or, if at all possible, directly over the graves of martyrs.[69] St. Peter's Basilica is one of the first examples of this practice. To satisfy the desire of the faithful to venerate the remains of those who fought for Christ, the so-called *fenestrella confessionis*, small openings of marble or metal lattice work, were constructed beneath the altar (later in the sides of the altar) and on the sides of the area containing the tomb. Thus the people were able to see the burial place and even insert objects of devotion and touch them to the tomb of the martyr.

When it became necessary to remove the bodies of martyrs from the catacombs to avoid the danger of their being desecrated by invading marauders, special crypts were often constructed behind the altar and beneath the sanctuary floor to receive them. As a later development we find such relics interred within the altar itself. These solutions were thought satisfactory in the early Middle Ages, and thus the shape of the altar—a table or cube shape—was not interfered with. But the piety of certain localities did not find this sufficient. Soon we see the bodies of saints placed *on* the altar table in just the same spot where today the tabernacle rests. In order to make up for space lost through this innovation, the altar table, hitherto almost square, now became oblong. The altar thus acquired a front and back, and another reason was at hand for the priest's celebrating Mass on the front of people's side of it.

Shrines built to house the relics of saints placed on top of the altar gradually increased to such size that the ciborium had to be done away with. Since admission to the sanctuary was normally forbidden to the laity, and their desire to get close to the relics was always strong, architects of the later Middle Ages found a solution for this dilemma by creating deambulatories that went around the sanctuary and by placing the altar near or against the back wall of the sanctuary. This, unfortunately, took the altar farther away from the congregation assisting at Mass.

Understandably, small and poor churches were not always able to obtain the body of a saint or the major portion of a saint's relics. This did not prevent them from imitating their "betters." Shrines could still be built over the altar to house statues or pictures of the saints. As devotion to individual martyrs and saints grew rapidly, special altars were erected here and there in the church to honor them, and this pious tendency, together with the desire on the part of priests to celebrate privately, gave rise to a multiplicity of altars in the same church.

The advent of the Renaissance and baroque periods only served to emphasize the shrine built on the altar. The superstructure became higher and higher, and the altar, when not lost in the maze of decora-

[69] Cf. Lechner-Eisenhofer, 98.

tion, assumed the form of a sarcophagus, whether it actually enclosed a saint's body or not.

This whole process of development comes to a close with the union of tabernacle and altar. Though there were already scattered instances of the tabernacle being placed on the altar from the tenth century on (in England and France), it was not until the sixteenth century that the practice became a general custom. This more modern usage can be traced back to the novel idea of Matteo Ghiberti, bishop of Verona (1524-1543), who, in order to enkindle the devotion of his clergy and people toward the Blessed Sacrament, had a tremendous tabernacle, made of marble and crystal and borne by four brass angels, suspended above the main altar of his cathedral. Other bishops followed suit. But the practice of placing the tabernacle on the altar did not actually become required until the Roman Ritual of Paul V in 1614 made it obligatory for all the churches of Rome and recommended its adoption by all other dioceses. It was left to baroque and rococo to make the whole altar subservient to this "house of God," often turning the already monstrous superstructure or retable into a radiant monstrance for the Blessed Sacrament.

Today, of course, the union of the tabernacle and altar is required by universal Church law. But it is a healthy sign of return to a more balanced view of the relationship of sacrifice and sacrament when modern architects reduce the size of the tabernacle, eliminate the gigantic rear superstructure, and emphasize the altar as a table of sacrifice.

Church law

The fundamental law concerning the altar is to be found in the *Missale Romanum*:[70]

> The altar, on which the most Holy Sacrifice of the Mass is to be celebrated, should be of stone and consecrated by a bishop or an abbot having faculties from the Apostolic See; or at least there should be a stone insertion large enough to support the Host and the greater part of the base of the chalice, and it should be likewise consecrated as above. This altar should be covered with three cloths, or clean coverings, blessed by a bishop or some other person having authority,[71] the upper cloth being at least long enough to reach to the ground at the end sides of the altar, the other two cloths shorter, or consisting of one folded cloth. It should be adorned with a frontal of the color suitable to the feast or office, in so far as it is possible. On the altar should be placed a crucifix,

[70] *Rubricae generales Missae*, XX.
[71] According to canon 1304, pastors and religious superiors may give the blessings necessary for vestments and other linens destined for divine worship within their own churches or religious houses. Local Ordinaries and religious superiors may delegate other priests for this.

in the middle, and at least two candlesticks with lighted candles, on either side. At the foot of the cross should be placed the altar card. On the Epistle corner there should be a cushion for the support of the missal, at the same side the wax candle to be lighted at the elevation of the Sacrament; a small bell, glass cruets for wine and water, together with a small dish and a clean towel should be prepared in a niche or small table near the Epistle corner of the altar. On the altar nothing whatever should be placed which does not appertain to the Sacrifice of the Mass, or to the adornment of the altar itself.

There are two kinds of altar according to canon law: (1) a *fixed* or immovable one, which consists of a table (*mensa*) [72] and legs (*stipites*). These two parts are consecrated as one whole.[73] (2) The other kind of altar is a portable one which consists of a stone, generally of small proportions, which alone is consecrated, or the same stone with its support which is not consecrated. [74] The Congregation of Rites seems to refer to a third type of altar, "*ad modum fixi.*" It consists of a consecrated altar stone (portable altar) inserted into the top of an altar made of solid and more or less permanent material (brick or stone).[75] There must be at least one fixed altar in a consecrated church, and it must be consecrated at the same time as the church.[76]

The table of the fixed altar or the altar stone of a portable altar must be of a single natural stone, integral and unbreakable (comparatively durable);[77] e.g., marble, granite, limestone, slate, sandstone, or schist.[78] This would certainly seem to exclude any artificial stone; e.g., brick, pumice,[79] concrete, and gypsum.[80] This table-top made of natural, integral stone must extend over the whole top of the altar and be firmly attached to the support or legs.[81] So that the priest will not mar the bottom of the altar front, should it be a cube, it is recommended that the table-top extend about two inches beyond the front support.

[72] Hence, when the Holy Father, Pius XII says that "one would be straying from the straight path were he to wish the altar restored to its primitive table-form," *Mediator Dei*, par. 62, he cannot be interpreted as forbidding the building of the altar in the form of a table, for thus it is defined in canon law. Rather he is against the use of an ordinary dinner table, which certainly would not comply with all the regulations set down in law concerning the altar. The word "primitive" indicates this.

[73] Can. 1197, 1, 1.

[74] Can. 1197, 1,2. Cf. also SCR, 3674; 4032. These latter decrees also make it plain that the consecrated stone must be durable (it must not be pumice or gypsum) and contain the relics of saints buried in the middle of its top side.

[75] SRC, 3162, ad 1.

[76] Can. 1197, 2; 1165, 5.

[77] Can. 1198, 1.

[78] Schist is explicitly permitted by SCR, 3674, ad 2.

[79] Explicitly forbidden in SCR, 4032, ad 2.

[80] Explicitly forbidden in SCR, 4032, ad 2; 3674, ad 3.

[81] Can. 1198, 2.

The supports, or legs, can be of any form as long as they are of the same material as the *mensa*.[82] The support may be one solid block of stone extending under the entire *mensa*, or one large stone block just under the middle of the *mensa*,[83] or four or more supports placed under the corners and elsewhere under the *mensa*.[84] In the consecration of an immovable altar, the *mensa* is ritually joined to the supports by means of four anointings.[85] The space between the supports may be filled in with brick, stone or cement, or it may be left open. Though the body of a saint may be placed in this open space, the Congregation of Rites forbids such a space to be used for storage.[86] In the spirit of this legislation and to preserve the sanctity of the altar, one should not place a crib below the *mensa*. Anything placed below or above the *mensa* which has nothing to do with the celebration of Mass or the simple adornment of the altar detracts from the altar's primary purpose and therefore ought to be avoided.

Also necessary for the consecration of an immovable altar is what is called a sepulcher, a small cavity, square or oblong, in the top [87] of the *mensa* in which relics of the saints are placed. This is to be covered by a single piece of stone of the same material as the *mensa* which is cemented in place during the consecration ceremony. For the validity of the consecration it is sufficient to place within the sepulcher the relics of one martyr and of another saint.[88] The relics are to be placed in a reliquary of lead, gold, or silver; this is tied with a ribbon and sealed after the insertion of three grains of incense and a certificate concerning the consecration of the altar.[89]

Since during the consecration of the altar the bishop must walk around it seven times, incensing it, it should stand free of the back wall. As for its measurements, nothing is prescribed, but experience suggests that it be from three feet three inches to three feet six inches high. A good length, allowing three distinct positions for the celebrant in a regular parish church, would be about seven feet six inches. If there is a tabernacle on the altar *mensa*, a minimum width for the latter would be approximately four feet.

According to the Congregation of Rites, there must be at least one step in front of the altar called the *predella* or *suppedaneum*.[90] It

[82] Can. 1198, 2.
[83] The Code itself often uses the word *stipes* in the singular: cf. can. 1198, 2; 1200, 1.
[84] Though the Code often uses the word *stipes* in the singular, a decree of the Congregation of Rites, some argue, seems to insist that there be at least *four* supports: 4145. It is very doubtful that this is still in force now that the Code has made its appearance.
[85] SCR, 4145. Also cf. the Rite of Consecration of an altar (towards the end) in the Roman Pontifical.
[86] SCR, 3741; 4225.
[87] It should be in the middle of the top, according to SCR, 4032, ad 3.
[88] SCR, 4180.
[89] Cf. the consecration ceremony in the Roman Pontifical.
[90] SCR, 1265, ad 4.

ought to have breadth enough to allow the priest to genuflect without his right foot falling off it, hence about three feet nine inches. To give the main altar dignity two more steps might be added, for the deacon and subdeacon in a Solemn Mass are supposed to stand on different levels.

An altar loses its consecration if the table becomes separated, even for a moment, from its support.[91] This does not necessarily mean that the altar cannot be moved—it may be, as long as the union of *mensa* and supports is not interrupted. A considerable break in any part of the altar or at the points of anointing, the removal of the relics from the sepulcher or the removal or breaking of its cover (except with authorization from the bishop) will bring about a loss of consecration.[92]

It must always be remembered that the altar is the most sacred object in the church. Great reverence should be shown to it. Those who must clean it, prepare it, or otherwise adorn it should always act in a becoming manner. They should not lean on it nor place anything on it which does not belong there.

3. Altar accessories

Tabernacle

In the early Church the Blessed Sacrament was not reserved in church except for the sake of the sick, and then it was usually kept in an appropriate place in the sacristy. A small cabinet in the wall beside or behind the altar served this purpose in the early Middle Ages. In France and England it became customary to reserve the Blessed Sacrament in a pyx resembling a dove and to hang this above the altar, while in Germany niches were cut into the wall for it. In richer churches a highly decorated house or tower was built. Already in the tenth century we begin to find ecclesiastical decrees requiring that the pyx containing the Blessed Sacrament be placed on the altar. In 1215 the Fourth Lateran Council insisted that the pyx be locked. In 1614 the Roman Ritual made it obligatory on all churches of Rome to keep the sacred species in a regular tabernacle on the altar. Finally the Code of Canon Law extended this obligation to the entire Church. Although the Roman Ritual enjoined the use of a tabernacle veil,[93] observance of this rule was more or less limited to Italy until the Congregation of Rites in 1866 made it an obligation for all.[94]

The Blessed Sacrament may habitually be reserved on only one altar in the church.[95] And it must be kept in a tabernacle that is im-

[91] Can. 1200, 1.
[92] Can. 1200, 2.
[93] Tit. IV, 1, 6.
[94] SCR, 3150.
[95] Can. 1268, 1.

movable and placed in the *middle* of an altar,[96] never anywhere else.[97] Canon law wants the tabernacle with the Blessed Sacrament to occupy a very excellent and noble place in the church, and states that it should *normally* be kept on the main altar, unless some other altar is considered more convenient and fitting.[98] The Code actually mentions some instances in which it would be better to reserve the Blessed Sacrament on an altar other than the main one—in cathedrals, collegiate and conventual churches. And the reason it gives for this preference is noteworthy, namely, that the Blessed Sacrament will not interfere with or hinder the sacred functions.[99] And Pius XII, in his allocution to the Assisi Congress for Pastoral Liturgy, used the same reasoning when he spoke of devotion to the Blessed Sacrament: He hoped that specialists would devise some way of arranging the tabernacle so that it would not hinder the celebration of Mass facing the people.[100]

A. Bugnini, a consultor of the Congregation of Rites, does not hesitate to say that where there is a desire to celebrate Mass facing the people the tabernacle may be transferred to another altar, as long as the altar is suitable for such a purpose.[101] Thus it is recommended that, in such a case, a special Blessed Sacrament chapel be built, or another altar be erected, behind and slightly higher than, the main altar and furnished with an appropriately decorated tabernacle. This latter arrangement would seem preferable, because it keeps the Blessed Sacrament in a centralized position, and therefore is in accord with canon law's direction that the Blessed Sacrament be given a very excellent and noble place in the church.[102] Where, however, only one altar is found in a church, it may not be *versus populum*, for the tabernacle with the Blessed Sacrament must be placed on and in the middle of the altar.[103]

The tabernacle must be well made and safely locked.[104] Any strong material may be used, but not transparent crystal,[105] and if

[96] Can. 1269, 1.

[97] SCR, *Decretum de Forma et Usu Tabernaculi*, nn. 4 and 8. *Ephem. Liturg.*, 71 (1957), 441.

[98] Can. 1268, 2: "Custodiatur in praecellentissimo ac nobilissimo ecclesiae loco ac proinde regulariter in altari maiore, nisi aliud venerationi et cultui tanti sacramenti commodius et decentius videatur. . . ."

[99] Can. 1268, 3. Cf. also the Roman Ritual, Tit.V, cap. 1, n.6: "ita ut nullum aliis sacris functionibus aut ecclesiasticis officiis impedimentum afferatur." The *Caeremoniale Episcoporum* says the same: "ad aliud altare transferatur, ne ritus et ordo caeremoniarum turbetur." Lib. I, c. XII, n.8.

[100] *AAS*, 48 (1956), 722.

[101] "Commentarium super decretum *De Forma et Usu Tabernaculi*," *Ephem. Liturg.*, 71 (1957), 443.

[102] On the whole question see Heinrich von Meurers, "Altar und Tabernakel," *Liturgisches Jahrbuch*, 3 (1953), 10-28.

[103] SCR, *De Forma et Usu Tabernaculi*, n. 4. *Ephem. Liturg, loc. cit.*

[104] Can. 1269, 2.

[105] SCR, 2564, ad 2.

wood is used it should be appropriately decorated.[106] It must be covered with a veil.[107] No special type of cloth is indicated; it may be either white or correspond to the liturgical colors, the latter procedure being preferred.[108] Violet, however, must be used for Requiem Masses.[109] In order to veil the tabernacle properly on all sides, it should not be built into the gradines, if there be such.

It should also be remembered that some sort of canopy is required over the Blessed Sacrament altar.[110] This canopy may take various forms. It may, for example, be a ciborium, i.e., a solid structure of stone, marble, metal, or wood supported over the altar by four or more columns. It might take the form of a baldachin, a smaller canopy of metal, wood, or cloth supported over the altar and predella by two columns at the rear of the altar or two chains from the rear wall, or it may be what is called a tester or a canopy, usually made of wood or cloth suspended directly from the ceiling.

A lamp burning day and night before the Blessed Sacrament is also prescribed.[111] It may be placed anywhere in the sanctuary: "before" does not necessarily mean immediately in front of the tabernacle door. The substance to be burned is either olive oil, beeswax, or some other vegetable oil.[112] No special color is prescribed for the lamp.[113]

Altar cloths and antependium

In early times the altar was covered only during Mass and was stripped afterward.[114] This covering originally reached to the bottom of the altar on all four sides.[115] Its reduction to a strip of cloth stretching only over the top and down the two sides may find a possible explanation in the impossibility of covering the whole altar when it was placed against the back wall. However, P. Anson suggests that the change was due rather to the fact that it was awkward to cover the whole structure with one large piece of cloth, since large cumbersome folds resulted at each corner.[116] At any rate when this cloth came to be

[106] SCR, 3697, ad 13.
[107] *Conopaeum* is the word used: Roman Ritual, tit. V, cap. 1, n. 6; SCR, 3520, 3150, 4137 and *De Forma et Usu Tabernaculi*, n. 6. *Ephem. Liturg.*, 71 (1957), 441.
[108] SCR, 3035, ad 10.
[109] SCR, 3562.
[110] SCR, 1966: over all altars; 2912: *omnino* over the Blessed Sacrament altar.
[111] Can. 1271.
[112] *Ibid.*; Roman Ritual, tit. V, cap. 1, n. 6.
[113] SCR, 3576, ad 5.
[114] Cf. *Acta Thomae* 49 (46). J. Quasten, *Monumenta*, 343; Optatus of Mileve, *De schismate Donatistarum* VI, 1. *MPL*, 11: 1068.
[115] In the church of St. Vitale in Ravenna there is a mosaic showing such an altar covering. The mosaic dates from the sixth century; see reproduction in Righetti, *op. cit.*, I, 445, fig. 124.
[116] *Op. cit.*, 115.

limited to the top and two sides, reverence to the altar as a symbol of Christ led many to decorate the altar front with silk or some other rich cloth and sometimes with carved wood or precious metals.[117] This was the beginning of the *antependium* or frontal, which in later times was changed according to the liturgical colors. From the Renaissance period on, when altars were so highly decorated, such frontals began to disappear.

The rubrics of the Roman Missal still require that the altar be adorned with an *antependium* which, as far as possible, should change according to the color of the liturgical office.[118] No particular material is indicated. Modern rubricians are inclined to dispense from this law whenever the front side of the altar is of precious or ornate quality. Though no Church law makes this distinction, custom would seem to countenance it.

The altar must also be covered with three altar-cloths.[119] And according to the Congregation of Rites, these must be made of linen or hemp; no other material may be used.[120]

Crucifix and candles

Both of these items are comparatively modern additions to the appurtenances of the altar. Originally neither stood on the altar itself; only the oblation and the missal were placed there. In the seventh century we find that seven candles were carried before the bishop as he entered the church; they were then placed on the pavement around the altar.[121] This custom was taken over from the practice of the Roman Imperial Curia where persons of high rank were so honored.[122] Evidence for the candles being placed on the altar *mensa* dates from the eleventh and twelfth centuries.[123] Innocent III says that the Rome of his day observed the custom of having two candles only on the altar for papal Masses.[124] From a study of documents of this period, Ed-

[117] Sometimes even with precious gems, as with Constantine's gift to the Basilica of St. Peter: *Liber Pontificalis* (ed. L. Duchesne), I, 177. In this text and many others from this same period, it is said that the altar is of gold or silver. Righetti (*op. cit.*, I, 430) suspects that this refers to the frontal only. Later references are more explicit in this matter: Gregory III (d. 741) dressed the front of the altar with silver. *Lib. Pont.*, I, 418.

[118] *Rubricae Generales*, tit., XX.

[119] *Ibid.*

[120] SCR, 2600, 3868.

[121] *Ordo Romanus* I, n. 46 and 52; *Ordo Romanus* II, n. 7. M. Andrieu, *Les Ordines Romani*, II, pp. 82, 84, 158.

[122] Cf. T. Klauser, *Der Ursprung der bischöflichen Insignien und Ehrenrechte* (Krefeld, 1953), 18.

[123] There is a fresco in the Basilica of St. Clement in Rome, which dates from the eleventh century, showing candles on the altar. There is also a marble plaque, from the eighth century, inserted into the superstructure of the baptismal font in the Baptistery of Cividale dal Friuli; it represents a cross with two candles on either side seemingly resting on a table. However, H. Leclercq rejects any Eucharistic implications: "Cividale en Frioul," *DACL*, III, 1833.

[124] *De sacro altaris mysterio* II, 21. *MPL*, 217: 811.

mund Bishop concludes that a change from two to seven candles on the altar was made between the years 1198 and 1254.[125] This same number of candles is still required for a Pontifical High Mass.[126] But on the altar where solemn functions take place only six are needed;[127] and at least two must be used for an ordinary low Mass.[128]

Long before the cross took its place upon the altar-table, there hung a cross from the ceiling of the church, usually between the apse and the nave. Sometimes it was simply a cross without the image of the crucified; sometimes it was covered with gems, the *crux gemmata*. Often, after Christians began to depict the Savior nailed to the cross, His image was vested in regal or priestly robes, and a crown of jewels was placed on His head. It was relatively late that the sufferings of the Savior were brought out in all their striking realism; this was done about the thirteenth century, the age of the Passion mystics.[129] At the end of the twelfth century we hear of the processional cross being placed *against* the altar once the bishop's procession had wound its way to the sanctuary.[130] A little later we are finally told that it was a regular thing to place a cross *on* the altar between two candles.[131]

The first time there is mention of an obligation to have a crucifix on the altar is in the Roman Missal of Pius V in 1570. This is still required,[132] but it does not mean that the crucifix cannot hang above the altar. All rubricians recognize the validity of such an arrangement. In fact, a hanging crucifix is much more desirable for an altar *versus populum*; it does not get in the way of the people's vision. And it would seem more fitting that in such a case the *corpus* be on the people's side. There is no law concerning which direction it should face; the rubrics of Mass simply state that the celebrant should bow to the cross. When other rubrics say that the celebrant is to glance upward towards heaven, i.e., towards the cross, this is only an indication of about how high he should raise his head.

After the appearance of the encyclical *Mediator Dei* some have thought that the so-called Christ the King crucifix was forbidden, since the Pope says, "one would be straying from the straight path were he to . . . order the crucifix so designed that the divine Redeemer's body shows no trace of His cruel sufferings." [133] But as long as such a crucifix allows the wounds in the hands and feet to be visible, it is still in accord with the Pope's wishes.

[125] *Liturgica Historica*, 310-311.
[126] *Caeremoniale Episcoporum*, I, XII, 12.
[127] SCR, 1615 ad 7.
[128] SCR, 2673.
[129] Cf. O. Marucchi, "Cross," *The Catholic Encyclopedia*, IV, 529.
[130] *Ordo Romanus* XI (according to Mabillon's *Museum Italicum*), n. 29. *MPL*, 78: 1037.
[131] Innocent III, *op. cit.*, II, 21. *MPL*, 217: 811.
[132] *Missale Romanum, Rubr. gen.*, tit., XX.
[133] Par. 62.

Secondary elements

Altar cards came into use in the sixteenth century. In order to assist the priest's memory, Pius V ordered that there should be a card in the middle of the altar containing certain formulas recited there. The use of two other cards, one at each end of the altar, began to spread in the course of the seventeenth century. Normally a priest should have all these prayers memorized; nevertheless the rubrics prescribe the center card. If the altar is so built that the priest can face the congregation as he celebrates Mass, this card (or cards) ought to be small enough to lie flat on the altar-table and not interfere with the view of the people. At the same time they should be practical: clear, legible, not smothered with decorative borders and frames.

A source of much abuse in churches is the use of flowers to decorate the altar. Before 1600 there was no official law concerning them. Before this time it was the custom to hang garlands on the walls and columns of the church and, if cut flowers were employed, to place them on the floor around the altar. In 1600, however, the *Caeremoniale Episcoporum* permitted the placing of flowers on the altar itself.[134] But here restraint and good taste must be employed. One should be careful not to make the altar just an occasion for arranging floral displays. And if the priest celebrates facing the people, the presence of anything on the altar-table except very low candles will defeat the purpose of this procedure.

Large churches seem to warrant the use of microphones on the altar, in order to make what the priest says there sufficiently understandable in the rear of the church. They ought, however, to be small and unobtrusive, perhaps even buried in the top of the altar.

4. Church furnishings

Communion rail

The sanctuary today is usually separated from the nave by means of a communion rail. Some maintain that this is a compromise between the medieval rood screen, which, not only separated sanctuary from nave, but completely cut off the people's view of the altar, and the long wall which enclosed the choir in the Roman basilicas.[135] But the rood screen was a late medieval exaggeration, comparable to the Oriental iconostasis. The communion rail more probably is derived from the enclosure for the choir or the low entablature of the *pergula* which, when the enclosure was lacking, separated the sanctuary from the people in the Roman basilicas. Neither the enclosure, which was high enough to conceal the singers, nor the low entablature of the *pergula*

---

[134] I, XII, 12.
[135] P. Anson, *op. cit.*, 136. It is difficult to see how Anson can argue that the rood screen or some such grill is demanded by the spirit of the Liturgy: cf. pp. 138-139.

ever obstructed the view of the altar; the *pergula*, to all appearances, was simply intended to mark off the space for the clerics.

The communion rail, while demarcating the sacred area of the church, also serves a higher purpose. It is an extension of the altar, the table of the Lord, since here the people enjoy the closest possible participation in the Holy Sacrifice by receiving Holy Communion, the fruit of that Sacrifice. To emphasize this fact, some have broadened the top of this rail, so that it has taken on more of the appearance of a narrow table. It seems ideal to construct the rail in such a way that it resembles somewhat the altar (same material, style, decoration).[136] In keeping with its sacred function, the communion rail must be covered with a clean white cloth during the distribution of communion.[137]

Pulpit

The word pulpit comes from the Latin *pulpitum*, a tribune or platform. The German uses the word *Kanzel*, which is derived from *cancelli*, the enclosure for the choir in the early Roman basilicas where the ambos were built for the singing of Epistle and Gospel. In French the word is *chaire*, seat, a usage that goes back to the time when the bishop addressed the faithful from his throne at the head of the apse. In early times when a bishop celebrated Mass, he would preach from his throne, but when an ordinary priest celebrated in the absence of pope or bishop, he would not dare preach from the episcopal throne; rather he spoke from the ambo built in the *cancelli*. With the advent of the mendicant orders pulpits were built out in the nave amid the faithful; it was at this very time that a separation of the sermon from the theme of the Mass occurred—before then, the sermon was a homily or commentary on the scripture readings of the Mass. At first the pulpit was a movable platform, while in the fifteenth century it was attached to or built as part of a column or the wall of the nave. At the same time, in order to favor acoustics, a shell-shaped canopy was placed above and to the rear of the preacher.

Actually there is no law governing the pulpit. However, with the ever increasing insistence on the homily type of sermon, that is, one which continues the proclamation of the word of God by explaining what is read in the lessons of the Mass, it is advisable to have some sort of lectern or small pulpit as part of the sanctuary in order to bring out the connection between the sermon and the Mass action. Care should be taken that the pulpit is not of a size to block the people's view of the altar.

[136] Cf. J. O'Connell, *Church Building and Furnishing* (Notre Dame, 1955), 13.

[137] Roman Ritual, tit. V, cap. 2, n. 1.

Confessional

Public confession of sin was a rare thing even in the early Church. Though the absolution, or reconciliation, as it was then called, was given in public, the penitent confessed his sins in private, usually in the residence of the bishop or priest. Because of the obvious dangers of hearing confessions in private dwellings, bishops insisted, from the eleventh century on, that they be heard in the church itself. The priest sat in the open church, either in the sanctuary or a more private part of the church, and the penitent knelt beside him. After the penitent had accused himself, the priest would then pronounce sentence, give a penance, impose his hand upon him, and give absolution. Only in the course of the seventeenth century was a grille introduced, probably due to the prescriptions laid down by St. Charles Borromeo for his own diocese of Milan in 1565. These prescriptions were taken over by the Roman Ritual in 1614. And present canon law insists that confessions of women be heard in an open and conspicuous place (in a public or semi-public oratory at least),[138] and that all confessionals have an immovable screen separating priest and penitent.[139]

For St. Jerome [140] and Tertullian [141] the sacrament of Penance was like a second Baptism, *secunda post naufragium tabula*; it was a second chance, a readmission of the sinner to the sacramental life of the Church. Others called it a *baptismus laboriosus*.[142] This function of Penance as a second Baptism could be well brought out by placing the confessionals in the Baptistery, or at least in a special Penance chapel near the Baptistery. Thus both sacraments would regain in the consciousness of the faithful the place and significance they should have as the means of purification before being admitted to the table of the Lord, the gateway to the other sacraments.

Lustral water stoups

Righetti connects the use of Blessed Water from the stoups which contain it at the entrances of churches, to the practice of sprinkling the faithful during the Sunday Asperges.[143] Since the custom of the faithful taking water upon entering the church certainly antedates the introduction of the Asperges, another opinion [144] sees the origin of the use of Blessed Water and its containers in the early Latin basilica's *cantharus*, or fountain, at which the faithful were wont to wash themselves before entering the church, and in the *impluvium* of the Roman

---

[138] Can. 909, 1.

[139] Can. 909, 2.

[140] *Epistola* 130 *ad Demetriadem de virginitate* 9. MPL, 22: 1115.

[141] *De poenitentia* IV. MPL, 1: 1343.

[142] Cf. R. Garrigou-Lagrange, *De Eucharistia* (Rome, 1946), 340.

[143] *Op. cit.*, I, 484. Cf. also Lechner-Eisenhofer, *op. cit.*, 109; J. O'Connell, *op. cit.*, 84.

[144] Cf. H. Leclercq, "Bénitier," *DACL*, II, 758-771; P. Anson, *op. cit.*, 152; also H. Reinhold's footnote in the same work, p. 153.

house. When the atrium ceased to be a part of the church structure, such fountains were replaced by smaller vessels and put inside the church. Two early documents allude to the practice by the faithful of using lustral water at the entrance of the church. The fifth century Church historian, Sozomen, reports an incident in which Valentinian, a captain of the Emperor Julian's guards, became violently angry when some of the lustral water, sprinkled by the priest on him and his entourage as they entered the church, fell upon his garments.[145] And Synesius, also of the fifth century, claims that the lustral water placed at the entrance of the Christian temples can do more good than the sword of the civil authorities.[146] Hence, the second opinion above seems more probable.

Sacred vessels

Since the ritual cups used by the Jews in the time of Augustus were made of glass, it is conjectured that our Lord Himself used one of this sort during the Last Supper.[147] The chalices used by the early Christians were also of glass, but silver and gold ones were also common. The oldest chalices known to have existed had small handles on either side of the cup. In the gothic period the height of chalices was increased, while in the baroque and rococo eras the cup was transformed until it took on the appearance of a fully opened tulip, and lavish decorations were added to the base and stem.

The paten originally was like a large platter—it had to be, for the celebrant broke the consecrated bread upon it for distribution in Communion. The dish referred to in the account of the Last Supper was very likely the forerunner of the paten (Matt. 25:23).

According to present legislation, the cup of the chalice must be of gold or silver, and, if the latter, at least the inside of the cup must be gold-plated. The paten also must be of gold or silver, or at least the upper surface gold-plated.[148] These vessels must be consecrated by someone having faculties for this.[149]

At first the paten was used for the distribution of Communion, unless a silk bag[150] took its place. Today we use a ciborium shaped very much like a chalice. It came into use about the thirteenth century.

The chalice veil became universal in the Church through prescriptions laid down by Pius V in the Roman Missal. It takes its origin from the *pannus offertorius*[151] which, out of reverence, was used to cover

---

[145] *Historia Ecclesiastica* IV, 4. *MPG*, 67: 1116.
[146] *Epist. ad Anastasium* 121. *MPG*, 66: 1501.
[147] Cf. Righetti, *op. cit.*, I, 461.
[148] SCR, 3136 ad 4.
[149] Formerly, according to SCR, 3042 ad 1, chalice and paten had to be reconsecrated when they were replated, but can. 1305, 2 abrogates this.
[150] Cf. *Ordo Romanus* I, n. 101. Andrieu, *Les Ordines Romani*, II, p. 100.
[151] *Ordo Romanus* I, nn. 84, 89. Andrieu, *Les Ordines Romani*, II, pp. 94, 96.

the chalice while it rested on the altar and to cover the priest's hand when he raised or otherwise touched the chalice during Mass.

To satisfy the people's growing desire to see the Blessed Sacrament, Eucharistic processions were often held in the late Middle Ages. Some vessel was needed to carry the sacred species in such a way that they could be easily seen by the faithful. Thus in the fourteenth century we see the beginnings of the monstrance or ostensorium (from the Latin *monstrare, ostendere,* meaning "to show"). At first it was made like a cylindrical glass reliquary; in the sixteenth century it took on the flat ray-like shape that it still has today.

Vestments

In spite of the attempt of some medieval writers to see in the liturgical prescriptions of the Old Testament the origin of our liturgical vestments, history very emphatically forces us to trace the derivation of these vestments from the ancient Greco-Roman civil dress. Dionysius Exiguus gives evidence that in 530 there was no difference between liturgical and lay dress.[152] From John the Deacon, biographer of Gregory the Great, we learn that during Gregory's lifetime he had frescoes of himself and his father painted for the benefit of his monks;[153] from John's description we can see that the only distinction between the dress of father and son is the pallium worn by Gregory. Finally, the pictures in the catacombs and ancient churches speak the same language: no distinction is indicated between the dress of the celebrant and that of the ordinary Christians standing about the altar.

Gradually, out of reverence, clerics were led to reserve their finer apparel for use in the Liturgy. The author of the *Liber Pontificalis* states that Pope Stephen, in the third century, decreed that clerics should not use their liturgical vestments outside the church.[154] But this may simply be a reflection of a practice true only of the author's own day, the sixth century. As a matter of fact, it is about this same time that we notice similar decrees being made in various places. The Council of Narbonne in 589 warned deacons and lectors not to remove the alb until the Mass was finished.[155]

While the Roman civil dress was already changing, under the influence of style, in the fourth and fifth centuries, the Church retained the use of the traditional garments. Thus began the slow process which led to a difference between liturgical and street dress, not only in the costliness and beauty of fabric, but also in the very cut and number of garments worn. The Carolingian period brought a further development in that the form and purpose of the multiple vestments

---

[152] See the way he interprets, through his title, the letter of Celestine I to the bishops of Gaul: *Epist.* IV, c. 1, 2. *MPL,* 50: 431; *Collectio decretorum PP. RR.,* XIV. *MPL,* 67: 274.

[153] *Vita Gregorii* IV, 83-84. *MPL,* 75: 229-231.

[154] Ed. L. Duchesne, I, 154.

[155] C. 12. Hefele-Leclercq, *Histoire des Conciles,* III, 230.

became determined, not so much by reason of clear-cut ecclesiastical laws, which were few, but through custom. The twelfth century fixed the liturgical colors, while the thirteenth century began to cut down the size of the chasuble; the baroque period pushed this process to an extreme until the chasuble no longer resembled a genuine garment.

Although originally there was no particular difference in color specified for the various feasts of the Church, the chasuble was normally dark and the dalmatic bright. However, the Romans were noted for wearing white togas on special occasions. This might easily have influenced the primitive Church in selecting white, the natural color of linen, as the predominant color of her vestments, though other colors were not unknown. The first traces of the tendency to set down rules concerning liturgical colors is found in the ninth century, a tendency which ends in specific prescriptions, at least as far as Rome is concerned, in the twelfth century.[156] Five colors are accepted: white, red, green, violet, and black. A missal of Naples dating from the thirteenth century mentions the use of rose. In other localities still other colors were used. The missal of Pius V in 1570 prescribed uniformity in the use of rose and the five colors mentioned by Innocent III. The use of gold vestments in place of white, red, and green was finally allowed in 1868 by the Congregation of Rites.[157]

Since the liturgical vestments were originally the actual attire worn by Roman citizens, it is rather difficult to see any grounds for giving the vestments a dogmatic or figurative meaning. Attempts to do so could only have arisen once the everyday clothing of the man in the street had departed definitively from the styles used in early centuries. Writers who were not acquainted with the vestments' true origin explained them by reference to Old Testament liturgical apparel or by pure allegory. And the prayers in use today for vesting before Mass spring straight from the pen of medieval allegorists; these prayers make their appearance in the ninth century and become general in the eleventh and twelfth centuries.[158]

The amice. The origin of the amice is still obscure. Some authors maintain that it appears as a liturgical vestment for the first time in the ninth century in the Frankish kingdom as a simple scarf for the neck.[159] But it was most certainly used in Rome by, at least, the beginning of the eighth century.[160] Righetti claims that its origin is to be found in an oblong piece of material falling over the shoulders from the neck in two parts and passing under the arms, the purpose of which was to hold the clothing close to the body and thus render the

[156] Cf. Innocent III, *De sacro altaris mysterio* I, 65. MPL, 217: 799-802.

[157] SCR, 3191 ad 4.

[158] J. Braun, *Die liturgischen Paramente in Gegenwart und Vergangenheit* (Freiburg, 1924), 48; cf. also idem, *Die liturgische Gewandung im Occident und Orient* (Freiburg, 1907), 701-707.

[159] Lechner-Eisenhofer, *op. cit.*, 116; E. Roulin, *Vestments and Vesture* (St. Louis, 1933), 21-22.

[160] *Ordo Rom.* I, n. 34. Andrieu, *Les Ordines*, II, p. 78.

movement of the arms unencumbered.[161] As a matter of fact, Cassian, who wrote in the early part of the fifth century, reports that the monks in Egypt wore such a garment, and he calls it *amictum*, or in Greek *anabolàs*.[162] And the *Ordo Romanus Primus* indicates that the Pontiff placed the amice (*anagolaium*) over the alb.[163] Even today this is still the custom in the Ambrosian Rite. In the Frankish kingdom, however, the amice always appears as the first garment;[164] this practice gradually became almost universal.

In the ninth century the amice begins to be worn in another way: over the head as a hood, being thrown back over the shoulders only after all the vestments have been put on.[165] It was worn this way universally in the West around the thirteenth century, and all those religious orders which came into existence during this period maintain the custom even today: Dominicans, Franciscans, Trinitarians and Servites. Since the amice thus thrown back did not always make for a neat appearance, a small strip of stiff ornate material was attached to its top edge. This was called an *aurifrisium* and gave to the amice when thrown back the appearance of a cowl. While disappearing generally once the Romal Missal was promulgated by Pius V, it is still used today in the Ambrosian Rite.

The alb. This vestment is simply the Greco-Roman *tunica talaris*, an indispensable garment of daily use reaching to the feet and worn by everyone.[166] It was called *tunica alba* because of its color, though *linea*, or *tunica linea*, seems to have been the earlier Roman name for it, since it was normally made of linen. In the Middle Ages bands of colored material were sewn around the bottom and on the extremities of the sleeves; sometimes this decoration appeared in the form of square pieces sewn on the back and front of the bottom. In the seventeenth century lace was introduced. Out of this long flowing gown came the surplice. Not quite as long as the alb and having wide, long sleeves, the surplice was in use already in the eleventh century as a choir-dress. In the fourteenth century all clerics used it for services which did not require the alb. The Roman cotta with sleeves reaching only to the elbows is a later development. The rochet (from the German *Rock*, coat) also comes from the alb but has tight sleeves and is used by prelates when they assist at liturgical functions. The cincture, an obvious necessity for the Roman costume, was intended simply as a means of gathering the folds of the alb close to the body. Sometimes it appears in the form of a cord with tassels at each end, sometimes as a flat band of linen. Though sashes were used in some

[161] *Op. cit.*, I, 494.
[162] *De coenobiorum institutione* I, vi. MPL, 49: 71-72.
[163] Cf. *supra*, note 160.
[164] Cf. Braun, *Die liturgische Gewandung*, 28.
[165] *Ibid.*, 29-30.
[166] *Ibid.*, 63.

localities, they are no longer permitted.[167] Though the cincture is normally white, like the alb, it may follow the color of the liturgical office.[168]

The chasuble. Originally, this was the Greco-Roman *poenula,* used for protection against bad weather as an overcoat or raincoat. In the third century it began to be used habitually as a topcoat or mantle. It was round-shaped, somewhat like a bell, with a hole in the top for the head to go through. Hence it covered the whole body like a little house (whence the Latin name *casula*). The Romans also called it by another name, *planeta,* since, it went around the body, like a planet. It is this word which the *Ordo Romanus Primus* uses.[169] According to the frescoes in the catacombs, the chasuble was worn by all the clergy, from bishop to those in minor orders. We still see a remnant of this practice on penitential days when the deacon and subdeacon put aside their dalmatic and tunicle and use the *planeta plicata,* or folded chasuble. With the introduction of the dalmatic and tunicle as special vestments for deacons and subdeacons, they ceased to use the chasuble, except as mentioned, on penitential days, and it became the distinctive garb of the priest. However, even today in some places all the assisting clergy, whether priests or not, wear it.

Since the chasuble was such a large and heavy garment, when the celebrant had to use his hands during Mass, it was necessary for him to let the front part of the chasuble rest on his forearms, thus causing an oval flow of folds. Despite many changes in color, material, and decoration, the chasuble preserved the essentials of its original form until the baroque period made of it little more than a meaningless ornament. It is true, the type of chasuble which today we call "gothic" is more akin to a later medieval development; still it is closer to the original bell-shaped chasuble than the baroque product, called very incorrectly the Roman chasuble. It would be better dubbed the placard or sign-board type. Not content to introduce the medieval "gothic" vestment, many regions have gone back to the original bell-shaped chasuble.[170]

The cope. Unlike most of our liturgical vestments, the cope does not come down to us directly from ancient civil dress. Most liturgical authors agree that it is nothing more than a transformation of the original bell-shaped chasuble, cut in the front to allow free movement of the arms.[171] This evolution does not seem direct, even though it would appear that the cope originally was bell-shaped and completely closed like the chasuble. Very probably the chasuble was adapted as

---

[167] SCR, 4048 ad 6.
[168] SCR, 2194 ad 3.
[169] N. 34. Andrieu, *Les Ordines,* II, p. 78.
[170] See the interesting articles of E. J. Sutfin, "The Chasuble in the Roman Rite," *Liturgical Arts,* 24 (August, 1956), 76-104; "How to make a Chasuble," *Liturgical Arts,* 25 (May, 1957), 66-86.
[171] Cf. J. Braun, *Die liturgische Gewandung,* 348-350; M. Righetti, op. cit., I, 510.

an ordinary cloak or cape for monks, first of all, for it was precisely in monasteries of the eighth century that it made its first appearance.[172] While bishops and priests continued to use the chasuble for most liturgical ceremonies, even for anointings and absolutions, monks began to use the cope on solemn occasions for certain parts of the Divine Office and for processions. With the help of Cluny its use spread rapidly, so much so that by the eleventh century it became a normal liturgical vestment almost everywhere. Originally a hood was part of the cope. Beginning with the fourteenth century the hood developed into a shield-shaped hanging sewn on the back of the cope.[173]

The dalmatic. In the second century Rome imported from Dalmatia another garment which took its name from its place of origin, the dalmatic. It was worn by important persons, and the Church gradually adopted it. According to the *Liber Pontificalis*,[174] Pope Silvester (314-335) granted its use to his own deacons. Later we see popes extend this privilege to churches outside Rome. Thus we read in the life of St. Caesarius of Arles that Pope Symmachus (498-514) gave him the privilege of permitting his deacons to wear dalmatics just as the Roman deacons did.[175] It must have become a general practice by the ninth century, for we read in Walafrid Strabo (died 849) that not only bishops and deacons used it, but even priests wore it under their chasubles.[176] From then on it was reserved to the use of the person acting as deacon during a liturgical function. From pictorial representations we know that this vestment was a long, wide tunic reaching to the feet and having long, wide sleeves. From the eleventh century on it became shorter and shorter until today it hardly reaches the knees, and what were once sleeves are now flaps hanging over the shoulders. Some attempt has been made to restore the sleeves to their original form.

The tunicle. In imitation [177] of the dalmatic worn by deacons, another vestment was fashioned for subdeacons called the tunicle (*tunicella*). It was originally worn by the pope himself, however, according to the *Ordo Romanus* I.[178] Gregory the Great says that one of his predecessors had permitted subdeacons to wear it; he, however, withdrew the permission.[179] But outside Rome it was in general use certainly by the ninth century.[180]

The maniple. The use of the maniple is one of the many marks of honor copied from the Roman court ceremonial. When Church and

---

[172] J. Braun, *Die liturgische Gewandung*, 310.
[173] Cf. Edmund Bishop's excellent treatment of this subject in *Liturgica Historica*, 260-275.
[174] Ed. L. Duchesne, I, 171.
[175] *Vita* I, 4. *MPL*, 67: 1016.
[176] *De rebus eccl.* 24. *MPL*, 114: 952.
[177] J. Braun, *Die liturgischen Paramente*, 93.
[178] N. 34. Andrieu, *Les Ordines*, II, 78.
[179] *Epist.* lib. IX, 12 *ad Joannem Syracusanum. MPL*, 77: 956.
[180] Cf. J. Braun, *Die liturgische Gewandung*, 283.

State entered into alliance, the Roman Emperor felt obliged to accord the pope and his officials the marks of honor due those holding high positions in civil administration.[181] Originally it was a napkin or hand-kerchief held in the left hand by dignitaries, just as today a folded handkerchief in the lapel pocket gives the air of being fully dressed. It was a common thing for officials to wave it as a signal to begin plays and races. We are told by the *Liber Pontificalis*, that Pope Silvester permitted the Roman deacons to carry the maniple in their left hands as a badge of honor.[182] The technical term originally used was *mappula*, or napkin;[183] later it was called *manipulus* because it was held in the hand. Among ecclesiastics, it was the exclusive privilege of the pope and his deacons until the sixth century, when Pope St. Gregory, against the wishes of his clerics, extended its use to the chief deacons of Ravenna upon the request of their bishop; he expressly refused the same prerogative to anyone else.[184] But by the ninth century its use had become so general that Rabanus Maurus states that his subdeacons were given the maniple at the time of their ordination.[185]

Thus we see that the maniple normally served as a mark of distinction for clerics, especially in major orders.[186] This is further brought out by the fact that in the twelfth century on certain very special feasts, in order to be "fully dressed up," some monasteries had all the monks, even lay brothers, wear albs and maniples during liturgical functions.[187] The earliest report of a change in the maniple, from an ordinary white kerchief to a decorative strip of material, comes from the tenth century,[188] and in the twelfth century we see the beginning of the practice of wearing the maniple on the forearm instead of carrying it in the left hand.[189]

The stole. The origin and purpose of the stole as a liturgical vestment has been controverted for some time.[190] Duchesne was probably

---

[181] *Ibid.*, 517, 523-530.

[182] Ed. L. Duchesne, I, 171: "pallia linostima leva eorum tegerentur."

[183] *Ordo Rom.* I, nn. 37, 38. Andrieu, *Les Ordines*, II, 79.

[184] *Epist.* III, 56 *ad Joannem episcopum. MPL*, 77: 653-654.

[185] *De clericorum institutione* I, 8. *MPL*, 107: 304. However, he uses the word *mantile*. That this means maniple can be seen by the fact that later, when he describes the maniple in his list of vestments, it is the word *mantile* he employs: I, 18. *MPL*, 107: 307. His contemporary, Amalar, does not mention the rite of giving the maniple to the subdeacon at the time of his ordination: *De ecclesiasticis officiis* II, 11. *MPL*, 105: 1086.

[186] Not always, however, for Amalar mentions it being used to wipe perspiration from the face: *Ibid.*, II, 24. *MPL*, 105: 1099; III, 19. *MPL*, 105: 1131.

[187] Cf. Rupert of Deutz, *De divinis officiis* II, 23. *MPL*, 170: 54; Lanfranc, *Epist.* 13 *ad Joannem Rotomagensem. MPL*, 150: 520.

[188] Cf. J. Braun, *Die liturgische Gewandung*, 532.

[189] Rupert of Deutz, *op. cit.*, I, 33. *MPL*, 170: 29.

[190] J. Wilpert has claimed that the stole was not always primarily intended as a distinctive mark of priests and deacons, but was also used as a towel: *Die Gewandung der Christen in den ersten Jahrhunderten* (Cologne, 1898), 51. J. Braun, on the other hand, tries to sustain the theory that the stole was purely a mark of distinction, which is, we believe, correct; but he adds that it was in use

correct when he stated that the stole was unknown in Rome as late as the tenth century but universally adopted elsewhere.[191] According to him, there is no Roman representation of the stole until the twelfth century.[192] It was first used in the East and from there found its way into the Gallican Liturgies and thence finally was accepted in Rome. The first mention of the use of the stole in the East is met with in the Council of Laodicea, held in the latter part of the fourth century, which reproaches those in minor orders for wearing it.[193] In the West we hear of the stole for the first time in 563 when the Council of Braga decreed that deacons were to wear it hanging from the left shoulder and outside the dalmatic in order to be distinguished from the sub-deacons.[194] According to the Council of Toledo, in 633, for bishops, priests, or deacons to be reinstated in their office they had to receive, among other things, the stole at the hands of an authorized prelate.[195] Later, at a Council held at Mainz in 813, it was decreed that priests were always to wear the stole, so that people would know they were priests.[196] They were even to wear their stoles on journeys.[197] It seems that only from the twelfth century on do we find the word "stole" itself used; formerly it was called *orarium*, which was taken from the Greek and designated a scarf worn about the neck. The custom of deacons wearing the stole over one shoulder, from left to right, also seems to stem from the twelfth century. Though the rule of having the priest cross the stole over his breast is already found in the seventh century,[198] especially in Spain, it became universal only with the Missal of Pius V.

B. The Baptistery

The significance of Baptism as the means of incorporation into the Mystical Body, as the gate to the other sacraments, found striking

---

even in Rome as early as the latter part of the eighth century and worn by *all* clerics: *Die liturgische Gewandung*, 618, 574-575. The principal basis for this latter assertion is the evidence afforded by the III (VI in Andrieu) and VIII Roman Ordos. But Andrieu has conclusively shown that these Ordos were not Roman: cf. *Ordo Rom.* VI, n. 11, *Ordo Rom.* VIII, nn. 1-6. Andrieu, *Les Ordines*, II, 243, 321-322 and his commentary on pp. 235, 312. Hugh Menard's Gregorian Sacramentary (*MPL*, 78: 222) has the deacon receive the stole at his ordination. But it is well known that this edition of the Gregorian is mixed with Gallican elements and therefore unreliable as a witness to pure Roman practice. This is especially so since *Ordo Rom.* I, n. 34 (Andrieu, II, 78 ff.) makes no mention of the stole. What Braun reports from Amalar and Rabanus Maurus may be true, but it is more probable that their evidence is unreliable.

[191] *Christian Worship* (London, 1949, 5th edit.), 390.
[192] *Ibid.*, 391.
[193] Can. 22, 23. Hefele-Leclercq, *Histoire des Conciles*, I, 1012.
[194] Can. 9. Hefele-Leclercq, *op. cit.*, III, 180.
[195] Can. 28. Hefele-Leclercq, *op. cit.*, III, 271.
[196] Can. 28. Hefele-Leclercq, *op. cit.*, III, 1141.
[197] Ratherius of Verona, *Synodica ad Presbyteros*, can. 11. *MPL*, 136: 562.
[198] Council of Braga in 675, can. 3. Hefele-Leclercq, *op. cit.*, III, 315.

emphasis in the architecture, location, and decoration of the Baptistery [199] and the over-all importance given to it. The very fact that a special edifice was built for the administration of Baptism, not simply a special room set aside in the church proper, but a building distinct and separate from the church building, certainly tended to add great dignity to this sacrament.

One of the principal motives for separating the place of Baptism from that of the Eucharist was undoubtedly the Church's desire to separate penitents and non-Christians from the main body of the faithful in the House of God. If Christians who fell into grievous sin were excluded to some degree from the fellowship of the faithful, *a fortiori* should those who had not yet washed themselves of the impurities of paganism be excluded from the fellowship. In keeping with this idea, there was every reason not to celebrate in one place those rites which were destined to cast out darkness and death and those rites intended for the living. A separation of church and baptistery was known to exist already in the third century in the domestic churches. The *impluvium*, located in the atrium, was the place for Baptism, while the family quarters of the house was the scene of the Eucharistic mysteries. When peace finally came and the Church began to construct her magnificent basilicas, the same motif was maintained: Baptism was conferred in the atrium or in a special compartment near the entrance of the church proper.

One of the earliest baptisteries built is that of the Basilica of St. John Lateran in Rome; Pope Sixtus III (432-440) had the baptistery constructed in an octagonal form where formerly one of circular shape had stood. Though baptisteries of many sizes, shapes, and designs are found dating from this period, the forms which seem to predominate by far are the octagonal and circular. There are two explanations of this fact. One holds that the Christians simply adopted the two forms which had received such favorable acceptance at the hands of the Romans in the construction of their baths.[200] A second opinion, however, sees in the octagonal form, at least, a certain symbolism.[201] The Fathers of the Church had given the number eight a special significance: it symbolized redemption. Very striking is the inscription found in the octagonal baptistery attached to the church of St. Thecla in Milan and reputedly composed by St. Ambrose. It reads in part:

[199] The word *baptisterium* was used by the Romans to designate both their bathrooms as well as their bathtubs. From the fourth century on, however, the word came to be employed exclusively, or at least predominantly, for that special edifice near the church in which the sacrament of regeneration was conferred. Christians also used other words, words that were more or less current in the parlance of their fellow Romans: *alveus, balneus, concha, fons, lavacrum, piscina, tinctorium*. Nevertheless, *baptisterium* ultimately prevailed.

[200] H. Leclercq, "Baptistère," *DACL*, II, 394.

[201] F-J. Dölger, "Zur Symbolik des altchristlichen Taufhauses," *Antike und Christentum*, 4 (1934), 153-197.

Octachorum templum sanctos surrexit in usus,
Octagonus fons est munere dignus eo.
Hoc numero decuit sancti baptismatis aulam
Surgere, quo populis vera salus rediit.[202]

In many of his writings St. Ambrose speaks of this deeper meaning of the number eight; the reason it had the meaning was that Christ rose on the eighth day [203]—"the number eight is the fulfillment of our hope." [204] He refers to this same mystical interpretation of the number, when he compares the prescription of the Mosaic Law that a male child was to be circumcised on the eighth day after his birth with the resurrection of Christ, which occurred on the eighth day.[205] In other words, since eight comes after seven (the great weekly festival of the Jews was observed on the seventh day of the week), it stood for the fact that the resurrection of Christ was the fulfillment of Old Testament hope. And since Baptism is the sacrament of resurrection, the Fathers thought it appropriate that the Christian soul should rise from the death of sin in the eight-sided baptistery. And Ambrose was not alone in preaching this mystical interpretation; many other Fathers likewise accepted it.[206]

Another feature of the most primitive baptisteries was the special arrangement whereby the baptismal font or pool was sunken into the floor and surrounded by several steps. The candidate for Baptism had to descend these steps to reach the pool and had to ascend them after the ceremony. Also, Baptism was conferred by immersion; the candidate entered the water at least to his waist, and when the names of the Holy Trinity were spoken he was completely immersed three times. This whole arrangement afforded an easily understood symbolic expression of the Pauline doctrine that in Baptism the new Christian is baptized into Christ's death (and burial) and rises with Him to a new life of grace.[207] This same theme is naturally taken up by the patristic writers.[208]

Baptisteries were not attached to every church. In fact, at first they were limited to the principal churches, even to cathedral churches. Candidates for Baptism had to travel to cities where the bishop resided to receive the sacrament from his hands, or at least from a priest delegated to confer it. It is only in the eleventh century that we find all priests permitted to baptize and all parish churches possessing their own baptisteries. Even today only parish churches are required to

---

[202] *Ibid.,* 155.

[203] *Ibid.,* 160-165.

[204] *Expositio in evang. sec. Lucam* V, 49. MPL, 15: 1735.

[205] *De Abraham* II, 11, 79. MPL, 14: 494.

[206] Cf. Dölger, *op. cit.,* 165-182.

[207] Rom 6: 3-11.

[208] Cf. L. Bouyer, *The Paschal Mystery* (Chicago, 1950), 314, n. 48.

have baptismal fonts; others may have them with the permission of the local Ordinary or because of a long tradition.[209]

The separation of the place of Baptism from the church proper continued in Italy as late as the thirteenth century. In northern Europe, however, Baptism by infusion began to appear as early as the sixth century. Hence, the former baptismal pools were no longer necessary, and simple fonts began to take their place. The reason given by many for this development is the fact that northern Europe was much colder; Baptism by immersion was in such circumstances very inconvenient.[210]

Infant Baptism likewise contributed to the change in design of both baptistery and font. When a small child is to be baptized, a baptismal tank or pool is hardly necessary. In place of it, stone or metal basins began to appear from the sixth century on. And when Baptism by infusion became firmly established, large basins gave way to small structures that resemble more the ordinary holy water stoups found at the entrances to churches. And since no one relished the idea of being baptized with water that had been used for others, the baptismal fonts became nothing more than mere receptacles for the baptismal water, and another basin with a shell-like spoon was actually used in the baptismal ceremony.

We need not return to the primitive practice of baptism by immersion, with a separate building for the administration of the sacrament, in order to reaffirm its proper dignity and significance. Yet, it is certainly a deplorable fact that our lack of appreciation for the full import of Baptism is so often betrayed by our neglect both of the place as well as the ceremonies of this gateway to the other sacraments. A sincere Catholic might well be ashamed to see the condition of this sacred womb of the Church in many places; so often it is simply a storeroom, a place for brooms and mops, pre-dieus and candelabras— and at that not too clean.

According to the Roman Ritual, the baptismal font is to be kept in a proper place and is to be of a suitable shape, made of solid material which can hold water and fittingly decorated. It should be surrounded by a railing, closed with lock and key, and so well covered that dust and dirt cannot enter it. On it, or at least near it—therefore some place in the baptistery—there should be a representation of St. John the Baptist baptizing our Lord.[211]

We might recall once more the suggestion that the baptistery be large enough to contain the confessionals and placed near the main entrance of the church, so that the relation of these two sacraments, their common role and their full meaning, will be once more placed

209 CIC, can. 774.

210 For a more complete history of the baptistery and the decoration used in it cf. H. Leclercq, art. cit., DACL, II, 382-469; Lucien de Bruyne, "La décoration des baptistères paléochrétiens," Miscellanea Liturgica Cuniberti Mohlberg, I (Rome, 1948), 189-220.

211 Tit., I, cap. 2, n. 46.

before the eyes of the faithful in a psychologically effective way. We lay such stress on catechetics; here is a living catechetics. It will do little good to teach the holiness and significance of Baptism, if we deny all of this practically in the way we treat the sacred womb of Holy Mother Church.

C. The Cemetery

The cemetery is not less sacred to the Christian than the church edifice. He firmly believes that the human body is holy, for through Baptism it has become a member of Christ, through the Holy Eucharist it comes into closest contact with the most pure body of Christ; indeed it is the dwelling place of the Blessed Trinity. What is more, the Christian belief in the resurrection engenders a respect and care for what now may be but a mere corpse but in the day of the Lord shall take its place in heaven with the company of the saints and, reunited with its soul, shall enjoy the Beatific Vision. Hence the resting place of the mortal remains of Christians is also held to be a sacred area. The cemetery, therefore, merits our attention, so that, well acquainted with its historical development, we may continue the loving care expended by generations of devout souls who appreciated the sanctity of "God's Acre" and honored the saints who died in the Lord.

Even the pagan Romans considered the burial places as sacred and inviolable. And Roman law protected the tombs and sepulchral monuments; it threatened violations of their precincts with stiff penalties. The free citizen, when providing for his and his family's burial, would purchase a piece of property outside the walls of Rome, for cemeteries were forbidden within the walls of the city. Once his title was established and the frontage and depth indicated on a small stone marker stuck into the property, it was called his *area*. Once a corpse was buried on the site, the spot became inviolable, and Roman protective law became operative.

The Romans used several kinds of burial. A freeman might simply dig a grave into the surface of his property, and this was called a *forma*. Another might desire to have a coffin on top the ground; this would be made of stone and called a *sarcophagus*. A rich Roman might have a large structure built atop the ground to house one or several sarcophagi, and this would be called a *mausoleum*. Still another might have a chamber dug out underground to hold the sarcophagi; this was called a *hypogaeum* (from the Greek υπο γη, under ground). Such sepulchral monuments still dot the countryside as one approaches Rome from the south on the Via Appia Antica.

Often the pagans cremated their dead and placed the ashes in terra-cotta or stone urns, more or less precious depending on family circumstances. The urns were very often placed in niches which lined the walls of the underground chambers or *hypogaea*. Sometimes the bases of the niches had small round openings resembling pigeonholes (whence the term *columbaria* for them) into which the ashes could be placed.

The Christians, however, were opposed to cremation; they committed the bodies of their dead to the ground intact. For rich Christians there was no problem; they owned burial plots outside the city walls. The poorer Christians, however, had no means for providing appropriate interment. The generous rich came to their assistance. Where they possessed a tomb above ground, they could easily have a *hypogaeum* dug under their property for the benefit of the poor. Or where they already had a *hypogaeum* filled with sarcophagi of their own family, they could either dig below it and construct another chamber or dig galleries or corridors from the sides of their *hypogaeum*. When the persons who owned contiguous burial plots were all Christian, they could pool their land, extend these underground galleries or corridors in such a way that they reached out for miles. Thus they established genuine community cemeteries. The above-mentioned galleries were regularly at least a yard wide and two yards deep; on either side tomb after tomb was hewn into the tufa walls. These tombs were called *loculi*. If after all such tombs had been filled more space was needed, they simply had to dig down further. Thus often the original height of two yards was doubled or even tripled, or galleries were dug to intersect each other at different levels. In this way, from simple family burial plots with a single underground chamber, the Christians, motivated by a concern for their poorer brethren, gradually dug veritable underground funereal cities called catacombs.

As a general name for the Roman underground cemeteries the word catacomb came to be used accidentally. The Christians called their burial places *coemeteria* meaning dormitories,[212] because death to their way of thinking was simply a period of sleep until the resurrection. Each cemetery had a proper name, sometimes the name of the original proprietor, sometimes a name indicative of its location; e.g.: *coemeterium inter duas lauros* (cemetery between the two laurels), *coemeterium Callixti* (cemetery of Callistus), *coemeterium ad clivum cucumeris* (cemetery at cucumber hill), *coemeterium in catacumbas* (cemetery in the hollow).

So we see that the name catacomb was originally proper to only one such cemetery, namely, one on the Via Appia where there was a slope or hollow. It was indeed a particularly famous locality, since it held within its environs, not only a group of subterranean tombs, but a shrine to St. Sebastian, the famous soldier-martyr, and above all a shrine to the Princes of the Apostles, Sts. Peter and Paul. Hence, even when the other cemeteries of Rome fell into oblivion during the Middle Ages, the one "in the hollow," "in the catacombs," was still popu-

---

[212] Tertullian is our earliest witness for the use of this term: cf. *De anima* 51. *MPL,* 2: 782.

lar. And so, when the sixteenth century rediscovered the other cemeteries, the name "catacomb" was given to them also.

Gradually the Church itself became the legal owner of these
cemeteries, either by outright donation on the part of the rich, or
because when the original owners died, she took possession of the
cemeteries as a legally registered funeral association. In time the
tombs and galleries were decorated with fresco work; precious coins
and stones were attached to these. Here we find some of the most
beautiful primitive Christian symbolism and art.[213]

The Church has always endeavored to maintain her community
cemeteries, to keep the bodies of her faithful departed separated from
those not of the faith. In the Middle Ages this was achieved principally by surrounding the church edifice with a yard for burial of
the dead; it was considered part of the church and it was expected
that Christians would come there, after they assisted at divine
service, to visit their dead. Where circumstances prevented such an
arrangement, a chapel would always be built in the middle of the
cemetery (usually in honor of St. Michael the Archangel or St. Sebastian). And when this was not possible, at least the cross was
erected, for it was expected that the Christian was to sleep in the
shadow of the cross.

Today the Catholic Church still asserts her right to possess her
own cemeteries, so that her faithful may be accorded full Christian
burial in consecrated ground. Whether the cemetery surrounds the
church or not, if it is possessed by the Church it is to be consecrated
or solemnly blessed. When this is not possible, each individual tomb
is to be blessed at the time of burial.[214] And canon law warns Ordinaries and pastors to guard and protect the genuine Catholic character of their cemeteries, so that no inscription or decoration will be
introduced that is not in keeping with sound piety and the true Christian outlook on death.[215] Inscriptions on tombs should not express
bitterness or hopeless grief. These are vain and foolish. The cemetery
is a place apart from the world of business, luxury, theatre, and
noise. It is just as far from the pagan outlook that makes death
the supreme tragedy. For the Catholic, the cemetery is a place in
which the bodies of the just repose until the day of the resurrection,
which he knows with the certainty of faith will come. Death for
him is not a tragedy; it is a truly happy event, the greatest moment
of his life, when he is called from this vale of tears to meet his Creator face to face and to begin that eternity of happiness which is the
reward of an earthly life well spent in the work of the Lord. *Beati*

---

[213] For a more detailed description of the Catacombs see. L. Hertling — E.
Kirschbaum, *The Roman Catacombs and their Martyrs*. Milwaukee, 1956.
[214] CIC, can. 1204, 1206.
[215] Can. 1211.

mortui qui in Domino moriuntur. Requiescant a laboribus suis; opera enim illorum sequuntur illos.[216]

D. Liturgical Art

"One picture is worth a thousand words." We have learned this lesson remarkably well today. What wonderfully clever teachers are the movies, television, the comic books! But this is a principle the Church has always followed, not only in dramatic liturgical action itself, but in the sacred adornment with which she outfits the sacred edifice and prepares it for the celebration of the mystery of redemption.

Pius XII, in his address to Italian artists on April 8, 1952, admirably expressed the connection between art and religion:

> It is not necessary to explain to you — who feel it within yourselves, often as a noble torment — one of the essential characteristics of art, which consists in a certain "affinity" of art with religion, which in certain ways renders artists interpreters of the infinite perfections of God, and particularly of the beauty and harmony of God's creation. The function of all art lies in breaking through the narrow and tortuous enclosure of the finite, in which man is immersed while living here below, and in providing a window on the infinite for his hungry soul. Thus it follows that any effort — and it would be a vain one, indeed — aimed at denying or suppressing any relation between art and religion must impair art itself. Whatever artistic beauty one may wish to grasp in the world, in nature and in man, in order to express it in sound, in color, or in plays for the masses, such beauty cannot prescind from God. Whatever exists is bound to Him by an essential relationship. Hence, there is not, neither in life nor in art — be it intended as an expression of the subject or as an interpretation of the object — the exclusively "human," the exclusively "natural" or "immanent." The greater the clarity with which art mirrors the infinite, the divine, the greater will be its possibility for success in striving toward its ideal and true artistic accomplishment. Thus, the more an artist lives religion, the better prepared he will be to speak the language of art, to understand its harmonies, to communicate its emotions.[217]

Though this is not the place for a detailed history of Christian art, a fleeting acquaintance with the art of the past ages will show just how close religion and art really were. The first Christian art we know of, that of the catacombs, was dominated by this "noble torment" to express the faith. Understandably, because of persecution, this art had to be symbolic to some degree: the fish, the cross, the dove, the olive branch, the anchor were to be seen everywhere. But there were

[216] Apoc. 14:13.
[217] Translation from *The Catholic Mind,* 50 (Nov. 1952), 697-698.

also the beautiful simple Madonnas, the Christs, the figure of the Christian at prayer called the *Orans,* certain figures from the Old Testament typifying Christ the Redeemer, etc. In either case, the purpose of this art was to make the invisible visible, to express the fervent faith and devotion of the Christian soul. With the coming of peace and the building of large, spacious basilicas, the Christian adorned his church with mosaics and frescoes depicting the great, majestic and glorious *Kyrios* and *Pantocrator,* the Lord and Ruler of all; the martyrs were also represented as having followed Christ in His victorious combat with death. With the number of conversions increasing daily, not only from noble and educated classes, but also from among the poor and the slaves, who were not particularly well educated, the teaching function of art came more to the fore.

As Pius XII says, "In truth, artistic masterpieces were known as the 'Bible of the people,' to mention such noted examples as the windows of Chartres, the door of Ghiberti (by happy expression known as the Door of Paradise), the Roman and Ravenna mosaics and the facade of the Cathedral of Orvieto. These and other masterpieces not only translate the Christian truths into easy reading and universal language; they also communicate the intimate sense and emotion of these truths with an effectiveness, lyricism, and ardor that, perhaps, is not contained in even the most fervent preaching." [218]

The dominant theme of this type of church decorative art was the story of redemption. Greater emphasis was of course laid on the birth and passion of our Lord, but other didactic scenes from His life do not escape notice. And Holy Scripture was a veritable mine for subjects of sculpture and painting. Yet early, and particularly medieval, art preferred to depict those themes which stood in the foreground of the liturgical life of the Church. At first it was the Easter theme, the consummation of redemption; later, in Carolingian times, Christmas begins to receive particular attention.[219] An instruction of the Holy Office of June 30, 1952 states: "It is the function and duty of sacred art, by reason of its very definition, to enhance the beauty of the house of God and to *foster the faith and piety* of those who gather in the church . . ." [220]

In contrast to this glorious Christian tradition stand some corrupt and errant forms of sacred art. Because of the lack of creative ability and artistic technique, stereotyped and second-rate statues and paintings are often absurdly exposed to the veneration of the faithful. On the other hand, however, the desire to break with this stale and empty commercialism, though good in itself, sometimes allowed itself to be captive of false philosophy and the search for novelty, and produced works which were a deformation and debasement of sane

[218] *Ibid.,* 698.
[219] For the reasons behind this shift of emphasis see J. Jungmann, "Church Art," *Worship,* 29 (1955), 68-82.
[220] *The Catholic Mind,* 50 (Nov. 1952), 699.

art; works which openly contradicted Christian truth, grace, modesty, and piety, were ugly and tended to destroy the beauty of man and nature.[221] Hence, ecclesiastical authority had to raise its voice more than once to disapprove of such works and to ban them from churches. Some canons on sacred art were obviously needed.

Let it suffice here to sum up the main points to be found in the pronouncements of the Church and in the discussions of reliable and tradition-minded authors.

1. A distinction must be made between architecture and art, or between the art of building and the art of decorating. While this distinction is valid, it does not mean that decoration is independent of architecture; it is subordinate to it. Both must join hands to produce one work of art that is organically fitted together. Whatever is placed in the church edifice by way of decoration must fit into the over-all architectural plan and design. And both architecture and art must serve the purpose of the church building; nothing must interfere with it. Hence, artistic building and decoration must be organically accommodated to the primacy and dominion of the Liturgy. Beauty in the church must have as its end the fostering of the faith and devotion of God's people; it must not only not be a hindrance to liturgical worship, but positively lead souls to a more intimate and meaningful participation in the sacred mysteries.

2. To do this the work of art must be orthodox, it must represent genuine Catholic dogma and morality.

3. It must spring from authentic religious and Christian inspiration. It must not be sentimental or overly emotional. Sacred art must learn how to be silent and reserved in the portrayal of sacred truth and not descend to an overemphasis of the petty, the ornamental, the gaudy, the ostentatious. Its great virtue must be simplicity and pure vitality of spiritual ideals. And this rules out the stereotyped trash.

4. Sacred art must be a community art, not simply the expression of the artist's subjective interior. True, all art must, to a degree, be subjective, for it must be the product of the artist's experience and appraisal of reality. Nevertheless, were this subjectivity to be stressed to the detriment of what must objectively be portrayed, the work of art simply could not *serve* the community.

5. To serve the community it must be intelligible, readable, so to speak, by the people. The esoteric gives rise to derision. Whatever is shocking, enigmatic, too novel, or styles that are anticipated must all be avoided. Sacred art must speak a living language, if it is to reveal the divine effectively to the human beings it is commissioned to teach.

[221] Pius XI, "Tante opere d'arte," *AAS*, 24 (1932), 355; Pius XII, *Mediator Dei*, 195; Instruction of Holy Office on Sacred Art, *The Catholic Mind*, 50 (Nov. 1952), 700.

6. And it must do the above reverently. Mimicry, sensuality, *excessive* deformation of the human figure are out of place.

7. Finally, sacred art must be honest; it must respect the integrity of the materials it uses. Wood or plaster painted to look like marble is deceitful.

If sacred art is faithful to these points, it will not merely give esthetic pleasure, but it will fulfill its primary purpose of raising the heart and mind to God within the liturgical context. And to insure the attainment of this ideal, the Holy Office urges bishops to entrust the execution of works of painting, sculpture and architecture only to men who are outstanding for their technique and at the same time capable of expressing sincere faith and piety—the purpose of any sacred art.[222]

[222] *The Catholic Mind,* 50 (Nov. 1952), 702. For a more lengthy treatment of the above notions see the following: the May-June issue of *Art Sacré,* 1952; H. de Montrand, "Art sacré et théologie," *Etudes,* 271 (1951), 314-321; P. Doncoeur, "Lessons of Eucharistic History," *Orate Fratres,* 23 (1949), 409-417; "An Order of Values in Sacred Art," *ibid.,* 24 (1950), 446-449; "Confusions et clartés dans le débat sur l'art sacré," *Etudes,* 273 (1952), 29-39; "L'architecture de l'église," *Etudes,* 275 (1952), 83-92; "La querelle de l'art sacré," *Vie Intellectuelle, n.* 11 (1951), 3-48; A. Durand, "Church Goods Statues and Good Church Statues," *AER,* 124 (1951), 190 ff.; J. Jungmann, "Church Art," *Worship,* 29 (1955), 68-82; J. LaFarge, "Catholic Religious Art," *National Liturgical Week,* (1948), 53-60; M. Lavanoux, "Parish Worship: Its Artistic Expression," *National Liturgical Week* (1940), 202-207; "Liturgical Art," *National Liturgical Week,* (1944), 74-81; "A Practical Aspect of Liturgical Art," *Orate Fratres,* 10 (1936), 570-574; C. Perkins, "The Perennial Art of the Liturgy," *National Liturgical Week* (1945), 99-107; P. Regamey, *Art Sacré au XXe Siècle,* Paris, 1952; H. A. Reinhold, "Copyrighted Churches," *Orate Fratres,* 20 (1946), 464-467; P. Roques, "Signification du baroque," *La Maison-Dieu, n.* 26 (1951), 125-142; D. Tucker, "Church Art in the Service of Praise," *National Liturgical Week* (1942), 148-160; F. Vandenbroucke, "Rome et art sacré," *QLP,* 34 (1953), 24-29; K. Frank, *Kernfragen Kirchlicher Kunst.* Vienna, 1953; T. Bogler, *Christliche Kunst als Verkündigung.* Maria Laach, 1953; Anthony Lauck, "Modern Sacred Art? Rome Speaks," *Ave Maria,* September, 1954.

CHAPTER FIVE

Structural Elements of the Liturgy

The peak of human existence is the communication of self. It would indeed be insufferable were a man to be deprived of every faculty for expressing himself, were he unable to speak or to signal in some way. Add to this the possibility of being totally incapable of receiving any communication from others, of being bereft of the powers of sight, hearing and touch. Man would be a prisoner within himself—a truly horrifying experience! For man is not self-sufficient; he needs others to complete and round out his own personality. And to be deprived of all social intercourse would spell utter isolation from the world about him. How much more tragic would be the consequences in his relationship with God; he could not speak to God in a way connatural to his own nature. For, after all, even God must treat man as man, according to his human condition and lot, and man learns through his senses. Where these are deficient, his knowledge limps. Hence God would have to resort to a completely supernatural manner of communicating Himself to man, which, of course, we know He does—but not as the normal pattern. While man in his relations with God uses signs to express himself, so God in sharing Himself with man uses symbols, words, actions, things—*"verbis et signis exterioribus perficitur sacramentum* — the sacrament is effected by means of external words and signs." [1]

The normal tools of human communication, then, are precious means of achieving the perfection of our existence, both natural and supernatural. Ordinary things like words and gestures play a tremendously important role in life; they are the medium of knowledge and growth, of love and life. Very naturally, they will exercise a similar role in the realm of divine communication and life which is the sacred Liturgy. It is only right that we devote some time to understanding the words and actions which teach us of God, give us His life, and through which we express our love and devotion to Him and communicate our knowledge and love of Him to others. Should we fail to understand them, we run the risk of going through empty motions, of saying things we really do not mean, of performing actions

[1] Council of Trent, Sess. xxiii, cap. 3. Denz. 959.

which in no way express our interior sentiments. In short, without an understanding of the words and actions of the Liturgy, our worship is in danger of being insincere.

A. Word

As Guardini says, "The word is a thing of mystery. It is so volatile that it vanishes almost on the lip, yet so powerful that it decides fates and determines the meaning of existence." [2] Aside from the fact that words must be used to instruct us, they play a particular part in relation to the gestures used in worship. They are, as it were, the soul of the gesture. The words used in the sacramental actions determine the meaning and direction of the gestures employed. Gestures, on the other hand, accompany the words to make them more graphic and to impress their meaning more clearly on the minds of others.

1. Vocal prayer

Answering the question whether prayer must always be vocal, St. Thomas makes a distinction between common and private prayer.[3] Common prayer, he says, since it is offered in the name of all the people, should be understood by them. Therefore, such prayer is spoken out loud so that the people might hear it. Private prayer, on the other hand, since it affects only a particular person, need not be said out loud; others need not hear. Nevertheless, St. Thomas offers three reasons why even private prayer uses the voice on occasion, and what he says applies just as well to common prayer. All the reasons flow from the nature of man as a composite of body and soul. Words, and even actions, are used: (a) to excite and arouse interior devotion, (b) to allow the body a chance of paying its debt of service to Almighty God, and (c) as an overflow of the interior joy and emotion of the soul.

Of necessity common prayer is somewhat different from private prayer. And this difference is a source of scandal to some. The Liturgy is too formalized for one person; it is too cold, impersonal for another. Then, too, when we compare the formulas of the Liturgy with the spontaneous outpourings of private prayer, we find that the former do not possess that same directness of expression, may even be meaningless for us in any given spiritual condition. This is truly a problem. How can we justify praying in ready-made formulas, formulas which may not immediately satisfy our concrete, momentary, completely personal spiritual disposition (or indisposition)?

Guardini says that:

[2] *Meditations before Mass* (Westminster, Maryland, 1955), 7.
[3] *Summa Theologica*, II-II, q. 83, art. 12.

It is hardly permissible to play off the spiritual life of the individual, with its purely personal bearing, against the spiritual life of the Liturgy, with its generalizing bias. They are not mutually contradictory; they should both combine in active cooperation. When we pray on our own behalf only we approach God from an entirely personal standpoint, precisely as we feel inclined or impelled to do so according to our feelings and circumstances. That is our right, and the Church would be the last to wish to deprive us of it. Here we live our own life, face to face with God. . . . The language we speak on these occasions suits us entirely, and much of it apparently is suited to us alone. We can use it with confidence because God understands it, and there is no one else who needs to do so. However, we are not only individuals, but members of a community as well; we are not merely transitory, but something of us belongs to eternity, and the Liturgy takes these elements into account. In the Liturgy we pray as members of the Church; by it we rise to the sphere which transcends the individual order and is therefore accessible to people of every condition, time and place. For this order of things the style of the Liturgy — vital, clear, and universally comprehensible — is the only possible one. The reason for this is that any other type of prayer, based upon one particular set of hypotheses or requirements, would undoubtedly prove a totally unsuitable form for a content of different origin. Only a system of life and thought which is truly Catholic — that is to say, actual and universal — is capable of being universally adopted, without violence to the individual. Yet there is still an element of sacrifice involved in such adoption. Each one is bound to strive within himself, and to rise superior to self. Yet in doing so he is not swallowed up by, and lost in, the majority; on the contrary, he becomes more independent, rich and versatile.[4]

Adhering more closely to the thought of St. Thomas as exposed at the beginning of this section, R. Hoornaert puts the relationship betweeen private and liturgical prayer in a slightly different way. Proceeding from the primacy of interior cult, he shows that the Liturgy is the exterior expression of the same. The contemplative is compelled towards this exterior manifestation. Adoration and praise become a formidable urge within the contemplative and make him say in the words of St. Theresa, "Would that I were transformed into a thousand tongues to praise the Lord." Contemplation gives rise to adoration, and the powerful force of adoration explodes, so to speak, into external praise. The more a soul is truly contemplative, the more it is compelled to be genuinely liturgical, for it finds in the rites and formulas of Holy Mother Church the most adequate expression of its interior praise.[5] And, on the other hand, the Liturgy compels towards

[4] *The Spirit of the Liturgy* (New York, 1940), 159-160.
[5] "Liturgie ou contemplation," *Etudes Carmélitaines,* 17 (1932), 197-198.

a deeper search for God. Liturgical prayer starts the contemplative on his way, hungry for a more intimate rendezvous with his God.[6] What Hoornaert says by way of conclusion is especially noteworthy: "Liturgy and contemplation, far from being two types of prayer which exclude one another, are therefore really two moments of one same and unique movement of love, for prayer is one. These two moments are so little separated from each other, that, in certain phases, they can even be superimposed.[7]

So for the Liturgy to have a truly universal appeal and usefulness, its thought content and form of expression must be purely objective and above the level of merely individual interests. Yet at the same time the genuinely interior soul will give itself generously to such "stylized" expression for two reasons: to nourish its own spiritual life with the objective values and truths coming from Christ through the Church, and to grow in spiritual breadth and richness by praying together with other souls devoted to Christ.

There is, of course, a certain danger of formalism in the Liturgy. Aside from the fact that formalism can arise in any spiritual exercise, liturgical prayer is particularly susceptible to it. This is so mainly because the Liturgy has been permitted to "grow old," to petrify. In many respects it has ceased to be functional, and, because of the natural tendency to enrich the Liturgy with the "best of everything," sometimes the basic meaning and reason of the ceremonies have been violated. The people's parts of the Mass have been taken over by the choir, and as a result the congregation has become a group of mute spectators, outsiders to an action which is really their own. With disuse, of course, comes lack of understanding and appreciation—the plague of most congregations today. When we do not understand, when we are left out of what is going on, we lose interest—formalism sets in. The outmoded forms of expression and the lack of functionalism can be and are being remedied by the pruning and inventive reforms on the part of Church authority. But the lack of understanding and appreciation can only be remedied by personal study and instruction from the pulpit.

2. A special liturgical language?

It is difficult to see how anyone can seriously believe in the principle of sacred languages so unhesitatingly asserted by Dom Prosper Guéranger: "We do not hesitate to affirm that until the fourth century of Christianity these three languages (which appeared in the title nailed to our Lord's cross)—Syriac, Greek and Latin—were the only ones used at the altar. This confers upon them à special liturgical dignity and marvellously confirms the principle of sacred, not vernac-

---

[6] *Ibid.*, 198-201.
[7] *Ibid.*, 202. For further discussion of this matter cf. J. Miller, *The Relationship between Liturgical and Private Prayer* (Trier, 1955), 102-110.

ular, languages in the Liturgy." [8] Such an assertion can only rest upon a lack of historical knowledge. The venerated founder of Solesmes pushes this principle so far as to interpret the Council of Trent as having pronounced a *dogmatic* definition in favor of Latin.[9] A little historical evidence will clear away this cloud.

There can be little doubt that our Lord Himself used Aramaic at the first Mass in the upper room the evening before He was taken prisoner. And nowhere do we find, either in Scripture or Tradition, that He left instructions concerning the language to be used in the celebration of the Eucharist. In fact, if St. Paul's words are to be taken as representative of the mind of all the Apostles, it would follow that both for preaching as well as for the Holy Sacrifice and the public prayers, the language of the people to whom the Apostles went was used. Writing to the Corinthians, Paul has this to say:

> He who prophesies [teaches] is greater than he who speaks in tongues . . . for he who speaks in a tongue edifies himself, but he who prophesies edifies the Church . . . speaking to men for edification, encouragement and consolation. . . . If I pray in a tongue, my spirit prays, but my understanding is unfruitful. What, then, is to be done? I will pray with the spirit, but I will also pray with the understanding; I will sing with the spirit, but I will sing with the understanding also. Else if thou givest praise with the spirit alone, how shall he who fills the place of the uninstructed say "Amen" to thy thanksgiving? For he does not know what thou sayest. For thou indeed givest thanks well, but the other is not edified. I thank God that I speak with all tongues; yet in the church, I had rather speak five words with my understanding, that I may also instruct others, than ten thousand words in a tongue.[10]

In Palestine itself Hebrew was without question the language of the Christians as long as they continued to frequent the synagogue services. We may infer that the Judeo-Christians insisted on maintaining the same language in their specifically Christian services even after the separation from the synagogue. Their attitude to Hellenism is well known. In fact, it was their narrow-mindedness in this regard which sparked one of the first conflicts within the Christian fold, between the Hebrew-speaking Christians and the Christians who, though originally Jews, spoke Greek. The latter protested that they were being neglected in the daily distribution of goods. As a result the seven deacons were appointed to take charge of an equitable service to all.[11] An even more serious division arose due to the aloofness of the Judeo-Christians towards the Gentile-Christians. The

[8] *Institutions Liturgiques,* 2nd edition (Paris, 1883), III, 52.
[9] *Ibid.,* 156.
[10] 1 Cor. 14: 5-19.
[11] Acts 6: 1-3.

former would not eat with the latter;[12] they considered them unclean [13] and demanded that they be circumcised.[14] It is hardly likely, therefore, that, with such an attitude towards Greeks, the Judeo-Christians would adopt their language in preference to their own native Hebrew or, at that time, Aramaic.

With the outbreak of the Jewish war, these Judeo-Christians were dispersed and died in oblivion. After the destruction of Jerusalem, the new Christian communities that arose there were composed of converts from the Hellenic Gentile stock which peopled the new city built by Hadrian and called Aelia. From that time on the Liturgy of Jerusalem was celebrated in Greek.[15] However, alongside the converts from the Gentiles, there were others from the remaining Jews, so that even at the end of the fourth century the Bible was read in Greek but explained in Syriac.[16] But with the fifth century a special Syriac version of the Bible makes its appearance and is used in the Liturgy. From that moment on the character of the Palestinian communities ceases to be exclusively Hellenic and becomes increasingly Syrian.

Though everything east of Antioch, even the immediate vicinity, was Syrian, the city itself was naturally drawn into the Hellenic orbit. This was true of the entire Mediterranean world including Rome itself. Strange as it may seem, though defeated by the Romans and subjugated to their rule, the Greeks succeeded in imposing on the Romans, to a great extent, Greek culture and language. To begin with, Rome swarmed with Greek and Oriental slaves. The schools of the Greek rhetoricians received the highest acclaim and were the most frequented by Roman students. The patricians even had a Greek maid take care of their children.[17] This should, perhaps, be taken in conjunction with what Quintillian says concerning the education of children. He desires that the child be taught Greek before he learns his native tongue, because, as he says, the Latin culture came from that of the Greeks. However, he does not want the child to speak Greek for a long time exclusively, even though such was the custom among most of the nobles.[18]

[12] Gal. 2: 11-13.
[13] Acts 10 and 11.
[14] Ibid., 15: 1.
[15] Cf. Gustave Bardy, La Question des Langues dans l'Eglise ancienne (Paris, 1948), 14.
[16] Ethérie, Journal de Voyage (Edit. Hélène Pétré; Paris, 1948), n. 47, pp. 260-262.
[17] Tacitus, Dialogus de Oratoribus, 29. C. Cornelii Taciti Opera Omnia (London: Delphin Classics, 1821), V, 3717: "A nunc natus infans delegatur Graeculae alicui ancillae."
[18] Institutio Oratoriae, I, 1, 12-13 (Edit. Eduard Bonnell; Leipzig, 1896), p. 8: "A sermone Graeco puerum incipere malo, quia Latinum, qui pluribus in usu est, vel nobis nolentibus perbibet; simul quia disciplinis quoque Graecis prius instituendus est, unde et nostrae fluxerunt. Non tamen hoc adeo superstitiose fieri velim, ut diu tantum Graece loquatur aut discat, sicut plerisque moris est."

In addition to the cultural attraction that Greek exercised over the Roman mind, Rome was the center of civilization and consequently became the melting pot of the world. Anyone who wanted wordly advancement travelled to and installed himself in Rome. The constant importation of slaves from conquered nations brought with it the vices as well as the virtues of those same nations.[19] Rome also became the capital of trade as well as government. And Greek was the idiom of commerce. The city was becoming so Greek in character that Juvenal threw up his hands in disgust, "I cannot bear this Greek city, O Romans!" [20] Thus the city of Rome was dominated by a Greek culture even as late as the period of silver Latin (96-125 A.D.). Nor was this the end of the dominance of the Greek language in Rome, for in 245 Plotinus could go to Rome, set up a school, live and teach there for twenty-five years (until 270) without knowing a word of Latin.[21]

Such, therefore, was the medium the Church used in her Liturgy in the city of Rome. After all, her first converts were among the class of Jews who spoke Greek, as well as from among the other Orientals whose maternal tongue was Greek. The list of the first thirteen popes contains but two Latin names, Clement and Pius. In 155 Polycarp of Smyrna paid a visit to Pope Anicetus to discuss with him the date of Easter and was invited to celebrate the Eucharist before the community.[22] At the time of Anicetus, then, the language of the Liturgy must have been Greek. Another proof that the Liturgy was celebrated in Greek in the first part of the third century is that Hippolytus wrote his *Apostolic Tradition*, a liturgical book, in Greek.

Approximately a hundred years later we find Marius Victorinus, a Roman writer, discussing the Nicene formula which makes Christ consubstantial with the Father. Though writing in Latin, he quotes a fragment of the Roman Canon in Greek.[23] This is a sure sign that Greek was still the language of the Mass—at least of the Canon. T. Klauser compares this quotation with one from another Roman author who wrote about fifteen or twenty years later and cited the Latin words *summus sacerdos* of the Roman Canon.[24] Klauser concludes from this that between 360 and 382 the Church officially changed her liturgical language from Greek to Latin.[25] Since the pontificate of Damasus (366-384) falls within this period, Klauser ascribes to him

---

[19] *Annales* 15, 44. *C. Cornelii Taciti Opera Omnia* (London: Delphin Classics, 1821), III, 1963-1964: "urbem . . . quo cuncta undique atrocia aut pudenda confluunt celebranturque."

[20] *Satira*, III, 60. *D. Junii Juvenalis Opera Omnia* (London: Delphin Classics, 1820), I, 222: "Non possum ferre, Quirites, Graecam urbem."

[21] G. Bardy, *op. cit.*, 156.

[22] Cf. Eusebius, *Historia Ecclesiastica* 5, 24, 17. GCS, 9(1), 496, 16-17.

[23] *Adversus Arium* 2, 8. MPL, 8: 1094.

[24] Cf. "Der Übergang der Römischen Kirche von der griechischen zur lateinischen Liturgiesprache," *Miscellanea Giovanni Mercati*, I (Vatican City, 1946), 467. The unknown Roman writer is called Pseudo-Augustinus, and his work, *Quaestiones Veteris et Novi Testamenti* 109, 21. CSEL, 50: 268.

[25] *Ibid.*, 469.

the initiative for changing the liturgical language in Rome, given the fact that Damasus was a pope of extraordinary energy and progressiveness—qualities certainly needed to put through such a reform.[26] He sees further evidence for his opinion in the fact that during the pontificate of Damasus debate concerning the liturgical language was particularly heated. By this time the liturgical language had already been at variance with the language of the people for about 120 years, for Latin began to predominate again in Rome roughly about 250, the time when the popes began to put Latin inscriptions on the tombs of their predecessors.[27] Klauser interprets Ambrosiaster's commentary on 1 Cor. 14 as indicative of the fact that, though the language of the Liturgy had recently been changed in order to coincide with the vernacular, certain factions were not content, especially the new converts from the mystery religions who wanted to veil the meaning of the words of the Liturgy in an obscure foreign language.[28] If we add to this evidence the extraordinary coincidence that Damasus was the man behind St. Jerome's translation of the Bible, there seems little doubt that it was with his authority that Latin was introduced into the Liturgy of Rome.[29]

The other countries of the West never succumbed to the allure of Greek culture. Egypt, of course, looked to Alexandria, which in turn came under the direct influence of Greece. But outside the civilized areas the north central part of Africa had its own national language, Berber.[30] At the end of the second century Tertullian was the first Christian to write in Latin. True, he had put some of his writings in Greek, but these he himself translated into Latin, and thus they have come down to us. Therefore, the influence of Greek in Africa was not great; it was limited to the cities, and even there to the elite and to foreign merchants. At the beginning of the Christian era in Africa, Latin culture clearly dominated the scene.[31] In fact, Africa possessed its Latin version of the Bible long before Rome did, even before the time of Tertullian, in the *Afra* version. Its Latin was not elegant; it

---

[26] *Ibid.*, 473.

[27] T. Klauser, *The Western Liturgy and its History*, 21.

[28] "Der Übergang," 477.

[29] Another important addition must be made to the above observations. In the same article Klauser summarizes the work done by Odo Casel in tracing the terminology of the Roman Canon to St. Ambrose, Bishop of Milan. Since according to Casel the only linguistic parallel in the West to "oblatio rationabilis" is to be found in Ambrose's work *De sacramentis*, Klauser accepts the conclusion that the text of the Roman Canon officially introduced by Damasus in Rome was first used in Latin in Milan under Ambrose: *ibid.*, 480-481. The original work of Casel may be found in "Ein orientalisches Kultwort in abendländischer Umschmelzung," *JLW*, 11 (1931), 1-19; "Oblatio rationabilis," *Theologische Quartalschrift*, 99 (1917-1918), 429-438. However, more recently Christine Mohrmann has rejected this thesis for the simple reason that Ambrose's use of the word "rationabilis" differs greatly from the way the word is used in the Roman Canon; the latter is based on the New Testament use of the word: cf. *Liturgical Latin — Its Origins and Character* (Washington, D.C.: The Catholic University Press, 1957), 65.

[30] Bardy, *op. cit.*, 52-53.

[31] *Ibid.*, 56.

was not the work of cultivated men, but of those whose concern it was to have a text capable of being read in liturgical gatherings and understood by the common people. The conclusion, therefore, seems inescapable that Africa was the first country to possess a Latin Liturgy.[32]

Though in Gaul, as in Rome, Christianity was first preached to Greek-speaking people, already towards the end of the second century its character is more Latin than Greek.[33] Everywhere else—in the northern part of Gaul, in Spain and Britain—the language of the Liturgy was exclusively Latin.[34]

For centuries Latin remained the language of cultured people in the West. Though Celtic and Basque certainly existed from a very early date, as did the Teutonic languages, only Latin was considered a universal literary language. The Romance tongues took several centuries to develop, and then were not universal or homogeneous within given countries until a relatively late time. It is a well known fact that even today, if a Genovese and a person from the hills of Lazio were to speak to each other in their own dialects, they would understand precious little. The day of national languages was a long time coming. What was needed was a literature which could weld the disparate elements of dialect into a unified whole and propagate it throughout the land with attractive force. In Italy, for example, Dante answered this call with all his literary genius. Though he certainly was not the first to write in Italian—the poets of the "sweet new style," Guittone and Guido Guinezelli, were his immediate forerunners—it was chiefly due to the *Divine Comedy* that Italian became respected as a literary language. And how late this appeared—not much before the end of his life in 1321. Even then he was forced to write another work, *De Vulgari Eloquentia*, a Latin treatise, to defend his use of Italian as a literary medium.

One might have expected these languages of newly found respectability to work their way into the Liturgy. Any such hopes were quickly disillusioned. The birth of the Renaissance smothered the new trend in a cloud of enthusiasm for the glory of ancient Rome, its architecture, its classics. The initiates of this new cult of the "good old days" tended to consider all else as barbaric. And their influence reached far and wide. As late as the sixteenth and seventeenth centuries we find a Pole, Copernicus (1473-1543), and an Italian, Galileo (1564-1642), writing their scientific works in Latin. This same attitude was often discernible in the proceedings of the Council of Trent. In their discussions, some of the Fathers of the Council gave as their reason for rejecting a vernacular Liturgy that they did not consider modern languages suitable literary media.[35]

[32] *Ibid.*, 60.
[33] *Ibid.*, 74.
[34] *Ibid.*, 78.
[35] Cf. H. Schmidt, *Liturgie et Langue Vulgaire* (Rome, 1950), 127.

When ecclesiastics of truly Catholic persuasion finally did recognize the usefulness of a vernacular Liturgy and began to petition for the introduction of at least some vernacular in the services of the Church, the issue was obscured by the outright heretical intent of the Protestant innovators, who made the same cry one of the principal points in their so-called reform. The Mass was, so the latter claimed, nothing more than a catechetical service—not at all the propitiatory sacrifice the Papists wrongly interpreted it to be. Therefore, to celebrate Mass in Latin thwarts its whole purpose. In principle only the vernacular can be used, otherwise the Mass has no effect—the people cannot understand it.[36] It logically follows that, if the essential characteristic of the Mass is the preaching of the word of God, or the "eating of the Bread of heaven received through faith," the whole procedure is of no value whatsoever when the word is spoken in a foreign tongue.

To counteract the Protestant menace, the Church convened the Council of Trent. At Trent the Fathers of the Council weighed each demand and thesis of the Protestants and clearly defined the doctrine of the Catholic Church. Among the canons decreed we find one touching directly on the matter of the vernacular. It reads: "*Si quis dixerit . . . lingua tantum vulgari Missam celebrari debere . . . anathema sit—* Should anyone say that the Mass must be celebrated in the vernacular language only, let him be anathema." [37] How is this to be understood? Is it true that in this canon the Council of Trent passed a *dogmatic* definition concerning the use of Latin in the Liturgy as Dom Guéranger believed?

The only possible way to answer these questions is to examine the decisions of the Council and to see whether the discussions preliminary to the final vote shed any light on the exegesis of the definitive canon.

The tentative draft drawn up by theologians prior to the first general discussion of the vernacular question in December of 1551 (eleven years before the final decision was reached) read thus: "*missamque non nisi in lingua vulgari, quam omnes intelligant, celebrari debere—* one must celebrate Mass only in the vernacular which all understand." [38] The words "*quam omnes intelligant*" indicate clearly that the theologians aimed the canon directly against the Protestant reformers who explicitly taught that the language of the Mass had to be understandable, since it was only a memorial intended to instruct.

A general discussion ensued, and from its minutes we learn that, of the sixteen Fathers who offered comment, two saw no reason whatsoever to condemn the use of the vernacular, while two others clearly stated that the Council should declare nothing dogmatic about Latin

[36] *Ibid.*: for Luther pp. 49-51, for Zwingli pp. 61-62, for Calvin p. 69.
[37] Sess. xxii, can. 9. Denz. 956.
[38] Schmidt, 98.

and the Liturgy. Three more urged the utmost caution lest it seem that the practice of the Oriental Church be thereby condemned. Another cited the words of Paul (1 Cor. 14) against the proposed condemnation. And two suggested branding the Protestant statement as false instead of as heretical.[39] The upshot of this discussion was that, though many of the Fathers were in favor of a condemnation, many others objected to the form in which it was expressed, because it did not take into account the rights and privileges of particular Churches and did not make it clear enough that the insistence on keeping Latin in the Liturgy was but a relative and contingent prescription. It would be interesting to see what the Fathers would have said about the dogmatic exposé subsequently submitted by the theologians of the Council. It invoked the principle of sacred languages: "Lingua enim latina, quae in titulo crucis Domini tamquam quoddam divinum instrumentum est consecrata . . . maxime convenit." [40] Unfortunately there was not enough time for the Fathers to debate the matter. Neither dogmatic exposé nor the condemnatory canon became official. An epidemic broke out in Trent. The Council was forced to discontinue its sessions, and it did not reconvene until ten years later.

Although the principal point gained in the discussion of 1552 was that the question of the language of the Liturgy was simply a matter of what the Church here and now considers more suitable, the reconvened Council of 1562 saw the attempt to dogmatize about Latin crop up again. The promoters of this tendency were supported by a Romanizing school of thought which placed a halo of sanctity around the Latin language. Under this type of influence, theologians prepared a brand new dogmatic exposé: "The Latin language, in which Masses in the Western Church are celebrated, is very appropriate, since it is common to many nations; nor can it be doubted that, if Masses were to be celebrated in the vernacular languages of each people, the divine mysteries would receive less reverence. There would also be a very great danger that various errors would creep into the many translations." [41]

This phrasing alerted the majority of the Fathers of the Council to the fact that the Romanizing faction, instead of being satisfied with a refutation of Protestantism, was actually attempting to push through a dogmatic condemnation of the vernacular as such. Those who did not have a purely Western outlook and whose views were broad enough to embrace the Church Universal reacted vigorously. What would the Orientals think? Was their age-old custom merely

[39] *Ibid.,* 108-109.
[40] Schmidt, 110: "The Latin language, which in the title of our Lord's cross was consecrated as a divine instrument, is most fitting."
[41] *Ibid.,* 135: "Lingua etiam latina, qua missae in occidentali ecclesia celebrantur, maxime congruit, si quidem ea pluribus nationibus communis est; neque videtur esse dubitandum, quin, si missae vulgari cuiusque gentis idiomate peragerentur, divina mysteria minori reverentia colerentur. Esset etiam magnopere periculosum, ne varii in multis translationibus errores nascerentur."

tolerated by the Church? Were they thereby being irreverent to the
sacred mysteries they celebrated? Were they to think themselves
suspect as regards orthodoxy? More Fathers than ever rose to speak
against the dogmatic exposé. Some rejected any condemnation whatsoever. Others, seeing that some statement was necessitated by the
doctrine of the Protestants, simply demanded that both the canon
and dogmatic exposé be clear enough so as not to give rise to the interpretation that the vernacular as such was condemned.[42]

On September 17, 1562, the Fathers finally approved a canon and
a dogmatic exposé in which the theologians had carefully omitted any
reference to the arguments for Latin so clearly rejected as false in
the previous general discussions.

As for the canon, a careful reading of it should be sufficient to
show that the Fathers did not aim their condemnation at the vernacular itself. "Si quis dixerit . . . lingua tantum vulgari Missam celebrari
debere . . . anathema sit." The word tantum, "only" is extremely important. The canon does not say that anyone who says the Mass should be
celebrated in the vernacular is a heretic. It indicates very clearly that
he is heretical who claims the Mass must be celebrated in the vernacular only, tantum. And who would say such a thing? As already indicated, some Catholics of this period had indeed requested the use
of some vernacular in the Mass; they never dreamed of saying that
Mass could not be celebrated except in the vernacular. This canon
must obviously be understood in terms of the error it intended to
combat. The Protestants, to repeat, had claimed that the Mass had
to be offered in a vernacular which the people understood, for otherwise the Mass, a mere instruction service, would be pure nonsense.
The condemnation, accordingly, touches only on the reason given by
the Protestants for the celebration of the Mass in the vernacular.[43]

Furthermore, the doctrinal chapter finally approved by the Fathers of the Council clearly shows that there is no dogmatic connection
between the Mass and any particular language. "Even though the Mass
does contain a great deal of instruction for the faithful, it does not
seem expedient (expedire) to the Fathers that it be celebrated indiscriminately in the vernacular." [44] The word expedire could hardly have
been used had the Council intended to write a dogmatic condemnation
of the vernacular as such. Expedire implies that it is a question of

---

[42] Ibid., 138-143.
[43] Cf. Schmidt, 98-99.
[44] Sess. xxii, cap. 8. Denz. 946: "Etsi Missa magnam contineat populi fidelis
eruditionem, non tamen expedire visum est Patribus, ut vulgari passim lingua
celebraretur. Quamobrem, retento ubique cuiusque ecclesiae antiquo et a sancta
Romana Ecclesia, omnium ecclesiarum matre et magistra, probato ritu, ne oves
Christi esuriant, neve parvuli panem petant et non sit, qui frangat eis: mandat
sancta Synodus pastoribus et singulis curam animarum gerentibus, ut frequenter
inter Missarum celebrationem vel per se vel per alios, ex his, quae in Missa
leguntur, aliquid exponant atque inter cetera sanctissimi huius sacrificii mysterium
aliquod declarent, diebus praesertim Dominicis et festis."

pragmatic, contingent circumstances and *not* one of dogma. In other words, the mind of the Council, according to this doctrinal chapter, is that the use of any particular language in the Mass is not a question of faith, bears no essential or necessary relation to the essence of the Mass, but rather is a matter which must be decided according to circumstances: Here and now is it advisable to use this or that language for the celebration of Mass. Nothing more can possibly be read into the decision of the Council.

Let us sum up our conclusions on the Council of Trent's teaching regarding the vernacular:

1. There is certainly a dogmatic question involved, but it does not concern the vernacular itself. The doctrinal chapter makes this quite clear; the matter of language used in Liturgy is entirely accessory: *expedire*. Any decision as to which language shall be employed will depend on adaptation to circumstances.

2. The negative meaning of the dogmatic canon is that the essence of the Mass does not demand the use of the vernacular; or that whoever demands the use of the vernacular out of Protestant persuasion is a heretic. Positively it means that there is no positive theological *convenientia* between the Mass and any particular language (Latin included); it is only a question of negative fitness, of expediency, of response to circumstances. In other words, as far as the essence of the Mass is concerned, it is *per se* indifferent to the use of any particular language.[45]

3. The principle of "sacred languages" cannot be admitted; the Council positively excluded this reason for the retention of Latin. Nor can it be admitted that the use of the vernacular necessarily brings with it a danger to faith or an increase of error; these too were expressly rejected in the general discussions of the Council.

4. It can be said that the Council, practically speaking, had to maintain the use of Latin at this time, because the Protestant reformers had linked the use of the vernacular with their heretical doctrine concerning the Mass: that it was only a catechetical memorial service, and must be celebrated in a language which the people understand.

5. The Mass is more, it is a sacrifice. In its essence, it is indifferent to language. Yet, parts of the Mass are obviously intended for the instruction of the faithful, and the Council, not being able to grant the full use of the vernacular at the moment, commands pastors of souls to explain in the vernacular the rites and texts of the Mass frequently.

This was not the first time heretics took up the cry for the vernacular. Many before the Protestants demanded the use of the mother tongue in the Liturgy; the Albigensians (1150), the Waldensians (1173), the sects begun by Wyclif (d.1384) and Huss (1415). The same was true after the Protestant revolt. In the eighteenth century,

---

[45] Cf. Schmidt, 153-155.

the jansenistically inclined Scipio Ricci [46] and his illegal synod of
Pistoia evoked another condemnation from Rome.[47] Still imbued to
a degree with the spirit of the Enlightenment, Winter, Werkmeister [48]
and Hirscher [49] worked towards the same goal. Sailer [50] and Moehler,[51]
pleading for the vernacular at first, were finally caught up in Romanticism and turned against the movement. Their age was one of excessive
nationalism and exaggerated independence of local bishops. To have
granted the use of the vernacular could have easily spelled disaster.

Admittedly the modern promoters of the vernacular feel uncom-
fortable in such tendentious company. Both heretics and modern liturgiologists often make the same proposals. But the relationship ends
there; the ends, reasons, and means are entirely different. On the one
hand, we have heresy, schismatic tendencies, and naturalism seeking
self-expression, on the other, orthodoxy, devotion to the Church, and
the earnest desire to supernaturalize and sanctify the faithful. The
modern movement for the vernacular rests solidly on a strong conviction of the Catholic priesthood, the sacrificial-sacramental-banquet
character of the Mass, the deep pastoral concern to nourish the faithful on the "solid meat" of the truths of the faith—sacraments, grace
and authentic spirituality, the orientation of Christ's members in the
common life of the Mystical Body in closest union with Christ's ministers and His Vicar on earth. This is uncommonly un-Protestant.

The case for the vernacular as presented by modern liturgiologists is quite simple. It is nothing else than a development of St. Paul's
admonition to pray with the understanding (1 Cor. 14). In vocal
prayer the ideal to be aimed at is for the worshipper to understand as
completely as possible the meaning of the words he is using. We usually define prayer as the raising of the heart and mind to God, or as a
conversation with God. Does not this imply that the person praying
should know what he is talking about? Normally does not a man
pray better if he understands what his prayer means?

We have already seen that St. Thomas says common prayer
should be vocal in order to make known to all taking part what is
being said. If they do not understand the language used to inform
them of what is being said, will they be informed? Prayer is vocal
and said out loud for a reason. Language is used for a reason, and
that is to communicate with one another and with God intelligently.
Just as there is little object in a man mumbling unintelligibly a message to another, so there is little point in speaking to another in a
language he obviously does not understand.

[46] Cf. W. Trapp, *Vorgeschichte und Ursprung der liturgischen Bewegung*
(Regensburg, 1940), 21-22.
[47] It came in 1794: Denz. 1533, 1566.
[48] Cf. Trapp, 22-42.
[49] *Ibid.*, 216-229.
[50] *Ibid.*, 205-216.
[51] *Ibid.*, 230-233.

Of late there has been much insistence on active participation in the Liturgy. This movement was spurred on by Pius X who said that "the active participation in the most holy mysteries and in the public and solemn prayer of the Church is the primary and indispensable source of the true Christian spirit." It is difficult to see how a person can have active participation in the Liturgy without taking part intelligently, that is, with understanding. And we will not fully achieve this unless the faithful understand the language spoken in Liturgy.

True, the faithful now have at their disposal missals which offer good translations of the words of the Mass. But why read what is spoken to you? This is an unnecessary duplication. An understandable vernacular suits better the original and present form of the Liturgy, for the Liturgy supposes *direct* communication and understanding between priest and people. It supposes active, vocal, congregational participation with understanding of the words *heard* and *spoken*.

Furthermore, one's mother tongue is the natural language of the soul and therefore the logical mode of expression for the soul's innermost spiritual sentiments. Rare is the man who uses Latin when he prays to God in private. The vernacular is capable of stirring the heart and mind (internal participation) more easily, more quickly, more deeply than Latin, even when both languages are known. And when Latin is not known (true for the majority of the faithful), it cannot stir at all. This principle is admitted and followed in the case of popular devotions; why not for the Liturgy also?

There are, of course, many objections against the vernacular. To use the vernacular, some say, might open the door to heresy. But we say, if the vernacular will do this, why do we teach catechism in the vernacular, why do we translate papal encyclicals into the vernacular? Whatever the layman knows of theology, moral, and Scripture, he has learned from being taught in his own language. The vernacular does not seem to harm doctrine in these cases. But we dare not translate our common prayers; we must say these prayers in Latin. Those opposed to the vernacular readily see the utility of vernacular missals for the people—they can read the Mass prayers from their missals. But the minute the priest would attempt to speak these translated words at the altar, heresy is knocking at the door.

Is it so hard to see that orthodoxy of faith does not depend so much on the language in which the doctrine is enshrined as on the personal knowledge and comprehension of that doctrine? Perhaps we are afraid to admit this because Pius XII, in his encyclical *Mediator Dei*,[52] said that Latin "is an effective antidote for any corruption of doctrinal truth." We should bear in mind, when interpreting this encyclical, that the Council of Trent rejected such an argument for Latin, precisely because of the danger of being misunderstood. It does not seem likely that the Pope would give as a reason for the retention

[52] Par. 60.

of Latin one which Trent expressly rejected. Certainly his words cannot refer to the mere speaking of the texts of the Mass or of other
parts of the Liturgy in the vernacular. Would it not be more appropriate to interpret the Holy Father's words in the sense that we should
keep Latin texts of the Liturgy, maintain them as the official version,
just as the official text of all doctrinal pronouncements is in Latin, and
that the orthodoxy of the vernacular translations should be judged on
the basis of their correspondence with the official Latin version? Otherwise the Pope's words would equally condemn the translations we
make of his encyclicals. A dead language, when maintained as the
official vehicle of the Church's teaching, will certainly help in safeguarding orthodoxy, but it will not protect the general faith of the
members unless they understand the language in which they are
taught.

Likewise the Council of Trent did away with the objection based
on the idea that there are "sacred languages." We need not go into
this again, except to point out that objectors should not interpret the
Church as holding views she has explicitly excluded as without foundation.

Latin is, as Pius XII states, a sign of unity. But again we must
not try to make him say more than he intended. Latin is a *sign* of
unity, not its *cause*—and even then it is a sign only for the Western
Church. Fundamentally, a deep comprehension of the faith will be
the ultimate cause of Church unity. A sign may help, but this can,
according to the principles of Trent, cede to other considerations,
such as the maturity of modern languages today, their nobility as
literary media, and the not unimportant fact that Latin is not really
universal any more.

The attempt of some to keep the Liturgy "mysterious" by means
of this dead language is entirely out of place. The early history of the
Church should dispel such a notion. Christianity is certainly based on
divine mysteries, but it is not mysterious about them. It teaches them,
explains them as far as possible, demands that its followers live them.
Such a notion as the "mysteriousness" of the Liturgy does violence to
the function of the Mass of the Catechumens, the whole purpose of
which is to instruct—not to hide.

Pius XII clearly admits the utility of the vernacular. "In spite of
this [that Latin is a sign of unity and a safeguard against error], the
use of the mother tongue in connection with many of the rites may be
of much advantage to the people. But the Apostolic See *alone* is empowered to grant this permission." [53] The import of this last sentence
is clearly shown in the many concessions granted by the Holy See.
Whenever the hierarchy of any given country is united in its appeal
for the vernacular, serious consideration is given the request and it
is sometimes granted.

[53] *Ibid.* Emphasis added.

A summary of such concessions on the part of the Holy See will prove this. Sts. Methodius and Cyril were permitted by Pope Hadrian II in 867 to celebrate the Liturgy in Old Slavonic. In 1947 permission was granted to the dioceses of France, and in 1950 to those of Germany, to use the vernacular for the rites connected with the administration of the sacraments—the sacramental forms and certain other prayers excepted. Like concessions were made to the missions in New Guinea, China, Japan, Indo-China, Indonesia, and Africa in 1941 and 1942. The bishops of Bavaria in 1929 and those of Austria in 1935 secured an unprecedented amount of the German language in the sacramental rites. The bishops of the United States obtained a similar permission in 1954. And now many other countries are taking steps to seek approval for vernacular rituals.

There are even some instances in which the Holy See has permitted the use of the vernacular in the Mass itself. The dioceses of Germany and Austria have had for a long time the faculty of having the faithful sing appropriate German hymns during High Mass instead of the Latin propers. The restored Easter Vigil allows the use of the vernacular for the renewal of baptismal promises. In 1949 permission was granted for China to employ Mandarin Chinese for the Mass, the Canon alone being excepted. And finally the dioceses of the Dutch East Indies obtained permission in 1954 to let the people sing the Ordinary chants of the Mass in their own language.

Thus we have shown that the decrees concerning the vernacular of the Council of Trent as well as of the popes are purely of a disciplinary character and not unchangeable. We have also seen how the attitude of the Holy See has become increasingly sympathetic to the use of the vernacular. If the Holy See has not yet seen fit to grant a more liberal use of the mother tongue in the Mass and other parts of the Liturgy, it is because the question is an extremely difficult one, its solution one of far-reaching consequences. Patience and understanding for those in authority is necessary, and, above all, respect and obedience.[54]

3. Music in worship

Just as it is natural for man to use speech in his worship of Almighty God, so is he naturally inclined to express the movements of his heart and soul in song. As St. James says in his Epistle, "Is anyone sad? Let him pray. Is anyone in good spirits? Let him sing a hymn" (5:13). How often do we not find ourselves humming or sing-

[54] For further arguments and history cf.: S. J. Gosling, "The Vernacular in the Liturgy," *Clergy Review*, 33 (1950), 361-375; Cyril Korolevsky, *Living Languages in Catholic Worship*, Westminster, Md., 1957; H. A. Reinhold, "The Vernacular in our Liturgy," *The Priest*, Feb., 1949; H. Schmidt, "The Problem of Language in Liturgy," *Worship*, 26 (1952), 276-292; C. M. Travers, *Valeur Sociale de la Liturgie*, Paris, 1946; *La Maison-Dieu*, n. 11 (1947), entitled: *Langues et Traductions Liturgiques*.

ing catchy tunes in our brighter moments? Tears express sorrow; joy
erupts into song. Man is simply made in such a way that happiness
and love—even sorrow at times—cannot be fully expressed except in
song.

There is an intimate relationship between word and music. The
spoken word is simply a noise which contains music, for every noise
has a certain pitch and intensity. A group of spoken words, the phrase
or sentence, adds the quality of rhythm, and with it inflection and
modulation of the voice become more apparent. A fine piece of oratory will show how language, even in its spoken form, is genuinely
musical.

But this symphony of sound reaches its zenith when it enters into
harmony with that sublime combination of thought and emotion,
prose and poetry, art and naïveté where all is song—even when not
spoken—for it is the expression of utmost completion, a many-stringed
instrument fingered by God: the soul at prayer. Prayer and music are
intimately connected. They are both animated by love. The soul in-
flamed with love of God cannot keep quiet, for, as St. Augustine says,
"It is a must for the lover to sing. The very voice of the singer is the
fervor of holy love." [55] Religious music, then, is but the life of prayer
taking its complete form of expression.

So strong were St. Augustine's convictions on this score, that,
despite his misgivings regarding certain abuses, he did not hesitate to
declare: "I feel that our souls are moved to the ardor of piety by the
sacred words more piously and more powerfully when they are sung
than when they are not. All the various affections of our soul have
modes of their own in chant and song by which they are stirred up as
by an indescribable and secret sympathy." [56] St. Thomas Aquinas
agrees with him in this and accepts it as the chief reason for the
Church's practice of using music in divine worship. He says: "It is
clear that the diverse melodies provoke different dispositions in the
human soul . . . And for this reason, it is opportune that we use chant
in divine praise, so that the souls of the weak be still more enkindled
to devotion." [57] It was this very chant that so moved St. Augustine
prior to his acceptance of the faith: "How I did weep in thy hymns
and canticles, touched to the quick by the sweet singing of the
Church. Those sounds flowed into my ears, and the truth streamed
into my heart; so that sentiments of piety overflowed, and the tears
ran from my eyes. And I was happy in them." [58]

This intimate marriage of music and prayer is also effective from
a social point of view. Music is pre-eminently the social art. After the
spoken word itself, it is the best agent of unity. In certain respects it is

[55] *Sermo* 336, 1. *MPL,* 38: 1472: "Cantare amantis est. Vox huius cantoris,
fervor est sancti amoris."
[56] *Confessions* X, 33. *MPL,* 32: 799-800.
[57] *Summa Theologica,* II-II, 91, 2.
[58] *Confessions* IX, 6. *MPL,* 32: 769.

even more effective than the merely spoken word. In singing the parts of the Mass, the faithful are forced to pay greater attention, using a means extremely well calculated to impress upon their minds the meaning and spirit of the words. In singing, the faithful not only speak together, but use melodies which arouse their souls to vibrate together, as it were. Providing them with a common interpretation of the words they utter, the chant brings about a marvellous fusion of their souls in the communal expression of the religious sentiments thus engendered.

In an inspired manner the true worshippers of God in the Old Testament spontaneously expressed their wonderment and gratitude in strains of song. Upon their victorious deliverance from the land of Egypt, the Chosen People sang a canticle to the Lord, while Mary, the sister of Moses and Aaron, accompanied their singing on her timbrel.[59] When the Jews recovered the Ark of the Covenant from the house of Abinadab, David and his people played before it with all sorts of instruments to express their joy.[60] And before his death David made certain prescriptions for the worship in the Temple, among which were those concerning the singers and musicians.[61]

The infant Christian Church continued the pràctice of singing in its worship, as the many exhortations of St. Paul prove. "When you come together each of you has a hymn." [62] And to the Ephesians he writes, "Be filled with the Spirit, speaking to one another in psalms and hymns and spiritual songs, singing and making melody in your hearts to the Lord."[63] It was substantially the same thing that he wrote to the Colossians. [64] Pliny indicates that this was true of the Christians with whom he came into contact: "Their greatest fault was that they were accustomed to gather before dawn on a certain day and sing a hymn to Christ as God." [65] And Eusebius says that the singing of psalms was a widespread custom.[66]

Many other early Christian writers offer evidence of the singing of the faithful. Tertullian says that in the gatherings of the Church the Scriptures are read, psalms are sung and sermons preached.[67] Cassian speaks of the night office as containing (in some localities) some twenty or thirty psalms which were prolonged by antiphonal singing and other melodies.[68] And this is in harmony with what St. Basil writes: "People go into church at night, and, divided into two

---

[59] Exod. 15: 1-20.
[60] 2 Kings 6:5.
[61] 1 Paralip. 25: 1-6.
[62] 1 Cor. 14: 26.
[63] 5: 18-19.
[64] 3: 16.
[65] *Epistularum liber* 10, 96. C. Kirch, *Enchiridion Fontium Historiae Ecclesiasticae Antiquae* (Barcelona, 1947), 30.
[66] *Historia ecclesiastica* 10, 3. *GCS,* 9(2), 860-862.
[67] *De anima* 9. *MPL,* 2: 701.
[68] *De inst. coen.* II, 2. *MPL,* 49: 78.

sections, they sing antiphonally, becoming masters of the Scriptural passages and at the same time directing their attention and the recollectedness of their hearts." [69]

Origin and history of Gregorian Chant

The evidence already brought forth clearly indicates that the Christian Church took over the singing of psalms from the Jewish synagogue. Not always, however, were they used as prayers or hymns; often they appear to have been employed by the early Church in much the same way that we use the historical and prophetic books of the Old Testament, as a reading in the Divine Office.[70] It also seems probable that the Church maintained the Jewish rules for cantillating lessons.[71] The same is true of early hymnody and the melismatic chants of the Christians. A third century "Hymn to the Holy Trinity," written by Greek-speaking Christians in Egypt, shows strong characteristics of Semitic melody construction.[72] Some melismatic melodies of the Alleluia (a word never translated from the Hebrew) were also derived from Hebrew music—a view borne out by the musical structure of the Alleluias in the Ambrosian rite.[73] And several other parallels between Hebrew and Christian music have been discovered, among them a *Kyrie* melody almost identical to a Babylonian Jewish Pentateuch melody.[74]

However, it was not exclusively the Jewish chant which influenced Christian music, for other examples have been found which indicate a Greek influence; for example, the melody for the *Hosanna filio David*, the music of which is the same as that found on the Greek epitaph of Seikilos.[75] The rarity of ancient melodies makes it almost impossible to determine which parentage was predominant. Certainly both influences were at work.

While responsorial singing [76] was taken over from the beginning because of its habitual use in the synagogue service, it was only later that antiphonal [77] singing was adopted, from the Temple service. We have already noted the mention made of this latter method of singing

[69] *Letters*, n. 207. *The Fathers of the Church*, 2 (New York, 1955), 83-84.
[70] Cf. Balthasar Fischer, *Die Psalmenfrömmigkeit der Märtyrerkirche* (Freiburg, 1949), 3.
[71] Cf. Egon Wellesz, "Early Christian Music," chapter 2 of *Early Medieval Music up to 1300*, vol. II of the New Oxford History of Music (New York, 1954), 1.
[72] *Ibid.*, 4-5.
[73] *Ibid.*, 5; cf. also Wellesz, *Eastern Elements in Western Chant* (Boston, 1947), 179-184.
[74] See G. Reese, *Music in the Middle Ages* (New York, 1940), 114.
[75] *Ibid.*, 115.
[76] In which a leader or precentor sings the first verse of a psalm, which the congregation repeats as a refrain as the precentor continues to sing the rest of the psalm.
[77] Alternate singing of choirs.

by St. Basil and Cassian.[78] It is generally agreed that antiphonal chant was introduced into the monasteries of Syria and Palestine at the beginning of the fourth century because of the influence of the Jewish communities in these regions, particularly those in Antioch.[79] From Palestine antiphonal chant passed to the West through the initiative of St. Ambrose of Milan and Pope St. Damasus.[80]

Ecclesiastical chant seems to have reached a point of high development long before the time of Gregory the Great. First of all, the frequent occurrence of the Itala version of the Bible in the Gregorian melodies seems to indicate this, for it does not seem likely that, after Pope St. Damasus had St. Jerome make the Vulgate translation, the older version would still continue to be used in composing liturgical texts—at least officially. Secondly, when the Gregorian melodies are compared with the Ambrosian ones, the latter exhibit a more ancient character. Indeed, many believe that the so-called Ambrosian chant was the common ecclesiastical music of Italy prior to Gregorian chant.[81] Egon Wellesz maintains that both Ambrosian and Gregorian chant, if not successive adaptations, are at least derivatives of a common stock, which he believes to have been the chant of the Church of Jerusalem.[82]

It has been an almost constant tradition that the liturgical chant in Rome took definitive form during the pontificate of Gregory the Great (590-604). Attacks on the tradition have come when Pierre Goussainville in 1675 and Georg von Eckhart in 1729 (and more recently A. Gevaert in 1890) questioned Gregory's part in the development of chant. Though it has never been proved that he himself composed any melodies or that he had even been a musician, sufficient evidence has been uncovered to warrant our adhesion to the old tradition. In view of all the well-founded scientific study of the parallelism among Gregorian, Ambrosian, Byzantine, and Hebrew music, there can be no question of claiming for Gregory a great (if any) degree of personal authorship of Gregorian chant. What foundation, then, is there for calling Roman chant Gregorian? What part did Gregory really play in its development?

Here is what historical evidence has to say. John the Deacon, ninth century biographer of Gregory, states that the latter collected

[78] The pilgrim Etheria also uses the expression *antiphonae,* but she does so in a context which makes it difficult to consider it the method we know: *Ethérie, Journal de Voyage* (Edit. Hélène Pétré, Paris, 1948), 24, 1 (p. 188), 3 (p. 190), 4 (p. 192). H. Leclercq seems correct in interpreting it as an independent piece of music: "Antienne," *DACL,* I: 2291-2292.

[79] Cf. Wellesz, "Early Christian Music," p. 6.

[80] Cf. Higini Anglès, "Gregorian Chant," chapter 4 of *Early Medieval Music up to 1300,* vol. II of the New Oxford History of Music, pp. 94-95. There are some authors, however, who claim that it was Pope St. Celestine I (422-432) who first introduced it in Rome: Reese, *op. cit.,* 106.

[81] Cf. Righetti, I, 556; Reese, 106-109; Anglès, 61, 69.

[82] *Eastern Elements in Western Chant,* 126.

material for an Antiphonary.[83] Egbert, bishop of York from 762-766, claimed that Gregory had sent to the English an Antiphonary and Missal.[84] And Bede the Venerable (d.735) describes Putta, bishop of Rochester from 669-676, as a man very skilled in the Roman manner of singing which he learned from disciples of Pope Gregory.[85] As can be seen, John's words are the clearest. According to them, Gregory made a compilation of already existing melodies. It is understood, of course, that he used the same organizing prudence which he exercised in compiling his Sacramentary. When we compare the existing Gregorian melodies with the allegedly more ancient Ambrosian ones, we must confess that he simplified the Ambrosian chant a great deal.

Also, according to John the Deacon, Gregory founded a school for chanters.[86] Despite the fact that many references can be adduced for the existence of groups of singers prior to the time of Gregory,[87] there is no documentary evidence that Gregory's institution was an outgrowth of some similar pre-existing school. His was a genuine original creation, according to John, intended to provide a sort of apprenticeship for the training of young boys to sing for liturgical functions.[88] This school of liturgical chant seems to have been put under the management of monks, and it acquired a well-founded reputation. Several popes came from the school. Bishops from various dioceses sent promising young clerics to it, that they might learn the Roman chant.[89] The school also sent skilled singers all over Europe to insure the propagation and exact rendition of the melodies collected by Gregory. We have seen that Bede spoke of Putta having been trained by disciples of Gregory. Later in the same work, Bede writes of John the Precentor of St. Peter's, who, while he sojourned in England, spent much of his time training young men to sing the liturgical chant.[90] The training afforded the students of this international Roman school of chant must have been altogether superb, for how else can we possibly account for the extraordinary uniformity and purity of Gregorian tradition all

[83] *Vita beati Gregorii* II, 6. *MPL*, 75: 90: "*Antiphonarium centonem, cantorum studiosissimus, nimis utiliter compilavit.*"

[84] *De institutione Catholica* xvi, 1-2. *MPL*, 89: 441. It may reasonably be doubted whether Augustine actually brought Gregory's books with him to England: cf. H. Ashworth, "Did St. Augustine bring the Gregorianum to England?" *Ephem. Lit.*, 72 (1958), 39-43; but it is certain that England did have Roman chant books by Egbert's time: cf. can. 13 of the Council of Cloveshoe in 747 (Hefele-Leclercq, *Histoire des Conciles*, III, 907), which commands the use of Roman books.

[85] *Historia Ecclesiastica* IV, 2. *MPL*, 95: 175.

[86] *Vita Greg.* II, 6. *MPL*, 75:90: "*Scholam quoque cantorum, quae hactenus eisdem institutionibus in sancta romana ecclesia modulatur, constituit.*"

[87] Cf. J. Quasten, *Musik und Gesang in den Kulten der Heidnischen und Christlichen Frühzeit* (Münster, 1930), 133-141.

[88] Cf. L. Duchesne, *Christian Worship*, 348-349; Enrico Josi, "Lectores—schola cantorum—clerici," *Ephem. Lit.*, 44 (1930), 282-290; H. Leclercq, "Schola," *DACL*, XV: 1008-1010.

[89] Letter of Paul I to Pepin, *MPL*, 89: 1187.

[90] *Op. cit.*, *MPL*, 95: 200.

over Europe, as found in the chant manuscripts made in such varied circumstances and times and by so many different people—especially given the fact that it was not until centuries later that any satisfactory method had been devised for indicating on paper the exact interval between the melodic notes. The melodies were all memorized.

True enough, even in the time of Gregory there must have been some type of notation. The oldest extant manuscripts date from the eighth century; the notation employed in them is already quite developed. It seems safe to assume that Gregory had at his disposal some sort of musical script, otherwise how could he have "collected" melodies, how could he have had these same melodies transcribed and sent to England?

But what kind of notation did he have, and how did it originate? The majority of musicologists are agreed that the Gregorian neums find their origin in the Latin and Greek oratorical accents: the acute (∕) and the grave (∖), which were used to indicate the subtle raising and lowering of the human voice in elocution.[91] It is from the various combinations of these two accents that we get our many Gregorian neums: *virga* (∕), *punctum* (∖), *clivis* (∧), *podatus* (∖∕), *porrectus* (∧∕), *torculus* (∖∧), *scandicus* (∖∖∕), and *climacus* (∧∖). These were essentially signs indicating an ascent or descent in the pitch of the voice. Reading from left to right, the acute accent would indicate a rise, while the grave would require a lowering of the voice. As such, they could not possibly indicate the interval between notes in the melody, but only the number of notes over a given syllable and the general direction which they were to take. The interval, or exact relationship of note to note, as has been mentioned, had to be memorized. Once the melody had been memorized, the sight of these strokes in their particular arrangement above a given context of words, the hand movements (cheironomy) of the director helping all the time, would bring back to mind the exact intervals in the melody without too much difficulty.[92] Such notation was written in either a straight or cursive manner as late as the thirteenth century. Only in the fourteenth and fifteenth centuries do the neums take on definitely their block-shape appearance with which we are familiar today.

Up until the eleventh century the neums were written "*in campo aperto,*" that is, in the open space above the words without lines of any sort to help the singer arrive at exact pitch. At that time the use of lines to determine the intervals between notes was suggested, according to Sunol,[93] by the common practice of employing a line to write the text evenly. At the beginning of the eleventh century we find the practice of using a red line to indicate *fa* and sometimes a yellow line for *do*. Guido d'Arezzo in about 1027 perfected this system

    [91] Cf. G. Sunol, *Introduction à la paléographie musicale grégorienne* (Paris, 1935), 23-28.
    [92] *Ibid.,* 37-45.
    [93] *Ibid.,* 58.

and used four lines. Thus, once Guido's system became generally adopted, there was no longer any difficulty in reading and preserving the Gregorian neums according to their tonality, or relative elevation.[94] This system is called "diastematic" notation, or one which indicates the intervals or relative pitch of notes by means of a stave, as opposed to the cheironomic, or "hand-movement" notation.

Strangely enough, it was at the very moment when musical knowledge had reached the stage in which it was able to express and hand on in definite written fashion the exact Gregorian melodies that liturgical chant began to decay. Though the growing popularity of the newly discovered harmony, leading eventually to the classic creations of polyphony, had something to do with this, it would be a mistake to lay the full blame at its door. The most basic cause of this decay is to be found in the spirit of the age, its very creativeness.

It is a natural human tendency to try to make divine worship as beautiful as possible. But sometimes this zeal is not prudently controlled. We have already seen that Pope St. Gregory's reform was basically one of pruning, of clearing away the excessive growth. And now once again, the desire to decorate gained the upper hand. Composers wrote tropes, sequences, and other verses (conductus and processional hymns) to make sure that there wasn't one empty space left in the liturgical action, that all the melismatic notes were provided with texts—whether this made sense or not. The melismatic chant itself became more involved and difficult. And it is hard to escape the impression that many a choir relished such pieces simply for the sake of showing off its virtuosity.

Obviously the more difficult a piece of music becomes, the fewer persons will there be who can execute it. Thus, as Gregorian chant became more florid, the people were reduced to silence during the solemn offices of the Church, and the number of choirs capable of singing the chant became all too scarce. This, of course, provided fertile ground for the development of harmonic singing and for anything new that might give the choir something to do, since it could no longer manage the Gregorian chant.

Finally, with the growing maturity of the Romance languages, we find travelling minstrels and troubadours in the late Middle Ages singing of the deeds of great men of the past and the loves of men of the present to popular and catchy tunes. This was no sudden development — the first name recorded in this connection was that of Guillaume of Aquitaine, Count of Poitiers (1071-1127), and later, Johannes de Grocheo (about 1300), a lecturer in Paris, wrote a treatise on the *Chansons de geste*.[95] The troubadours made their art felt in Spain too, but the religious hymn adopted their general style, and the

---

94 Cf. Reese, *op. cit.*, 138.
95 Cf. J. A. Westrup, "Medieval Song," *Early Medieval Music up to 1300*, 220-260.

magnificent collection of *Cantigas de Santa Maria* made by Alfonso X soon overshadowed them.[96] The religious vernacular hymn, called *laude spirituale*, was even more powerful in Italy, due, at least in part, to the impetuous outbreak of the popular religious movements characterized by the *flagellantes*. Though checked to a degree in Italy, these movements spread north of the Alps; in Germany fuel was added to the penitential fervor by the outbreak of the Black Death.[97] The result was the *Geisslerlieder* (flagellants' songs).

The Protestant reformers, as is well known, capitalized on the popular appeal of the vernacular hymn to spread their errors. The Catholics, in turn, had to use the same weapon (as once before the Church had done under Ambrose and Hilary) to make the Catholic doctrine palatable and known. With individualism and baroque emotionalism at large, many hymnodic compositions of the last centuries are of dubious spiritual quality. But the people had to be given something to take the place of the beautiful and authentically religious chant which once belonged to them in the liturgical services of the Church.

Trent had realized that something needed to be done but did not succeed in achieving anything. At about that time Pier Luigi da Palestrina had made a name for himself with his magnificent polyphonic pieces. Having been persuaded of the need for a reform, Gregory XIII entrusted Palestrina and Annibale Zoilo, composers for the papal chapel, with a radical correction of the Gregorian melodies according to the laws of the music of the time. Fortunately, Fernando de las Ynfantas, knowing something of Gregorian chant, protested this uncalled for mutilation of the traditional Gregorian and the work was suspended.[98] A little later, Raimondi, the director of the Medicean printing establishment, requested permission to publish a new edition of the *Graduale*. Paul V, in 1611, assigned Cardinal del Monte to oversee the work. To help the Cardinal, he chose Anerio and Soriano, two musicians who, though talented, knew little about the true spirit and nature of Gregorian chant. As a result, in 1614 there was given to the Christian world a book of utter arbitrariness, whose underlying principles were to suppress or transplant the neums until they uniformly corresponded to the quantity of syllables in the Latin text, and to eliminate entirely, or at least reduce to an absolute minimum, all the melismas, since they were nothing but a senseless redundance.[99] And such a monstrosity held sway as the official chant until Pius X in 1903 put an end to this unfortunate deformation.

It was Dom Guéranger, in 1860, who gave impetus to a scientific renovation of the original Gregorian chant when he charged two of his monks with this work: Dom Jaussions and Dom Pothier. In 1883

[96] *Ibid.*, 261.
[97] *Ibid.*, 266-267.
[98] Cf. Righetti, I, 573.
[99] *Ibid.*, 575, note 149.

Pothier published the first results of his labors with the *Liber Gradualis,* based on a painstaking investigation of all available manuscripts. Later there appeared the *Liber Antiphonarius.* Leo XIII publicly acknowledged the work of these French Benedictines in his Brief *Nos quidem* of May 17, 1901, and Pius X confirmed it in a *Motu proprio* of April 25, 1904; the latter gave to the Benedictines of Solesmes and other Gregorianists, under the presidency of Dom Pothier, the task of re-establishing the rest of the Church's ancient chants.[100]

With Pope Pius X we definitely come upon a turning point in the history of chant as well as Liturgy as a whole. He brought to the writing of his *Motu Proprio* on the Liturgy and Sacred Music all the pastoral experience and zeal of a priest who himself had undertaken to instruct his people in the Liturgy and to train his own choir boys. And he knew what a tremendous means for good it was in their spiritual lives. With deepest conviction he could write that "the primary and indispensable source of the true Christian spirit is the active participation of the faithful in the sacred mysteries and in the public and solemn prayer of the Church." And he made it clear once and for all that the singing of the people was an integral part of the sacred Liturgy: "musica sacra, utpote solemnis liturgiae pars necessaria. . . ."[101]

According to this pronouncement, Gregorian chant is to be considered the supreme model of Church music,[102] and its use by the people must be restored.[103] All sacred music must possess the qualities of holiness and goodness of form; it must be true art, and it must be universal. Polyphony, especially that of the school of Palestrina, is considered to enjoy these characteristics, because it approximates the ideal which is Gregorian Chant; it should therefore be restored in basilicas, cathedrals, seminary churches and other institutions where the necessary means of performing it are available.[104] Modern music too may be used, as long as it really possesses these same qualities.[105] It is noteworthy that the substance of this *Motu proprio* on Sacred Music is already to be found in the pastoral letter which Pius X wrote when still Patriarch of Venice in May of 1895.[106] This only serves to make it all the more clear that, as pope, he spoke from practical experience and genuine pastoral conviction.

Subsequent popes could do nothing more than reaffirm what Pius X had already said. Thus were added the voices of Pius XI in his Apostolic Constitution, *Divini Cultus,* December 20, 1928, and Pius XII in the encyclical *Mediator Dei,* November 20, 1947, and the encyclical *Musicae sacrae disciplina,* December 25, 1955. In the latter,

[100] *Acta Sanctae Sedis,* 36 (1903-1904), 586-589.
[101] *Tra le sollecitudini,* 5. *Documenta Pontificia ad Instaurationem Liturgicam Spectantia,* Edit. A. Bugnini (Rome, 1953), 13.
[102] *Ibid.,* 11. *Documenta,* 15.
[103] *Ibid.,* 13. *Documenta,* 16.
[104] *Ibid.,* 14. *Documenta,* 16.
[105] *Ibid.,* 15. *Documenta,* 16-17.
[106] *Documenta,* pp. 1-9.

Pius XII, while reiterating all the exhortations of his predecessors regarding the importance of having the faithful take an active part in the song of the Church, suggests that more attention be given to the quality of the vernacular hymn and that it be used more effectively.[107] He also approves the use of instruments other than the organ during liturgical services, particularly stringed instruments, so long as nothing strident or at variance with the sacred services is played.[108]

According to the spirit of these papal pronouncements, then, we should take care to afford the faithful the opportunity of singing the Ordinary chants of the Mass. The faithful, however, cannot possibly sing polyphonic or four-part renditions of these chants. Therefore, Gregorian chant, or simple modern music intended for unison singing, should be used exclusively for these parts of the Mass. Extraordinary occasions may motivate the desire to use a polyphonic arrangement of the Ordinary of the Mass. But this should not be done too frequently; the people, who are not yet prepared to sing the Ordinary, must hear it sung often to simple melodies or they will never learn to do it themselves.

There are even some parts of the Proper chants of the Mass which have traditionally allowed for the participation of the faithful: the Gloria Patri of the Introit, the Alleluias after the Epistle, as well as a suitable psalm sung on an easy psalm tone as a Communion processional, after the Communion antiphon. The same thing may be done at the Offertory.

Care should be taken to preserve the function of the different chants: the Introit as an entrance hymn, begun as soon as the clerical procession leaves the sacristy; the Sanctus and Benedictus sung together, without a break, and as the people's acclamation at the end of the Preface; the Communion antiphon as a genuine Communion processional. A good exhilarating vernacular hymn at the end of Mass helps the faithful carry over into the world the sentiments of adoration, praise, gratitude, and spiritual joy engendered during the Mass.

Finally, music must not be allowed to take over the Liturgy; it exists to help the Liturgy. The people should be permitted a little breather now and then; they need not be always singing. Nor should the person directing them act in a theatrical manner, thus violating the sacred character of the place and circumstances.

4. Liturgical formulas

What Guardini has to say about the Mass is also true of the entire Liturgy. "Holy Mass is an act; it is not, however, enacted mutely, but combines doing and speaking. It includes several varieties of words, and it is helpful not only to our understanding but also to our effective participation in the liturgy to realize this multiplicity and

---

[107] Par. 63 (NCWC Edition).
[108] *Ibid.*, 59.

learn to distinguish between the different kinds of words employed."[109]
Time and usage have consecrated certain liturgical formulas in both
meaning and function, and the Church employs a variety of them—
obviously not all in the same way. To gain, therefore, an appreciation
of the whole liturgical mosaic, we need to see all the precious stones
in their right perspective.

Our purpose here, however, is not to discuss each text and formula used in the sacred Liturgy, but rather to consider a few of the
main, recurring combinations of words, with an eye to appreciating
their function. Other specific texts will be taken up in their proper
place in the Mass, Divine Office, sacraments and sacramentals.

Prayer of the People

All the formulas of the Liturgy can be divided into three classes:
(a) those which belong to the people or their voice, the choir, (b)
those read or sung by the minor ministers specially deputed for this
task, and (c) those said by the head of the liturgical assembly, the
priest. In general, the prayer of the people can be said to be acclamatory in character. An acclamation, in the strict sense of the word, is a
short cry protesting good wishes, approval, consent, praise, greeting,
faith, and even petition.[110] In the broad sense, we can also call acclamations all formulas which in a standardized, brief, and repetitious
manner express a religious sentiment.[111] There are other formulas
which, though longer, still have this acclamatory quality, since they
are mere concatenations of briefer acclamations. For this reason, therefore, we group all the prayers of the people under this category; the
title "acclamation" aptly epitomizes the character of their prayers:
they greet (Christ or His ministers), they respond, they protest their
faith, praise and consent.

The Church did not invent this method of prayer. Acclamations
similar to the Church's are to be found in the cults of all ancient
peoples. For the most part, however, the Church was never satisfied
simply to accept them as they were; she usually adapted them to the
needs of popular participation in the sacred mysteries. A great many
of them came from the Old Testament Liturgy; some of them have
not even been translated from the Hebrew.

Laudes

A form of acclamation already in use among the pagans of ancient
Rome for purely civil and festive occasions, the laudes were shouts
of joy or applause. Sometimes they were spontaneous, sometimes well

---

[109] *Meditations before Mass*, 65.
[110] Cf. Righetti, I, 172; Oppenheim, *Tractatus de Textibus Liturgicis* (Rome,
1945), 25; Lechner-Eisenhofer, 64.
[111] Lechner-Eisenhofer, *loc. cit.*

organized, rehearsed, and modulated. For example, to acclaim the Emperor, the following were used: "Auguste Claudi, dii te nobis praestent [dictum sexagies]; vivas, floreas, valeas, vincas, multis annis imperes."[112] The same was true of weddings ("Io Hymen!"), for triumphal processions (Io Triumphe!), and pleasing speeches ("Belle et festive! Belle et praeclare!") in theatres and in the circus.[113] The Christians continued this custom for papal elections ("Dignus est!"), for Councils, the consecration of bishops, the crowning of Kings. We still have a remnant of the practice in the Roman Pontifical, when during the consecration of a bishop, the newly consecrated prelate is directed to genuflect three times on the predella of the altar towards his consecrator and sing "Ad multos annos!" Another instance is the singing of the "Ecce sacerdos Magnus" for the reception of the bishop at the door of the church.[114]

Et cum spiritu tuo

With the Dominus vobiscum and its reply, we come to one of the most important acclamations in our present day Liturgy. "Dominus vobiscum" is a greeting which harks back to pre-Christian times. Booz greets his reapers with it.[115] The reply, "et cum spiritu tuo," is at least paralleled by St. Paul, when he uses it as a conclusion to several of his Epistles.[116] Its adoption by the Church as a greeting in her Liturgy is attested to already in the earliest anaphoras. It always precedes the strictly sacerdotal prayer and is meant as a sign of union between the celebrant and the congregation. It is intended to attract the attention of the faithful and to bind them spiritually to the prayer which follows. This is no ordinary greeting:

> It is stamped through and through with the spirit of the communal action for which priest and people have assembled. Union with Him who said: "Where two or three are gathered in my name, there am I in the midst of them"— is what the priest wishes the faithful. . . . The faithful wish the celebrant the same union with Christ, but notice the fine nuance in the formulation of their reply. They do not, as we might expect, answer: 'And with you too;' they say rather: 'And with thy spirit.' [117] For centuries more than just a mere Semitism has been understood here. It is a recognition of that special indwelling or possession by the Holy Ghost which takes place through the imposition of hands and the prayer of the bishop,

---

112 F. Cabrol, "Acclamations," *DACL*, I, 240.

113 Cf. Righetti, I, 170.

114 For other examples see H. Leclercq, "Laudes Gallicanae," *DACL*, VIII, 1898-1910; J. Hanssens, "De laudibus Carolinis," *Periodica* 30 (1941), 280-302.

115 Ruth 2:4; it is often met with in other places: Judges 6:12; 2 Paralip. 15:2; Luke 1:28; 2 Thess. 3:16.

116 2 Tim. 4:22; Philemon 25; Gal. 6:18; Philip. 4:23.

117 Jungmann says that this is but a Semitism. *Spiritus tuus* means your person, you: *Mass of the Roman Rite*, I 363.

in other words, through the sacrament of Holy Orders. Only one who has received at least the diaconate can use the greeting *Dominus vobiscum* and be answered *et cum spiritu tuo*. There is obviously a difference in whether I wish a baptized or an ordained person union with Christ. Their mystical representation of Christ is always connoted.[118]

Certainly St. John Chrysostom understands the word "spirit" as referring to the spirit given in Holy Orders.[119] So the Church does not use the expression as a Semitism. As an objectively efficacious prayer of the Church, this liturgical greeting obtains for both priest and people the fruitful union with Christ in the solemn oration which follows. United to Christ and to one another, priest and people act as a unit in worshipping the Father in Christ's name.

Amen

This is not simply a formalistic, regularly recurring conclusion to the liturgical prayers. Though not going so far as Protestants who claim that it is the most important word of the entire Liturgy, it is emphatically true that the Amen is the most important word which the faithful speak in divine worship. A Hebrew word, actually translated in only a few modern languages, it was consistently used in Jewish worship, and its importance can be gathered from the words of St. Paul: "If thou givest praise with the spirit alone [in a language not understood by others], how shall he who fills the place of the uninstructed say 'Amen' to thy thanksgiving? For he does not know what thou sayest."[120] In the Rome of his day, says St. Jerome, the Amen resounded like a peal of heavenly thunder and shook the empty pagan temples.[121] St. Augustine also speaks of the Amen and indicates its meaning: "By answering Amen, you consent" to what has been said.[122] Its original Hebrew sense was "certainly," "truly." It signified agreement to a statement regarded as true. In worship it is used to manifest assent to what is said in prayer. When used in private prayer, when we answer ourselves, it has an intensifying sense: "Amen, I mean it!" Certainly, therefore, in liturgical prayer it indicates that the faithful are one with their priest in praising God or in begging some favor of Him.

St. Justin describes its place in the Mass of his day: "When he [the celebrant] has finished the prayers and thanksgiving, the whole congregation stands by and cries out in agreement: 'Amen.' In Hebrew

---

[118] Balthasar Fischer, "Zu den Akklamationen bei der Eucharistiefeier," *Liturgisches Jahrbuch*, 5 (1955), 17-18.

[119] *Sermo in die Pentecostes*, n. 4. *MPG*, 50: 458, ff.

[120] 1 Cor. 14:16.

[121] *In epist. ad Galat*. II, praef. *MPL*, 26:381.

[122] "Amen respondetis, et respondendo subscribitis," *Sermo* 272. *MPL*, 38: 1247.

it means 'So be it.'" [123] This particular Amen at the end of the Canon of the Mass is by far the most important of all, for it is the expression of the people's consent to the principal priestly prayer. If there is one moment during the liturgical celebration at which we wish the faithful to be active, attentive, spiritually cooperating, it is here at the *Actio*, the most sacred act of the entire Liturgy from which all else flows, the solemn Eucharistic prayer of thanksgiving.

So solicitous was the Church during the Middle Ages that the people use this opportunity of making their own the sentiments of this great prayer, that the final words of the Canon were not included in the silence which gradually came to prevail during the rest of its length.[124] Even today the concluding "per omnia saecula saeculorum" is said or sung aloud (often giving, it is true, the mistaken idea that it is an introduction to the Pater). In many of the Oriental Rites, where the silent Canon has also made inroads, the audible part starts at the beginning of the final doxology and is called the *ecphonesis* (something said aloud), so that the people will know what they are answering Amen to.[125]

It is to be hoped, then, that pastors will teach the people the true meaning of this response and its importance, so that, far from being a mere lame and feeble rhetorical ending, it will become a bright and fresh cry, the expression of an assent that comes from the heart, a deep and heartfelt association and participation in the sacred action.[126]

Deo gratias

A concept familiar already to the Jews,[127] and basic to the Passover theme, thanksgiving is perhaps mentioned more often in the New Testament than any other type of prayer.[128] The idea of thanksgiving became so much a part of the life of early Christians that they used a "Deo gratias" to greet one another. In some instances, the phrase was even a mark of orthodoxy, as in the Donatist controversy when Christians would shout "Deo gratias!" while the Donatists shouted "Deo laudes!"[129] Sometimes the martyrs shouted it repeatedly as a pledge of their fidelity to Christ.[130] It was even employed by the faithful to signify that they had heard and understood the various

---

[123] I *Apology* 65. J. Quasten, *Monumenta*, 17.
[124] Cf. J. Jungmann, *The Mass of the Roman Rite*, II, 273.
[125] Cf. F. E. Brightman, *Liturgies Eastern and Western* (Oxford, 1896), I, 337 for Byzantine Rite, 134, 179-180 for Coptic, 96 for Syrian.
[126] Cf. Fischer, "Zu den Akklamationen," 17.
[127] Tobias 2:14; 11:17.
[128] Matt. 15:36; 26:27; Mark 8:6; Luke 17:16; 18:11; John 6:11, 23; 11:41; Acts 27:35; 28:15; Rom. 6:17; 14:6; Philip. 1:3; Col. 1:3, 12; 3:17; 1 Tim. 1:12; 2:1; Apoc. 11:17; etc.
[129] H. Leclercq, "Deo Gratias, Deo Laudes," *DACL*, IV, 652.
[130] *Ibid.*

announcements made during the liturgical ceremonies.[131] This latter practice gives us a clue to the understanding of its use in the Mass after the Epistle and Ite missa est. Certainly it is fitting to thank God for the chance to hear His word, but this does not seem to be the function of the phrase in the Mass. The frequency with which it was employed as a mere signal in the early centuries of the Christian era leads Jungmann to interpret it in this way when it is used in the Mass and the Divine Office.[132] Fischer insists, however, that the Deo gratias after the dismissal takes on grander proportions and repeats the theme of the whole celebration—thanksgiving—as the faithful are about to pass over the threshold of the church into their different walks of life; it becomes a final cry of dedication in joy and thanksgiving.[133]

Gloria tibi Domine—Laus tibi Christe

It is somewhat peculiar that at the beginning of the Gospel the people should give forth with an acclamation and interrupt its singing. This does not happen in the Divine Office or, in the Mass, even for the reading of the Epistle. The ancient Roman Liturgy would not have done it.[134] We have here a feature which is assuredly non-Roman. The earliest mention of this response appears in a Gallican Ordo for Holy Week dating from the beginning of the ninth century.[135] The critical text of the first Roman Ordo, edited by Michel Andrieu, does not even have the Dominus vobiscum precede the Gospel.[136] The acclamation originates with the Gallican Mass of the seventh century.[137]

The fact that the Laus tibi Christe is not sung by the choir but merely spoken by the acolyte indicates a relatively recent origin, also Gallican.[138] Both acclamations must therefore be interpreted according to the spirit of the times in which they originated. Christ Himself speaks in the Gospel. With these responses the faithful show their faith and veneration for the Savior, ever present and active in His sacred word.

Alleluia

This is another word of obvious Jewish origin. It is composed of two Hebrew words: *Hallelu* (praise ye) and *Yah* (an abbreviation of

---

[131] F. Cabrol, "Deo gratias," *DACL*, IV, 651.
[132] *The Mass of the Roman Rite*, I, 421.
[133] "Zu den Akklamationen," 20.
[134] *Ibid.*, 18.
[135] *Ordo* XXVIII, n. 3. Andrieu, *Les Ordines*, III, 391. A similar phrase is found in the *Historia Francorum* of Gregory of Tours: viii, 4. *MPL*, 71:451: "*Gloria Deo omnipotenti.*"
[136] *Ordo Romanus* I, n. 62. Andrieu, *Les Ordines*, II, 89.
[137] J. Jungmann, *The Mass of the Roman Rite*, I, 447, note 34. Cf. *MPL*, 72: 91.
[138] *Ibid.*, note 35.

Yahwe, God). Most of the time these two words are contracted in this manner to form Alleluia, a sort of liturgical acclamation.[139] In all instances in which it is reported in the Old Testament, it appears as a joyful and triumphant acclamation. It is for this reason that, like the Amen, it is seldom translated either in versions of the Bible or in Christian liturgical practice. The psalms which contain the Alleluia all belong to the fifth book of the Psalter, which is considered to have been intended in particular for use in the Temple liturgy. And here the Alleluia is not an integral part of the psalm text, but appears at the beginning or end, giving the impression that it was used either as an antiphon or as a constantly recurring refrain shouted by the people. One group of these psalms is called the Hallel psalms and was sung on the great feasts of the Passover, Pentecost, Tabernacles and others.[140] The fact that the Holy Eucharist was instituted and first celebrated during the Jewish Passover meal, which was concluded with the last part of the Hallel (Ps. 135), indicates one point of concrete Jewish influence on the Christian use of the Alleluia. The only text in the New Testament which speaks of the Alleluia is a passage in the Apocalypse of St. John.[141] And here again it is used as a triumphant refrain or acclamation in direct connection with the nuptials of the Lamb—a fulfillment of the Hebrew Passover meal.

Though references to the use of the Alleluia in the early fathers are rare, we do fiind a few. Tertullian tells us that the Christians used it as a refrain to orations and the regular Alleluia psalms.[142] It was also used as a refrain in a fourth century papyrus.[143] And St. Augustine informs us that the Alleluia is a song of joy and praise.[144] In his day it was sung everywhere during Paschal time, but some places followed the custom of also singing it every Sunday; in other places it was sung at different times.[145] Unfortunately, Augustine does not indicate exactly when it was sung during the liturgical services.

From early times the Alleluia was sung independently of any texts and with a great variety of melismas; out of these the Sequence later developed as an attempt to furnish the rich melodies with words. The Alleluia was also used at the end of different parts of the Liturgy, notably the antiphons, as a special mark of joy during Paschal time; its frequent repetitions celebrated in an almost unrestrained outburst of triumphant jubilation the victory of the Lamb over sin and death. This same attitude was particularly apparent in the early Church's

---

[139] Cf. F. Cabrol, "Alleluia—Acclamation liturgique," *DACL*, I, 1230.

[140] Pss. 112-117, 135. A reference to this last psalm, which concluded the Hallel, is probably meant in Matt. 26:30, "And after reciting a hymn, they went out to Mount Olivet."

[141] 19: 1-7.

[142] "Subjungere in orationibus alleluia solent, et hoc genus psalmos quorum clausulis respondeant qui simul sunt." *De oratione* 27. *MPL*, 1:1301.

[143] Cf. Cabrol, *art. cit.*, 1232.

[144] *Sermo* 254, 4. *MPL*, 38: 1184.

[145] *Epist.* 55, cc. 15 and 17. *MPL*, 33: 218, 220.

manner of burying the dead. Up until the fifth century, her loved ones were laid to rest amid the chant of alleluias,[146] so joyfully confident was she that her Savior's resurrection would some day become operative for her children too.

Kyrie

The Kyrie eleison was known as an acclamation in heathen cults as well as in the honors paid to civil rulers, especially great conquerors.[147] It was of widespread use in the Jewish religion also, mostly in the psalms,[148] but also in other books of the Old Testament.[149] It is frequently to be found in the New Testament too.[150] None of these latter cases, it is true, present the same verbal construction as our Kyrie, but as Jungmann points out,[151] the divergence was not so great as to prevent the transition to the Kyrie eleison.

The first document attesting to the Kyrie's use in Christian worship is the *Apostolic Constitutions*. There we read that after the sermon the deacon began the various prayers for the different categories of catechumens and faithful. After each petition spoken by the deacon, the faithful were to reply "Kyrie eleison." [152] Since modern scholars are agreed that the *Apostolic Constitutions*, at least in its eighth book, evolved from the Roman third century *Apostolic Tradition*,[153] it is quite possible that the Kyrie was used at the earlier time in the same way. This same diaconal litany is reported in the second century *Apology* of Justin, but he fails to say exactly how it was recited,[154] and whether or not the Kyrie was a part of it. A modified form of this litany is reported by Etheria in the fourth century for Jerusalem, where the deacon read a list of names after each of which a group of boys shouted "Kyrie eleison!" She adds that in her own country, northern Spain or southern France, "miserere Domine" was said instead.[155]

From these early documentary references, we see that the original function of the Kyrie was that of an acclamation made by the people, or by the choir in their stead, to the various intentions or petitions read out by priest or deacon.[156] This is what is called a litany;

[146] Cf. Jerome, *Epist.* 77, 11. *MPL*, 22: 697.
[147] Cf. F-J. Dölger, *Sol Salutis. Gebet und Gesang im christlichen Altertum* (Münster, 1925), 60-103; see especially 75-77.
[148] E.g.: 4, 2; 6, 3; 9, 14; 25, 11, etc.
[149] Tobias and Isaias.
[150] Mark 9:27; 15:22; Matt. 20:30, etc.
[151] *The Mass of the Roman Rite*, I 334.
[152] 8, 6, 4. J. Quasten, *Monumenta*, 199, 200, 205.
[153] Cf. J. Quasten, *Patrology*, I, 184.
[154] 65. J. Quasten, *Monumenta*, 16.
[155] *Ethérie, Journal de Voyage*, Edit. Hélène Pétré, 24, 5-6, p. 192.
[156] It seems that "Amen" originally supplied this function: cf. Anton Baumstark, *Liturgie Comparée* (Chevetogne, 1953), p. 51, for the practice among the Jews; cf. Brightman, *op. cit.*, 198-201 for its use in the ancient Nestorian Liturgy.

it is nothing else than a special type of intercessory prayer consisting of a list of petitions for various categories of people and for different intentions. After each petition or intention is read, the people make a response using some standardized phrase. The solemn orations on Good Friday are a vestige of such an ancient litany, in this case without the Kyrie, recited at the beginning of the Mass of the Faithful. Such orations at this point of the Mass were called the *Oratio Fidelium, Communis Oratio,* the general prayer of the Church, and, by the Greeks, *ektene* or *synapte.* Apparently this type of prayer underwent a change in the Roman Mass during the fifth century. An abbreviated type then appears, but this time at the beginning of the Mass, called the *Deprecatio Gelasii,*[157] much like the final part of our modern Litany of the Saints, and here again the Kyrie appears as the people's response. And in the time of Gregory the Great, another change takes place. While some sort of a litany as that of Gelasius was still recited on occasion, the normal daily Mass saw the use of only Kyrie eleison and Christe eleison without the litanic petitions.[158]

It is precisely from this ancient Oratio Fidelium that we get our modern litanies, an essential part of which is the Kyrie, but now more as an introduction rather than a response recurring throughout the prayer. So much was the Kyrie a part of this litanic prayer, that St. Benedict considers the terms interchangeable.[159] In time this litanic type of prayer became the main feature of processions, and a strictly Western feature.[160] And on Rogation Days, and other stational days, since the litany was sung in procession, it was customary to omit the singing of the Kyrie after the Introit.[161]

Another development of this litanic prayer with the Kyrie is its use as *Preces* in the Divine Office.[162] St. Benedict had already ordered his monks to say the litany at the end of certain hours of the Office.[163] And the second Council of Vaison, held in 529, observing that the Kyrie was a venerable custom introduced in Rome, Italy, and the Orient, commanded its recitation at Matins, Vespers, and during Mass.[164]

[157] See text in Jungmann, *The Mass of the Roman Rite,* I, 336-337.

[158] Gregory, *Epist. ad Joannem Syracusanum,* 9, 12. *MPL,* 77, 956: "apud nos a clericis dicitur et a populo respondetur. . . . In cotidianis autem missis aliqua, quae dici solent, tacemus, tantummodo Kyrie eleison et Christe eleison dicimus. . . ."

[159] *Regula,* c. 9. *MPL,* 66, 424.

[160] Baumstark, *op. cit.,* 84.

[161] *Ordo Romanus* XXI, n. 18. Andrieu, *Les Ordines,* III, 249.

[162] For general history, see S. Bäumer, *Histoire du Bréviaire* (Paris, 1905), II, 429-441; for recommendations for reform, see Balt. Fischer, "Litania ad Laudes et Vesperas. Ein Vorschlag zur Neugestaltung der Ferialpreces in Laudes und Vesper des Römischen Brevier," *Liturgisches Jahrbuch,* 1 (1951), 55-74.

[163] *Regula,* c. 9 and 17. *MPL,* 66: 424, 460, 459.

[164] Hefele-Leclercq, *Histoire des Conciles,* II, 1113-1114. With this early evidence of Benedict and the Council of Vaison, it is hard to believe Edmund Bishop when he says that Gregory the Great was the first to introduce the Kyrie in the Roman Rite: *Liturgica Historica,* 134-135.

Except for its part in the litanic *preces* in the Divine Office, the Kyrie has the role of an opening rite, more particularly in the Mass as the beginning of the solemn oration in which the priest speaks to God on behalf of the entire liturgical assembly. Thus, it still retains the characteristics of an acclamation shouted by the people in praise of their Lord and King, the glorious and triumphant conqueror, Whose favor and blessing they beseech.[165]

Sanctus

Unquestionably the Sanctus comes from the vision of Isaias [166] in which he beheld the Lord sitting upon a throne surrounded by seraphim who cried out to one another: "Holy, holy, holy, the Lord God of hosts, all the earth is full of his glory." The threefold repetition of "holy" indicates the superlative holiness of God.[167] Sometimes in Christian use the repetition was given a Trinitarian significance.[168] The word "sabaoth" as used in our liturgical text means the armies of angels and all beings which God made in the six days of creation.[169] As for its use in the Liturgy, St. Clement of Rome says that the Christians of his day sang this hymn in common,[170] but this does not necessarily mean that it was part of the Liturgy.[171] The first clear-cut witness to its liturgical use comes to us in the third century Liturgy of the *Papyrus Dêr Balyzeh* [172] and in the fourth century *Euchologion* of Serapion of Thmuis.[173] And in the *Apostolic Constitutions* from the last decade of the fourth century we are told that the people sang the Sanctus: "et omnis populus simul dicat: Sanctus, etc." [174] The Benedictus is also found in the *Apostolic Constitutions* but as a response before Communion to the Sancta sanctis.[175] While the *Ordo Romanus* I does not mention the Benedictus as being sung together with the Sanctus (this is not to be wondered at, for it rarely gives the complete text of formulas),[176] it was certainly joined in the Roman Mass to the

---

[165] Cf. T. Schnitzler, "Zu den Volksgesängen bei der Eucharistiefeier," *Liturgisches Jahrbuch*, 5 (1955), 22.

[166] Is. 6:1-3.

[167] *The Catholic Commentary on Holy Scripture* (London—New York, 1953), p. 545, 425 L.

[168] Cf. Jungmann, *The Mass of the Roman Rite*, II, 134, note 28.

[169] *Ibid.*, 134.

[170] After quoting the song of the seraphim, Clement adds: "Et nos ergo conscientia ducti, in concordia in unum congregati, tamquam ex uno ore ad ipsum continuo clamemus, ut magnarum et gloriosarum promissionum eius participes fiamus," *Epist. ad Corinthios*, c. 34. J. Quasten, *Monumenta*, 330.

[171] Cf. Jungmann, *The Mass of the Roman Rite*, II, 132, note 24.

[172] J. Quasten, *Monumenta*, 41.

[173] *Ibid.*, 61.

[174] 8, 12, 27. J. Quasten, *Monumenta*, 220.

[175] 8, 13, 13. *Ibid.*, 230.

[176] N. 87. Andrieu, *Les Ordines*, II, 95.

Sanctus as one canticle by the seventh century, for most of the early manuscripts contain it.[177]

By singing the Sanctus the faithful take their place at the very heart of the solemn Eucharistic prayer, joining with the celebrant to praise and thank the divine Majesty, welcoming His coming at the moment of consecration. The participation, active and vocal, of the laity is not restricted to the reading service of the Mass, but is exercised in the Mass of Sacrifice, in that, with lifted heart and mind, the faithful break out in song at the very core of the Eucharistic service. At the same time, the faithful should be conscious of their tremendous dignity: they should realize that in singing the Sanctus they already begin to share in their heavenly vocation—taking the place of the fallen angels and singing God's glory together with the seraphim and cherubim and the entire celestial court. Indeed, as God's holy people, they already have heaven on earth, for something far greater happens at the altar than happened to Isaias. He saw a vision; the faithful have God in their midst once those powerful words of consecration are spoken. Is that not heaven on earth, God present sacramentally in the "mystery" of the Church?[178]

Agnus Dei

The threefold repetition of the "Agnus Dei" together with the conclusion, "miserere nobis," constitutes a sort of litany based, obviously, on the testimony given by John the Baptist to his disciples regarding Christ: "Behold the Lamb of God, who takes away the sin of the world!",[179] as well as on the vision in the Apocalypse of the Lamb seated on the throne.[180] Both of these, in turn, have as their point of departure the divinely instituted Jewish rite of slaying and consuming the Paschal lamb.[181] The use of the Agnus Dei in the Liturgy is of Eastern origin; parallel elements can be found there as early as the sixth century.[182] It was a pope of Syrian origin who introduced it into the Roman Mass. The *Liber Pontificalis* tells us that Pope Sergius I (687-701) decided that the chant of the Agnus Dei should be sung by clergy and people to accompany the breaking of the leavened bread for distribution in Communion.[183] Its use in the same way in the Roman Mass is first attested to in the *Ordo Romanus* I.[184] Originally the chant was repeated for as long as it took to complete the confraction; when the latter fell into disuse (about the ninth

---

[177] See the apparatus in B. Botte, *Le Canon de la Messe Romaine* (Louvain, 1935), 30, note II, 17.

[178] Cf. T. Schnitzler, *art. cit.*, 33-34.

[179] John 1: 29.

[180] 5: 6 ff.

[181] Exod. 12.

[182] Cf. Jungmann, *The Mass of the Roman Rite*, II, 301, 334; for its use in the modern Byzantine Liturgy see Brightman, *op. cit.*, 15, 357.

[183] Ed. L. Duchesne, I, 376. Cf. M. Andrieu, *Les Ordines*, II, 48.

[184] N. 105. Andrieu, *Les Ordines*, II, 101.

century), the repetition was limited to three times and the chant began to occupy other positions in the Mass. In some places it was employed to accompany the kiss of peace (by the ninth century), and this occasioned the change in the conclusion of the third repetition from "miserere nobis" to "dona nobis pacem" (twelfth century). For Masses of the dead, of course, it was used as a prayer for eternal rest (eleventh century).[185] Today the Agnus Dei is also used as a conclusion to all our modern litanies.

Following John the Baptist, the Christian people salute their Savior, their Paschal Lamb, present in the Sacrament. Having re-enkindled in their hearts the joy and thanksgiving that come from the memory, sacramentally re-enacted before them, of the Paschal Victim ("Victimae Paschali laudes!"), who by dying overcame their death and by rising restored once again their life (Preface for Easter), they approach the Holy Table to consummate the renewal of life through union with the resurrected Christ.

Psalms

Every book of the Bible has its special purpose and value. The Book of Psalms is above all a book of sung prayer. It was used as such by the Jews and, in time, also by Christians. The word *psalm* comes from the Greek ψαλλειν, meaning to sing a hymn to the accompaniment of a stringed instrument. The Psalter, or book of psalms, contains 150 compositions which were originally thought to be the exclusive work of David but now, due to closer study of the text, are seen to be the handiwork of different writers (principally of David, however) of various periods and brought together for liturgical and musical reasons into one collection.[186] It is practically certain that the period of composition extended over some six or seven hundred years—from the time of David (about 1,000 B.C.) to some date in the post-exilic era (after 538 B.C., the first return of the exiles from Babylon).

Until the second century, the Psalter was used in Christian worship not as a prayer book, but for reading, because of its prophetic character which was acknowledged by the New Testament writers and the later apologists. It was principally because of the misuse of original hymnodic compositions in the hands of Gnostics and other heretics that the Church turned to the Psalter as a song book.[187] The psalms began to be used in ever greater measure, whether in whole, as hymns of praise, or in part, as versicles and responses of one type or another.

[185] Cf. Jungmann, *op. cit.*, II, 337-339.
[186] Decree of the Pontifical Biblical Commission, May 1, 1910. *Rome and the Study of Scripture* (St. Meinrad, Indiana, 1946), 115-117.
[187] Cf. Balthasar Fischer, *Die Psalmenfrömmigkeit der Märtyrerkirche* (Freiburg, 1949), 3; *idem*, "Christ in the Psalms," *Theology Digest* 1 (Winter, 1953), 53.

Their importance grew to such a degree that there were ecclesiastical synods which attempted to make their use exclusive.[188]

According to the manner in which the psalms are sung in the Liturgy, they too have an acclamatory character. This is especially true of those parts of psalms used as versicles and responses and those used for the processionals: Introit, Offertory, and Communion. Though the psalms used for Graduals, Tracts, and Responsories of the Divine Office are more meditative in character, they are still acclamatory by reason of the refrain by which the people, or at least the choir, answer the smaller group of chanters. Even the recitation of whole psalms in the Divine Office, though strictly speaking not acclamatory, may be called such *reductively*—by reason of the way they are chanted: antiphonally, or responsorially. It should be remarked that the short versicles taken from psalms have as their purpose to introduce or begin a liturgical service, or to form a transitional link between the various parts of any given service. In either case, they also serve to draw the attention of those assisting to a stirring religious thought and to enliven their devotion; e.g.: "Deus in adjutorium meum intende" from Ps. 69, 2 (God's special assistance for a worthy recitation of the Hours), "Adjutorium nostrum in nomine Domini" from Ps. 123, 8 (God is the origin of the grace flowing through the sacraments and sacramentals), "Sit nomen Domini benedictum" from Ps. 112, 2 (God's name the source of all blessings), "Domine exaudi orationem meam" from Ps. 101, 2 (a fervent plea that the prayer which follows may be accepted and granted by God).

Since the psalms are used in such a variety of ways and circumstances, it is important that we have a few principles for understanding them correctly in their given liturgical context. In interpreting the psalms our point of departure. must always be their *literal* scriptural sense, for this sense gives the natural signification of the words as intended by the inspired writer. We must always seek to discover this sense first and principally, for it is the foundation of a sensible, solid, and sober use of the spiritual sense in all its aspects and applications. When this primary sense of the psalm is properly understood, it is already capable of offering us sublime thoughts which excite sentiments of adoration, praise, thanksgiving, petition, and atonement and thus lend expression to every spiritual disposition of the soul, to all our external needs, and to the liturgical life of the Church.

The psalm must also, however, be taken in the *fullest* sense intended by God. Sometimes we will see that the psalm as spoken by the inspired singer was intended by God to foreshadow a future person, event, or doctrine. But we can know this only with the help of

---

[188] Council of Laodicea held between 343 and 381, can. 59. Hefele-Leclercq, *Histoire des Conciles,* I, 1025; Second Council of Braga in 563, can 12. Hefele-Leclercq, III, 180; Fourth Council of Toledo in 633 decreed otherwise: can. 13. Hefele-Leclercq, III, 270. And centuries later Agobard of Lyons (d.840) insisted on the earlier position: *Liber de divina psalmodia. MPL,* 104: 327.

a subsequent revelation on God's part and through the teaching authority of the Church. Then we must take into consideration the particular use or application which the Church makes of the psalm in her liturgical system of prayer; therefore, the way she *accommodates* the psalm. This we call the *accommodated* sense, a meaning given to the psalm by the Church but not necessarily intended by Scripture itself. Finally, we must take into consideration the peculiar "typological" interpretation of the psalms (called by some the spiritual sense) consecrated by the practice of the primitive Church, the Fathers, and the present-day Liturgy. This does not at all mean that we want to go back to the exaggerations of the Alexandrian school and those of certain of its followers. But it does mean that the so-called "Christological" interpretation of the psalms cannot be rejected as of no consequence; this has a solid foundation in the manner in which Christ and the Apostles interpreted the psalms to prove His own messiahship, in the manner in which the Fathers understood even the non-messianic psalms as referring to Christ, and in the fact that the Church is the fulfillment of the Synagogue. For the Church of the martyrs and the Fathers, the psalter was a book about Christ, and each psalm was either *vox de Christo, vox Ecclesiae ad Christum,* or finally, *vox Christi ad Patrem.*[189]

The typological interpretation can follow the literal, the fuller, or the consequent sense (a meaning of Scripture derived through a reasoning process); sometimes it will only be an accommodation. In the last case, as mentioned, we have not a real Scriptural sense. It is nonetheless a meaning which the Church gives the psalm in her particular liturgical use of it, and is therefore not to be spurned but to be used as the Church does, to nourish and build up the spiritual life in prayer.

Doxologies

The doxology is a formula of praise directed immediately to God as one or triune. As such it is already used in the Old Testament to separate the five books of the psalms.[190] St. Paul frequently used doxologies either to begin or to conclude his Epistles.[191] The *Didache* employs "Tibi gloria in saecula" as a refrain in liturgical prayers.[192] Origen suggests that every prayer be concluded with such an act of praise of God the Father, through Christ in the Holy Spirit.[193] As a matter of fact, Hippolytus has most of his prayers conclude in this

---

[189] Cf. Balthasar Fischer, *Die Psalmenfrömmigkeit der Märtyrerkirche;* "Christ in the Psalms," *Theology Digest,* 1 (Winter, 1953), 53-57; P. Oppenheim, *Tractatus de Textibus Liturgicis* (Rome, 1945), 194-195; Lechner-Eisenhofer, *op. cit.,* 59.

[190] "Blessed be the Lord, the God of Israel, from eternity to eternity. So be it, so be it." Ps. 40, 14; cf. also the end of Pss. 71, 88 and 105.

[191] Rom. 9:5; 16:27; 2 Cor. 1:3; Eph. 1:3, etc.

[192] C. 10. J. Quasten, *Monumenta,* 11-12.

[193] *De oratione* 33. *Ancient Christian Writers,* 19 (Westminster, Md., 1954). 139.

way in his *Apostolic Tradition*.[194] Philostorgius tells us that, about 350, Diodor of Tarsus and Flavian became the center of the Catholic reaction to the Arian heresy in Antioch and, in order to combat the attempt of the heresy to make the Son appear subordinate to the Father, introduced in the recitation of the psalms and in other parts of the Liturgy the doxology, "Glory be to the Father and to the Son and to the Holy Spirit." [195] And from Theodoret we learn that the ending "for ever and ever" was also in use about the same time.[196] By the end of the fourth century we have evidence that both the Gloria Patri and its ordinary conclusion were in use also in the West.[197]

Thus far we have been speaking of what is commonly called the "little doxology." The term "greater doxology" is applied to the Gloria in excelsis Deo. The latter, too, is trinitarian in form: simply an extensive grouping of acclamations in honor of the Father, Son, and Holy Spirit. It is not originally Roman,[198] nor was it intended for the Mass; in the time of St. Athanasius its position seems to have been at the end of Lauds.[199] The hymn apparently came to the West with St. Hilary of Poitiers about the fourth century and became firmly established in the Mass of the Roman Liturgy at least by the end of the fifth century.

The Te Deum, another extended doxology, was formerly thought to be the work of St. Ambrose or St. Augustine. The majority of critics are agreed, however, that most of the evidence stands in favor of Niceta of Remesiana as author (died 414).[200] Even this thesis must be altered to a degree, for the Te Deum, from internal criticism, does not seem to be the work of one man. Indeed we find the phrase "Illic apostolorum gloriosus chorus, illic prophetarum exultantium numerus, illic martyrum innumerabilis populus . . ." among the writings of S. Cyprian.[201] It would, then, be better to say that Niceta brought different hymns together and reshaped them into one. In the sixth century, the recitation of the Te Deum at Matins for Sundays had already been prescribed by St. Benedict.[202]

---

[194] ". . . per quem tibi gloria et potentia et honor, Patri et Filio cum spiritu sancto, et nunc et in saecula saeculorum. Amen." *La Tradition Apostolique*, Edit. B. Botte, n. 4, p. 30; cf. also: n. 6, p. 35.

[195] *Historia ecclesiastica* III, 13. *GCS*, 21: 43.

[196] *Historia ecclesiastica* II, 24, 3. *GCS*, 19:153.

[197] The Gloria Patri ended all antiphonally sung psalms, according to Cassian, *De institutione coenobiorum* 2, 8. *MPL*, 49: 94-95. And in 529 the second Council of Vaison decreed that since the conclusion of the Gloria Patri, *sicut erat*, etc., was in use in Rome and elsewhere, it should also be sung in Gaul: Can. 5. Hefele-Leclercq, II, 1114.

[198] See original Greek text from the *Apostolic Constitutions* 7, 47 as well as that of the older Syrian Nestorian version and that from the Codex Alexandrinus of the New Testament in Jungmann, *The Mass of the Roman Rite*, I, 347-349.

[199] Cf. S. Bäumer, *Histoire du Bréviaire*, I, 122-123.

[200] Cf. Righetti, *op. cit.*, I, 199-200.

[201] *De mortalitate* 26. *MPL*, 4: 624.

[202] *Regula* c. 11. *MPL*, 66:436.

The Trisagion (*Hagios ho Theos*) is a doxology of widespread use in the Oriental Rites. In the Byzantine, Armenian, Maronite, and Chaldaic Rites it immediately precedes the readings of the Foremass, while in the Syrian, Coptic, and Abyssinian Rites it is placed at various spots between the readings.[203] In the Roman Rite it was formerly used at the *Preces* for Prime of the Divine Office. It is still used in the Roman ceremonies for the veneration of the cross on Good Friday. This connection with the Holy Week Passion services seems to stem from the time when Peter Fullo, monophysite Patriarch of Antioch, added to the Trisagion the phrase, "Who was crucified for us." [204] The Trisagion makes its appearance in the Roman Rite in the papal Pontifical of the twelfth century and got there through the influence of the Romano-Germanic Pontifical of the tenth.[205]

The hymn may also be called a doxology, at least reductively, for always, as used in the Liturgy, it concludes with a doxology, strictly speaking. It may be considered a special formula of praise and glorification of God even when its theme concerns a particular saint, the idea being that the saint is the motivation of our divine praise, for he shows what God can and will do to a human being if that human being cooperates. The purpose of such hymns in the Liturgy seems to be to set the exact meaning of feasts and offices.

There is hardly a formula of greater dogmatic value in the whole Liturgy than the doxology. In a sharp, devout cry of adoration, the Christian community acknowledges its fervent faith in the central mystery of redemption. The frequent repetition of doxologies during the liturgical services gives to the entire worship a strictly trinitarian imprint; the simple form enables all the faithful to take part in an acclamation which sums up the whole God-ward movement of worship. It is a résumé of the plan of redemption, a prelude of that heavenly Liturgy in which human creation stands side by side with the angelic hosts to glorify (*doxein*) the Alpha and Omega of the Heavenly Jerusalem where all shout with a loud voice: "Salvation belongs to our God who sits upon the throne, and to the Lamb . . . Amen. Blessing and glory and wisdom and thanksgiving and honor and power and strength to our God forever and ever. Amen." [206]

Creeds

Out of the need to teach the neophytes the basic doctrines of Christianity, condensed into an easy and manageable formula, arose the primitive creeds. Some of the early writings call them *regula veritatis, tessera*, but the most widespread and long-lasting term is *sym-*

[203] Cf. A. Raes, *Introductio in Liturgiam Orientalem* (Rome, 1947), 78-79.
[204] Cf. A. Baumstark, *Liturgie Comparée*, 96-97.
[205] Cf. B. Capelle, "Problèmes de pastorale liturgique: le Vendredi Saint," *Questions Liturgiques et Paroissiales*, 34 (1953), 257-259.
[206] Apoc. 7:10, 12.

bolum. The creed was indeed the password of the Christians, for it served as a sort of easy identification and at the same time as a protection against heresy. At present there are in use in the Roman Rite three creeds: the Apostles', Nicene and Athanasian.

Our Apostles' Creed does not seem to antedate the sixth century. In its present form, it is first found in the writings of St. Caesarius of Arles.[207] Thus it is with a smile that we read in one of Augustine's sermons that each of the Apostles composed a verse of the Creed: "Peter said, I believe in God the Father almighty, Creator of heaven and earth. . . .Andrew said, And in Jesus Christ His only son, our Lord, etc. . . ."[208] Even as late as the beginning of the fifth century Rufinus records a version of the Creed which differs in many respects from our own.[209] It is a combination of two earlier credal forms, a trinitarian one and a Christological one. The trinitarian formula seems to be the older; it appears already in the second century *Testament of our Lord Jesus Christ*: "I believe in the Father almighty, and in Jesus Christ our Savior, and in the Holy Ghost, in the Holy Church and in the remission of sins."[210]

The Christological creed was clearly influential in the baptismal formula contained in Hippolytus' *Apostolic Tradition*. After the candidate had descended into the water, the priest inquired, "Do you believe in God the Father almighty?" Upon answering "I do believe," the candidate was immersed once. Again the priest inquired, "Do you believe in Jesus Christ, the Son of God, who was born of the Holy Ghost and the Virgin, crucified under Pontius Pilate, died and was buried, arose on the third day live from the dead, ascended into heaven and sits at the right hand of the Father, to come again to judge the living and the dead?" Upon answering, "I do," the candidate was immersed a second time. Again the priest inquired, "Do you believe in the Holy Ghost and the holy Church and the resurrection of the body?" After answering, "I do," the candidate was immersed for the third and last time.[211] The second question, just before the second immersion, gives us a good idea of what the primitive Christological creed was like. Very possibly, it was precisely from just such a baptismal formula that our combination of the trinitarian and Christological forms developed.

The Apostles' Creed as we have it today seems to have entered the Liturgy by the eighth century,[212] appearing first in the Divine Office and the rite for Baptism. Later its recitation shows up in the rites for Confirmation and Holy Orders. And now, because of the

[207] Cf. J. Quasten, *Patrology*, I, 27.
[208] *Sermo* 240. *MPL*, 39: 2189-2190. This was falsely attributed to him.
[209] Denz., 2.
[210] Denz., 1.
[211] *La Tradition Apostolique*, Edit. B. Botte, n. 21, pp. 50-51.
[212] Cf. S. Bäumer, *Histoire du Bréviaire*, I, 377.

decree of the Congregation of Rites, dated March 23, 1955, simplifying the rubrics of the Office, the creed no longer appears there.

To refute the Arian heresy a council was held in Nicea in 325. The Fathers of the Council drew up a formula of faith stressing the consubstantiality of the Son with the Father.[213] This was not yet the text of the creed which we use in the Mass, for it ended with "et in spiritum sanctum." According to the Council of Chalcedon (451), the creed which we recite at Mass today is an enlargement of the Nicean Creed made by the Fathers gathered for the Council of Constantinople in 381.[214] Unfortunately, we have no way of verifying this statement since the acts of the Council of Constantinople have been lost. Originally, it was the formula proposed by Eusebius which Nicea adopted.[215] Practically the same formula is to be found in other writings of the time. And the almost complete formula of Constantinople was already used by Epiphanius (374) for catechizing neophytes.[216] St. Cyril of Jerusalem also followed a similar creed in teaching the basic truths of Christianity to his catechumens.[217] This leads scholars to conclude that this Credo originally had the same use in the East as our Apostles' Creed in the West; namely, a profession of faith during the administration of Baptism. It was not, therefore, intended for recitation at Mass. Its use for this latter circumstance must have started in the Frankish territory under Oriental influence, for when Henry II went to Rome in 1014, he was surprised that no Credo was said during Mass. Pope Benedict VIII granted his request and had it chanted thereafter.[218]

Once thought to be the composition of St. Athanasius, but now no longer, the *Quicumque,* or Athanasian Creed, is also used in the Liturgy, at Prime of the Divine Office on the feast of the Holy Trinity. It contains direct allusions to the errors of Nestorius and Eutyches, which prove that its date of composition must be placed after the Councils of Ephesus and Chalcedon (431 and 451). But St. Athanasius lived at the beginning of the fourth century, 295-373. The first sure references to this creed are that of the council held at Toledo in 633, which quotes certain verses of the creed,[219] and that of Isidore of Seville (died 636), who speaks of it in his epistles.[220] Its introduction into the Liturgy seems to be due to Hetto, Bishop of Basel who died in 836.[221] In form and style, the *Quicumque* is less a creed than a theological exposition of the doctrines of the Trinity and Incarnation.

[213] Denz., 54.
[214] Cf. Hefele-Leclercq, *op. cit.,* II, 700.
[215] *Ibid.,* I, 436.
[216] Denz., 13.
[217] Cf. *Catechesis* 6-18. *MPG,* 33: 535 ff.
[218] So reports Berno of Reichenau, *Libellus de quibusdam rebus ad missae officium pertinentibus* 2. *MPL,* 142: 1060.
[219] Cf. Hefele-Leclercq, *op. cit.,* III, 267, note 4.
[220] *Epist.* VI, 4 and VII, 3. *MPL,* 83: 903, 908.
[221] *Hettonis Capitulare* IV. *MPL,* 105: 763.

Apologies

All the formulas found throughout the Liturgy which have as their purpose to make us aware of our unworthiness to take part in such a sacred mystery and thereby to awaken sentiments of contrition and humility and to help us beg God for purification are called Apologies. In some writings they are called *excusationes, confessio, indulgentia*.[222] In reproving the Corinthians for their behavior in the liturgical gatherings, St. Paul reminds them of the sacredness of the mystery they celebrate and urges them to realize that "whoever eats this bread and drinks the cup of the Lord unworthily, will be guilty of the body and blood of the Lord. But let a man," he continues, "*prove* himself, and so let him eat of that bread and drink of the cup; for he who eats and drinks unworthily, without distinguishing the body, eats and drinks judgment to himself." [223] The author of the *Didache* lays down the same rule when he says, "Gathered together on Sunday, break bread and give thanks, after you have confessed your sins, in order that your sacrifice may be clean."[224] Yet it is strange to see how long it took the Church to insert formulas of personal unworthiness and of desire for forgiveness into the Mass itself. They begin to appear in the seventh century and reach their heyday in the ninth and tenth centuries. This long interval between the *Didache* and the first evident traces of the apologies leads us to believe, contrary to the opinion of J. Quasten,[225] that what St. Paul and the author of the *Didache* were referring to was a sacramental cleansing of the soul previous to and apart from the Mass.

The apologies are definitely not of Roman origin; they appear for the first time in Gallican liturgical books: the Missal of Stowe, the Book of Cerne, the *Missa Illyrica*, the Mozarabic *Liber Ordinum*, the Bobbio and Gothic Missals.[226] Because of certain Oriental parallels,[227] many authors claim a dependence of these apologies on the Eastern Rites.[228] But Jungmann prefers to see as a common root for the practice in both East and West the weakening of the genuine concept of the mediatorship of Christ in liturgical prayer.[229] In addition to this, an added impetus for the introduction of myriad private prayers on the part of the celebrant was to be found in the Frankish concept of the Liturgy which abhorred any silence during the liturgical action.[230]

[222] F. Cabrol, "Apologies," *DACL*, I, 2591.
[223] 1 Cor. 11: 27-29.
[224] C. 14. J. Quasten, *Monumenta*, 12-13.
[225] He sees in the words of the *Didache* an allusion to a purely ceremonial confession of sin similar to our modern Confiteor. *Patrology*, I, 33.
[226] Cf. F. Cabrol, *art. cit.*, 2592. See other examples in *MPL*, 78: 226-231, 245.
[227] Cf. Brightman, 316, 11; 144, 20; 144, 4.
[228] Cf. Lechner-Eisenhofer, 70; P. Oppenheim, *Tractatus de Textibus Liturgicis*, 6.
[229] *Die Stellung Christi im liturgischen Gebet*, 224.
[230] Cf. Jungmann, *The Mass of the Roman Rite*, II, 53.

This custom of making self-accusations during the liturgical service increased to such an extent that as late as the twelfth century the celebrant was led to fill every so-called "pause" of the High Mass, when he was not singing along with the choir or people and was not otherwise engaged, with every sort of apology. Thus he busied himself with prayers to remedy his unworthiness to offer sacrifice during the Introit, Gloria, Credo, Gradual, etc. It was due to this combination of trends that in the ninth century the Confiteor with the preceding *Iudica* psalm made its appearance at the beginning of the Mass in Gallican lands. The first evidence of such insertions in the Roman Mass comes from the eleventh century,[231] but they became obligatory on all only with the Missal of Pius V in 1570.

In the twelfth century we find the Confiteor placed before the Communion of the faithful, even in the administration of Communion to the sick with previous sacramental Confession. At approximately the same time there appear the prayers to be recited while the celebrant ascends the altar steps, the *Aufer a nobis* and *Oramus,* also the *Munda cor meum,* the *Per evangelica dicta,* many of the Offertory prayers, the longer prayers before Communion—*Domine Jesu Christe* and the *Perceptio*—the *Placeat* at the end of Mass, yes, even apologies for vesting and unvesting.[232] So far did this preoccupation with personal unworthiness go in interrupting the liturgical sequence of rites and prayers that in German territories of the tenth century another confession of faults for the people was introduced at the beginning of the Mass of the Faithful. It was called *Offene Schuld,* public accusation.[233]

Given the peculiar origin of these prayers as private devotions of the celebrant, and the unfortunate manner in which they succeeded in marring the natural unfolding of the liturgical action and overshadowing the primary liturgical emphasis, we should not attach so much importance to them as to neglect the more communal features of the Liturgy which from the earliest times played a functional social role: the Introit, Offertory and Communion antiphons, the Agnus Dei and the chants in between the Epistle and Gospel.

The Lord's Prayer

Reverencing everything coming from Christ, the Church recommended to her children the recitation of the Our Father from the very beginning. The *Didache* says that Christians were to recite it thrice daily.[234] In his instructions to converts prior to their reception of Baptism, St. Cyril of Jerusalem indicates that the Our Father is recited

---

[231] Bernold, *Micrologus* I. *MPL,* 151: 979.
[232] Cf. J. Jungmann, *The Mass of the Roman Rite,* Index to the second volume under *Apologiae.*
[233] Cf. Jungmann, *op. cit.,* I, 492, ff.
[234] 8, 3. *Ancient Christian Writers,* VI, 19.

between the Consecration and the Communion of the Mass.[235] A generation later, Augustine is a witness to this same custom in Africa.[236] Finally, St. Gregory the Great gives evidence of the recitation, in Rome, of the Our Father immediately after the concluding doxology of the Canon.[237] And St. Benedict includes its recitation at the end of the Hours of the Office.[238] In this manner, the Our Father summed up all of the prayer intentions of the service. In the Middle Ages,[239] however, it came to be used too often (at the beginning and at the end as well as several times during the Hours). Thus it lost its role as the peak and summation of liturgical prayer.

The Hail Mary

The first time this prayer is mentioned is in the twelfth century, when a synod of Paris (1198) encourages its recitation immediately after the Our Father. This appears to have been a general practice among the Dominicans.[240] A combination of the two greetings of the angel [241] and of Elizabeth,[242] it is used in the Greek Liturgy of St. James,[243] which goes back at least to the sixth century, and as the Offertory antiphon for the fourth Sunday of Advent in the Antiphonary of St. Gregory the Great.[244] The last part of the prayer, "Holy Mary, Mother of God etc.," begins to make its appearance in the second half of the fifteenth century.[245] Its recitation at the beginning of the Hours of the Divine Office was made obligatory by Pius V, but in the decree simplifying the rubrics by the Congregation of Rites on March 23, 1955, this order was rescinded.

Exorcisms

Following in the footsteps of Christ and His Apostles, the Church knows with divine faith that she has power over the devils. There is hardly an ecclesiastical writer of early times who does not refer to the Church's exercise of this power. Tertullian, for example, tells how even pagans brought their obsessed relatives to the Christians to be exorcised, thus acknowledging the peculiar power of Christianity over evil.[246] Even layman, he says, enjoyed power over the devil.[247] Origen speaks of the strange power the various names of God had over the

---

235 *Mystagogical Catechesis* 5, 11. *MPG,* 33: 1118.
236 *Sermo* 227 *ad infantes. MPL,* 38: 1101.
237 *Epist.* IX, 12 *ad Joannem Syracusanum. MPL,* 77: 956.
238 *Regula* c. 13. *MPL,* 66: 448.
239 Lechner-Eisenhofer, 63.
240 *Ibid.*
241 Luke 1:28.
242 Luke 1:42.
243 Brightman, *op. cit.,* 56.
244 *MPL,* 78: 645.
245 Lechner-Eisenhofer, 63.
246 *Liber apologeticus* 23. *MPL,* 1: 475.
247 *Ibid.,* 472.

devils: God of Israel, God of Hosts, etc.[248] And Justin relates that devils were cast out by the holy name of Jesus.[249] As indicated by Tertullian, every Christian possessed the power of casting out devils. It
was exercised by all until the third century, when the minor order of
exorcist was especially entrusted with this task.[250] It is about the year
251 that we find the first reference to this order in a letter of Pope
Cornelius to Fabius.[251] In modern times, however, the exercise of this
office is limited to priests specially delegated by the local Ordinary,
when it is a case of possession by the devil. Many other exorcisms are
pronounced during the administration of the sacraments and sacramentals. In Baptism, the power of the devil over the candidate is
loosened before the latter is made a child of God. This is also true of
the consecration and blessing of various objects; the devil is always
cast out before the object is dedicated to God, e.g., in the consecration of churches, holy oils, bells, the blessing of baptismal water during the Easter Vigil and the ordinary Asperges water on Sundays, etc.
The exorcism, therefore, as generally applied in liturgical rites, is a
dispository purification making way for the advent of God, for the
power of good and evil are incompatible and contradictory.

The Readings

From the very beginning, Christian worship was divided into two
parts, prayer and doctrine. The Acts of the Apostles tell us that the
first Christians "continued steadfastly in the teaching of the Apostles
and in the communion of the breaking of the bread and in the prayers." [252] The same combination of the Service of the Word and the
Service of the Eucharist is to be found in the documents of the sub-
apostolic period. St. Justin, for instance, says that on Sunday the
Christians gathered together, and the writings of the Prophets and
Apostles were read; then followed the prayers and the oblation.[253]
Just as the format of the Eucharistic part of the Mass was derived
from the framework of the Jewish Passover meal, as we shall see when
we speak of the Preface, so the Service of the Word came from the
Jewish synagogue Sabbath service, which was primarily a reading of
the Scriptures.

The primitive Christian tie with the synagogue is attested to by
the Acts: "And continuing daily with one another in the temple. . . ." [254]
Again we are told that, after passing through Perge, Paul and his
companions came to Antioch in Pisidia where they entered the synagogue on the Sabbath and sat down. "After the reading of the law

[248] *Contra Celsum* iv, 34; v, 45. *GCS*, 2, 304-305; 3, 50-51.
[249] II *Apologia* 6. *MPG*, 6: 454.
[250] Cf. H. Leclercq, "Exorcisme, Exorciste," *DACL*, V, 974.
[251] *MPL*, 3: 767. Cf. also Cyprian, *Epist.* 16. *MPL*, 4: 276.
[252] 2:42.
[253] I *Apology* 67. J. Quasten, *Monumenta*, 19.
[254] 2:46.

and the prophets, the leaders of the synagogue sent to them, saying, Brethren, if you have any word of exhortation for the people, speak." [255] After preaching to them about Christ, Paul was invited to return the following Sabbath at which time "The whole city gathered to hear the word of the Lord." [256] And this was Paul's general practice, to address the Jews during their Sabbath synagogue service.[257] In doing this, he and the first Christians only followed the example of their Master,[258] making use of already existing places of worship.[259] It was only after the break with the synagogue consequent upon the persecution of the year 44 that the Christians moved their doctrinal service out of the synagogue and united it to their Eucharistic service.[260]

Already at an early date a special reader was appointed to read to the whole assembly, and he was someone other than the president of the gathering.[261] In the fourth century in Rome, this position was usually given to young boys, while in the seventh century it shifted to the subdeacon.[262] Special locations and ambos were provided for the reading of different sections of Scripture to bring out their relative importance and dignity. Today, of course, all the readings are taken care of by the celebrant himself in a Low Mass. But in a Solemn Mass the distinction of offices is still maintained to a degree, and even in a High Mass it is recommended that a lector sing the Epistle.

All of this is designed to set off the special place the word of God occupies in divine worship. The people do not read together; they are read to by a specially ordained cleric to emphasize the character of the readings as an announcement, "the good tidings," coming from God to man. At the same time, the celebrant does not normally read to the people in a solemn service, and this is to bring out his supreme role as official representative of the people in *prayer* and of Christ in *consecrating*. He does, however, explain the readings. This should make clear the fact that the readings are intended for the instruction of the people and not simply as a formalistic mumbling of mysterious words. Trent lays it upon the shoulders of the priest to explain the scriptural word to the faithful. All the readings of whatever nature or form should be brought into direct relation with our prayer, inspire it, direct it, nourish it. Our prayer, when rightly understood, is supposed to flow as a response evoked by God's speaking first to men.[263]

[255] 13: 14-15.
[256] 13:44.
[257] See Acts 17:2; 18:4; etc.
[258] ". . . and according to his custom, he entered the synagogue on the Sabbath and stood up to read." Luke 4:16.
[259] Cf. J. Nielen, *The Earliest Christian Liturgy* (St. Louis, 1941), 104.
[260] Cf. J. Srawley, *The Early History of the Liturgy* (Cambridge, 1947), 14, 34.
[261] "After the reader had finished, the one presiding . . ." Justin, I *Apology* 67. J. Quasten, *Monumenta*, 19.
[262] J. Jungmann, *op. cit.*, I, 410.
[263] Cf. L. Bouyer, *Liturgical Piety* (Notre Dame, Indiana, 1955), 99-114.

Prayer of the Priest

As head of the liturgical assembly and representative of Jesus Christ our High Priest, the celebrant has as his role the accomplishment of the central parts of the Liturgy. These comprise, besides the positing of the matter and form of the other sacraments, the orations and consecratory Prefaces, both of which, not only as regards their content, but also their very form and style are extremely ancient.

Orations

A specialty of the Roman Rite is its short, pithy orations which recur during the Liturgy as the conclusion or high point of liturgical prayer. In classical times *oratio* signified the movement of the mouth in speaking, but in classical times, too, poets used the word in reference to prayer to their gods. As opposed to the short quick tempo of the Roman orations, the Oriental and Gallican types are long, contemplative, sometimes repetitious. The Roman oration usually consists of only one sentence, the Oriental and Gallican usually more than one.

There are two types of Roman oration: the simple and the enlarged. The simple type contains three elements: an invocation, a petition, and the conclusion; while the enlarged type, though consisting of the same basic elements, adds a *qui* clause after *Deus*, a relative clause intended to praise God or give Him grounds for granting the petition, usually based on the theme of the feast. An example of the simple type is:

Omnipotens sempiterne Deus,	(invocation)
dirige actus nostros in beneplacito tuo: ut in nomine dilecti Filii tui mereamur bonis operibus abundare.	(petition)
Per Dominum nostrum Jesum, etc.	(conclusion)

An example of the enlarged type is:

Deus,	(invocation)
qui hodierna die Unigenitum tuum gentibus stella duce revelasti	(with *qui* clause)
concede propitius: ut, qui iam te ex fide cognovimus, usque ad contemplandam speciem tuae celsitudinis perducamur.	(petition)
Per Dominum, etc.	(conclusion)

This latter type is to be found more often in the first Collect of days of special solemnity as well as of the feast days of saints, but seldom in the Secrets and Postcommunions. The simple type usually occurs on ferias and even Sundays without any special commemorative character, and nearly always in the Secrets and Postcommunions. The relative clause present in the enlarged type of oration is clearly a device used to insert the predominant thought of the feast. In more modern feasts of saints, however, it has become overburdened with data from the saint's biography or with lengthy theological considerations; see, for example, the Collects for the feast of St. Jane Francis de Chantal and the feast of the Seven Dolors.

The style of the orations is also worthy of note, for they are characterized by their beautiful flow of rhythm, a feature which certainly adds to their dignity and majesty as vehicles of the Church's solemn prayer. This rhythm is brought about by their fidelity to the *cursus*, or the rhythm of the cadences produced by arranging the accents of the phrases according to the rules of classical prose of the fourth or fifth centuries. There are three forms of cadences:

cursus planus: ˈ - - ˈ -   (beneplacito tuo)

cursus velox: ˈ - -(ˈ)- ˈ -   (operibus abundare; celsitudinis perducamur)

cursus tardus: ˈ - - ˈ - -   (fide cognovimus)

Here we see a beautiful combination of prose and poetic style. And this is typical of all priestly orations of the Roman Rite; they are never written in verse like certain hymns, but remain prose. The same thing is observed in the chant the priest uses for his strictly priestly prayers; it is hardly more than a solemn recitative tone, nothing like the highly developed melodies used for the rest of the liturgical texts. This method of chanting brings out the more solemn and sacred character of these specifically sacerdotal prayers in which the celebrant truly enters upon his role as mediator between God and men, speaking on behalf of all the faithful before God.

All orations are introduced by the exhortation "Oremus." We find this rule already set down in the *Ordo Romanus Primus.*[264] In the Oriental Rites much longer introductions are to be found, e.g., "Stand for prayer," etc.;[265] sometimes the intention of the prayer is announced: "Pray for the bishop," "pray for the emperor." It is very likely that our present Oremus in the Roman Rite is a remnant of a much longer introduction similar to those in the Oriental Rites and to the still extant solemn orations on Good Friday in the Roman Rite; its survival follows the law formulated by Anton Baumstark: that which is ancient

[264] N. 53. Andrieu, *Les Ordines,* II, 85.
[265] See Brightman, *op. cit.,* 113, 115, 117.

in what is liturgically a season of high value (Holy Week) survives.[266] If this be true, then in ancient times the deacon or celebrant announced the intention thus: "Oremus pro ecclesia sancta Dei"; the celebrant then said "Oremus" (meaning this time "Let us pray in silence") and finally summed up all the private prayers in a solemn oration.[267]

As for the conclusion of the orations, "Per Dominum nostrum Jesum Christum, etc.," this was the practice, already well established in literary form, of the *Apostolic Tradition* of Hippolytus. There we read at the end of the bishop's consecratory prayer: "offerentem tibi odorem suavitatis per puerum tuum Iesum Christum, per quem tibi gloria . . . et nunc et in saecula saeculorum. Amen." [268] This prayer through Christ to the Father is fundamental to Christianity, for it is precisely Christ's role and mission to be a mediator between us and the Father. This is already apparent in St. Paul's Epistles: "Through Him also rises the 'Amen' to God unto our glory. . . .[269] I give thanks to my God through Jesus Christ. . . .[270] To the only wise God, through Jesus Christ, be honor forever and ever. Amen." [271] St. Paul gives the doctrinal basis for this approach to God through Christ in his treatment of Christ's priesthood in chapters 7-10 of the Epistle to the Hebrews, and he summarizes his teaching on this point by saying, "Therefore He is able at all times to save those who come to God through Him, since He lives always to make intercession for them." [272] At the Last Supper our Lord Himself said, "If you ask the Father anything in my name, He will give it to you."[273]

The Church, therefore, has always directed her sacrifice and prayer to God through Christ, her Mediator and High Priest. In fact, the early Church insisted that prayer always be directed to the Father, not to Christ. At the Council of Hippo in 393 and again at Carthage in 397 it was decreed that at the altar all prayer be offered to the Father.[274] So closely did the Church adhere to this rule that even today there are only twenty-seven orations addressed to the Son in the Roman Missal, and almost all of these date from the thirteenth century or later.[275] This more recent development was due to the introduction of Gallican elements into the Roman Rite. Such emphasis on the Son arose out of reaction to the Arian heresy, which denied

---

[266] Cf. "Das Gesetz der Erhaltung des Alten in liturgisch hochwertiger Zeit," *JLW*, 7 (1927), 1-23; see the same author's treatment of the question in *Liturgie Comparée*, 30.

[267] Cf. Jungmann, *The Mass of the Roman Rite*, I, 367-370.

[268] *La Tradition Apostolique*, Edit. B. Botte, n. 3, p. 30. A similar conclusion is also found for the prayers in the *Didache*, c. 9. J. Quasten, *Monumenta*, 11.

[269] 2 Cor. 1:20.

[270] Rom. 1:8.

[271] Rom. 16:27.

[272] 7:25.

[273] John 16:23.

[274] Cf. J. Jungmann, *Die Stellung Christi im liturgischen Gebet*, 150, 198.

[275] Cf. G. Lefebvre, *Catholic Liturgy* (St. Louis, 1954), 40.

the divinity of Christ. In this reaction we again see the influence of the Orient, for it was from there that the anti-Arian struggle, with its consequent effects on the Liturgy, was transplanted to Gallican soil.[276]

According to Lefebvre:

> The chief reason why the Church addresses herself to the Father is because we are so united to Jesus, Son of the Father, as to form with Him, according to the teaching of St. Paul, one great living body of which Christ is the Head and Christians of all times and countries are the members. . . . Through our intimate union with Jesus Christ we too are admitted as sons into the bosom of the divine family and become children of the Father. Christ is the way: *Ego sum via.* He is the door, *Ego sum ostium,* through which we must pass to go to the Father. "Through Christ as man," says St. Augustine, "we go to Christ as God." And this is what the Liturgy endeavors to make us realize. . . . This official prayer is infinitely pleasing to the Father, for, said as it is in union with our Lord Jesus Christ, it has an infinite value communicated to it by the Word . . . The Man-God is the intermediary or indispensable mediator between men and God. That is why liturgical prayers addressed to God the Father invariably conclude through Jesus Christ our Lord . . . The Church desires that we should contemplate Jesus Christ as man, the supreme Pontiff who, as Head of the Mystical Body, in the name of and together with all its members, adores God in the person of the Father.[277]

This brings out again the beautiful thought expressed in our first chapter on the nature of the Liturgy. Liturgical prayer is not simply human, but rather, in a certain sense, divine. It is the prayer of Christ Himself. And it is through our priestly baptismal character that we are enabled to make Christ's prayer our own and speak in His name when we take part in the Liturgy, the worship of the entire Mystical Body, both Head and members.

The Preface

The word "Preface" in the context of the Mass-Liturgy does not mean "foreword," as though it were but an introduction placed before the Canon of the Mass. True, the Latin term in question, *praefari,* had several significations in classical literature.[278] But among them appears the sense of a solemn prayer of praise addressed to, spoken before (*prae*: before, *fari*: speak) a god.[279] It was in this manner that the word was used in the most ancient Roman Sacramentaries and other liturgical books. It was not limited to the introduction of the

[276] J. Jungmann, *Die Stellung Christi,* esp. pp. 151-168, 188-211, 217-233.
[277] *Op. cit.,* 41-42.
[278] Cf. F-J. Dölger, *Sol Salutis,* 286-295.
[279] Cf. J. Jungmann, *Gewordene Liturgie* (Innsbruck, 1940), 76-79.

Canon, as it is today, but rather it and the Canon were synonymous. Preface meant the entire Eucharistic act of consecration, from the beginning with "Sursum corda" to the final doxology, "Per ipsum, et cum ipso, etc." [280]

Here, then, we have a solemn prayer of praise addressed to God, spoken before Him and the assisting community of the faithful. And this is a *Eucharistic* prayer, a prayer of thanksgiving which relates all the wonderful things God has done for mankind, the *magnalia Dei*, for which we are grateful. Here preface, eucharist, bear the same meaning as *contestatio* and *praedicatio* (as in "Laudate Dominum omnes gentes, praedicate eum omnes populi!"), a protestation of man's praise and thanksgiving for the great things God has done to him. It is in the context of this narrative of the *wonders of God* that the priest accomplishes the act of consecration. Whence the name Eucharist for the Mass.

In the oldest formula for the Canon of the Mass which has come down to us, that of the third century *Apostolic Tradition* of Hippolytus, we find a clear-cut expression of this theme. After beginning the Canon in the same manner as we do with "Sursum corda, etc.," the celebrant continues:

> We give thee thanks, O God, through thy beloved son, Jesus Christ, whom thou hast sent to us recently as savior, redeemer and messenger of Thy will; who is Thine inseparable Word and in whom Thou hast placed Thy good pleasure; whom Thou hast sent down from heaven into the womb of the virgin, and who, having been conceived, became incarnate and showed himself as Thy son, born of the Holy Ghost and the virgin; who, accomplishing Thy will and acquiring for Thee a holy people, extended his hands, when he suffered, in order by his passion to deliver those who believed in Thee; who, as he handed himself over to a voluntary passion in order to destroy death, break the chains of the devil, trample on hell, illumine the just, establish the testament and show forth his resurrection, taking bread into his hands and rendering thanks to Thee, said, "Take, eat; this is my body which is broken for you." In like manner the chalice, saying, "This is my blood which is shed for you. When you do this you remember me." Being mindful, therefore, of his death and resurrection we offer Thee the bread and the chalice, giving thanks to Thee . . .[281]

As we can see, the whole first part of this prayer—and the same theme is taken up again at the end—is but a grateful commemoration, a *thanking-thinking*, to use an expression of Jungmann's.[282] Hence, the

[280] See Jungmann's arguments, *ibid.*, 53-87.
[281] *La Tradition Apostolique*, Edit. B. Botte, n. 4, pp. 31-32.
[282] *Das Eucharistische Hochgebet* (Würzburg, 1954), 18. The English translation, *The Eucharistic Prayer* (Chicago: Fides, 1956), 7, has "thanking remembrance."

Canon of the Mass is called a Eucharistic preface, or the solemn prayer of thanksgiving *par excellence*. We recall God's plan of redemption for us, thanking Him the while, and we, in that very process, renew the greatest act of the whole plan, the sacrifice of the cross.

This same prayer of *thanking-thinking*, this same Eucharistic form of prayer, or preface, is used to consecrate bishops, ordain priests and deacons, to bless abbots and abbesses, to consecrate virgins, to crown kings, to bless chrism and baptismal water, to consecrate churches, altars and, formerly, the Paschal Candle.

This form of prayer, like so many others, did not originate with Christianity. We find its prototype in the so-called *Chabûrah* suppers. The *Chabûrah* was a small group or society of friends who gathered approximately once a week, usually on the eve of the Sabbath, for a religious meal.[283] This was precisely what our Lord and His Apostles did prior to the passion. He gathered about Him His beloved friends, with whom He desired to celebrate the sacrificial Passover meal before He died.

This was the religious meal above all others, observed each year on the eve of the Passover in observance of Moses' command [284] to eat the Paschal lamb within the family circle. At such a meal no food of any kind was taken without first giving thanks, without offering up a eucharist. The meal opened with the Kiddush, or announcement of the holiness of the feast, in the form of prayers of praise to God. After certain ceremonies, the reading of the Haggadah took place; this was simply a narrative of the Jews' liberation from Egypt, the first Passover. The first part of the Hallel was sung towards the end of the Haggadah. The eating of the Paschal lamb then followed; in later times, as today, the Afikoman, or the central matzah, seems to have replaced the lamb at the Passover meal. After the lamb or Afikoman is eaten, the leader says a solemn prayer of thanksgiving over the third cup of wine, called the cup of benediction. After it is drunk, the meal concludes with the singing of the rest of the Hallel.

The blessings pronounced over the Afikoman and the cup of benediction are of particular interest to us, for it was these two elements which played such an important part in the institution of the Holy Eucharist. Recall that our Lord at the Last Supper took bread (the Afikoman), blessed, broke and gave it to His disciples, saying, "This is my body." The words of the blessing are not recorded in the Gospels, for they were well known to all Jews. "Blessed art Thou, Lord our God, Ruler of the universe, who bringeth forth bread from the earth. Blessed art Thou, Lord our God, Ruler of the universe, who hast sanctified us with Thy commandments and enjoined on us the

[283] See the explanations of G. Dix, *The Shape of the Liturgy* (Westminster, England, 1952), 50; and of L. Bouyer, *Liturgical Piety*, 115-128.
[284] Exod. 12.

eating of unleavened bread."[285] And after they had eaten the meal, our Lord took the cup of benediction and consecrated it as His blood. But before He did so we are told that He gave thanks and blessed it; this too was provided for in the Passover ritual. The formula of His thanksgiving must have been:

Blessed art Thou, Lord our God, Ruler of the universe. Thou dost sustain the whole world with Thy goodness, loving favor and kindness. Thou givest food to all flesh, for Thy mercy endureth forever. In Thy great goodness our sustenance has never yet failed. May it never fail us, for the sake of Thy great name. Thou providest nourishing food and sustenance for all, and art beneficent to all, preparing food for all Thy creatures that Thou hast created. Blessed art Thou, Lord who providest food for all.

We thank Thee, Lord our God, for the goodly and ample land of our desire which Thou gavest to our fathers to inherit. We thank Thee, Lord our God, that Thou didst bring us forth from the land of Egypt and redeem us from the house of bondage. We thank Thee for Thy covenant sealed in our flesh, and for Thy Torah which Thou hast taught us, making us know Thy precepts. We thank Thee also for life which with loving favor Thou hast bestowed graciously on us, and for the food we eat with which Thou does nourish and sustain us at all times, daily, at every season, at every hour.

For all these blessings, Lord our God, we thank Thee and bless Thee. May Thy name be blessed in the mouth of all living at all times and for all time! Thus we fulfill Thy command, 'Thou shalt eat and be satisfied, and bless the Lord thy God for the goodly land which He has given thee,' Blessed art Thou, Lord, for that land and for our sustenance.

Lord our God, have mercy on Israel Thy people, on Jerusalem Thy city and Sion the dwelling place of Thy glory, on the royal house of David Thy anointed, and on the great and holy Temple called by Thy name. Our God, our Father, be Thou our Shepherd. Sustain us, support us and provide for all our needs, and, Lord our God, give us speedy surcease of all our troubles. Lord our God, may we not be brought to need gifts or loans from the hand of flesh and blood, but only from Thy hand so generous, so open, so bountiful. Thus shall we never be put to shame.

Our God, God of our fathers, on this day of the festival of unleavened bread may there come before Thee the remembrance of us and our fathers, Jerusalem Thy holy city, the Messiah son of David Thy servant, and all Thy people of the house of Israel. May this remembrance be presented to Thee and in tenderness, grace and mercy be heard and accepted with favor by Thee for life and peace, for our

[285] Rabbi David and Tamar de Sola Pool, *The Haggadah of Passover* (New York, 1952), 57, 59.

> deliverance and happiness . . . May the All-merciful adjudge
> us worthy of seeing the days of the Messiah and the life to
> come.[286]

In this blessing over the third cup of wine we see the plan of God neatly outlined: His giving life to man in creation, His delivering of the Chosen People from Egypt and the donation of a new land of inheritance, the covenant, the law—these latter types of a new creation—for all of which Israel thanks the Lord. And we catch a note of eschatological hope expressed in the petition that Israel will soon see fulfilled the messianic promises of old. When we compare this with the Eucharistic formula of Hippolytus, we see the same insistence on the plan of redemption, but only this time the outline begins with Christ, the fulfillment of the Israelites' hope. And just as the Passover Eucharist reviews the works of God in grateful memory, so the plan of redemption is commemorated by Hippolytus precisely as a form of thanksgiving.

This same *praefatio*, or solemn prayer of praise and thanksgiving, effective of the Christian sacrifice, is still discernible in our Preface and Canon, in spite of the additions which had been made already before St. Gregory the Great's time.[287] Of course, in the Missal there is the artificial division created between Preface and Canon by the page with the picture of the crucifixion on it and by the fact that the Preface is sung aloud and the Canon is then read silently (a practice dating from the ninth century). The content of the Preface likewise has suffered, since in the course of time the full story of redemption has been parcelled out according to the different feasts of the Church year, while the Common Preface, leaving out all mention of the plan of salvation, retained only the beginning and end of the original schema.

Were we to piece together once again the individual parts of this redemptive outline as found in the Proper Prefaces and place them within the framework of the Common Preface, we would have a more faithful reproduction of the primitive idea:

> It is right and just that we thank Thee at all times and in
> all places, O Lord, holy Father, almighty and eternal God,
> that Mary, without losing the splendor of her virginity, con-
> ceived through the overshadowing of the Holy Ghost Thine
> only begotten Son (Preface for feasts of the Blessed Virgin),
> in Whose flesh the light of Thy glory has once more shone
> upon us (Christmas), Who, establishing our salvation on the
> tree of the cross (Holy Cross), and by dying as our Paschal
> Lamb, took away the sins of the world, overcame our death,
> and by rising restored life (Easter), Who, by being lifted up
> into heaven, made us sharers in His Godhead (Ascension) and

[286] *Ibid.*, 65, 67, 71.
[287] See B. Botte, *Le Canon de la Messe Romaine*. Louvain, 1935.

poured out upon us the Spirit of adoption (Pentecost).
Through Him the angels praise Thy majesty, the dominations
adore it, the powers stand in awe, the heavens and the
celestial hosts and the blessed seraphim join together in
celebrating their joy. With their voices we beg Thee join ours,
saying in humble praise . . .[288]

Then follows the hymn of the seraphim, the Sanctus. Overlooking, for
the purposes of discerning the original lines of the Preface, the intercessory prayers (introduced into the Canon about the middle of the
fourth century to emphasize the sacrificial character of the Mass in
opposition to heresy [289]), the Preface would mention next the words
of institution and in the Unde et memores state that in commemorating these words the Church offers Christ's sacrifice again. It would
conclude with the words of the final doxology, "Per ipsum, et cum
ipso, etc."

Little wonder that this solemn prayer of sacrificial praise and
thanksgiving is reserved to the priest himself, who directly represents
Christ the Head of the Mystical Body in renewing His redemptive
act for contemporary mankind.

B. Action

No less than words, actions or gestures are also a type of language; they too hold a message for us. They have a meaning which
the person who sincerely wishes to pray the Liturgy must get to
know. Whether used by man for practical or symbolical reasons, gestures or ceremonies help man to express himself better, make his
thought and intent clearer and more vivid.

This is true, not only of the Liturgy, but of the whole of life. In
every phase of his activity man, the composite of matter and spirit,
will use some sort of ceremonial to express himself. Such ceremonial
is made up of signs, both natural and conventional, as old as man himself. Some of these have grown up and developed with man as a necessary part of his social intercourse. A gentle bow of the head will
normally denote respect and honor towards another; a shake of the
hand or a pat on the back will speak his friendship. We salute our
flag to show our devotion to our country; we tip our hat, rise and
stand erect to display our respect and reverence for others.

This is no less necessary for man in his relations with God. Every
ceremony gives body to a religious idea or attitude. And ceremonies
are to be found in every religion known to man—a proof of their nat-
uralness.[290]

[288] Cf. Jungmann, The Eucharistic Prayer, 8.
[289] Ibid., 22, 24.
[290] Cf. the excellent work of T. Ohm, Die Gebetsgebärden der Völker und
das Christentum. Leiden, 1948.

But how shall we arrive at a correct explanation of the different ceremonies, all the gestures and signs found in Christian worship? Many attempts have been made to interpret these actions, but they so often contradict each other. Where does the truth lie? The modern criteria of historical research and the principle of functionalism were not always the inspiration behind explanations of liturgical ceremonial. Very often, quite oblivious of the true historical origin of many rites, medieval authors resorted to an allegorizing method similar to that employed by some of the early Church Fathers in their biblical exegesis.

By liturgical allegorism we mean an interpretation of liturgical action based, not on historical origins, nor on the official declaration of the Church, but upon a purely arbitrary symbolism, extraneous to the true reasons for the institution of any given rite, but nevertheless seen in it by later writers. When we ignore the true historical circumstances and reasons for the introduction of a ceremony into the liturgical sphere and foist upon the faithful our own explanations, we fall into pure subjectivism. We run the risk of doing violence to the Liturgy itself by introducing other things into it which do not belong there, or we turn and twist ancient rites into positions and roles which are incompatible with their basic symbolism and the proper unfolding of liturgical prayer. In the absence—or rejection—of any objective norms of interpretation, there will be as many meanings as there are commentators, any similarity to actual reality or historical fact being purely coincidental. In short, we will turn the Liturgy into a mysterious play.

This is actually what happened in the Middle Ages, and unfortunately this tendency has survived even to the present time in some pietistic manuals of devotion.[291] For Amalar of Metz (or Trier), who died in 850, many of the actions of the Mass have a mystical relation to Christ's life. When the bishop ascends his throne during Mass he does so in memory of Christ's Ascension.[292] The entrance of the bishop at the beginning of Mass recalls Christ's coming into the world.[293] The deacon and celebrant lift the chalice and host during the final doxology of the Canon in imitation of Joseph of Arimathea and the disciples who took the body of Jesus down from the cross and carried it to the sepulcher.[294]

Bernold of Constance says that the celebrant extends his hands during the Canon because Christ's arms were stretched out on the

---

[291] A good example of such a pietistic manual is Martin von Cochem's *Explanation of the Holy Sacrifice of the Mass* (New York: Benziger, 1896), which was reprinted as late as 1925 and offers a series of allegorical interpretations of the Mass which lay claim to no higher authority than Martin himself: they are a pure projection of his own lively imagination.

[292] *De ecclesiasticis officiis* III, 10. *MPL*, 105:1117.

[293] *Ibid.*, 1108.

[294] *Ibid.*, 1144.

cross;[295] the five prayers of the Canon which end with "Per Christum Dominum nostrum" recall the five wounds of Christ;[296] and the priest bows before the altar at the Supplices te rogamus because Christ gave up His spirit with a bow of the head.[297] In the loud voice of the celebrant at the Nobis quoque peccatoribus he hears the voice of the centurion at the foot of the cross confessing Christ's divinity,[298] while in the three articles of the Pater Noster (introduction, Pater, and embolism), he sees symbolized the three days Christ lay in the tomb.[299] And finally, for the sake of one more example, Rupert of Deutz also finds many hidden meanings in the rites of the Mass: in the Sanctus and Benedictus the confession of Mary Magdalen anointing Christ's feet in Bethany and the cries of the children at His triumphal entry into Jerusalem,[300] in the silence of the Canon the agony of the Passion,[301] in the Agnus Dei Christ's Ascension.[302] As can be seen, the primary and natural meaning of the rites was no longer sought.

A saner interpretation was a necessity. In reaction to such extremes as those mentioned above (which were just a few among many others), Florus, a deacon of Lyons, took up the battle in the Synod of Thionville in 835. Unfortunately his truculence turned the assembled clergy away from his cause and made them sympathetic to Amalar and his ilk. Thus the cause for sound liturgical interpretation was lost. And later, through the Pontifical of William Durand of Mende (died in 1296), some of this allegorism crept into the Liturgy itself.

Centuries later Dom Claude de Vert attempted once more to shake off the abuse of allegorism,[303] and composed his *Explication simple, littérale et historique des cérémonies de l'Eglise*, in which, proposing a motive of purely natural necessity, practicality, or decorum for all the rites, he carefully eliminated every consideration of a symbolical nature. This, of course, was a swing in the opposite extreme, for symbolism does play some part in the Church's ceremonial. After him came the effort of the Oratorian, Pierre LeBrun, who tried to coordinate both points of view in his *Explication littérale, historique et dogmatique des prières et des cérémonies de la Messe*. This was published in 1716.

There is only one way of determining the true meaning of ritual actions, and that is by going back to the originator, or at least to his times, to see what he meant by the actions, unless the Church has subsequently *officially* changed the original meaning. And so, in this general section on liturgical gestures and actions, we will try to indi-

---

[295] *Micrologus* 16. MPL, 151: 987.
[296] *Ibid.*
[297] *Ibid.*
[298] *Ibid.*, 17. MPL, 151: 988.
[299] *Ibid.*
[300] *De divinis officiis* II, 4. MPL, 170: 37.
[301] *Ibid.*, 5. MPL, 170: 37.
[302] *Ibid.*, 17. MPL, 170: 46.
[303] He died in 1708.

cate the true nature of the gestures in general use throughout the Liturgy. The rest will be treated in the sections on individual parts of the Liturgy: the Mass, the Office, the Sacraments, Sacramentals, and the Liturgical Year.

Standing

This was the customary position at prayer among the ancient peoples,[304] as it was considered normal to stand, out of reverence, before a person in authority. This was true of the Jews in their Temple and synagogue services.[305] And the Christians followed suit.[306] Apart from the many pictures in the catacombs depicting Christians standing at times of prayer, we also have the testimony of documents. Justin says that they stood up for the orations after the readings of the Mass.[307] Tertullian sees in this practice of standing a special sign of joy, for it was the position assumed during Easter time and the Pentecostal season; kneeling was a sign of penance and atonement.[308] In fact, he says that it was against Church discipline to kneel on Sundays.[309] And much later the Council of Nicea explicitly decrees that all should stand at prayer on Sundays and in Paschal time,[310] and this position seems to be the normal one in the *Apostolic Constitutions* for the orations.[311] For St. John Chrysostom standing is a sign of priestly ministration, for the priest stands at the altar,[312] and St. Benedict makes this a rule for the chanting of psalms.[313]

Sitting

While standing for prayer was the common practice for the Jews and Christians, Scripture suggests that both were accustomed to be seated during the readings and the sermon.[314] And we see the same thing in Justin and in the *Apostolic Constitutions*.[315] However, St. Augustine indicates that when he spoke to the people, he sat and they stood listening.[316] Sitting is the normal position of the official teacher. We often hear of "the chair of philosophy" in such and such a university. In French the pulpit is even called *la chaire*. But such is also the

[304] Cf. F-J. Dölger, *Sol Salutis*, 22; T. Ohm, *Die Gebetsgebärden*, 323-324.
[305] 1 Kings 1:26; Ps. 134:2; Matt. 6:5; Mark 11:25; Luke 18:11.
[306] Our Lord even made mention of this position "When you stand for prayer . . ." Mark 11:25.
[307] I *Apology* 67. J. Quasten, *Monumenta*, 19.
[308] *De oratione* 23. *MPL*, 1: 1298-1299.
[309] *De corona* 3. *MPL*, 2: 99.
[310] Can. 20. Hefele-Leclercq, op. cit., I, 618.
[311] 8, 10, 22. J. Quasten, *Monumenta*, 209.
[312] *Homilia* 18 *in Hebr.*, n. 1. *MPG*, 63: 135.
[313] *Regula* 19. *MPL*, 66: 476.
[314] Luke 4:20; John 8:2; Acts 20:9; 1 Cor. 14:30.
[315] I *Apology* 67. J. Quasten, *Monumenta*, 19; *Apost. Const.*, 8, 6, 2. Quasten, 199.
[316] "Ego sedens loquor; vos stando laboratis." *Sermo* 17, 2. *MPL*, 38: 125.

position of the listening and attentive student, or hearer, unless the dignity of the speaker be such that it would be disrespectful to sit in his presence. That is why all stand for the reading of the Gospel.

As remarked above, St. Benedict insisted on standing during the recitation of psalms. But by the eleventh century some clerics began to give into human infirmity and sit, judging from the reproaches that Peter Damian (died 1072) heaped upon them.[317] In many Benedictine monasteries, in order to maintain the prescriptions of St. Benedict and yet reduce the tedium of long hours in choir, small wooden seats are so attached to the under side of the choir benches, that when the latter are pulled up the monks may still stand and yet rest themselves on the small seat. This ingenious device, motivated by solicitude for human weakness, is aptly called a *misericordia*.

Kneeling

This position was not unknown either in the Old or New Testaments;[318] it seems to have been a sign of intensified prayer, sometimes of humility, reverence, and consciousness of sin. And it is found with this same symbolism in many pagan religions.[319] In the Liturgy, as we have seen, kneeling was usually associated with fasting and was a penitential and suppliant posture.[320] In the same spirit the *Apostolic Constitutions* has the catechumens kneel during the prayers said for them;[321] the faithful, too, are told to kneel to pray for the various intentions of the *Oratio fidelium*.[322] In the latter instance, however, after a few moments of private prayer said kneeling, the faithful rose for the solemn oration pronounced by the bishop. Instead of assuming the standing position as the regular one for liturgical prayer and limiting kneeling to penitential and other special occasions, in recent centuries it has become customary to kneel almost always for prayer. Ohm sees as the cause of this the Counter Reformation attempt to emphasize the Catholic belief in the Real Presence through humble adoration. Because of this, he believes, we have become somewhat one-sided and left out the important aspect of joy and hope so well expressed by standing.[323]

Genuflection

This was originally a sign of adoration in Roman civil usage, especially towards the Emperor. When it lost its significance of adora-

[317] *Opuscula* 39, 2. *MPL*, 145: 644.
[318] 3 Kings 8:54; 19:18; Daniel 6:10; Luke 22:41; Matt. 20:36; Acts 9:40.
[319] Cf. T. Ohm, *Die Gebetsgebärden*, 345-352.
[320] Tertullian, *De oratione* 23. *MPL*, 1: 1298-1299.
[321] For the deacon tells them to rise after the prayers, 8, 6, 8. J. Quasten, *Monumenta*, 200.
[322] 8, 10, 2. Quasten, 206. For a discussion of this passage and book 2, 57, 14, see F-J Dölger, *Sol Salutis* 326-327.
[323] *Op. cit.*, 354.

tion and came to be looked upon merely as an act of respect for a high personage, it found its way into the Church. Since the pope and other bishops were on a par with the Emperor and high subordinate officials, they too were honored by means of a genuflection.[324] Its use as an expression of adoration of God is conspicuously absent from the Oriental Rites. In the Roman Rite it is of relatively recent introduction for this purpose. The occasion for its introduction was the Catholic reaction to the Eucharistic errors of Berengarius in the eleventh century, but it was by no means a general practice. It was John Burchard (1502) who included it in his *Ordo Missae* for papal ceremonies; whence it found its way into the Roman Missal of Pius V and became obligatory for all who follow the Roman Rite. Prior to this development, the customary act of adoration prescribed by the Liturgy was the profound bow. Today people are often confused when they see the genuflection used to pay respect to bishops; in their mind it belongs only to our Lord present in the Blessed Sacrament. We would do well to point out the two uses of the genuflection, especially the fact that its native and original significance was simply respect and honor for our spiritual rulers.

Bows

The bow has been employed in a variety of ways. One was to receive the blessing of the bishop in this position.[325] During Lent in our present day Liturgy, the deacon cries "Humiliate capita vestra Deo" just before the Oratio super populum. This is obviously a remnant from the time when the Oratio super populum was the final blessing given at the end of Mass,[326] in the same manner followed by the *Apostolic Constitutions*. The bow is also used for adoration; for instance, the *Ordo Romanus Primus* indicates that a bow accompanies the recitation of the Sanctus at Mass.[327] The same *Ordo* prescribes a bow as a mark of reverence and respect for the altar.[328] Today we employ the bow in the same variety of ways: adoration and reverence at the mention of the holy name, during the Gloria Patri and Sanctus, etc.; respect for God's representative, the priest; and for holy things, the altar and crucifix; penance at the Confiteor, Munda cor meum, etc.; and humble supplication at the Suscipe sancta Trinitas, Oremus, In spiritu humilitatis, Supplices te rogamus, Te igitur, etc.[329]

[324] Cf. T. Klauser, *The Western Liturgy and its History*, 27.

[325] The *Apostolic Constitutions* has the catechumens, the obsessed, those to be baptized in the near future, the penitents at the end of the Mass of the Catechumens, and the faithful at the end of the Mass of Sacrifice, bow to receive the bishop's blessing: 8, 6, 8; 7,3; 8,4; 9,6; 15,6. J. Quasten, *Monumenta* 200, 202, 203, 205, 232.

[326] Cf. J. Jungmann *The Mass of the Roman Rite*, II, 428-429.

[327] Nn. 87-88. Andrieu, *Les Ordines*, II, 95.

[328] N. 49. Andrieu, *Les Ordines*, II, 83.

[329] For its use in pagan religions, see T. Ohm, *Die Gebetsgebärden*, 340.

Prostration

Abraham, we are told, fell flat on his face before the appearance of God and worshiped Him;[330] and our Lord fell prostrate on the ground in prayer before his capture in the Garden of Gethsemani.[331] In the first instance the prostration seems to imply a quality of awe in adoration, in the second intense supplication. So common was this prayer posture among the Sumerians and Babylonians, that their words for prostration (make-oneself-little, make-the-nose-flat) were the regular expressions for "to pray." [332] Tertullian tells us that the prostration was a form of penance in his day.[333] And in the fifth century, Sozomen describes the public penitents who prostrated themselves on the ground, and the bishop with them, at the end of Mass to beg forgiveness of their sins.[334] A prostration before the altar at the beginning of Mass is found in the Roman Rite, perhaps for the first time, in the *Ordo Romanus* XV,[335] which was composed after the middle of the eighth century in Gaul. Here the author describes a papal Mass in which he had seen the Pope prostrate himself before the altar until the end of the Introit. Lechner-Eisenhofer believe that this was introduced under the influence of Byzantine ceremonial.[336] This same body position is used on Good Friday at the very beginning of the liturgical action. We find it also in the rites of ordination, the blessing of Abbots, etc., always with the idea of penance.

Orientation

Praying faced in the direction of the rising sun was a feature found in many pagan religions of East and West, most especially those whose adepts adored the sun as a god.[337] Christians observed the same custom, but for a different reason: the sun was the symbol of the light of Christ. While both Tertullian and Augustine speak of the practice,[338] the *Apostolic Constitutions* speaks of it being done for the orations after the readings of the Mass; the reasons for this were the memory of our Lord's Ascension in the East and the desire for heaven symbolized in the Garden of Paradise, which was supposed to have been located in the East.[339] To this Dölger adds another motive, the ex-

---

[330] Gen. 17:3.
[331] Matt. 26:39.
[332] T. Ohm, *op. cit.*, 359.
[333] *De poenitentia* 9, 2. *MPL*, 1: 1354.
[334] *Hist. eccl.* 7, 16. *MPG*, 69: 1459.
[335] N. 15. Andrieu, *Les Ordines*, III, 98.
[336] *Op. cit.*, 73.
[337] Cf, F-J. Dölger, *Sol Salutis*, 20-60.
[338] Tertullian, *Ad nationes* 1, 13. *MPL*, 1:650; Augustine, *De sermone Domini* 2, 18. *MPL*, 34: 1277.
[339] "Deinde cuncti pariter consurgentes, et in orientem contemplantes . . . orent Deum, 'qui ascendit super coelum ad orientem,' ac recordantes antiquam possessionem paradisi ad orientem siti." 2, 57, 14. Quasten, *Monumenta*, 184-185. Cf. Dölger, *Sol Salutis*, 220-242.

pectancy of Christ's second coming in the East.[340] This custom, however, does not seem to have penetrated the Roman spirit. Its presence in the *Ordo Romanus Primus* [341] is definitely a Gallican interpolation.[342]

The raising of the eyes and hands

These are two other practices natural to man when praying. In the *Aeneid* we read that "Anchises, raising his eyes to the stars and extending his hands toward heaven, prayed, 'Almighty Jupiter . . . .' " [343] Jesus Himself did likewise: "And Jesus, raising His eyes, said, 'Father, I give Thee thanks that Thou hast heard me.' " [344] And the Christians followed suit, for Tertullian informs us that they looked to heaven while praying.[345] To find the reason for this we need only to look at Psalm 122. There the psalmist says, "To Thee I lift up my eyes, O Thou who dwellest in heaven." It is a universal popular view that God has His dwelling place in the skies, His throne in the clouds. In order to centralize God's presence for himself and thus to intensify his prayer, man directs his eyes to God as though He were above more so than here below, for height more or less symbolizes superiority. And it is a remarkable fact that as often as the priest during the Liturgy gives a blessing, that action is normally preceded by a glance to heaven, as though, looking first to the throne of mercy, he brings down upon man or things celestial favor and protection.

Connected with this practice is the action of raising one's hands, then bringing them together to form a sort of circle before lifting the right hand in blessing. St. Luke (24:50) tells us that our Lord, before ascending into heaven, blessed His disciples after raising His hands: "elevatis manibus benedixit eis." The priest, imitating our Lord perhaps, seems to encompass within the grasp of his hands the blessings he imparts to the faithful. Yet he also makes this same encircling movement with his hands at the Gloria and Credo; at other times he simply raises his hands to the level of his shoulders (at the Sursum corda). At another he stands praying with his hands outstretched, lifts them in offering, opens them out to the people in greeting. We meet this same variety of usage in the Old Testament as well as in patristic writers.[346] The gesture, obviously, does not always have the same connotation. Yet, basically, we see therein a powerful expression of the soul's de-

---

[340] *Op. cit.*, 198-219.
[341] N. 53. Andrieu, *Les Ordines*, II, 84.
[342] *Ibid.*, p. 7.
[343] "At pater Anchises oculos ad sidera laetus extulit, et coelo palmas cum voce tetendit: Jupiter omnipotens . . ." II, 688. *P. Virgilii Maronis Opera Omnia*, I (London: Delphin Classics, 1819). 549.
[344] John 11:41.
[345] "Illuc (coelum) suspicientes oramus." *Liber apologeticus* 30. MPL, 1:503.
[346] Exod. 9:29; Isaias 1:15; Pss. 27:2; 62:5; 133:2; Lamentations of Jeremias 2:4; 3 Kings 9:54; 8:22; Tertullian, *Liber Apol.* 30. MPL, 1:503; *De oratione* 14. MPL, 1: 1273; Clement of Rome, *Epist.* I ad Cor. 29. MPG, 1: 270.

pendence on God, man's confident awaiting of God's answer and help, the lifting of man's heart in prayer to his Maker, his joy in praising God, his openness of heart and communication of self when greeting others living the same inner life as he, and, of course, the offering of a gift.[347]

The custom of praying with folded hands, though found occasionally in the early Church (perhaps for private prayer only), did not become popular until about the thirteenth century.[348] Righetti believes that the action was probably derived from the manner in which a vassal paid his homage to his feudal lord in the Frankish realm.[349] With hands folded, he went before his lord, placed them in between the lord's legs, and received from him a sign of his enfeoffment. This was a way of manifesting his submission and subjection to the lord, and, in the sphere of religion, a sign of his reverence for God. It is noteworthy that it is precisely this gesture that is employed by the celebrant at Mass while reciting those prayers which stem from Frankish lands. This does not mean that such a gesture was proper only to the Franks; it is to be found in other lands and among many other peoples.[350]

Imposition of hands

Again this is not strictly a Christian gesture. Sophocles has Oedipus lay his hands on his children in blessing before he dies.[351] Its use in revealed religion, in general, seems to denote the might and power of God, for in His hands "are the depths of the earth."[352] In the Old Testament as well as the New, we see it used to impart a blessing.[353] With it sin was passed on to the scapegoat,[354] Christ and His disciples cured the sick,[355] administrative authority was handed on,[356] priestly and other ministerial powers were conferred,[357] and the Holy Spirit was given.[358] Tertullian is a witness to the administration of Confirma-

---

[347] Cf. the beautiful article of B. Mullahy, "The Raising of my Hands," *Orate Fratres*, 21 (1947), 241-249. In the ancient manner of praying, not simply with outstretched hands but outstretched arms as well, so often found in the frescoes of the Catacombs, now for the most part no longer in vogue except among the older Religious Orders, Tertullian likes to see a symbol of Christ's passion: "nos vero non attollimus tantum, sed etiam expandimus (manus) et dominica passione modulati, orantes, confitemur Domino." *De oratione* 14. MPL, 1: 1273.

[348] Lechner-Eisenhofer, 77.

[349] *Op. cit.*, I, 310.

[350] Cf. T. Ohm, *op. cit.*, 268-269.

[351] *Ibid.*, 290.

[352] Cf. Pss. 94:4; 88:22, 26.

[353] Gen. 48:;4 ff; Lev. 9:22; Mark 10:16.

[354] Lev. 16:21.

[355] Luke 4:40; Acts 9:17.

[356] Numbers 8:10; 27:23.

[357] Acts 6:6; 13:3; 1 Tim. 4:14; 5:22; 2 Tim. 1:6.

[358] Acts 8:17; 19:3.

tion through imposition of hands.[359] Pope St. Stephen, writing to Cyprian, states that the sacrament of Penance was conferred with an imposition of hands.[360] And Hippolytus reports that a newly-consecrated bishop, in offering his first Mass (the Mass in which he was consecrated), would lay his hands on the oblation brought to the altar by the deacons and recite the Preface.[361] The gesture was even used, according to Origen, for exorcizing unclean spirits;[362] in the exhortation to future exorcists, the ordaining bishop even today speaks of the use of imposition of hands in exorcizing the possessed: "Accipis itaque potestatem imponendi manum super energumenos; et per impositionem manuum tuarum . . ." [363]

Beating the breast

This gesture signifies contrition for sin, the ultimate root of which lies in the misplaced affections of the heart. Though this meaning was not always attached to it in pagan practice,[364] no other significance can logically be read into it as used in revealed religion. The publican standing far off beating his breast cried, "O Lord be merciful to me a sinner." [365] When our Lord finally expired on the cross, the Jews walked away slowly to their homes beating their breasts.[366] And St. Augustine takes the time to explain this action. "What does it mean to beat the breast except to accuse what lies hidden there and with a visible stroke to castigate the invisible sin?" [367] To beat one's breast, therefore, is to acknowledge one's sinfulness. To make it an act of adoration is to weaken it. To beat one's breast at the elevation of the Host or at "And the Word was made flesh" during the Angelus is not very meaningful. It shows that we have not grasped the true nature of the gesture.[368]

The Sign of the Cross

According to the teaching of St. Paul, the cross is the center of our faith[369] and the means of our reconciliation with God.[370] Our Lord

[359] "Dehinc manus inponitur per benedictionem advocans et invitans spiritum sanctum." De baptismo 8, 1. MPL, 1: 1316.
[360] "Nihil innovetur nisi quod traditum est ut manus illis imponantur in poenitentiam." Epist. 74, 1. MPL, 3: 1175.
[361] La Tradition Apostolique, Edit. B. Botte, n. 4, p. 30.
[362] "et exorcistarum manus impositione vehementius imposita super immundos spiritus . . ." In librum Jesu Nave hom. 24. MPG, 12: 940.
[363] Roman Pontifical.
[364] Cf. T. Ohm, op. cit., 281.
[365] Luke 18:13.
[366] Luke 23:48.
[367] "Tundere autem pectus quid est, nisi arguere quod latet in pectore, et evidenti pulsu occultum castigare peccatum?" Sermo 67, 1. MPL, 38:433.
[368] Cf. R. Guardini, Sacred Signs (St. Louis: Pio Decimo Press, 1956), 31.
[369] 1 Cor. 1:18.
[370] Col. 1:20; Eph. 2:16.

made it a mark of His followers that they should bear their cross bravely in imitation of Him.[371] Hence we may expect a rather profuse use to be made of it in Christian liturgical practice. Taking the words of John the Baptist too literally (that one was coming who would baptize with fire and the Holy Spirit), Carpocrates *branded* the sign of the cross on the ear lobe of his initiates;[372] in those days the ear lobes were considered the seat of the memory.[373] Cabrol believes that the word *sphragizein* meant originally to mark a person with the cross; later on it became synonymous with Baptism.[374] The early Christians attached such importance to the sign of the cross, Tertullian tells us, that they made it before doing anything.[375] By the fourth century it was used in many sacramental rites, according to St. Augustine: the Mass, consecration of oils, the ordination of priests and other ministers, etc.[376] It was also a sign of faith for the Christian who made it.[377]

According to the words of Tertullian, referred to above, the sign of the cross was made only on the forehead. In the eighth century Alcuin mentions the signing of the lips.[378] And in the middle of the tenth century, the *Ordo Romanus* V, of Gallican origin, says that the deacon signs himself on the forehead and the breast at the words "Sequentia sancti evangelii. . . ."[379] The large sign of the cross, though mentioned as early as the sixth century,[380] does not seem to have become common until the tenth.[381] The sign of the cross is the usual gesture of blessing in all sacramental actions. Yet, it is difficult to see how the signs of the cross made over the consecrated Body and Blood of our Savior during the Mass can be interpreted as blessings. Because of so much parallel evidence, Jungmann considers them to be nothing more than a stylized pointing gesture, indicating the objects mentioned.[382]

[371] Matt. 10:38; 16:24; Gal. 2:19.

[372] Cf. F-J. Dölger, "Die Sphragis als religöse Brandmarkung im Einweihungsakt der gnostischen Karpokratianer," *Antike und Christentum*, 1 (1929), 73.

[373] *Ibid.*, 75.

[374] "Imposition des mains," *DACL*, VII, 397; also H. Leclercq, "Sphragis," *Ibid.*, XV, 1637.

[375] "Ad omnem progressum atque promotum, ad omnem aditum et exitum, ad calciatum, ad lavacra, ad mensas, ad lumina, ad cubilia, ad sedilia, quaecumque nos conversatio exercet, frontem crucis signaculo terimus." *De corona* 3. *MPL*, 2:99.

[376] *Tract. in Joan.* 118, n. 5. *MPL*, 35: 1950.

[377] *Tract. in Joan.* 2, n. 3. *MPL*, 35: 1390.

[378] *De usu psalmorum* I, n. 1. *MPL*, 101: 468.

[379] N. 35. Andrieu, *Les Ordines*, II, 216. Amalar mentions the fact that deacon and people sign themselves at this point, but only on the forehead: *De eccl. off.*, III, 18. *MPL*, 105: 1126.

[380] Eugippius, *Vita Severini* 11, 53. *MPL*, 62: 1196.

[381] Righetti, *op. cit.*, I, 302.

[382] *The Mass of the Roman Rite*, II, 145-146.

The liturgical kiss

"Greet one another with a holy kiss," Paul instructs the faithful in Rome.[383] The kiss so often used in the Liturgy is a symbol of the supernatural love which all Christians should bear towards one another, though it was also employed in pagan religions.[384] We find the kiss mentioned in a strictly liturgical context already in Justin's I *Apology*. After the congregation had finished the prayers which normally followed upon the Mass of the Catechumens and before the oblation was brought forth, the faithful greeted one another with a kiss.[385] Exactly how this was done is not indicated, though it is likely that it was done with the mouth, for this method was expressly prescribed in the *Apostolic Tradition* for the Kiss before the Mass of the faithful after the Baptism of a new candidate.[386] The same thing was true of the Mass for the consecration of a bishop.[387] Dölger claims that such a kiss with the mouth is to be found also in Cyprian,[388] and that it was a sign of welcome of the newly baptized into the brotherhood of Christians. Eventually Christians were led to venerate sacred objects with a kiss. Long before the seventh century the Gospel book was kissed as well as the feet of the pontiff.[389] Today this sort of veneration is extended to the altar, a symbol of Christ, the hands of the celebrant, the vestments, cruets, etc. The kiss of peace continued to be extended to the faithful up until the end of the Middle Ages. Innocent III attests to it.[390] Sometimes the paten would be kissed by the celebrant then passed around; later a board inscribed with a cross, called the osculatorium, or peace-board, was used in the same manner.[391]

Insufflation — Exsufflation

In the Roman Ritual for the administration of Baptism to adults we read that the priest is to blow, *exsufflat*, upon the face of the candidate three times, saying: "Exi ab eo, spiritus immunde, et da locum Spiritui Sancto Paraclito." And then he breathes, *halat*, upon the face of the candidate in the form of a cross, saying: "N. accipe Spiritum bonum per istam insufflationem. . . ." [392] Here we have clearly distinguished two actions. The first is an exsufflation, or vehement blowing, signifying the expulsion of the devil. The second is an insufflation,

---

[383] Rom. 16:16.
[384] Cf. T. Ohm, *op. cit.*, 213.
[385] I *Apology* 65. Quasten, *Monumenta*, 16.
[386] "Et cum oraverint, de ore pacem offerant." *La Tradition Apostolique,* Edit. B. Botte, n. 22, p. 53.
[387] *Ibid.*, n. 4, p. 30.
[388] "Der Kuss im Tauf- und Firmungsritual nach Cyprian von Karthago und Hippolyt von Rom," *Antike und Christentum*, 1 (1929), 189.
[389] *Ordo Romanus* I, n. 59. Andrieu, *Les Ordines*, II, 87.
[390] *De sacro altaris mysterio* VI, 5. MPL, 217: 909.
[391] J. Bona, *Rerum liturgicarum libri duo* (Paris, 1672), bk. II, c. 16, 7, p. 478.
[392] Tit. II, cap. 4, nn. 8 and 9.

or gentle breathing upon the candidate, and signifies a breathing of the Holy Spirit into the candidate.

We find our Lord performing a similar action when He gives His Apostles power to forgive sins: "He breathed upon them, and said, 'Receive the Holy Spirit. . . .'"[393] Exsufflation, or blowing out, was an action common among the early Christians denoting disgust and abhorrence of the pagan temples in which the devil was worshiped.[394] It was a logical step to introduce some such action into the Liturgy with which to express their hatred of the cause of all evil and to make sport of the devil's defeat at the hands of Christ.[395] After expelling the devil from the person or object to be baptized, blessed, or consecrated, there normally follows an insufflation, a breathing in of the Holy Spirit, and with Him divine power of life. Sometimes when the exsufflation is omitted or replaced by some verbal exorcism, the priest or pontiff proceeds immediately to the breathing in of the Spirit.[396] However, the terminology of our liturgical books is not always clear and precise. Though the word *halare* normally means to breathe and is used for insufflations, in the Pontifical this word is used for the exorcism of the oil to be blessed as chrism, and therefore certainly indicates an exsufflation.

Processions

These actions are a wonderful expression of the processes, changes of states, and inner sentiments of the spiritual life. Basically man needs to share his religious feelings with others. Processions are a means to this. But all prayer is a movement towards God; it is a continual "passover," a departure from the land of Egypt, the life of sin and defection from God, to the promised land, a life of union with our Creator. Processions should serve to bring out this fact. Yet more, our spiritual life consists in following Christ, rather than "walking after strange gods."[397] A procession should be an image for us of the Church in pilgrimage here below, following Christ and His cross to our home of eternity. And there we walk with God, as our first parents did in

[393] John 20:22.

[394] Cf. F.-J. Dölger, "Heidnische Begrüssung und christliche Verhöhnung der Heidentempel. *Despuere* und *Exsufflare* in der Dämonenbeschwörung," *Antike und Christentum*, 3 (1932), 192-203.

[395] Augustine's words are very much to the point: "Sicut vidistis hodie, sicut nostis, et parvuli exsufflantur, et exorcizantur, ut pellatur ab eis diaboli potestas iniqua, quae decepit homines. Non ergo creatura Dei in infantibus exorcizatur, aut exsufflatur, sed ille, sub quo sunt omnes, qui sub peccato nascuntur." *De symbolo ad catechumenos 1. MPL,* 40: 628. And in another place: ". . . omnes baptizandi infantuli non ob aliud exsufflantur nisi ut ab eis princeps mundi mittatur foras." *Contra Julianum opus imperfectum V,* 64. *MPL,* 45: 1504.

[396] As is the case for the blessing of baptismal water during the Easter Vigil. Here the priest breathes three times over the water in the form of a cross, saying: "Tu has simplices aquas tuo ore benedicito . . ."

[397] Jeremiah 7:6.

the Garden of Paradise. Yet this walking with God has already begun here below, for, says St. Paul, "our conversation is in heaven"; [398] prayer is a walk with God.[399] With all this powerful symbolism of the *ecclesia peregrinans* behind her, was it not natural that the Church should express this movement of prayer and salvation by means of the gesture we call "procession"?

Many processions, of course, are of practical necessity: we must go from one place to another. During the times of persecution, the only procession which the Church could have was the funeral cortège. But afterwards her processions became more frequent as manifestations of her joy, or to strengthen the spiritual dispositions of the faithful, or to manifest her faith. Thus in the time of the Arian controversy, both factions held processions through the streets of Constantinople shouting their respective mottos and singing their hymns.[400] From the fourth to the sixth century, processions were formed to transfer relics, receive popes, bishops and kings, as a means of thanksgiving, penance, or petition. And more recently (in the fourteenth century), the Eucharistic procession arose as a means of heightening the faith of the people in the Real Presence, of giving them a chance to see the host.[401]

C. Things

The Church has always been plagued by people who assume two extreme, opposed views in regard to matter. The one group tends to an unfounded spiritualism, looking upon material things as evil, or at most tolerating them as a necessary evil. This group seems to forget that man is human, not angelic; that he has, not only a spirit, but also a body, the two in a composite unity. They will harp on "worship in spirit and truth," will consider the use of material things as a perversion and degradation of their intercourse with God, and will endeavor to eliminate the material element as far as possible. "Enter into thy chamber, close the door, and pray to thy God in secret," they will say.

The other extreme is one of materialism; it tries to escape from thought and the spirit, runs from the angelic and embraces the brute animal in man, confuses spirit with matter. In its most extreme form, it divinizes nature; it is pantheistic. In less extreme manifestations, it gets entangled in matter, sinks itself into externalism. It mistakes the symbol for the symbolized; it never seems to arrive at the spiritual terminus behind the sign. In worship this would be called ritualism.

The Church has strenuously resisted both extremes. She recalls that "God saw all the things that He had made, and they were

[398] Philip. 3:20.
[399] Cf. T. Ohm, "Die Gebetgebärde des Gehens," *Benediktinische Monatschrift*, 25 (1949), 35.
[400] Sozomenus, *Hist. eccl.* 6, 8. *MPG*, 67: 690.
[401] Cf. E, Dumoutet, *Le Désir de voir l'hostie* (Paris, 1926), 82-83, 88.

good." [402] But she also insists with St. Paul that "since the creation of the world God's invisible attributes are clearly seen—his everlasting power also and divinity—being understood through the things that are made." [403] She asks us not to forget that all things were made through the eternal Word,[404] and that this same Word was made flesh and dwelt among us. But she adds: It was in this man like unto ourselves that we saw the glory, grace, and truth of the only begotten of the Father; in Him the Father was revealed to us.[405] Her stand, therefore, is one of *integral* humanism. It is only when we realize this that material things can become for us symbols of supernatural reality.

As Guardini puts it:

> The liturgy is reality throughout. It is this which distinguishes it from all purely intellectual or emotional piety, from rationalism and religious romanticism. In it man is confronted with physical realities — men, things, ceremonies, ornaments — and with metaphysical realities — a real Christ, real grace . . . The whole of nature must be evoked by the liturgy, and the liturgy, seized by grace, must take hold of it all, refine and glorify it in the likeness of Christ . . . Thus the liturgy embraces everything in existence, angels, men and things; all the content and events of life, in short, the whole of reality. And natural reality is here made subject to the supernatural; created reality related to the uncreated . . . Hence, the liturgy is *creation, redeemed and at prayer*.[406]

There is hardly a material thing for which the Church does not provide a blessing. She thus redeems all with man and consecrates all to the glory of God. But it is not with all material things that we are concerned here; we shall treat them later when we consider the Church's sacramentals. Here we will look into the symbolism of only a few elements, and this the better to understand the symbolic language of the Church. As Dom Cabrol says:

> In all times a symbolic meaning in harmony with their natural use has been attached to the great phenomena of nature and to material elements of universal utility. Water, which has the power of cleansing and refreshing, is, in the language of signs as well as that of religion, the symbol of purification. Fire not only burns, it also purifies like water; and again, it gives light. Oil softens, soothes, strengthens, renders supple. Salt gives flavor to food and preserves it. Every language contains expressions or metaphors derived from these words and based on these primitive ideas. For instance, we speak of fiery zeal, of the salt of wisdom; men

[402] Gen. 1:31.
[403] Rom. 1:20.
[404] John 1:3.
[405] *Ibid.*, 1:14, 18.
[406] Romano Guardini, *The Church and the Catholic* (New York, 1940), 29-31.

endowed with a certain kind of eloquence are said to speak
with unction.[407]

Bread and wine

The most important of all material elements used in the Liturgy
are bread and wine. Their symbolism should be obvious. As the staple
foods, at least in much of the world, of man's natural life, it was most
fitting that our Lord should choose them as the channels of His greatest grace to man, His Body and Blood, the food of the soul. By divine
revelation these same two foods had been employed for ages in the
Jewish rite of the Passover to commemorate in a spirit of thanksgiving
the deliverance of the Chosen People of God from a land of oppression
and slavery. They were also intended by God as a pledge of hope, an
image and prototype of the spiritual liberation of mankind to be accomplished by the promised Redeemer. He, the true Paschal Lamb,
the night before He was taken prisoner, took the matzah, or piece of
unleavened bread, that remained from the Passover meal, and the
wine of the cup of benediction and with them inaugurated that spotless and holy sacrifice through which He would rebuild and renew a
decadent and perverted human race.

This bread and wine, now His Body and Blood given for the
remission of sins, He bequeathed to His disciples in ratification of
the new and eternal testament or pact between God and men and as a
sacred banquet in which to renew the effects of His holy passion, as a
source of grace, as food for the soul, and as an earnest of future glory.
This same bread and wine marvelously express man's part in this
new and spotless sacrifice, for bread and wine are products of human
work: man must grind the wheat and bake the flour to have bread;
he must pick and crush the grapes and ferment their juice to obtain
wine. When offered to God through the hands of the priest at Mass,
they symbolize man's work, his life, himself given, dedicated, consecrated to God—a sign of his subjection to God's dominion as well as of
his hope of final return to the Source and Sire of his being in whom
alone his heart will find rest.

Incense

According to the words of the psalmist, incense is a symbol of
prayer: "Let my prayer be directed as incense in Thy sight." [408] And
St. John sees in vision a bowl of incense held before the Lamb by the
twenty-four elders; it is the prayers of the saints.[409] At the very moment when the drama of the New Testament redemption unfolds, we

[407] *Liturgical Prayer. Its History and Spirit* (Westminster, Md., 1950), 218.
[408] Ps. 140:2.
[409] Apoc. 5:8.

find Zachary officiating at the altar of incense,[410] complying with one of the many prescriptions regarding the use of incense in Jewish worship laid down by Moses under the inspiration of God.[411] But to use incense in worship was natural, as is proved by its frequent mention in ancient pagan writings. The Romans, particularly, used it, considering no sacrifice complete without it.[412] They also used it profusely at funerals and as a protection against calamities.[413] Although the Christians maintained the use of incense at funerals,[414] they did not offer it to God.[415] They refrained from employing incense as an act of worship probably because of their hatred of the idolatrous use made of it by the pagans.[416] After the decline of paganism, however, the Church did not hesitate to adopt incense as another help in giving God fitting adoration. Our first witness for its use in the Mass comes from the East. Pseudo-Dionysius reports that the bishop began the celebration of Mass by incensing the altar and sanctuary.[417] And this was at least before the end of the fifth century. But in Rome incense was employed in quite a different manner. It seems that it was carried in civil ceremonial before persons of high office or rank simply as a mark of honor.[418] And this is exactly how it makes its debut in the Roman Rite, where we find it carried before the pope as he makes his entrance into the basilica to begin Mass and also before the Gospel book.[419] The first mention of the incensation of the oblation at Mass is in the eleventh century.[420] Though in the East, specifically at Jerusalem, incense was used during the night vigils as early as the fourth century,[421] in the West we must wait until the eighth century to find it used at Lauds and Vespers.[422] As used by the Church today, incense is intended as a mark of adoration to God (in the Blessed Sacrament), or of reverence and respect for persons and things: the celebrant, ministers, clergy and people (who are temples of the Holy Spirit), the Gospel book, oblation, altar, crucifix, etc. In the thirteenth century

[410] Luke 1:9-11.

[411] Exod. 30:1-9; Lev. 16:12.

[412] Cf. E. Fehrenbach, "Encens," *DACL*, V, 4-5; J. Quasten, *Musik und Gesang in den Kulten der heidenischen Antike und christlichen Frühzeit* (Münster, 1930), 29 ff., 43, 55, 202.

[413] *Ibid.*

[414] Cf. Tertullian, *De idololatria* 11. MPL, 1: 752; *Liber Apol.* 42. MPL, 1: 558.

[415] *Ibid.*, 30. MPL, 1: 504.

[416] E. Fehrenbach, *art. cit.*, 8.

[417] *De ecclesiastica hierarchia* III, 2. J. Quasten, *Monumenta*, 294.

[418] Cf. P. Connolly, "The Use of Incense in the Roman Rite," *Ephem. Liturg.*, 43 (1929), 173.

[419] *Ord. Rom.* I, nn. 46, 59. Andrieu, *Les Ordines*, II, 82, 88.

[420] Bernold, *Micrologus* 9. MPL, 151: 983.

[421] Ethérie, *Journal de Voyage*, n. 24, 10, p. 196.

[422] *Epist. Gemmuli ad Bonifacium.* MPL, 89: 755.

we even find Innocent III attaching an exorcistic significance to its use,[423] an idea which continues to our own day.[424]

Light

The use of lights in divine worship is not peculiar to Christianity. A seven-branched candlestick was commanded by God to be set up in the Temple.[425] The pagans too made a practice of burning lamps before their idols and above all in their funerals.[426] At first the Christians were opposed to the use of lights in worship, except, of course, for purely practical needs. And this opposition stems again from the idolatrous connotation attached to them. To offer lights to the dead was regarded as a religious act; the dead were considered by the pagans as living in the tomb.[427] Hence, the Council of Elvira (306) severely condemned the burning of lights before the graves of deceased Christians.[428] And the Christian writer Lactantius spoke out vigorously against all use of lights in worship. Candles and torches, he said, were necessary in pagan worship, for their idols dwelt in darkness, but our God, the maker of light, has no need of them.[429]

But just as in the case of incense, once paganism had been overcome and all the idolatrous connotation behind lights broken, their use steadily increased. Before the end of the third century there is sufficient evidence to show that their use was popular as a means of honoring the dead.[430] Later, in the fourth century, Jerome clearly says that lamps were burned by pious women before the tombs of martyrs even in the daytime, not as the pagans burned lamps before their idols, but simply as a mark of honor and respect; and that lights were carried at the singing of the Gospel in the Orient, not to dispel darkness, but as a sign of joy.[431] A custom of somewhat later introduction,

[423] "Ob hoc etiam incensatur altare, quatenus ab eo omnis daemonis nequitia propellatur. Fumus enim incensi valere creditur ad daemones effugandos." *De sacro altaris mysterio* II, 17. *MPL*, 217: 808.

[424] See the prayer for blessing incense for the erection of a new cross in the Roman Ritual: "dignare respicere, benedicere, et sanctificare hanc creaturam incensi, ut omnes languores, omnesque infirmitates, atque insidiae inimici, odorem eius sentientes, effugiant, et separentur a plasmate tuo . . ."

[425] Exod. 25:31-40.

[426] Propertius speaks of living between two torches, one used in the rites of marriage, the other for funerals: "Viximus insignes inter utramque facem." *Elegiae* iv, 11, 46. *Sexti Aurelii Propertii Opera Omnia*, II (London: Delphin Classics, 1822), 739. So many were the torches carried in the funeral procession in honor of Germanicus that they illuminated the streets of the entire city, says Tacitus: ". . . plena urbis itinera collucentes per Campum Martis faces." *Annales* iii, 4. *C. Cornelii Taciti Opera Omnia* (London: Delphin Classics, 1821), I, 465.

[427] Cf. A. Rush, *Death and Burial in Christian Antiquity* (Washington, 1941), 221-228.

[428] C. 34. Hefele-Leclercq, *op cit.*, I. 239.

[429] *Divinae institutiones* 6, 2. *MPL*, 6: 637-639.

[430] See the inscriptions in T. Klauser, *Die Cathedra im Totenkult der heidnischen und christlichen Antike* (Münster, 1927), 127, note 104.

[431] *Contra Vigilantium* 7. *MPL*, 23: 361.

that of carrying lights before the pope as he entered the basilica,[432] is traced again to the Roman civil ceremonial which included the bearing of torches before persons of high rank.[433]

Though so many of these practices developed under the influence of pagan or civil customs,[434] the Christians read into them a new symbolism. Light became a symbol of Christ, referred to so often in Scripture as the light of the world.[435] Light was also a symbol of life. The pagans often referred to birth as a wandering out of darkness into sun and light.[436] Even today we follow the custom of putting candles on the birthday cake, as many small ones as the years one has lived and in the middle a larger one as the light of life, a symbol of the many more years still hoped for.[437] But while the pagan regarded death as the snuffing out of life or the going down of one's sun, the Christian considered the day of death as the *dies natalis*. Though the earthly sun may no longer shine for him, a greater light illumines his life, the *lux perpetua* which knows no night. Thus, the candle or the lamp lighted in the cemetery is no sign of despair for the Christian because his beloved deceased now dwell in darkness; rather it is a sign of hope and faith, a symbol of the eternal light and life which the souls of the departed now enjoy. It is truly a sign of joy, harking back to Baptism in which we were "made light in the Lord." [438] "O Orient, splendor of eternal light and Sun of justice, come and enlighten those who sit in darkness and in the shadow of death!"

Water

In the Book of Exodus (30:18-20) Aaron and his sons were required to wash before approaching the altar. And in Psalm 50 we read, "Sprinkle me with hyssop and I shall be cleansed; wash me and I shall be made whiter than snow." Here water is used as a symbol of purification and expiation. And John the Baptist, in preparation for the coming of the Savior of the world, preached a Baptism of repentance.[439] Our Lord willed to continue this symbolic practice, but He infused into it a real supernatural purification of the soul in the sacrament of Baptism. A purificatory use of water along with a worship of water is to be found in the pagan rites of the Greeks and

---

[432] See *Ord. Rom.* I, n. 46. Andrieu, *Les ordines*, II, 82.
[433] Cf. T. Klauser, *Der Ursprung der bischöflichen Insignien und Ehrenrechte* (Krefeld, 2nd edit., 1953), 18.
[434] For the origins of the Paschal Candle and blessing, see F-J. Dölger, "Lumen Christi," *Antike und Christentum*, 5 (1936), 1-43.
[435] Isaias 9:2; 49:6; 60:1-3; 60:19-20; Luke 1:79; 2:32; John 8:12; Apoc. 1:12-20; 1 Tim. 6:16.
[436] Cf. Dölger, *Sol Salutis*, 385.
[437] *Ibid.*, 386.
[438] Eph. 5:8-9.
[439] Luke 3:3; John 1:25-26.

Romans.[440] Tertullian tells us that Christians of his time washed before praying.[441] Clement of Alexandria reports the same practice,[442] but, he insists, this must not be an empty ritual—a genuine spiritual purity of heart must be sought. So much was the practice a part of the life of the early Church, that in the period after Constantine the *cantharus,* or water fountain, became a standard fixture in the court-yard before the basilica to permit the faithful to purify themselves before entering the presence of God.[443]

Our present custom of taking blessed water upon entering the church is a continuation of this earlier practice. A like purification is performed during Mass at the end of the Offertory in the Lavabo.[444] All these lustral uses of water in the Liturgy help maintain us in the spirit of our Baptism, in which, through the instrumentality of this earthly element, Almighty God cleansed our souls from the impurity of original sin and adorned it with that essential supernatural purity, sanctifying grace.

Oil

Oil is used liturgically in the Old Testament for the anointing of the tabernacle and Aaron[445] and the Jewish kings.[446] None of these, however, inspired the Church's primitive use of oil. It was only later that she began to employ oil for the consecration of the altar, the bishop's head, and the priest's hands. Originally she was motivated rather by the healing effects of oil in profane use. It is only with this implication that an anointing with oil is mentioned in the New Testament. St. Mark relates how the Twelve cast out many devils and anointed with oil many sick people and healed them.[447] And St. James urges the presbyters to go to the sick, pray over them, and anoint them in the name of the Lord.[448] Even the sacrament of Confirmation originally did not seem to contain an anointing, for in all the pertinent texts of the Acts only an imposition of hands is mentioned. Tertullian records an anointing at the time of Baptism, however.[449] Oil was also used to drive out the devil.[450]

[440] Cf. F-J. Dölger, "Nilwasser und Taufwasser," *Antike und Christentum,* 5 (1936), 153-187.

[441] *De Oratione* 13. MPL, 1: 1271.

[442] ". . . dicunt oportere nos ablutos ad sacrificia et preces ire mundos et splendidos." *Stromata* 4, 22. MPG, 8: 1351.

[443] Cf. Eusebius, *Historia eccl.* 10, 4, 40. GCS, 9 (2), p. 874.

[444] Cf. J. Jungmann, *The Mass of the Roman Rite,* II, 76-82, for the weighty evidence attesting to the symbolic interpretation of this washing.

[445] Exod. 30:24-31; Lev. 8:10-12.

[446] 1 Kings 10:1; 16:12-13.

[447] 6:13.

[448] Epistle of St. James 5:14.

[449] *De baptismo* 7. MPL, 1:1315. See a similar reference in *La Tradition Apostolique,* n. 21, p. 50. However, Hippolytus has Confirmation immediately follow with an anointing: n. 22, p. 52.

[450] Cf. *La Tradition Apostolique,* n. 21, p. 49; *Euchologion* of Serapion of Thmuis, XVII. Quasten, *Monumenta,* 66.

Oil, therefore, is the symbol of divine healing, the giving of strength and priestly power. Since the giving of grace is appropriated to the Holy Spirit, oil is also a fitting symbol of the giver of divine gifts.[451] Whence the name "unction of the Holy Spirit": "Qui diceris Paraclitus, Altissimi donum Dei, Fons vivus, ignis, caritas et spiritalis unctio."

Salt

As the Roman proverb has it, "There is nothing as useful as sun and salt." [452] There is no kitchen without salt; hardly a food we eat is not seasoned with it, so much so that in ancient times it was regarded as a symbol of hospitality.[453] It was also used to prevent decay, to preserve meat, as an antiseptic, to harden the skin of new-born babies among the Orientals.[454] It was used in sacrifice by both Jews [455] and Romans alike.[456] Eliseus cast salt into a well to cure the water and make it fruitful once more.[457] And remembering our Lord's words, "You are the salt of the earth, etc.," [458] the Church uses it to dispel the devil in her exorcisms and as a symbol of the divine wisdom of revealed truth which preserves the newly baptized unto everlasting life. In this spirit the Church used to give salt to her catechumens all during the year in preparation for their Baptism.[459]

[451] Cyril of Jerusalem, *Mystagogical Catechesis*, 3, 3. *MPG*, 33: 1089.
[452] Dölger, *Sol Salutis*, 383.
[453] Dölger, "Salz der Freundschaft," *Antike und Christentum*, 5 (1936), 143.
[454] Ezech. 16:4.
[455] Lev. 2:13.
[456] ". . . illi ad surgentem conversi lumina solem dant fruges manibus salsas." *Aneid*, XII, 172. *P. Vergilii Maronis Opera Omnia* (Leipzig, 1894), 794.
[457] 4 Kings 2:19-22.
[458] Matt. 5:13.
[459] Council of Hippo in 393, can. 7. Hefele-Leclercq, *op. cit.*, II, 86.

CHAPTER SIX

The Mass

With a treatment of the Mass we have arrived at the very heart of Christianity, for, as Pius XII says, "the mystery of the most Holy Eucharist is the culmination and center of the Christian religion; it is the crowning act of the sacred Liturgy." [1] It stands at the very core of the soul's relationship to God, for it is the chief source of redemption, being the same redemptive act which Christ wrought on Calvary. It is Calvary applied to contemporary mankind. Just as Calvary is the starting point from which flows the entire current of salvific grace, so the Mass is "the source and center of Christian piety." [2]

Let us recall that Catholicism is not a natural religion, but a supernatural one. As such, its warp and woof is made up of divine acts productive of supernatural life in its adherents. And at the center of these acts stands the Eucharist. Everything in the spiritual life must, if we are to be truly Catholic, take its meaning and direction from the Mass. Whatever religious activity we engage in must be understood either as a preparation for immersing ourselves in the redemptive action of the Mass, or as a prolongation and extension of that same action. Pius XII clearly tells us that "if the private and interior devotion of individuals were to neglect the sacrifice of the altar and the sacraments, and to withdraw them from the stream of vital energy that flows from Head to members, it would indeed be sterile and deserve to be condemned." [3] Such devotion would be unable to make the soul grow in the spiritual life, for that growth must come from Christ. But, on the other hand, the Mass and the other sacraments will never produce their proper effect of Christ-likeness in our souls, unless our hearts are genuinely disposed to receive the sacraments. As intelligent beings, we must put our own "lips to the fountain and drink, absorb for ourselves the life-giving water, and rid ourselves of anything that might hinder its nutritive effect." [4] Works of asceticism, therefore, should be regarded as preparation for the Mass, with our apostolic

[1] *Mediator Dei*, 66.
[2] *Ibid.*, 201.
[3] *Ibid.*, 32.
[4] *Ibid.*, 31.

work being our effort to carry Christ's redemptive activity (begun in the Mass) to the world.

It is traditional in theology to divide the Eucharist into sacrifice and sacrament. Without desiring to break with conventional terminology, we would point out that this division often gives rise to misunderstanding, as though Communion were a sacrament in itself, totally independent and distinct from the Eucharistic Sacrifice. This, however, is false. As theology teaches, the words of consecration spoken over bread and wine confect the sacrament of the Eucharist. Holy Communion is the reception of the fruit or the effect of the sacramental consecration. This distinction ought to bring out the dependence of Holy Communion on the sacrificial action of the Mass, put in relief its role as an integrating part of the sacrament, and preclude any false dichotomy between the two.

A. The Nature and Forms of the Mass

1. The meaning of the Mass

A Mystery-Memorial

At the Last Supper, after having spoken those powerful words over bread and wine, our Lord said, "Do this in memory of me!" [5] And to this St. Paul adds by way of explanation, "As often as you shall eat this bread and drink the cup, you proclaim the death of the Lord until He comes." [6] The Mass, then, is a celebration dedicated to the memory of Christ and His redemptive work.

When someone close to us dies, we do everything we can to keep his memory alive in our minds. We zealously collect and preserve the things he used during his life. We set up his portrait in a place of honor where we will often see it. We recount his virtues and various good deeds. We may write his biography, even erect a monument to his memory. Yet, try as we may, this memory will live in our minds and hearts only; we cannot bring him back or make him truly live physically anymore in our midst. And the great power or influence which he may have exerted among men, the works he may have started, might still live on in some fashion aided through our efforts, but they are no longer his power, works, or actions. They are now performed by others.

This is not the case with Christ's memory. It is not only His memory that lives on; that very memory brings Him and His work to us in all their original vitality, freshness, and reality.

We who have come so late on the stage of human history were not privileged to see and touch the Son of God made man. Yet He is here: His flesh, His blood, His soul, His divinity. We were unable to

[5] Luke 22:19; 1 Cor. 11:25.
[6] 1 Cor. 11:26.

witness the great drama of redemption wrought for us by Christ's heroic sacrifice on the cross and accepted by God through the Resurrection and Ascension. Little worry, for in the Mass we have the same body and blood as they were once immolated on Calvary, arose from the dead on Easter morning and ascended into heaven forty days later. We have not simply the empty sepulcher present, nor just a picture of our heroic Savior. Our memorial rite of the Mass re-enacts sacramentally what it commemorates.

That is why right after the Consecration we pray: "Unde et memores beatae passionis, nec non et ab inferis resurrectionis, sed et in caelos gloriosae ascensionis. . . ." Note that this prayer stands in intimate relationship with the Consecration, bound to the final words, "Haec quotiescumque feceritis, in mei memoriam facietis," as though dependent on them. In other words, we offer this holy victim in memory of His Passion, Resurrection and Ascension, as He commanded us to do.

This prayer, the Unde et memores, called the *Anamnesis* (Greek for remembrance), is to be found in every Liturgy of the Church, both Eastern and Western. This fact serves to bring out a very basic aspect of the Mass, recognized clearly and explicitly by the entire Church, that it is a memorial of Christ and His salvific acts. Indeed it is almost as important as the sacrificial aspect of the Mass. It is a theme that we find constantly recurring in the writings of the Fathers of the Church, at least as frequently as the sacrificial theme.[7]

Such a memorial of the facts of redemption is both essential and basic to Christianity, Jungmann insists.[8] Christianity is an historical religion based on the coming of God's Son who redeemed man at a certain time and place. Our spiritual life depends completely on a special intervention of the Divinity in human history. And it is extremely important that we always bear this in mind. The temptation is all too great to succumb to a religious naturalism. We are very prone to make religion the religious apostolate revolve about our human qualities—our personality, our administrative ability, our human cleverness. We act sometimes as though we can lift man up to God without the latter's help.

This was the attitude of the Renaissance period: its basic theme was a sort of pagan humanism, human nature glorified through its own inventiveness. And how much we still think that way today, especially with the marvelous advances of technology. This idea of mere human goodness, the mere natural perfectibility of man, is entirely foreign to Christianity. While man certainly has powers proper to himself,

[7] Cf. the article on the Mass, "Messe d'après les pères, jusqu'à S. Cyprien," *Dictionnaire de Théologie Catholique,* I, 864-964: Justin, Irenaeus, Origen, Hippolytus and Cyprian.
[8] *The Eucharistic Prayer. A Study of the Canon Missae* (Chicago: Fides, 1956), 3.

whereby he can improve himself, he is absolutely incapable of bridging the gap between himself and God, between his nature impaired by sin and imperfection and the divine life according to which alone he will find true happiness. Hence, a memorial of the supernatural events of our redemption serves to elevate Christianity far above the type of religion it would be were we to give in to the temptation to naturalize it. It is not simply a support for natural morality. Sanctifying grace makes us sons of God, and supernatural morality is a consequence of this divine fact. This memorial forever keeps before our mind the fact that God's love made us a new race.

Such a memorial is also essential to man in his religious endeavor, for man is a rational creature; he must consciously relate himself to God through the primary source of salvation. Such a memorial is basic to Christianity, for our religion is presented by Christ Himself as the advent of a new kingdom; it must be preached so that men know what is happening, can prepare for it and accept it when it comes. Just as man cannot supernaturalize himself without God's intervention, so neither can God save man unless man knows what is expected of him and willingly cooperates.

This memorial takes the form of a mystery-rite, in the sense of that term used by the ancient Christian writers; i.e., the re-enactment of the work of our salvation under a symbolic veil. In the words of Odo Casel, "The mystery is a holy ritual action in which a salvific act is made present in the rite and brings salvation to the cult-community which participates in it." [9] According to the Secret of the ninth Sunday after Pentecost, "as often as the commemoration of this Victim is celebrated, there is wrought the work of our redemption."

What is this work of redemption that is made present? Certainly the sacrifice of Christ, but not in its historical reality: it is not a death that takes place, but the sacrifice achieved through that death. This is the meaning of the sacramental signs; the sacrificial body and blood of Christ, therefore the *Christus passus*,[10] not the *Christus patiens*, is made present. However, the work of redemption did not stop with the death of Christ; that would have been a purely negative ending. He came, He died to bring a new life of grace, achieved in His Resurrection, a life of grace blossoming into eternal life in heaven, exemplified in His Ascension. These two mysteries, therefore, are made present, at least as far as their virtue or effects are concerned, for it is not the dead Christ who is made present through the transubstantiation, but the glorified Christ, who can die no more. These three mysteries— Passion, Resurrection, and Ascension—make up the central work of redemption.

[9] "Mysterienfrömmigkeit," *Bonner Zeitschrift für Theologie und Seelsorge*, 4 (1927), 104.
[10] *Summa Theol.*, III, 73, 6.

This presence of the redemptive mystery in the Mass, when it is a question of the sacrifice wrought by Christ on the Cross, is a real, objective presence in the sacrament. It is the same, identical sacrifice as offered on Calvary, *idem actus numero*;[11] not a repetition, but a perpetuation of it through sacramental efficacy. The *manner* of offering alone is different. It is not a physical, bloody immolation, but a symbolic, unbloody one.

The other mysteries pertaining to the central work of redemption are made present, not objectively in their proper substantial reality, but in the objective virtue and power flowing from the humanity of Christ bringing about our conformity and union with Him under the aspect exemplified by those same mysteries.[12] As Pius XII clearly states, these mysteries "are shining examples of Christian perfection, as well as sources of divine grace, due to the merit and prayers of Christ; they still influence us because each mystery brings its own special grace for our salvation."[13] Furthermore, the Pope goes on, "holy Mother the Church, while proposing for our contemplation the mysteries of our Redeemer, asks in her prayers for those gifts which would give her children the greatest possible share in the spirit of these mysteries through the merits of Christ."[14]

Thus this mystery-memorial actually takes a threefold form. After the Church has placed these mysteries before our mind's eye, allowing us a mental review of the work of redemption, she asks for the graces peculiar to them for us in her sacramental prayers of the Mass, and then re-enacts in the sacrament the same identical sacrifice of our Savior. The so-called Mass of the Catechumens, or instruction period of the Mass, constructs the mental review, the Orations and Preface of the Mass ask for the graces of these *magnalia Dei*, and the Consecration, at the very heart of the Mass, produces and applies to contemporary mankind Christ's sacrifice.

We must bring to Mass the vivid realization that, as we commemorate the magnificent plan of redemption devised by God's loving mercy, we are not simply reading or playing out a cold and lifeless representation of the dead past, or a simple and bare record of a former age.[15] We bring the past back into the present and make it so real in our liturgical action (not always substantially real) that we actually achieve our salvation; we experience, go through the whole drama of redemption, as we participate in it.

No wonder we say that the Mass is the center, core, and source of Christian piety. Here is Christ in person, and here is His entire

[11] Cf. the profound article of M. Matthijs, O. P. "Mysteriengegenwart secundum Sanctum Thomam," *Angelicum*, 34 (1957), 393-399, esp. 398-399; R. Garrigou-Lagrange, *Eucharistia* (Rome: Marietti, 1946), 289, 298.
[12] *Ibid.*, 396.
[13] *Mediator Dei*, 165.
[14] *Ibid.*
[15] *Ibid.*

redemptive activity, working on us, transfiguring us, divinizing us, reshaping us into His own image and likeness. What a phenomenal change could take place within us as we participate in Mass—if only we would cooperate!

A Sacrifice

There can be no doubt that the Mass is a sacrifice. Nor is there any question of an idea of sacrifice which evolved gradually in the life of the Church. According to Mark, our Lord said, "This is my blood of the new covenant, which is being shed for many." [16] Thus did He deliberately relate His actions at the Last Supper to the sacrificial blood of the Paschal Lamb; thus did He fill with reality the figurative sacrificial Passover meal. And in the earliest patristic document still extant, the *Didache*, we find the word *thusia*, Greek for sacrifice, used in reference to the Mass.[17] The same text considers the Mass the fulfillment of the prophecy made by Malachias: "From the rising of the sun even to the going down of the same, my name is great among the Gentiles, and in every place there is sacrifice, and there is offered to my name a clean oblation." [18]

In response to attacks on the Mass made by the would-be reformers, the Council of Trent dogmatically defined it to be a true sacrifice instituted by Christ.

> Our Lord . . . at the Last Supper, the night He was betrayed, wishing to leave His beloved Spouse, the Church, a visible sacrifice such as the nature of men requires, that would represent the bloody sacrifice offered once on the cross, and perpetuate its memory to the end of time, and whose salutary virtue might be applied in remitting those sins which we daily commit . . . offered His body and blood under the species of bread and wine to God the Father, and under the same species allowed the apostles, whom He at that time constituted priests of the New Testament, to partake thereof, commanding them and their successors in the priesthood to make the same offering with these words: "Do this in memory of me." [19] Should anyone say that in the Mass there is not offered a true and genuine sacrifice, or that to be offered means nothing more than that Christ is given to us to eat, *anath.sit.*[20] Should anyone say that the sacrifice of the Mass is only one of praise or thanksgiving, or but a bare commemoration of the sacrifice offered on the cross, and not propitiatory . . . *anath.sit.*[21]

[16] Mark 14:24.
[17] J. Quasten, *Monumenta*, p. 13.
[18] Mal. 1:11.
[19] Sess. 22, c. 1. Denz. 938.
[20] Sess. 22, c. 1. Denz. 948.
[21] Sess. 22, c. 3, Denz. 950.

In their attempt to show that the Mass is a true sacrifice, many theologians of the past few centuries appear to have overlooked the sacramental quality of the Consecration. For some, in order to have a genuine sacrifice in the Mass, the victim had to be destroyed; others claimed that any alteration in the victim or a simple presence of the victim in a less noble state would suffice.[22] But all of this would seem to be unnecessary, if it is kept firmly in mind that the Mass is a *sacramental* sacrifice, a sacrifice whose whole essence consists in *sacramental signification*. The essence of the sacrifice of the Mass is that it *represents* the bloody sacrifice on the cross. The twofold Consecration is, formally speaking, a sacrifice inasmuch as it *sacramentally* separates (that is, by *signs* or *symbols*) the body from the blood of Christ. This sacramental immolation is joined to the offering which Christ once made on the cross and is now actually made present again.[23] Thus, while the offering by Christ is real and actual, the immolation is only symbolic: it vividly represents the real or physical immolation, or separation, of body and blood which once took place on Calvary.[24]

Beyond showing that in the Mass the priest and the ends of the sacrifice are the same as on Calvary, Pius XII centers his whole argument around sacramental signification to show the sacrificial character of the Mass, and thus he recapitulates the whole of the Thomistic tradition:

> Likewise the victim is the same, namely, our Divine Redeemer in His human nature with His true body and blood. The manner, however, in which Christ is offered is different. On the cross He completely offered Himself and all His sufferings to God, and the immolation of the victim was brought about by the bloody death, which He underwent of His free will. But on the altar, by reason of the glorified state of His human nature, "death shall have no more dominion over Him",[25] and so the shedding of His blood is impossible; still, according to the plan of divine wisdom, the sacrifice of our Redeemer is shown forth in an admirable manner by external signs which are the symbols of His death. For by the "transubstantiation" of bread into the body of Christ and of wine into His blood, His body and blood are both really present: now the eucharistic species under which He is present symbolize the actual separation of His body and blood. Thus the commemorative representation of His death, which actually took place on Calvary, is repeated in every sacrifice of

[22] All these opinions are described and discussed in the work of M. Lepin, *L'idée du sacrifice de la Messe d'après les théologiens depuis l'origine jusqu'à nos jours.* Paris, 1926.

[23] Cf. Garrigou-Lagrange, *op. cit.*, 290-298.

[24] *Ibid.*, 284-289; *Summa Theol.*, III, 74, 1. The magnificent book of A. Vonier is essential for a genuine understanding of this problem: *The Key to the Doctrine of the Eucharist* (Westminster, Maryland: Newman, 1946), esp. 108-133.

[25] Rom. 6:9.

the altar, seeing that Jesus Christ is symbolically shown by separate symbols to be in a state of victimhood.[26]

But the celebration of Mass means more than simply making Christ's sacrifice truly present; it is also our sacrifice, the sacrifice of the Church. While on the cross Christ offered His sacrifice alone, in the Mass it is no longer Christ alone who offers or who is offered: now it is the whole Christ, the Mystical Body of Christ, both Head and members. Unfortunately this is a truth that is often passed over in silence in our catechetics. We hold firmly that the Mass is Christ's sacrifice; the Church teaches this very explicitly. But the fact that we, as members of Christ, offer this sacrifice and are offered together with Christ, is rarely mentioned; yet it is nonetheless true. In fact, it is of utmost importance for our spiritual lives that we keep this truth firmly in mind and put it into practice.

In the Council of Trent, as we have already seen, the Church officially teaches that, in instituting the Mass, Christ bequeathed His Spouse, the Church, a visible sacrifice such as the nature of man requires, in order to apply its salutary virtue to men of all times, in order to afford to all peoples the opportunity of ratifying Christ's sacrifice, of making it their own, of offering it together with Christ, of joining and cooperating in the supreme act of glorification of God which Christ performed on the cross.

As a matter of fact, the Church teaches this doctrine very explicitly in the texts of the Mass. There the sacrifice of Christ is only hinted at; it is enshrined, contained, in the sacrifice of the Church, our sacrifice. What we see and hear at Mass is almost exclusively what the Church is doing, what, if you will, Christ the Head is doing through and together with His Mystical Body. We hear continually the words: "*We* bring gifts," "*We* offer this oblation," "*Our* sacrifice," "*We* offer this host, this victim," "*We* beg for the acceptance of *our* sacrifice," "*We* prepare *our* sacrifice," etc. The sacrifice of Christ is present as though wrapped up in the sacrifice of the Church; He has given His sacrifice to us to offer.

If this were not true, how could the priest during Mass beg God to accept benignly "this holy victim, this spotless victim, this pure victim?" What sense would it make to ask God to deign to accept it as He had done the sacrifices of Abel, Abraham, and the Melchisedech? Surely the priest knows that this victim we offer is Christ, that it is His sacrifice. Is this not blasphemy? How could God not accept it? Christ is the Son of God; His sacrifice is infinitely pleasing to the Father, and therefore always acceptable and accepted by the Father. There can be question of an unfavorable acceptance or reception only when it is a matter of *our* sacrifice. And it is; that is precisely what the priest refers to. In the Mass, not only Christ on Calvary is

[26] *Mediator Dei,* 70.

offered, but now the whole Christ—Christ and His members, His Mystical Body.

While Christ the Head is always pleasing to God, we cannot say the same of His members. We are filled with imperfections, inordinate attachments; we therefore are not always pleasing to God, not accepted by Him without further ado. The object of our pleas during Mass is that God accept us as part of Christ's sacrifice, that He look favorably upon this association of ourselves with Him, this addition to the infinitely pleasing act of redemption once performed by Christ alone and now re-offered by us in the Mass.

And when will God accept our part in this sacrificial Mass? Only if and when we offer it in a worthy manner, when we possess that inner disposition of which this sacrifice is the sign.

This is the precise meaning of the Mass as a sacrifice. A sacrifice is, after all, nothing but a sign. We give God an object, we make Him a present which stands for ourselves, which represents, symbolizes the giving of ourselves. A young man who gives a girl an engagement ring does not do so simply to decorate her hand. This gift symbolizes his fidelity to her, his devotion, his dedication, his giving of himself. If these sentiments really do not stand behind the ring, no girl in her right mind will accept it. So in sacrifice, we give God a gift, not as though He needed it, but because we feel the need of showing our allegiance to Him. We would, of course, do this most perfectly by taking our lives; but this He forbids. Hence, we must search for something else that will stand for us, be a vicarious victim for us.

The very material elements of the sacrifice of the Mass already symbolize our self-dedication. We place bread and wine on the altar. These are products of human labor. We must plant the grain of wheat, till the soil, reap the harvest, grind the wheat into flour, then bake it in order to produce bread. As for the wine, we obtain it only after planting a vineyard, pruning the vine, picking the grapes, crushing them, and helping their juice to ferment. And so they represent a great amount of human labor. At the same time they are food; by presenting them to the priest to be made into sacrifice, we give God something essential to our life, that which nourishes and supports it.

But we do not stop here. It isn't bread and wine, merely natural things, that we offer God. No, they are transubstantiated; they become the body and blood of a divine person, a Person who represents us in a unique way, for He is the second Head of the human race, the only victim really capable of satisfying God.

Thus we place ourselves on the altar, we offer up ourselves as victims through a representative sign, someone who takes our place, since we cannot take our own life. Christ becomes a victim for us; He substitutes Himself for sinful man.

And so Christ is the sign of our sacrifice. And our participation in this sacrifice is meaningful only when it truly expresses what is in our hearts, only when it is in fact the symbol of a genuine spirit of obedience and reverence on our part towards God. Only when this sentiment is realized can we hope that God will accept our sacrifice as favorably as He did that of Abel, Abraham, and Melchisedech. When such is not the case, when we do not actually stand behind the celebration with genuine interior preparation, then the sharp words of the prophet can be applied to us: "Your sacrifice is an outrage in my eyes, because your hands are stained with blood and sacrilege!"

Indeed the ideal should be far different. Our sentiments must be far purer and more elevated than those of the holy men we have just mentioned, precisely because the sign of our sacrifice is purer and more elevated. It isn't just any sign, not just any gift of esteem, that we offer to God, but the very flesh and blood of Jesus Christ, the Son of God. Hence, Christ's sentiments must be ours, if we really want Him to represent us at the altar, a victim in our stead.

This thought stands before us at least as a challenge, as a high ideal, and it is a thought which is clearly expressed in the words of the Mass itself. Right after the Consecration we say through the mouth of the priest that prayer, Unde et memores, "Wherefore being mindful of Christ's passion, resurrection and ascension, we offer!" We offer fitly—and we admit it through this prayer—only when we do so with the awareness that we are thereby continuing Christ's work of redemption, that we are entering into *His* offering and praying. It is a genuine sacrifice on *our* part only if beforehand we have truly entered into the world of Christ's principles and spirit, only if we have made our own the dispositions with which He went to His death. As St. Paul says, when speaking of Christ's complete self-abnegation, "Let this mind be in you which was also in Christ Jesus." [27] And in another place, "As often as you eat and drink of this bread and wine, you proclaim the death of the Lord. . . ." [28] We are supposed to show it!

Pius XII insists on this point very vigorously. The fact that Christ substitutes Himself for us as a victim requires:

> . . . that all Christians possess, as far as humanly possible, the same dispositions as those which the divine Redeemer had when He offered Himself in sacrifice: that is to say, they should in a humble attitude of mind, pay adoration, honor, praise and thanksgiving to the supreme majesty of God. Moreover, it means that they must assume to some extent the character of a victim, that they deny themselves as the Gospel commands, that freely and of their own accord they do penance and that each detests and satisfies for his sins. It means, in a word, that we must all undergo with Christ a mystical death on the cross so that we can apply to ourselves

[27] Col. 2:5.
[28] 1 Cor. 11:26.

the words of St. Paul, "With Christ I am nailed to the cross." [29]

In accordance with Peter's words, "Be ye . . . a holy priesthood, to offer up spiritual sacrifices acceptable to God through Jesus Christ," [30] the Pope says that it is precisely at Mass, when with and through our High Priest Christ we offer ourselves as a spiritual sacrifice, "that each one's faith ought to become more ready to work through charity, his piety more real and fervent, and each one should consecrate himself to the furthering of the divine glory, desiring to become as like as possible to Christ in His most grievous sufferings." [31]

If, therefore, we do not want God to look with disdain upon us during Mass, as though we were hypocrites, we must do sincerely, in our hearts, what we are at that moment claiming to do. We must closely unite ourselves to Christ, our priest and victim, and consecrate our lives, as He did, to the service of God. When we stand at the altar, under the symbol of Christ, it is our duty so to transform our hearts, that every trace of sin may be completely blotted out, and zealously intend to foster whatever promotes our supernatural union and likeness to Christ. This is the center which gives meaning to the whole of spirituality, for at this moment we proclaim in symbolic fashion (through Christ's body and blood as the victim) that our whole day will be God's, that whatever we do during the rest of the day will be done precisely as a consecrated sacrifice, a gift of our own flesh and blood, tears and sweat, work and joy, through Him and with Him and in Him, for the greater glory and honor of the Blessed Trinity. We vow at this moment that our entire day will be spent in reproducing within ourselves a faithful image of Christ Jesus, the symbol of our self-sacrifice, the model of our divine sonship, the pledge of our union with God in glory.

A Banquet

"With great desire have I longed to eat this Passover with you before I die," exclaimed the Savior at the Last Supper.[32] And St. John adds that "having loved His own who were in the world, Jesus loved them to the end." [33] A meal is a sign of friendship and love. In fact, there is an old German saying to the effect that more is accomplished at the white table than at the green table: more accomplished over a meal than at a conference, for at a meal the atmosphere is one of love and friendship; a spirit of sharing dominates the scene.

[29] *Mediator Dei*, 81.
[30] 1 Peter 2:5.
[31] *Mediator Dei*, 99.
[32] Luke 22:15.
[33] John 13:1.

The Mass too is a banquet. All the old names for the Mass bring out this fact. St. Paul calls it the Lord's Supper.[34] The Acts of the Apostles speak of it as "the breaking of bread."[35] And the early Christians used to celebrate Mass together with another meal, a love-feast called the Agape. After all, it was in the course of the Passover meal that our Lord Himself celebrated the first Mass. The Evangelist Mark tells us that "While they were eating, Jesus took bread, and blessing it, He broke and gave it to them, and said, 'Take; this is my body.' And taking a cup and giving thanks, He gave it to them, and they drank all of it; and He said to them, 'This is my blood of the new covenant, which is being shed for many.' " [36] Our Lord consecrated the bread and wine as part of a holy meal, and He did so by means of a blessing or eucharist—the grace spoken at the meal.

The very name Eucharist means a thanksgiving pronounced over food. And that thanksgiving, or, as the Jews called it, blessing, today consists in the Preface and Canon of the Mass. Notice, it is pronounced over food; bread and wine lie there on the altar. The altar itself is nothing but a table, holy to be sure, but nevertheless a table. And finally, around the table, there is the community which eats and drinks. Again it is in the context of this holy meal that the sacrifice of our Lord is made present, just as it was on the night He was taken prisoner.

The basic form of the Mass, therefore, is that of a meal, with the symbols of bread and wine changed into the body and blood of our Redeemer. The fact that Christ specially chose food for symbols and in His words of institution directly related the Eucharist to the Passover meal evidently indicates that He willed this meal character for His sacrifice. It would be unrealistic to reverse this form, saying that through bread and wine a sacrifice is represented and, since the symbols of sacrifice are food and are eaten, this sacrifice has a secondary character of a meal. On the contrary, we know that the Mass is a sacrifice only through faith; its meal character is something obvious. Here, then, is a meal which is sacrificial.

The question at hand is the visible format and the symbolism willed by Christ. Under this form is hidden the sacrifice of Christ and the life that flows from the sacrifice in Holy Communion. Obviously, the sacrifice of Christ is the basis for the communication of life. The sacrifice is the primary reality, the most important thing; the meal character is secondary, but nevertheless the primary or basic form of this sacrifice. These two aspects, though distinct, are not separate. Just as the Passover meal was sacrificial, so in the Mass we have a sacrificial meal. Nor should we limit this meal character only to the reception of Holy Communion. The Mass is basically a meal from the

34 1 Cor. 11:20.
35 2:42.
36 14:22-24.

moment we place food on the table of the altar and pronounce a blessing over the food. In the Mass the Church continues the Passover of the Jews and infuses into it a new content, the new Paschal Lamb prefigured long ago by the lamb slain in Egypt and consumed before the Jews departed on their flight. Here is the New Testament Passover sacrificial meal; Christ is our Pasch, our sacrificial victim whom we eat as we fly from the death of sin to the life of grace.

The sacrifice is made present, we know, as soon as the sacramental symbolism is effected and not at Communion time; the validity of the Mass as a sacrifice certainly, therefore, does not depend upon the reception of Holy Communion. Nevertheless, the Church holds the Communion of at least the celebrant to be a very important part of the whole procedure, so much so that, were it lacking, the Mass would be, so to speak, mutilated; it would be a meal without eating. Theologians call the Communion of the celebrant an integral part of the Mass. We must not forget, however, that the Communion of the faithful is also a part of the Mass and not simply something stuck on to it. True enough, it can be lacking and the nature of the Mass remains, but when it is present the form of the Mass celebration is more complete: its basic symbolism is carried out in its entirety. That is why Pius XII, though permitting the reception of Communion outside of Mass (people still take part in the Mass through such a Communion), urges us not to neglect the directions of the Liturgy so long as there is no great difficulty involved; he says that we "should aim that all our actions at the altar manifest more clearly the living unity of the Mystical Body."[37] The Mass is a banquet of the children of God, Communion its natural climax. At the Lord's Supper we dine with Him, we break bread with Him.

Even more, the Council of Trent exhorts the faithful "when they attend Mass to communicate, not only by a spiritual communion, but also by a sacramental one, so that they may obtain more abundant fruit from this most holy sacrifice." [38] And Pius XII, quoting his predecessor, Benedict XIV, with approval, adds:

> . . . although in addition to those to whom the celebrant gives a portion of the Victim he has himself offered in the Mass, they also participate in the same sacrifice to whom a priest distributes the Blessed Sacrament that has been reserved; however, the Church has not for this reason ever forbidden, nor does she now forbid, a celebrant to satisfy the piety and just request of those who, when present at Mass, want to become partakers of the same sacrifice (by receiving hosts consecrated at the same Mass), because they likewise offer it after their own manner; nay more, she approves of it and *desires that it should not be omitted* and would rep-

[37] *Mediator Dei*, 122.
[38] Sess. 22, c. 6. Denz., 944.

rehend those priests through whose fault and negligence this participation would be denied to the faithful.[39]

Another fact serves to bring out the banquet form of the Mass. As Christ presided over the Passover meal with His disciples, He took the place of the father of the family who breaks the bread with His children, and the disciples took the place of the children of the family. For the Passover meal, according to Jewish law, was supposed to be eaten within the family circle. When a group of friends were away from home at the time of the Passover, they could then eat it together, one of them presiding as the father of the family. Thus Christ, the head of the household, created a new holy meal, for with His all-powerful word He made the food truly holy and thereby used His high-priestly power to consecrate a sacrifice. And at the same time, in saying to His Apostles "Do this in memory of me," He handed on to them the role of head of the Christian family, so that they could break bread with their spiritual children.

This same sublime drama is continued in the Mass, for the priest acts as Christ, and the faithful are the children about the table of their father. The priest is able to do this because he has the radical interior power to be another Christ. Through his ordination he is equipped with a certain inner Christ-likeness. Because of this he is able to represent the Lord in His sacramental efficacy, so that his words are Christ's and have the power to make present again the sacrificial banquet enacted by Christ at the Last Supper.

But just like the priest, the faithful too possess a configuration, coming from their baptismal character, that enables them to act as the Apostles at the Last Supper. They too represent Christ, therefore; not Christ the Head, but Christ in His members, just as the disciples at the Last Supper showed themselves to be members of Christ as children are members of their father's family. This is more than play-acting. Were it only that, then a pagan could belong to this sacrificial meal brotherhood just as well as the Christian. But this we know he cannot do. No unbaptized person can come into Mass and take part in it. He might pray aloud with us; he might sing. But he simply cannot offer the Mass with us nor partake of the bread of life. He does not belong to our Father's table.

This group of the faithful surrounding the altar is a beautiful and realistic symbol of the family of God gathered about His table to enjoy His sacred nourishment. This little group is an efficacious symbol, we may say the organ, of the Mystical Body, for right here and now it does what is commanded for the entire Mystical Body; it does so in union with it, in its name and for it. Here is the source of unity in Christ's Body, for in the words of St. Paul, "because the bread is one, we, though many, are one body, all of us who partake of the

[39] *Mediator Dei,* 118.

one bread." [40] It is here, Pius XII says, that Christians learn to live together as brothers, who, breaking the same bread, sit down to the same heavenly table to partake of the elixir of immortality.[41] Indeed, this banquet of God's family is, in the words of St. Augustine, "a sacrament of filial piety, a sign of unity and a bond of love." [42]

Let us go a step further. As we have already mentioned, this whole banquet appearance of the Mass is a symbol of the sacrifice offered during it. The sacrifice of the Mass is, properly speaking, a sacrificial banquet. The sacrifice takes place as we make holy the food lying on the table of the altar. Then, just as the faithful help constitute the holy brotherhood around the Lord's table, so they offer with the priest the sacrifice thus effected—though obviously not in the same manner as the priest. The activity of the faithful at Mass is not as vital or as essential as that of the ordained priest, but they do have an important role to play.

The priest alone, says Pius XII, consecrates as the representative of Christ the Head,[43] as the role of father of the household implies— a role exercised by the priest in Christ's stead alone. But what the priest alone has consecrated the faithful, as members of Christ's Mystical Body, children of His family, offer *through* or *by* the hands of the priest.[44] And they, let us recall, are especially equipped to make this offering: the priestly character imprinted on their souls in Baptism involves them in the official priestly action of the Church, performed externally, of course, only by the ordained priests. But this does not mean that the offering made by the faithful through the priest is unreal; it is very real, but is performed only through him and never independently of him.

In addition to this offering made *through* the hand of the priest, the faithful are also supposed to offer *in union with* the priest. They are to unite themselves consciously, wholeheartedly with him. By an intentional, interior, and personal act, they unite their hearts in praise, impetration, expiation, and thanksgiving with the prayers and intentions of the priest.[45] The priest is supposed to be expressing their spirit of religion. Unless the faithful who assist at Mass make this offering with the priest, he stands alone—we do not back him up, we do not mean what he says and does in our name.

All that we have said regarding the communal character of the Mass must not be pushed to extremes. The people do not have to ratify publicly what the priest does, for the priest does not act in virtue of an office committed to him by the community; he is the rep-

---

[40] 1 Cor. 11:17.
[41] *Mediator Dei*, 120.
[42] *Tract. 26 in Joann.*, 13. *MPL*, 35: 1613.
[43] *Mediator Dei*, 92.
[44] *Ibid.*
[45] *Ibid.*, 93.

resentative of Christ alone.[46] A Mass celebrated by a priest without
a congregation present, though not ideally performed, is still by its
very nature a public and social act, inasmuch as he who offers it acts
in the name of Christ and in the name of the faithful as members of
Christ's Mystical Body.[47] Nevertheless, as a sign that she does not
treat lightly the importance of symbolism in achieving more effectively
the tremendous realities of grace and unity brought about by the Mass,
the Church insists rigorously that "no priest should say Mass unless
a server is at hand to answer the prayers," [48] and that the manner in
which Mass is celebrated should aim at manifesting "more clearly the
living unity of the Mystical Body" [49] and at helping the people "to
take part more easily and more fruitfully." [50]

Hence, it is not without reason that we pray immediately after
the Consecration: "*Unde et memores, Domine, nos servi tui, sed et
plebs tua sancta . . . offerimus.*" Here the Church consciously includes
as cooperators in this holy sacrificial meal all those who have been
made children of God's family, members of Christ's Mystical Body
and bearers of His sacerdotal dignity through the character of Baptism. No wonder St. Thomas Aquinas could exclaim, "O sacrum convivium—O sacred banquet in which Christ is eaten, His passion commemorated, our souls filled with grace and given a pledge of future
heavenly glory!" [51] Note that he did not limit the meal character only
to Communion: "recolitur memoria passionis eius."

The Mass is a sacred sacrificial banquet, then, in which we continue Christ's saving activity among men, share God's life by eating
a divine food, become assimilated to Him, transformed into Him for
the glorious sharing of God's intimate life in heaven. The Mass is a
real image and prelude of the eternal feast of heaven, the consummation of our love for God in the festive, nuptial banquet of the Lamb
slain for our sins.[52]

2. Names for the Mass

Throughout the history of the Church the Holy Sacrifice of the
Mass has received a variety of appellations each of which tends to
bring out particular aspects of one and the same action. The very first
title we find in Scripture is "the breaking of bread";[53] it also occurs

[46] *Ibid.*, 83-84.
[47] *Ibid.*, 95, 96, 106.
[48] *Ibid.*, 97.
[49] *Ibid.*, 122.
[50] *Ibid.*, 105.
[51] Adopted by the Church as an antiphon for the feast of Corpus Christi.
[52] For a more lengthy treatment of the importance of the meal character of
the Mass and how necessary it is that we make our concept of this meal a living
one, see: J. Pascher, *Eucharistia. Gestalt und Vollzug* (Münster: Aschendorff,
1953), 18-40; R. Guardini, *Meditations before Mass* (Westminster, Maryland:
Newman, 1956), 150-159; 168-174.
[53] Acts 2:42, 46; 20:7.

in the *Didache* [54] and many other places. That this expression actually refers to the Holy Eucharist itself and not simply to any preliminary meal can be clearly seen in the fact that St. Paul says: "And the bread that we break, is it not the partaking of the body of the Lord?" [55] Such a use of this expression was undoubtedly bound up with the fact that during Mass the sacred species were broken in order to be distributed to those in attendance, just as our Lord had broken the matzah during the Last Supper in order to give each Apostle a piece of it. This expression serves to accentuate the meal character of the Mass, as do the names "the Lord's Supper," used by St. Paul,[56] and *dominicum convivium*, "the Lord's banquet," used by Tertullian.[57]

The same is true of the term "Eucharist." Its use in the post-Apostolic era is very frequent. Sometimes, as in the *Didache*, the word is used in reference to the gifts offered during Mass and later consumed in Holy Communion.[58] But it is also used to designate the thanksgiving prayer, the Preface-Canon, which consecrated these gifts.[59]

The Mass was also called "Liturgy," for example, by Clement of Rome.[60] This name survives even today in the Oriental Rites, where, for instance, we hear of the Divine Liturgy of St. John Chrysostom, and others.

To bring out the sacrificial aspect of the Mass, the term "sacrifice" is to be found as a name for the Mass, as in Tertullian and Cyprian.[61] And the memorial character of the Mass was also indicated by the name *dominicum*, either used alone, as in Cyprian's statement, "Numquid ergo dominicum post coenam celebrare debemus?" [62] or in conjunction with some noun, as in Tertullian's words, "Quomodo dominica solemnia celebrabimus?" [63]

Another term frequently used in the language of pagan cult, *actio* or *agere*, is also to be found as a name for the Mass. Victor Vitensis, for instance, employs *agere missas*,[64] while the so-called Leonine Sacramentary has the combination *actio mysterii*: "Sit nobis, Domine, operatio mentis et corporis coeleste mysterium, ut cuius exequimur

---

[54] XIV. J. Quasten, *Monumenta*, 12.
[55] 1 Cor. 10:16.
[56] 1 Cor. 11:20.
[57] *Ad uxorem*, 2, 4. *MPL*, 1:1407.
[58] IX. Quasten, 11.
[59] *Didache*, XIV. Quasten, 13; Justin, *Apologia*, 65 and 67. Quasten, 17, 20; *Acta Thomae*, 27 and 49. Quasten, 343; c. 158. Quasten, 345; Ignatius of Antioch, *Ad Ephesios*, 13, 1. Quasten, 335; *Ad Philadelphenses*, 4, 1. Quasten, 335; *Ad Smyrnaeos*, 7, 1; 8, 1. Quasten, 336.
[60] *Ad Corinthios*, 40, 2. *MPG*, 1: 288-289.
[61] Tertullian, *De cultu feminarum*, II, 11. *MPL*, 1:1444; Cyprian, *Epist.* 63, 9. *MPL*, 4:392; *De lapsis*, 25-26. *MPL*, 4:499, 501.
[62] *Epist.* 63, 16. *MPL*, 4:398.
[63] *De fuga*, 14. *MPL*, 2:141.
[64] *De persecutione Vandalica*, II, 2 and 13. *MPL*, 58: 203, 213.

actionem, sentiamus effectum." [65] And in the *Liber Pontificalis* the term *actio* is used as meaning the Canon of the Mass: *actio sacrificii.*[66]

While it is understandable that the Mass could be called *collecta* or *synaxis*, expressions which found passing acceptance in early writings and which mean the coming together or gathering of the Christian community, it is certainly strange that the word *missa* should have become so prevalent as a name for the Holy Sacrifice, since it means dismissal or the departure of the members of the community. In Ambrose we find it used, not in the sense of the entire liturgical service, but as the ritual dismissal of those not yet baptized: "Ego tamen mansi in munere, missam facere coepi. Dum offero, raptum cognovi a populo . . . ." [67] (He tells us that the Arians had just invaded the church in an attempt to occupy it, as he began to dismiss those who were not yet baptized.) Etheria too uses *missa* to refer to the dismissals after the vigil service, Vespers and the morning service.[68] This is precisely the sense of the *Ite, missa est* at the end of Mass: "Go, the Mass is over," or "the gathering is dismissed." But gradually the word came to be used for the entire service. Sometimes it is even employed in the plural and together with other words; e.g., *solemnia*: *missarum solemnia.*[69]

Jungmann thinks that the reason *missa* became applied to the whole Mass was because it came to be synonymous with blessing. As a matter of fact, together with the announcement of dismissal went a blessing; we find this, not only at the end of Mass, but also for each category of catechumen as the groups, one after the other, were dismissed before the beginning of the Mass of the Faithful.[70] The reasoning behind the transferal was probably that a blessing is found *par excellence* during the Mass when bread and wine are blessed and changed into the body and blood of Christ.[71]

3. Forms of the Mass

Pontifical

When one reads the early Fathers and the oldest liturgical documents, he cannot but be struck by the insistence of the early Church on a hierarchical arrangement of the Mass celebration. It belonged to the bishop, in the first place, to celebrate the sacred mysteries. Form-

---

[65] K. Mohlberg, *Sacramentarium Veronense* (Rome: Herder, 1956), p. 75, n. 580; see also *actione mysterii*, p. 101, n. 806.

[66] L. Duchesne, I, 239.

[67] *Epist.* 20, 4. *MPL*, 26: 1037. Avitus of Vienne defines the word *missa* when he says: "in ecclesiis palatiisque sive praetoriis missa fieri pronuntiatur, cum populus ab observatione dimittitur," *Epist.* 1. *MPL*, 59: 199.

[68] *Journal de Voyage*, 24, 2 and 6, pp. 190, 192; 25, 2, p. 198.

[69] Gregory of Tours, *De gloria confess.*, 65. *MPL*, 71:875; Gregory the Great, *In evang. hom*, 8, 1. *MPL*, 76:1103.

[70] *Apostolic Constitutions*, VIII, 6-9. *MPG*, 1:1075-1086.

[71] J. Jungmann, *The Mass of the Roman Rite*, I, 174-175. For a more complete

ing a unit of priesthood with him were the members of his clergy, according to their various orders. Present too were all the faithful of the locality uniting themselves to their chief shepherd.

St. Ignatius of Antioch is a glorious witness to this primitive tradition:

> You must all follow the lead of the bishop, as Jesus Christ followed that of the Father, and the presbytery as you would the Apostles; reverence the deacons as you would God's commandment. Let no one do anything touching the Church apart from the bishop. *Let that celebration of the Eucharist be considered valid which is held under the bishop or anyone to whom he has committed it.* Where the bishop appears, there let the people be, just as where Jesus Christ is, there is the Catholic Church. It is not permitted without authorization from the bishop either to baptize or to hold an agape; but whatever he approves is pleasing to God.[72]

And again to the Ephesians he writes:

> . . . You are in the habit, through grace derived from the Name, of meeting in common, animated by one faith and in union with Jesus Christ . . . of meeting, I say, to show obedience with undivided mind to the bishop and the presbytery, and to break the same bread, which is the medicine of immortality, the antidote against death . . .[73]

And in the same vein he addresses himself to the Philadelphians:

> Take care, then, to partake of the one Eucharist; for one is the flesh of the Lord Jesus Christ, and one the cup to unite us with His blood, and one altar, just as there is one bishop assisted by the presbytery and deacons, my fellow servants.[74]

This same hierarchical arrangement of all the faithful, together with the clergy headed by the bishop, at the Eucharistic celebration is also clearly indicated by Justin,[75] Hippolytus,[76] the *Apostolic Constitutions*,[77] and Narsai.[78]

The ancient Roman Ordinals likewise provide us with papal Masses in which the faithful and clergy of Rome gather around the pope, and which call for a change of locale of the celebration for the different stational days and feasts. Here the spirit of unity and hierarchy was so strong that the whole of Rome, so far as was possible, fol-

history of the question, see the same author's *Gewordene Liturgie,* 34-52.

[72] *To the Smyrneans,* 8. *Ancient Christian Writers,* I, 93.
[73] 20. *Ancient Christian Writers,* I, 67-68.
[74] 4. *Ancient Christian Writers,* I. 86.
[75] I *Apology* 65. Quasten, pp. 16. 19-20.
[76] *La Tradition Apostolique* (Ed. B. Botte), pp. 26-35.
[77] II, 57 and VIII, 5-15. *MPG,* 1:723-738, 1075-1114.
[78] *Homily* 17. R. H. Connolly, *The Liturgical Homilies of Narsai* (London, 1909), p. 4.

lowed the pope from place to place in order to be with him as a community when he celebrated.[79] Since Rome gradually dominated the liturgical practice of the West, its norms regarding such communal and hierarchical celebrations were followed all over Europe.[80] The episcopal service became the ideal, not only in Rome, but in all the principal See cities of West and East. The Pontifical Mass, in which all the clergy as well as the faithful took their respective parts, was the norm.

Since, however, the clergy formed with the bishop the ruling and sanctifying group in the Church, their participation in the Pontifical Mass was expressed in a more hierarchic, a more sacerdotal manner. This has been called concelebration. And of this history offers many examples and types.

In the *Apostolic Tradition* of Hippolytus we read that, after the new bishop had been consecrated, the deacons brought the oblation to the altar, then he together with the whole *presbyterium* imposed hands on the oblation; the bishop alone, however, pronounced the words of consecration.[81] While Bernard Botte [82] and Karl Rahner [83] consider this a true co-consecration, Georges Frénaud raises doubts.[84] However, in his address to the Assisi Congress on Pastoral Liturgy, Pius XII definitely rejects the validity of such action. The mere will, even shown by some external action, to make one's own the words and actions of the celebrant does not suffice for genuinely consecratory concelebration. For the latter to be had the concelebrants must each pronounce the words of consecration over bread and wine. Otherwise the concelebration is purely ceremonial.[85]

Botte cites the interesting circumstance from the *Didascalia Apostolorum* in which the celebrating bishop allows a visiting bishop to consecrate the chalice of wine.[86] And then there is the report of Eusebius concerning Polycarp's visit to Pope Anicetus. Eusebius says, ". . . they communicated with each other, and in the church Anicetus conceded the celebration of the Eucharist to Polycarp, obviously out of

[79] *Ordo Romanus*, I, II, and at least part of III. Andrieu, *Les Ordines Romani du Haut Moyen-Age*, II, 67-108, 115-116, 131-133.

[80] This can be seen from the fact that other Ordinals, though bearing the title "Roman", in point of fact describe the rites of other dioceses, intending indeed to follow the practice of Rome as far as posible; e.g., the *Ordo of St. Amand* which appears as *OR IV* in Andrieu, II, 158-170.

[81] *La Tradition Apostolique* (Ed. B. Botte), p. 30.

[82] See Botte's remark in the above edition of the *Apostolic Tradition*, p. 30, note 3; also his more lengthy defense of this interpretation in "Note historique sur la concélébration dans l'Eglise ancienne," *La Maison-Dieu*, n. 35 (1953), 11-12; "Décret de la Congrégation des Rites sur les ordinations," *ibid.*, n. 25 (1951), 134-139.

[83] "Dogmatique de la concélébration," *QLP*, 36 (1955), 119-135, esp. 128-129.

[84] "Remarques doctrinales au sujet de la concélébration eucharistique," *QLP*, 37 (1956), 119.

[85] *AAS*, 48 (1956), 718.

[86] "Note historique," *loc. cit.*, p. 13.

respect for him." [87] Botte explains: "Polycarp and Anicetus are standing at the altar. The Pope invites the Asian bishop to pronounce the formula for the prayer of thanksgiving (therefore, the words of consecration), which normally belongs by right to the bishop of the place . . . Then they partook of the same eucharist." [88] In other words, according to Botte, Anicetus, while celebrating Mass, invited Polycarp to do the actual consecrating.

There are other instances which more obviously concern concelebration in the strictly consecratory sense. In *Ordo Romanus* III we read that on certain more solemn feasts the cardinal-priests of Rome surrounded the pope and held corporals upon which the archdeacon had placed three particles of bread. All recited the Canon together with the pope, but only the pope, apparently, had the chalices of wine before him.[89] We read of the same rite in the *Ordo of St. Amand.* [90] For other days which do not enjoy such solemnity the Ordo specifies that only the pope consecrates;[91] the participation of the attending clergy was limited to the Offering, Fraction and Communion. Somewhat the same practice must have still been in vogue in the thirteenth century, for Innocent III takes up the question of several priests pronouncing the words of consecration together.[92] While in the Roman Rite such consecratory concelebration is today limited to the Masses accompanying the ordination of priests and the consecration of bishops, in the various Oriental Rites there is still a frequent use made of the different types of concelebration.[93]

Solemn

Though one might be tempted to consider the Solemn Mass as an elaboration of the Low Mass of a simple priest,[94] in reality it is closer to being a simplification of the bishop's Mass. Jungmann finds the ultimate historical reason for this in an addition to the *Ordo Romanus* I, which appears in Andrieu's collection as *OR* II. Allowing for occasions when the pope himself might not be able to celebrate, the rubrics di-

[87] *Historica ecclesiastica*, 5, 24, 17. *GCS*, 9 (1), p. 496.

[88] "Note historique," loc. cit., p. 15. It seems to me, however, that another interpretation of Eusebius' text is perfectly in order: Anicetus did not begin to celebrate Mass, but immediately offered Polycarp the privilege.

[89] N. 1. Andrieu, *Les Ordines*, II, 131.

[90] *OR* IV in Andrieu, n. 52, vol. II, p. 163.

[91] N. 53. *Ibid.*

[92] *De sacro altaris mysterio*, IV, 25. *MPL*, 217: 873-874.

[93] Cf. A. Raes, "La concélébration eucharistique dans les rites orientaux," *La Maison-Dieu*, n. 35 (1953), 24-47. For further discussion of the history and forms of concelebration see: Cardinal Bona, *Rerum liturgicarum libri duo* (Paris, 1672), I, 18, 9, pp. 151-152; A. Fortescue, "Concelebration," *The Catholic Encyclopedia*, IV, 190; P. DePuniet, "Concélébration liturgique," *DACL*, III, 2470-2488; J. Hanssens, "De concelebratione eucharistica," *Periodica*, 16 (1927), 143-154, 181-210; 17 (1928), 93-127; 21 (1932), 193-219.

[94] Righetti seems to infer this: cf. *Storia Liturgica*, III (Milan: Ancora, 1949), 112-113.

rect that a bishop in Rome who takes the pope's place should do certain things differently, but that bishops in their own See cities should do everything just as the pope. It also foresees an occasion when a simple priest will take the place of the pope at a stational service. In this case we do not find what we might expect: there are no radical changes. The simple priest does exactly as the bishop with the sole exception of not singing the Gloria.[95] Here was the stepping-stone—an official one at that—to the ceremonial of the Solemn Mass which a priest would follow anywhere on more festive occasions.

Up until the eleventh century the number of deacons and subdeacons varied at Solemn Mass.[96] The first clear and definite evidence of only one of each is a section of the *Liber de divinis officiis*, appearing under the name of Alcuin, but which Mabillon ascribes to Remigius of Auxerre who died in 908.[97] After Remigius, Jean d'Avranches (died 1065) is an indisputable witness to this form of the Mass,[98] as is also Uldaricus, who wrote the *Custom Book of Cluny*.[99] From then on the Solemn Mass began to drop more and more of those ceremonies which have come in time to be regarded as peculiar to the Pontifical Mass.

High

It is obvious that even in early times some provision in regard to Mass had to be made for localities distant from the episcopal cities and for even those numbers of Christians within the chief cities who exceeded the capacity of the principal church. We know that in the time of Pope Marcellus (died 309) there were twenty-five titular churches in Rome, churches, therefore, with their own congregations which had to be cared for.[100] And Eusebius tells us that at the time of Pope Cornelius (died 253) there were fifteen hundred widows alone who were supported by the Church.[101] Certainly, therefore, the community at Rome even in those days numbered so many that it could not possibly fit into one church for papal Mass.

This brings us to another basic form of Mass, namely, High Mass or *Missa Cantata*—not that our present High Mass existed then as it does now, but in the sense that our present practice can ultimately be traced back to some such original type. True, *explicit* testimony that simple priests actually celebrated Mass is rare. Cyprian's remark stands out in this matter: "mando vos ut . . . vice mea fungamini circa gerenda

[95] *OR* II, n. 9. Andrieu, *Les Ordines*, II, p. 116.
[96] Cf. J. Jungmann, *Mass of the Roman Rite*, I, 201-202 for the diverse customs.
[97] *MPL*, 101: 1247, 1250, 1251; see Mabillon's note (j) under col. 1246.
[98] *De off. eccl., MPL*, 147: 32, ff.
[99] *Consuet. Cluniac.*, II, 30. *MPL*, 149: 716, ff.
[100] *Liber Pontificalis*, (Ed. L. Duchesne), I, 164.
[101] *Hist. eccl.*, 6, 43, 11. *GCS*, 9 (2), 618.

ea quae administratio religiosa deposcit." [102] Of course, there is the statement of Ignatius of Antioch to the effect that only that Eucharist is to be considered valid which is held under the bishop or anyone to whom he has committed it.[103] Yet there are no extant accounts of priests celebrating without pontifical ceremonies. Perhaps this is so because it was such a commonplace occurrence that there was no need for setting down a description of such a service in writing.

In the absence of such documentary evidence, Jungmann does not hesitate to attempt a reconstruction of this original type, at least as far as general lines go.[104] Besides congregation and priest, there was usually another cleric of a lower order in attendance. He could be a deacon;[105] he might also be a lesser cleric: a lector or an acolyte.

It was the duty of this cleric to assist the celebrant in the parish (titular) Mass. He was to sing one of the readings, and in some places, should he be a deacon, he was also to sing the Gospel (otherwise the celebrant did so). Assistance was also offered the celebrant as he collected the offerings of the faithful and arranged them on the altar-table. A cleric again helped with the breaking of the consecrated hosts and the distribution of Communion. It was to answer the need of small parishes, country parishes, and those on large private estates, that even lesser clerics were ordained for the service of individual churches.[106] It is in the light of this tradition that a prescription of the ninth century *Admonitio Synodalis* is to be understood: "Every priest should have a cleric or boy [*scolarem*] to read the epistle or lesson, answer him at Mass and with whom he can chant the psalms." [107] Note the transition from cleric to altar boy: our present altar boys continue the service of the clerics of old who were specially ordained for this purpose in particular churches.[108]

Since the Introit and other processional chants proper to the feast were not used (they were needed only for Pontifical services),[109] the only changeable chant which the cleric had to sing was the psalmody between the lessons to which the people responded. And the people themselves, of course, performed the chants of the Ordinary of the Mass.

[102] *Epist.*, 5, 2. *MPL*, 4: 438.
[103] *To the Smyrneans*, 8, 1. *Ancient Christian Writers*, I, 93.
[104] *Mass of the Roman Rite*, I, 208, ff.
[105] This seems implied by Gregory the Great's anxiety that churches without bishops should be provided with presbyters and deacons: *Epist.*, I, 15 and 78; II, 43. *MPL*, 77: 461, 532, 581. Remigius of Auxerre was also insistent on this point: "presbyter sine diacono nomen habet, officium non habet," *De div. off.*, 40. *MPL*, 101: 1247.
[106] Cf. Jungmann, I, 209, notes 7 and 8.
[107] *MPL*, 132: 456.
[108] This should be pointed out to the young men and boys who serve Mass, so that they might know the tremendous dignity which is theirs.
[109] Cf. Jungmann, I, 209, note 10.

Low

Though it was the general rule in the early Church that Mass should be offered only for the sake of the congregation, nonetheless we do find instances in which this congregation was more or less small. The early Christians "broke bread in their houses," [110] and we may rightly suppose that Paul did the same during his missionary journeys as he came upon small groups of people newly converted to Christianity. Many authors interpret the Eucharistic prayers of the *Didache* as a "domestic" celebration of Mass.[111] And in the time of persecution it was always difficult to gather the whole flock together for Mass. Victor of Vitensis says that the Christians celebrated the divine mysteries in whatever manner they could and wherever they could.[112] Cyprian speaks of the priests and deacons who visited the prisoners in order to celebrate Mass for them in their cells.[113] And there were even cases in which priests who were forbidden to hold public services because of some fault they had committed were nevertheless allowed to offer their priestly services in private homes.[114]

This practice of celebrating Mass alone or in private homes grew to such a point that it often entailed abuses and became the object of synodal restrictions. In the fourth century the Council of Laodicea decreed a general prohibition against it.[115] In other regions of the Christian world, it was only necessary to ask and obtain episcopal permission in order to celebrate this way. Private Masses were occasioned in Rome by the presence of many domestic shrines to the memory of the martyrs,[116] while in Frankish lands large estates frequently had their own chapels served by priests who actually belonged to the manor in some way or other.[117] Again and again various Church synods tried to stem the tide of the private Mass with varying success and ever decreasing strictness. The Synod of Agde in 506 made it obligatory to attend the episcopal or parish Mass on all feast days;[118] in 541 the Fourth Synod of Orleans reduced this obligation to the

[110] Acts 2:46.

[111] See a discussion of this hypothesis in the introduction to the *Didache* by James Kleist: *Ancient Christian Writers*, 6, p. 7 ff; also Jungmann, *Mass of the Roman Rite*, I, 13, notes 27 and 28.

[112] "Qualiter poterant, et ubi poterant . . . ." *De persec. Vandal.*, I, 5. MPL, 58: 188.

[113] *Epist.*, 5, 2. MPL, 4: 438.

[114] Basil, *Epist.* 199. *The Fathers of the Church*, 28 (New York, 1955), 47.

[115] Can. 58. Hefele-Leclercq, *Histoire des Conciles*, I, 1025.

[116] Cf. J. P. Kirsch, "I santuari domestici di martiri," *Rendiconti della Academia Romana di Archeologia* (1924), II, 27-43 cited by Jungmann, *op. cit.*, I, 214, note 12.

[117] Archbishop Agobard of Lyons (died 840) complained that in his day there was hardly a man of wealth who did not have a private chaplain whom he used in all sorts of ways, both legal and illegal: now for the celebration of Mass, now as a stable-hand: *De privil, et iure sacerdotum*, II. MPL, 104: 138.

[118] Can. 21. Hefele-Leclercq, *op. cit.*, II, 990.

feast of Easter.[119] Finally the Council of Trent forbade all Masses in private homes.[120]

Although the Masses described above still were orientated towards the welfare of souls—few though they may have been in concrete circumstances—they nevertheless provided a precedent for Mass celebrated with no popular attendance at all—even without a server. Personal devotion of the priest played a large part in the spread of this practice, for during a long period of time Sunday was the only occasion on which a public service was held. There are examples of the celebration of Mass in private from the sixth century on. Bishop Cassius of Narni is said to have celebrated Mass daily.[121] With the ordination of monks this tendency reached its peak. And it left its marks on the very physical plant of monasteries: altar after altar was added, as was side chapel upon side chapel, in order to facilitate private celebration for large numbers of monastic priests. By the ninth century daily private celebration had become a general rule.

But the desire on the part of the faithful for votive Masses like our modern Requiem Mass also assisted this growth. Like the faithful today who offer the priest a stipend to celebrate Mass for some special intention (vota), the medieval Christian found solace in knowing that his deceased relatives or special interests were being promoted before the throne of God.[122]

It is thus that there developed a distinct form for private Mass— a form that often tended to go to extremes. It was thought that since Mass was said alone the plural forms were out of place. Hence, a quantity of "I" prayers entered the Roman Mass. This was a trend that practically engulfed the Gallican Mass. As we have seen and will see more at length later on, most of our Roman singular prayers were introduced under Gallican influence. The Church, however, intervened just in time to stave off this encroachment on the spirit of the Roman Rite. Renewed endeavors were made to stop priests from celebrating alone. In the *Capitular* of Theodulf of Orleans (died 821) we read that "the priest must never celebrate Mass alone; there must always be present [*qui ei circumstent*] those whom he greets and by whom he is answered." [123] Burchard of Worms reports a prescription which has been attributed to Pope Soter: "Let no priest presume to celebrate Mass unless there are two people present to answer him." [124] Other-

---

[119] Can. 3. *Ibid.*, II, 1166.
[120] Sess. xxii. H. J. Schroeder, *Canons and Decrees of the Council of Trent* (St. Louis, 1941), p. 151. The Code of Canon Law allows the local ordinary to permit the celebration of Mass *per modum actus* in a private room: cf. Can. 822, n. 4.
[121] Cf. Gregory the Great, *Dialogues*, IV. 56. *MPL*, 77: 421; also see Leontius, *Life of John the Almoner*, 41. *MPL*, 73: 375.
[122] Cf. Jungmann, *op. cit.*, I, 217-219.
[123] I, 7. *MPL*, 105: 194.
[124] *Decretum*, III, 74. *MPL*, 140: 689.

wise, the Synod of Mainz (813) asks, "how can a priest say, 'Dominus vobiscum,' or 'Sursum corda,' if no one else is there present?" [125]

The reasoning behind these statements is the same which Pius XII insistently taught: We should see that all our actions at the altar "manifest more clearly the living unity of the Mystical Body." [126] Of course, the various externals of the Mass are not at all necessary "to constitute it a public act or to give it a social character." [127] They are, however, important to bring out the community character of the Church's sacrifice, to set it clearly before the minds of the faithful, and to help them to profit the more by it. [128]

Our present Low Mass, then, grew out of the practice of celebrating private Mass. The most obvious feature of the Low Mass is that, instead of being sung, it is read. There would have been a much greater difference, of course, had the Church given in to the attempts to "individualize" all the prayers of the Mass (as some wish to see happen to the prayers of the Breviary, dropping every trace of its choral character). Low Mass today is anything but private; it has become the basic form of celebration for parish worship. And all too often, departing from the mentality so evident in the past history of the Church, people think of the sung, or High, Mass and the Solemn Mass as mere gorgeous appendages. Pius XII, on the contrary, looked upon the sung Mass as the ideal; [129] therefore the present conventional view is not the traditional, or official, view of the Church.

4. Frequency of celebration

From Sunday to daily Mass

Though in the early Church Mass may have been celebrated on other days of the week, the only documentary proof that we have is for the Sunday observance. In the Acts of the Apostles we read: "And on the *first* day of the week, when we had met for the breaking of bread, Paul addressed them. . . ." [130] The *Didache* [131] and Justin [132] likewise mention Sunday as the day for Mass. And gradually attendance on the part of all became a clearly defined obligation. [133]

Later, other liturgical days were added. There were, first of all, the anniversaries of martyrs—at least for the churches to which they

---

[125] Can. 43. Hefele-Leclercq, *op. cit.*, III, 1141. Many other appeals to collective formulas of the Roman Mass may be found in J. Hanssens, "Fungiturne minister missae privatae diaconi et subdiaconi vicibus?" *EL*, 48 (1934), 406-412; e.g.: *Oremus, Orate pro me, circumstantes*, etc.
[126] *Mediator Dei*, 122.
[127] *Ibid.*, 106.
[128] *Ibid.*, 101, 105, 97, 104.
[129] *Ibid.*, 106.
[130] 20:7.
[131] C. 14. Quasten, *op. cit.*, 12.
[132] I *Apology* 67. Quasten, *op. cit.*, 19.
[133] For the history of this obligation cf. J. Guiniven, *The Precept of Hearing Mass* (Washington: The Catholic University Press, 1942), p. 18 ff.

had belonged when living or in which they were interred. Easter and its period of preparation, Lent, soon came into the liturgical calendar as a season during which Mass would be offered frequently if not daily. In some places it was even considered obligatory to attend Mass daily during Lent.[134] In nearly all of Christendom the stational days, Wednesday and Friday, were observed by means of a fast concluded with Mass. Saturday was added to these, at least in the Ember weeks, when the Mass of the vigil terminating the Ember week observance, formerly celebrated on Sunday morning, was moved back to Saturday morning.

But there is no conclusive evidence for daily Mass with an external public character until the fourth century. References to a daily Eucharist before this time seem rather to have in mind only a reception of Communion at home.[135] About the end of the fourth century Augustine is a clear witness to daily Mass in Africa [136] and in some other regions.[137] Ambrose leads us to believe that this was true of Milan also.[138] And as for Rome, such a practice may certainly be implied in the fact that Innocent I (died 417) says that the sacred mysteries are not to be celebrated on Fridays and Saturdays.[139]

The same two factors hastening the development of private Mass also aided the practice of daily Mass. The attractiveness of having a priest offer Mass for one's personal intentions, for a stipend, naturally led the pious laity to attend this particular Mass. Furthermore, with an ever deepening appreciation of the value of Mass and growing holiness among the clergy, the desire to celebrate out of personal devotion spread, regardless of whether or not a stipend for a particular intention was at hand. Daily Mass has now become almost an essential part of the priest's spiritual life. Thus is made available for the laity the opportunity of assisting at one of the many Masses celebrated each day in the parish church.

Polyliturgy

The repetition of the Holy Sacrifice at different hours of the same day is called for by the rubrics on certain feasts; this is called "polyliturgy." There are four concrete examples of such a practice in the Roman Rite: the three Masses on Christmas and All Souls Day, the two Masses on Holy Thursday, and the two Masses on Easter. Though

---

[134] Cf. Theodulf, *Capitulare*, I, 39; Burchard of Worms, *Decretum* 19, 5. *MPL*, 105:204; 140:962.

[135] Tertullian, *De idololatria*, 7. *MPL*, 1: 745; Cyprian, *De dominica oratione* 18. *MPL*. 4: 549. See further references in P. Browe, *De Frequenti Communione*. Rome: Gregorian University, 1932. True, Cyprian speaks of "sacerdotes qui cotidie sacrificia Dei celebramus," *Epistola Synodica*, 3. *MPL*, 3: 884, but Jungmann claims that this must refer to private Mass: *op. cit.*, I, 213, note 4, and p. 247.

[136] *Epist.* 228,6. *MPL*, 33: 1016.

[137] *Epist.* 54, 2, 2; in *Joann. tract.*, 26, 15. *MPL*, 33:200; 35:1614.

[138] *De benedictionibus patriarcharum*, 9, 38. *MPL*, 14: 686.

[139] *Epist.* 25 ad *Decentium*, 4. *MPL*, 20: 556.

today we celebrate these Masses in the same church, originally (in the case of Christmas and Holy Thursday; the other two instances are modern introductions), they were intended to be offered at different localities with specific purposes in view. In early medieval times Rome had a threefold celebration for Christmas. The first Mass was meant to be celebrated at the Basilica of St. Mary Major at the altar of the crib; the second was offered at the Church of St. Anastasia, whose memory was kept on this day of her death by the Byzantine colony of Rome, as the pope passed on his way from St. Mary Major's to St. Peter's Basilica for the main celebration of the day, the third Mass. It was only at the end of the Middle Ages that this practice was extended beyond Rome and each priest was permitted to celebrate the three Masses. Somewhat the same thing occurred on the feasts of certain martyrs in Rome: one Mass would be offered at the church where the martyr was buried (or in each church which possessed a major relic of the saint) and a second Mass, this one enjoying a more public quality, would be offered in the martyr's basilica. Again, Rome followed the same practice on Holy Thursday, with one Mass celebrated in the morning for the reconciliation of penitents and another in the evening to commemorate the Lord's Supper. Outside Rome there was still a third Mass for the consecration of the Holy Oils, this being done in Rome during the evening Mass, *In coena Domini.*

Bination—Trination

Somewhat similar to polyliturgy is the permission accorded by authority for priests to celebrate more than one Mass on Sundays and feast days of obligation in order to accommodate the large numbers of the faithful, who otherwise would have to go without Mass because of lack of space in the church edifice. Although in the beginning the Church followed the rule of having only one celebration in the sacred building on any given day, Pope St. Leo I, moved by the thought of so many pious Christians being turned away from the churches because of lack of space, did not hesitate to change the earlier discipline.[140] Of course, this did not always involve the celebration of more than one Mass by a particular priest. This practice was not unknown in the Middle Ages, though. And we have one practical example of it as early as the fifth century with Gerontius, the chaplain of the monasteries governed by St. Melania, who had to celebrate three Masses on Sundays, one in each of the monasteries in his charge.[141]

Abuses, however, came with the practice of the faithful offering a stipend for the Mass said for their intention. Walafrid Strabo (died 849) reports that some priests of his day celebrated twice, thrice,

[140] *Epist.* 9, 2. *MPL*, 54: 626-627.
[141] M. Cardinal Rampolla, *The Life of St. Melania* (New York: Benziger), p. ix.

some as often as they wanted, in one day; Pope Leo III offered Mass from seven to nine times on the same day [142]—simply out of devotion. But from this practice (still not in complete harmony with the spirit of the Liturgy) it was an easy step to the same practice based on commerce in Mass stipends. Peter the Chanter laments the greed of his contemporary clergy in this respect.[143] In fact, so bad was the situation that Pope Alexander II felt obliged to state categorically that one Mass was enough, and that "whoever presumed to offer several Masses for monetary or other worldly considerations would not escape damnation." [144] A genuine celebration of Mass being allowed only once a day, some clerics did not hesitate to repeat the Mass of the catechumens several times, while reciting the Canon only once, in order to acquit several intentions. This has been called *Missa bifaciata*, or *trifaciata*,[145] a monstrous arrangement which was quickly condemned by Church authority.[146]

Dry Mass

One more step was to be made in order to simulate the Mass as closely as possible in circumstances in which a true sacrificial Mass was prohibited. The Middle Ages developed a ceremony called the *Missa sicca*, or Dry Mass. H. Leclercq claims that its origin is due to Guy de Mont-Rocher in 1333,[147] but P. Browe holds for an earlier introduction.[148] As a matter of fact, the Pontifical of Prudentius of Troyes (ninth century) contains rubrics concerning it.[149] It seems that it was originally intended to be a sort of framework for distributing Communion to the infirm. Later it was used for funerals and marriages held in the afternoon, since Mass could not be celebrated at such an hour. It consisted in reading (or singing) all the texts of the Mass except the Canon. This was practiced by priests in many places and for a long time without contradiction on the part of authority, for as long as the faithful knew that they were not assisting at a real Mass, it was considered by theologians and liturgiologists alike to be a pious exercise. It is reported, in fact, that in Carthusian monasteries, for a time, the monks would retire to their cells after their community Mass and go through the Dry Mass out of devotion. However, abuses did finally creep in, especially when an unconsecrated host would be ele-

[142] *De exordiis et incrementis.*, 21. *MPL*, 114: 943.
[143] *Verb. abbrev.*, 28. *MPL*, 205: 102.
[144] Quoted in *Decretum Gratiani*, III *De consecrat.*, Dist. I, c. 53. *MPL*, 187: 1723.
[145] Peter the Chanter, *op. cit.*, 29. *MPL*, 205: 104.
[146] John, Archbishop of Prague, *Statut Synodal*, 12. Hefele-Leclercq, *op. cit.*, VI, 958.
[147] Cf his article, "Messe," *DACL*, XI, 772.
[148] "Messa senza consacrazione e communione," *EL*, 50 (1936), 129.
[149] Cf. M. Righetti, *Manuale di Storia Liturgica*, III (Milan: Ancora, 1948), 120.

vated to make the ceremony look more like a real Mass. Some priests even "communicated" with simple bread and wine. Because of the dangers inherent in such extremes, the Dry Mass was finally condemned by theologians and ecclesiastical synods.[150] Yet one trace of this practice lasted even till our own day: the entire ceremony of blessing the Palms on Palm Sunday was enframed in just such a "Mass" without consecration, before Pius XII promulgated his new Holy Week Ordo.

5. Time of celebration

As we have seen, when St. Paul joined the faithful of Troas for the "breaking of bread," it was an evening service.[151] It is true that the actual celebration of the Eucharist took place after midnight, but this was because Paul prolonged his address since he was to leave the next morning. Likewise his discussion of the Eucharist in his First Epistle to the Corinthians [152] indicates that it was celebrated in the context of an evening meal.

In sub-apostolic times, on the other hand, we find that a morning Mass was the normal thing. In a report written about 111-113 to the Emperor Trajan, Pliny the Younger says that the greatest fault of the Christians was their custom of "coming together on a determined day before daybreak and singing a hymn to Christ as God." [153] The author of the *Epistula Apostolorum*, which dates from about the middle of the second century, depicts Christ speaking with His Apostles and supposing as an ordinary thing that they celebrated His memory and the Agape at cock-crow after the all-night vigil.[154] And in the same century Justin tells us that after Mass a deacon would carry Communion to those absent, a thing quite difficult if it were question here of an evening Mass.[155]

[150] Cf. P. Browe, *art. cit.*, 130-131. A type of dry mass is still continued by the Carthusians out of devotion: cf. A. King, *Liturgies of the Religious Orders* (London, 1955), 35-37.

[151] Acts 20:7.

[152] 1 Cor. 11:18ff. E. Dekkers claims that, far from being a proof of the custom of celebrating Mass in the evening, this text of Paul's is actually a condemnation of the practice: "L'Eglise ancienne, a-t-elle connu une messe du soir?" *Miscellanea Mohlberg*, I (1948), 235-237. This opinion, however, does violence to the Pauline statement, relating the condemnation to the meal as such, whereas Paul seems rather to be disapproving the factions that result from each one eating his own meal in small groups: vv. 18-22.

[153] "stato die ante lucem convenire carmenque Christo quasi deo dicere," text in C. Kirch, *Enchiridion Fontium Historiae Ecclesiasticae Antiquae* (Barcelona: Herder, 1947), n. 30, p. 23. For the interpretation of this text in the sense of a morning celebration of the Eucharist, see K. Mohlberg, "Carmen Christo quasi Deo," *Rivista di Archeologia Christiana*, 14 (1937), 93-123; J. H. Srawley, *The Early History of the Liturgy* (Cambridge, 1947), 28-30.

[154] Text in J. Quasten, *Monumenta*, 337.

[155] I *Apology* 65. Quasten, 17.

We have similar testimony coming down to us from the end of the second and first part of the third century. Though Tertullian says that in times of persecution it was opportune to offer Mass during the night,[156] he also states that on fast days some people were afraid to receive Communion at Mass lest they break their fast [157]—which must mean, at least, that Mass was celebrated early in the day, for they could eat in the evening. And Cyprian rebukes those Christians who are afraid to attend Mass in the morning, *sacrificiis matutinis*, lest on returning from it the odor of wine betray the fact that they had been at a Christian reunion. He further insists that the morning hours are a good time for Mass, for thus the Christians celebrate the Resurrection of the Lord.[158]

The fourth century reveals a change in ecclesiastical discipline, for now we find Mass celebrated just after noon as well as in the evening. On certain fast days, and they were many, Ambrose tells us *plerique sunt huiusmodi dies*, Mass was celebrated immediately after noon: *statim meridianis horis*, while on certain others we find it placed in the evening: *non longe est finis diei . . . sacrificium vespertinum . . . in occasu diei.*[159] And on Holy Thursday it was offered after supper: *post coenam.*[160] At about the same time Etheria wrote a report of her pilgrimage to the Holy Land and described many of the liturgical services held there. Though the text of her diary is confused in many spots, it seems that on Sundays Mass was generally celebrated at about the third hour, or nine o'clock in the morning,[161] on Wednesdays and Fridays except during Lent at the ninth hour, or three o'clock in the afternoon,[162] and on Saturdays during Lent early in the morning before daylight.[163]

Mass on feast days and, of course, Sundays, at the hour of Tierce was a common practice all through the Middle Ages. This was already looked upon as the normal thing in the fifth and sixth centuries both in Rome [164] and in Gaul.[165] Thence it was taken over by all the lead-

[156] *De fuga in persec.*, 14. *MPL*, 2: 141-142.
[157] *De oratione*, 19. *MPL*, 1: 1286-1287.
[158] *Epist.* 63, 15 and 16. *MPL*, 4: 398. Often a story related by Hippolytus (*Contra Artemon*, reported by Eusebius in *Hist. eccl.*, V, 28, 12. *GCS*, 9 [1], pp. 503-505) is cited in reference to Mass in the morning: a certain schismatic, Natalis, after being buffeted during the night by angels, awoke early in the morning and went and prostrated himself before Pope Zephyrinus and the assembled clergy and people in church. But this could just as well refer to Lauds of the Divine Office.
[159] Ambrose, *In ps.* 118 *sermo* 8, 48. *MPL*, 15: 1383-1384; cf. also Paulinus of Nola, *Carm.* 23, 112. *MPL*, 61: 610: *libatis vespere sacris*.
[160] Council of Hippo of 393, can. 32. Hefele-Leclercq, *op. cit.*, II, 88.
[161] Ethérie, *Journal de Voyage*, n. 25, 6, p. 200.
[162] *Ibid.*, n. 27, 6, p. 210; n. 27, 7, p. 212.
[163] *Ibid.*, n. 27, 7, p. 212.
[164] Gregory the Great, *Homil.* 37, 9. *MPL*, 76: 1280.
[165] Gregory of Tours, *Vitae Patrum*, VIII, 11. *MPL*, 71: 1050; III Council of Orleans in 538, can. 14, cited by J. Mabillon, *De liturgia gallicana*, I, 6. *MPL*, 72: 142.

ing liturgiologists,[166] and canonists.[167] The principle remains even in our present Roman Missal.[168]

Mass on fast days was another matter. What we found to be true of the fourth century according to Ambrose, the Council of Hippo, and Etheria, was continued in the Middle Ages. On fast days during Lent Mass was offered in the evening at the Vesper hour.[169] But actually there were different types of fast days: some complete, some half-way between feast and fast days, and so the hour of Mass varied accordingly. Walafrid Strabo states: "The time of the celebration of Mass differs according to the quality of the solemnity. Sometimes it is celebrated before noon, sometimes at the ninth hour, sometimes at vesper time, even sometimes at night." [170]

One thing that should be brought out, however, is the fact that in the Middle Ages it was not the hours of the Office that changed on such occasions, but rather the hour of Mass. On feast days Mass was to be offered *post horam tertiam*, on full fast days *ad vesperas*, on the days of partial fast *post horam sextam*. This was certainly the understanding even in the days of St. Thomas Aquinas.[171] How then does it happen that today, even though the rubrics of the Missal use the same terminology, we find that it is the common practice to fix the hour of Mass and let the hours of the Office move about it as the quality of the feast or feria changes?

Such a tendency to rearrange the hours of the Office so that Mass might be celebrated at the same time every day was first noticed in the fourteenth century. According to P. Boeri, the monks of his day were always finished with Mass before Sext and then recited Vespers before they took their noon meal—and this in Lent.[171a] The Eucharistic fast was the basic cause of this practice, but more immediately the monks had a rule that the principal meal was not to be taken until after Vespers. Since it was a gruelling task to work in the fields all day long without anything in their stomachs, the monks moved Mass and Vespers up so that they could take refreshment at noon and be the better able to carry on their work.

Here is a classic example of the tendency, so often noticed in ecclesiastical discipline, whereby insistence on keeping the law has rendered liturgical practice meaningless. It is here that we find the explanation of the notice found so often in our modern Ordos that

[166] Walafrid Strabo, *De exord. et increm.*, 23. MPL, 114: 951; Amalar, *De eccl. off.*, III, 42. MPL, 105:1160; Bernold of Constance, *Micrologus*, 58. MPL, 151: 1019.

[167] Regino of Prüm, *De eccl. discipl.*, I, inq, 29. MPL, 132: 188; *Decretum Gratiani*, III, 1, 48. MPL, 187: 1721.

[168] *Rubr. gen.* XV, 2.

[169] III Council of Orleans, can. 29, cited by J. Mabillon, *art. cit.* MPL, 72: 142; Theodulf of Orleans, *Capitulare*, I, 39. MPL, 105: 204.

[170] *De exord. et increm.*, 23. MPL, 114: 951.

[171] Cf. *Summa Theol.*, III, 83, 2, ad. 3.

[171a] *Regula s. Benedicti commentata*, c. 48. MPL, 66: 710.

during Lent it is a laudable custom to recite Vespers before noon. It is anything but a laudable custom. Vespers are an evening office. If the former law that obliged monks to wait until after Vespers for their principal meal on fast days was found impossible, it should have been changed, rather than deprive the hours of the Office of their true meaning.

So much had this unrealistic compromise taken hold in the West by the time Pius V promulgated his *Missale Romanum*, that a recitation of the hours of the Office at the correct time indicated by their titles had become a dead letter. A few years before, Pius V had even dubbed the celebration of Mass in the evening an attempt to pervert the ancient practice of the Church, and he forbade it for the future.[172] If he had had a copy of Gratian's *Decretum*, it is difficult to see how he could say that evening Mass was contrary to the ancient discipline of the Church, unless the common practice of his time obscured the meaning of the decrees Gratian had so carefully transcribed.

Recently pastoral considerations have led the Church once again to permit evening Mass. This first occurred during the Second World War, when Rome granted such permissions to various military ordinariates. Such a practice was given wider extension through the Apostolic Constitution, *Christus Dominus*, of January 6, 1953.[173] Accordingly, local Ordinaries were able to permit evening Mass (not to begin before four o'clock in the afternoon) on holy days of obligation presently and formerly in force, on the First Friday of each month, on all those solemnities of the year which are normally celebrated with a great concourse of people, and also, in addition to the before-mentioned days, once a week. Finally on March 19, 1957, Pius XII made this concession even broader in a new Constitution, *Sacram Communionem*, wherein local Ordinaries were empowered to grant permission for evening Mass every day where pastoral reasons call for it.[174] Apart from such considerations, Mass must be celebrated according to the norms of canon law: it must begin not earlier than an hour before the aurora and not later than one hour after twelve o'clock noon.[175]

6. Manner of popular participation

As we have already seen, the Holy Sacrifice of the Mass is the re-offering of the redemptive act of Christ. Since it is Christ's own action, then, it is "truly capable in itself of conveying and dispensing grace from the divine Head to the members of the Mystical Body of Christ." [176] So important does the Church consider the Mass for our

---

[172] *Sanctissimus in Christo*, March 29, 1566. *Fontes iuris canonici*, I, 196.
[173] *AAS*, 45 (1953), 22-23.
[174] *Ibid.*, 49 (1957), 177-178.
[175] *CIC*, 821, 1.
[176] *Mediator Dei*, 31.

sanctification, that she has made assistance at it obligatory once a week. Thus the Church is unequivocally telling us: The Mass is the chief and indispensable source of sanctification; if you neglect it, you do so at your own risk.

But regular attendance at Mass will do little good for us, if we do not use the Mass correctly. This divine reservoir of grace and life, though infinite in itself, is conditioned in its efficacy by the devotion and fervor which the faithful bring to its celebration. As Pius XII has said, "Observe that these members [of the Mystical Body] are alive, endowed and equipped with an intelligence and will of their own. It follows that they are strictly required to put their lips to the fountain and drink and absorb for themselves the life-giving water, and rid themselves personally of anything that might hinder its nutritive effect in their souls. Emphatically, therefore, the work of redemption, which in itself is independent of our will, requires a serious effort on our part if we are to achieve eternal salvation." [177]

It is precisely in order to help the faithful absorb the life-giving water, to reap the fullest possible fruit from the Mass, that the Church has surrounded the essential matter and form of the sacrifice of the Mass with so many ceremonies. Pius XII tells us:

> The prescriptions of the sacred Liturgy aim, by every means at their disposal, at helping the Church to bring about this most holy purpose in the most suitable manner possible. This is the object, not only of the readings, homilies and other sermons given by priests, as also the whole cycle of mysteries which are proposed for our commemoration in the course of the year, but it is also the purpose of vestments, of sacred rites and their external splendor. All these things aim at "enhancing the majesty of this great sacrifice, and raising the minds of the faithful by means of these visible signs of religion and piety, to the contemplation of the sublime truths contained in this sacrifice." [178]

How should the faithful use these means which the Church has placed at their disposal? Can they safely ignore them? Certainly the devout Christian must make some effort to drink of the grace coming from this great act of sacrifice. Since the ceremonies of the Church are based on our human nature and are intended to aid that nature in accommodating to itself the fruits of the Mass, a conscientious observance of the ceremonies in their entirety would seem to be the ideal approach to assistance at Mass, the ideal way of preparing the soul for the grace proper to this sacrifice, of opening it to the saving influence of the Mass.

We certainly cannot admit that every method of participation in the Mass is as good as the other. If the Church prays in one manner

177 *Ibid.*
178 Council of Trent, sess. 22,5. Denz. 943, cited in *Mediator Dei.* 101.

in our name, is it not natural to expect that we should go along with that prayer as intelligently and meaningfully as possible? But not all methods enable us to follow the Mass and unite ourselves to it as completely as possible. For instance, it would seem contradictory for us to be reading a book while the priest is speaking to us, either from the pulpit or at the altar, when he announces the Gospel to us. And how can we be said to be entering into the spirit of the prayers at Mass intelligently and with the fullest amount of cooperation if we insist on making the Way of the Cross while those prayers are being said? Certainly if we go to Church for an evening devotion, the priest expects us to pray and sing along with him. Or if we attend October devotions, it would be very odd for us to be making our private novena to St. Philomena as the Rosary is being recited.

In the same way, such devotions are quite distinct from the Mass; we simply cannot call them the Mass. It's perfectly understandable that a person might engage in these devotions if he is unable to do anything else. But this certainly is not the ideal which the shepherd of souls, or the teacher in the classroom, should hold out to his charges. That method which aims at keeping us always attentive and fully alive to what is taking place at the altar, that helps us to be closely united with every prayer and action the priest performs, is ideally the best.

Notice, we say *ideally* the best, for this method is based on man's nature as he performs a distinct act of religion. But what is ideally the best may in certain circumstances not be suitable for any given individual. As Pius XII says, "So varied are men's talents and characters that it is impossible for all to be moved and attracted to the same extent by community prayers, hymns and liturgical services. Moreover, the needs and inclinations of all are not the same, nor are they always constant in the same individual." [179] But what is based generally on the nature of man at prayer does help him. Generally, therefore, all men should offer the Mass in the words and actions of the Church herself. This certainly should be taught people as the ideal, but it should never be forced upon them. Older people, for instance, because of a lack of training, very often experience difficulty with community singing. Another person may feel quite indisposed on some particular morning. Still another may feel the need for something altogether special at given point of spiritual development. Nonetheless, what is ideally the most perfect should be taught and urged as such.

However, since the ideal is not always applicable, and since, as Pius XII says, souls may certainly use methods that are easier for them as long as these methods are essentially in harmony with the sacred rites,[180] let us discuss the various ways of assisting at Mass and,

[179] *Mediator Dei*, 108.
[180] *Ibid.*

beginning with the minimum necessary for devout participation and ending with what is ideally more perfect, evaluate them. The more perfect method, after all, is not the only way of obtaining the fruits of the Mass. The ideal method, since it is most in harmony with the sacred rites, ought to be the normal manner of celebration; it should at least be made available, even though given individuals may be allowed the freedom to adopt something more suitable for themselves.

Self-offering and Communion

Immediately it must be remarked that we are not discussing the qualities of assistance at Mass which are necessary for the fulfillment of one's Sunday obligation.[181] Here we are concerned with what a devout Catholic will do in order to derive as much benefit as possible from the specifically distinct religious act he is presumably performing. The act he is performing by attending Mass is one of sacrifice, an act of self-offering symbolized by the sacramental sign—Christ in the form of a victim; this is the central and essential act of the Mass.

The very minimum, therefore, that is to be expected for devout assistance at Mass from a Catholic capable of doing no more is that he actually make an internal act of self-offering at the moment of consecration. Without at least this, the symbolic action taking place does not express him in an actual, conscious manner. While less than this may be all that is necessary for complying with one's Sunday obligation, it is certainly not to be recommended for the devout performance of the act of the virtue of religion called sacrifice. No one can claim that we get the most by doing the least; it is a truism that one gets out of something exactly what he puts into it. And so Pius XII says, "In order that the oblation by which the faithful offer the Divine Victim in this sacrifice to the heavenly Father may have its full effect, it is necessary that the people add something else, namely, the offering of themselves as a victim." [182] And what is the effect for the individual concerned? The merit of having personally performed an act of sacrifice. To this is coupled the special merit of having united that act of sacrifice to the infinitely meritorious sacrifice of Christ, of having enabled Him to be the bearer of one's personal self-offering.

Along with this act of sacrifice there should also be present the will to be personally united with the Savior. Let us remember that the Mass is a sacrificial banquet, a banquet symbolizing a union of love. Whenever possible, this ought to be expressed through the actual reception of Holy Communion. When not possible, we should at least, by means of a spiritual Communion, become partakers of the fruits of

181 For a treatment of this question see J. Guiniven, *The Precept of Hearing Mass* (Washington, D. C.: The Catholic University Press, 1942), 103-109.
182 *Mediator Dei*, 98.

the sacrifice.[183] This desire to share, to communicate in Christ's life is the natural outcome of sacrifice. We give ourselves to God in order to be divinized! He does not need our gift; it is we who need Him. And the giving of Himself to us is accomplished in Communion.

Internal attention and devotion [183a]

A still more intimate participation in the Mass is had when, in addition to making an oblation of self, of uniting oneself with Christ the Victim, and receiving Him as the source of the new life given to man as a consequence of His act of atonement and ours, we enter into the Church's own preparation for these two most important parts of the Mass by a sincere and intelligent attention paid to the rest of the prayers and actions. The very ritual of the Mass shows that certain readings are addressed to the people, certain prayers are said in their name, and often the priest greets the people to unite them more closely with his strictly priestly action. It is, therefore, a mark of a more intimate association with the Mass-action when we endeavor to follow its meaning, when we try to give genuine interior assent to what is spoken and done in our name.

We should bear in mind that the whole first part of the Mass, the so-called Mass of the Catechumens, is an instruction period. It is regrettable that so much, if not most, of the doctrine taught to the people by this means goes over their heads simply because they cannot understand the language in which it is clothed. Nevertheless, they can be helped to a great extent by a sermon or homily which, in a language and in terms which meet their needs, explains the doctrine or mystery celebrated. The people can also meditate on the mystery of the day, or, if this is too difficult (and often it is for the uneducated), they can ponder on the mystery of redemption itself centralized in the sacrifice of the cross. This is certainly one appropriate way of preparing for the moment of sacrifice and communion, a way which allows for a full reception of the grace of this action and the other fruits of the sacrifice.[184] This is what we mean, therefore, by internal attention and devotion: First of all, the application of the mind to the words and actions of the priest with an effort to understand them and make them one's own, or to the sacrifice itself, or to the passion and death of Christ; secondly, an application of the will to the pious affections which normally flow from such mental considerations of God's greatness and mercy.

Use of the Missal [184a]

Undoubtedly the best means for fostering this internal attention to the Mass is the use of the Missal, for it enables a person to pierce

[183] *Ibid.*, 117, 118.
[183a] *Instr. on Sacred Music and Liturgy,* 22a. AAS, 50 (1958), 637-638.
[184] *Mediator Dei,* 108.
[184a] *Instr. on Sacred Music and Liturgy,* 29. AAS, 50 (1958), 641.

the veil of foreign language and follow each word of the priest in the person's own language. It associates us more closely with the prayer of the Church for each particular day and thus nourishes the mind with the solid dogmatic truth and moral exhortation which form the warp and woof of the spiritual life of the Church. Offering as it does the entire riches of the Church's liturgical prayer and sacrificial action, it provides us with a firm basis for a sane and balanced spiritual life as opposed to the often bizarre sentimentalism promoted by some manuals of devotion written by individuals who all too frequently allow their imaginations to take precedence over the true, objective Catholic spirit.

The use of the Missal on the part of the laity is of comparatively recent origin in the Church. For centuries it had been forbidden to translate the Latin Mass; for an even longer period it was considered unlawful to print vernacular versions of the Canon of the Mass. This was due to the connection of certain French Missals with heretical groups, especially the Jansenists. Then there was the play of politics that succeeded in getting Rome to condemn Voisin's Missal in 1661 because, so the French politicians alleged, it resulted from a plot of the Jansenists.[185] Though vernacular Missals were in evidence all over Europe, Rome as late as 1857 was still writing decrees against a translation of liturgical prayers: "It is not permitted to translate the Ordinary of the Mass . . . into the vernacular, and print the same for the use of the faithful, nor can such a work get the approbation of the bishop." [186] Later Pius IX slackened this rigidity and allowed bishops to authorize such translations, and Leo XIII put this on the ordinary imprimatur basis. But it was left to a pope of personal pastoral experience, Pius X, to be the first to issue a complete translation of the Ordinary and Canon of the Mass as a supplement to his catechism. From then on vernacular Missals for the laity multiplied and, through the efforts of the liturgical movement, have become a genuinely popular item in the Christian life. This is particularly true of Monsignor Stedman's Sunday Missal, of which millions of copies have been placed in the hands of the laity and in the pews of churches all over the world—and this because of its simple arrangement, easily followed by people who have little formal liturgical training.[187]

The objection, therefore, that many people cannot use the Missal should eventually lose its foundation with the ever increasing simplicity of arrangement of these popular Missals. For instance, the simplest conception to date has been the *Leaflet Missals* published

[185] For an interesting account of this whole episode, see Henri Brémond, *Histoire littéraire du sentiment réligieux en France* (Paris: Bloud et Gay, 1932), IX, pp. 177-192.

[186] Cf. G. Ellard, *The Mass of the Future* (Milwaukee: Bruce, 1948), 128.

[187] Cf. the interesting dissertation of P. Bussard, *The Vernacular Missal in Religious Education* (Washington, D. C.: The Catholic University Press, 1937), especially the chapter on "The History of the Vernacular Missal," pp. 10-39.

by Fr. Paul Bussard, which obviate all unnecessary page-turning and confusion by printing each Sunday Mass in a few pages and as a separate leaflet, so that all the prayers and actions of the Mass follow each other in their proper order: the parts of both Proper and Ordinary appear in the sequence in which they are actually recited at Mass. This increasing popularity of the vernacular Missal will in time rectify the sad situation in which so many of the faithful find themselves today, not being able to understand the rites and prayers of the Liturgy. They will the better be able to unite themselves, *ceteris paribus*, as intimately as possible with the prayer and action of Holy Mother Church as expressed and performed by her delegated minister, the celebrating priest.

• *Bodily posture and gestures* [187a]

Though insufficient in themselves (i.e., apart from genuine internal devotion), a suitable bodily posture and the use of certain gestures can heighten as well as better express the inner participation of the faithful at Mass. If we are to accept seriously the consequences of man's composite nature, we must admit the value of external movements in prayer. A cursory reading of Thomas Ohm's book on the use of such bodily expression among both Christians and pagan peoples will reveal how universally this concept is accepted by all religions.[188] We have already seen how convinced Catholicism has always been of the utility of prayer-gestures for the faithful at Mass.[189]

Such gestures have been faithfully practiced by all the Rites of the Church. There has always been care to give the faithful a part in the Offertory by means of a gift of some sort. In the early Church, the faithful presented bread and wine to the celebrant,[190] while today this oblation takes the form of a collection of alms. But the faithful were encouraged to go even further than this: they often imitated the gestures of the celebrant. Just like the priest, they turned and faced the East[191] and lifted their hands [192] in prayer during the oration. They bowed at the Sanctus [193] and exchanged the kiss of peace as well.[194] And even today rubricists recommend that the faithful follow the same rubrics for standing, sitting, and kneeling observed by the clergy assisting at High Mass in the sanctuary.[195]

[187a] *Instr. on Sacred Music and Liturgy*, 22b. AAS, 50 (1958), 638.
[188] *Die Gebetsgebärden der Völker und das Christentum*. Leiden: Brill, 1948.
[189] Cf. our treatment of liturgical actions in Chapter 5, pp. 191-201.
[190] *Ord. Rom. I*, 69-76. Andrieu, *Les Ordines*, II, pp. 91-92.
[191] *Didascalia Apostolorum*, II, 57. Quasten, *op. cit.*, 35; *Apostolic Constitutions*, II, 57. MPG, 1: 734; J-F Dölger, *Sol Salutis*, 136 ff.
[192] See evidence in J. Quasten, *op. cit.*, 174, note 4.
[193] *Ord. Rom. XVII*, n. 48. *Andrieu*, III, p. 181.
[194] *Ibid.*, n. 57. Andrieu, III, 183.
[195] Cf. J. O'Connell, *The Celebration of Mass* (Milwaukee: Bruce, 1941), I, appendix, pp. 281-282.

The Dialogue Mass

When, in addition to all the above methods of taking part in the Mass, we also make the responses, we have the most liturgical manner of assisting at Low Mass. Why? Because this method brings out better the hierarchical nature of the Mass, activates more perfectly the power issuing from the sacramental character of Baptism, and knits the congregation into the closest possible union with the celebrant. If the foregoing use of gestures is so important and useful, the use of the voice is even more so, for thus we employ the highest power of self-expression proper to man as a human being. In this way the people are transformed from mute spectators to communicative, human co-offerers.[196]

Though the modern practice can possibly be traced back to Dom Gerard von Caloen of the Belgian Benedictine Abbey of Maredsous in 1880, the idea behind it is not new. In our treatment of liturgical formulas we saw that from earliest times the Christian faithful were not only allowed but urged to respond at Mass. Their doing so was considered very important. St. Paul speaks of the faithful saying "Amen" to the prayers of thanksgiving;[197] Justin Martyr expects the faithful to answer the same at the end of the Canon.[198] And Jerome remarks how the Amens of the faithful resounded like heavenly thunder and shook the pagan temples.[199] This practice continued throughout the Middle Ages, and the people's sharing in other formulas is also noted — besides the Amen,[200] the Et cum spiritu tuo,[201] the Gloria tibi, Domine,[202] and the dialogue before the Preface.[203] Burchard of Worms reports that it was even considered a fault when the people failed to respond.[204]

Of course, the above formulas were *sung* by the people; the Dialogue Mass puts the traditional idea of participation into a new form: simple speech without music. Though the Congregation of Rites at first showed reserve toward this new practice, it finally left its use up to the discretion of the local Ordinary in a decree of November 30,

---

196 Cf. G. Lefebvre, "La question de la messe dialoguée," *Cours et Conférences des Semaines Liturgiques*, XI (1933), 153-196.

197 1 Cor. 14:16. This is possibly a reference to thanksgiving prayer as the Canon of the Mass.

198 I *Apology* 65 and 67. J. Quasten, *op. cit.*, 17 and 20.

199 *In epist. ad Gal.* II, praef. *MPL*, 26: 381.

200 Amalar, *De eccl. off.*, III, 19. *MPL*, 105: 1128; Rabanus Maurus, *De instit. cleric.*, I, 33. *MPL*, 107: 323; Bernold, *Micrologus*, 2, 7. *MPL*, 151: 979 and 981; Remigius, *Expositio*. *MPL*, 101: 1252 ff.

201 *Expositio* "Primum in ordine," *MPL*, 138: 1175 and 1185: *Ord. Rom.* XVII, n. 29. Andrieu, III, 179.

202 Amalar, *De eccl, off.*, III, 18. *MPL*, 105: 1125.

203 *Ibid.*, III, 19. *MPL*, 105: 1131; Caesarius of Arles, *Sermo* 281, 2. *MPL*, 39: 2277; Remigius, *Expositio*. *MPL*, 101: 1252 ff.

204 *Poenitentiale eccl. Germ.* n. 145. *MPL*, 140: 970.

1935.[205] And the new *Instruction on Sacred Music and Liturgy* of September 3, 1958, gives full approbation to the practice. In fact, it speaks of the Dialogue Mass as "the most perfect manner of participation" in the read Mass.[205a]

The *Instruction* itself outlines several forms of the Dialogue Mass: (a) the faithful may simply make the responses ordinarily made by the server; (b) in addition to these, they may also recite together in Latin those parts of the Ordinary of the Mass normally sung at High Mass: the Gloria, Credo, Pater Noster together with its Amen, the Agnus Dei; also the Confiteor and Domine non sum dignus before they receive Holy Communion; (c) in some places for a worthwhile change on special occasions the Proper parts of the Mass, sung by the choir at High Mass, are also recited: the Introit, Gradual, Alleluia or Tract, Offertory and Communion antiphons—or at least someone is chosen to read these texts aloud in English; (d) the custom is also growing of singing four vernacular hymns during the Dialogue Mass: at the beginning of Mass a hymn of preparation or one having a direct connection with the theme of the feast day or season, at the Offertory a hymn of offering, during the distribution of Communion a Eucharistic hymn, and at the conclusion of Mass a jubilant recessional hymn. This last practice is certainly commendable; for, allowing as it does for a periodic musical expression of fundamental ideas of the Mass, it helps greatly to lift the congregation to a higher level of participation at the most climactic points.[206]

Community Sung Mass

Unquestionably the highest form of active participation is obtained when—always presuming the vital presence of internal attention, devotion, and genuine sentiments of self-offering and communion —the entire congregation takes its rightful part in the singing of the Ordinary of a High Mass. The very impressiveness of the ceremonies and the chant incline Pius XII to see in this form a dignity and effectiveness which other forms of the Mass cannot replace.[207] Even more than the Dialogue Mass, the High and Solemn Masses bring out the hierarchical character of the Church's worship and give fullest expression to "the living unity of the Mystical Body." [208]

---

[205] *Collectio Decretorum ad sacram liturgiam spectantium ab anno 1927 ad annum 1946* (Rome: Edizioni Liturgiche, 1947), pp. 36-37.

[205a] Nn. 31-33. *AAS*, 50 (1958), 642-643.

[206] The World Library of Sacred Music in Cincinnati, Ohio, has published several Mass Cards for the Dialogue Mass containing hymns. *Mass Card II* offers by far the better choice of hymns and has become very popular. And even wider selection of hymns and psalms, both in English and Latin, is provided in the *Parish Mass Book*, Cincinnati: World Library of Sacred Music, 1958. This latter also contains simple Gregorian chants for High Mass.

[207] *Mediator Dei*, 106; cf. also *Instr. on Sacred Music and Liturgy*, nn. 24, 26. *AAS*, 50 (1958), 639-640.

[208] *Ibid.*, 122.

As we have already noted, the evidence brought forth in favor of the basic principle behind the Dialogue Mass is specifically pertinent to this sung form of the Mass. In fact, all of tradition attests to the community sung Mass as the normal manner of celebrating the sacred mysteries. That the singing of the faithful was not limited to a musical rendition of simple responses is proven by the fact that already in the *Apostolic Constitutions* all the faithful were to sing the Sanctus.[209] And this practice lasted until and through the Carolingian era, for we find Charlemagne stipulating that the people were expected to sing the Sanctus; he also urged them to sing the Gloria Patri.[210] Furthermore, Pope Sergius I, at the end of the seventh century, introduced the Agnus Dei into the Mass and wanted it sung by both clergy and people together.[211] And now the *Instruction on Sacred Music and Liturgy* insists that every effort be made that the faithful of the entire world learn how to sing the simple responses and at least Mass XVI, the Gloria and Ite missa est-Deo gratias of Mass XV, and the Credo I and III of the Roman Gradual.[211a]

Let us recall what was said in our present treatment on the use of music in worship:[212] the sung Liturgy is the highest type of spiritual expression, most capable of moving the soul to fervent devotion and of giving fullest articulation to social prayer. For this reason, the Dialogue Mass is considered by many authors as being only a stepping-stone in preparing the people for the day when they will be spiritually and musically capable of accepting the sung Mass as the normal form of the prayer-life of the Mystical Body (always allowing, of course, for circumstances in which song is simply out of the question.)

Of course, it is entirely possible that a person does not like to sing. That is unfortunate, for singing is so natural to man that, when he cannot sing, he must consider himself deprived of a basic power of self-expression. It might be well to remind him that Mass is a sacrifice. We go to the Mass in order to give, not just to be flattered by our own feelings, and to do only what we like. By joining with the Church in her song to Almighty God, we willingly sacrifice ourselves, make ourselves a more dedicated part of the glorious choir of singers, both human and angelic, and to that degree allow ourselves to be transformed into worthy members of Christ, who are called to take the place of the fallen angels. For that matter, all these methods are simply the practical, human, reasonable steps one takes to open his heart and allow the torrential stream of grace to do its work of trans-

---

[209] VIII, 12. *MPG*, 1: 1102.
[210] *Capitulare ecclesiasticum*, 69. *MPL*, 97: 175.
[211] *Liber Pontificalis* (Ed. L. Duchesne), I, 376: "Hic statuit ut tempore confractionis dominici corporis *Agnus Dei, qui tollis peccata mundi, miserere nobis* a clero et populo decantetur."
[211a] N. 25 a, b. AAS, 50 (1958), 639-640.
[212] Chapter 5, pp. 147-149.

figuring him into the likeness of the Christ who is commemorated, sacrificed, and eaten.

B. History of the Ordinary of the Mass

1. In the first six centuries

The Mass as we have it today is greatly different from the simple ceremony followed by Christ and His Apostles. Christ Himself celebrated the first Eucharist in the context of the Jewish Passover meal. The ritual of the Christian sacrifice proper consisted in:

> consecration of bread,
> breaking of bread,
> communion,
> consecration of wine,
> communion.

The words of the blessing which Christ pronounced over the bread and wine have already been described in our treatment of the Preface.[213] It was this same simple ritual which the Apostles performed in their Christian reunions after our Lord's ascension into heaven. And these essential phases of the Eucharistic Liturgy were faithfully adhered to throughout the ages regardless of what other embellishments were added.

Though the faithful in apostolic times did attend a service of instruction similar to our own so-called Mass of the Catechumens, this we know took place in the Jewish Synagogue at first. Only later did Christians hold this service of instruction completely apart from the ordinary Jewish Sabbath service. It was not united to the Mass of sacrifice until later, therefore.[214] When this fusion occurred and how often before it occurred the Christians actually held both services together is not so certain. But in the second-century work of Justin Martyr, his I *Apology*,[215] we find both these services definitively linked together.

According to his account, the Mass in his day comprised the following elements:

---

[213] Chapter 5, pp. 185-186.
[214] It is difficult to see how this can be so completely denied by E. Siegman, "Teaching in the Liturgy according to the New Testament," *Education and the Liturgy*, Proceedings of the Eighteenth North American Liturgical Week of 1957 (Elsberry, Missouri: The Liturgical Conference, 1958), p. 53, following Oscar Cullmann, *Early Christian Worship* (London: SCM Press, 1954), pp. 26-31, who calls the separation of these two services a "textbook dogma." This original separation is correctly insisted on by J. Jungmann, *op. cit.*, I, 20, who bases his position on a text from the Acts of the Apostles (2:46) which clearly indicates that the Christians frequented the Jewish reading service, and also on the imitation of the old Jewish Sabbath service as found in the two-fold division of the Law and the Prophets and the intervenient chants of the Mass of the Catechumens; see also I, 391-395.
[215] 65 and 67, J. Quasten, *op. cit.*, 16-21.

Didactic part

> Readings from Apostles or Prophets
> A homily (based on these readings)
> Common prayers (presumably similar to the Oratio Fidelium)
> The kiss of peace

Sacrificial part

> Presentation of bread and wine mixed with water
> Prayers and thanksgivings over these oblations (Consecration)
> Breaking of the consecrated bread
> Distribution of Communion under both species
> A collection taken up for the poor.

In the third century, Hippolytus offers us a detailed example of the consecratory prayer of the Mass; this we have already reprinted in full in our treatment of the Preface.[216] In addition he provides prayers of blessing for oil, cheese, and olives to be said towards the end of the Canon.[217]

In the *Apostolic Constitutions*[218] of the fourth century we find a more highly developed form of Mass. There is the same didactic part as found in Justin, but now for the first time the Oratio Fidelium, the prayers for various categories of the faithful, is reported in minute detail. Here we find special orations for catechumens in different stages of preparation for Baptism, others for possessed persons, for penitents. Each group is told to bow in order to receive the pontiff's blessing and is then dismissed. Upon this follows prayers for the faithful themselves. After the kiss of peace, there is a washing of hands and the presentation of the oblation. The celebrant then begins the Eucharistic prayer (Preface and Canon) which climaxes in Communion, during which a psalm is sung. The Mass comes rapidly to a conclusion with a short prayer of thanksgiving, our Postcommunion, the celebrant's blessing and the deacon's "Ite in pace!"

At about the same time the Canon of the Roman Mass was receiving a lasting and definite literary form. St. Ambrose is the first to cite a considerable portion of the Roman Canon,[219] and he claims to be following Roman usage.[220] From Pope Innocent I, who wrote in 416, we learn that the diptychs were read during the Canon.[221] Furthermore, the Secret seems to be implied when Innocent says that "first the oblations are to be commended" to God and only then the names re-

---

[216] See Chapter 5, pp. 183-188.
[217] Cf. J. Quasten, 30-31.
[218] VIII, end of chapter 5 to chapter 15 inclusive. *MPG*, 1:1075-1114.
[219] *De sacramentis* V-VI. J. Quasten, 160-162.
[220] *Ibid.*, III, 1, 5. J. Quasten, 152.
[221] *Epist.* 25 *ad Decentium.* MPL, 20: 553-554.

cited. Certain parts of the Canon, however, were still wanting in the beginning of the fifth century: Communicantes, Hanc igitur, Memento (of the dead) and the Nobis quoque peccatoribus. The Communicantes and Nobis quoque both belong to the period of St. Leo the Great.[222] The Memento of the dead existed most probably at the same time, but it was used only in Masses for the dead; later it was inserted into the text for all Masses by Alcuin.[223] The authentic version of our present Canon (with the exception, of course, of the Memento of the dead) goes back at least as far as Pope St. Gelasius I (died 496).[224]

Pope Gelasius seems to have gone one step further. He moved the litanic type prayer normally used for the Oratio Fidelium from the beginning of the Mass of the Faithful to before the first Collect. Many of the petitions of the former Oratio Fidelium are included in the deacon's part of the dialogue Gelasius instituted at the beginning of Mass; this dialogue-litany has come down to us under the name *Deprecatio Gelasii*.[225] It consisted in the recital of a short prayer petition followed by the acclamation, Kyrie eleison. Even as late as Gregory the Great, we know, there were two ways of singing the Kyrie: either as a simple repetition of Kyrie eleison, Christe eleison, etc., or the singing of Kyrie as a reply to a petition announced by the deacon.[226]

Though the antiphons for the Introit and Offertory processions probably did exist long before, we find the first explicit mention of them in the *Ordo Romanus* I, which we know stems substantially from the time of Gregory the Great. After the pontiff had vested and all were ready for the procession to the altar, the schola, arranged on either side of the entrance to the presbytery, started the *antiphonam ad introitum*.[227] And during the Offertory, though we are not told when the antiphon began, once the oblations had been collected the pontiff nodded to the *schola* for silence.[228]

So by the reign of Gregory the Great the Mass had attained to a certain definitive form—not that the actual formulas of the Mass were invariable, but the framework or schema of the Mass ritual had achieved a certain fixed determination. And this basic form of the Mass has lasted even to our own day. In the centuries following St.

[222] C. Callewaert in "S. Léon, le Communicantes et le Nobis quoque peccatoribus," *Sacris Erudiri*, I (1948), 123-164, claims that Leo's own pen was at work here; but see reservations by H. Frank, "Beobachtungen zur Geschichte des Messkanons," *ALW*, 1 (1950), 110 and 119.

[223] B. Botte, *L'Ordinaire de la Messe* (Louvain: Abbaye de Mont César 1953), 24.

[224] Cf. Jungmann, I, 55; B. Botte, *Le Canon de la Messe Romaine* (Louvain, 1935), 32.

[225] Jungmann reproduces it in full, *op. cit.*, I, 336-337.

[226] Gregory, *Epist. ad Joannem Syracusanum*, 9, 12. *MPL*, 77: 956.

[227] Nn. 42-44. Andrieu, *Les Ordines*, II, 81.

[228] Nn. 85. *Ibid.*, 95.

Gregory other prayers were to find their way into the Roman Mass, but for the most part they concerned only what the priest prays silently—and this happened under the influence of the Gallican rites.

2. The Gallican Mass

Though the Gallican Liturgy did not last (except in a very mitigated form in a few places), it nevertheless exercised considerable influence on the Roman Rite when the latter was fused with it in Frankish territory. In order to understand our own Roman Mass, it is important to get a good picture of what the Gallican Mass was like from about the seventh to the tenth centuries. Already, it is true, in the eighth century the Roman Mass was becoming known in France and Germany, especially through the efforts of Pepin and Charlemagne. Nonetheless, as late as the tenth century we still find evidence of the Gallican influence working itself out and being inserted into the already mixed affair that was the current Roman Liturgy of Frankish lands.

The following survey is based upon a comparison of the most important documents pertaining to the Gallican Rite.[229] Such a survey was first worked out by Louis Duchesne in 1881.[230] The research since that time will allow us to make certain additions and retouches to the picture as he first conceived it.

The opening rite of the Mass consists of four chants. There is a piece of psalmody for the entry of the bishop similar to our Introit; it is called the Officium in the Mozarabic Rite and corresponds to the singing of the Monogenes in the Byzantine Liturgy. After the celebrant has greeted the people with "Dominus sit semper vobiscum," and the people have replied with "Et cum spiritu tuo," the pontiff intones the Trisagion, sometimes called the *Ajus*, from the Greek *Hagios*; it is sung in both Greek and Latin. Then comes the Kyrie sung by three boys, which, unlike its counterpart in the Roman Rite, has no connection with the original diaconal litany. Finally, the Benedictus is sung. The opening rite is concluded with an Oration, but only after the celebrant has spoken a short allocution, called *praefatio*, announcing the theme of the feast.

A service of reading then follows consisting of three Lessons: the first from the Old Testament, the second from the Acts or Epistles, and the third from the Gospels. After the first lesson, the Canticle of the Three Young Men is sung, called the Benediction because of the frequently recurring "Benedicite." A responsorial chant, the Psalmulus, comes next. The singing of the *Ajus* is again introduced between the Epistle and Gospel and after the Gospel. During this singing, a solemn

---

[229] Recorded in Chapter 2.
[230] In his *Christian Worship. Its Origin and Evolution* (5th edit. London, 1949), 189-227.

procession takes place led by seven candle-bearers, climaxed with cries of "Gloria tibi, Domine!" as the deacon ascends the Gospel ambo. A homily is given after the chanting of the Gospel. And the Foremass is brought to a close with a diaconal litany. At first this diaconal litany had two parts: a section for the catechumens, after which they were dismissed, and another for the faithful, which was considered to open the Mass of the Faithful. However, with the disappearance of the catechumenate, both sections of the diaconal litany were fused to such a point that often only one petition concerns the catechumens. These litanies are exactly of the same type as those found in the Oriental Liturgies beginning with the Liturgy of the *Apostolic Constitutions*: each petition is announced by the deacon, and the people reply with "Kyrie eleison" or "Domine, miserere." In fact, very often the sequence of petitions and even the wording indicate that they were mere translations of Greek originals. This reading service is finally concluded with a *collectio post precem* recited by the celebrant, summing up all the petitions of the litany.

The Mass of the Faithful begins with another solemn procession in which the clergy carry the gifts to the altar. This oblation was already prepared before the entry of the celebrant at the very beginning of Mass—an Oriental and Gallican peculiarity which has passed over into the Dominican Rite. If the people offered any gifts, this too was done before Mass. During the Offertory procession and after the oblation is laid on the altar, chants similar to the Byzantine Cheroubicon are sung. Various names have been given to these chants: *sonus, Laudes, Alleluia, Antiphona post Evangelium, Sacrificium, Offertorium* or *Offerenda*. While the choir is executing these chants, the celebrant recites privately numerous prayers; this is the origin of the Apologies. They stand out quite obviously as silent prayers of the priest in the Mozarabic *Missale Mixtum*.[231] Though these prayers achieve their closest resemblance to our present Roman Offertory prayers in the Sacramentary of Amiens,[232] striking parallelisms, sometimes exact verbal likenesses, occur already in the *Missale Mixtum*. In some Gallican documents we also see for the first time an incensation of the oblation once it is placed on the altar.[233] The counterpart of our Secret is called a *collectio* but is preceded by an invitatory allocution called the *praefatio missae*—not to be confused

[231] *MPL*, 85: 112-113.

[232] Cf. V. Leroquais, "L'ordo missae du sacramentaire d'Amiens," *EL*, 41 (1927), 435-445.

[233] *Missale Mixtum, MPL*, 85: 113; certain Ordos from the ninth and tenth centuries coming from Frankish territory: *OR* V, n. 55. Andrieu *Les Ordines*, II, 220; *OR* X, n. 46. Andrieu, II, 360. These instances seem due to the influence of Amalar, according to Andrieu, II, 202 and 220, note *b*. In *OR* X, m. 14. Andrieu, II 354, we even find an incensation of the altar when the officiant arrives there for the first time at the beginning of Mass. This, as we know, was untrue of the Roman Rite, in which incense was used only in the procession before Mass when it was carried before the pontiff.

with the Preface of the Mass. After this collect comes the reading of
the diptychs which inlcude the name of those offering the Mass or
for whom it is offered, along with a commemoration of certain saints—
all this similar to the various commemorations of the Church militant,
triumphant, and suffering made in our Roman Canon. The reading of
the diptychs is closed with another oration called *collectio post nomina.*
The kiss of peace is then given, preceded by a *collectio ad pacem* and
the salutation: "May the grace of God the Father Almighty, the peace
and love of our Lord Jesus Christ, and the communication of the Holy
Spirit be always with all of us."[234] While the kiss is being exchanged
the choir sings the antiphon, "Pacem meam do vobis, etc."

At last we arrive at the Eucharistic prayer. The customary dialogue between celebrant and people precedes it: "Sursum corda, etc."
The first part of the Canon, which we call the Preface, is called in
Gallican service books *Illatio, immolatio* or *contestatio.*[235] Like our
Roman Preface, its basic motif is thanksgiving, though sometimes it
turns to petition. It likewise issues in the singing of the Sanctus. The
collectio post Sanctus serves merely as a transitional link to the words
of institution, forming, as in our Rite, the Consecration. Immediately
upon this follows the Anamnesis (like our Unde et memores); a
prayer, called *Post mysterium* or *Post pridie,* is then recited with the
intention of calling down the Holy Spirit on the oblation. The breaking
of the host is a complicated matter and is governed by careful regulations. The particles are to be specially arranged on the paten. At
first such an arrangement was supposed to represent the human body,
but later it assumed the form of a cross, once the former was condemned as an abuse by the Council of Tours.[236] An antiphonal chant
or the Credo accompanies this ceremony; if the former, it is usually
called the *Confractorium.* The Pater Noster is then recited by the
whole assembly; it is preceded by a short preface and followed by a
frequently changed embolism similar to our Libera. The rite of commixtion follows as one or more particles are let fall into the chalice
with the prayer *Sancta sanctis,* etc. A culminating point may be seen
in the blessing spoken over the bowed heads of the congregation, and
it is preceded by the diaconal warning, "Humiliate vos benedic-
tioni!"[237] Though the practice was not looked upon with favor by
ecclesiastical authority, it was here that many of the faithful who
did not intend to receive Communion left the church. The Communion
of those who remained was accompanied by the chant called the
Trecanum. And at this point, just before Communion, we notice the

234 *Missale Mixtum, MPL,* 85: 115.

235 Cf. *Missale Mixtum, MPL,* 85: 116 ff; *Missale Gothicum, MPL,* 72: 225,
279.

236 This complicated ordering of the sacred particles is to be found in the
pre-Mass preparation of the oblation in some Oriental Rites today.

237 Compare our Roman "Humiliate capita vestra Deo" used during Lent
before the *Oratio super populum,* which was originally also a blessing.

preoccupation of the celebrant with the recitation of many apologies similar to the prayer spoken privately by the celebrant in the Roman Rite before he consumes the consecrated host.[238] A thanksgiving prayer follows the distribution of Communion, just as in the Roman Rite we have a *Post-communio*. And here again a short preface is spoken before the collect. The Mass is concluded by a simple announcement of the fact: "Missa acta est—In pace," or "Solemnia completa sunt, etc." The celebrant then gives his blessing.

3. Fusion of the Roman and Gallican Mass

A comparison between the Roman and the Gallican Mass shows sufficiently well that the latter was imprinted with a genius entirely different from that of the former. The Roman Ordinary, as has often been remarked, was characterized by a sober, almost puritanical brevity; the Gallican Ordinary, on the other hand, was inspired by the temperament of the northern peoples which expressed itself chiefly in a love of the dramatic and a delight in long prayers. We have called attention to the "playful" use of incense, the multiplying of silent prayers on the part of the celebrant. There is yet more. The fact that the liturgical language of the West was strange to the northern folk likewise had its effect in their understanding of the Liturgy and subsequently in the Liturgy itself.

Because of this linguistic veil, the Mass became more of a clerical reserve; the rites were *hidden*, they became truly mysterious. This difficulty, coupled with a shifting focus of attention from sacrifice to adoration of the Real Presence, gave rise to explanations of the Mass which, though intended to bring the people to a deeper understanding, were based, not on the word content, but rather on what struck the people's eye, the ceremonies. Thus developed the allegorical interpretation of the Mass, which in turn influenced the introduction of newer rites aimed at enhancing this "mystery play." The contact, therefore, of this Gallican mind with the old, restrained Roman one, brought a new Mass rite into existence which in its first appearances proved to be a confused and inorganic hybrid.

Attempts at a fusion of these two disparate rites were apparent over a broad area of time and place in the Frankish realm. They begin as early as the eighth century and last well into the tenth. New Ordos and Sacramentaries appear, now in Switzerland, now along the Rhine, now in Alsace and Paris, in episcopal sees in Normandy, in the center and south of France. The mixture resulting from such attempts is represented by various manuscripts which, though going under the name of Roman Ordos, are in reality not Roman documents but adaptations of Roman ones to circumstances peculiar to the

---

[238] Cf. *Missale Mixtum, MPL,* 85: 120.

Frankish realm.[239] Another example of this endeavor is the so-called *Ordo Romanus Antiquus*, which, because of its obvious German origin, Michel Andrieu has renamed the *Romano-Germanic Pontifical*.[240] Still another instance of this mixture is to be seen in a group of manuscripts called the Séez group, so named because they all reproduce in greater or lesser degree the Mass Ordinary of the city of Séez in Normandy,[241] an Ordinary peculiarly close to our modern Mass. This form itself, however, had as its point of propagation St. Alban in Mainz and originated in the monastery of St. Gall in Switzerland.[242]

It is in this last named Mass formulary that we find, combined with Roman elements for the first time, the vesting prayers, Psalm 42 ending with the *Aufer a nobis* (as prayers to be recited by the celebrant on his way to the altar), the various texts recited silently during the Offertory, the prayers for the Offertory incensation which we still use today, the series of prayers before Communion still in use and, finally, the Benedicite to be recited by the celebrant on his way back to the sacristy after Mass. It was this new form which found its way back to Rome and was subsequently adopted and adapted there.

However, this was not the only form current at the turn of the first thousand years. As the various religious orders became more centralized and saw the need of regulation of divine worship, they decided on one or the other current form. Thus was propagated for their own religious establishments the Mass-Ordos proper to the Carthusians, Carmelites, and Dominicans. The fact that these orders usually adopted the Mass-Ordinary of the locale where they were founded or had their central government explains the similarity of their rites to those local Liturgies which have come to us; e.g., the Carthusians and the Rite of Lyons, the Dominicans and the thirteenth century Rite of Paris, etc.

4. The Ordinaries of Innocent III and Pius V

Once the Romano-Germanic liturgical books reached Rome, the Romans went to work at transcribing them and, in doing so, adapted them. However, there must have still been alive a spirit alert against the intrusion of foreign rites into the Roman, for as late as the end of the eleventh century Bernold of Constance remarks that there were no apologies in the Roman Offertory.[243] About a century later there appears in Rome an official Mass-Ordinary which is full of such apologies: all of our modern Offertory prayers are present. A manuscript in the Vatican Library, *Cod. Ottobon. lat. 356,* composed sometime

---

[239] Often these adaptations turn out to be sad miscarriages of ceremonial; see in particular *OR* IV, V, VI, VII, VIII, IX, X in Andrieu *Les Ordines*, II.

[240] Composed at Mainz around 950: M. Andrieu, *Les Ordines*, I, 454-545.

[241] Reprinted in *MPL*, 78: 245-251.

[242] Cf. J. Jungmann, *Missarum Sollemnia*, I (4th edition, Freiburg: Herder, 1958), 123-124, esp. note 9.

[243] *Micrologus*, XI. *MPL*, 151: 984.

during the second half of the thirteenth century, is considered by most
authors to contain the reform of Pope Innocent III.[244] Though under
Innocent's orders certain Gallican elements had been admitted (e.g.,
the Offertory prayers), the many Gallican greetings, blessings, and
longer apologies were left out. This new Missal of the Roman Curia
was indeed an attempt at simplification to meet the needs of the time.

Though Bernold stated that there were no prayers in the Roman
Offertory, he does say that an apology was placed at the very beginning of the Mass, the Confiteor.[245] Neither were there incensations
either of the altar or the oblation.[246] But around 1143, Benedict, a
canon of St. Peter's, composed the *Ordo Romanus* XI (Mabillon's
numeration) in which we find a incensation of the altar at the beginning of Mass.[247]

In addition to the Gallican insertions spoken of by Bernold and
Benedict, we find the Ordinary of Innocent III giving official acceptance for the first time to an incensation of the oblation and altar at the
Offertory together with all the prayers for the offering of bread and
wine and the incensations just as they appear in the Missal of Pius V.
The apologies before Communion also appear and are identical to
those of today. And while the prayer *Placeat* does appear, the Gospel
of St. John at the end of Mass is not mentioned.

Another point of rubrics that was introduced here for the first
time officially and that proved to be symptomatic of the whole late
medieval trend, is that the celebrant had now to *read* the Introit with
his ministers even though it was being sung by the *schola*. The practice
of the celebrant repeating what was sung by others at Mass seems to
have started with Cardinal Bernard's insisting on it for the Lateran
Basilica in 1170.[248] Though Innocent had introduced this reading only
for the Introit, once the principle was admitted the same rubric was
extended to all the chants executed by the *schola*. We find this happening in the *Ordo Romanus* XIV which is attributed to Cardinal
Stephaneschi;[249] thence it passed into the *Ordo Missae* of Johannes
Burchard [250] (died 1506) and the Missal of Pius V.

We see, then, that the Mass-Ordinary of Innocent III gave official
sanction to the introduction of Gallican elements into the Roman
Rite. Because of the handiness of the Roman Curia's liturgical books,
they were subsequently adopted by the Franciscans for their missionary journeys throughout Europe, thus making them known and

[244] It is described in full by J. Brinktrine, "Ordo et Canon Missae," *EL*, 51
(1937), 198-209.
[245] *Micrologus*, I. *MPL*, 151: 979. There were also several psalms indicated
for the vesting of the celebrant.
[246] *Ibid*. I, IX, *MPL*, 151: 979, 983.
[247] C. 18. *MPL*, 78: 1032.
[248] *Ordo Eccl. Lat*, ed. Fischer, 121. Righetti, *op. cit.*, III, 151.
[249] *MPL*, 78: 1121-1274.
[250] *Ordo Missae, auctore Ioanne Burckardo*, appearing as a supplement to
Ephemerides Liturgicae 38 (1924), 10. Cf. *OR* XV, n. 121. Andrieu, III, 120.

popular everywhere. The later Ordo of John Burchard (in which the
Last Gospel of St. John appears for the first time) and the Missal of
Pius V made very few changes. Essentially we have today the Mass-
Ordinary as established by Pope Innocent III.

C. The Present Roman Mass: Historical, Functional, Symbolic and Ascetical Explanation

Though in the Middle Ages many divisions of the Mass were
proposed, these for the most part were products of a special predilec-
tion for symbolism, or rather allegorism. The only division of the Mass
that is truly justified from the point of view of history and functionalism is that between the Mass of the Catechumens and the Mass of the
Faithful. Both of these major parts, as we know, have come from the
Jewish system of worship: the first from the synagogal reading service
on the Sabbath, the second from the religious meal of the *Chabûrah*—
both, of course, filled with a new internal reality. It seems that this
structural division was first employed by Ivo of Chartres, who died in
1117: he used the terms *Missa catechumenorum* and *Missa sacramentorum.*[251]

The term "Mass of the Catechumens," however, is historically
justified only for a certain period of time when the discipline of the
catechumenate was still in force. Even apart from this institution, both
in the earliest history of the Church as well as after the fourth century,
this first part of the Mass had as its objective, not only the instruction
of the catechumens, but also the edification of the faithful. A more
adequate term, transcending the temporal limitations of the other,
is used by many authors today—the "Foremass," or, even better, the
"Didactic Mass." The term "Mass of the Faithful" is not entirely satisfactory either, for the first part of the Mass pertains to the faithful just
as much as the second part. Mass of Sacrifice, or Sacrificial Mass,
would more perfectly express its true function.

1. Mass of Instruction

Opening rite

The Mass begins with the prayers at the foot of the altar. This is
a private preparation of the priest and his ministers which formerly
took place either in the sacristy or as they approached the altar—
"Introibo ad altare Dei." This verse of the psalm *Iudica me* was chosen
for this function, for it pleads for recognition on the part of God of
his servant, the priest, as he dares draw nigh to the altar. God's mercy
and grace lead him on to His altar and encourage him in praising God
despite the celebrant's personal unworthiness. Since God is readily

[251] *Epist.* 219. *MPL,* 162: 224.

disposed to grant pardon and look down graciously on our prayer when we admit our guilt and unworthiness, the priest confesses that, because of his faults, he should not present himself before God: "Confiteor Deo omnipotenti . . . omnibus sanctis et vobis, fratres, quia peccavi nimis. . . ." With great humility he implores all redeemed creation to beg of God the grace that will make him more "presentable" in God's sight: "Ideo precor beatam Mariam semper virginem . . . omnes sanctos et vos, fratres, orare pro me ad Dominum Deum nostrum." These prayers for internal purification are concluded by further versicles, responses, and other short acclamations asking God directly for His favor. As pointed out, these initial prayers are of Gallican, not Roman, origin; the first evidence we have of their insertion into the Liturgy of Rome is of the eleventh century.[252] They became obligatory for all following the Roman Rite only with the Missal of Pius V in 1570.

Another element taken over from the Gallican rites is the incensation of the altar as soon as the celebrant ascends its steps after the initial prayers. The pure Roman Mass allowed for the use of incense here only insofar as it was carried before the pope during the procession to the altar simply as a mark of respect for him. An emphasis on the altar would not have been looked favorably upon by the original Roman spirit, for the first part of the Mass, since it is one of instruction and not of sacrifice, does not concern the altar but the person of the official teacher.[253]

The real beginning of the Roman Mass was the Introit antiphon and psalm. The institution of this opening chant is usually attributed to Pope Celestine I, who died in 432. But this attribution is based on a report of the Liber Pontificalis,[254] whose historicity is doubted by some authors.[255] However, it does tell us that at the time of the book's composition, about the middle of the sixth century, the Introit existed.

The Introit was originally intended as a processional chant as the Roman pontiff made his way to the sanctuary,[256] and its length depended on his will: he nodded to the schola when he felt it was time to end it.[257] Though it was the schola which was charged with the execution of the Introit, some attempt was made to include the participation of the people through the singing of the Gloria Patri.[258] Our modern Introit is a greatly reduced remnant of its original form, for in former times the schola was supposed to sing an entire psalm, or as much of one as the pontiff desired, using one of the psalm verses as a constantly recurring refrain. This ancient custom is again countenanced

[252] Bernold, Micrologus, I. MPL, 151: 979.
[253] In the earliest Roman Ordo, after a reverence towards the altar, the pontiff went immediately to his throne and stayed there for the entire Foremass: OR I, nn. 50-51. Andrieu, Les Ordines, II, 83.
[254] L. Duchesne, Liber Pontificalis, I, 230.
[255] E.g., J. Jungmann, Mass of the Roman Rite, I, 322.
[256] OR I, nn. 44-51. Andrieu, II, 81-83.
[257] Ibid., n. 50.
[258] Charlemagne's Capitulare ecclesiasticum, n. 69. MPL, 97: 175.

by the *Instructio de Musica sacra et Liturgia* promulgated by the Congregation of Rites on September 3, 1958.[259]

On ordinary days the Introit was chosen in sequence from the list of psalms as they appear in the Bible psalter. But on special feasts on which a particular mystery was celebrated this normal sequence was broken by a specially chosen psalm or some other composition; e.g., *Gaudeamus, Salve, sancta Parens,* etc. Regardless of the make-up of the Introit, its purpose was to set the mood or tone that should dominate the assembly during the celebration of Mass, somewhat in the manner as the overture of a musical concert. The celebrant originally did not recite this song of entrance, but rather, with the faithful, listened to it as it was executed by the *schola.* Since it is not a specifically sacerdotal prayer, the rubric of Innocent III's *Ordinarium* imposing its recitation on the celebrant constitutes an anomaly.

Before this opening rite is brought to a close by means of an official priestly prayer, the Oration, the people are given an opportunity for vocal prayer, according to a regularly recurring rule of all liturgical prayer. This is the function of the Kyrie. It stems from the Oriental litany first introduced into the Roman Rite as the Oratio Fidelium. As has been pointed out, this general prayer for all the categories of the faithful consisted of a list of petitions spoken by the deacon and answered by the people with "Kyrie eleison." In the fifth century this had been moved from the point of junction between the Foremass and the Sacrificial Mass to its present place. The *Deprecatio Gelasii* seems to have been the original form of this transferred Kyrie-litany; it was a much shorter form of the litany, having eighteen petitions similar to the last part of our present Litany of the Saints. We learn from St. Gregory the Great that already in his time the Kyrie was no longer always sung with its petitions: sometimes only the Kyrie and Christe were repeated over and over again.[260] The Kyrie, then, was and is an acclamation of the people, either as a response to the diaconal litany or alone. Gregory explicitly says this: "It is said by the clergy and answered by the people."[261] Here, after the preliminary overture sung by the *schola,* the people become vocal and greet their invisible priest represented by the visible liturgist.

Since the number of times the Kyrie and Christe were repeated varied indefinitely, it is difficult to give credance to any attempt at reading into our modern ninefold repetition a Trinitarian significance. This interpretation again is due to Gallican allegorists. After all, not only is the title Christe appropriately directed to Christ, but also

---

[259] N. 27a. *AAS,* 50 (1958), 640: If the ministers make their way to the altar by means of a longer procession, the antiphon of the Introit may be repeated after every one or two verses of the its psalm.

[260] *Epist. ad Joannem Syracusanum* 9, 12. *MPL,* 77: 956.

[261] *Ibid.: apud nos a clericis dicitur et a populo respondetur.*

Kyrie, "Lord," has in the whole of tradition been applied to the Redeemer.[262]

On feast-days the celebrant recites the Gloria. Here, for the first time in the Mass, we come across the strains of a genuine hymn. It is not a litany like the Kyrie, nor a psalm like the Introit, but a hymn of ecclesiastical composition. Originally it must have occupied a place similar to that of the Te Deum. Not until late as the sixth century did it become firmly established as part of the Mass.[263] Even then its use was limited to bishops; priests could recite it only on Easter.[264]

Unlike the Kyrie, the Gloria does bear a Trinitarian significance. In the first part we direct our praise of God's majesty to the Father: *Deus Pater omnipotens;* this majesty or glory has, in the process of being revealed, become grace for us, and we thank Him for it. The acclamations to Christ in the next section take the form of a litanic prayer with three petitions ending in *miserere nobis* or *suscipe*. The phrases beginning with *Tu solus* have an anti-pagan ring and lead directly to the glorious Trinitarian climax: *Cum sancto Spiritu in gloria Dei Patris.*

After the Kyrie-litany an oration traditionally followed to bind together, as it were, all the petitions mentioned in the litany. The separation of the Kyrie and oration was only gradually and begrudgingly permitted, as can be seen from the rarity of the Gloria. Introit, Kyrie and oration or Collect constitute a whole opening rite. The fact that in the oration, for the first time in the Mass, the celebrant prays aloud publicly in the name of all indicates that the first high point in the Mass has been reached, the conclusion of the opening rite. After having greeted the faithful with "Dominus vobiscum" and thus bound them into a close union of prayer with him, the celebrant "collects" or sums up all the petitions of the entire Church as well as the various chants and prayers that have thus far been executed. It is, therefore, in every sense the climax of the overture of the liturgical service.

This should bring out the incongruity of having more than one oration at Mass, a practice that was not always followed. Even in cases where the old Sacramentaries provide more than one formulary for the oration, only one was recited. The modern practice of appending one oration on another stems, it would seem, from a twofold circumstance: the dropping of the Oratio Fidelium, although the need to express these various petitions in some way was still felt, and the search for some solution to provide for a plurality of votive offerings once it became forbidden to offer more than one Mass for a stipend

[262] Cf. J. Jungmann, *Mass of the Roman Rite,* I, 341-342; Balt. Fischer, "Liturgiegeschichte und Verkündigung," in B. Fischer-F. X. Arnold, *Die Messe in der Glaubensverkündigung* (Freiburg: Herder, 1953), 11.

[263] Duchesne, *Liber Pontificalis,* I, 263. There is apparent here an attempt of the compiler of the *Liber* to make the hymn seem traditional by claiming that Pope Telesphorus had it sung on Christmas: I, 129.

[264] *OR* II, n. 9. Andrieu, II, p. 116.

and thereafter to read a Dry Mass or a *missa bifaciata* for these intentions. Happily the Church is returning to the single oration and thus
restoring it to its proper function.

Reading service

If the Foremass is essentially a period of instruction, the readings
bring us to its very core, just as the Canon is the center of the Mass of
Sacrifice. As we have seen, it would appear that the reading service was
for a time separate from the Mass of Sacrifice,[265] but later they were
united.[266] As L. Bouyer points out, the union of these two distinct
forms of worship was the natural thing to expect, for "the Word of God
tends to evoke thanksgiving, not only as a normal response to it, but
also as the natural product of it."[267] And this thanksgiving is expressed
in the most sublime manner in the solemn thanksgiving prayer, the
Eucharist, instituted by Christ at the Last Supper. The didactic part
of the Mass fits well into the scheme of the Mass as a memorial of our
Lord; it provides us with a review of the great deeds of redemption
and thus conditions our souls for a deeper participation in the sacramental renewal of the redemptive act. Just as faith and the preaching
of the word of God always precede justification or the infusion of
grace, so also here God speaks to us first, and we listen to Him with
open hearts and minds in order to know how He wishes us to live,
before we accomplish the act of sacrifice from which flows all sanctity,
justification, all power to live according to God's will.

The origin of this reading service goes back to the same type of
worship held by the Jews in their synagogues on the Sabbath. The
Apostles grew up in this environment, and the early Christians regularly took part in this Sabbath service, before they were expelled from
the Synagogue. Hence, if we are to understand the didactic part of
the Mass, we must study the synagogue service. There were two readings at each meeting: one from the Law, or *Torah*, the other from the
Prophets. While the first formed a continuous reading from one service
to the other, the lesson from the Prophets was usually chosen at will.
The service opened with a sort of profession of faith based on the
words of Scripture.[268] Inserted in the meeting either after the first or
second readings was a homily. And the service ended with a blessing,
if there was a priest present, or with a prayer.

Upon examining the early liturgical documents of Christianity,
we find that these same essential elements were included in the Foremass.[269] Justin speaks of the readings from the Apostles and Prophets,

[265] Acts 2:46.
[266] Acts 20:7 is perhaps evidence of this; certainly this fusion had taken place
by the time of Justin, *Apology* I, 67. J. Quasten, 19.
[267] *Liturgical Piety* (Notre Dame, Indiana, 1955), 115.
[268] Deut. 6:4-9; 11:13-21; Num. 15:37-41.
[269] Cf. J. Nielen, *The Earliest Christian Liturgy* (St. Louis, 1941), 241-250.

commented on by the presiding priest or bishop, and the concluding prayers.[270] That there were also some chants inserted in between these readings is borne out by the mention made in the *Apostolic Constitutions* of a psalmist who sang Old Testament hymns to which the people responded.[271] Nor was this the first time such chants were introduced, for Tertullian refers to the singing of psalms during the Foremass right after the readings.[272] This same combination of readings, chants, homily (when the occasion presented itself), and prayers has been traditional in the liturgical services of the Church. It is even employed in the Divine Office after the recitation of the designated number of psalms; there the sequence is lesson, short response or hymn, and oration.

A great variety has always existed in the Church as far as the number of lessons is concerned. While Justin speaks of the readings from the Apostles and Prophets, he gives no indication of the exact number of these readings. Both Tertullian [273] and the *Apostolic Constitutions* [274] seem to say that there were four: the Law, the Prophets, the Apostolic Epistles (or Acts) and the Gospels. The West Syrian Rite contains as many as six: three from the Old Testament and three from the New.[275] In the Occident, however, the prevailing custom among both Gallican and Roman Liturgies was to have three lessons: the Old Testament, the Epistles, and the Gospels. That this was true of the Roman Rite is shown by several indications. The older liturgical days, such as Ember Wednesdays, the Wednesday of the fourth week of Lent, the Wednesday and Friday of Holy Week, still have three lessons. The same arrangement is evident for most days in the older books of the Roman Liturgy. Furthermore, the presence of two meditative chants—the Gradual and Tract, or Alleluia verse—in between our present Epistle and Gospel, founds the suspicion that at one time the first chant was placed between the Old Testament lesson and the New Testament Epistle, while the Tract or Alleluia verse was sung between the Epistle and Gospel.[276]

The primitive Church followed the practice of reading the Scriptures in a continuous fashion in such a way that the various books of

[270] I *Apology* 67. J. Quasten, 19.

[271] II, 57. *MPG*, 1: 727.

[272] *De anima* 9. *MPL*, 2: 701: "inter dominica solemnia . . . prout scripturae leguntur aut psalmi canuntur aut allocutiones proferuntur aut petitiones delegantur." Here he is speaking of Mass: *dominica solemnia*, and makes reference to the regular succession of readings, intervenient chants, homily and the Oratio Fidelium.

[273] *Liber de praescriptione* 36. *MPL*, 2: 60.

[274] VIII, 5. *MPG*, 1: 1075.

[275] Cf. A. Raes, *Introductio in Liturgiam Orientalem* (Rome, 1947), 76, 78.

[276] This suspicion is confirmed by the fact that in some churches of Italy before the fifteenth century these chants were apportioned precisely in this manner; cf. J. Jungmann, *Mass of the Roman Rite*, I, 396, note 18.

the Bible were read right through, either in one or successive gatherings. This was called the *lectio continua*, and some remnants of it are still at hand in our Roman Rite. The very form of the Gospel announcement, *Sequentia sancti Evangelii secundum . . .*, originated in this way. And if we examine the list of Epistles read at Sunday Masses after Pentecost, we see that they are taken from the letters of St. Paul with almost no interruption of the Scripture canon. The Gospels of these same Sundays, on the other hand, follow no Scripture order, but rather were chosen with the idea of constructing a parallel with the Epistle theme.[277]

In the Solemn Mass the apportionment of readings to various clerics, which is the ideal method, is maintained. While all the readings exclusive of the Gospel may be announced to the people by a lector or subdeacons, the Gospel is always reserved to the deacon (or in a High Mass to the priest). This is obviously intended to bring out the greater dignity of the Gospel. Thus it is recommended that even in High Masses a lector be employed for the first lesson. And in the *Instructio de Musica sacra et Liturgia* of the Congregation of Rites of September 3, 1958, the use of a commentator who would read the lessons in English during a Low Mass is recommended.[278]

The instruction period of the Mass, however, is not given over entirely to readings. There are meditative chants, joyful or sorrowful as the character of the day or season may demand, to be inserted between the readings. And by their nature these chants are intended to be of a responsorial type; the people used to repeat the initial phrase as a refrain since only one or more specially chosen singers rendered the continuous text. In the Gradual it was the first verse that was thus used as a refrain, and this was repeated after each verse of the psalm. In the case of the Alleluia, it was the Alleluia itself that was intended as the refrain, while the chanters would sing the verse part. Of this ancient practice the only thing that remains is the "V" in the middle of the Gradual and after the Alleluia, thus marking off the part that was to be sung by the chanters alone. This older manner of singing the Gradual and Alleluia, of course, may still be employed.

The Gradual gets its name from the fact that a singer chanted his verses of the psalm, not from the top of the ambo or pulpit, but from one of its steps, *in gradu*. And as we have pointed out, it seems most probable that the original place of the Gradual was in between the lesson and the Epistle, while the Alleluia was sung in between the

---

[277] This original correspondence between Epistle and Gospel for the Sundays after Pentecost has unfortunately been destroyed by the fact that, beginning with the 4th Sunday after Pentecost, the Gospels are advanced by one Sunday; cf. my paper "The Formation of the Cycles of Epistles and Gospels," *Proceedings of the North American Liturgical Week of 1958*. Elsberry, Missouri: The Liturgical Conference, 1959.

[278] N. 96. AAS, 50 (1958), 657.

Epistle and Gospel. On days of penitential character, however, the Tract replaces the Alleluia, and it gets its name from the type of melody used for it, that is, a plain, unchanging melody that goes on for several verses of a psalm without an intervening refrain. Since the ninth century, on days of especial joy the *schola* has added a variety of melismatic notes to the end of the Alleluia, and when extra words were attached to these notes, the newer compositions were called Sequences (from *sequentia,* meaning what *follows* upon the Alleluia).

In the early Church the normal conclusion to the service of the word was reached with the Oratio Fidelium, the prayer for the various categories of the faithful. This was gradually dropped once the various intercessory prayers were added to the Canon. Yet, even today we feel the need of making mention of current intentions at this point of the Mass. On Sundays the celebrant usually invites the faithful to pray for the souls of those who have recently died and often he makes specific mention of their names. Hence, it would not be surprising if eventually some modified type of the Oratio Fidelium is reintroduced by the Church at this point in the Mass.

Since the service of the word is devoted to a study of God's revelation, at least on Sundays and more important feasts a homily is supposed to be given by way of commentary on the Biblical texts read. By more zealous priests this practice is extended even to the daily parochial Mass, where circumstances permit. In such cases the homily is not very long, but the important thing is that the faithful are briefly instructed in the meaning of the sacred texts, so that they are the better prepared to cooperate in the sacred sacrifice that follows and at the same time take into their workaday world the inspiration that will aid them in supernaturalizing the most ordinary aspects of their life.

After the homily there follows, on Sundays and feast days, the recitation or singing of the Nicene Creed. Such creeds as this were originally intended for Baptism and other occasions where a profession of faith was required. That the Credo does not necessarily belong here in the Mass is shown by the varying positions it has occupied: now before the Offertory, now before the Preface, or even before Communion. Whether in Oriental, Gallican, or Roman Rites, its introduction in the Mass is of relatively late date, and, in practically every instance, its insertion was by way of antidote and reaction to heresy. Its presence in the Roman Mass, however, is due to the influence of the German Emperor Henry II. When he went to Rome in 1014 he was surprised that the Romans did not recite it at all during Mass and prevailed on Pope Benedict VIII to do so.[279] Even so, its use at Mass has always been limited to certain days (as with the Gloria) and will probably become even more limited.

[279] Cf. Berno of Reichenau, *De quibusdam rebus ad missae officium spectantibus,* 2. MPL, 142: 1060.

2. Mass of Sacrifice

Preparation of gifts

As in the Foremass, the Mass of Sacrifice also has an *opening* rite, and it is the so-called Offertory. For such a rite, which comes before the real moment of sacrifice, we can conceive *a priori* two fundamental purposes: (1) the preparation of the material of sacrifice—bringing gifts to the altar, placing them and arranging them there; (2) a more immediate preparation of the offerers before they enter the "holy of holies," the most sacred moment of the sacrificial action. The Offertory is not an *offering* of gifts to God except in so far as they are intrinsically ordered to sacrifice or they are "antitypes" of what is truly offered, and only thus acquire a dedication to God. Theologically speaking, the Church has no interest in the bread and wine expect in so far as they are the "sacraments," symbols of the true sacrificial victim, Christ; it is not the bread and wine which are sacrificed, but the Body and Blood of Christ. Only at the moment of transubstantiation are these gifts transformed into the *immediate* matter of sacrifice, and only after that, in the Unde et memores, can and does the Church speak in the strict sense of offering the sacrificial Victim. If the Offertory prayers speak of offering when the celebrant raises the bread and wine heavenward, they speak in an anticipatory sense: the grace asked for is looked forward to, not by reason of the presentation that is being made at this moment, but rather by virtue of the Eucharistic sacrifice that is to take place. Thus also must be understood such terms as *hostiam immaculatam, calicem salutaris;* we are speaking as though the true sacrificial victim were present.

What is demanded by strict theology is also brought out by liturgical history. The question is, exactly what is the essential liturgical act performed at the Offertory? This can only be answered by determining which particular act during the Offertory has remained constant in all Liturgies of all times. And the only act which can stand this test is the *setting of gifts on the altar*—the bread and the wine. In Justin this action is very informal; only the bare statement is made: "bread, wine and water are brought forth." [280] Hippolytus elaborates slightly: "Deacons bring the oblation to the bishop, and he, imposing his hands on it with the entire presbytery, offers thanks [this latter is the Preface-Canon]." [281] With the *Apostolic Constitutions,* it would seem, we make another step towards embellishment; we are told that, after the gifts are brought to the altar, the pontiff prays by himself: "Orans igitur apud se pontifex. . ." [282] Unless we are mistaken, this has a connection with the prayer before the Preface called the

[280] I *Apology* 65 and 67. J. Quasten, 16 and 19.
[281] *La Tradition Apostolique* (ed. B. Botte), n. 4, p. 30.
[282] VIII, 12. *MPG*, 1: 1091.

Secret. This simple rite, then—the bringing forth of gifts and the placing of them on the altar—is to be found in every Liturgy, both Eastern
and Western. In some Rites this setting of the gifts on the altar may
take place at the very beginning of Mass, but they are not taken notice
of until this moment, when by means of some prayer the initial step is
taken towards sacrifice.

This action, constant in all Liturgies, indicates, therefore, that,
from a liturgical point of view, the nature of the Offertory rite consists in preparing the remote matter of sacrifice. All other ceremonies
or prayers that have been added in the course of time have as their
purpose to make this opening rite of sacrifice more solemn, to bring
out the dignity of this remote sacrificial matter which will soon become
the Body and Blood of Christ, to emphasize the human operation and
share in the sacrifice proper, to express the participation of the faithful and to prepare the offerers to perform this sacrifice with great internal devotion. But they are not the essential Offertory action. In fact,
in some cases they have led to a blurring of the essential lines of this
rite and to error as to its true nature. Specifically, the prayers recited
by the celebrant as he raises the bread and wine, prayers originally intended only for him and no one else, have led some to think that the
Church is truly offering at this moment. But we cannot say more
than that the Church is here preparing for the real offering, both by
arranging the remote matter on the altar and by instilling sentiments
of self-offering in the hearts of those who participate.

The oblation on the part of the faithful has not been at all constant in liturgical history, although, generally speaking, it has been
favored and expressed by the Church in several ways. The Roman
Rite has known from earliest times an offering by the faithful of bread
and wine, candles, oil, honey and, of late, money.[283] It has never known
an Offertory procession strictly so-called: i.e., a well-formed and order-
ly movement of lines of the faithful from nave to sanctuary with
gifts.[284] Though the Oriental and Gallican Liturgies did possess an
Offertory procession strictly so-called, this was a ceremonial procession
on the part of the clergy.[285] And this type of procession lives on today
in the Roman Rite for the consecration of a bishop and for canonizations.

Even though some such Offertory procession on the part of the

[283] See Jungmann, II, 1-26 for details.
[284] Cf. V. Kennedy, "The Offertory Rite," *OF*, 12 (1938), 198; G. Booth,
The Offertory Rite in the Ordo Romanus Primus (Washington: The Catholic
University Press, 1948), 39-42, which is unsatisfactory both as regards evaluation
of detail and general conclusions; the review of the latter by Alan Clark, "The
Offertory Rite: a recent study," *EL*, 67 (1953), 242-247; the excellent dissertation
of Alan Clark, "The Function of the Offertory Rite," *EL*, 64 (1950), 311-344.
[285] See L. Duchesne, *Christian Worship*, 203-205; J. Hanssens, *Institutiones
Liturgicae de Ritibus Orientalibus*, III (Rome, 1932), nn. 1110-1123, 1143-1154;
A. Raes, *Introductio in Liturgiam Orientalem*, 72-75, 84-85.

faithful is definitely a valuable pastoral practice, its exact nature must be understood. Is it not a presentation of gifts to God. The gifts are presented to the celebrant; he then commends them to God. Even in the case of the modern Offertory collection, whether of money or kind, we must remember that the faithful do not offer directly to God, but only through the priest. And such offering which might be read into the rite is only such by way of anticipation or preparation. Here the clergy and faithful make an initial step toward sacrifice; by presenting gifts, they unite themselves to the *Christus passus* who is the real matter of sacrifice. The offering implied in such an Offertory rite is essentially dependent upon and orientated to the only true oblation which takes place once the Victim has been made present.

It was certainly in connection with the Offertory oblation, whether a procession or a mere collection of gifts, that the Offertory antiphon originated. The first textual reference made to it is in the *Ordo Romanus* I.[286] From this document it is obvious that the Offertory chant was intended to accompany the collection the pontiff made of gifts of bread and wine from the attending clergy and laity, first from the men then from the women. Like the Introit, it was first an antiphonal chant: a psalm sung alternately by two choirs with an antiphon as prelude and postlude. However, already at an early period this chant appears as a responsorial piece: the choir or *schola* singing the psalm and the people singing a simple antiphon as a refrain. And this chant was protracted according as the collection of gifts required. Of this processional chant only the antiphon remains today, and an examination of the various texts used as the Offertory antiphon shows that normally it follows the theme of the feast or season, just as the Introit.

In the original Roman Rite the only prayer recited by the celebrant during the Offertory was the so-called Secret. Just as the opening rite of the Foremass was brought to a climax by an oration spoken by the celebrant, so here the initial step in the sacrificial part of the Mass is concluded by a priestly prayer. The Roman service books formerly called this prayer the "Oratio super oblata," prayer over the offerings, and it concluded the placing of the gifts on the altar. As such it was intended to connect these material gifts with the sacrificial action soon to be accomplished. The offering which the Church will make together with Christ at the moment of sacrifice is clearly emphasized here, for the material elements laid on the altar are a token of the members of the Church uniting themselves through them to the Victim, Christ. The prayer usually begs God to accept our human offering joined to that of Christ and, in order that we may be less unworthy thus to be associated with Christ and His sacrifice, mercifully to dispose us to imbue ourselves with His inner sacrificial outlook. In this way, the intrinsic ordering of the gifts to Christ the

[286] Nn. 85-86. Andrieu, II, p. 95.

Victim and of ourselves to Christ the Priest inherent in the Offertory *action* is made explicit in the Offertory *prayer*.

The term "Secret" is not a Roman one; it comes from the Gallican Rite. Since in the Roman Rite this prayer was, like all strictly sacerdotal prayers, recited aloud, it seems highly probable that the term was used in Gallican circles to indicate that the prayer was to be said quietly.[287] The name itself begins to appear in Roman documents only after they are fused with Gallican elements on Gallican soil. Our present practice, therefore, of reciting the Secret silently also comes from the Frankish custom, for in spirit it is quite contrary to Roman style. An incongruous effect of such a practice is that the concluding "per omnia saecula saeculorum," since it alone is said aloud, seems more like the beginning of the Preface than the end of the Secret.

In the primitive plan for the Roman Offertory rite the only formulas spoken (or sung) were the antiphon and the Secret, the first to accompany the people's oblation, the second to conclude and orientate this oblation to the sacrifice. All else is Gallican addition—at least as far as use at this particular moment of the Mass is concerned. The Lavabo, for instance, seems to have taken place in the Roman Rite after the oblation of the faithful but before the oblation of the clerics; however, it was not the pontiff who washed his hands, but rather the archdeacon, who had to arrange the oblation on the altar.[288] From the very beginning the whole purpose of such an action was symbolic: purification before beginning the Canon. In fact, other documents have the celebrant wash his hands several times: once at the very beginning of the Offertory before accepting the oblation,[289] again before receiving the oblation of the clergy.[290] In other words, the closer one approached the "holy of holies" the more one felt the need of purification.

The prayer recited for the blessing of water before it is poured into the wine also has a claim to antiquity in the Roman Rite, but it was not intended for use at this point. We find it originally used as the oration for the Christmas Mass in the so-called Leonine Sacramentary,[291] without, of course, the reference to water and wine. It has been successfully shown that, in its original form, it was the composition of Pope St. Leo I.[292] Along with all the other Offertory prayers,

---

[287] Having at hand a term of Gallican invention, it is quite proper to turn to strictly Gallican sources for its explanation. And Amalar tells us that the prayer is called Secret because it is to be recited secretly: *De officiis*, III, 20. *MPL*, 105: 1132.

[288] *OR* I, n. 77. Andrieu, II, 92. N. 76 GA, which has the pontiff wash his hands, is a variant reading which is not primitive.

[289] *OR* IV, n. 36; *OR* XV, n. 27. Andrieu, II, 161; III, 100.

[290] *OR* IV, n. 44 (here it is the archdeacon who washes his hands); *OR* XV, n. 30. Andrieu, II, 162; III, 101.

[291] Mohlberg, *Sacramentarium Veronense*, p. 157, n. 1239.

[292] Cf. A. Lang, *Leo der Grosse und die Texte des Altgelasianums mit Berücksichtigung des Sacramentarium Leonianum und des Sacramentarium Gregorianum* (Steyl, 1957), 57-59.

aside from the antiphon and the Secret, it was introduced into the Mass of the city of Rome through the Mass-Ordinary of Innocent III.

From this same document, too, comes the introduction into the Roman Rite of an incensation of the gifts and the altar. Though this is Gallican in origin we must admit that, unlike the incensation of the altar at the beginning of Mass, at this point it is in place; for now, as we prepare the sacrificial material, it is appropriate to call attention to the role of the altar.

Preface and Canon

Preparations completed, the celebrant now begins the Eucharistic prayer, the priestly prayer *par excellence* that stands at the very core of the whole Mass. Up until now the various prayers and actions of the Mass have been parcelled out to be performed by persons of varying hierarchic power. But now the priest stands alone before God and His people. As mediator between God and men, he joins in his person all creation and in strains of glorious praise spells out the great deeds of God's mercy towards men and expresses the latter's consequent submission and homage in sacrifice. And even as the human priest attempts to bind together once again the two extreme poles of existence, this phenomenon assumes reality in the Incarnate God, the personal union of God and man, who once more, as Priest and Victim, offers Himself to God and brings God's life to men.

All the involved and minute preparations that have gone before now give way to the most sublime moment of the Mass. The supreme climax arrives when, in response to God's spoken word, His holy people through their priest immolates to His glory and in their own stead His Eternal Word. What was visible in Christ's earthly life now takes place in sacrament.[293] The great drama is about to be re-enacted again—but this time man consciously makes himself a part of it as he inserts himself into Christ's act of sacrifice, done and accomplished under signs representative of man's life, products of his work: bread and wine. As these are transformed into Christ, so man's life becomes transfigured into the divine.

As pointed out in our treatment of the Preface,[294] it and the Canon really constitute a whole. This is borne out both by history and by the nature of the Eucharistic prayer.

From the historical point of view, the earliest documentary evidence we have of the Eucharistic prayer, that of Hippolytus' *Apostolic Tradition*,[295] shows that it begins with the introductory dialogue: "Dominus vobiscum . . . Sursum corda . . . Gratias agamus . . .," and ends with the doxology, "per quem tibi honor et gloria . . ." and the people's "Amen." The same impression is to be had from the *Apostolic*

---

[293] Leo, *Sermo* 74, 2. *MPL*, 54: 398.
[294] Cf. Chapter 5, pp. 183-184.
[295] Reproduced in Chapter 5, p. 184.

Constitutions of the end of the fourth century.[296] The sixth century *Liber Pontificalis* [297] says the people should sing the Sanctus during the Canon ("intra actionem"). This unity is brought out even more by the fact that most of the ancient Sacramentary manuscripts have the title "Incipit canon actionis" at the very beginning of the Preface dialogue.[298] And in the ninth century Amalar still speaks of the Te igitur as being, not at the beginning of the Canon, but in the middle.[299]

However, a cleavage between the two parts set in, and this was due, according to Jungmann, to the Gallican Liturgies again. First of all, several Gallican writers proposed highly artificial divisions of the Mass. Isidore of Seville, for instance, called everything from the Sanctus to the Pater the "Oratio sexta" of the Mass.[300] In this scheme of things the Preface was understood as a solemn introduction to the Eucharistic prayer. Furthermore, the Canon, in Gallican hands, changes from a sung prayer to one spoken so low by the celebrant that no one can hear him. According to authentic Roman documents the Canon was to be sung aloud; [301] only in the Frankish documents do we read that the "pontiff continues the Canon silently." [302] And because of this, it had to be specifically mentioned that the Nobis quoque peccatoribus was to be said *aperta voce*.[303] It was about the middle of the tenth century that the silently read Canon became an established practice and thus helped to harden the dichotomy between Preface and Canon.[304] And this cleavage then became illustrated in the artistic arrangements of the Gallican Mass-books. The first letter of the Te igitur was enlarged and decorated, then portrayed as the crucifixion scene, and finally moved to the opposite, facing page. In such missals the title "Canon" or "Actio" was no longer to be found before the Preface but after it.

Considering the very nature of the Eucharistic prayer we are led to the same conclusion, that the Preface and Canon are a unity. In

---

[296] VIII, 12. *MPG*, 1: 1091-1107.

[297] Edit. L. Duchesne, I, 128.

[298] Cf. B. Botte, *Le canon de la messe romaine*, p. 30, footnote. This same manner of thinking is manifest in the *OR* I, nn. 88 and 91. Andrieu, II, 95-96; see his footnotes for paragraphs 88 and 91.

[299] *De officiis*, III, 27. *MPL*, 105: 1146.

[300] *De eccl. off.*, I, 15, 3. *MPL*, 83: 753.

[301] N. 88 of the *OR* I (Andrieu, II, p. 95) says simply that the pontiff begins (or continues) the Canon alone. Nothing is said about a change of voice or melody. Later, in n. 89 (Andrieu, II, p. 96), without any indication of a change of voice on the part of the celebrant, the subdeacons are to rise at "Nobis quoque peccatoribus." *OR* XV, n. 39 (Andrieu, III, p. 103) serves as an intermediary step in the transition from the loudly sung Canon to the completely silent recitation, when it says that the pontiff begins to sing in a different voice and melody, so that he can be heard only by those standing about the altar: "Et incipit canire dissimili voce et melodia, ita ut a circumstantibus altare tantum audiatur."

[302] *OR* V, n. 58. Andrieu, II, 221.

[303] *Ibid.*, n. 63. Andrieu, II, 222.

[304] For a more lengthy treatment of this question see J. Jungmann, *Gewordene Liturgie*, 53-119, or as originally published, "Praefatio und stiller Kanon," *Zeitschrift für katholische Theologie*, (1929), 66-94, 247-271.

all the early documents, the whole section of the Mass from the end
of the Offertory to the Pater was referred to as the thanksgiving prayer, or *Eucharistia, gratiarum actio.* A giving of thanks also characterized the Jewish prototype, the *berachah,* or prayer of praise and
blessing which was spoken over bread and wine during the Passover
or the *Chabûrah* meals. This thanksgiving theme ran through the
whole Eucharistic prayer, and while thanking God for His greatest of
all mercies, His only begotten Son, the celebrant recounted the great
deed He performed the night He was taken prisoner. Thus was
accomplished the Eucharistic (thanksgiving) Sacrifice.

The unity of the Eucharistic prayer was, of course, broken up
by other elements; namely, the intercessory prayers. Until the end of
the second century, as has been pointed out, the emphasis in the
Canon was on thanksgiving. But then the sacrificial aspect gradually
came to the fore. Besides the introduction of such words as "offerimus,"
"dona," "oblatio, etc.," various petitions were also inserted in the
course of time to bring out the impetratory character of the Eucharistic
Sacrifice. Jungmann ascribes this growing insistence on sacrificial terminology to the fact that an heretical group of this period, the Gnostics,
sought to de-emphasize the use of material things in religion and consequently to deny that the Church had a true sacrifice.[305] Though the
intercessory prayers did not all appear at once, we have certain evidence that some such prayers were recited at least by the beginning of
the fifth century.[306] Indeed, all the intercessory and sacrificial prayers
as we have them today in the Canon can be found in the oldest manuscripts of the so-called Gelasian Sacramentary.[307]

With the introduction of such intercessory prayer within the
Canon we must connect another change in the Liturgy. It is precisely
at the end of the fifth century (the time of Gelasius I) that the Oratio
Fidelium disappears from the end of the Foremass and appears in
greatly reduced form in the opening rite of the Foremass. And around
the time of Gregory the Great such prayers for the various categories
of the faithful completely disappear from the Kyrie. Was this because
they had already found another place within the Canon? Let us remember that one of Gregory's talents was that of abbreviating. If
we pray for all the faithful in the Canon, why duplicate the action
in the Foremass? This could also have been the reason which prompted
Gelasius to cause the first reduction of the prayers.[308]

One more preliminary remark before we discuss each prayer of
the Canon: Note the symmetry that characterizes the arrangement of
these prayers. Many authors point out that the Canon possesses all

[305] *The Eucharistic Prayer* (Chicago: Fides, 1956), 22.
[306] Innocent I, *Epist. 25 ad Decentium. MPL,* 20: 553; Boniface I, *Epist.* 7.
MPL, 20: 767; Celestine I, *Epist.* 23. *MPL,* 50: 544.
[307] Cf. B. Botte, *Le canon de la messe romaine,* 32-46.
[308] Cf. J. Jungmann, *The Mass of the Roman Rite,* I, 58.

the balance and literary sense of proportion that is true of the greatest Roman mosaics. P. Bussard tries to translate this appreciation of the Canon into visual form by means of the following diagram:[309]

The cross in the center indicates the Consecration, while the small arrow coming from the base of the cross is the offering prayer, the Unde et memores. The other four small arrows on either side of the cross stand for the pleas for acceptance immediately preceding and following the Consecration. The boxes are the intercessory prayers for the Church, her rulers, the faithful, the commemoration of the saints, and, after the Consecration, the memento of the dead, the prayer for ourselves, for sinners, and finally for all nature. The two slanting arrows at either end stand for the solemn prayers of praise—Preface and doxology—which open and conclude the Canon. We must speak a word of caution about this diagram, however. The symmetry the author sees in the Canon is often only an external one; it does not always correspond to the historical and functional rationale of the prayers. Therefore the diagram should be used circumspectly.

The very way in which the Canon begins indicates that something of the greatest importance is at hand. The celebrant does not rush into it, nor does he begin it with a simple "Oremus" or only with the usual greeting placed before priestly prayers, "Dominus vobiscum." Rather a solemn dialogue is prefixed to the Eucharistic prayer: a greeting to bind the faithful closely with the celebrant, a warning that they should raise their minds and hearts to God, putting out of their minds all distractions, and an invitation to offer God their best praise and thanksgiving. Note that this practice is not peculiar to the Roman Rite; it is common to every Rite in the Church, in more or less embellished forms. Here, then, the Church obviously wishes to set off this prayer above all others, declaring at once its importance and dignity. This dialogue can trace its textual form, for the Roman Rite, to the Apostolic Tradition of Hippolytus [310] and, for the Oriental Rite, to the Apostolic Constitutions.[311]

In its present form the Preface limits its theme, usually, to a very general sort of praise and thanksgiving, declaring that the purpose of the Church is to join herself to the heavenly chorus of praise offered to God by the angelic choirs. Only on major feasts and for major seasons is anything added to this simple plan. But formerly,

[309] The Meaning of the Mass (New York: Kenedy, 1942), 187. This appears to be based on Parsch's outline in The Liturgy of the Mass (St. Louis: Herder, 1936), 196.
[310] La Tradition Apostolique (edit. B. Botte), n. 4, p. 30.
[311] VIII, 12, MPG, 1:1091.

before the time of Gregory the Great, there was a special Preface
for practically every Mass. In the so-called Leonine Sacramentary we
count some 271, in the Gelasian Sacramentary about 232, but in the
Gregorian Sacramentary we find only 14. Jungmann sees this sharp
reduction caused by the danger of the manifold Prefaces straying
from the theme proper to them, namely, the story of redemption, by
placing in the foreground a secondary theme: the life of a saint, a
sermon on apostleship, an act of faith, or in fact a creed, in the case
of the Preface for the Trinity.[312] Though a certain poverty is preferable to such a denaturing overgrowth, a return to the full and proper
concept of the Preface is desired, wherein the main reason for such a
prayer of thanksgiving is clearly stated: God's plan of redemption.
From all the present Prefaces joined together we would obtain just
such a plan.

Solemn and strictly sacerdotal though the Eucharistic prayer may
be, the Church does not forget the faithful. From earliest times they
joined in the singing of the Sanctus together with the priest after he
had made mention of the angelic hymn of praise. And the celebrant
did not continue the Canon until after the Benedictus had been
completed. In this way greater unity between priest and people was
achieved at the most sacred moment of the Mass. The recent *Instruction* of the Congregation of Rites explicitly encourages the faithful to
sing the Sanctus and Benedictus.[313] Conscious of the fact that they
are destined to take the place of the fallen angels, the Christian
people approach the *Mysterium Fidei,* the divinely instituted means
for achieving their supernatural vocation, with this heavenly hymn
on their lips.

A continuation of Preface and Sanctus, the Te igitur turns more
specifically to the sacrifice to be accomplished through the Eucharistic prayer. The word "igitur" links it with the Preface. Thanksgiving
now becomes a plea for acceptance of the sacrifice, for the prayer of
thanksgiving culminates in the offering of sacrifice: We thank God
for His tremendous gifts to mankind by offering Him man's gifts in
return. May He accept them!

The present arrangement of the Roman Missal makes this plea
for acceptance appear as the beginning of the first intercessory prayer.
It seems quite probable that the original version of the Canon attached the prayer "Quam oblationem" directly to the first phrase of
the Te igitur.[314] This design was subsequently interrupted when the
prayers of intercession were inserted into the Canon.

The intercessory prayers begin with "In primis." Just as the an-

---

[312] Jungmann, *The Eucharistic Prayer,* 9.
[313] Par. 25, b. *AAS,* 50 (1958), 639. It is to be noted that when the Sanctus
and Benedictus are sung in Gregorian Chant, they are to be sung together at
their proper place; if other music is used, the Benedictus is to be sung after the
consecration: *ibid.,* par. 27, d. *AAS,* 50 (1958), 641.
[314] As a matter of fact, the present arrangement whereby the part from "in

cient Oratio Fidelium, this long intercession starts with a petition for the welfare of the Church and her rulers, the pope and the bishops. Some vernacular Missals translate the word "cultoribus" to mean those who profess the Catholic and apostolic faith. This does not seem correct, for the word stands in direct relation to the expression "una cum." The sense is, then, "may God deign to rule the Church throughout the world *together* with the pope, the local bishop, and all others who cultivate, or guard, the Catholic and apostolic faith." Furthermore, a tautology would result from the other translation, since there follows a special mention of "thy servants who stand about, or who offer this sacrifice with us, or for whom it is offered." This interpretation is corroborated by an analogy with the Oratio Fidelium which always began with a petition for the rulers of the Church and only then turned its attention to the needs of those governed. Arguing in this fashion, we would also see here the place to pray for civil rulers. Understandably such a prayer is left out of the Roman Canon, for the pope was the supreme ruler of Rome, but it is to be found in Missals stemming from other localities which did not come under the pope's temporal governance.[315]

After praying for the Church militant in both head and members, the Canon then invokes the memory of the Church triumphant, inviting these glorified members of the Mystical Body to take part in the Holy Sacrifice, the bond of unity in the Mystical Body. They have already attained the glory of which the grace of the Eucharist is the seed; let them, then, stand before God's throne and beg for acceptance of that sacrificial activity of which they are truly associates. We should note the hierarchical order in which the saints are mentioned. After the Mother of God, the prayer invokes the Apostles, six bishops, five of whom are popes, the last a non-Roman (Cyprian), then two clerics (Lawrence and Chrysogonus) and four laymen (John, Paul, Cosmas, and Damian). But why only these saints? The simplest and most obvious explanation is that since a *Roman* Canon is in question here, the saints especially honored in *Rome* will find a place in it.[316]

That the intercessory prayers before the Consecration come to an end with the Communicantes is shown by the concluding "Per

---

primis" to "apostolicae fidei cultoribus" is considered a part of the Te igitur cannot be too old, for there are older Missals in which "In primis" begins with a capital, thus indicating the fact that it begins something new: cf. Jungmann, *The Mass of the Roman Rite*, II, 152, note 21.

[315] See references in Jungmann, *op. cit.*, II, 157-158.

[316] *Ibid.*, II, 173-175. V. Kennedy, in his *The Saints of the Canon of the Mass* (Vatican City, 1938), 189, holds that Pope Gelasius gave the Communicantes its final form. H. Frank, on the other hand, claims that this cannot be proven and sees just as much, if not more, probability in Lietzmann's (*Petrus und Paulus in Rom*, Berlin, 1927, 82-93) assertion that the list of saints in question here was taken over from the Roman calendar of the fourth-fifth century: "Beobachtungen zur Geschichte des Messkanons," *Archiv für Liturgiewissenschaft*, 1 (1950), 111 ff.

eumdem Christum Dominum nostrum." But the Amen which appears in this place in our present Canon text is not at all primitive, for the "Per eumdem Christum, etc." is not a formal conclusion, but only the end of one part of the Canon. The "Amen" appears at this place for the first time in the ninth century Sacramentary of Saint-Thierry.[317]

The Hanc igitur has long posed a special difficulty for scholars. Its very ending, "Per Christum Dominum nostrum," would again indicate that here we have a prayer that was not part of the primitive Canon, but one added to the fundamental schema of the Eucharistic prayer. True, it was already part of the Canon in the days of Gregory the Great. In fact, we are told by the *Liber Pontificalis*[318] that Gregory commanded the phrase, "diesque nostros in tua pace dispone, etc.," to be added to the prayer. This addition, however, was not completely new. Something similar to it is to be found in the so-called Leonine Sacramentary for the anniversary of a bishop's consecration: "diesque meos clementissima gubernatione disponas."[319]

This last circumstance gives us a clue to the original purpose of the Hanc igitur. In perusing the Leonine and Gelasian books we discover that such a formula is not provided for every Mass. In the whole of the Leonine we find but ten such formulas, whereas in the Gelasian we discover only fifty-four. We find none for ordinary Sundays or regular feast days. This fact gives solid foundation to the opinion that we have here a variable formula, or rather the beginning and end of a formula into which could be inserted special phrases for different occasions. An examination of all the early formulas shows that they were really an expression of a special intention for, we might say, votive Masses; i.e. Masses offered for special intentions. At this point in the Canon, then, the special intention for which the Mass was being offered was expressed. Thus, in the old books we find Hanc igitur formulas provided for nuptial Masses, Masses for the deceased, newly-ordained priests, deacons, bishops, the newly-baptized, etc. This, then, is the fundamental purpose of the Hanc igitur: to mention specifically the person or intention for which the Mass is being offered. In fact, we find in the Gelasian book a rubric which directs that, for the scrutiny held on the Third Sunday of Lent, the names of the catechumens be read at this moment in the Mass.[320]

The reading of names in the Hanc igitur constitutes a certain parallel between it and the Memento of the living. But it is only external. In the Memento are read the names contained in the diptychs; i.e., the names of those people who were recommended to the prayers of the Church. But in the Hanc igitur we have a determination of the special fruit of this particular Mass celebration, the special intention for which this particular Mass is being offered.

[317] Cf. B. Botte, *Le canon*, 57, note 9.
[318] Edit. L. Duchesne, I, 312.
[319] K. Mohlberg, *Sacramentarium Veronense*, n. 958, p. 123.
[320] Edit. H. A. Wilson, n. 26, p. 34.

The action of Gregory, then, was to do away with all this diversity, insert a petition universally applicable, and to have the entire formula recited at every Mass. And so, historically, the view which treats the Hanc igitur as a plea for acceptance is really incorrect. Only since the formula lost its original purpose did it assume this secondary significance as a plea for acceptance.

The imposition of hands which accompanies this prayer has been interpreted variously by different authors. Some claim that it is in imitation of the Jewish practice whereby through a laying on of hands the sins of the people were figuratively loaded on to the scapegoat which was then driven into the wilderness. But the wording of the prayer does not at all warrant such an interpretation. Jungmann sees in it a stylized pointing gesture going together with the word "Hanc," just as he does for the signs of the cross over the consecrated species.[321] The same thing would be true of the signs of the cross during the Te igitur where the words "haec . . . haec . . . haec" call for such a pointing gesture. This certainly seems to be a more natural explanation.

A last plea for the sanctifying of the gifts lying on the altar is contained in the Quam oblationem. It is a formal introduction to the words of institution and begs God to bless, approve, ratify, make spiritual and acceptable our offering so that it may become the Body and Blood of Christ.

The word "rationabilem" is usually translated by modern authors as "worthy." However, as Bernard Botte has shown,[322] the original sense of this word is "spiritual"; it was the Latin equivalent for the Greek word "logikos" and was used as the translation of the latter in I Peter 2:2 and Romans 12:1. Despite other changes in this prayer (the insertion, for instance of "ratam," a juridical term of the Latins), he maintains that this word "rationabilem" retained its primitive meaning.[323] Therefore, the idea would be that here we beg God to raise this oblation above the material sphere, changing it into the Body and Blood of His beloved Son.[324]

This calling on God to begin His sacramental operation has been named the "epiclesis." However, this is not to be understood as certain orthodox Orientals understand it; that is, as having consecratory force. The existence of such an epiclesis has not at all been a constant

[321] *The Mass of the Roman Rite*, II, 186. Compare this with the use of a cross to mark the beginning of the Gospel in the missal.

[322] "Rationabilis," in *L'Ordinaire de la Messe. Texte critique, traduction et études* (Louvain: Abbaye de Mont César, 1953), 117-122.

[323] Jungmann himself has apparently changed his interpretation and now accepts the primitive meaning of the word also: see the fourth German edition of *Missarum Sollemnia*, II (Freiburg: Herder, 1958), 238.

[324] See the same interpretation made by Edmund Bishop in "The Moment of Consecration," an appendix to R. H. Connolly's *The Liturgical Homilies of Narsai* (Cambridge, 1909), 150-152.

thing even in the Oriental Liturgies.[325] The epiclesis in Catholic theology has no other sense than that of asking God to transform these elements of bread and wine into the Body and Blood of Christ, to bring it about that our human offerings become the true and sublime sacrifice of Christ.

That the words of institution stand at the very core of the entire Eucharistic prayer is a fact attested to by every known Christian Liturgy. But we should take notice that the account of the institution of the Eucharist as used in the Mass is never a simple restatement of the Biblical text. Jungmann sees in this a proof that the Eucharist was long celebrated before the Evangelists actually wrote their Gospels, and that the differences in the very Biblical accounts must themselves spring from differences in liturgical practice.[326] Furthermore, in practically every Liturgy our Lord's command, "Do this in memory of me," is repeated, thus showing that the narrative is used not as a mere historical record, but precisely in order to continue Christ's sacramental action over bread and wine. The priest even imitates Christ's own actions during the narrative. All of this serves to bring out the fact that this repetition of what Christ said and did is intended by its very nature to be consecratory.

Only when the Eucharistic prayer ceased to be regarded as a unified whole did acts of faith in the Real Presence and sacrificial action become prominent. Thus in some Liturgies the people shout "Amen!" after both Consecrations.[327] In the West the infrequency of reception of Communion led the faithful to seek other ways of satisfying their devotion to the Holy Eucharist. The simple gazing upon the Blessed Sacrament implied for them a special benediction. This popular desire to see the sacred host, which antedated the heresy of Berengarius (died in 1088), was finally permitted by Church authorities who became aroused to a vigorous reaction against Berengarius.[328] A basically popular movement, not a theological one, it was peculiar to the Gallican areas, coming as they did under the influence of the Oriental Rites. As a result, the elevation of the host immediately after the Consecration was introduced, at the latest, by the beginning of the thirteenth century.[329] But it was still unknown to the Liturgy of Rome as late as the end of the same century.[330] The elevation of the chalice was very rare; it was not made to correspond fully to that of the host until the appearance of the Missal of Pius V.

[325] Regarding the question of the epiclesis and its interpretations see Jungmann, *The Mass of the Roman Rite*, II, 190-194; also E. Bishop, "The Moment of Consecration," as above in note 324, pp. 126-163.

[326] *The Mass of the Roman Rite*, II, 195.

[327] See Brightman, 52, 385 ff., 437. Other acts of faith were also added: *ibid.*, 232 ff., 176 ff.

[328] Cf. E. Dumoutet, *Le désir de voir l' hostie*, p. 26.

[329] Cf. Jungmann, *The Mass of the Roman Rite*, II, 207.

[330] J. Brinktrine, "Ordo et Canon Missae," EL, 51 (1937), 204.

If what Christ did is re-enacted in the Consecration, in the Unde et memores that sacrificial activity of Christ is offered by the Church. The particle "unde" links this prayer with the Consecration and thus interprets it, orientates it. And in this prayer we read that the sacrificial action taking place is both a commemoration of what Christ did for mankind as well as a re-offering of it. If in the Offertory we can speak of an anticipatory offering of gifts, this is true only in dependence on the Unde et memores, for here for the first time, now that the true victim is made present, can we speak of the Church's offering in the strict sense of the word. Thus the Anamnesis, or commemorative offering, is truly a part of the central sacrificial action of the Mass.[331]

After this two prayers follow asking God to accept this sacrifice: the Supra quae and Supplices te rogamus. In their most primitive form they seem to have been one prayer as evidenced by the quotation given in St. Ambrose's De sacramentis.[332] As remarked above, it would be foolish to relate these two pleas for acceptance to Christ's sacrifice, for that is always acceptable to the Father. What we beg for here is that our participation in that sacrifice be graciously received by the Father; in other words, that we might truly be one with Christ in our subjective sentiments so that with Him we may find access to His Father.

The next two intercessory prayers—the Memento of the Dead and the Nobis quoque—are hinged together: the "quoque" obviously links the second with the first. And both are of late introduction as part of daily Mass. The best representative manuscripts of the original Roman Canon omit them.[333] The Memento of the Dead seems to be another remnant of votive Masses for the dead just as the Hanc igitur is a remnant of other types of votive Masses. The former had no place in Sunday and feast day Masses; only on ferial days could votive Masses be celebrated for the dead, or at least could their names be commemorated.[334] Jungmann is of the opinion that at first the Nobis quoque was also omitted on Sundays and feast days because of its close literary resemblance with the Memento of the Dead.[335] The fact that its present place and its list of saints' names form a parallel to the Communicantes would have furnished a reason for including it as a permanent part of the Canon. Though it is quite probable that both these prayers existed from the fourth century as at least an occasional insert within the Canon, the Memento of the Dead did not become a permanent part of the Canon text except in the revision of the Gregorian Sacramentary made by Alcuin around the beginning of

[331] For the import of this prayer we refer the reader back to our treatment of the Mass as a memorial; see also J. Jungmann, The Eucharistic Prayer, 1-13: the chapter entitled "Memores."
[332] IV, 6, 27. B. Botte, Le canon de la messe romaine, p. 43.
[333] See Botte, op. cit., pp 44 and 67.
[334] OR XV, nn. 128-129. Andrieu, III, 121.
[335] The Mass of the Roman Rite, II, 251.

the ninth century.[336] The raising of the voice at the beginning of the Nobis quoque is a Gallican element, introduced once the Canon was said silently, but it clearly depends on the earlier Roman rubric whereby the subdeacons, at the start of this prayer, went to their assigned places to prepare for the fraction of the consecrated bread.[337]

After the intercessory prayers two doxologies follow by way of conclusion to the Canon. The first takes up the ending of the Nobis quoque—"per Christum Dominum nostrum"—by means of the phrase "Per quem." That this is like the final formula, a doxology, is shown by the tense and mood of the verbs, the indicative present: Thou *dost* create, sanctify, enliven, bless and bestow: *creas, sanctificas,* etc. And the final formula, too, hinges on the "Per Christum dominum nostrum of the Nobis quoque, for it begins with "Per ipsum, cum ipso, et in ipso . . ." There is a contrast, however, between these two final doxologies. The first portrays God's gifts coming down to man, the second man's homage being offered to God—both movements taking place through Christ. Thus the Canon ends on that marvelous note, beautifully expressing the whole essence of liturgical prayer: the *Sacrum commercium,* the holy exchange between God and men.

But to what does the "haec omnia" in the first formula refer? The answer is to be found in the ancient liturgical books. In the *Apostolic Tradition* of Hippolytus we see that from the equivalent of our Supplices the Canon goes immediately to the concluding doxology, "per quem tibi gloria et honor . . ." Following this there appear two blessings provided for oil, cheese, and olives.[338] A similar blessing is to be found in the so-called Leonine Sacramentary for water, honey, and milk in the Mass for the solemn Baptism on Pentecost.[339] And the Gelasian has two blessings for new beans on the feast of the Ascension and for grapes.[340] In the latter two Sacramentaries the formulas end with "per quem haec omnia." This leads to the conclusion that the first doxology is actually a remnant of the unchanging conclusion for such blessings. The fact that Hippolytus also adds that after every blessing the doxology "Tibi gloria patri et filio cum sancto spiritu . . ." should be appended, shows that then as now the Canon was always concluded with the final trinitarian doxology even when there was occasion to insert a blessing of natural products.

But why were the fruits of the earth blessed at this particular

[336] *Ibid.,* II, 253 and note 25. The Nobis quoque is found in the earliest manuscripts; the Memento of the Dead is found only in the Paduan codex of the Gregorian Sacramentary with the rubric: "Si fuerint nomina defunctorum, recitentur dicente diacono: Memento . . ." (K. Mohlberg, *Die älteste erreichbare Gestalt,* p. 74, n. 885). Hence, even in the Paduan Codex it was not always used. It becomes a permanent part of the Canon text only with the revision made by Alcuin (H. Lietzmann, *Das Sacramentarium Gregorianum,* 1, 28).

[337] *OR* I, n. 89; *OR* V, n. 63; *OR* IX, n. 33; *OR* XV, nn. 40-42. Andrieu, II, p. 96; II, p. 222; II, p. 334; III, pp. 103-104.

[338] Edit. B. Botte, nn. 4, 5, 6, pp. 33-35.

[339] K. Mohlberg, *Sacramentarium Veronense,* p. 26, n. 205.

[340] H. A. Wilson, *The Gelasian Sacramentary,* pp. 107, 294.

point in the Mass? Most likely to show the relationship of such blessings to the greatest of all God's blessings, Christ Himself and His
work of redemption. This thought is emphasized by the very wording: "per quem [Christ] . . . semper bona creas . . . et praestas
nobis." We cannot help but think of the opening words of St. John's
Gospel: "All things were made through him [the Word], and without
Him was made nothing that has been made." But not only are all things
made through the Logos; through His incarnation, passion and resurrection all creation receives a new meaning: *sanctificas, vivificas et
benedicis.* It is precisely through His wholly marvelous work of redemption that God's creation is brought to a new head, recapitulated
in Him. And since we have just re-enacted the work of redemption and
consciously made ourselves part of it, we must prolong it with our
labors until everything redounds to the honor and glory of the
Blessed Trinity. Here the whole finality of the Incarnation and Redemption is recalled for us: through us, the members of Christ's Mystical Body, all things are to be brought back to God; our purpose as
Christians is to restore all things in Christ. What a magnificent ending
for the Eucharistic prayer, the great sacrificial banquet hymn of
praise that continues for contemporary mankind and all creation the
priestly work of Jesus Christ!

These concluding words of the Canon are furnished with a
gesture, a lifting up of both host and chalice. What is the significance
of this rite? Is it just another elevation (a more primitive one, to be
sure) like the elevations immediately following each Consecration?
Is it really a showing of the consecrated species to the people, as
Pius Parsch contends? [341] True enough, the rearrangement of the original Roman Rite effected on Gallican soil tended to make this the
sense of the gesture in question.[342] But when we compare this Gallican counterfeit with the rite as it appears in the *Ordo Romanus* I,
we gain quite a different impression. In Rome, at the words "Per
ipsum," the archdeacon took the chalice by its handles, having covered
his hands with a cloth, and raised it aloft, while the celebrating
pontiff took the two consecrated breads and touched them to the brim
of the chalice as he spoke the entire doxology.[343] Here it is clearly
seen that gesture and words go together; we have here a genuine offering.[344] In Gallican hands this expressive rite was curtailed until the
elevation was limited to the last words: "omnis honor et gloria." The
rite becomes further obscured with the addition of the signs of the
cross about the end of the eighth century.[345]

The Canon is concluded when the people, by means of the

[341] *The Liturgy of the Mass,* p. 255.
[342] *OR* IV, n. 55. Andrieu, II, p. 164.
[343] *OR* I, nn. 89-90. Andrieu, II, p. 96.
[344] See Andrieu's discussion of the rite, *op. cit.,* II, 146-147. The cloth with
which the archdeacon touched the chalice was called *offertorium.*
[345] Cf. Amalar, *De eccl. off.,* III, 26. *MPL,* 105: 1144.

"Amen!," shout their assent and union with the sacrifice and adoration offered to God. It is precisely to allow for a response that the final "per omnia" of the doxology even today is spoken aloud. Unfortunately this often gives the impression that the "per omnia saecula saeculorum" begins the preamble to the Pater Noster. This could partially be avoided if the genuflection were allowed after the "per omnia" instead of before it.

Communion

The sacrifice of the Mass reaches its climax in the reception of Holy Communion. The victim offered to God now returns to man as his spiritual food. This profound idea of communion or table comradeship with God was already foreshadowed in primitive pagan rites; it was basic to the Passover meal. Why then not also of the Mass, of which the Paschal meal was but a figure and in which the Last Supper is continued? Truly we have here a fellowship at table far surpassing what pagan or Jew might have dreamed of; Christ is not only the head of the table but also our food. "No nation has its gods so close to it as ours is to us!" [346]

In the earliest account we have of the Mass, Communion follows immediately upon the Eucharistic prayer: that is, the sacred species were distributed apparently without formality.[347] In the fourth century, however, an opening rite begins to make an appearance. St. Augustine explicitly speaks of a recitation of the Pater Noster.[348] With the *Ordo Romanus* I of the seventh century we attain the Communion rite practically as we have it today: Pater, embolism, fraction, commixtion, Pax Domini, Agnus Dei, the Communion antiphon with several verses of a psalm together with the Gloria Patri, and the Postcommunion.[349] The apologies, of course, were not present; they are Gallican additions which entered the rite with the *Ordinarium* of Innocent III.

Though the Pater did not always occupy the same place in the Communion service as it does today—Gregory the Great placed it in

[346] Responsory after the seventh lesson of Matins for the feast of Corpus Christi; it is based on Deuteronomy 4:7.

[347] Justin, *Apology* I, 65 and 67. J. Quasten, 17 and 20.

[348] "Ubi peracta est sanctificatio dicimus orationem dominicam," *Sermo* 227. *MPL*, 38: 1101. Though B. Botte places in his edition of the *Apostolic Tradition* certain prayers before Communion, all authors do not consider this authentic. Botte's inclusion of these prayers is based only on parallel ceremonial in the Ethiopic adaptation of the *Tradition* and in the *Apostolic Constitutions: La Tradition Apostolique*, n. 7, p. 35. The *Constitutions* offer as the Communion rite a diaconal prayer for various categories of Christians, a prayer of purification, the exhortation "Sancta sanctis," and an adaptation of the Gloria followed by distribution of Communion during which Ps. 33 is sung. This is followed by the Postcommunion thanksgiving prayer: VIII, 13-15. *MPG*, 1: 1107-1114.

[349] Nn. 94-124. Andrieu, II, 97-107.

its present position [350]—it did always possess a close connection with Communion. The Latin Fathers usually emphasize this connection when they comment on the petition, "give us this day our daily bread." [351] These commentaries lead us to believe that the faithful usually recited the Pater in preparation for Communion. Even the preamble to the Pater is found substantially quoted by Cyprian.[352]

There seems to be another reason why the Pater was used as a preparation for Communion, and that is its reference to forgiveness of sins. That this particular phrase was so appreciated is brought out by the embolism which is employed by most Liturgies: Roman,[353] Oriental,[354] and Gallican.[355] This is simply an enlargement of the "libera nos a malo" of the Pater. That this *malum* is to be understood primarily as sin is shown by the fact that a deliverance from sin is again mentioned in the Libera: "et a peccato simus semper liberi . . ."

Though the Pater in the Roman Rite has traditionally been sung or recited aloud by the priest alone, it was otherwise in the Oriental and Gallican Liturgies. Generally the Orientals have the people recite it together; e.g., the Byzantines [356] and the Syrian Jacobites.[357] While the Gallican Rites generally have the people do this,[358] the Mozarabic *Missale Mixtum* simply has the people answer "Amen" to each of the Pater's petitions.[359] Thus in these non-Roman Liturgies the communal preparation for Communion is enhanced. More recently, in the new Roman *Actio Liturgica* for Good Friday and the Instruction of the Congregation of Rites on *Sacred Music and Liturgy* [360] this principle has been accepted.

While today the breaking of the host occupies the short space of the concluding "Per Dominum" of the Libera, formerly this was a very long ceremony. In the *Ordo Romanus* I it extends for some time, for leavened bread was used in those days, and it had to be made small enough for distribution. For this reason Pope Sergius I began the practice of having the clergy and people sing the Agnus Dei during

[350] *Epist.* IX, 12. *MPL,* 77: 956; see the explanation of this passage in B. Botte, *Le canon,* p. 70.

[351] Tertullian, *De oratione,* 6; Cyprian, *De dominica oratione,* 18; Ambrose, *De sacramentis,* V, 4, 24. J. Quasten, 354, 356, 168; also in the passage of St. Augustine as cited in note 348.

[352] *Loc. cit.,* 2. *MPL,* 4: 537.

[353] As early as the Leonine Sacramentary: K. Mohlberg, *Sacramentarium Veronense,* p. 64, n. 483.

[354] With the exception of the Byzantine, which substitutes a doxology for it: Brightman, 339-340.

[355] L. Duchesne, *Christian Worship,* 221.

[356] Brightman, 339. The Armenians, however, have clerics recite it: *ibid.,* 446.

[357] *Ibid.,* 100.

[358] Duchesne, *op. cit.,* 221.

[359] *MPL,* 85: 559.

[360] Par. 32. *AAS,* 50 (1958),

the confraction.[361] Once unleavened hosts were introduced, this whole ceremony was rendered purposeless. Yet it has remained with us in reduced form mainly because of symbolic reasons which themselves are so varied and arbitrary that it is useless to put any faith in them.

There has been much discussion about the origin and significance of the commingling of the consecrated species. The particle of consecrated bread which was dropped into the chalice of wine was called the *fermentum*. This practice undoubtedly originated as a manifestation of unity within the Church. The pope would send such particles from his Mass to the priests in charge of the Roman titular churches when they, because of their pastoral charge, were prevented from participating in the papal Mass. That this is an historical fact cannot be denied, for there exists a letter from Pope Innocent I to Decentius of Gubbio specifically attesting to the practice. He writes: "Since the priests in charge of the titular churches are not able to be present with us on Sundays, they receive by the hands of acolytes the *fermentum* confected by us, lest they feel they are cut off from our communion especially on this day." [362] The recipients of the *fermentum* dropped it into the chalice during the Communion service of their Mass. A like custom was observed in the principal stational Masses in Rome when the pope himself could not celebrate them. To show that he was still involved he would send a *fermentum* to be added to the chalice by the bishop or priest who celebrated in the pope's stead.[363] Since it is to be presumed that the pope was quite frequently prevented from making a personal appearance at such public stational Masses in Rome, the people and clerics came to look upon the dropping of the *fermentum* into the chalice in such Masses as a regular occurrence. Therefore, reasons Andrieu, in order not to mutilate a ceremonial which had become the normal thing, the pope maintained the same practice when he celebrated in person.[364]

If we are to rely on the testimony of Eusebius, this must have been an ancient and frequent custom, for he reports a letter from Irenaeus in which the latter tells of the practice the popes followed of sending the Eucharist solemnly to other bishops to attest to the spirit of union among them.[365] This, then, must be the fundamental reasoning behind our use of it today, even though the *fermentum* is not sent but consecrated in the same Mass.

It seems altogether probable that this commingling of the *fermentum*, itself a sign of fraternal charity and unity, was kept and performed at the "Pax Domini sit semper vobiscum" because the Pax Domini was originally the greeting that accompanied the kiss of

---

[361] See discussion of this in Andrieu, II, 48-49.
[362] *Epist.* 25 *ad Decentium*, c. 5. *MPL*, 20: 556.
[363] *OR II*, n. 6. Andrieu, II, 115.
[364] *Op. cit.*, II, 63.
[365] *Hist. eccl.*, V, 24, 16. *GCS*, 9 (1), p. 497.

peace.[366] Even today this formula is used when the bishop gives the kiss of peace to the newly-ordained priests during the Mass of ordination. But as far as the regular Mass is concerned, in the course of time other elements came to separate the wish for fraternal charity and unity from the actual giving of the kiss of peace; namely, the Agnus Dei and the first of the three long prayers before Communion. This separation, however, did not appear until in the eleventh century the first of the three prayers was introduced in German territory. The arrangement did not become a definite part of the Roman Mass until 1570.

In placing the kiss of peace before Communion the Roman Rite really broke with the universal tradition of giving it before the Offertory. This is where it occurs in all the other Liturgies; this was also the primitive Roman custom, as is shown by the *Apostolic Tradition* of the third century.[367] By the time of Innocent I the custom had changed in Rome. In his famous letter to Decentius he speaks of it as being given after the Canon as a sign of assent, a seal and guarantee to all that had preceded.[368]

That the kiss of peace was also intended for the faithful and not limited to the clerics in the sanctuary is borne out by specific evidence in the *Ordo Romanus* I: "The archdeacon gives the kiss of peace to the first bishop, then the others on down the hierarchic line, and the people also." [369] As is apparent, according to this early manuscript, all *exchanged* the kiss of peace. Later documents, variations of this earlier one, effect a change of some import: "then *to* the others, and *to* the people." [370] Here the concept is that the sign of charity and unity proceeds from the hierarchical head to others. Other documents have the oldest priest receive the kiss from the celebrating bishop [371] then pass it on to others. Finally, we arrive at the point where the celebrant himself "receives" it by kissing the altar before he gives it to others,[372] the idea being that charity and unity come from Christ symbolized by the altar. In time, instead of the kiss being exchanged or given by means of an embrace, objects were passed around to be kissed; it was the "pax-board," however, which gained the ascendancy. This latter was a highly ornate plaque which was first used in England about the middle of the thirteenth century.[373] The use of such an in-

[366] *OR* I, n. 95-96. Andrieu, II, 98.

[367] Edit. B. Botte, n. 4, p. 30.

[368] C. 1. *MPL*, 20: 553.

[369] N. 96. Andrieu, II, p. 98: "Archidiaconus vero dat pacem priori episcopo, deinde ceteri per ordinem et populus similiter."

[370] Andrieu, II, p. 98, notes 4 and 5 to n. 96: *ceteris, populis or populo.*

[371] *OR* X, n. 55. Andrieu, II, p. 361.

[372] Bernold, *Micrologus,* 23. *MPL,* 151: 995.

[373] J. Braun, *Das christliche Altargerät* (Munich, 1932), 557-572; see illustrations on plates 116-120.

strument even for the laity is still provided for in the *Missale Roman-um* of Pius V.[374]

In the beginning the laity received Communion under both species: the consecrated bread would be placed in their hands, and they would drink of the Precious Blood from a chalice by means of a tube called the *pugillaris*.[375] At solemn papal Masses today the pope still uses such an instrument. But sometimes the consecrated host alone was placed in the hands of the communicant after it had been dipped into the Precious Blood.[376] Actually, the reception of the Precious Blood was practiced longer in the Roman Rite than the placing of the host in the hands of the communicant. It is in this last manner that Communion is usually distributed among Orientals today. Apparently the reception of the Precious Blood by the laity was still in vogue in some churches as late as the time of St. Thomas Aquinas,[377] though it had already begun to disappear in the twelfth century. This was due perhaps to the clearer understanding of concomitance. Yet, it was still to be seen on special occasions even as late as the fourteenth century.[378] After the Council of Trent, of course, the practice has been generally forbidden, though in isolated localities permission has been granted for a time.

The antiphon at the Communion was sung during the distribution of the sacred hosts. This is clearly attested to by the early documents.[379] It is a processional chant intended to remove distractions from the minds of the communicants and dispose them to receive with humble love and sentiments of fraternal union the source of Christian unity. According to the *Instruction on Sacred Music and Liturgy* of the Congregation of Rites, the antiphon is to be sung during the celebrant's Communion, if he alone communicates; if Communion is also to be distributed to the faithful, the antiphon should begin after the Domine non sum dignus before the Communion of the people.[380]

After the distribution of Communion the Mass comes rapidly to an end. From earliest times there existed an official thanksgiving prayer, the Postcommunion oration. Generally speaking, this has preserved, even until today, the theme of gratitude for the tremendous graces received through Christ, and it begs God that the graces thus received may fructify unto life everlasting by means of a holy life here below.

[374] *Ritus servandus*, X, 3. Since this rubric contains no restrictions, rubricists say that the kiss may be extended to the laity: Gavanti-Merati, *Thesaurus Sacrorum Rituum*, II, 10, 8. Jungmann, II, 329, note 45.

[375] *OR* I, n. 111. Andrieu, II, p. 103.

[376] Uldaricus, *Consuetud. Clun.*, II, 30. MPL, 149: 721; Jean d'Avranches, *De off. eccl.*, MPL, 147: 37; Bernold, *Micrologus*, 19. MPL, 151: 989. The latter argues against it.

[377] *Summa Theol.*, III, 80, 12.

[378] On Easter Sunday according to the papal Mass *Ordo* XV (Mabillon's numeration), n. 85. MPL, 78: 1332.

[379] E. g., *OR* I, n. 117. Andrieu, II, p. 105.

[380] Par. 27, c. AAS, 50 (1958), 640-641.

Dismissal

The Christian synaxis was too sacred and formal an affair for Christians simply to leave it as they liked. An official dismissal was provided for the end of Mass just as for the departure of the catechumens and penitents at the end of the Foremass. As we have seen, in fact, the Mass takes its name precisely from this dismissal.

Though our present concluding rites somewhat becloud the original lines of the dismissal,[381] the primitive design is extremely climactic. A blessing is invoked upon the faithful similar to the ones pronounced over the catechumens just before they were dismissed from the assembly. Before the blessing is imparted, however, the faithful are warned to bow for it: "Humiliate capita vestra!" or "Deo per Christum eius inclinate et accipite benedictionem!" [382] And the ancient form of the blessing was closer to a formal oration spoken over the bowed heads of the faithful than to the brief blessing we have today. Both the preliminary warning and blessing have passed over into what we call today the Oratio super populum of our Lenten Masses, with a change of content, of course. After this blessing the deacon announced the dismissal: "Ite in pace! Go in peace!" It finally became in our Roman Rite "Ite, missa est! Go, the assembly is dismissed!" By the sixth century [383] the Oratio super populum had become attached to the Postcommunion, and another briefer blessing was given by the bishop. In the eleventh century we find such blessings conferred by priests, too.[384]

[381] The "placeat" is a late-comer from Gallican sources. Of the same origin is the so-called Last Gospel, which was originally a blessing against ill weather, a use paralleled by the practice in modern France of reading Luke 11: 27-28 as a blessing over babies. St. John's prologue took its place at the end of the Mass as a refined summary of the whole drama of redemption spoken as a thanksgiving. That it was not originally meant specifically as a Gospel reading at Mass is borne out by the fact that the "Dominus vobiscum" which precedes it is never sung at High Mass — just as the text of the Prologue itself is not sung. In other words, even now it is not intended as an announcement of the Gospel of Christ. It is merely the private thanksgiving of the celebrant. In a pontifical Mass it is not even said at the altar, but once begun there, it is continued by the bishop as he walks to his throne.

[382] Apostolic Constitutions, VIII, 15. MPG, 1: 1111.

[383] Already the former blessings and warning appear in the so-called Leonine Sacramentary as formal orations: K. Mohlberg, Sacramentarium Veronense, p. 161, n. 1257.

[384] Cf. Jungmann, II, 440.

CHAPTER SEVEN

The Divine Office

The *élan* of the Christian virtue of religion is not spent with the celebration of the Holy Sacrifice of the Mass and reception of Holy Communion, for the Divine Master has enjoined us "that we must always pray and not lose heart." [1] No sincere Catholic is satisfied with simply performing one religious act; his ideal is to achieve the closest possible union with God. And that can be done only by means of a spirit of prayer, adoration, and praise that permeates his whole being and all of his activity. In her wisdom the Church has provided her children with a shining example of how they should imbue their daily life with a spirit of prayer and at the same time has given a mighty means towards achieving this goal. By means of her Divine Office each hour of the day receives its own special sanctification and consecration, so that the devout Christian, following the lead of Mother Church, can orientate all his apostolic endeavors as well as his pains, pleasures, and peaceful repose towards the greater glory of God; he can insert his entire earthly existence, hour by hour, into the unending chorus of angels and saints who stand about the throne of the Almighty exclaiming: "Holy! Holy! Holy!"

A. The Spirit of the Office

1. The Sacrifice of Praise and its relationship to the Mass

Though sacrifice was the conscious goal of all our Lord's efforts, He did not limit Himself to it. He prepared for it with prayer, and with prayer He prolonged and insured its effect. Thus His public ministry was begun with forty days of prayer and fasting. Thereafter He withdrew often from the crowd and even from His Apostles for brief moments of prayer. Often He spent whole nights on His knees speaking with His Father. And on the night He instituted the new Pasch His spirit soared to the very heights in His priestly prayer for unity.[2] After the paschal supper He went to the Mount of Olives and,

[1] Luke 18:1.
[2] John 17.

going a short distance from His disciples, threw Himself prostrate
before His Father. So intense was that prayer, and so worried and
laden with the sins and conscience of the world, that He underwent
a bloody sweat. Neither did He forget in His fearful agony on the
cross to pray for His persecutors. Indeed, He gave up His spirit
breathing a prayer.

Just as the central redemptive act of Christ's life was enshrined-
with prayer, so the renewal of that sacrifice is prepared for and followed up with the official prayer of the Church. As Pius XII says:
"The worship that the Church renders to God, and which is based
especially on the eucharistic sacrifice and the use of the sacraments,
is directed and arranged in such a way that it embraces, by means of
the divine office, the hours of the day, the weeks and the whole cycle
of the year, and reaches all the aspects and phases of human life." [3]

The Office and the Mass form a unit: the liturgical day, *officium
diei*. The sacrifice of the body and blood of Christ and its grace-effects
are begun, continued, and channelled off by means of the "Sacrifice of
Praise." In a comprehensive view of this unit, the Mass begins at first
Vespers of the preceding evening, continues through Matins, Lauds,
Prime, and Tierce, while its graces are applied to the rest of the day
as the remaining Hours echo and hark back to the theme of praise
and thanksgiving of the Eucharistic prayer. Thus the Office is the
handmaid of the queen, the Mass, serving the core of Christian worship; its Hours are like the surrounding stars and planets reflecting
the glory, light and warmth of the sacrificial sun.

2. The theology of the Office: *Vox Ecclesiae*, the Voice of the Spouse

By His very incarnation, our Lord, the Divine Word, says Pius
XII, "introduced into this earthly exile a hymn which is sung in heaven
for all eternity. He unites to Himself the whole human race and sings
with it this hymn to the praise of God." [4] Since we know not how to
pray of ourselves as we ought, "the Spirit Himself pleads for us with
unutterable groanings." [5] As St. Augustine says:

> God could give us no greater gift than that He made
> the Word, through Whom all was created, the Head of all
> of us and formed us as His members, so that He would be
> the Son of God as well as the Son of Man, one God with the
> Father and one man among men. Hence, when we speak to
> God in prayer we do not separate the Son from Him, nor
> when the Body of the Son prays does it separate itself from its
> Head. He prays for us, He prays in us, and we pray to Him.

[3] *Mediator Dei*, 138.
[4] *Ibid.*, 144.
[5] Rom. 8:26.

He prays for us as our priest, He prays in us as our Head,
and we pray to Him as our God. Thus can we recognize our
voice in Him and His voice in us . . . He is prayed to in the
form of God; He prays in the form of a servant: there as
Creator, here as created. Unchanged, He assumes created
nature to change it, and makes together with us one man,
head and body! [6]

In the same spirit Dom Marmion explains:

> The Word is the canticle that God inwardly sings to
> Himself, the Canticle that rises up from the depths of the
> Divinity, the Living Canticle wherein God takes eternal de-
> light, for it is the infinite expression of Himself and His perfec-
> tion . . . In becoming man the Word is not lessened, but
> continues to be the infinite glorification of the Father. . . .
> Through the incarnation His sacred humanity enters into this
> work of glorification. It is like a temple in which the Word
> sings the Divine Canticle to His Father. . . . This theandric
> activity remains that of a human nature; it glorifies God in
> a human fashion, but as it emanates from a Divine Person,
> as it depends upon the Word, the praises it supplies, human
> in their expression, become the praises of the Word, and
> acquire, on this account, an infinite value. [7]

The Mystical Body is the continuation of Christ; to it Christ has
bequeathed His mission and power of praising and adoring God. As
Christ in His members, the Church must continue this canticle of
praise which He began on earth. Christ pledged to His Church, as
it were by a mystical marriage, all His riches: His merits, satisfactions,
His precious Blood, His very divine personality. Thus the Church
becomes His bride by this mystical marriage of priestly power and
grace given her by Christ. And like the human two-in-one flesh,
whenever the bride speaks the bridegroom is sure to concur, or whenever the bridegroom does something the bride is always with Him, so
in the voice of this mystical Bride we hear the voice of Christ: when
the Church prays, the Father is infinitely pleased, for He really hears
the voice of His well beloved Son, Jesus Christ.

And so the Office is the official voice of the Spouse of Christ. By
her faith, and most especially by her priestly union with Christ, the
Church spans the abyss between God and creatures and sings His
praises like the very Logos in the bosom of the Divinity. It is under
God's gaze that, united to Christ, she sings that eternal canticle, and
because of her union with Christ, on which is based her title of Bride,
she merits always to be heard. Hence, when we recite the Divine
Office, we do not go before God as individuals with solely private

[6] *Enarratio in Psalmos*, 85, 1. MPL, 36: 1081-1082.
[7] *Christ the Ideal of the Monk* (St. Louis: Herder, 1926), 295 ff.

interests and purely human praise. No, we stand before Him as ambassadors of this heavenly Bride of His only begotten Son and speak
to Him of the cause of souls with every right to do so: We are officially invested with her dignity and priestly power. In God's sight this
praise surpasses, in value and efficacy, all other praise, all other prayer, even all other work. "This is truly the work of God, and pre-eminently so, for it is a work of praise that comes from God through the
Incarnate Word and is offered by the Church in Christ's name."[8]

How well the saints understood this profound truth is brought
out beautifully by St. Mary Magdalen of Pazzi, who put assistance in
choir before all the private devotions that a person could make. When
one of her nuns asked to be dispensed from choir in order to give
herself more time for mental prayer, she replied: "No, my daughter,
I should certainly deceive you in giving you such a permission, for it
would be making you believe that this private devotion of yours would
honor God more and render you more pleasing to the Divine Majesty,
while in comparison with this public office which you sing with your
sisters, private prayer is but a small thing."[9]

But when, precisely, can we consider the recitation of the Divine
Office as the prayer of the Church? Some maintain that any Catholic
may be considered as praying in the name of the Church when he
picks up the Breviary and recites the formulas contained therein.[10]
And for this, they allege, the general deputation received by way of
the character of Baptism suffices. This, however, is far from the truth.
Over and above the priestly power conferred in Baptism, a deputation
given by the Holy See is necessary. We must remember that the
priestly power of the baptized lay person is essentially passive and
dependent on the priestly power of the ordained. Should the Church
decide to activate this power of the layman and make him the minister
of other liturgical actions not reserved by Christ to the power of the
ordained, this is her right. But it is left to the Supreme Head of the
Church to do this, and no one may presume what is not granted by
law: The Church is not a democracy, but a divinely established hierarchy. No one can act in the name of the Church except the Head
of the Church, who alone is fully empowered to make such juridical
decisions, delegate such a person to the task.

And thus Christ Himself or Church law has decided that the
priestly power of lay people may be exercised in certain ways: They
are able to offer what the ordained priest has consecrated, they are
able to take an active part in the Mass and the sacraments in certain
prescribed ways, they are the ministers of the sacraments of Matrimony and (in case of necessity) Baptism. For all else the Church has

[8] *Ibid.*, 300.
[9] *Ibid.*
[10] E. g., L. Bouyer, "The Breviary and the Spiritual Life," *Orate Fratres*, 21
(1947), p. 147 and note 2.

decided the laity can exercise their power only in dependence upon the officially deputed minister. In other words, when they take part in a liturgical service in conjunction with a priest or other officially deputed minister, their prayer and action then take on the character of formal liturgical acts, otherwise not. Of course, they may perform a liturgical act or prayer, materially speaking; i.e., they may use in a purely private capacity what the Church concretely uses in her prayer, but this is not Liturgy formally speaking, done precisely in the name of the Church.

This conclusion is supported by official declarations of the supreme authority of the Church. Pius XII says: "The Divine Office is the prayer of the Mystical Body of Jesus Christ, offered to God in the name and on behalf of all Christians, when recited by priests and other ministers of the Church and by religious deputed for this by the Church." [11] And the *Instruction on Sacred Music and Liturgy* of the Congregation of Rites states that the Divine Office is an act of public cult, rendered to God in the name of the Church, when it is recited by those who are deputed for such recitation by ecclesiastical laws, whether it be done in choir, in common, or all alone.[12] Lay people, therefore, are excluded from performing a strictly liturgical act in this case without the ministry of one of these deputed officials. And who are these persons deputed for the recitation of the Office by ecclesiastical law? Canon law seems to indicate that there are three categories of persons enjoying this deputation: clerics in major orders (c.135), those bound by an ecclesiastical benefice for this purpose (c.414), and finally religious who are solemnly professed for the choir office (cc.610,#1 and 3; 640,#2).[13] It would also seem that this last category excludes those Sisters of modern religious communities who do not pronounce solemn vows or at least have not received the Consecration of Virgins.

Does this mean that all those thus excluded are to be discouraged from reciting the Divine Office? Not in the least, for even though they cannot perform a *formal* liturgical act, they certainly can nourish their spiritual life with this excellent prayer as well as join themselves to the Church in her prayer. But let us bear in mind that such a uniting of oneself to the Church, without the deputed use of the power of priesthood, is purely and simply an intentional union, not one that automatically brings with it all the value and efficacy of a true priestly action. However, the recitation of the Breviary on the part of the laity and modern religious is greatly to be urged, for they can deepen their

[11] *Mediator Dei,* 142.

[12] Par. 40. AAS, 50 (1958), 645: "Officium vero divinum, quovis modo absolvatur, sive *in choro,* sive *in communi,* sive *a solo,* si ab illis peragatur, qui per leges ecclesiasticas ad officium persolvendum deputati sunt, semper habendus est uti actus cultus publici, nomine Ecclesiae Deo redditi."

[13] This is also the opinion of C. Callewaert, *Liturgicae Institutiones: De Sacra Liturgia Universim,* n. 26; *De Breviarii Romani Liturgia,* n. 204.

spiritual lives immensely by using privately what the Church prays officially. But we must beware of believing that such a use is as great as their actual participation in the Office when led by one of the officially deputed ministers, either in a public service in church or chapel or together with him in other circumstances.

3. The Office and the spiritual life

If the Office stands in such close relationship to the Holy Sacrifice of the Mass and is intended by the Church to channel its effects and prolong its spirit of praise throughout the day, it plays an extremely important role in the spiritual life. We have already indicated what a great need there is to pray often during the day, to maintain in ourselves the true spirit of religion, one of adoration, thanksgiving, submission to Almighty God's will, in order to give all our efforts a truly supernatural value by orientating them towards the glory of God. In the Divine Office the Church gives us a handy tool by which we can effect this orientation of the whole day and consecrate each section of it to God. Even if our use of the Office is not strictly liturgical (in the case of those who do not enjoy a deputation to an independent ministerial role without the presence of a priest or other minister), our private use of it still retains its intended character as a prayer at certain hours. All can use it to unite themselves intimately with the entire Church, can breathe the spirit of her prayer and thus walk hand in hand with her during the day.

To do this, however, we must keep firmly in mind something that is of prime importance: the Office is the prayer of the hours, that is, prayer to be said at certain hours to dedicate them to God. Lauds is the official morning prayer of the Church, the first thing to be said in the morning. Prime is the prayer for the beginning of the day's work. Tierce is the prayer of the third hour or nine o'clock in the morning, and it is intended to break up our work and help us renew our purity of intention and direction God-ward. Sext is the prayer of the sixth hour or twelve o'clock noon; again it is a re-entering into ourselves to re-enkindle the fervor with which we began the day. None is the prayer of the ninth hour or three o'clock in the afternoon; it asks God to help us persevere in our good intentions as we finish our work. Vespers is the evening prayer to be said immediately before supper in order to dedicate the evening hours to God. And Compline is the retiring prayer which seeks God's protection for us as we sleep. Matins was originally a prayer said during the middle of the night, but since few of us can do that, it could be said sometime before retiring to fill our minds with thoughts of the following day and thus to prepare our meditation for that day.

Is this plan artificial? Hardly. This is the precise purpose of each Hour of the Office, derived both from their names as well as from the hymns sung during them which ask God for the graces proper to these specific times of the day. To use them in this way is to recite the Office in the most ideal way, according to its *raison d'être*. As far as possible, the Hours should not be lumped together, for this tends to rob them of their true function in our spiritual day. There are, of course, good and valid reasons why one may have to say much or all of his Office early in the day. He may foresee that, because of special demands of the apostolate later in the day, he will not be able to recite his Office at the proper times. This is perfectly understandable; indeed, the demands of modern apostolic action form one of the basic reasons for reform of the Breviary. But such necessity ought not be twisted into becoming a hard and fast rule, so that one develops the idea of simply "getting finished with the Office," so as not to let it interfere with the day's work. Rather the attitude of the zealous priest and religious should be the same towards the Office as to the other aspects of life: Let us do the best we can in our given set of circumstances, trying in every way to be faithful to the proper times of the Office, so that its Hours will be so many precious means to sanctify each moment of the day and the work we perform for God's glory.

Unfortunately, we do find priests and religious whose prayer-life begins when they close their Breviary. This tremendous objective and poetic prayer of the Church is not "pious"—in the sense of the prayers with which they have grown up, which give their hearts the customary tingle of sentimentality. This outlook is indeed a sad commentary on the state of the Church's leaders. A little planning of the day and a little study will be a great assist towards making the sacred obligation of reciting the Office a truly religious and meaningful experience. With effort and love, the Divine Office will help us grow in the spiritual life together with Holy Mother Church, expressing in terms of highest praise the zeal, devotion and loyalty we show in our apostolate.

B. Origin and General Historical Development

1. Roots of the Office in the early centuries

Vigils

The testimony of the earliest times may be vague, but it gives indubitable evidence of ecclesiastical reunions during the night hours. In the Acts of the Apostles we find a group of the faithful gathered in the house of Mary, mother of Mark, for prayer when Peter, just liberated from prison by an angel, comes knocking at the door in the middle of the night.[14] Sometimes during these nocturnal gatherings Mass was celebrated, as is evidenced by the vigil before St. Paul's departure from Troas.[15] That this practice of the apostolic church was continued

[14] 12:12.
[15] Acts 20:7.

is proved by later writings. Pliny the Younger wrote to Trajan that the Christians were accustomed to gather on a determined day before daylight and sing a hymn to Christ.[16] Mention of *nocturnae convocationes* and *coetus antelucani* as well as *vigiliae* occur frequently in the writings of Tertullian.[17] And Cyprian very clearly alludes to vigils in common.[18]

Righetti claims that such vigils were to be observed every Sunday.[19] Battifol, before him, also made this assertion, but wisely added that it was only a conjecture.[20] It is true, as we have seen, that the early Christians assembled every Sunday, but it is not at all so certain that such nocturnal reunions were concerned with anything more than the celebration of Mass without any particularly prolonged preparation. If Tertullian does give us explicit testimony to vigils, he also says that they were held only on occasion: *si ita oportuerit.*[21] Hence, any claim that a vigil properly so-called was held every Sunday in the early Church seems entirely unwarranted—at least until more evidence is discovered.

What, then, were the occasions of which Tertullian speaks? He himself speaks of observing stational days with a nocturnal vigil.[22] The expression "stational days" was not always used in the same way by all early writers. But we do find the Shepherd of Hermas saying that stational days were days of fasting,[23] while we learn from the *Didache* that Wednesdays and Fridays were fast days.[24] Since Tertullian wrote a century after the author of the *Didache*, we cannot conclude absolutely that Tertullian meant to say that every Wednesday and Friday was celebrated with a night vigil, though this may be possible. In addition to these days, the anniversaries of certain martyrs were celebrated by means of a vigil. Though Pontius tells us that such a vigil was kept the night before Cyprian underwent martyrdom,[25] we learn from the author of the *Passion of St. Saturninus* that such vigils normally took place on the anniversary.[26] There was a vigil for Easter, of course, and as far as we know this is the only one that lasted through the entire night.[27] Other vigils generally began an hour or so before daylight—*coetus antelucani*—or were held for a while during the night, after which the faithful were dismissed. But only the Easter

[16] C. Kirch, *Enchiridion Fontium Historiae*, n. 30.
[17] *Ad uxorem* II, 4; *De oratione* 29; *De corona* 3. *MPL*, 1: 1407, 1304; 2: 99.
[18] *De oratione dominica*, 29 and 36. *MPL*, 4: 556, 562.
[19] *Manuale di Storia Liturgica*, II, 416-417.
[20] *History of the Roman Breviary* (London: Longmans and Green, 1898), 4.
[21] *Ad uxorem* II, 4. *MPL*, 1: 1407.
[22] *De oratione*, 29. *MPL*, 1: 1304: *Die stationis nocte vigiliae meminerimus.*
[23] *Parables*, V. *The Fathers of the Church*, I (New York, 1947), 292.
[24] VIII. *Ancient Christian Writers*, 6 (Westminster, Maryland, 1948), 19.
[25] *Vita Cypriani*, 15. *MPL*, 3: 1554.
[26] Cf. S. Bäumer, *Histoire du Bréviaire*, I, 78: "Vigiliis . . . honoramus . . . sanctum diem . . . quo vir beatissimus Saturninus geminatam coronam promeruit."
[27] *Ad uxorem*, II, 4. *MPL*, 1: 1407: *solemnibus Paschae abnoctantem.*

vigil seems to have been of universal obligation.[28] St. Augustine calls it the "mother of all Christian vigils."[29]

The above-mentioned *Passion of St. Saturninus* gives us some inkling as to what took place during these vigils: hymns were sung, and very probably they were concluded with the celebration of Mass.[30] A comparative study of ancient Liturgies has enabled Anton Baumstark to conclude that the bulk of these vigils consisted in readings from Holy Scripture and that the hymns sung were most probably the Old Testament canticles.[31] The Easter Vigil, even as we have it today, would seem to be the direct heir of the arrangement proper to the ancient public vigils. This content of hymns (canticles or psalms), Scripture readings, and prayers was a universal phenomenon.[32]

To sum up, three types of public vigil were known to the primitive Church: one, if we can even speak of it as a vigil, consisting of little more than the celebration of Mass at an hour just before sunrise on Sundays; another for the anniversaries of martyrs and for stational days, which involved more extensive chants and readings before Mass; and a third for the eve of Easter which lasted all night and contained, principally, readings and canticles from Scripture. As we shall see, other elements were, in time, added to the above to produce what we today call Matins. Such elements, which came from the monastic and the private-home vigil, were increased frequency of the vigils, to the point that they become daily occurrences, and a more extensive use of psalms so that they gradually come to constitute the principal part of the night Office.

Prayer at appointed times

While assistance at the public vigils by and large was left to the option of the faithful, other prayers, said at certain hours of the day, took on a more obligatory quality, for they could usually be said in private and at home. Tertullian calls prayer in the morning and at night "legitimate" prayers, because they were of obligation.[33] Cyprian

[28] Cf. I Schuster, *The Sacramentary*, I (New York: Benziger, 1924), 28; also Bäumer, I, 66.

[29] *Sermo* 219. *MPL*, 38: 1088.

[30] Bäumer, I, 78: ". . . hymnis ac sacramentis etiam solemnibus honoramus . . ." Battifol is certainly in error when he takes as referring to the arrangement of the vigils the passage in Tertullian's *De anima* (c. 9) concerning a prophetess of the Montanist sect (*History of the Roman Breviary*, 5). In the text of Tertullian it is explicitly stated that the readings, psalms and prayers are those of the "dominica solemnia," an expression designating the Mass.

[31] *Liturgie comparée*, 39-40, 128-129.

[32] Cf., e.g., *Apostolic Constitutions*, VIII, 34. *MPG*, 1: 1135-1138; Ethérie, *Journal de Voyage* (edit. H. Pétré), n. 24, pp. 188-190; Cassian, *De coenobiorum institutione*, III, 18. MPL, 49: 144; for St. Basil see Bäumer, I, 118-121; see the excellent chapter "Der Typus älterer Gemeindevigil," in A. Baumstark, *Nocturna Laus* (Münster, 1957), 34-104.

[33] *De oratione*, 25. *MPL*, 1:1301.

also urges the Christian to pray at these times.[34] However, the third century *Apostolic Tradition* goes into more detail concerning the hours of prayer. The Christian the moment he rises should wash his hands and pray, but should there be a service of the word of God in the church, he ought to go there by preference. Let him also pray at the third, sixth, and ninth hour and immediately before retiring. He should also interrupt his sleep twice during the night for prayer: at midnight and at cockcrow.[35]

Even though such prayer periods were not unknown in the Old Testament,[36] early Christian writers repeatedly refer these practices, especially of praying at the third, sixth, and ninth hours, to the example of the Apostles. Such prayers, therefore, have been called "apostolic" prayers. "At the third hour," says Tertullian, "the Holy Spirit was infused into the assembled disciples (Acts 2:15). And Peter had just ascended to the roof of the house to pray at the sixth hour when he received that vision of the whole Church contained in a vessel (Acts 10:9-11). At the ninth hour Peter went with John into the temple where he cured the paralytic of his infirmity (Acts 3:1 ff)." [37]

As to what particular form such prayers were to take, we are given no explicit directions by these authors. However, the *Didache* informs us that Christians were supposed to recite the Pater three times a day,[38] but whether these three times were meant to coincide with the Jewish custom of praying at morning, noon, and evening, or with the hours mentioned by later Christian authors, is an open question. It is also undetermined whether these periods of prayer were spent in common or in private; the evidence is too vague. It seems reasonable, though, to agree with Bäumer when he speaks of prayer at the third, sixth, and ninth hour as private prayer.

This much is certain: By the first part of the third century, seven prayer periods are known—and these were ultimately to develop into the corresponding Hours of our Breviary. There was prayer during the night (some sources speak of two such periods: midnight and cockcrow), upon first rising in the morning, at the third, sixth, and ninth hours, in the evening, and before retiring. We know for certain that public church functions were sometimes provided for the vigils, and for morning and evening prayers, but popular assistance at them was not always obligatory, only recommended. If there were public ser-

---

[34] "Mane . . . recedente sole . . . necessario rursus orandum est," *De oratione dominica*, 35. *MPL*, 4: 560.

[35] B. Botte, *La Tradition Apostolique*, n. 35, pp. 68-73. Tertullian also seems to refer to private prayer during the night: *Ad uxorem*, II, 5. *MPL.*, 1:1408.

[36] Ps. 54, 18: "Evening and morning and at noon I will lament and groan, and he will hear my voice," 1 Par. 23, 30: "And the levites are to stand in the morning to give thanks and to sing praises to the Lord; and in like manner in the evening."

[37] *De oratione*, 25. *MPL*, 1: 1300. Cf. also Clement of Alexandria, *Stromata*, VII, 7. *MPG*, 9: 455; Cyprian traces the biblical foundations for prayer at the third, sixth and ninth hour in *De oratione dominica*, 34, 35. *MPL*, 4: 559-560.

[38] VIII. *Ancient Christian Writers*, 6, p. 19.

vices at the third, sixth, and ninth hours, we have no proof that, as such, they were ever obligatory on the faithful; Christians were simply expected to pray privately at these times. And again, when no public gathering was had for the vigils, and the morning and evening prayers,[39] the faithful were to devote themselves to prayer and reading at these specified times.

Prayer of ascetics and virgins

It is principally to the institution of monasticism that we owe the extraordinary development and diffusion of the Divine Office. If up until this point the vigils and the morning and evening prayers had been held only sporadically as public church functions—and the diurnal Hours (Tierce, Sext, and None) not at all as far as we know—these began to be sung regularly in common as a public function by groups of pious persons trying to lead a holier life.

Of course, there always existed in the Church souls who felt themselves called to do more and whose personal lives were always looked upon as beautiful examples of the perfect Christian life. But during the times of persecution such souls remained hidden for the most part. It was only after peace had been won that they could afford to become more conspicuous by banding together and by seeking the other-worldliness of the desert or woods. Thus it is only in the beginning of the fourth century that pious souls allow themselves to gravitate about persons of holy repute installed in out-of-the-way places.

Word was spread abroad of the severe life led by the anchorites in the Egyptian desert. People flocked to see them and to talk over their personal problems with them. Some remained behind to follow their example of extreme self-denial and dedication to higher things. Here were to be found the hermits Anthony, Paul, Macarius. In the lifetime of St. Anthony alone some five thousand solitaries were known to have lived in the valley of Nitria.[40]

But still the bond among these men was not strict. They lived in separate huts. There was no common rule, and each ordered his affairs as he thought best. It was only on Saturdays and Sundays that they met in a common church. Hence, their prayers for the most part were said in solitude.[41] Even virgins, though they had now to follow a set rule laid down by the bishops, could still live at home, and

---

[39] That such services were sometimes but not always held in church is clear from the *Apostolic Tradition* of Hippolytus, in which he says that *should* there be a service in church, the Christian should attend it: Edit. B. Botte, n. 35, p. 69. Cf also the *Canons of Hippolytus*, n. 26 in Bäumer, I, 71.

[40] Palladius, *Historia Lausiaca*, VII, *MPL*, 73: 1098.

[41] Cf. P. Pourrat, *Christian Spirituality*, I (Westminster, Maryland: Newman, 1953), 80-83.

the various night and day hours of prayer were spent in common only when they could get together. [42]

With Pachomius things change. The foundation of his monastery in 320 at Tabennesi in the Thebaid begins the cenobitic life in which the various monks who lived it were bound by a common rule of life and obeyed a single superior. Soon similar monastic establishments sprang up all over Asia Minor and later in the Occident too. Under such circumstances the hours of prayer formerly observed by all pious people in private could now be spent in common. In both the Pachomian and Basilian rule, all the religious exercises were to be performed daily and together; these included the nocturnal prayers and some of the diurnal ones. We find the same thing to be true of the *monazontes* and *parthenae* of whom the pilgrim nun Etheria speaks. They came together for their prayers in the Church of the Resurrection in Jerusalem and sang hymns and psalms. And here Church authorities intervened to give an official stamp of approval to these exercises for the first time: priests and deacons were always deputed by the bishop to conclude their singing with an oration. Thus their religious exercises were lifted to the sphere of *liturgical* prayer and became *canonical* Hours in the fullest sense of those words.[43] The bishop himself came to conclude some of these hours of prayer. And the same account narrates how even lay people joined the monks and virgins, not only for the day Hours, but also for the vigils.

Such religious exercises of monks took on an additional official appearance as more and more bishops took steps to house the monks near their cathedrals in order to have them chant their Hours in public. The religious who lived in these "cathedral" monasteries were then specially dedicated to chanting all the Hours, both day and night. They were officially deputed by ecclesiastical authority for this role in the life of the Church. Their activity was all the more important, since the cathedral and parochial clergy, devoted as they were to pastoral work, could not find the time to conduct anything more than the official morning and evening prayer in public. It was a later and quite a slow evolution that made the secular clergy assume the obligation of reciting in common all the Hours of the Office just as the monks did.

2. The Office from the fourth to sixth centuries

The Monastic Cursus

Eastern

According to John Cassian, the monks in Egypt assembled for daily Vespers and the night Office, as well as for Mass on Saturdays

---

[42] Athanasius, *De virginitate*, 12 and 20. *MPG*, 28: 266, 275.
[43] *Journal de Voyage* (edit. H. Pétré), n. 24, pp. 189-190.

and' Sundays; [44] all other prayers were said in private. In each of these public Offices the monks sang twelve psalms and read two lessons, one from the Old Testament and a second one from the New.[45] Only one monk chanted the psalms, while the rest of the community remained seated and listened to them. After each psalm all rose and with outstretched arms meditated on what had just been sung. All then prostrated themselves for a brief interval and rose for the collect sung by one of the monks.[46] It is noteworthy that the Gloria Patri was sung, not after the psalm, but after the antiphon.[47] Apparently the last of these psalms was always taken from one of the Alleluia psalms.[48] This manner of singing the psalms must have been very tedious, for, because of the danger of falling asleep while the lector sang, Pachomius wanted all his monks to keep themselves busy with light handwork during the night Office, such as weaving straw mats.[49]

In the rest of the monasteries of the East, those of Palestine, Syria, and Asia Minor, we find that the Office was more complete and each of its parts much longer than in Egypt. While most of these monastic centers observed publicly all of our present Hours: Vigils, Matins (Lauds), Prime, Tierce, Sext, None, and Vespers (there was even a faint trace of Compline), great disorder reigned among them as to the content and length of these Hours. For instance, in the vigils some monasteries sang eighteen psalms, others twenty, others thirty, and still others made the vigils even longer by means of all sorts of melodious antiphons.[50] In their Saturday and Sunday vigils there were three parts. First three psalms were sung antiphonally as all stood, after which three more were sung responsorially as all were seated; then came three readings from the Bible, most probably one from the Old Testament, a second from the Apostolic letters and a third from the Gospels.[51] Evidently this threefold order was meant to be repeated as often as necessary to fill up the long winter nights, for Cassian explicitly says that at this time of the year the vigil lasted from Vespers till the fourth watch; i.e., from about six in the evening till between three and six in the morning.[52] This would easily explain how in some places the monks sang as many as thirty psalms and fifteen lessons. Cassian tells us that Lauds (*matutina solemnitas*) were supposed to follow immediately upon the vigils and comprised Pss.148-150.[53] However, from the other sources [54] we learn that Psalms 50 and

[44] *De institutione coenobiorum*, III, 2. *MPL*, 49: 115.
[45] *Ibid.*, II, 4. *MPL*, 49: 83.
[46] *Ibid.*, II, 7. *MPL*, 49: 92-94.
[47] *Ibid.*, II, 8. *MPL*, 49: 94-95.
[48] *Ibid.*, II, 11. *MPL*, 49: 101.
[49] *Regula*, V and VII. *MPL*, 23: 69.
[50] Cassian, *op. cit.*, II, 2. *MPL*, 49: 78.
[51] *Ibid.*, III, 8. *MPL*, 49: 144.
[52] *Ibid.*, III, 8. *MPL*, 49: 140.
[53] *Ibid.*, III, 6. *MPL*, 49: 135-136.
[54] *Apostolic Constitutions*, II, 59. *MPG*, 1: 743; Basil, *Letter to the Clergy of Neo-caesarea*, n. 207. *The Fathers of the Church*, 28 (New York, 1955), 84.

62 were also sung in the morning Office. Perhaps the reason Cassian fails to mention them in connection with Lauds is that by his time a new Hour had been instituted, *novella matutina solemnitas* or our Prime, and for this three psalms were sung: 50, 62 and 89.[55] He gives as the reason for this new Hour the fact that some monks in the monastery of Bethlehem went back to bed for too long a time after Lauds; to get them up for their work the Abbot called them together for another prayer-hour first.[56]

Unlike the Egyptian monasteries, those in the rest of the East were accustomed to reciting Tierce, Sext, and None in common. Three psalms were sung at each of these Hours. And Cassian gives the same reason for such Hours as we came across in the writings of the early Fathers, namely, the practice of the Apostolic Church.[57]

Speaking of Vespers, which is called the *Lucernarium* in other documents, for it was the time when the lights of the house were lighted,[58] Cassian recalls the evening sacrifice commanded by Moses,[59] David's Psalm 140, "Dirigatur oratio mea sicut incensum in conspectu tuo," and our Lord's Last Supper; he thus provides the symbolic connection between this evening sacrifice of praise and the sacrifice of the Mass.[60] Unfortunately, he does not indicate how many or which psalms were chanted at this Hour, but from his *Collationes* [61] we learn that at least Psalm 140 was sung daily. And this is corroborated from other sources.[62] Sometimes, on Sundays, the monks came together to sing a few psalms before retiring, as those monks who waited on tables ended their weekly service by washing the feet of all the other brethren.[63] This may have been the beginning of Compline; on other nights of the week perhaps these same psalms were attached to Vespers.

Cassian certainly does not give us a complete account of the Divine Office recited in the monasteries of the East. From the *Apostolic Constitutions* we learn that after the morning and evening psalms a series of prayers were sung, and dismissals were pronounced similar to those at the end of the Foremass.[64] Perhaps these are the original form of the group of prayers which were later called *Capitella* in the rules of Caesarius of Arles and Aurelian and which form today our Preces.[65]

There are also indications that certain other canticles and hymns were part of the Office in the East. St. Athanasius, for instance, says that the Benedicite and the Gloria in excelsis Deo were to be sung at

---

[55] *De insti. coenob.*, III, 6. *MPL*, 49: 136.
[56] *Ibid.*, III, 4. *MPL*, 49: 127-130.
[57] *Ibid.*, III, 3. *MPL*, 49: 116-122.
[58] Cf. the *Oratio lucernalis* in the *Apostolic Constitutions*, VIII, 36. *MPG*, 1:1138.
[59] Numbers 28:8.
[60] *De institut. coenob.*, III, 3. *MPL*, 49: 122-125.
[61] IX, 34. *MPL*, 49: 818.
[62] *Apostolic Constitutions*, II, 59. *MPG*, 1: 743.
[63] *De institut. coenob.*, IV, 19. *MPL*, 49: 179.
[64] VIII, 35-41. *MPG*, 1: 1138-1143.
[65] Possibly it is to this that Cassian refers when he speaks of "illum trinae

the beginning of the day.[66] The hymn φῶς ἱλαρον (Joyous Light) was sung by all the people at Vespers according to St. Basil,[67] and therefore presumably by the monks; it is still a regular part of this Hour in the Greek Office today.

Western

Though the Office of the Oriental monasteries served to a great extent as the model for the monachism of the West, there were nevertheless some differences. Generally speaking, the moderation for which Cassian praises the Egyptian monks was a little too drab for the West, which tended rather to follow the example of Palestine and the rest of the Orient. In time, however, enthusiasm for Egyptian asceticism gained pace and was the dominant element in the fusion that ultimately resulted.[68]

Before treating of some of the peculiarities of the Western rules concerning the monastic Office, let us sum up what Cassian has to say about them. In the monasteries of his acquaintance, the prayer after each psalm was recited kneeling, whereas in Egypt it was recited standing.[69] Also many more psalms were said after the model of the non-Egyptian Oriental monks. At the end of each psalm the Gloria Patri was sung.[70] Again in imitation of the Oriental practice, Psalms 50 and 148-150 were sung at Lauds; however Psalms 62 and 89 were added.[71] In Gaul vigils were celebrated every day, Lauds also, but not following immediately upon the vigils; a short interval separated them.[72] Prime had been introduced from the East,[73] but the rest of the little Hours, contrary to Egyptian practice, were all recited in common.[74] Vespers concluded the daily cursus.

But now to the Rules of the great Western monastic founders. For what concerns the vigils, Caesarius of Arles indicates [75] that: (1) from Easter to September on Saturdays, Sundays, and feast days there were recited twelve psalms, three antiphons, and three lessons—one from the Old Testament, one from the Epistles and a third from the

---

orationis numerum, qui solet congregationibus fratrum ad concludendum synaxim celebrari . . . ." *Collationes*, IX, 34. *MPL*, 49: 816.

[66] *De virginitate*, 20. *MPG*, 28: 275.

[67] *De spiritu sancto*, c. 29, n. 73. *MPG*, 32:206.

[68] Compare, for instance, Cassian's preface to his *De instit. coenobiorum* (*MPL*, 49: 53-60) with the prefaces to the first and second part of his *Collationes* (*ibid.*, 477-482; 843-848).

[69] *De institut. coenob.*, II, 7. *MPL*, 49:91.

[70] *Ibid.*, II, 8, col. 94.

[71] *Ibid.*, III, 6, col. 136.

[72] *Ibid.*, III, 4, col. 127.

[73] *Ibid.*, III, 4, col. 131.

[74] Ibid., III, 2, col. 112-115.

[75] *Regula*, XX, XXI, XXV. L. Holstenius, *Codex Regularum* (Paris, 1663), II, pp. 92-93.

Gospels; (2) from October to Easter on ordinary days there were recited two nocturns (probably of twelve psalms each) and three
lessons, the psalms being taken in their Biblical order and recited, it
appears, first antiphonally, then responsorially, then antiphonally
again; (3) for Sundays of this latter period there were six lessons of
which the first was always about the Resurrection (certainly under the
influence of Jerusalem). The psalms to be sung at Sunday Lauds are
all set down: "Exaltabo te, Deus meus" (144), one of the *Confitemini*
psalms, the canticle "Cantemus Domino" (Exod.15), "Lauda anima
mea Dominum" (145), "Benedicite, Laudate Dominum de coelis"
(Pss.148-150?); to these were added the Te Deum, Gloria in excelsis
Deo and the *capitella* (Preces). In Aurelian's Rule, however, Psalms
62 and 42 also figure, and the Magnificat replaces the Te Deum.[76]

While Caesarius simply says that the day Hours exist,[77] Aurelian
offers some details. For Tierce, Sext, and None twelve psalms were
sung, three lessons read; upon these followed a hymn proper to each
Hour: "Iam surgit hora tertia," "Iam sexta sensum solvitur," "Ter hora
trina volvitur." After these came the capitella.[78] Vespers seems to have
been a double Hour: Vespers, then *Duodecima*. The first, Aurelian
tells us, comprised one psalm sung *recto tono*, two antiphonally sung,
a hymn (either "Deus qui certis legibus," or "Deus creator omnium"),
then a capitellum. The second comprised eighteen psalms, an antiphon, a hymn, a lesson and the capitellum.[79] Prime consisted of twelve
psalms, a hymn: "Fulgentis auctor aetheris," two lessons, and the
capitellum.[80] The day ended with Compline which was very simple:
Psalm 90 and the usual capitella.[81]

This brief description shows how heavy the Office had become.
The number twelve, so sacred to the Egyptians, figured everywhere.
But the tendency of the other Oriental monasteries was also felt in
that the number of psalms was on occasion indefinitely multiplied.

With St. Columbanus a slight respite is already to be found.
Though the vigils still remain incredibly long: on short nights there
were twelve psalms, on long nights from eighteen to thirty-six, on
Saturdays and Sundays in winter as many as sixty-five; the Little
Hours had only three psalms and Vespers twelve. Columbanus, like
the other religious founders, speaks of the capitella concluding the
various Hours.[82]

The most important religious rule for the history of the Roman
Office is undoubtedly that of St. Benedict. The Benedictine Office was
not a pure invention of its founder for his rule itself leaves no doubt

[76] *Regula*, LV. *Ibid.*, II, p. 110.
[77] *Recapitulatio*, n. IX. *Ibid.*, III, p. 37.
[78] *Regula*, LV. *Ibid.*, II, p. 111.
[79] *Ibid.*, 112.
[80] *Ibid.*, 111.
[81] *Ibid.*, 112.
[82] *Regula*, VII: *De cursu psalmorum.* Holstenius, II, pp. 157-159.

that he borrowed, or better, re-arranged the Office of Rome: "sicut psallit Ecclesia Romana." [83] After studying St. Benedict's rule, Callewaert lays down the following principle: The Rule of St. Benedict offers a detailed description of the Office only when it differs from the usage of Rome; otherwise it presupposes the arrangement of the Roman Office as known.[84] Benedict's ordering of the Office was considered so excellent that, in turn, the Roman Church as well as many others adopted it, at least along general lines. And this was due in large part to the fact that the popes founded monasteries in Rome for the Benedictines who were entrusted with the execution of the Divine Office in the neighboring basilicas. Gregory the Great relates that upon the destruction of Monte Cassino by the Lombards the monks took refuge in Rome and the Pope established them in the Lateran; Valentinian had been abbot of this group for many years by the time Gregory wrote his *Dialogues*.[85] Furthermore, Gregory himself made his own home over into a monastery, *ad clivum Scauri*,[86] of which he was a monk until his election as pope. He also called the Benedictines to take charge of the Church of St. Pancratius.[87] Gregory II did the same for the Basilica of St. Paul.[88] And we know from several sources that John, the abbot of the Benedictines installed at St. Martin's, was the director of chant for the Basilica of St. Peter's. From such vantage points—the episcopal church of Rome, the Lateran Basilica, and the city's two major monuments, the Basilicas of Sts. Peter and Paul—these monks would exercise a tremendous influence over the future development of the Liturgy of the eternal city.

Since this was the role played by the cursus of St. Benedict, it will be of definite value to outline its order. Before doing so, however, let us establish the principles which guided the Father of Western Monasticism in arranging the Office.[89] These principles can be reduced to five: (1) The entire Psalter should be recited once a week, the entire Old and New Testaments once a year with suitable commentaries. (2) The sacred number twelve makes its appearance again

[83] *Regula*, XIII. Holstenius, II, p. 24.

[84] *Liturgicae Institutiones*: II. *De Breviarii Romani Liturgia* (Bruges, 1931), p. 301. In various articles Callewaert has endeavored to piece together the information obtainable from Benedict's Rule in order to arrive at the original Roman cursus. These articles have been collected and reprinted in the work *Sacris Erudiri* (Bruges, 1940). See in particular the following: "De laudibus matutinis," pp. 53-89; "Vesperae antiquae in officio praesertim Romano," pp. 91-117; "De parvis Horis Romanis ante Regulam s. Benedicti," pp. 119-126; "De Completorio ante s. Benedictum," pp. 127-130; "De Capitulis in officio Romano ante s. Benedictum," pp. 131-133; "Les prières d'introduction aux differentes heures de l'office," pp. 135-144; "De Matutino in antiquo officio Romano," pp. 145-148; "Les offices festifs à Rome avant la Règle de saint Benoît," pp. 149-166.

[85] Lib. II, intro. *MPL*, 66: 126.

[86] *Liber Pontificalis*, ed. L. Duchesne, I, 312.

[87] *Epistola*, IV, 18. *MPL*, 77: 687-688.

[88] *Liber Pontificalis*, I, 397.

[89] For these and for the cursus in general see his *Regula*, VIII-XIX. Holstenius, II, pp. 24-31. Cf. also S. Bäumer, *op. cit.*, I, 243-245.

in that twelve psalms are to be recited in both the night and day Hours (though in the latter they are parcelled out in groups of three for each Little Hour. (3) In order to leave time for work during the day, the Little Hours would contain short psalms (or long ones divided into parts), and Matins during the summer months would have only one lesson (because of the shorter night); but on Sundays and feast days even in summer, when there was no work, all the long lessons would be read. (4) Guided by discretion, Benedict knew that his monks would be tired after a long day's work; at the end of the day there would be no long Office, but Vespers would be shorter and followed by supper before nightfall. (5) Every attempt would be made to have the Office equal on all the days of the week except Sunday, for harmony and a well-ordered life are important.

With these principles in mind St. Benedict decided upon the following arrangement of the various Hours:

Ferial night Office [90]

Introduction: "Domine labia mea aperies" (thrice).
    Ps. 3: "Domine, quid multiplicati sunt" (chosen because of verse 6: "I lay down and I slept, I arose . . . .").
    Ps. 94: "Venite, exultemus Domino" with an antiphon.
    Hymn.
Nocturn:
    Part I: Six psalms with antiphons.
      Versicle and response; blessing of abbot.
      Three lessons from Bible and Fathers (in summer only one: from the Old Testament) each followed by responsories, the Gloria Patri being added to the last.
    Part II: Six psalms with Alleluia.
      Capitulum or brief lesson from St. Paul.
      Versicle and response.
Conclusion: Litanies (Preces).

Sunday and Festive night Office [91]

Introduction: as above.
Nocturn:
    Part I: Six psalms with antiphons.
      Versicle and response; blessing of abbot.

[90] The traditional twelve psalms comes from Pachomius, but the 6-6 division stems from Byzantine practice, according to A. Baumstark, *Nocturna Laus* (Münster, 1957), 106-118, 154.

[91] The tripartite arrangement of the Sunday vigil Office is derived from the Syro-Palestinian Office, according to Baumstark, *op. cit.*, 145-150; the presence of the three canticles parallels their use in the popular vigils of Constantinople, Jerusalem, Milan, and Spain: *ibid.*, 142.

> Four lessons with responsories, the last with Gloria
> Patri.
> II: Same order as Part I.
> III: Three prophetic canticles with Alleluia.
> Versicle and response; abbot's blessing.
> Four lessons from the New Testament with respon-
> sories.
> Te Deum.
> Gospel.
> "Te decet laus."
> Conclusion: Abbot's blessing.
> *Lauds (Matutinorum solemnitas)*[*]

This Office was to begin with the coming of light. In winter the
interval between the vigil and Lauds was to be spent in meditation;
in summer only a brief interval was allowed, for at that time of the
year daylight comes earlier. On Sundays and feast days, however,
Lauds were to follow immediately, undoubtedly because the length of
the Sunday vigil brought it right to the break of day. This Office was
arranged thus:

Introduction: Ps.66, "Deus misereatur nostri."

Ps.50, "Miserere" with Alleluia or some other antiphon.

Two other psalms according to the day of the week: 117 and 62,
5 and 35, 42 and 56, 63 and 64, 87 and 89, 75 and 91, 142 and
the first part of the canticle from Deuteronomy.

A canticle varying according to the day (Benedicite on Sundays).
Pss. 148-150.

Brief lesson (Apocalypse on Sundays, St. Paul on weekdays).

Responsory, hymn, versicle, and response.

Benedictus, Preces, Pater.

Little Hours

Introduction: "Deus in ajutorium meum intende" and Gloria Patri.
Hymn.

Three psalms with one antiphon: at Prime on Sundays four parts
of Ps.118; at the other Little Hours on Sundays and Mondays
three parts of Ps.118. At Prime for the rest of the week Pss.1-19
are sung, omitting those recited at other Hours. At the rest of the
Little Hours during the remainder of the week Pss.119-127 are
recited. Each psalm is concluded with Gloria Patri.

Lesson, versicle, and response.

Litany (Preces) and Pater.

Vespers

Introduction: as above.
Four psalms with antiphons: from 109-116, 128-132, 134-141, 143-147, with Pss.138, 143, 144 being divided into two or more parts and Ps.116 added to Ps.115.
Lesson, responsory.
Hymn, versicle, and response.
Magnificat.
Litany (Preces) and Pater.

Compline

Introduction: same as above.
Three psalms: 4, 90, 133 without antiphon.
Lesson, versicle, and response.
Litany (Preces) and final blessing.

As we can see, Benedict put a very definite order into the monastic Office. Much of it, of course, he inherited directly from Rome. This is true, above all, of the already existing texts, for he alludes to the hymns customarily sung at certain Hours and often calls them *Ambrosianum*. He did not, it is generally believed, compose any new texts for the Office, but he did re-order it.

Secular Cursus

Eastern

Once having seen what type of canonical prayer was proper to monks, it remains for us yet to discuss the development of that same prayer as proper to the parish or cathedral church and therefore to the secular clergy. The monastic practice undoubtedly influenced public prayer. Nevertheless, there is a distinction, and the Office recited by monks was not always considered applicable to the needs of the ordinary parish church.

The only *daily* public prayer that was generally held in the East during the fourth century was Lauds and Vespers. Sozomen relates that Zeno, bishop of Majuma (Gaza in Palestine), who died in 380, never missed morning and evening services except when ill.[92] Socrates says expressly that Vespers were sung daily in all the Orient.[93] St. John Chrysostom is also clear on this matter of daily Lauds and Vespers.[94] About a century later Theodoret of Cyr states that, besides as-

[92] *Hist. eccl.*, VII, 28. *MPG*, 67: 1506.
[93] *Hist. eccl.*, V, 22. *MPG*, 67: 642.
[94] *Homily* 18 *on the Acts of the Apostles*, n. 5. *MPG*, 60: 147. He also urges the faithful to visit the church three times a day or at least to pray privately, but it is not clear to which Offices he is referring: *Serm. 4 on S. Anna. MPG*, 54: 667.

sisting at morning and evening services (*liturgias*) which took place in church, the people of his day also glorified the Blessed Trinity at three other times of the day.[95]

When Chrysostom speaks of vigils for the faithful, it is private prayer at home which is his concern,[96] but he does make specific reference to the Office of certain monks which contained a daily public vigil.[97] Though St. Basil is a very clear witness to public vigils for the faithful, unfortunately he gives no indication how often they were held:

> As to the charge regarding psalmody, the customs now prevailing are in accord with those of all the churches of God. Among us the people come early after nightfall to the house of prayer, and in labor, affliction, and continual tears confess to God. Finally, rising up from their prayers, they begin the chanting of psalms. And now, divided into two parts, they chant antiphonally, becoming master of the text of the Scriptures, and at the same time directing their attention and the recollectedness of their hearts. Then, leaving it to one to intone the melody, the rest chant in response. Thus having spent the night in a variety of psalmody and intervening prayers, when day at last begins to dawn, all in common, as with one voice and one heart, offer up the psalm of confession to the Lord, making each one his own the words of repentance.[98]

Hence, according to Basil, his people were accustomed to spend the whole night in both antiphonal and responsorial chanting of the psalms and to sing the "Miserere" at daybreak. This, he tells us, was the custom of the Egyptians, Libyans, Palestinians, Arabians, Phoenicians and Syrians.

As we have already seen on several occasions, the *Apostolic Constitutions*, a Syrian document, is fairly explicit regarding Lauds and Vespers: in Vespers, after Psalm 140, the people recite the prayers of the Oratio Fidelium led by the deacon, and after the Oratio lucernalis and the blessing of the bishop, they are dismissed with the diaconal announcement *Exite in pace*; in Lauds we find the same order followed except that Psalm 62 is sung instead of 140.[99] On the other hand, all that is said about the vigils is that, where possible, the faithful should come together at cockcrow; where not, each should recite psalms, read the Scriptures and pray.[100] If this text means what it

---

[95] *Epist.* 145. *MPG,* 83: 1378.

[96] *Homily 26 on the Acts of the Apostles,* n. 4. *MPG,* 60: 203-204. Sozomen reports Chrysostom's action taken against the Arians by having his people sing hymns early in the morning on Sundays and feast days (*Hist. eccl.,* VIII, 8. *MPG,* 67: 1535), but it is difficult to see how this could be called a vigil.

[97] *Homily 14 on Timothy,* 5, 4. *MPG,* 62: 575-577.

[98] *Letter 207 to the Clergy of Neo-Caesarea. The Fathers of the Church,* 28 (New York, 1955), 83-84.

[99] VIII, 34-39. *MPG,* 1: 1135-1142.

[100] *Ibid.* 34, col. 1135-1138.

seems to indicate, it is rather extraordinary that the bishop of Antioch, even at the end of the fourth century, could really expect his flock to come to church every night after midnight!

The *Diary* of Etheria is a most important document for the history of the Divine Office in the East towards the end of the fourth century, giving as it does a precise description of the celebration of the Hours in Jerusalem. Like the Rule of St. Benedict, Etheria's delineation of the Office holds a midway position between the strictly monastic Office and that of public secular churches. For one thing, the ascetics and virgins sustain the greater part of the prayer, while priests and deacons take turns being present to recite the concluding orations, thus giving the prayer of the religious an official character. The bishop himself attends only some of the Offices in their entirety; for others he comes only at the end. The attendance of the laity seems altogether voluntary, though their assistance at the Sunday vigils may be somewhat obligatory, since the number present is so great. Hence, we have here a case in point where specifically religious practice is used by local church authority for the welfare of the faithful at large, for all the services take place in a public church, the Anastasis or Church of the Holy Sepulcher, and a few priests are always there to take care of the faithful.

Every night at cockcrow the vigil begins. The monks and virgins sing hymns, responsorial and antiphonal psalms, and the laity who come may take part in the singing. After each hymn and psalm an oration is sung by a priest or deacon from among the local clergy. At daybreak the morning hymns (*hymni matutini*) are sung. At this moment the bishop comes with his clergy. He says a prayer for all (perhaps the Oratio Fidelium), blesses the catechumens, says another prayer, then blesses the faithful. All are then dismissed.[101]

Tierce is ordinarily not celebrated in any special way, except in Lent when there is a daily Office exactly like Sext and None. At the latter two Hours psalms and antiphons are sung until someone goes to get the bishop. Upon arriving he recites an oration and blesses the people. All are dismissed.

Another Office is held in the evening at the tenth hour (approximately four o'clock); it is called the "Lucernarium." At this service torches and candles are lighted during the chanting of the lucernal psalms and antiphons, which last for quite a long time (*diutius*). The bishop arrives with his clergy, and all sit while hymns and antiphons [102] are sung. The deacon then reads a list of names; after each name young boys (*pisinni plurimi*) shout "Kyrie eleison!" The bishop then recites an oration for all. The deacon warns the catechumens to bow

---

[101] *Ethérie, Journal de Voyage* (edit. H. Pétré), n. 24, pp. 188-190.
[102] Antiphons may refer to antiphonally sung psalms.

for the bishop's blessing. After another oration, the bishop blesses the faithful. All are then dismissed.[103]

On Sunday a great crowd comes for the vigil, and, in order to keep themselves busy until the doors of the Anastasis are opened, the faithful sing psalms, hymns, and orations. At cockcrow the doors are opened. The bishop is there with his clergy from that moment on. The first psalm is sung responsorially: a priest sings it while the people answer with a refrain. A second psalm is sung in the same way by a deacon, and a third by another cleric. Then follows what appears to be the Oratio Fidelium. Incense fills the church, and the bishop sings the Gospel of the Passion and Resurrection amid loud moanings of the people. Then all go to the chapel of the cross while hymns are chanted. Upon arrival there a psalm is recited, the bishop says an oration, pronounces a blessing, and all are dismissed. The monks and the virgins, however, return to the Church of the Anastasis and continue to chant psalms and antiphons, an oration concluding each, until daybreak. The laity may attend if they wish.[104] Evidently the latter service was supposed to be Lauds, but it was not a solemn Office, since all the solemnity was given to Matins on Sunday. Since Mass on Sunday was so long,[105] Sext and None were not held, but Vespers was celebrated at its regular hour.

Though Etheria does not mention precisely what psalms or antiphons were sung at the various Hours, undoubtedly a regular cursus had been established, for over and over again she mentions something which attracted her attention in a special way: psalms, hymns, and antiphons as well as lessons and orations always were appropriately chosen to fit the particular day and Hour.[106] From her report we also see that in Jerusalem at the end of the fourth century there were five canonical Hours: vigils, Lauds, Sext, None, and Vespers. A sixth Hour, Tierce, was celebrated only during Lent. The faithful together with all the clergy, the bishop at their head, assisted at the vigils of Sundays and feast days (also of Saturdays of Lent, it would seem) [107] and at daily Lauds and Vespers; but during the week the daily vigils were celebrated only by the monks and virgins with a few pious people present and a couple of priests or deacons to recite the concluding orations.

Summing up all the testimony regarding the East, therefore, we see that the cursus for secular churches takes as its point of departure

---

[103] *Journal de Voyage*, n. 24, pp. 190-192.
[104] *Ibid.*, pp. 194-198.
[105] It began, most likely, about nine o'clock in the morning and lasted well past eleven because of the many sermons.
[106] N. 25 and 43, pp. 200, 250. In other words this appears rather remarkable to our pilgrim nun; it indicates that in her home country (Spain or southern Gaul) such was not the case: the chants and prayers were apparently always the same.
[107] N. 27, p. 212.

the official morning and evening prayers—Lauds and Vespers. Vigils on very important occasions had been known for centuries; only later did they make their appearance every Sunday. In some centers vigils were ultimately observed each day of the week either with the help of monks or, more rarely, by the local bishop together with his presbyteral college.[108] The Little Hours as canonical services were known and practiced publicly in few places, and there with the help of monks, as in Etheria's report; more often they were hours of private prayer. And so, Lauds and Vespers were, generally speaking, the secular *Opus Dei*, with vigils figuring only on Sundays and special feasts.

Western

Concerning the Divine Office of Rome itself there has been much discussion. Battifol claims that the daily vigil constituted the entire Office of the Roman clergy in the fifth and six centuries,[109] and that the other Hours were formed only in the course of the seventh and eighth centuries in the monasteries attached to the Roman basilicas.[110] However, it seems altogether strange that Rome, unlike any other center in Christendom, would have taken the vigil, instead of the morning and evening services of Lauds and Vespers, as the point of departure in developing her Office. St. Benedict clearly alludes to the existence of Lauds in the Roman cursus when he says that at that Hour his monks are to sing one of the canticles "sicut psallit ecclesia Romana." [111] Battifol himself even quotes this statement, but he thinks it refers to the vigil. Yet it clearly had to do with *matutinorum solemnitas*—not Matins in our modern sense, but the *morning* office.

Furthermore, in the so-called Leonine Sacramentary are found several orations coming under the title "Orationes Matutinae vel ad Vesperum." [112] We find similar prayers in the Gelasian Sacramentary.[113] Besides, what of the still earlier testimony of the *Apostolic Tradition*? Actually Lauds and Vespers were the starting point of Roman development.

Vigils are indeed witnessed to, but not until later. In the *Liber Diurnus* we find an oath made by suburbicarian bishops to the pope on the occasion of their episcopal consecration. It dates from the end of the sixth or the beginning of the seventh century.[114] In it the bishop promised the pope that he would celebrate the daily vigil with his clergy.[115] The very fact that the pope had to insist on such an oath

---

[108] For more references see S. Bäumer, I, 114-115.
[109] *History of the Roman Breviary*, pp. 49, 50, 52.
[110] *Ibid.*, 72.
[111] *Regula*, XIII. Holstenius, II, 27.
[112] C. Mohlberg, *Sacramentarium Veronense*, p. 75, beginning with n. 587.
[113] Edit. H. Wilson, 291-293.
[114] Bäumer, I, 307.
[115] III, 7. *MPL*, 105: 71.

from newly consecrated bishops of his own Roman province would seem to indicate that we are faced here with an institution just recently introduced which did not at all sit well with the clergy. It is true that Jerome speaks of the Roman matron Laeta taking her daughter to the public vigils, but he does not indicate how often they took place.[116] The earliest reference we have to an obligation incumbent upon all clerics to assist at *daily* vigils is a decree of the Emperor Justinian dating about 530: All clerics were to chant each day in their proper churches the nocturnal, morning, and evening prayers; should anyone fail in this duty he would be expelled from the ranks of the clergy.[117]

What was the content of these Hours? For what concerns the vigils, the episcopal oath contained in the above-cited *Liber Diurnus* says that in summer three lessons, three antiphons (perhaps antiphonally sung psalms) and three responsories were to be recited; in winter four of each; in the Sunday vigils nine of each.[118] As for Lauds, Cassian tells us that in all churches of Italy Psalm 50 was sung after the morning hymns.[119] He also states that the morning hymns were Pss.62, 89, 148-150, but it is not certain whether he refers this practice to the whole of the West or only Gaul.[120] Arnobius the Younger, however, who wrote about 470, when commenting on Ps.148, says that it was sung throughout the whole world in the morning.[121] True, these allusions are somewhat vague, but we do get more help from an Irishman who probably lived in the last half of the seventh century and had seen both the Roman and Benedictine cursus. According to him the cursus of St. Benedict differed but little from that of Rome: "singulariter pauco discordante a cursu Romano."[122] Thus, in general, we may consider the description of the Benedictine Office which we have given above as valid also for Rome.[123]

One more question needs to be discussed regarding the Roman Office. Who was its author—in the sense of who was the principal moving spirit behind it? This is a difficult question, and no definitive

[116] *Epist.* 107 *ad Laetam,* n. 9. *MPL,* 22: 875.

[117] Justinian, *Cod.,* I, iii, 41 (al. 42), #10. J. Beck, *Corpus Iuris Civilis* (Leipzig, 1837), pp. 22-23.

[118] We must remember, however, that this is not conclusive evidence for the content of the Roman vigils, for this document does not really pertain to the practice of Rome itself; it is concerned with what should take place in the suburbicarian dioceses. We must not forget that the principal churches of Rome had monks to celebrate the Office, which could in this case be much longer than that demanded of the secular clergy.

[119] *De coenob. instit.,* III, 6. *MPL,* 49: 136.

[120] He uses the expression *in hac regione: ibid.,* col. 135.

[121] *MPL,* 53: 566.

[122] Haddan and Stubbs, *Councils and Ecclesiastical Documents,* I (Oxford, 1869), 140. Bäumer, I, 298, note 3.

[123] A more detailed idea of the Roman Office of the eighth century can be had from certain of the Roman Ordinals: *OR* XII for the antiphons, *OR* XIIIa and *OR* XIV for the readings. Andrieu, *Les Ordines Romani du Haut Moyen-Age,* II, 459-466; 480-488; II, 39-41.

answer can be given to it. The Frankish monk who compiled the St. Gall Codex 349 [124] in the latter part of the eighth century makes the claim that Pope St. Damasus (366-384), with the help of St. Jerome, imported the Office from Jerusalem.[125] This and a similar interpolation in the *Liber Pontificalis* [126] are based on an apocryphal letter of St. Jerome to Damasus and hence do not carry with them all the certitude we would wish for. All that we can say is that, since Damasus did have Jerome revise the Psalter, it is probable that he did so with an eye towards its use in the Office. Popes Leo and Gelasius are also credited with an interest in the Office. But above all, we must certainly attribute to Gregory the Great some activity in this matter. His biographer, John the Deacon, tells us that he was a man well informed in musical matters and had compiled an Antiphonary and founded schools for chant in Rome.[127] Let us also recall the important role, mentioned above, that the Benedictine monks played in Rome's Liturgy: by the eighth century there were some nineteen liturgical-monastic groups serving the churches of Rome.[128]

Regarding the Divine Office for the secular clergy outside Rome, there are scant and vague references. For the sake of completeness, however, we will mention some of them here. In Africa, about the year 383, Lauds and Vespers seem to have been observed, for Augustine recalls how his mother Monica went to church every morning and evening to hear the word of God and to say prayers.[129] Hilary of Poitiers speaks of Lauds and Vespers as daily public functions,[130] and though he urges his people to nocturnal prayer, it does not appear from his text that this was necessarily in public.[131] In the life of St. Ambrose we read that one night, in order to occupy the people who fled to the church during the Arian siege, he had them sing hymns and psalms in the oriental manner. This was so popular that it was continued even to the time of Ambrose's biographer and had spread to other cities.[132]

For Spain and Gaul there are also extant a number of synodal and conciliar decrees which indicate the existence of certain Hours in those regions at this date. The Synod of Vannes in 465 commanded all clerics who lived within the walls of the city to attend daily Lauds.[133] In 506, however, the Council of Agde demanded daily cele-

---

[124] *Ordines* XIV-XIX in Andrieu.
[125] *OR* XIX, n. 36. Andrieu, III, p. 223.
[126] Edit. L. Duchesne, I, 213; see note 17, pp. 214-215.
[127] *Vita Gregorii*, II, 6. *MPL*, 75: 90.
[128] Cf. Bäumer, L, 260-262; C. Callewaert, *Liturgicae Institutiones*, II: *De Breviarii Romani Liturgia*, n. 233; I. Schuster, *The Sacramentary*, III, 14-73.
[129] *Confessiones*, V, 9. *MPL*, 32: 714; *Epist.* 167 *ad Alypium*, 11. *MPL*, 33: 120.
[130] *Comment. in ps.* 64, 9. *MPL*, 9:420.
[131] *Comment. in ps.* 118, 55. *MPL*, 9:550.
[132] Paulinus of Milan, *Vita*, n. 13. *MPL*, 14:31; Augustine, *Confessiones*, IX, 7. *MPL*, 32: 770.
[133] Can. 14. Hefele-Leclercq, *Histoire des Conciles*, II, 905.

bration of Vespers in addition to Lauds; during these, after the psalmody, the Preces were to be said, and after an oration recited by bishop or priest, the blessing of the bishop was to be given.[134] While the Synod of Tarragona, held in 516, asks that priests and deacons arrange it so that one of them is always present for the Lauds and Vespers held daily in their respective churches,[135] the Braga Synod of 561 requires a uniform order for the celebration of Lauds and Vespers and for the feast day vigils.[136] Finally, the Fourth Council of Toledo, celebrated in 633, in addition to commanding daily Lauds and Vespers,[137] decreed that the use of hymns composed by Hilary and Ambrose was appropriate for the Divine Office.[138]

3. The Roman Office from the sixth to the eleventh centuries

With Gregory the Great the development of the Roman Liturgy reached a point of perfection; the essential lines of the Office, along with the rest of the Liturgy, were so well fixed that they were to remain in this condition for many centuries to come. This was true even of the texts used in the Office. There were, to be sure, certain additions and changes made by subsequent popes and others, but, for the most part, they kept to the already established forms.

In this period, apart from the introduction of new feasts due to the ever increasing cult of the martyrs and saints, the story of the Roman Office concerns mainly its diffusion throughout Europe. Here again the principal agents of this propagation were the Benedictine monks, sent here and there to Christianize the rest of the western world or to organize what had already been conquered for Christ. It is the story of Augustine of Canterbury, of Boniface, of John the Arch-chanter, of Alcuin and others. Everywhere they went they firmly established the Office they had known in Rome or which had been brought to them from Rome.

The first thrust towards expansion of the Roman Office was made when St. Augustine, along with forty of his monks, was sent by Gregory the Great in 596 to help evangelize England.[139] The chanting of these monks made a great impression, not only on the pagans of Kent, but on all England. Wilfrid, bishop of York, obtained the assistance of two monks from Canterbury to establish the Roman chant in his diocese.[140] In 668 Wighard, a monk of the same monastery, was consecrated bishop of Canterbury,[141] and later another monk, Putta, was

---

[134] Can. 30. *Ibid.*, 992.
[135] Can. 7. *Ibid.*, 1028.
[136] Cc. 1 and 2. *Ibid.*, III, 179.
[137] Can. 2. *Ibid.*, III, 268.
[138] Can. 13. *Ibid.*, III, 270.
[139] Bede, *Hist. eccl. angl.*, I, 22. MPL, 95: 52-54.
[140] *Ibid.*, IV, 2. MPL, 95: 174.
[141] Bede, *Vita S. Benedicti*, III, MPL, 94: 715.

named bishop of Rochester and was an expert in Roman chant.[142]
About a decade later Benedict Biscop founded a new monastery at
Wearmouth, and, in order to establish firmly there the Roman chant
and cursus, he obtained from Pope Agatho permission to bring back
to England with him the Abbot of the monastery of St. Martin near
the Vatican, John the Arch-chanter of St. Peter's Basilica.[143] While
there John taught the monks the Roman fashion of chanting the Office.
At the same time other monasteries profited by such an opportunity
and sent their young monks to learn under John's tutelage. Intending
to remain for only a few years, he undertook to render his efforts more
lasting by composing an Ordo for the ecclesiastical year, and this
many other localities copied.[144] Perhaps it was this Ordo which the
Council of Cloveshoe in 747 laid down as the model to be followed in
chanting the seven canonical Hours.[145]

The papacy had taken similar steps to insure the observance of
Roman chant for the Office in southern Germany. In 716 Gregory II
gave orders to his legates Martinian and George to see to it that each
church was provided with all that was necessary for Mass and both
the day and night Hours of the Office according to the order of the
Roman Church.[146]

For the rest of the Frankish territory, we know that St. Boniface,
an English Benedictine monk, exercised a great influence on the
Frankish court. About 768 Pope Paul I sent to Remedius, Bishop of
Rouen, the *secundicerius*, or second in command, of the Roman
schola cantorum, who was called Simeon. He was supposed to take
over the direction of the musical training of the Rouen monks. When,
however, the *primicerius*, or head of the Roman school, died, the
Pope had to recall Simeon. Remedius lost no time in having his
brother, Pepin, complain to the Pope that his own monks were not
yet well enough trained in Roman chant: Would the Pope please
receive some of the Rouen monks into the Roman school itself? Paul
I gladly acceded to this wish.[147] Furthermore, Chrodegang, Bishop
of Metz, had also introduced the Roman Office and chant into his
diocese upon his return from Rome [148] and so beautifully was it
executed in Metz that monks and clerics were sent thither to study.
And Charlemagne pursued the same goal as his father, Pepin, in trying
to establish effectively the Roman usage in all the churches of Gaul.
Besides providing his realm with copies of the Roman service books,

---

[142] Bede, *Hist. eccl. angl.*, IV, 2. *MPL*, 95: 175.

[143] *Ibid.*, IV, 18. *MPL*, 95: 199.

[144] *Ibid.*, col. 200.

[145] ". . . iuxta exemplar videlicet quod scriptum de Romana habemus Ecclesia," can. 15. Hefele-Leclercq, *Histoire des Conciles*, III, 908.

[146] *Capit. Gregorii II. MPL*, 89: 532.

[147] *Epist. 36 Pauli I ad Pippinum. MPL*, 98: 199-201.

[148] Cf. Bäumer, I, 328.

he saw to it that decree after decree was passed, obliging all to adopt them.[149]

Mindful, however, of the force of Gallican tradition and of the transformations effected in the Roman Sacramentaries when these were transplanted onto Frankish ground, we might well ask whether a like process did not occur when the Franks began to adopt the Roman Office. Such indeed is the truth of the matter, as facts will bear out. But it is also true that certain changes were already made in Rome itself by the eighth century. When, for instance, Amalar compared the Antiphonary which Gregory IV had given to Wala in the early part of the ninth century with that sent to Metz by Paul I in 768, he found that the two disagreed, not only as to their ordering, but also as to their formulas and the number of responsories and antiphons.[150] He discovered that the Antiphonary given to Wala carried an inscription to the effect that it had been corrected by Pope Hadrian I (died in 795).[151] The differences, then, between the Metz practice and Rome's were due, not to Gallican changes, but rather to a papal reform effected some time after 768.

But Amalar himself went ahead and made other changes. Aware of the different usages of the various Gallican churches, both he and (so he says) Helisachar attempted another revision of the Antiphonary, combining elements from both papal books and current Frankish custom.[152] The occasion of the changes which both these men made in their new books was the diverse manner of reciting the responsories. In Rome the entire responsory was repeated after the versicle had been sung, but in Gaul only a part repeated (the part marked in our modern books by an asterisk). The latter practice often did violence to the meaning of the text. While Helisachar undertook a radical reform, Amalar wanted to keep all that was traditional and thus reached a compromise between materials from Roman and Gallican sources. In order to indicate to the user the origin of the various antiphons and responsories in the revised book, Amalar set up his own peculiar apparatus. He marked with an R whatever came from the Roman Antiphonary corrected by Hadrian; with an M whatever material came from the older Roman book (sent by Paul I in 768) which was in use up until then in Metz; and finally with IC (for the

---

[149] In the *Capitulare Ecclesiasticum* of 789, for instance, it was strictly enjoined on all clerics to study with care the Roman chant both for the Mass and the Office: n. 79. *MPL*, 97: 180. In another such *Capitulare* (of 802) it is ordered that during ecclesiastical visitations it should be ascertained whether priests are able to celebrate the Office according to the Roman Rite: n. 7. *MPL*, 97:248. Finally, the Diet of Thionville in 805, under the direction of the Emperor, again decrees that Roman chant be taught and that the Office be executed in the Roman manner: n. 2. *MPL*, 97: 283.

[150] *De ordine antiphonarii*, prol. *MPL*, 105: 1245.

[151] *Ibid.*, col. 1243.

[152] *Ibid.*, col. 1244.

"indulgentia et caritas" which he begged of the reader) he set off his own new compositions.

In spite of the opposition to his work emanating from certain quarters,[153] the reputation of the Metz liturgical center was such as to assure the new book wide acceptance. It found its way into most of the Gallic churches and was even adopted later by the Cistercians and Premonstratensians. Nor did its diffusion stop there. Our present Roman Breviary shows that Amalar's work was also favorably received in Rome, at least as far as the responsories are concerned, for we now recite them in the Gallican fashion.

There were other changes too. In Rome during the eleventh century, we are told, the Office was in a deplorable state. Pope John XIX himself bemoaned the fact that in St. Peter's Basilica the ancient and majestic Offices of the Church were replaced in a disrespectful way with a mutilated and disfigured one.[154] As a consequence, John instituted a new ceremonial for both Mass and Office, at least during Holy Week. Gregory VII endeavored to push John's reform further to include the entire year. In his day the length of Matins was again proving to be a difficult burden for the secular clergy; they had substituted for the long Office just three psalms and three lessons. He lost no time in rectifying this situation, which, as he claimed, was due to nothing else but relaxation. During the Synod of his very first Lent as pope, that is in 1074, he reorganized Matins: on ferias twelve psalms were to be sung and three lessons read, on feast days nine psalms and nine lessons, on Sundays throughout the year eighteen psalms and nine lessons, but during the octaves of Easter and Pentecost only three psalms and three lessons.[155] This is practically the same order as described by Amalar. Energetic though Gregory's reforms were, the century that followed concentrated the attention of his successors elsewhere than on the Liturgy. Frequent political troubles kept the popes in constant exile. This must be the reason for the decadence described by Abelard, who complained that Rome herself no longer observed the ancient Office except in one church, the Lateran Basilica.[156]

4. The Office of Innocent III and the Franciscans

The political turmoil of the times and Abelard's letter set the stage for the future development of a ceremonial proper to the papal court. Pope after pope had to spend his pontificate "on the run," so to

[153] In particular Florus and Agobard of Lyons: cf. the latter's book against Amalar, *De correctione antiphonarii. MPL*, 104: 330.
[154] Appendix to Mabillon's *Ordo Romanus* XI in *MPL*, 78: 1055.
[155] *Decretum Gratiani*, III, *de consecratione*, IV, 15. *MPL*, 187: 1859-1860. Gregory also decreed that the feasts of all pope-martyrs were to be celebrated by the entire Christian world, according to Bernold of Constance, *Micrologus*, c. 43. *MPL*, 151: 1010.
[156] *Epist.* X. *MPL*, 178: 340.

speak; the papal court had no fixed residence. In such a state of affairs the order of the times was abbreviation of rites and a further development of ceremonial independent of the traditions of the great Roman basilicas. Thus evolved a rite proper to the papal curia; a shortened rite, divorced from its natural habitat.[157] Even when the court returned to Rome, the more recently developed ritual was retained. It is just such a papal Liturgy for both Mass and Office that we see set down in the *Ordo Romanus* XII of Mabillon's collection;[158] it was composed by Cardinal Cencius during the pontificate of Celestine III, before 1198.

We learn from Radulph de Rivo, who wrote towards the end of the fourteenth century, that an ordinary for the Office codified under Innocent III was still to be found in Rome in his own day.[159] This Office was an abbreviation made by the clerics of Innocent's court to suit the pope and the Cardinals. The Friars Minor, in turn, found this Office well adapted to their particular type of apostolic life. In his second rule, written about 1223, St. Francis had his sons recite the curial Office with the exception of the Psalter. Instead of adopting the Roman Psalter, Jerome's first revision, they adopted the so-called Gallican Psalter, Jerome's second revision which was followed throughout Christendom. In time the Franciscans, under their General, Haymon, saw the need for other corrections and, with the approval of Gregory IX, shortened the long lessons into simple excerpts. They also celebrated the feasts of simple rank as doubles and added a great number of new saints to the calendar. Since for such feasts they recited the Common of the saints, including lives and sermons proper to them, it followed that the weekly recitation of the Psalter became less and less common, and the reading of the regular *Scriptura occurrens* was reduced to an absolute minimum.[160] Since the Friars carried these Breviaries with them on their missionary journeys, they soon came to the attention of clerics the world over, and the latter were not long in adopting the easy new form. In fact, a Franciscan pope, Nicholas III (1277-1280), made this new form of the Office obligatory on all the churches of Rome.[161]

Thus we see the same process verifying itself again: a Roman form of Liturgy is adopted for use outside Rome; in turn it is reformed by those who adopted it and finds its way back to Rome in this changed form and becomes official there. In addition, the handiness of this particular Roman form recommended its adoption by clerics who could not assist at the Office in choir and still had to recite it in

[157] Cf. Bäumer, II, 19-21.
[158] *MPL*, 78: 1063-1102.
[159] See text in Bäumer, II, 22, note 1.
[160] Cf. Bäumer, II, 26-33.
[161] *Ibid.*, II, 24.

private—an obligation which had been gaining pace from the eleventh century on [162] and was repeated by council after council.[163]

5. Attempts at reform culminating in the Breviary of Pius V

While the above reforms of the Franciscans tended to lighten the burden of the Breviary, another movement aimed at doing just the opposite. More prayers and subsidiary psalms were added to the Office. Almost without exception they were all of non-Roman origin: the Quicumque, suffrages, the Office of the Blessed Virgin on Saturdays, the Little Office said in addition to the principal Office every day, the Office of the Dead for certain days, and during Lent the penitential and gradual psalms and litanies—all these started out as supererogatory devotions mainly in monasteries (of Cluny, the Carthusians, and Cistercians) but soon penetrated everywhere, some even being obligatory.[164]

At the same time when discontent was being engendered by these additions, as well as by the obvious deficiencies of the Franciscan Breviary, the uncertainty of the official text was allowing errors to creep into the Office; superstitious practices and fabulous stories were also cropping up and many new saints' feasts were being introduced, due to more numerous canonizations—and all of this brought forth new complaints.[165] There were occasional pleas for a complete revision of the Office, such as Radulph's, and one-sided reform projects as that of John Hagen, Abbot of Bursfeld from 1439-1469. The Humanists as a whole were shocked by the vulgar Latin of the liturgical books, even though some of them had even better reasons for asking for a reform: excess of sanctoral feasts, confused rubrics, insufficient scriptural content, apocryphal legends, an unbalanced recitation of psalms and the unseemly adjuncts to the Office.[166]

Armed with the approval of Pope Leo X, Zachary Ferreri undertook a revision of all the hymns. His new hymnal appeared in 1525, and Clement VII permitted the private recitation of its contents for the Breviary. According to the frontispiece of the hymnal, a complete revision of the entire Breviary by the same author would soon appear, but it never did.[167]

Much more significant by reason of its wide influence was the

[162] Cf. J. Jungmann, *Der Gottesdienst der Kirche*, 177; J. Pascher, *Das Stundengebet der römischen Kirche*, 56.

[163] E.g.: Cologne in 1280, c. 1. Hefele-Leclercq, VI, 259; IV Lateran in 1215, c. 17. H. Schroeder, *Disciplinary Decrees of the General Councils* (St. Louis: Herder, 1937), 257; Trier in 1227, c. 9. Hefele-Leclercq, V, 1462; Basel in 1435, c. 9. Schroeder, 477.

[164] Judging from the statement of Radulph de Rivo: "Officia mortuorum et Virginis gloriosae sunt obligatoria et ab omnibus servanda," Bäumer, II, 38, note 1.

[165] *Ibid.*, II, 100.

[166] *Ibid.*, II, 114-117.

[167] *Ibid.*, II, 117-124.

Breviary reform undertaken by the Franciscan Cardinal Quignonez at the order of Clement VII and finally published, after seven years of labor, under Paul III in 1535. So warmly was it received that a second edition appeared the following year incorporating all the suggestions made after the first edition. The Cardinal's primary guiding principle was the distinction between choral and private recitation of the Office. Since his purpose was to produce a Breviary exclusively intended for private recitation, all remnants of a choral character were eliminated: antiphons (though partially re-inserted in the second edition), responsories, versicles and hymns. Unfortunately, by pushing this principle to the extreme, he overlooked a more fundamental one: namely, that the Office is always recited in the name of the Church and therefore bears a public character regardless of whether or not it is recited in choir.

Quignonez set as his goal the recitation of the entire Psalter every week, the whole of Scripture once a year, and he gave an equal length to the Office of each day. With this in mind, he arranged the Breviary in the following manner: (1) each Hour was composed of three psalms (with the Benedictus at Lauds, Magnificat at Vespers and the Nunc dimittis at Compline in addition), the third psalm at Lauds being an Old Testament canticle; (2) the psalms were recited in such a way that none of them were repeated during the week; (3) lessons were reduced to three, while the brief lessons of the Little Hours, Lauds, and Vespers disappeared completely, and the readings for Matins were taken from the Old and New Testaments, the commentaries of the Fathers and the legends of the saints—the latter severely purged of fantasy; (4) the psalms were never to change according to the rank of the feast—but those assigned to each day of the week were always to be recited; (5) the Offices of the Blessed Virgin and of the Dead were restricted to certain few days of the year. Finally, all the rubrics necessary for this simplification were gathered together in one section of the book under the title "Rubricae Generales."

In spite of the tremendous popularity of this Breviary—in forty years it went through approximately one hundred editions [168]—harsh criticism of its plan was not lacking. The Church finally put it aside and forgot about it. Although its author claimed not to have created anything new but only to have returned to the *forma antiqua* of Christian prayer, the principal complaint against it was precisely the very radical fashion in which it broke with tradition. Nevertheless, the violent opposition which it excited did not hinder its wide diffusion and even later influence. And by supplanting most of the local Breviaries, it played a providential role in preparing the way for the reform of Pius V. Thus when the Pope suppressed all Breviaries with a tradition of less than two hundred years, the dioceses which had

[168] *Ibid.*, II, 126.

given up their older ones in favor of the Quignonez reform had no such tradition to fall back on and had to adopt the *Breviarium Pianum*.

Those who had opposed Quignonez' ill-fated reform did not hesitate to make known their desires to the Pope. For a long time before the Council of Trent convened, many Synods in different localities called for a universal reform. In fact, the Theatines in Rome had received orders to work towards such a reform from the same pope who had set Quignonez to work, Clement VII. Though both the co-founders of the Theatines, Gaetano and Giovanni Caraffa, cooperated on this project, it was especially the latter who energetically elaborated a new Breviary and presented it to Clement and his successors. But each pope in turn waited for further advice. The day finally came when Caraffa ascended the papal throne as Paul IV in 1556, but with only two years left to him he failed to achieve anything lasting.

From the very beginning of the Council of Trent in 1545 both the Fathers of the Council and their theologians turned their attention to the many demands and plans for liturgical reform. In the last years under Pius IV (from 1562 to 1563) they studied the problem more in detail, but it was soon apparent that they would get nowhere, for there were two clear-cut currents making themselves felt: the one desired complete uniformity within the Church, the other wanted each diocese to be allowed to determine its own course. Prudently the Council decided to place the whole affair in the hands of the Pope, asking him to see to a revision of the Breviary along with that of other liturgical books.

With the manuscripts of Paul IV's projected Breviary and the reports of the Council's commission before him, Pius established a special commission to work out a reform. After Pius IV's death, Pius V augmented the membership of this commission. Finally in 1568 the new Breviary was promulgated.

The guiding principle of this reform was diametrically opposed to that used by Quignonez. Paul IV, Pius IV, and Pius V all felt that nothing essential in the ancient Roman Breviary should be suppressed. And the commissions under their tutelage directed all their efforts to constructing the Divine Office, not changing it; they sought after the primitive state of this book, not after a new creation. It was the Divine Office as a *public* or choral prayer which they intended to re-instate. Towards this end the members of the commissions investigated all the ancient Sacramentaries, Antiphonaries, and other books which could shed light on the way this public character of the Office had been maintained throughout previous ages.

Most of the well-founded criticism anterior to the Council influenced the result of the commission's labors. Only those historical lessons were accepted which were best established and most characteristic of the feasts to be celebrated. A more judicious choice of

patristic homilies was made, and the scriptural readings were re-
divided and better grouped. For the rest, orations and smaller items,
the problem was simply to get the most authentic forms as they appeared in the ancient manuscripts. The feasts of saints were highly
restricted, leaving much room for local Propers, and even where accepted for the universal Church the only elements these feasts contained as proper to them were historical lessons, hymns, and orations.
The psalms were to be regularly taken from the Psalter as arranged
for the various days of the week—an arrangement coming from about
the seventh to eighth century—and the Gallican version of the Psalter
was authorized for general use. Octaves were reduced and newly
ordered, the rank of feasts differently appraised, and all the accessory
parts—Little Office, the Office of the Dead, Gradual and Penitential
Psalms and Litanies—were no longer obligatory except where it had
been the custom before to recite these parts on the first free day of
the month, on the Mondays of Advent and Lent, on certain vigils, and
on the Ember Days—but only when the Office was chorally recited.
The long ferial Preces were to be said only at Lauds, Prime, and Vespers during Advent and Lent, on vigils and Ember Days; for these
same occasions very brief Preces were provided in the Little Hours.
Something new was added, however: at the beginning of each Hour
the Pater and Ave, and at Matins, the Credo, were to be recited.

Though a few complaints were heard (about the historical lessons), satisfaction was expressed everywhere. Even many Orders and
dioceses which could have retained their traditional Offices according
to Pius' Bull of promulgation either accepted the new reform *in toto*
or corrected their own books to suit its spirit.

6. Reforms of Pius X and Pius XII

Since the time of Pius V's great reform other popes have put
their hand to the task of revising the Breviary—with more or less
liturgical foresight. Gregory XIII reformed the Julian Calendar in
1582 and the Roman Martyrology in 1584. Though Sixtus V had instituted the Congregation of Rites in 1588 and started commissions
working on the revision of the Vulgate and the Breviary, he died
before he could see his initiative bear results.[169] Gregory XIV continued this work but also died before its completion. Both projects
were completed under Clement VIII: the Vulgate in 1592 and the
Breviary in 1602. In his Breviary reform Clement authorized the use
of the revised text of the Vulgate, corrected many historical lessons,
substituted some new patristic readings for those formerly in use,
added the Common of Holy Women not Virgins, introduced the rank

---

[169] As for the Vulgate, the theologians he had commissioned to work on its
revision were offended and dissatisfied with his autocratic and one-sided corrections
of their work and after his death intervened to prevent the sale of the revised
text which had appeared in 1590.

of double of the second class and instituted about twelve new sanctoral feasts. Urban VIII, with great literary elegance but little liturgical sense, was embarrassed by the vulgar Latin of the hymns. He
"corrected" them and published the Breviary with his version of the
hymns in 1632. And during the reign of Clement X (1669-1676) the
Breviary was over-loaded with new saints' feasts of high rank, while
during the seventeenth and eighteenth centuries a crop of national
breviaries rose up everywhere due to the growth of Gallicanism and
Jansenism.

Though Benedict XIV, in 1740, saw the great need there was for
another revision of the Breviary—some ninety new sanctoral feasts had
been instituted since the time of Pius V, overshadowing the temporal
Offices and making the recitation of the entire Psalter a very rare
thing—he died before he could approve the work of the commission
he had set to work.[170] Subsequent popes failed to bring his labors to
fruition; in fact, the situation was only aggravated by the introduction
of an even more astonishing number of new feasts in the sanctoral
order under Pius IX and Leo XIII.[171]

Once again, this time on July 2, 1911, another pope, Pius X, established a commission to try to restore order to the Breviary. The two
major disorders caused by the many feasts with special Offices were
that the Psalter was seldom recited in its entirety and the Scriptural
readings, too, were often excluded. And so the same old problem of
reconciling the rights of temporal and sanctoral cycles had to be
faced. The commission set two objectives before itself: (a) make the
ferial Office once again functional, (b) maintain the feasts of the
saints.

These two objectives were achieved by means of a compromise
or a mixture of the two. Each would have its own function within the
same Office. First of all, Sunday had to be restored to its dignity. In
the new reform the ordinary Sunday Office excluded all feasts of the
sanctoral cycle with the exception of those which enjoyed a rank of
double of the first or second class and the octave days of feasts of
our Lord. All other feasts were reduced to a mere commemoration and
could not be transferred to other days. On weekdays the ferial Office
would cede to the sanctoral but in such a way that the psalms would
no longer be taken from the Proper or Common of the Saints, but
from the occurring feria with its own antiphons, versicles, Scripture
readings, and responsories—exception being made of course, for
feasts of greater importance. Thus was achieved a mixed Office, satisfying the demands of both temporal and sanctoral cycles. In order to
facilitate this combination, the arrangements of psalms proper to the
ferial and common Offices had to be reordered, for in the old system
ferial Matins comprised from twelve to eighteen psalms, whereas the

<hr>

[170] See the interesting account of his plans in Bäumer, II, 324-326; 372-401.
[171] Cf. Bäumer, II, 410-419.

proper or common Matins always counted nine psalms. As a result, the traditional number of twelve was abandoned; Matins was always to have nine psalms.

However, this entailed an additional difficulty: quite a few psalms would be left out altogether if the whole Psalter were not given a new arrangement. Matins, Lauds, and Vespers contained practically all the psalms, while the Little Hours were almost always the same: Ps. 118 was repeated every day. And so the number of psalms in Lauds had to be reduced, for there were regularly eight every day (Pss. 148-150 were an unchangeable part of Lauds). Besides this regrouping of psalms, new canticles from the Old Testament were added and those formerly in use were relegated to second Lauds for penitential days. Finally, the Little Hours and Compline were given different psalms for each day.

To complete this lightening of the Office, many accessories were no longer obligatory: the Offices of the Blessed Virgin and the Dead, as well as other votive Offices which had made their appearance; the gradual and penitential psalms. Even the Preces were shortened, and the Litany of the Saints was relegated to Rogation Days.

In order to give a clear idea of the differences in the arrangement of the psalms occasioned by Pius X's reform, we reprint here both the new and old disposition:

Arrangement of Pius X

	Sunday	Monday	Tuesday	Wednesday	Thursday	Friday	Saturday
	1	13	34	44	61	77	104
	2	14	34	44	65	77	104
	3	16	34	45	65	77	104
	8	17	36	47	67	77	105
Matins	9	17	36	48	67	77	105
	9	17	36	48	67	77	105
	9	19	37	49	68	78	106
	9	20	37	49	68	80	106
	10	29	38	50	68	82	106
	92	46	95	96	97	98	149
	99	5	42	64	89	142	91
	62	28	66	100	35	84	63
Lauds	Cant. Bened.	Cant. David	Cant. Tobias	Cant. Judith	Cant. Jerem.	Cant. Isaias	Cant. Eccles.
	148	116	134	145	146	147	150
	117	23	24	25	22	21	93
Prime	118	18	24	51	71	21	93
	118	18	24	52	71	21	107

Arrangement of Pius X

Tierce	118	26	39	53	72	79	101
	118	26	39	54	72	79	101
	118	27	39	54	72	81	101
Sext	118	30	40	55	73	83	103
	118	30	41	56	73	83	103
	118	30	41	57	73	86	103
None	118	31	43	58	74	88	108
	118	32	43	58	75	88	108
	118	32	43	59	75	88	108
Vespers	109	114	122	127	132	138	143
	110	115	123	128	135	138	143
	111	119	124	129	135	139	144
	112	120	125	130	136	140	144
	113	121	126	131	137	141	144
Compline	4	6	11	33	69	76	87
	90	7	12	33	70	76	102
	133	7	15	60	70	85	102

Old arrangement

	Sunday		*Monday*	*Tuesday*	*Wednesday*	*Thursday*	*Friday*	*Saturday*
Matins	a)1	b)15	26	38	52	68	80	97
	2	16	27	39	54	69	81	98
	3	17	28	40	55	70	82	99
	6		29	41	56	71	83	100
	7		30	43	57	72	84	101
	8	c)18	31	44	58	73	85	102
	9	19	32	45	59	74	86	103
	10	20	33	46	60	75	87	104
	11		34	47	61	76	88	105
	12		35	48	63	77	93	106
	13		36	49	65	78	95	107
	14		37	51	67	79	96	108
Lauds	92		50	50	50	50	50	50
	99		5	42	64	89	142	91
	62		62	62	62	62	62	62
	66		66	66	66	66	66	66
	Cant. Bened.		*Cant. Isaias*	*Cant. Ezechias*	*Cant. Anna*	*Cant. Exod. 15*	*Cant. Habacuc*	*Cant. Deut. 32*
	148		148	148	148	148	148	148
	149		149	149	149	149	149	149
	150		150	150	150	150	150	150

Old Arrangement

	53	53	53	53	53	53	53
	117	23	24	25	22	21	118
Prime	118	118	118	118	118	118	118
	118	118	118	118	118	118	118
	118						
Tierce	118	same	same	same	same	same	same
	118						
	118						
Sext	118	same	same	same	same	same	same
	118						
	118						
None	118	same	same	same	same	same	same
	118						
	109	114	121	126	131	137	143
	110	115	122	127	132	138	144
Vespers	111	116	123	128	134	139	145
	112	119	124	129	135	140	146
	113	120	125	130	136	141	147
	4						
	30						
Compline	90	same	same	same	same	same	same
	133						

With the Bull which promulgated the new Breviary on November 11, 1911, Pius X announced a more ample revision of the Office sometime in the future. Unfortunately, his death prevented this. Pius XII, however, pushed the reform a bit further with the introduction into the Psalter, in 1945, of a new Latin translation of the psalms and, in 1955, a simplification of the rubrics of the Breviary and an effective shortening of its length. In the decree of simplification the special importance of Sunday was again emphasized by the fact that all Sundays were made doubles and those of Advent and Lent doubles of the first class. Most vigils and octaves were abolished. The rank of semi-double was suppressed; all feasts formerly of that rank are now simples, while all feasts formerly simples are now only commemorated. Thus the Office is much shorter, and the feria has once more come into its own. The ferias of Lent are given their rightful prominence in that whenever a feast falls on those days one has a choice of either the Office of the feria or of the feast. The number of commemorations has also been strictly limited—never more than two. The opening Pater, Ave, and Credo are abolished. All Preces are omitted except those of Lauds and Vespers of the ferial Office on Wednesdays and

Fridays of Advent and Lent and on Ember Days (except during the octave of Pentecost). Finally, the more frequent recitation of the entire Psalter is further guaranteed through the provision that in all feasts, except those of double of the first class, the psalms for the Little Hours are to be taken from the feria on which the feast falls.

7. Projected future reform

With this history behind us we are forced to admit that the Divine Office is a compromise between, papal, basilical, episcopal, parochial, and monastic worship. This can hardly be denied. And this fact is the root of our present difficulties: the compromise does not fully correspond to the exigencies of each of the above categories. The secular clergy are no longer monks. Their way of life is necessarily quite different. Neither is the parish church a cathedral—even less a Roman basilica. To attempt to force a type of worship proper to one set of circumstances on another is to doom the service to inevitable failure, because it is a misfit. And the end result of this procedure can be nothing less than that dreaded formalism: observing certain forms only because we have to do so, not because they really express our concrete spiritual condition or way of life.

Furthermore, the conditions of the parochial ministry have changed since the Middle Ages. The Church is no longer the absolute master and center of social life. In the Middle Ages she was able to set the pace and rhythm of human life; she can no longer pretend to anything of the kind. She has many competitors today: the cinema, the dance hall, the stadium, and television. Even the school, once the child of the Church, has developed quite independently of her rhythm of life. And the parish priest is torn between those things which are strictly sacerdotal and the endeavor to insert his guiding hand into the social institutions about him, either to Christianize them or to keep them Christian. And these apostolic labors place unavoidable demands on his time; much of the day—even till late hours of the night—finds him about his Father's business. It is extremely difficult, if not impossible, for a man of such activity to say each Hour of the Office at its proper time of the day. He usually finishes by having much or most of his Office to say late at night when the tardiness of the hour and the fatigue from the day's work are little conducive to long prayer.

Monasticism itself has changed considerably since the time of Benedict and Pachomius. Modern monks are neither hermits nor always or continuously cenobites. They often conduct schools, which must meet certain academic standards just as all other institutions of learning. They are also missionaries and parish priests. And even when they live in monasteries, Sundays find them going to the aid of pastors who must provide more Masses and facilities for confession

than he has priests to dispose of. What St. Benedict and the other
founders of monasticism once held to be true—that, since Sunday was
a day without work, the Office should be longer and more solemn—is
no longer entirely applicable. The monk, in other words, is no longer
exclusively dedicated to the contemplative life, but finds himself
drawn more and more into the feverish work of pastoral activity.

Contemporary pleas for a radical reform of the *pensum* and arrangement of the Office are founded, not on a spirit of relaxation but
upon the realization that we no longer live in the Middle Ages and
that the Office itself, as history shows, is a fusion of so many diverse
elements that it cannot fully express the spiritual life of all those
obliged to say it. The very practice of the medieval popes of bringing
monks to Rome to provide the solemn ceremonies of the basilicas
shows that it was impossible even then for the secular clergy, primarily involved in the care of souls, to accomplish this task. And it is
an unquestionable fact that the Roman Liturgy was never completely
accepted in any region outside of the province of Rome; when Roman
service books were transplanted to non-Roman soil they were inevi-
tably transformed by the recipients so as to be more applicable to
their circumstances.

It is even doubted by some whether any given form can ever be
suitable for all. However, a word of caution is in place here. Uniformity is good only so long as it does not do violence to the various
parts which it seeks to unify. But violence can hardly occur when
it is a question of the basic or minimum expression of ecclesiastical
prayer, for all must be truly Catholic. It is a different matter, however,
when we come to the maximum expression, for here racial traits,
institutional spirit, the exigencies of diverse apostolates—all these
factors and more come into play. And since these are legitimate considerations they must be respected or harm will result. But in all this
we must avoid two extremes: antiquarianism, or excessive attachment
to the past with no regard for the needs of the present; and a policy
of mere expediency with no respect for the tradition of the Church.

Both *Mediator Dei* and the reforms undertaken by Pius XII show
that this balanced approach is the mind of the Church. The Pope
says: "The Church is without question a living organism, and as an
organism, in respect to the sacred Liturgy also, she grows, matures,
develops, adapts and accommodates herself to the needs and circumstances of the times, provided only that the integrity of her doctrine
be kept intact. This notwithstanding, the temerity and daring of those
who deliberately introduce novel liturgical practices, or call for the
revival of obsolete rites inconsistent with existing laws and rubrics,
must be condemned." [172] In preceding paragraphs [173] the same Pope
shows that the Church did not hesitate to modify what she considered

---

[172] *Mediator Dei*, 59.
[173] *Ibid.*, 49-50.

did not give honor to God in the most fitting way or that did not instruct and stimulate the faithful to greatest advantage. He insists that the human components of the Liturgy admit of change as the needs of the age, circumstance, and the good of souls require. This is the reason, he points out, why in due time religious practices were introduced which were only faintly discernible in earlier periods of history, why some things were abolished, and why older customs were revived. From the teaching of Pius XII, then, it must be concluded that whatever reforms are undertaken they must always be faithful in taking into account both the pastoral needs of our day and the traditions of the past.

Three basic principles which must prevail in a reform of the Breviary are: (1) its nature as a prayer at *certain hours* must be restored and maintained, (2) its character as *public* prayer must be respected and (3) that certain Hours were instituted as the prayer, not of all, but of only special categories of the faithful ought to be kept in mind. Many excellent articles concerning Breviary reform have appeared in recent years; [174] let us summarize the more outstanding and realistic proposals.

History shows that Lauds and Vespers were the original liturgical Hours, intended as public morning and evening prayer in the church, even for the faithful. Let these, then, form the basis for the canonical Office for the secular clergy. They should be recited at determined times: Lauds preferably the very first thing in the morning before Mass, but at least sometime between five o'clock and noon; Vespers as a prayer beginning the evening hours, preferably before supper, but at least between five o'clock and eight o'clock. The Benedictus and Magnificat form the high point of these Hours and should remain that. The other psalms used at Vespers should be the Alleluia psalms —in general all those from 109 to 144, excluding 118—while those for Lauds should be taken from the Laudate psalms and others which speak of morning praise or the Kingship of God. While there seems to be no sufficient reason for changing the sequence of the elements in these Hours, perhaps the Capitulum could more profitably be a continuation of the readings begun at Matins or at least a repetition of their essential thoughts.

Sunday vigils were practiced on and off in various localities throughout the history of the Church. If this vigil was made principally a service of the word, consisting mainly of readings from the Old and New Testaments with patristic commentaries having fitting

[174] Besides the reports of two enquiries on this matter: *Lauda Jerusalem Dominum*, a special issue of *La Vie Spirituelle*, 76 (January, 1947), and that of A. Bugnini, "Per una riforma liturgica generale," *EL*, 63 (1949), 166-184, there are also the excellent essays of T. Klauser, "De ratione reformandi Breviarium Romanum," *EL*, 63 (1949), 406-411, and of P. Salmon, "Presuppositi storici di una riforma del Breviario," *EL*, 63 (1949) 412-418; see also the editorial comments on the latter, pp. 418-420.

biblical canticles dispersed among them (and if these readings had a genuine liturgical character to satisfy for the priest's obligation to recite Matins), it would be a useful means of giving the faithful a genuine love of Scripture and helping them weave it into the make-up of their life. It seems impractical to hold such "vigils" in the middle of the night, but the Saturday evening hours do not present the same difficulty. Perhaps they could be held simultaneously with the hearing of confessions on Saturday evening, and thus the people would be exposed to their salutary influence. It would be important, of course, to emphasize their character as a weekly echo of the chief vigil of the year, that of Easter.

As for Matins during the rest of the week, which presumably the cleric (and others who are willing) will recite in private, the length of this Hour ought to be reduced to at most a half-hour. It should always be anticipated and recited sometime between noon and midnight. It is to be hoped that its primitive character as a *lectio divina* will be restored.[175] Like the public vigil, it should consist mainly of biblical readings and patristic commentaries, accompanied by suitable, but few, canticles. This would be the priest's real spiritual reading for the day.

After all, the priest needs a substantial period of spiritual reading each day. Often such a period is devoted to modern works of definitely second-rate quality. Why not bring him back to Scripture and the Fathers? If these were offered him in his own language, and if the readings were well chosen—over a period of from two to four years— from the point of view of the spiritual life and the divine plan of salvation, it would be of profound benefit for spirituality. Perhaps one psalm could be recited as an introduction to this reading, and still others could be used as background for meditations on the readings. In all, there might be three readings: one from the Old Testament, another from the New (parallel passages always to be used, preferably), a third from a patristic commentary on the first two. These patristic homilies, however, ought to be of use for the spiritual life, not simply a cold exegesis of Scripture. Since it is hoped that the feasts of the saints will be radically restricted to local celebration (the universal calendar would contain only those feasts of truly universal significance), the lives of the saints would be read only rarely, as the third lesson, and would contain only what meets the requirements of true hagiography and what is especially characteristic of their sanctity. If the reading of Holy Scripture as the principal and proper content of Matins is to be insured, it is desirable that all other formulas of little or no import be dropped (absolutions, bless-

---

[175] This was excellently brought out by J. Jungmann, "Die Psalmodie als Vorstufen in den Horen" and "Der Umfang der Lesungen im Offizium," *Zeitschrift für katholische Theologie*, 72 (1950), 223-234.

ings); the psalms, as mentioned above, being used, for the sake of variety, as introduction and meditation in between readings.

Historically, the rest of the Hours are proper to monasticism. They cannot be recited by the active clergy at the prescribed times. Accordingly, three suggestions have been made: either (a) have the obligation to recite them cease when they cannot be recited at their proper times because of apostolic duty, or (b) let them be omitted entirely by those who are not monks, or (c) let them be reduced to a mere Pater,[176] or to the hymns presently in use at these Hours, or to a very brief psalm, all of which, taken singly, can be recited at the determined hours and in any place, for they can be easily memorized.

The hymns used at Lauds and Vespers might very profitably return to their original text before the "correction" made by Urban VIII. They ought always to have as their theme the idea of morning and evening praise. Our present hymns for the ferial Office actually have this theme, but they are seldom used because of the occurrence of so many festal Offices. This situation could be remedied, were such proper hymns limited to very special feasts only and the hymns assigned to various ferias used for all other feasts.

The suggestion has also been made that the antiphons be recited in their entirety before as well as after the psalms. It is to be hoped that in any future reform they will be brief and their chant very simple so that even the faithful can sing them, using them as a responsorial refrain. They should likewise express the topical idea of the psalms they accompany, so that their use will explain clearly the meaning of the psalm. Antiphons proper to a feast would, of course, be quite rare, being limited to feasts of the highest rank.

An abbreviation of the Office can hardly be accomplished if it is insisted upon that the entire Psalter be recited every week. Hence, various suggestions have been made concerning a redistribution of the psalms. Perhaps the long established practice in the Ambrosian Rite of reciting the Psalter every two weeks might be worth trying. To recite the entire Psalter every week is of monastic origin and, unfortunately is more a question of quantity than quality. Not all psalms have the same value of nourishing the spiritual life or of helping the soul in its praise of God. Why not choose the psalms most appropriate for the purposes of Matins, Lauds, and Vespers over a period of a week or two and use the rest just as we do other books of the Bible— as readings? Or perhaps the psalms, still in keeping with the *rationale* of Matins, Lauds, and Vespers, could be chosen according to the changing seasons of the liturgical year.

Regardless of the details that will be decided upon in any future reform, the fundamental principle behind it will unquestionably be the nature of the Office as a prayer for well-defined hours of the day. It is most important to avoid reciting several Hours of the Office

176 Going back to the tradition of Book 8 of the *Didache*.

together, for this violates their purpose, their role in our spiritual day, and thus kills their meaning and the spirit of prayer. The integrity of the Office as functional prayer will be facilitated if a clear distinction is kept in mind between the secular and the monastic Office. It is not at all contrary to the spirit of unity for each way of life within the Church to have its own type of Office. This desire to accommodate the needs and exigencies of various cultural groups has always been regarded as quite legitimate in the matter of distinction of Rites within the Church (Oriental, Roman, Ambrosian, etc.). Why not also in the case of different walks of life?

Such a solution could be reached if more power were granted to local Ordinaries and the major Superiors of religious institutes to regulate the length of the Office for their respective subjects within well-defined limits. This was the practice of the past. True, certain drawbacks are inherent in such a procedure; this has also been proven by the past history of the Office. However, any difficulties in this regard could be avoided if, once the initiative were taken by local authority, individual plans were then submitted to the Holy See for *final* approval. This would afford the various institutions within the Church more opportunity for self-expression and at the same time give the highest authority of the Church the prerogative of safeguarding and maintaining the general pattern of ecclesiastical prayer. It would be expected, for example, that the Holy See determine the over-all schema of the various Hours of the Office, but bishops and religious superiors could then suggest what their subjects, the intensity and type of their work being taken into consideration, could prayerfully and meaningfully accomplish. It might also be a good thing were bishops and superiors granted the authority to dispense from the obligation of the Office or even to change the texts of the Office *per modum actus,* i.e., on given occasions and for special reasons.

Such a solution, it would seem, should result in a higher calibre of prayer. It should also serve to undo the supposed opposition between liturgical and private prayer, for the prayer we have been describing would at once be liturgical, prayed in the name of the entire Church, and also more personalized, corresponding more immediately to the character and needs of the faithful. And it would certainly go a long way towards reducing the danger of formalism.

C. Individual Hours of the Office

1. Matins

The name Matins for the first Hour of the Office seems to date back to the twelfth century. It was then that clerics began to chant this Hour later in the morning. Until that time it was called the Vigil, being celebrated during the night, while the name Matins formerly designated our present Lauds, which were the first prayer of the morning.

Though, as we have seen, early references to the Vigils are scarce and vague, once the Church was able to elaborate her system of official worship, the Vigil changed from a purely private practice of praying during the middle of the night to an all-night service of prayer and reading called the *Pannuchis* (Greek for "all night"). The Easter Vigil seems to come close to the original type except for the comparative brevity of the present-day Vigil. Such all-night Vigils were mainly services given over to the word of God, the reading of which was interrupted by occasional chants and orations. From only an occasional service (for anniversaries of martyrs, and more important feasts), the Vigil was extended to every Sunday in some localities, and monasticism made it a daily affair.

Since the Easter Vigil seems to have been the prototype of the Sunday Vigil, it is to the former that we must look for the underlying meaning. Though the Easter Vigil was commemorative of the night of the Resurrection, according to St. Augustine,[177] it also looked to the future. It was filled with the live expectancy of the Parousia, Christ's second coming: "Let your loins be girt about and your lamps burning, and you yourselves like men waiting for their master's return from the wedding; so that when he comes and knocks, they may straightway open to him. Blessed are those servants whom the master, upon his return, shall find watching. . . .You also must be ready, because at an hour that you do not expect, the Son of Man is coming." [178] As Lactantius says, "This is the night which we celebrate with a nightlong vigil because of the coming of our God and King. This night has a twofold significance: in it Christ received life after dying, and in the future He will come into possession of the kingdom of the whole earth." [179] And Jerome, after him, connects this holy expectation with that of the Jews as they celebrated their Passover. The Messiah, they believed, was to come to deliver them while they were observing the night of the Pasch. For this same reason, the Christians "held fast to a tradition of apostolic origin, that during the Easter Vigil no one was to leave before midnight, for all awaited the coming of Christ. But after the middle of the night, when they felt sure that He would not come, they were then to celebrate the feast." [180]

Since Sunday was considered a weekly celebration of the Resur-

[177] "We observe the night in which our Lord arose by watching; we contemplate that life in which there is no death nor sleep, and which Christ began for us in His own flesh by raising it from the dead . . . Nor is it incongruous for us thus to stay awake in vigil, for He slept that we might remain awake, He who died that we might live." *Sermo* 221. MPL, 38: 1090.

[178] Luke 12: 35-40.

[179] *De div. insti.,* 7, 19. MPL, 6: 796.

[180] *Comm. in evang. Matt.,* 25, 6. MPL, 26:192. The Gospel text upon which he is commenting is: "Behold, the bridegroom cometh. Go ye forth to meet him!"

rection,[181] the same mystical considerations must lie at the root of the Sunday Vigil. The Church and the Christian are essentially *in via ad Patrem*; they must always wait in holy and anxious expectation for the coming of their Deliverer, the Bridegroom who shall usher in the Day of eternal spring! And the monks pushed this idea to its ultimate ascetical application by means of a vigil every night.

Matins of the Divine Office, then, come undoubtedly from the ancient vigil services, although our modern Hour is a mixture of the public church service and the private devotions performed at home during the night.[182] It is a distinct Hour of the Office and not, as J. Hanssens would have it, simply an elongated introduction to Lauds.[183] Even St. Benedict, who had so much to do in the formation of the Roman Office, indicates in his *Regula* [184] a pause between Matins and Lauds. It was only with the twelfth century practice of delaying the recitation of Matins till later in the morning that there necessarily resulted the grouping together of Matins and Lauds. Once this had become habitual in private recitation, it was only to be expected that Lauds would be transplanted along with Matins, when in the sixteenth century the latter were anticipated the evening or afternoon before—a custom which does utter violence to the meaning and function of Lauds, a morning prayer.

The component parts of Matins are an introduction or invitatory, and, on feast days, three nocturns consisting of three psalms, three lessons, and three responsories, the last followed by the Te Deum. On ferias there is only one nocturn consisting of nine psalms and three lessons with their responsories. The invitatory psalm is certainly not a primitive feature of the Office; it is lacking even in some of the late Ordinals, and even today it does not figure in Matins of the last three days of Holy Week. We find it first mentioned, at least in the West, by St. Benedict.[185] The recitation of the psalms in their numerical order comes from monasticism, while the oldest component of Matins is the biblical reading.[186] The reading is by far the more important thing, the psalms playing the role of a preparation for that reading

---

[181] The Gospel of the Resurrection was read every Sunday at Matins by the Bishop of Jerusalem: *Ethérie, Journal de Voyage* (Edit. H. Pétré), n. 43, p. 246; n. 44, p. 252. For a detailed discussion of this relationship between Easter and Sunday and their vigils cf. J. Miller, "The Easter Vigil: Climax of the Week and the Year," *Proceedings of the North American Liturgical Week of 1956* (Elsberry, Missouri, 1957), 132-145.

[182] Cf. the profound work of A. Baumstark, *Nocturna Laus. Typen frühchristlicher Vigilienfeier und ihr Fortleben vor allem im römischen und monastischen Ritus.* Münster, 1957.

[183] *Nature et Genèse de l' Office des Matines.* Rome: Gregorian University 1952.

[184] VIII. Holstenius, II, 24-25.

[185] *Regula*, IX. Holstenius, II, 25.

[186] Cf. J. Jungmann, "Die Psalmodie als Vorstufe in den Horen" and "Der Umfang der Lesungen im Offizium," *Zeitschrift für katholische Theologie*, 72 (1950), 223-234.

together with its accompanying responsories. All of this reaches its climax in the oration.

2. Lauds

The name Lauds comes from the Laudate psalms which always conclude this Hour. The ancient name for this part of the Office was Laudes matutinae, or simply Matutinum, which brings out the function of the Hour and points to the correct time for reciting it. Here is the morning prayer of the Church, her first service of praise as the sun begins to rise. While it is understandable that we often anticipate Matins the afternoon or evening of the preceding day, it is better not to do so with Lauds. For such a practice really runs counter to the meaning of the psalms of Lauds. The Church wants the new day begun with songs of praise to Christ the King, the Sun of Justice, in honor of His Resurrection, symbolized by the rising sun. This is the Church's "morning offering."

Lauds and Vespers were the first Hours of the Office to receive a liturgical character. They were the kernel from which the other Hours gradually evolved. And from the beginning Lauds and Vespers took on a public and popular form, intended as they were to be the official morning and evening prayer of the entire community. To fulfill this purpose, unlike Matins and the other Hours (with the exception of Compline), they were provided with special psalms chosen for their connection with the time of the day or their portrayal of the kingship and triumph of Christ. And accordingly, they are usually characterized, when sung in choir, by a more solemn and impressive ceremonial.

In Lauds we find five psalms, the fourth of which is an Old Testament canticle; a short reading from Scripture called the *Capitulum;* a metrical hymn (instead of a responsory); a versicle and response; the Benedictus with its antiphon; and a concluding oration. The psalms, again, are a less ancient feature, but what follows upon the psalms belongs to the typical arrangement of all the Hours: *reading, song* (a hymn in the case of Lauds and Vespers, a responsory for all other Hours), and *prayer.*

Particularly noteworthy is the climactic disposition of the psalms for Lauds. Let us take the psalms for Sunday Lauds as an instance. In Psalm 92 we praise God first as King and Lord of creation. Then in Psalm 99 we turn to a consideration of Him as having dominion over man, the greatest of God's creatures here below, and we speak of those attributes of God which have special meaning from man's point of view: mercy and fidelity. With Psalm 62 we let the human soul speak its ardent longing for God. Then, with the realization that we are limited in our ability to praise God as we ought, we invite, in the Benedicite and Psalm 148, the rest of creation to join with us in praising the Creator and King—first the material creation about us in the Benedicite, then the creation above us, the angels and heavenly bodies, in Psalm 148.

In the last psalm we mention the law which God has made, and this serves as a transition to the Capitulum—an excerpt from His law, His message to mankind. The metrical quality of the hymn aids the people in singing of their passing from darkness to light, from death to life, from slumber to wakefulness. And both the Capitulum and the hymn provide an opportunity on feast days to bring in the theme of the festal celebration. Lauds reaches its climax in the Benedictus, which once more allows us to use the passing of night into the brightness of day as a symbol of the triumphant rising of the Sun of Justice from death and with Him our own passage from the death of sin to the life and light of grace: the "Oriens ex alto, illuminare his qui in tenebris et in umbra mortis sedent!" Thus the Church ushers in the new day, consecrates it to the glory of God and reminds us to walk as children of light, reborn in grace through the victory of Christ over sin and death.

3. The Little Hours

The primitive root of the Hours of Tierce, Sext and None was the ancient practice of the so-called Apostolic prayers. In imitation of the prayer of the Apostles at the third, sixth, and ninth hours, the faithful were urged to recollect themselves and renew themselves in the spirit of prayer. And the custom of reciting the Pater three times a day, as recorded in the *Didache*,[187] may have been a reflection of the earlier Apostolic practice. But it was left to monasticism to make of these prayer-times formal liturgical periods of prayer.

Unlike Lauds and Vespers, these Hours begin straightway with a hymn, which gives them their special connection with the times of the day at which they are recited. At Tierce the descent of the Holy Spirit upon the Apostles is recalled: courage in the profession of faith and an increase of charity are requested. At Sext the sun at its zenith is taken account of, and God, who moderates all the changes of heat and light, is asked to temper the heat of human passion. Finally, at None we notice that the sun has already begun to decline, and we connect this with our own decline in death and beg of God the grace of a holy death, the reward of perseverance in good works. The remaining parts of these Hours follow the usual schema: psalmody, reading, responsory, and prayer. The psalms, however, are taken in their biblical order without special attention to the time of day or the theme of the feast.

We saw that the youngest of the Little Hours, Prime, was first spoken of by Cassian in his description of the canonical Hours of the

[187] VIII. *Ancient Christian Writers,* 6, p. 19.

monks in Bethlehem.[188] And St. Benedict includes it in his cursus. But in the eighth century it receives an addition at the hands of Chrode-gang of Metz, or at least the addition is recorded by him for the first time.[189] While the *officium chori*, a regular office of prayer existed from the time of its institution in the monastery of Bethlehem, now it is lengthened to include an *officium capituli*, or a monastic chapter meeting. The latter includes the reading of the martyrology, the distri-bution of the day's work, a reading of a chapter of the Rule (for us, to-day, of Scripture) and the blessing by the Abbot. It was also a normal thing for the Abbot to speak a few words of commentary on the por-tion of the Rule read during this chapter. The practice of distributing the work to the monks during this chapter actually gave this Hour its specific meaning and significance, which is beautifully expressed in the opening hymn: it is a consecration of the day's work and ac-tivity. The history of the Hour indicates, then, that it is a duplication of Lauds and is proper to the monastic life.

4. Vespers

Vespers are the official evening prayer of the Church, said at the moment when darkness approaches and the evening star, Vesper, appears in the heavens. A perfectly correct English name for this Hour would be Evensong. It is neither an afternoon nor a night Hour, but one which coincides with the waning of daylight and the cessation of work. Formerly, because of the failing light, candles and lamps had to be lighted, and so we often find this evening prayer called the Lucernarium in the early Church.

Just as Lauds made use of such a natural thing as light and turned it into a symbol of Christ, so Vespers see in the evening lamps a figure of the *Lumen Christi*, the light that never wanes.[190] The Lu-cernarium made the most of the natural need for candles and lamps in the evening and afforded an opportunity of giving thanks for the blessings of the day and of consecrating the evening hours to Christ, the source of light. This is the origin of the beautiful ceremonies con-cerned with the blessing of the Paschal Candle at the beginning of the Easter Vigil. In the early Church, whenever an all-night vigil, a *Pannuchis*, was held, it would begin with Vespers or the Lucernarium, of which the blessing of the candles was a prominent part. The Easter Vigil was the chief of such *Pannuchis* and today is the only occasion on which we find a remnant of this rite.

This ceremony of illuminating the church was often referred to as the *Eucharistia lucernaris*, for the lamps were lighted and blessed as the head of the liturgical assembly pronounced a beautiful prayer

---

[188] *De insti. coenob.*, III, 4. *MPL*, 49: 127-130.
[189] *Regula Canonicorum*, 18. *MPL*, 89: 1067-1068.
[190] Cf. F-J. Dölger, "Lumen Christi," *Antike und Christentum*, 5 (1936), 1-43.

of thanksgiving bearing the same structure as the Preface of the Mass. In the *Apostolic Tradition* of Hippolytus we find an excellent example of this prayer:

> When evening is come, let the deacon bring forth a lamp. The bishop, standing in the midst of the faithful, offers thanks, saying: "The Lord be with you." The people answer, "And with thy spirit." The bishop: "Let us give thanks to the Lord." The people: "It is right and just." The bishop then continues: "We give Thee thanks, O God, through Thy Son, Jesus Christ, our Lord, that Thou hast enlightened us, giving us an incorruptible light. We have brought the day to an end and have come to the beginning of the night. Filled as we have been with the brightness of day which Thou hast created for our satisfaction, even now do we not lack illumination for the night. Therefore we sanctify Thee, we glorify Thee through Thine only Son, our Lord, Jesus Christ, through Whom and with the Holy Spirit Thine is the glory, the power and the honor now and forever." The people answer, "Amen." [191]

We find these same basic thoughts expressed in the *Praeconium Paschale,* sung before the Paschal Candle during the Easter Vigil.

The Lucernarium, however, was not exactly identical with Vespers; it was only the preliminary. And this is brought out very well in the same chapter of the *Apostolic Tradition* which we have just quoted. After supper (this was an Agape) the deacon rises and takes some bread and the chalice which contains wine—an oblation in *imitation* of the Holy Eucharist—and recites some of the Alleluia psalms, those psalms which even today constitute the bulk of our Vesper psalms. Etheria also describes the service of Vespers with a preliminary Lucernarium in Jerusalem. At the tenth hour (about 4:00 P.M.) a great multitude has already assembled at the Anastasis. The service begins with what is called in Jerusalem the *licinicon* (Greek for Lucernarium). All the lights and candles are lighted to make a *lumen infinitum.* For this a light is brought forth from inside the Holy Sepulcher. And while the lamps are lighted with this fire a great number of psalms and antiphons are sung. When the bishop finally comes with his clergy, more hymns and antiphons are sung—the second part of the service evidently—after which follow the commemorations of all the faithful, the prayer of the bishop and the final blessings.[192] And this same distinction between Lucernarium and Vespers appears over and over again.[193]

In addition to the lighting and blessing of the evening lamps, a ceremony which is ultimately derived from the Jewish practice of the

[191] *La Tradition Apostolique* (Edit. B. Botte), n. 26, p. 61.
[192] *Ethérie, Journal de Voyage* (Edit. H. Pétré), n. 24, pp. 190-192.
[193] E.g., Aurelian, *Regula, Ordo psallendi.* Holstenius, II, 112.

same sort at the close of the Sabbath feast, incense was also offered; this was suggested by the traditional Vesper Psalm 140: "Dirigatur, Domine, oratio mea sicut incensum in conspectu tuo; elevatio manuum mearum sacrificium vespertinum." Such a use of incense was likewise part of the Jewish ritual, for in the evening was celebrated the hour of incense.[194] But, it would seem, it took quite a long time for incense to be introduced into the Church's Vespers. Amalar is the first to mention the practice.[195] He says that incense was offered during the recitation of the above verses of Psalm 140, whereas now this is done during the singing of the Magnificat.

The Fathers liked to see in Psalm 140 an image of the crucified Redeemer who at the hour of evening sacrifice of incense in the Temple stretched out His arms on the cross of Calvary and thus celebrated the first Vespers of the New Law. The burning and sweet-smelling evening incense was for them a symbol of the sacrifice of Calvary where the Pontiff of the New Covenant offered up His first oblation like incense in the sight of God.[196] It was at approximately the same hour that our Lord ate the Last Supper with His disciples. It was, then, the thought of the first Eucharistic Sacrifice and that of the cross which dominated the Vesper rite. It was aptly called, therefore, the *Eucharistia lucernalis,* for both the Hour and the prayers of thanksgiving spoken during it commemorated the sacrifice of the Lord: for the Church this was truly an evening sacrifice of light, incense, and thanksgiving.[197]

Thus originally Vespers comprised three phases: (a) the Lucernarium, (b) the evening Agape meal, (c) the chanting of psalms and antiphons and sometimes a sermon. First the Agape fell into disuse. Then the Lucernarium (still part of the Easter Vigil) gradually became fused with the third phase and, in Gallican lands, replaced by the offering of incense. Yet the themes proper to all these elements still can be found. Vespers are still imbued with the spirit of the Eucharist, whose heaven-ward glorification it prolongs amid strains of thanksgiving, praise, and the aroma of incense; it celebrates the triumph of divine sacrificial love, rejoicing with gratitude and humility (the Alleluia psalms and the Magnificat) over the redemption of liberty, life, and light thus acquired, even as it recalls *magna opera Domini,* the *justitia, fidelitas,* the *divitiae* and *munificentia* and *misericordia*—all combined in the glorious *nomen* of the great and victorious King who can and has done all things, *quaecumque voluit fecit* (Pss. 109-144).

The arrangement of the content of Vespers is the same as that of Lauds. However, coming as they do midway between the day and

[194] Luke 1:8-10; Exodus 30:8.
[195] *De eccl. off.,* IV, 7. *MPL,* 105: 1181.
[196] See I. Schuster, *The Sacramentary,* II, 255.
[197] *Ibid.,* 245.

night Hours, Vespers can have a festal theme of the occurring day or of the following day, if the solemnity of the latter is such that an anticipation of it is desired. Thus arises the possibility of first and second Vespers. First Vespers—that is, those celebrated on the evening preceding a feast—seem to have received the greater emphasis for many centuries. But the question of which service was the original Vesper observance is controverted. J. Jungmann and J. Brinktrine consider first Vespers to be more primitive,[198] while J. Pascher brings forth solid and cogent arguments in favor of second Vespers as the original Roman Office.[199] In point of fact, the recent decree simplifying the Divine Office follows the second view by providing only Sundays and feasts of the first and second class with first Vespers.

5. Compline

Vespers is an evening prayer, Compline a night prayer, one intended for retiring. Its very name in Latin, *Completorium*, indicates this. And, again unlike Vespers, Compline is of monastic origin. The first time we hear of this prayer period is in Cassian's account of monastic practices of his day. He tells us that the Oriental monks were accustomed to gather in their dormitory on Sunday nights and sing a few psalms before retiring.[200] And in the Rule of Aurelian we are told that, when the monks were about to go to bed, they recited Psalm 90 and Preces.[201]

Compline is made up of two distinct parts. The first consists of a period of spiritual reading, and the second is dedicated to prayers for the night's rest. We meet this practice of spiritual reading for the first time in the Rule of St. Benedict, who prescribes, not the short lesson we recite today, which was inserted into the Roman Breviary with the reform of Pius V, but four or five pages of the "collationes et vitas patrum." [202] It was also the custom in some monasteries, to judge from the Rule of St. Fructuosus,[203] for the monks to accuse themselves of the faults committed during the day and to receive an absolution before chanting the three psalms of Compline. The monastic quality of these customs was recognized clearly for a long time; even after

---

[198] Jungmann, *Der Gottesdienst der Kirche*, 195; Brinktrine, *Das römische Brevier* (Paderborn, 1932), 97 ff. It is noteworthy, however, that in the English edition of his work, *Public Worship — A Survey* (Collegeville, 1957), 175, Jungmann has changed his opinion. He admits that the emphasis on first Vespers appeared for the first time in the Gallican Liturgy, but that in the older Roman tradition there was an emphasis on second Vespers.

[199] *Das Stundengebet der römischen Kirche*, 163-170. And more recently V. Raffa has again examined the problem and likewise concluded to second Vespers as the more primitive in the Roman Rite: "Più antichi i primi o i secondi Vesperi?" *EL*, 69 (1955), 313-335.

[200] *De insti. coenob.*, IV, 19. *MPL*, 49: 179.

[201] *Regula, Ordo psallendi*. Holstenius, II, 112.

[202] *Regula*, 42. Holstenius, II, 43.

[203] *Regula*, 2. Holstenius, II, 232.

Compline was accepted by seculars, the introductory reading and accusation were left out—and this as late as Durandus' time, in the thirteenth century.[204]

The second part of the Hour consists of the regular choral Office of three psalms, a hymn, a lesson and a responsory, the Nunc dimittis, an oration, and a final blessing. Benedict indicates that Pss. 4, 90 and 133 were sung daily; a hymn, lesson and responsory were also contained in his Rule. Most authors also believe that the Nunc dimittis was already a part of the Hour in Gregory the Great's time. All of the elements of this second part of Compline speak of confidence in God, ask His help and protection during the night. The basis for the confidence we have in God is given in the lesson in a particularly striking fashion: God is in us, and we are called by His Name, meaning that we are His children, He our Father. With perfect trust, we place ourselves in His hands, thanking Him once again for all His graces, the salvation which we saw coming to us from His bounty during the day.

D. *Excursus:* The Little Office of the Blessed Virgin and The Office of the Dead

It was out of the extraordinary devotion of monks in the Middle Ages that the Little Office of the Blessed Virgin arose. The long hours spent at the recitation of the Divine Office were not enough for them. During the Middle Ages we notice the trend to add to the Office. Some of these additions were the penitential psalms, the gradual psalms, litanies, and all sorts of votive Offices—one, several, or all of them recited after the Divine Office. The Little Office of the Blessed Virgin was only one of them. Cardinal Bona wrote that he had found a manuscript penned by Peter the Deacon, a monk of Monte Cassino, which stated that Pope Gregory II (d. 731) had composed this Office, and that Pope Zachary (d. 752), when he lived in the above monastery imposed its recitation on the monks there.[205] However, a statement in the *Liber Pontificalis* [206] to the effect that it was Pope Gregory III (d. 741) who made its recitation obligatory on the monks of the monasteries located near St. Peter's Basilica, makes Bäumer suspicious of the authenticity of Peter the Deacon's testimony. At any rate, we find Bernerius, Provost of the Cathedral of Verdun two centuries later, daily reciting such an Office in Mary's honor.[207] St. Ulrich, Bishop of Augsburg (d. 973), pursued a similar practice.[208] Later, a little before 1072, St. Peter Damian corrected and reorganized the Office. This daily Office spread from monasteries even to secular churches, and by the twelfth century it was already very general.

---

[204] *Rationale divinorum officiorum*, V, 10, 6. M. Righetti, II, 600.
[205] *De divina psalmodia*, XII, 2. Bäumer, I, 375.
[206] I, 422.
[207] Lechner-Eisenhofer, *Liturgik des römischen Ritus*, 370.
[208] See text from his life in Bäumer, I, 376.

Pius V put an end to any general obligation in this matter and limited the obligation only to certain monastic groups. Finally Pius X lifted even this duty. Since then it is simply a supererogatory devotion—one often practiced by congregations of Brothers or Sisters founded since the Reformation.

The origins of the Office of the Dead, according to C. Callewaert,[209] go back to at least the end of the seventh century and may even antedate the reign of Gregory the Great. Such a conclusion is based on the fact that the Office is purely Roman in the arrangement of its psalms and lacks all trace of monastic and Gallican elements: introductory prayers, hymns, little chapter, final doxology after each psalm. Its schema is practically the same as the Office for the last three days of Holy Week, itself very primitive. Amalar supports the purely Roman origin of the Office when he states that it was contained in the very first liturgical books to be introduced into Gaul from Rome.[210] He goes on to say that this Office was celebrated on the third, seventh, and thirtieth day after death and on the anniversary, but not on the eve of the burial.[211] In its original form it comprised only Matins, Lauds, and Vespers; except in a few localities, the Little Hours were not added until the time of Pius X. Like the Office of the Blessed Virgin during the Middle Ages, this Office was said frequently in addition to the Divine Office. But Pius V abolished all obligation in this regard, leaving, however, a twofold Office for the feast of All Souls. Finally, Pius X made the Office of the Dead the regular Office for November 2 and thus did away with this duplication.

[209] "De Officio Mortuorum," *Sacris Erudiri* (Steenbrugge, 1940), 169 ff.
[210] *De eccl. off.*, IV, 41-42. *MPL*, 105: 1237-1240.
[211] Cf. also the *Ordo of St. Riquier* edited by E. Bishop, *Liturgica Historica*, 328.

CHAPTER EIGHT

The Liturgical Year

Just as the Divine Office was especially designed by the Church to give each hour of the day its own consecration, so a system of feasts and cycles has been instituted to bring each season of the year the hallowing grace of Christ the Redeemer. And as we celebrate these holy times, we are afforded the opportunity of calling to mind the various mysteries of Christ and of taking part in them "so that the Divine Head of the Mystical Body may live in all of us with the fulness of His holiness." [1] If, as St. Augustine says, "the perfection of religion is to imitate him whom we adore," [2] then it will be of great help to the spiritual life to know the true meaning of the method used by the Church above all others to configure us ever more intimately to the likeness of Christ through a participation in the grace of His mysteries.

A. The Theology of the Liturgical Year

1. The Christian meaning of time

Since the coming of Christ, time has a Christian meaning. It is not simply the measure of *prius et posterius*, nor even less the tick-tock of the clock. As the inch on the ruler does not exhaust the mysteries of space, so the minute cannot disclose the full significance of time. Time is indeed measured, yet it transcends any measure. Time is colored by the way we look at it. For one it will mean the daily routine of punching the clock, for another the clatter of dishes, for the young the endless drudgery of pushing off to school early in the morning, and for the teacher the never diminishing stacks of class-work to correct. But for all its humdrum monotony it has its special religious meaning: one for the ancient pagan, one for the modern pagan, still another for the thinking Christian.

Time is forever changing and yet remains the same. Minute succeeds minute, and hour follows upon hour. Yet they all go to make

---

[1] *Mediator Dei,* 152.
[2] *De civitate Dei,* 8, 17. *MPL,* 41: 242.

up regularly recurring periods of days, weeks, months, and years. And
life, too, the progress of which is thus counted out, is really the same.
It is the same rise and fall of the sun, the same awakening and falling
asleep—together with the work and repose that accompany both.
There is the same death and rebirth of nature's vegetative life. And
so, though minutes fly quickly by, they simply count out the coming
and going of identical natural phenomena.

We mechanical moderns tend to lose sight of the sameness in
time for all our preoccupation with clock-watching and minute-count-
ing. We are inclined to look upon time as an unending straight line
which one day will break off abruptly. The ancients lived closer to
nature; they stood within its cycle of waning and reviving life. Because
of this they looked upon the year as a circle. Hence the expression:
anni circulum, the circle of the year. For them time was a circular
movement which returned upon its own beginnings and within which
all the marvelous feats of nature were constantly being worked anew.

Both conceptions can have a fatalistic ring, however: man might
possibly be going nowhere. Man could either be living a totally dis-
connected life, or be going around in circles. Time, in reality, is quite
different: it has purpose, it is headed somewhere, even though in circular fashion. Man living in time has an end, a supernatural end,
which crowns and rewards his earthly life. For this reason, it would
be better to conceive of time as a spiral movement—circular but going
always higher until it brings man to God.

It is with Christ, of course, that the ancient circular concept of
time becomes definitively a spiral one, for He stands at the end of
man's past and effectively joins to it the hope of a glorious future. As
one from outside of time, He lived in time, worked in time, died in
time, in order to bring man from time to eternity. "Jesus Christ, yester-
day, today, and the same forever." [3] Like an ever constant present,
Christ gradually reshapes man in the course of his cyclic natural life
from what he was to what his Designer wants him to be.

Thus Christ has sanctified time, making it a symbol or sacramental
of spiritual regeneration, growth, and maturity. [4] Using the natural
rhythm of the "circle of the year," Christianity, urged on by the *magnum mysterium* of redemption, has constructed a system of feasts and
seasons to insert that mystery into man's life. And man, in turn, is
thus gradually caught up into the current of Christ's life and bit by
bit transfigured into His likeness. Come once into time, Christ is continued in time, uses time, gives time a power of sanctification that
makes man live for himself the great wonders of redemption wrought
by Christ long ago.

What is true of time is also true of the spiritual life of man. It is

[3] Hebr. 13:8.
[4] See the beautiful article of Odo Casel, "Le sens chrétien du temps," *La
Vie Spirituelle*, 76 (January, 1947), 18-26.

always changing and yet remains the same. It is the same life of Christ that finds myriad concretizations as different men absorb and apply it to themselves according to their daily changing dispositions. And the liturgical year takes this into account as it changes, during the course of the natural seasons, the aspect under which it presents the mystery of Christ to men. This is important, for in the spiritual life there are no plateaus: man must either advance or retreat; he cannot remain static. And the annually recurring mysteries of Christ's life force him to take another step, make him change pace, give him reason to try harder to climb the spiral of a supernaturalized time that leads him to likeness with Christ.

Even though all days are holy since the coming of Christ, there are, nevertheless, certain days which are pre-eminently holy, special days which heighten man's attention to Christ and the spiritual life and thus keep him free of that killer of true devotion, routine. That such holy days are a real need in the spiritual life is well attested to by the universal practice of all religions, both natural and revealed. This is a need that corresponds to the time-rhythm of human life. Man cannot live in a rut; neither can he always live on the excitement of quickened emotion. He has ups and downs in his personal dispositions. This is his human condition, and the liturgical year, with its changing seasons and more outstanding solemnities, is especially well suited to provide for it.

2. Notion of a Christian feast

While it is all very good and important to insist on the "natural-ness" of the liturgical year, it is no less necessary to bring out its other-worldly character, its supernaturalness. Christianity is not just another form of religious naturalism. It rests on the solid conviction that man, left to himself, can in no way lift himself out of his human condition. He may contrive to improve society, reform customs, invent devices that make life more pleasurable. But man will be deceived if he thinks his empire is not purely human—and mortal. He has neither a higher objective nor the power to achieve it. Both must come from God. Christianity is a supernatural religion based on a supernatural event that left man transfigured and redeemed. Though the Church has conscientiously endeavored to adopt in her worship the seasons of the natural year as well as the solemn occasions of civil society, she has done this, not because these institutions were of themselves sacred, but in order to make them sacred and thus the more easily to sanctify man who uses them. Every feast of the Church is a com-memoration of a *supernatural* event that happened among men to transform men into God. It is the work of redemption that the Church brings to man and inserts into the orbit of time which man uses and in which he lives.

And yet today we often get the impression that particular feasts are celebrated purely in honor of this or that saint. This is simply not true. Regardless of the immediate title of a feast, it is always celebrated as leading to or flowing from the central mystery of our religion, Christ's act of redemption. "Among all the feasts held sacred by Christian devotion," St. Leo tells us, "none is more excellent than the paschal feast. All other solemnities of God's Church find their dignity consecrated in it." [5] Easter was in fact the first and, for about a century, the only feast. Only later were other feasts introduced, and even then only as a preparation for or a prolongation of this central feast. Sunday is a weekly reverberation, throughout the year, of the great Sunday. Christmas and its cycle—introduced in the middle of the fourth century—is a prelude to the work of redemption. The feasts of the martyrs and many of the other saints are examples of the grace of the Resurrection already become operative. [6]

But what kind of a commemoration of the work of redemption takes place in the liturgical feast? Is it merely a cold and lifeless *mental* review of the mysteries of Christ, as some would have it? Or is the very reality of the Christ-mystery made present in some way? Pius XII emphatically rejects the first view: "The liturgical year, devotedly fostered and accompanied by the Church, is not a cold and lifeless representation of the events of the past, or a simple and bare record of a former age. It is rather Christ Himself who is ever living in His Church." [7] Dom Odo Casel insists that it is not sufficient to look upon the liturgical year as a pious contemplation of the details of Christ's earthly life—a non-baptized person could do that. [8] In our celebration of the liturgical year we are not simply pious antiquarians interested in studying about the historical Jesus. Christ is not only a fact to be known; He is also the "way and the life." [9] In the Liturgy, Christ represents and renews His life precisely as a way of salvation, [10] the realization of the mystical and ontological union of us with Himself which is the end and essence of the Christian life. [11]

We, of course, do not deny that fundamental to the liturgical year is a mental review of the various mysteries of Christ. If, as Augustine says, "the perfection of religion is to imitate Him whom we adore," [12] then it is important that the Liturgy teach us about Christ. From knowledge flows love, and love, in turn, prompts imitation. This is the

---

[5] *Sermo* 48. *MPL*, 54:298.

[6] For the theological arguments and patristic and liturgical evidence in support of these ideas see my paper, "The Easter Vigil: Climax of the Week and the Year," *Proceedings of the North American Liturgical Week of 1956* (Elsberry, Mo., 1957), 133-137, 139-141.

[7] *Mediator Dei*, 165.

[8] *Le Mystère du culte dans le christianisme* (Paris, 1946), 134.

[9] John 14:6.

[10] Casel, *op. cit.*, 135.

[11] *Ibid.*, 132.

[12] See note 2.

whole meaning of the Foremass, the Service of the Word; it teaches us about Christ, His life, His work, with the obvious intent of feeding our minds with strong spiritual food for meditation and contemplation, of "giving us examples of virtue to imitate, of pointing out treasures of sanctity for us to make our own, since it is fitting that the mind believe what the lips sing, and that what the mind believes should be practiced in public and private life." [13]

This mental review or memorial is basic to Christianity. We can never emphasize enough the fact that Christianity has sprung from an historical event, that it was from the injection of "divine blood," so to speak, into man that a new priestly people has arisen. We are children of the Second Adam, and like all good children we like to know about our father, so that we may be like him. If the ability to become sons of God depends on this supernatural event, the intensity of our conscious living as sons of God will depend on how well we co-operate with the picture God presents us of Himself. Here, then, in the didactic part of the Mass we are presented with the story of salvation and the virtues of the Savior. This presentation evokes a response: willingness to accept salvation through becoming like the Savior, the image of man saved.

But the power of the liturgical commemoration is not exhausted by our mental agility in assimilating Christian doctrine or in mulling over salvific events of the past. The power behind the liturgical year is rather "Christ Himself who is ever living in His Church. Here He continues that journey of immense mercy which He lovingly began in His mortal life, going about doing good, with the design of bringing men (first) to know His mysteries and (second) *in a way to live by them*." [14] This twofold design of Christ in working through the liturgical year for men's salvation is actually brought about through some sort of a *presence* of His mysteries in the liturgical commemoration. Pius XII speaks of their being present in two ways: first, as shining examples of Christian perfection; secondly, "as sources of divine grace, due to the merits and prayers of Christ; they still influence us because each mystery brings its own special grace for our salvation." [15] Now we are in Christianity proper; we are in a sacramental system which, not only shows Christ to us, but actually effects His likeness within us. Not only is the higher objective placed before man; he is given the power to attain it.

But we are not yet speaking of the sacraments properly so-called. Pius XII continues: "Our holy Mother the Church, while proposing for our contemplation the mysteries of our Redeemer, asks in her prayers for those gifts which would give her children the greatest possible share in the spirit of these mysteries through the merits of

[13] *Mediator Dei,,* 153.
[14] *Ibid.,* 165. Emphasis added.
[15] *Ibid.*

Christ." [16] The part of the sacramental system of which we are now speaking is the *sacramental prayer* of the Church. It is sacramental because it is said through the power of priesthood. It is Christ, therefore, who is praying, although using the Church, i.e., His members, as His instrument. And Christ's prayer is always pleasing, always acceptable to the Father, always heard. The effect of the sacramental prayer of the Church is infallible, in the sense that it always makes present and available for us the grace of the mystery commemorated. It is there for us to take or leave.

There is more. This liturgical commemoration is not only a sacramental, it is also a *sacrament*. During the Consecration of the Mass the act of redemption—Christ's sacrifice and the new life He gained for us through it—is made really present. Thus Pius XII: "This mystery is the very center of divine worship since the Mass represents and renews it every day." [17] He continues: "The august sacrifice of the altar is no mere empty commemoration of the passion and death of Jesus Christ, but a true and proper act of sacrifice wherein, by means of an unbloody immolation, the High Priest *does again what He already did on* the cross, offering Himself a most acceptable victim to the Eternal Father." [18] As we read in the Secret for the Ninth Sunday after Pentecost, which the Pope quotes, "as often as this commemorative sacrifice is offered, there is wrought the work of our redemption." [19]

During the course of the liturgical year all the mysteries of Christ's life are individually celebrated. This gives the human mind an opportunity of taking in the whole mystery of redemption according to its various aspects.[20] Each feast permits us to contemplate more minutely the mystery of salvation and to drink more deeply of the current of grace and life flowing from our Head. After all, the Christian mystery, an infinite one, is much too vast, for the human mind to grasp all at once, just as grace itself cannot be adequately assimilated in its proper infinite mode by a human soul with strictly finite faculties of intellect and will. A human being needs to break down the single mystery of redemption into a pattern of cycles and feasts which allows him to be introduced slowly and gradually into the details of the mystery revealed and effected in Christ, and only thus to be transfigured into the likeness of Christ.

Does this mean that the individual mysteries of Christ's life are made truly present as separate entities during the liturgical year? Though this opinion has been imputed to Dom Odo Casel, he emphatically states the contrary. The only historical salvific event of Christ's

[16] *Ibid.*
[17] *Ibid.*, 164.
[18] *Ibid.* (A. Bugnini, *Documenta Pontificia ad Instaurationem Liturgicam Spectantia*, Rome, 1953), par. 67. Emphasis added: *id agit, quod iam in cruce fecit.*
[19] *Ibid.* (America Press Edition), 79.
[20] Cf. L. Bouyer, *Liturgical Piety* (Notre Dame, Indiana, 1955), 192-198.

life which breaks the bonds of time and is made present under our ritual symbols is the central act of redemption.[21] By the central act of redemption Casel means Christ's sacrifice and its acceptance on the part of the Father as demonstrated in the Resurrection. Not that the historical circumstances of Christ's being put to death and actually dying are made present; these took place only once in history. It is what was clothed in those historical circumstances that is important: the New Passover, the transition from earthly life to a glorified state.[22] This transition obviously implies the Resurrection as the terminus of this salvific act, in the same sense that St. Thomas Aquinas sees the Resurrection as a necessary part of the central act of redemption.[23] According to him, the death of Christ is, properly speaking, the efficient cause of the removal of the obstacle to our justification, namely, sin; the Resurrection is the efficient cause of justification itself, namely, the life of grace.

What then of the other mysteries of Christ's life? Casel answers that the mystery of redemption is one unbroken unity. The other mysteries of our Lord's life are never present separately, for the different phases of our Lord's redemptive work cannot in actuality be separated from the whole mystery which is Christ the Risen Lord.[24] They are present from the viewpoint of Christ's central salvific act, therefore, only as presupposed (the Incarnation) or as resulting therefrom (the Ascension)—not in their individual reality.[25] If the Church has appropriated the different elements and phases of this Mystery [26] to the various festivals and seasons of the liturgical year, it was only because, as we have said, that the Mystery includes a very involved process (Christ's own earthly life as well as the preparation of Israel for His coming), and it can only be brought to man by way of a concrete, factual reproduction of the major events that go to make up the work of redemption. Bringing the Mystery to man is, again, the problem of bringing the eternal decrees and plans of God into the realm of time, which is a successive thing. Man is so bound up with the limitations of time, that he simply cannot be taken up into the divine, transformed into the likeness of Christ, unless time, which is so con-

---

[21] "Glaube, Gnosis, und Mysterium," *Jahrbuch für Liturgiewissenschaft,* 15 (1941), 266.

[22] "Art und Sinn der ältesten christlichen Osterfeier," *JLW,* 14 (1938), 19-20; V. Warnach, "Zur Problem der Mysteriengegenwart," *Liturgisches Leben,* 5 (1938), 37. See, too, the interesting study of M. Matthijs, O. P., "Mysteriengegenwart secundum Sanctum Thomam," *Angelicum,* 34 (1957), 393-399.

[23] Summa Theol., III, 53, 1; 56, 2, ad 4; *Comm. in Epist. ad Rom.* IV, 25.

[24] "Art und Sinn der ältesten christlichen Osterfeier," *JLW,* 14 (1938), 52; "Mysteriengegenwart," *JLW,* 8 (1928), 204, 207.

[25] "Das Mysteriengedächtnis der Messliturgie im Lichte der Tradition," *JLW,* 6 (1926), 204.

[26] It must be borne in mind that nowhere does Casel speak of Mystery as a *Lehrgeheimnis,* as a truth or doctrine. He insists over and over again that the Mystery of Christ, both in its historical phase as well as in its liturgical commemoration, is an *action* effecting salvation.

natural to him, is also in some way taken up and, so to speak, eternal-
ized. And this surely means all the natural rhythm of time: the days,
seasons, and years through which time flows and man lives.

Here, then, in the liturgical year we witness a wedding of time
and eternity. Man, the finite and time-bound, stands face to face with
the divine, eternal *mysterium tremendum* of salvation as it is offered
to him in a concretized, itemized form by means of a mental review
of the deeds of redemption and through a sharing in their specific
graces with the help of the Church's sacramental prayer; and, finally,
as it is offered to him in the whole unbroken form of the central salvific act as found in the Eucharist. Thus he is led bit by bit up the
spiral that flowers into the glory of definitive and final configuration
to the Eternal Logos, the Image of the Father.

3. Consequences for the spiritual life and pastoral ministry

The Church insists on the value of daily mental prayer, and rightly so, for man must reflect on the truths possessed by faith if he is to
build up convictions strong enough to attach him irrevocably to a love,
imitation, and service of the Christ known through faith. Regardless
of what method a person may use, mental prayer needs to feed on the
wholesome objective truth of revelation as proposed and interpreted
by the divine authority of the Church. Otherwise, instead of bringing
man out of himself and leading him to the supernatural goal of likeness to Christ, it will only tend to falsify religion with emotionalism
and sentimentality; it will only shape Christ to our way of thinking.
Instead of supernaturalizing us, it will naturalize Christ.

Every day the Church holds out to us her objective teaching
about Christ. She intends very specifically to *instruct* us during the
Foremass and effectively brings us the grace of each mystery she thus
explains. She is very clearly, then, offering us matter to absorb and
apply to our own lives as well as the grace to do so. But how can we
better prepare to receive this grace in all its fulness and make an intelligent application of her teaching to ourselves and our condition than
by opening our hearts to that grace through reflection, meditation,
through an attempt to understand what the Church is saying? As
Pius XII says, "We must put our lips to the fountain, imbibe and
absorb for ourselves the life-giving water." [27] The work of redemption is taught to us and made present for us throughout the liturgical
year; for it to have its full effect, however, we must put forth a
serious, interior, mental and voluntary effort to experience the Christ-
mystery in our souls.

By thus meditating on the Church's teaching contained in her
liturgical year we are guaranteed of orthodoxy and purity of devotion,
of proportion, harmony, and homogeneity, in that we learn the *whole*

[27] *Mediator Dei*, 31.

Christ. We also become more conscious of the fact that we are members of His Mystical Body and live its life, and the danger is thereby lessened of divorcing ourselves from the body without which we cannot live. It is also an effective antidote against routine and formalism, for the Foremass comes to life for us in proportion as the mysteries of the liturgical year become more vital and real to us. We no longer simply go through so many Epistles and Gospels, feasts and seasons, automatically, as through so many formalities, but we begin really to experience them, to relive them. And thus the Liturgy becomes what it should be: "the primary source of the true Christian spirit." It truly forms us to the image and likeness of the God-man, and we accept all the formative influence it wishes to exert on us. It becomes a vivifying immersion in the Mystery of Christ, a sharing in the eternal life of God, a veritable transfiguration through grace to glory.

Such meditation could give tremendous meaning to our preaching. We have already seen that the true nature of the homily at Mass implies that we preach on the teaching of the Church contained in the Foremass, the Scripture readings, and the other aspects of the liturgical feast. If we have meditated wisely and have thoroughly imbibed the spirit of these feasts and seasons, our duty as priests of bringing this same spirit to the faithful will be rendered all the more easy. The priest, more conscious of his role as the intermediary teacher between Church and people, will see to it that he enriches the lives of the people day by day and season by season with the solid meat of spirituality which the Church in her feasts offers her children. Pedagogue and spiritual guide, the priest will fulfill ever more effectively his sublime calling as he molds his flock into conformity with the spirit of Christ vitally seen and experienced in the mysteries of a redemptive liturgical cycle.[28]

B. General Development of the Liturgical Year

1. Genesis of the liturgical calendar

It should be obvious from the outset that the liturgical year was not something created all at once, nor was it designed according to a clear-cut plan; it grew and developed over a period of many centuries. As we have already mentioned, the liturgical year grew from its center, the feast of Easter, which in point of fact was the very first Christian festival. The observance of Easter by Christians is not explicitly mentioned in the New Testament, but when the date for its

[28] A word of caution. The Holy Spirit leads some souls along special paths in the spiritual life. We must respect His action and not push this *normal* path to extremes by forcing it upon souls who are called to special ways. The liturgical year holds something for everybody, and all must use it, but all cannot use it in the same way or to the same degree. We need prudence, therefore, and fidelity to discernment of spirits.

celebration came up for discussion in the second century, the followers of the Quartodeciman practice claimed the authority of the
Apostles Philip and John for their usage.[29] And Sunday, as a weekly
commemoration of the Christian Pasch, is already reported in Acts
20:7 and 1 Cor. 16:2. Though it is generally held that the feast of
Pentecost was instituted by the Apostles, we have no uncontroverted
evidence for this. However, both Easter and Pentecost figure as well-
established festivals in the writings of Tertullian [30] and Origen.[31] As
a matter of fact, these are the only feasts known to these two writers.

With the coming of peace to the Church, all obstacles to a rich
development of her liturgical life were removed. One of the first
things Constantine did to facilitate Christian worship was to forbid
all legal business on Sundays.[32] This same prohibition was repeated
by his successors and was gradually extended to include new feasts
celebrated by the Church on weekdays. And Valentinian II, in 389,
even decreed the seven days preceding and following Easter to be
legal holidays.[33]

One of the first official ecclesiastical documents to ennumerate all
the feasts celebrated is the *Apostolic Constitutions*. There, in addition
to all the Sundays of the year and the fasts to be observed every
Wednesday and Friday and the forty-day fast of Lent, we find the
following festivals: Christmas, Epiphany, Holy Week, Easter and its
octave-day, the Ascension (*Assumptio Domini*), and Pentecost.[34]
Christmas and Epiphany are, of course, mentioned earlier, before the
time of this document, which is from the end of the fourth century.[35]
In the latter half of the fifth century, Perpetuus, sixth Bishop of Tours
(461-491), provides us with a list of feasts celebrated in that city. In
addition to the feasts already mentioned in the *Apostolic Constitutions*,
we also find the birthday of John the Baptist, the episcopate of St.
Peter on February 22, the passion of John the Baptist, the birthdays of
Peter and Paul, as well as the feasts of several other martyrs.[36]

The Roman Sacramentaries of the sixth and seventh centuries,
Leonine, Gelasian and Gregorian, show an even greater increase in
the number of feasts, both temporal and sanctoral.[37] Furthermore, in

---

[29] See the letter of Polycrates to Pope Victor dating from about 190, and the
report of the conference held around 150 between Polycarp and Pope Anicetus,
written by Irenaeus to Pope Victor, in Eusebius' *Hist. eccl.*, 5, 24. *GCS*, 9 (1), pp.
491-497.
[30] *De baptismo*, 19. *MPL*, 1: 1331.
[31] *Contra Celsum*, 8: 22. *MPG*, 11: 1550.
[32] Sozomen, *Hist. eccl.*, I, 8. *MPG*, 67: 882.
[33] *Cod. Theod.*, 2, 8, 1, 19. H. Kellner, *Heortology* (London, 1908), 18.
[34] V. 13-20. *MPG*, 1: 858-907.
[35] Christmas is explicitly listed in the Philocalian Calendar of 354, and a
celebration of Epiphany by the gnostic Basilidian sect before 215 is mentioned by
Clement of Alexandria, *Stromata*, I, 21. *MPG*, 8: 887.
[36] Gregory of Tours, *Historia Francorum*, 10: 31, 6. *MPL*, 71: 566-567.
[37] Apart from the many festivals of the local Roman martyrs, there are celebrations indicated for the following:
Jan. 1: Oct. of Christmas (G, Gr)   June 30: Birth of Paul (G, Gr).

the Gregorian Sacramentary according to the Paduan Codex edited by K. Mohlberg, all the Sundays of the year—in Advent, after Epiphany, Lent, after Easter and after Pentecost—receive their special Mass formularies. We can truly say, then, that the temporal cycle achieved a stage of definitive completion at the hands of Gregory I. In the sanctoral cycle, however, which was traditionally a matter of local concern, the feast days of six Apostles are still lacking.

Such feast days were not always days on which servile work was forbidden, and when servile work was forbidden it was not necessarily a feast day. It is somewhat difficult to determine when the two finally went together. In 425, however, Thedosius II promulgated a list of all the days on which public spectacles were forbidden, and they were: all Sundays of the year, Christmas, Epiphany, and the entire period from Easter to Pentecost.[38] In the seventh century, Sonnatius, Bishop of Rheims (614-631), indicated thirteen feast days, in addition to all Sundays of the year, on which no servile work could be done.[39] This totaled, therefore, sixty-three days. But this number was greatly to increase in the following centuries. In 821 Bishop Hetto of Basel decreed that his people should refrain from servile work on eighty-eight days of the year.[40] And between the thirteenth and eighteenth centuries there were some dioceses in which such days exceeded a hundred,[41] the diocese of Bamberg, for instance, having fifty-four holydays of obligation over and above the fifty-two Sundays of the year.

Once the most important component parts of the Mystery of redemption were provided with fitting celebrations, the chief reason for the tremendous increase in the number of feasts was undoubtedly the fact that bishops exercised their canonical right in introducing new festivals within their provinces of influence. Canon law in the Middle Ages left to the bishops the duty of watching over the veneration paid to martyrs; it was up to them to decide whether a particular

---

Jan. 5: Vig. of Theophany (G)	July 6: Oct. of the Apostles (G, Gr)
Jan. 6: Theophany (G, Gr)	Aug. 9: Vig. of Laurence (G, Gr)
Feb. 2: Purification (G)	Aug. 10: Laurence (L, G, Gr)
Hypapante (Gr)	Aug. 15: Assumption (G, Gr)
Mar. 25: Annunciation (G, Gr)	Sept. 6: Nativity of BVM (G)
April 25: Greater Litanies (Gr)	Sept. 14: Exaltation of Cross (G, Gr)
May 1: Philip and James (G, Gr)	Nov. 29: Andrew's Vigil (G, Gr)
May 6: John at Latin Gate (Gr)	Nov. 30: Andrew (L, G, Gr)
May 3: Finding of Cross (G)	Dec. 21: Thomas (G)
May 13: Mary at Martyrs (Gr)	Dec. 24: Vig. of Christmas (G, Gr)
June 23: Vig. of John Bapt. (G, Gr)	Dec. 25: Christmas (L, G, Gr)
June 24: Birth of John Bapt. (L, G, Gr)	Dec. 26: Stephen (G, Gr)
June 28: Vig. of Peter and Paul (G)	Dec. 27: John Evang. (L, G, Gr)
June 29: Peter and Paul (L, G)	Dec. 28: Innocents (L, G, Gr)
Peter (Gr)	

[38] *Cod. Theod.*, 15, 5, no. 5 compared with 2, 8, no. 24. H. Kellner, *op. cit.*, 19.

[39] *Statuta*, 20. *MPL*, 80: 446.

[40] *Capitulare*, 8. *MPL*, 105: 763.

[41] Cf. H. Kellner, *op. cit.*, 25.

martyr should receive liturgical *cultus* in their dioceses. With the spread of the religious orders, the calendar of martyrs and saints venerated by the orders found acceptance in various localities throughout the world. If the Holy See intervened, the holydays thus established were considered fully sanctioned. But until such authoritative sanction came, there often reigned confusion and uncertainty, so much so that in 1642 Pope Urban VIII warned bishops not to use their rights in this regard any longer.[42] Kellner rightly observes that the use of such episcopal prerogatives was a basic factor in the whole question; it should never be lost sight of, for without it the institution and development of even a single feast cannot be understood, much less the historical development of the whole festal cycle. After this principle had been acted upon for more than a thousand years, it is truly remarkable that the end result is as harmonious and systematic as it is.

Nevertheless, unlimited multiplication of holydays led to hardship—especially for the poor who were thus prevented from gaining their livelihood. Men like Jean Gerson in 1408 and Nicholas de Clemangiis in 1416 spoke out boldly against the introduction of any new feasts. In short, it was the same story with which we are already familiar from our study of the Breviary. Synod after synod and pope after pope attempted to reduce the number of feasts, while other popes or bishops only established new ones or re-introduced the old ones.

The recent decree on the simplification and abbreviation of the Office has done much to assuage the situation, but a more complete and thoroughgoing reform of the calendar is needed. Any passing acquaintance with the Gregorian Sacramentary will show how Gregory the Great tried to solve the problem of reconciling the temporal and sanctoral cycles. He grouped the feasts of saints around typical solemnities of the temporal order and then, in turn, grouped certain Sundays about the major saints' feasts. Whether this is the solution or not, some attempt has to be made to prevent the feasts of saints from endangering the integrity of the temporal cycle; the latter's primacy, as representing the redemptive mystery in itself, should be definitely assured.

It should also be kept in mind that the celebration of the majority of saints' feasts was a strictly local affair. While a certain number of saints bear such a universal character that their *cultus* will normally be spread over the entire Church (e.g.: certain historical feasts of the Blessed Virgin, the *natalitia* of the Apostles and other personages directly connected with the plan of redemption, as well as the feasts of the Fathers and Doctors of the Church), other saints enjoy only a local and restricted popular significance, and hence their liturgical veneration will also be restricted. Possibly, last of all, when the doctrines bound up with the historical feasts of the temporal cycle

---

[42] *Ibid.*, 28-29.

are *fully* exploited, we may no longer feel the need of the more recent "idea-feasts."

2. Classification of feasts

A first general criterion for the classification of feasts is whether the object immediately celebrated is a mystery of our Lord's life or the sanctity of a particular saint. In more recent times a third object of veneration has appeared: the mystery of *doctrine*, not as an historical phase of the plan of redemption, but as something to be learned, loved, and adhered to: the Holy Trinity, the Sacred Heart, the Maternity of Mary, the Kingship of Christ, etc.

Mysteries of our Lord's life are celebrated either as movable feasts on no determined day of the month, such as Easter and Pentecost, or as immovable feasts, such as Christmas, Epiphany, the Transfiguration. And at least some of these historical mysteries of Christ's life are celebrated on the actual day on which they occurred, or as close to it as the historical knowledge of the Church makes possible.

Within their respective categories the many feasts of the Church are set off from one another by a whole series of gradations of rank. The days on which no feast occurs are called *feriae*, but they are not separated from the rhythm of the Church year, for they are always caught up into the festal character of the season in which they fall. Feasts themselves are divided according to their importance: simples, doubles (semi-doubles were abolished in 1955), double majors, doubles of the first and second class, some of the latter enjoying even greater distinction by reason of their octave—Easter, Pentecost, and Christmas.

Although originally this nomenclature had real significance, today it indicates no more than a distinction in rank. Formerly, when a feast fell upon a weekday, a double night office was sung: one of the feria in question and another of the feast. Eventually, though the double recitation of the office disappeared, the title "double" for more important feasts remained.[43] And when in the thirteenth century the rest of these ranks appeared, the original meaning was lost sight of. Formerly all saints' feasts were celebrated as simples and enjoyed only one proper lesson. But Gregory VII (1073-1085) ordered that the feasts of all pope-martyrs were to be celebrated as doubles. Boniface VIII, in 1298, elevated the feasts of Apostles, Evangelists and the four great Doctors of the West to this rank. And the Franciscans brought about a thorough revolution in this regard by observing all saints' feasts as doubles. Subsequent popes, such as Pius V, Pius X and Pius XII, reduced the rank of many of these feasts once again.

Octaves, too, was observed differently in the ancient Church. In the early times an octave meant only that a feast was commemorated

[43] Lechner-Eisenhofer, 183.

in the office on the eighth day after the feast. No notice was taken of
the intervening days. Another transformation is to be seen in the
matter of vigils. Formerly if a feast was of a high rank, it was celebrated with a night service, sometimes beginning at sundown the
evening before and lasting till morning, as on Easter; this was called
the *Pannuchis*—all-night vigil. More often such night services began
at midnight. When this became too difficult for the laity (around the
fourth century), a vigil service was celebrated before the fall of night.
Gradually this service was moved forward to noon and then to morning
of the day before the feast, and from being the solemn celebration of
the festal office itself, it became, as today, a type of fore-feast or
preparation for the feast.

3. Origin of the cycles

As we have already seen, the basic division of the Church year
into temporal and sanctoral cycles has really been accentuated as such
only from the end of the Middle Ages on, from the time that our missal and breviaries set up the clear-cut *Proprium de tempore* and
Proprium de sanctis. In the oldest calendars and service books, as exemplified, again, by the Gregorian Sacramentary, the feasts of the
saints are found mixed in with the feasts of the temporal cycle. The
present division is only a mechanical device intended to facilitate our
use of the liturgical books.

According to the deepest spirit and meaning of the saints' feasts,
they are intimately and thematically connected with the liturgical
commemorations of the mysteries of our Lord. There is really only
one liturgical cycle, that of Easter. We are accustomed to speak of
the Christmas cycle also, but in reality, according to the plan of
divine providence and the thought of the Church, this cycle of the
Incarnation is subordinated to the Easter cycle as a part to the whole,
because it is only the prelude to the act of redemption. As Pope St.
Leo I reminds us, Christ had no other purpose in being born of a virgin than that He should be nailed to the cross for our salvation.[44]
Every time we recite the Credo we say quite explicitly "propter nos
homines, et propter nostram salutem descendit de caelis." And the
feasts of the Blessed Virgin, the confessors, and the martyrs are not
less orientated towards the Christological cycle. They belong to it
integrally, for the bloody sacrifice of the martyrs and the unbloody
self-sacrifice of the other saints finds its prototype and motive in the
Passion and Resurrection of Christ. They have followed Christ in dying to self in order to rise with Him to the new life of glory. And it is
thus that their liturgical commemorations are most properly to be
understood.

It is true that certain saints' feasts are more particularly orientated

[44] *Sermo* 48, *MPL*, 54: 298.

towards either the Easter or Christmas cycle according to their role in the plan of redemption. Mary, Joseph, John the Baptist, Anna, Joachim, and the Archangel Gabriel—all these played their role in the drama of the Incarnation and therefore are most logically grouped about the Christmas theme. On the other hand, the Apostles, Evangelists, martyrs, confessors, and virgins were either directly connected with the propagation of the work of redemption or were shining examples of its efficacy, and for that reason belong to the Easter theme. Therefore, although we will keep the late medieval distinction between temporal and sanctoral cycles in our treatment, we will discuss the saints' feasts in their proper perspective—as related either to the incarnational prelude or to the paschal climax of the redemptive work.

There is another cycle of which we must speak, the weekly one. This was taken over from Judaism and is a commemoration of the six days of creation and the seventh day of rest. St. Ambrose, in his beautiful Vesper hymns, was the particular exponent of the work of the days of creation. In spite of these hymns and the carry-over from Judaism of the idea of a day of rest commemorating the completion of creation, the predominant theme of the week for at least a thousand years was, again, the plan of redemption; the weekdays were dedicated to the Passion and Sunday was seen as its conclusion, just as the Resurrection climaxed our Lord's sufferings. Thereafter other ideas begin to creep in, ideas centering on the doctrines of the Trinity and the Incarnation. These are, however, expressed for the most part in the votive Masses for the week, and so the older conception must be said to be more fundamental.

With all these different cycles before us, we may rightly ask where the liturgical year begins. The only answer we can truthfully give is that various points of departure for the annual cycle can be discerned as new feasts and cycles were introduced at different times during the historical development of the Church year. At the very beginning there was only Easter, which was subsequently extended into a cycle of feasts; the liturgical year began with the Easter Vigil and ended on Holy Saturday morning. When, however, the ancient Roman Rite began its biblical readings with Genesis in March (*mensis primus*), this was considered the beginning of the liturgical year.[45]

With the institution of the feast of Christmas in the fourth century, however, a new logical point of departure for the *anni circulum* was at hand—the very beginning of the earthly life of Christ Himself. And the liturgical books actually began with this feast, that is, with its vigil, even after the introduction of Advent. The Epistle-list of the Würzburg Lectionary is the first Roman document to begin the Church

[45] Cf. A. Chavasse, "Le calendrier dominical romain au vi siècle. L'epistolier

year thus.[46] The Sundays of Advent are found in the rear of this and similar books.

This arrangement may seem strange to us who are brought up with the idea that Advent is the beginning of the liturgical year, but there were reasons for this ancient, or rather medieval view. At first Advent was regarded merely as a period of penance and mortification established out of imitation of Lent. Then in some regions the idea of the Parousia was inserted,[47] and this gave the Advent season more of the appearance of the conclusion to the year. But in the eighth and ninth centuries Advent, for the first time, came to be regarded as the beginning of the year, when allegorists saw in the four [48] Sundays of Advent a commemoration of the four thousand years which elapsed from Adam to Christ.

What we have said has served to point out that the liturgical year is at present not a unified whole—at least from the viewpoint of beginning and end. The Sundays of the pre-Lenten season speak to us of the beginning of the world, the Fall, the Patriarchs and other types of the promised Redeemer, the second Head of the human race. Now Advent places before us again the same messianic hope, but starts out with a Gospel selection speaking of the end of the world, as the very last Sunday after Pentecost also does. This duplication would seem to call for a reform in the liturgical calendar, and the modern emphasis on the didactic aspect of the Church year supports this desire.

Perhaps a suitable way of eliminating this duplication and of bringing out better the actual unfolding of the redemptive plan would be to move the Breviary lessons concerning Adam, Noe, Abraham (leaving those about Jacob, Joseph, and Moses for Lent) to before Christmas and to weave them into a unity with the lessons from Isaias (Advent) concerning the person of the Messias. Possibly this could best be done by extending the number of Advent Sundays to seven, depicting the anxieties of fallen man encouraged by the hope of the Promised One. From Christmas till Easter there could be a more factual presentation of the childhood and public ministry of Christ (using Jacob, Joseph, and Moses, still, as types for this latter part)

---

et l'homiliaire prégrégoriens," *Recherches de Science Religieuse,* 38 (Oct. 1952), 235. The beginning of this reading was eventually (middle of seventh century) affixed to what we call today Septuagesima Sunday.

[46] Cf. G. Godu, "Epîtres," *DACL,* V: 312, also A. Chavasse, *op. cit.,* 236.

[47] This is not originally Roman, but is due to the missionary activity on the continent of Europe of the Irish monks of St. Columbanus. True, we find Luke 21:25 as the basis for Gregory the Great's homily for the First Sunday of Advent, but it seems he intended its use for this one occasion during his pontificate and not as an annually recurring pericope. See W. Croce, "Die Adventsliturgie im Licht ihrer geschichtlichen Entwicklung," *ZkTh,* 76 (1954), 258-296, esp. 274-275 and 290-292.

[48] This number was not at all a constant in history, and the Liturgy gives no support to this number-allegory. The messianic theme of Advent, however, is undeniably the correct interpretation.

culminating in the central act of redemption. This would do away with the lack of unity between the Christmas and Easter cycles and satisfy modern demands for a more didactic and pedagogical emphasis on the life and work of Christ, who fulfilled the messianic promises of old.

C. The Weekly Cycle

1. Observance of Sunday

Though we have no New Testament record of our Lord's having abrogated the Sabbath, Justin Martyr insists that it was in fact our Lord who determined that Sunday should be a day of weekly religious observance.[49] Sunday already appears as a stable institution in the Acts of the Apostles,[50] St. Paul,[51] and the Apocalypse,[52] and it is in the latter that it is first called the Lord's Day. The *Didache* also sets Sunday aside as the day for the Eucharistic Sacrifice,[53] and the *stato die* on which Pliny the Younger says the Christians met to "sing a hymn to Christ as God" [54] is commonly regarded by scholars as Sunday. Yet there is good reason to believe that a specifically Christian celebration of Sunday existed side by side, for a while, with a continued observance of the Jewish Sabbath.[55]

Why did the Christians choose Sunday for their weekly service? There is hardly room for doubt that it was precisely because they saw in the institution of Sunday a weekly commemoration of the Resurrection of Christ—a weekly Easter, as it were. All the Patristic texts dealing with Sunday insist that it is held especially sacred, for on the first day of the week Christ arose from the dead. St. Ignatius of Antioch tells us that because our life arose together with Christ on this day it was called the Lord's Day.[56] And Justin says that Sunday is "the day on which God transforming darkness and matter created the world and on which Jesus Christ our Savior arose from the dead." [57] Because of this close connection with Easter there was to be no fasting, genuflecting, or kneeling, according to Tertullian,[58] for these were all signs of sorrow and penance. The paschal quality of the Sunday was so deeply felt in the Jerusalem of the fourth century that it was the custom, according to Etheria, there to read the Gospel of Resur-

---

[49] I *Apology* 67, 7. J. Quasten, *Monumenta*, 20-21.
[50] 20:7.
[51] 1 Cor. 16:2.
[52] 1:10.
[53] 14,1. J. Quasten, 12.
[54] Cf. Kirch, *Enchiridion Fontium Historiae Ecclesiasticae Antiquae* (Barcelona, 1947), n. 30, p. 23.
[55] Cf. Acts, 2:46; 13:14; 17:2; 18:4.
[56] *Ad Magnes.* IX. *The Fathers of the Church*, I (New York, 1947), 99.
[57] I *Apology* 67, 7. J. Quasten, 20.
[58] *De corona militis*, 3. MPL, 2: 79; cf. also Irenaeus, *Fragmenta* VII. MPG, 7: 1234.

rection at Matins every Sunday of the year.[59] Finally, a practice very much in vogue today, the Asperges, was begun in imitation of the great Christian initiation rite, Baptism, which was conferred during the Easter Vigil.[60]

The Jews called Sunday the first day of the week since it was on this day, according to Genesis, that God began the work of creation; the Christians, though accepting this, went a step further and regarded Sunday as the first day of the second creation. Thus in Eusebius of Alexandria we read: "It was on this day that the Lord began the first-fruits of the creation of the world, and on the same day He gave to the world the first-fruits of the resurrection." [61] St. Ambrose has beautifully enshrined this parallelism in his hymn for Sunday Matins:

> Primo die quo Trinitas
> Beata mundum condidit,
> Vel quo resurgens Conditor
> Nos, morte victa, liberat . . .

The Fathers also exploit the symbolism based on the Greco-Roman (originally Egyptian) name for the first day of the week, dies solis, from which the Anglo-Saxon term came, Sonntag, Sunday. Justin apparently was the first to make mention of this, since he considered it his vocation to be an apologist to the Greco-Roman world. He expressly constructs a parallel between the dies solis and the action of God on that day, the creation of light. As he says, "On the day of the sun on which God changing darkness and matter. . . ." [62] Much the same idea is expressed by Clement of Alexandria: "From this day wisdom and knowledge shine out on us. It is indeed the light of Truth which is the true Light without shadow, sharing indivisibly the Spirit of the Lord with those who are sanctified by Him." [63] And in Eusebius of Caesarea: "It was on this day that at the time of creation when God said, 'Let there be light,' there was light; and on this day also the Sun of Justice arose on our souls." [64]

So well known to the pagans was the Christian observance of Sunday that some considered the Christians just another sect of sun-worshipers, since it was customary for the pagans to offer sacrifice to Apollo, the sun god, on this day. Tertullian had to defend the Church on this score. He writes: "If we give ourselves to rejoicing on the day of the sun, it is because of an entirely different reason." [65] And at that, in the canticle of Zachary, the Redeemer was called the Orient from

---

[59] *Journal de Voyage* (Paris: Editions du Cerf, 1948), n. 43, p. 246; n. 44, p. 252.
[60] Rupert of Deutz, *De divinis officiis*, VII, 20. MPL, 170: 200.
[61] *Sermo 16 de die dominica*, 1. MPG, 86: 416.
[62] *I Apology* 67, 7. J. Quasten, 20.
[63] *Stromata*, VI, 16. MPG, 9: 363.
[64] *On the Pasch.* MPG, 23: 1172.
[65] *I Apology* 67, 7. J. Quasten, 20.

on high,[66] and in this only followed the Old Testament prophecy of the Messias as a rising light.[67] St. Jerome gladly accepts this coincidence between revelation and pagan terminology when he says: "The day of the Lord, the day of the resurrection, the day of Christians is our day. And if it is called the day of the sun by the pagans, we willingly accept this name, for on this day arose the light; on this day shone forth the sun of justice." [68]

There is still another symbolic explanation of Sunday; some of the Fathers spoke of Sunday as the *eighth day*. Pseudo-Barnabas was probably the first Christian writer to undertake an explanation of why Sunday was observed by Christians in preference to the Sabbath. He has God speak: "The present Sabbaths are not acceptable to me, only the Sabbath which I have made, in which, after giving rest to all things, I will make the beginning of the eighth day, that is, the beginning of another world." Therefore, says Barnabas, "we . . . celebrate . . . the eighth day on which Jesus arose from the dead, was made manifest and ascended into heaven." [69] Though we find allusions to this idea in Jewish apocalyptic literature; e.g., the Second Book of Hennoch, since this writing dates from after the beginning of the Christian era, we must conclude that the symbol of the eighth day is of purely Christian origin.[70] As Pseudo-Barnabas indicates, the substitution of the eighth for the seventh day is an expression of the substitution of Christianity for Judaism.[71] But there is also a sort of eschatological symbolism in Pseudo-Barnabas, and this is brought out more explicitly by Origen: "The number eight, which contains the virtue of the resurrection, is the figure of the future world." [72] St. Ambrose too gives to the number eight the meaning of redemption: "The number eight is the fulfillment of our hope [73] . . . . for according to the Mosaic Law a male child was to be circumcised on the eighth day after his birth, while in the New Testament Christ arose from the dead on the eighth day." [74] So important was this day that the early Fathers gave it a new number, in order to bring out its entirely special character as a day made by the Lord, the *dies quam fecit Dominus*, completely outside the natural order of time, a substitution for Judaism, the beginning of the new world order established by Christ and at

---

[66] Luke 1:78.

[67] Isaias 9:1 ff.

[68] *In die dominica Paschae*. J. Quasten, 20, note 2. See also the beautiful chapter: "Der Sonntag" Hugo Rahner, *Griechische Mythen in christlicher Deutung* (Zürich: Rhein Verlag, 1945), 141-148.

[69] *Letter of Barnabas*, XV, 8-9. *The Fathers of the Church*, I (New York, 1947), 216.

[70] Cf. J. Daniélou, *The Bible and the Liturgy* (Notre Dame, Indiana, 1956), 256.

[71] See also, in this regard, Hilary, *Prologus in librum psalmorum*, n. 12. MPL, 9: 239.

[72] *Selecta in Psalmos*, Ps. 118, 164, MPG, 12: 1624.

[73] *Expositio in evang. sec. Lucam*, V, 49. MPL, 15: 1735.

[74] *De Abraham*, II, 11. MPL, 14: 494.

the same time prognostic of the world to come as *gratia est semen gloriae!* [75]

As for the obligation to assist at Mass on Sundays, we find no hard and fast rule in the primitive Church. In the *Didache* [76] we read the bald statement that Christians gathered on Sundays to break bread. It was, then, generally expected that the faithful would attend Mass on the Lord's Day. But just when this became expressed in a written law is a matter of dispute. Many authors see in the twenty-first canon of the Council of Elvira, held in 306, such a precept.[77] But J. Guiniven claims that the specific object of this legislation was, not the obligation of attending Mass, but rather that of participating actively in the religious life of the local parish.[78] As a matter of fact, subsequent councils either ignored or variously interpreted this canon. Only in the sixth century do we find a positive written law imposing such an obligation; it came from the Council of Agde held in 506.[79] However, this does not mean that no obligation existed at all. There was certainly one imposed by tradition. The *Didascalia*, composed in the first half of the third century, seems to rely on just such custom when it admonishes the faithful to put aside everything on Sunday and to gather in church; it asks what excuse he will offer to God who does not go to church to hear the word of salvation and to be nourished by the Divine Food.[80]

Nor does it seem to have been an early rule in the Church to abstain from servile work on Sunday. For one thing, most Christians, until freedom was granted to the slaves, were obliged to render service to their masters and could not very well have risked being absent from such duties. It is only around the year 244 that we discover the first traces of an attempt on the part of the Church to urge her faithful to dedicate Sunday to rest as the Jews had done with the Sabbath. Origen writes: "On Sunday none of the actions of the world should be done. If, then, you abstain from all the works of this world and do not engage in any worldly affair but keep yourself free for spiritual things, go to the church, listen to the readings and divine homilies, meditate on heavenly things. . . ." [81] Constantine made this pious ad-

---

[75] Cf. Daniélou, chapter 16: "The Eighth Day," *op. cit.*, 262-286; 255-261; F-J. Dölger, "Zur Symbolik der altchristlichen Taufhauses," *Antike und Christentum,* 4 (1934), 153-197. Even the baptisteries in which the sacrament of the Resurrection was conferred were built in an octagonal shape: see Ambrose's inscription in Dölger, 155.

[76] 14, 1. J. Quasten, 12.

[77] Thus A. Villien, *History of the Commandments of the Church* (St. Louis: Herder, 1915), 28: "Si quis in civitate tres dominicas ad ecclesiam non accesserit, tanto tempore abstineat ut correptus esse videatur."

[78] *The Precept of Hearing Mass* (Washington, D. C.: The Catholic University Press, 1942), 19.

[79] *Ibid.*, 23.

[80] II, 59. *Ibid.*, 21.

[81] *Homil. 23 in Numeros,* 4. *MPG,* 12: 749-750.

monition a law by forbidding all business on Sundays.[82] And he gave special permission to the Christian soldiers to be absent from their duty in order to attend divine services.[83] Finally, in the *Apostolic Constitutions*,[84] this prohibition of servile work becomes an ecclesiastical law.

Thus we see that Sunday was especially set aside as the heir of the legacy of the Sabbath for the worship of God and the weekly commemoration of the work of redemption whose fruits were applied to the faithful in order to prepare them for the great Sabbath rest of eternity.

2. Stational days

Besides Sunday, two other days of the week were singled out for religious observance—for fasting, specifically. Just as Sunday was substituted for the Jewish Sabbath, so Wednesday and Friday took the place of the two Jewish weekday fasts: Monday and Thursday. The *Didache* expressly mentions this substitution: "Let not your fasts be made with the hypocrites. They fast on Mondays and Thursdays. You, however, should fast on Wednesdays and Fridays." [85] It was also easy to see in these fasts a connection between the betrayal by Judas and our Lord's Passion; in fact, Isidore of Seville says that some people fasted on Fridays because of our Lord's Passion.[86] Such weekday fasts were called "stations" by the Shepherd of Hermas.[87] This expression is commonly explained as a military term used among the Romans to mean "stand guard." The reason for the Church's adoption of this term is disputed, but the most favored explanation seems to be that of P. Kirsch, who, basing his argument on Tertullian's use of the term,[88] concludes that it meant "place of gathering" as well as the assembly itself.[89]

These days were not observed everywhere in the same fashion. Tertullian leads us to believe that the fast was not really obligatory, and that Mass would normally be celebrated on such days.[90] And further, the fast was not a full one but continued only until the ninth hour.[91] In Alexandria, however, if the Wednesday and Friday of Holy Week are to be taken as typical of the rest of the year, though regular

[82] Sozomen, *Hist. eccl.*, 1, 8. *MPG*, 67:882.
[83] Eusebius, *Vita Constantini*, 4, 19. *GCS*, 7: 124.
[84] VIII, 33. *MPG*, 1: 1134.
[85] VIII. *Ancient Christian Writers*, 6, 19.
[86] *De eccl. off.*, I, 43. *MPL*, 83: 775.
[87] *Parables*, V. *The Fathers of the Church*, I (New York, 1947), 292.
[88] *Liber Apologeticus*, III. *MPL*, 1: 331: "locus conventiculorum et stationum suarum."
[89] P. Kirsch, "L'origine des Stations Liturgiques du missel romain," *Ephemerides Liturgicae*, 41 (1927), 136.
[90] *De oratione*, 19. *MPL*, 1: 1286.
[91] *De jejunio*, 2 and 10. *MPL*, 2: 1007, 1017.

synaxes were held, the Eucharistic Sacrifice was not offered.[92] And, according to Pope Innocent I, this was also the custom in Rome.[93]

Although Saturday at first enjoyed no special observance precisely because of the opposition to Jewish practice,[94] by the time of St. Augustine certain churches, notably Rome and others in the West, dedicated the day to fasting[95] because of the memory of Christ's death.[96] Duchesne, however, believes that this Saturday fast was due to a continuation, in some churches, of the Friday fast through Saturday.[97] This practice was called *continuare jejunium* or *superponere jejunium*.[98] Fasting on Saturdays was continued in Rome and other churches of the West up until the eleventh century, when it gave way to simple abstinence. This change was sanctioned by Gregory VII in 1078, but in the end even this requirement was abolished by Pius X in 1908.

3. Ember Days

The fact that the Ember Days are always the same stational days may lead one to believe that they are only the remnant of the primitive Roman liturgical week. In fact, L. Duchesne holds, when the rigid discipline of fasting three times every week was finally dropped, Rome wanted to retain this practice at least four times a year, at the beginning of the four seasons.[99] But such a contention runs headlong into serious historical objections: the weekly Saturday fast, for instance, is later, as an institution, than the Ember Days. Furthermore, the Ember Days were already observed in the Roman Church long before the suppression of the weekly fasts. In fact, Pope Leo I attributes the institution of these Ember Days to the time of the Apostles.[100] The *Liber Pontificalis*, however, attributes the institution to Pope Callistus, who died in 222.[101]

It is noteworthy that both the *Liber* and Leo[102] regard this Christian practice as a revival of an old Jewish custom recorded in the book of Zacharias (8:19). There we read: "Thus saith the Lord of hosts, 'The fast of the fourth month, and the fast of the fifth, and the fast of the seventh,[103] and the fast of the tenth[104] shall be to the house of Juda joy and gladness and great solemnities; only love ye truth and peace!'" This fact, however, need not necessarily mean that the Chris-

---

[92] Socrates, *Hist. eccl.*, V, 22. *MPG*, 67: 635-638.
[93] *Epist.* 25 *ad Decentium*. 4, *MPL*, 20: 555.
[94] Ignatius of Antioch, *Ad Magnes.*, 9-11. *The Fathers of the Church*, I (New York, 1947), 99.
[95] Augustine, *Epist.* 36 *ad Casulanum*, XIII, 31. *MPL*, 33: 150.
[96] Victorinus, *Fragmenta de fabrica mundi*. *MPL*, 5: 306.
[97] *Christian Worship*, 231.
[98] Tertullian, *De jejunio*, 14; Victorinus, *op. cit. MPL*, 2: 1024; 5: 304, 306.
[99] *Christian Worship*, 233.
[100] *Sermo* 93, n. 3. *MPL*, 54: 457.
[101] Edit. L. Duchesne, I, 141.
[102] *Sermo* 90, n. 1. *MPL*, 54: 447.
[103] These first three are found in Jeremias also, 52: 6, 12; 41:2.
[104] 4 Kings 25:1.

tian practice was a direct outgrowth of the Old Testament fasts, but only that the Old Law provided a precedent.

As a matter of fact, the above decretal of Callistus speaks of fasts on three Saturdays of the year: *frumenti, vini et olei.* Now the Romans knew three pagan solemnities during the year under the name of *feriae messis, feriae vindemiales* and *feriae sementivae,* and these were celebrated, respectively, in June-July at the time of the grain-harvest, in September at the collecting of the grapes for the making of wine, and in December for the sowing of seed. It is, therefore, difficult to escape the conclusion that the Ember Days were really a Christian adaptation of these pagan feasts—and this is not the only instance of such adaptations. The days were, therefore, a specifically local and Roman custom of a rural character, a feast of the seasons, intended to call down God's blessing and to thank Him for a good harvest.[105] Several homilies of Pope Leo I make express mention of the theme of these fasts as being a means of making the faithful more conscious of God's providence and at the same time of thanking Him for all the products of the land.[106] And this same theme recurs consistently in the Leonine [107] and Gelasian [108] orations for these occasions.

As we have seen, Callistus instituted only three Ember periods: summer, autumn and winter. Just when the fourth Ember season was added has been a matter of dispute. It is true that both Leo [109] and Gelasius [110] speak of a fast in Lent, but this could not be the Ember fast, for in later documents, which certainly testify to the existence of the spring Embertide—the *Liber Diurnus* and the Gelasian Sacramentary, both from the latter part of the sixth century—we see that this Ember season was not at all identified with Lent, but rather was called *jejunium mensis primi*: the March Ember Days.[111] Gregory I definitely made this fast coincide with the first week of Lent.[112] And so it results that the Spring Ember Days were instituted no earlier than the latter part of the sixth century.

Where did we get the name Embertides? At first the four fasts were simply named according to the months in which they fell: *jejunium mensis primi, quarti, septimi, decimi.* Later the fact that they corresponded to the four seasons of the year was brought out by means of a new name: *Quattuor Tempora,* the four times or seasons. Our English "ember" is a corruption of *tempora.*

[105] This is the opinion of G. Morin, "L'origine des Quatre-Temps," *Revue Bénédictine,* 1897, pp. 337-346.
[106] *Sermo* 13 *de jejunio mensis decimi; Sermo* 16; *Sermo* 12. MPL, 54: 172, 176, 170-171.
[107] K. Mohlberg, *Sacramentarium Veronense,* 109-118; 166-169.
[108] H. Wilson, *The Gelasian Sacramentary,* 126-127; 200; 220.
[109] *Sermo* 19, n. 2. MPL, 54: 186.
[110] *Epist.* 9 *ad Episc. Luc.,* 11. MPL, 59: 52.
[111] See a discussion of these texts in A. Chavasse, "Les messes quadragésimales du sacramentaire Gelasien," *Ephemerides Liturgicae,* 63 (1949), 260-267; 270-275.
[112] *Ibid.,* 260-261.

Though these four fasts were originally a purely local Roman usage, they spread throughout the entire West, although slowly. They were introduced into Great Britain in 747 by the Council of Cloveshoe [113] and into the Frankish empire under Charlemagne in 769.[114] In Milan they were not inserted into the annual cycle until the time of Charles Borromeo, according to H. Kellner.[115] However, Mario Righetti insists that Borromeo only restored an earlier practice, since he has found evidence that the Embertides already existed in Milan in the thirteenth century.[116]

An obvious consequence of the uneven propagation of the Ember seasons throughout the West was the uncertainty as to the exact weeks in which they were to be celebrated. In one place they would be observed during the first week of the month, in another during the last week, sometimes before Pentecost, sometimes after. It must be admitted, however, that this was also a difficulty in Rome itself. Although their celebration was in general attached to the months of March, June, September, and December, they were not directly connected with any specific week. The reason for this was that they normally followed the planting and harvesting dates, which were variable. A special announcement had to be made each season of when they would fall. A formula for this purpose can still be found in the Gelasian Sacramentary: *Denuntiatio jejuniorum quarti, septimi, et decimi mensis.* . . .[117] Although Gregory the Great had fixed the March Ember Days for the first week of Lent, confusion still reigned as to the others until Gregory VII [118] determined that they were to be observed in the week of Pentecost, the third week of September and the third week of Advent.

Although originally all the Ember seasons were of a festive character designed to thank God for the produce of the earth and to beg His continued temporal assistance, later they came to be regarded solely as days of penance and prayer. In the formulas of the Roman Missal today, hardly a trace can be found of their primitive quality. The September Ember Days alone preserve the original spirit: *Exsultate Deo adjutori nostro, jubilate* . . . (Wednesday), *Laetetur cor quaerentium Dominum* . . . (Friday), *Venite, adoremus* . . . *Venite exsultemus Domino: jubilemus Deo* . . . (Saturday). All the other Embertides have acquired either a purely penitential theme or have joined to this the dominant thought of the major feast of the season in which they fall: the Ember Day Masses of Advent, for instance, speak of the coming of Christ, those of Lent of the suffering caused

---

[113] Can. 18. Hefele-Leclercq, *Histoire des Conciles,* III, 908.
[114] Can. 11. *MPL,* 97: 124.
[115] *Op. cit.,* 186.
[116] *Op. cit.,* II, 413-414.
[117] Edit. H. Wilson, p. 124.
[118] *Micrologus,* 24. *MPL,* 151: 995.

by sin and the need for its atonement, and those of Pentecost week of
the descent of the Holy Spirit.

The Liturgy itself of these days manifests the great antiquity of
their institution. On each Wednesday, for instance, not just two, but
three lessons are read at Mass in the older schema. On all the Ember
Days of Advent and Lent special churches are assigned for the *collecta* in addition to the regular stational church, which means that a
special penitential procession was held on these days beginning at the
ecclesia collecta, or the church where the faithful gathered, and ending at the *ecclesia stationalis,* or the church where Mass was celebrated. Finally, the Saturday of each Ember season has six readings
at Mass. This is a remnant of the original twelve lessons, for in the
old Sacramentaries the title of these Saturdays was *Sabbatum in XII
lectionibus.* On such occasions the Foremass constituted the first part
of the all-night vigil extending from Saturday evening till early Sunday
morning, with Mass itself celebrated at its conclusion. It is because
of this phenomenon that we find in both the Gelasian and Gregorian
Sacramentaries no Mass formulary provided for the Sunday after the
Ember Saturdays: we read only the rubric *Dominica vacat.* In other
words, Saturday itself was without Mass; the Ember Mass was actually celebrated early on Sunday morning. Whence today we have the
custom of reading the same Gospel of the Ember Saturdays of Advent
and Lent on the following Sundays.

Actually in the old manuscripts, even though we find the title
Sabbatum in XII lectionibus, there are only seven orations: one to be
recited before each lesson and one before the Gospel. This lends support to the view that the original number of twelve lessons was arrived at due to the repetition of each lesson in Greek after it had been
read in Latin.[119] And that there were six pericopes to be read finds its
explanation in the fact that Holy Orders were conferred [120] between the
various lessons. Therefore, then, even as now, the order of Porter
was conferred after the first lesson, Lector after the second, Exorcist
after the third, Acolyte after the fourth, the Subdiaconate after the
fifth, the Diaconate after the Epistle and the Priesthood just before
the final verse of the Tract or Alleluia.

These ordinations, according to Cardinal Schuster,[121] also explain
the special choice of the stational churches for all the Ember Days.
It was customary to hold the final scrutiny or examination of the
candidates for Holy Orders in the Basilica of St. Mary Major on
Wednesday, make the official announcement of the names of the
newly chosen candidates in the Basilica of the Twelve Apostles on
Friday, and finally confer the various priestly powers over the tomb

---

[119] A practice still followed at all solemn papal Masses.
[120] It was in 494 that Pope Gelasius attached the ordinations to the Ember
Saturday celebration: *Epist.* 9 *ad Episc. Lucaniae,* 11, MPL, 59: 52.
[121] *The Sacramentary,* II (London: Burns, Oates and Washbourne, 1925),
pp. 64, 71, 73.

of the Prince of the Apostles, the High Priest and Vicar of Jesus Christ, source of the Priesthood—namely, in the Vatican Basilica during the solemn vigil service.

D. The Easter Cycle

1. Easter

As the principal and oldest festival of the Church, Easter is the very basis of the entire liturgical year as well as its connecting link with the feasts of the Old Testament. We have already seen that the early Church regarded Easter as the central feast of the annual cycle just as the Resurrection is the chief mystery of redemption. The Fathers of the Church could not find enough superlatives to describe its dignity. For Pope St. Leo I it is the *dies inclyta atque egregia.*[122] St. Gregory Nazianzen says that it is the "solemnity of solemnities, far exalted above all others, even those celebrated in honor of Christ," [123] yes, the "queen of days." [124] And Commodianus calls it the *dies felicissimus.*[125]

Our English name "Easter" comes from the Anglo-Saxon *Eastre,* in German *Ostra,*[126] the name of the Spring goddess worshipped by the ancient peoples who inhabited the north-west section of Germany. It was their custom to enkindle fires in honor of her and other deities in the Spring; this is the probable origin of the ceremony of the new fire at the beginning of the Easter Vigil. The original Latin name for Easter was *Dominica Resurrectionis.* Later the word *Pascha* was taken up by the Christians. It is Aramic for *pesach,* to pass over. It is in this sense that we find it used in Exodus (12:11) and Numbers (28:16): the *phase* or *transitus*—the passage—of the Lord. Easter celebrates the Passover as fulfilled by Christ; not simply the deliverance of the Jews from the hands of the Pharoah, but the passage from death to life effected by Christ.

Easter is indeed the Christian Passover, and the very name suggests the connection, both historical and ideological, between it and the Jewish feast. Historically, Christ died on the very first day of the Jewish Passover. Ideologically the connection is very real, for what happened to the world through Christ's death and Resurrection found its type and figure in the Jewish feast.

What was the Jewish Passover? It was the memorial of what occurred on the eve of the exodus of the Jews from Egypt. The Lord had commanded the Jews to kill a lamb, mark their doorposts with its blood and then, dressed for journey, to consume the lamb at a family

---

122 *Sermo 9 de resurrectione. MPL,* 54: 497.
123 *Oratio 45, n. 2. MPG,* 36: 623.
124 *Oratio 18 at the death of his father, n. 28. MPG,* 35:1018.
125 *Instructiones,* n. 75, v. I, *MPL,* 5: 257.
126 Bede, *De ratione temporum,* 15. *MPL,* 90: 357.

ceremonial meal. When the angel of death approached to execute God's command to kill the first-born of each Egyptian family, the houses thus marked with the blood of the lamb were saved from the devastating visit. Thereafter, at God's express command, the Jews were to commemorate their hard-won freedom by means of this same ceremonial meal repeated every year on the same day, the fourteenth day of Nisan.

Now all of this was the prophetic type of the final redemption to be wrought by Christ. The lamb itself symbolized Christ, through whose blood and atoning death the God-fearing were to be delivered from the death of sin and brought into the promised land of eternal life. Isaias took up this idea when he spoke of the suffering Messias as the lamb chosen by God to bear the iniquity of others.[127] Later St. John the Baptist exclaimed to his followers: "Behold the Lamb of God who takes away the sins of the world." [128] And St. John the Evangelist sees in the fact that the Roman soldiers would not break any of Christ's bones but only pierced His side a fulfillment of the prophecy contained in the regulation in Exodus that no bone of the Paschal Lamb's body should be broken.[129] And the Fathers of the Church followed this example as they explained the death of Christ as the realization of all the typological prophecies implicit in the Passover lamb of the Jews.[130]

This typological and historical connection between the Jewish Passover and Christ's sacrificial death and Resurrection led the early Christians to celebrate Easter and the events leading up to it on the very days on which they had occurred. But right away an insurmountable difficulty was discovered. Christ had died, according to one tradition at least, on the fourteenth day of Nisan. But what did this mean to people who used a solar year? For them the fourteenth day of Nisan, calculated according to the Jewish lunar year, could fall anywhere in March or April. The matter was further complicated by the fact that the Sanhedrin's caprice often introduced additional days and months for a variety of reasons. H. Kellner quotes an astounding letter written by the Rabbi Gamaliel and preserved in the Talmud. It shows the kind of considerations which ruled the Sanhedrin. "We herewith inform you that we, in conjunction with our colleagues, have deemed it necessary to add thirty days to the year, since the doves (to be offered in sacrifice) are still too tender, the lambs (for the Passover) too young, and the time of Abib (the barley harvest) has not arrived." [131] Bearing this in mind, we must conclude that any attempt

---

[127] 53:7 ff.
[128] John 1:29.
[129] John 19:36; Exodus 12:46.
[130] Cf. e. g.: Tertullian, *Adv. Marcionem*, 4, 40; 5, 7. *MPL*, 2: 490-493; 518; Justin, *Dialogus contra Tryphonem*, 40. *MPG*, 6: 562. See the interesting chapter of J. Daniélou, "Easter," in *The Bible and the Liturgy*, pp. 287-302.
[131] *Op. cit.*, 49-50.

to reconcile the Jewish Calendar with the Julian is doomed to failure, precisely because no one can be sure that such and such a year was a leap year with the Jews.

It was to be expected that converts from Judaism would follow their own calendar in fixing the date of Easter. Regardless of the day of the week on which it fell, the death of our Lord was always commemorated by them on the fourteenth day of Nisan. Whence came the name *Quartodeciman* for this practice. However, another consideration demanded a departure from such Jewish methods. The Resurrection, not the death of our Lord, was the central event to be commemorated by Christians, and this originally occurred on a Sunday. Hence the desire to remain faithful to fixed days of the week. This latter desire, coupled with the above-mentioned difficulty of arriving at a synchronization of the Jewish and Julian Calendars, led to a wide divergence in determining the date of the Easter celebration. Where the converts to Christianity came principally from among the Jews and the Jewish Calendar was in vogue, it was followed for this matter. But where the majority of converts were from among the Gentile nations another method of fixing the date for Easter had to be used.

Thus it is quite understandable that the Apostles are reported to have made conflicting decisions on this matter in different parts of the world. In Syria and Asia Minor, we are told, the Apostles John and Philip fixed the date of Easter according to Quartodeciman principles.[132] The Romans, however, appealed to a tradition stemming from St. Peter, which forbade them to go beyond March 26 and April 21.[133] And in this matter the Africans, along with Alexandria, followed the practice of Rome.[134]

After lively debate on this issue, Pope Victor in 190 decided in favor of the more widespread custom of celebrating Easter on the first Sunday after the full moon which followed upon the vernal equinox. Thus the date of Easter can oscillate between March 22 and April 25. And so, the variable Jewish lunar calendar has left its mark on Christianity and given practical expression to the relationship between it and Christianity.

2. Holy Week

The importance of Holy Week is brought out by some of the names given it. We find the term "holy week" used by St. Athanasius in his Festal Letters announcing the date of Easter.[135] It was called "greater week" in Jerusalem towards the end of the fourth century.[136]

[132] Eusebius, *Hist. eccl.*, V, 24. GCS, 9 (1), p. 491.
[133] *Athanasii Epistolarum Festalium Chronicon Praevium*, 9. MPG, 26: 1355.
[134] Athanasius, *Epist. ad Afros Episcopos*, 2. MPG, 26: 1031.
[135] *Epist. festalis*, 2, 8. MPG, 26: 1371.
[136] Ethérie, *Journal de Voyage* (Edit. du Cerf, 1948), n. 30, p. 218.

This designation is proper, as St. John Chrysostom remarks,[137] because our Lord has done truly marvelous things in it. Without doubt this week occupies the chief place in the liturgical year, for within it are celebrated the principal mysteries of man's redemption: the Last Supper, at which Christ instituted the Eucharistic Sacrifice and the priesthood; His death on Calvary, through which He removed the death of sin and purchased us from the power of the devil; and His resurrection, through which He gave us the new life of grace.

In the same way as the Church year itself grew and developed through the centuries, so in particular did Holy Week enjoy a variety of observances throughout the world in different periods. From earliest times, perhaps even in the days of the Apostles, Friday and Saturday of this week were observed by means of an especially rigorous fast.[138] At a later date still another day was added—Wednesday, the day on which the Jews made their decision to capture and execute Jesus, at least according to one tradition.[139] And by the third century Christians in many localities fasted during the entire week.[140] Not everywhere, however, was Mass offered on all these days.

It is to Jerusalem that we must look for the origin of many of the liturgical specialties of this week. Since that city contained so many places sanctified by the memory of our Lord's life, it was only natural that the Christians there should try as best they could to re-enact the more important episodes of Christ's last days on the very ground where they had originally occurred. The pilgrim nun Etheria, who wrote the diary of her travels through Palestine towards the end of the fourth century, has left us a minute description of each day's liturgical ceremonies.[141] From Palestine these rites found their way into Gallican lands and thence to Rome itself. There they were fused with the already existing Roman Holy Week ritual.

Palm Sunday

In the course of time this Sunday has received many names. The original Roman name seems to have been Passion Sunday, simply because the story of the passion was read during Mass this day.[142] But the title Palm Sunday appears already in the Gelasian [143] and Gregorian Sacramentaries.[144] Finally, Rome combined both the commemora-

[137] Homil. 30 in Genesim, 1. MPG, 53: 273-274.
[138] Innocent I, Epist., 25, 4. MPL, 20: 555; Tertullian, De jejuniis, 2. MPL, 2: 1006: in quibus ablatus est sponsus.
[139] Peter of Alexandria, Epistula Canonica, 15. MPG, 17: 507.
[140] Apostolic Constitutions, V, 18. MPG, 1: 890.
[141] As in note 136, nn. 30-38, pp. 218-240.
[142] Cf. e.g., Leo I, Sermo de passione Domini, 1, 5. MPL, 54: 314.
[143] Yet it still bears the subtitle De Passione Domini: H. A. Wilson, The Gelasian Sacramentary (Oxford, 1894), p. 60.
[144] K. Mohlberg, Die älteste erreichbare Gestalt des Liber Sacramentorum anni circuli der römischen Kirche (Münster, 1927), p. 22.

tion of our Lord's triumphal entry into Jerusalem with the chanting of the Passion.[145] Today it is called Palm Sunday or Second Sunday of the Passion.

There is little doubt that the procession of palms originated in Jerusalem. Christ's entry into the Holy City was a fulfillment of a prophecy made in the Old Testament: "Behold thy king shall come to thee, the just and savior; he is poor and riding upon an ass and upon a colt, the foal of an ass." [146] Since the fulfillment of this prophecy was of such great apologetic value, showing as it did that Christ was the promised Messias, the people of Jerusalem were led to re-enact the episode. They gathered about their bishop at one o'clock in the afternoon on the Mount of Olives. Having sung hymns and listened to readings of the Old Testament and the Gospel account of our Lord's entry, at five o'clock the faithful, carrying olive or palm branches, led the bishop, seated on an ass, to the Church of the Resurrection. All the while they chanted psalms and hymns, constantly interjecting the refrain: "Blessed is he who cometh in the name of the Lord!" The service concluded with the singing of Vespers.[147]

It is not certain just when this rite was brought over to the West. Rome knew nothing of it for many centuries. True, the Gelasian and Gregorian Sacramentaries contain the title Palm Sunday, but this is only the title; no blessing of palms is provided,[148] nor is there any mention of a procession. The presence of such a title in these books remains unexplained.[149] It is quite possible that the mere memory of the original historical event which took place on this day was sufficient to call forth such a title. The fact remains, however, that no trace of any palm ceremony has been found in official Roman books until the twelfth century.[150] It is reasonable to conjecture that the ceremony of the palm blessing and the procession made its way to Rome from Gallican lands during the time of the Ottos, just as so many other Gallican elements did.[151]

---

[145] In many Gallican service books the title given this Sunday is *In symboli traditione* (*Missale Gothicum*, 27; *Vetus Missale Gallicanum*, 15; The Bobbio Missal. *MPL*, 72: 263, 354, 487), for it was on this day that the Gallican Church had its catechumens taught the Creed. Rome, however, left this for another day in Lent.

[146] Zacharias 9:9.

[147] See the whole account in Etheria, *Journal de Voyage*, n. 31, pp. 220-222.

[148] *Codex Ottob.* 313, written about 850 for use in Paris, is the first Gregorian type Sacramentary to contain a blessing for palms: Cf. H. Wilson, *The Gregorian Sacramentary*, p. 46, note 3; H. Lietzmann, *Das Sacramentarium Gregorianum nach dem Aachener Urexemplar* (Münster, 1921), n. 73, p. 42, note 9.

[149] It is not too convincing to say that its presence is due to Gallican influence, as does Noële Maurice-Denis Boulet, ("Le dimanche des Rameaux," *La Maison-Dieu*, n. 41 (1955), 25.) for it is found even when no special ceremonial is indicated and in the most genuine of Roman books.

[150] M. Andrieu, *Le Pontifical Romain au moyen-age* (4 vols. Vatican City, 1938-1941), I, 210-214.

[151] Andrieu shows that most of the formulas contained in the Roman Pontifical

That these rites existed from a relatively early time in the territories using the Gallican Liturgy is beyond doubt. Though Isidore of
Seville speaks of the *dies palmarum*, it is not certain that he is really
speaking of a liturgical ceremony.[152] And we may say the same of what
the Venerable Bede relates.[153] The Mozarabic *Liber Ordinum*, which
contains traditions of the fifth and sixth centuries, seems to be the first
Western service book to describe such ceremonies.[154] After this these
rites are clearly attested to in Gaul and Germany by Theodulf of
Orleans, who composed the famous hymn, "Gloria, laus et honor,"
before 821,[155] and by Amalar of Metz, who alludes to a procession of
palms.[156] And we find a formula for blessing palms in the seventh
century Bobbio Missal.[157]

Throughout the Middle Ages the dramatic possibilities of Christ's
triumphal entry into Jerusalem found a variety of concrete expressions in the many countries of Europe. Instead of having their bishop
ride a donkey in the procession, the populace would represent the
person of the Messias by means of the Gospel book covered with a
purple cloth placed upon an improvised carriage borne by deacons.
This was the custom in some French localities.[158] In northern Italy
people were accustomed to decorating a large cross with green foliage
and would carry this in procession. Arriving at the gate of the city,
they would cast their garments and palms before the carriage with
the cross and shout the same acclamations as the Jews who hailed the
advent of their messianic King and Redeemer. A cleric would then
knock on the gate of the city, and, as the gate opened and the cortege
entered, everyone would sing the antiphon *Ingrediente Domino in
sanctam civitatem*. Finally, in England from the time of Lanfranc
(1089) on, as well as in Normandy, it was the custom to carry the
Blessed Sacrament in procession.[159]

The present rite for the blessing and procession with palms is a
simplification, with some new additions, of the ritual which obtained
until 1955. In earliest times, of course, there was no blessing provided
for the palms.[160] It appears for the first time in the above-mentioned
Liber Ordinum of the Mozarabic Rite. At the end of the Middle Ages

of the twelfth century stemmed directly from the Romano-Germanic Pontifical of
the tenth century: *ibid.*, 210-214.

[152] *De eccl. off.*, I, 28. *MPL*, 83: 763.
[153] *Homil.* 23. *MPL*, 94: 125.
[154] M. Férotin, *Le liber ordinum en usage dans l'Eglise visigothique et
mozarabe d'Espagne* (Paris, 1904), col. 73.
[155] *Carmina*, lib. II, 3. *MPL*, 105: 308.
[156] *De off. eccl.*, I, 10. *MPL*, 105: 1008.
[157] *MPL*, 72: 572.
[158] A similar practice employing the Gospel book to represent Christ is also
to be found in the thirteenth century *Ordo Romanus* XII of Mabillon: n. 18. *MPL*,
78: 1071.
[159] Cf. E. Bishop, *Liturgica Historica*, 286.
[160] Cf. Etheria, *op. cit.*, n. 31, p. 222.

this blessing was removed from the Mass proper. Still it was desired that the rite resemble a Mass as much as possible, and thus an almost complete *Missa sicca* was developed, that is, a Mass-formulary without consecration. Such a framework for this ceremony was introduced into the official Roman Rite at least by the twelfth century, though it had already been in existence in Germany centuries before.[161] Unfortunately such an involved rite laid so much emphasis on the palm itself as a sacramental that the central theme of the rite, the messianic kingship of Christ, was overshadowed. This is why, in the Holy Week Ordo of Pius XII, the blessing is reduced to a single oration, while everything else centers around the joyous acclamation of Christ the King. And to stress this theme even more, the Ordo prescribes that regal red vestments be worn during the whole service before Mass and provides many more psalms and antiphons with a messianic content for singing by the faithful.

After the procession, the mood of the celebration changes radically. From the boisterous and joyful acclaim of the Chosen People upon seeing their King we turn to the jeers of the bewildered mob as it decrees the crucifixion of its God. Here the fickleness of the Jews is brought out, but even more the true nature of the Messias is made manifest. According to the prophets of old, the Holy One, the Christ, was to gain His glory through suffering.[162] The gorgeous red vestments are exchanged for the somber violet, and the theme of the Mass proper is the Passion of Christ. With this we have arrived at the original Roman Liturgy for Palm Sunday which had always centered around the chanting of the Passion according to St. Matthew.[163]

At first the Passion was sung by the deacon, whose office it always was to chant the Gospel. But the length of the Passion as well as the dramatizing tendency of the northern peoples of Europe led, at least by the tenth century, to the practice of having three chanters sing it.[164] But Rome was slow in accepting this usage. As late as the fourteenth century the Passion was still sung by the cardinal-deacon alone.[165] One of the results of the reform of Pius XII was a shortening of the Passion; now it begins with the agony in the garden instead of with Christ's prediction of His own crucifixion and the meeting of the Sanhedrin at which the chief priests and elders reached their decision to apprehend Jesus.

[161] Everything belonging to this quasi-Mass rite is already to be found in the Romano-Germanic Pontifical of the tenth century with the exception of the Preface and Sanctus; cf. M. Andrieu, *Le Pontifical Romain*, I, 210-214.

[162] Luke 24: 25-27.

[163] Pope St. Leo I is the earliest witness to this custom; he always explained the account of the Passion on this day: *Sermo de pass. Domini*, I ff. *MPL*, 54: 314.

[164] H. Thurston, *Lent and Holy Week* (London: Longmans, 1904), 230.

[165] *Ordo Rom.* XV, n. 60. *MPL*, 78: 1303-1304.

Holy Thursday

While the first three days of the week are not without their special contribution to the overall theme of the week, that of the Passion, it is only natural to expect that the Church has placed greater emphasis on the last three days through more solemn services because it was on these days that the redemptive work of Christ was brought to completion.

The first of the days, Holy Thursday, has received in the course of time a variety of names which serve to put in relief its special theme. From earliest times it has been called *feria quinta in coena Domini*, since it principally commemorates the institution of the Holy Eucharist. The same theme is brought out by the title given it in the Calendar of Polemius Silvius, namely, *Natalis Calicis*.[166] To underline the idea that on this day our Lord was betrayed by His trusted disciple Judas and also began to offer Himself up for the sins of mankind, some called the day the *dies traditionis*.[167] A common English name is Maundy Thursday, which is derived from the ceremony for washing the feet, called in Latin *mandatum* (commandment) and done in imitation of our Lord when He washed the feet of the Apostles, saying to them: "A new commandment I give to you, that you love one another. . . ." [168]

Besides commemorating the mystery of the Eucharist and the fraternal love which it should beget, Holy Thursday was also the day on which two other ceremonies took place: the reconciliation of penitents and the consecration of Holy Oils. At first sight these ceremonies might seem entirely accidental to the theme of the day. And generally authors give as the reason for holding them on this day the desire to shorten the Easter Vigil.[169] Nevertheless, when the sacrament of Penance is seen as the second gateway to the communion of saints, with its source in the Eucharistic Sacrifice, it is altogether fitting that this relationship be expressed on the feast of the Holy Eucharist. Our first witness to this union is the letter of Pope Innocent I to Decentius of Gubbio written at the beginning of the fifth century.[170] And the old Gelasian Sacramentary provides special formulas for this ceremony. According to it, the reconciliation of penitents replaced the normal Foremass, as the following rubric states: "Eodem die non psallitur, nec salutat, id est non dicit Dominus vobiscum; et Reconciliatio." [171] After the penitents were reconciled, the Mass proper started with the Offertory.[172] However, by the time of Gregory the Great this

---

[166] *MPL*, 13: 678.
[167] Thurston, *op. cit.*, 286.
[168] John 13:34.
[169] Cf. e.g., H. Schmidt, "Geist und Geschichte des Gründonnerstags," *Liturgisches Jahrbuch*, III (1953), 243.
[170] *Epist.* 25, 7. *MPL*, 20: 559.
[171] Edit. H. A. Wilson, p. 63.
[172] *Ibid.*, p. 67.

rite had already fallen into disuse, for there is no ceremony and no mention of the practice in the Gregorian Sacramentary.[173]

We must also admit that the consecration of Holy Oils on this Thursday is appropriate, for it serves to emphasize the fact that all sacraments and blessings flow from the Eucharistic Sacrifice.[174] However, the oils were not always blessed on this day. Though a special blessing for oil (apparently oil for the infirm) figures among the blessings provided for other natural products before the concluding doxology of the Canon of the Mass in the *Apostolic Tradition*,[175] Chrism and the Oil for Catechumens were blessed in the early Church immediately before the conferring of Baptism.[176] The first trace of all the oils being consecrated together during the Mass on Holy Thursday appears in the Gelasian Sacramentary.[177]

Did the ancient Roman Rite have a special Mass for the Consecration of Oils on Holy Thursday? There are three documents which profess to offer the Roman usage: the Gelasian Sacramentary, the Gregorian Sacramentary according to the Paduan Codex, and the same Sacramentary as exemplified in the copy sent by Pope Hadrian to Charlemagne. The Gelasian offers us three Masses: one for the reconciliation of penitents, a second for the Consecration of Oils, and a third, in the evening, to commemorate the Last Supper.[178] On the other hand, the Paduan Codex contains the partial formularies of two Masses: one with no special designation and another intended as an evening Mass.[179] Lastly, in the Hadrian text we find but one Mass, during which the Oils were consecrated.[180]

Leaving aside for the moment what the Gelasian Sacramentary contains, for it is so often gallicanized that we cannot always trust it, we must take the Paduan Codex and the Hadrian book as being the sole secure witnesses to pure Roman practice. A comparison of these two books shows that the one Hadrian Mass is really a combination of the two formularies appearing in the Paduan Codex. But both of these latter are incomplete. H. Schmidt [181] reasons that the first, which lacks the Foremass, is a remnant of the ancient Mass for the recon-

[173] Edit. K. Mohlberg, pp. 23-24. However, two Mass-formularies are provided: one begins with the Communicantes, and this may possibly be the remnant of the Mass for the reconciliation of penitents; the other is for an evening Mass.
[174] This is, after all, the origin of the *Per quem haec omnia* of the Canon of the Mass, as seen in the *Apostolic Tradition*: see following note.
[175] Edited by B. Botte (Paris: Editions du Cerf, 1946), n. 5, p. 33.
[176] *Ibid.*, n. 21, p. 49.
[177] Edit. H. A. Wilson, pp. 69-72. In some places, however, the Consecration of Oils took place on other days: the seventh century Parisian Liturgy had it on Palm Sunday, whence the name *dies unctionis;* St. Caesarius of Arles (d. 542) kept it till the Easter Vigil, a more ancient practice: cf. G. Morin, "Une particularité arlésienne de la liturgie du samedi saint," *Ephemerides Liturgicae*, 49 (1935), 146-149.
[178] Wilson, pp. 63-73.
[179] Mohlberg, pp. 23-24.
[180] Lietzmann, pp. 44-47.
[181] "Geist und Geschichte des Gründonnerstags," p. 245.

ciliation of penitents, for, as we know, this reconciliation itself took the place of the Foremass. The second formulary of the Paduan Codex bears the title *Item de ipsa die Missa sero*—an evening Mass, and one which lacks its proper ending. This lack is explained when we remember that the ritual of the Consecration of Oils would naturally take the place of the ending.[182] And as a matter of fact the Oils were consecrated in the Hadrian Mass, which was formed by joining the two partial formularies of the earlier Paduan codex.

So, as far as genuine and uncontroverted Roman documents go, we cannot prove that Rome ever had any more than two Masses on Holy Thursday: one for the reconciliation of penitents, another in the evening, as a commemoration of the Last Supper, in which the Oils were consecrated. Finally, when the earlier Roman penitential practice died out, only one Mass was offered, in the evening; there was no special Mass for the Consecration of the Oils. As for the evidence in the Gelasian Sacramentary, it has been suggested that these latter rites are a good example of how Holy Thursday was observed *outside* of Rome.[183] If this is true, then we must see in the institution of the special Mass for the Consecration of Oils in the new Holy Week Ordo of Pius XII a re-introduction of a specifically Gallican usage. As a matter of fact, all the orations and the Preface for this Mass were taken from the same Mass in the Gelasian book, while all the material for the evening Mass was taken from the Paduan and Hadrian books.

The ceremony of the Mandatum, or the washing of the feet, was originally a simple act of charity very common in the Church—especially in monasteries. St. Paul lists this act among the good works of a saintly widow.[184] The first evidence of the ceremony being a liturgical rite for Holy Thursday comes from the seventeenth Synod of Toledo, held in 694, which speaks of it as having already fallen into desuetude in some places but recommends its restoration.[185] The rite had certainly been adopted in Rome by the eleventh century, for at that time we find the pope washing the feet of twelve subdeacons at the end of the evening Mass.[186] When during the fourteenth century all the ceremonies were held in the morning hours, the Mandatum remained a separate service which usually took place in the afternoon.[187] Pius XII had this ceremony restored to its place of honor in the evening Mass; according to his Ordo it comes immediately after the Gos-

---

[182] *Ibid.*, 246.

[183] *Ibid.*, 244. We consider Schmidt's conclusion, not as certain, but only as highly probable. Unfortunately, he does not base it on arguments which would show that these three Masses could not have existed in Rome. Rather it seems based entirely on his assumption that the Gelasian Sacramentary is an out and out Gallican document. For a refutation of this assumption see our treatment in Chapter 3. A. Chavasse claims that the Gelasian book represents the Holy Thursday rite proper to parish churches of Rome: *Le Sacramentaire Gélasien*, pp. 126-135.

[184] 1 Tim. 5:10.

[185] Can. 3. Hefele-Leclercq, *Histoire des Conciles*, III, 586.

[186] *Ord. Rom.* X, n. 12. *MPL*, 78: 1013.

[187] *Ord. Rom.* XV, n. 65. *MPL*, 78: 1307.

pel. Thus we are the better able to imitate the ritual of the original Last Supper at which our Lord washed the feet of His disciples *during the meal.*[188]

During the Mass on Holy Thursday enough extra hosts are to be consecrated for the general communion on Good Friday. After Mass they are carried in solemn procession to a specially prepared altar and repository. As might be expected, it took time for this arrangement to develop. At first—from the seventh century— [189] the Blessed Sacrament was reserved in the sacristy, and it was brought there in the simplest possible manner. All the earliest references to such reservation on Holy Thursday indicate this by the bald statement: *et reservantur sancta usque in crastinum.*[190] The first mention of a formal procession is by Jean d'Avranches in the eleventh century.[191] And this was due to the increasing devotion of the faithful towards the reserved Sacrament.

In a short time another influence made itself felt. The allegorists saw in the depositing of the hosts in a special repository a symbol of our Lord's burial, and thus in some countries the repository came to be known as the *sepulcrum.*[192] And there the people kept watch. But this watch, originally quite distinct from any Eucharistic devotion, was to last for forty hours beginning on Good Friday. However, the desire to keep a full forty-hour watch, coupled with the development which brought the Easter Vigil farther into the morning hours of Holy Saturday, effectively fused two distinct devotions into one: veneration for the reserved Sacrament and the Forty Hours Devotion—a pious watch before the tomb of Christ.[193]

The idea of the *sepulcrum* was, of course, in sharp conflict with the chronology of these last three days: Christ was not placed in the tomb until the evening of Good Friday after His crucifixion. In time all the funereal [194] processional drama connecting Christ's burial with the solemn reservation of hosts consecrated on Holy Thursday was sharply curbed by the Holy See, and the name *sepulcrum* for the repository was only grudgingly permitted by the Congregation of Rites. The true spirit behind this nocturnal adoration on Thursday is to keep watch—as the Apostles failed to do—with Christ during His long hours of agony before His arrest in the Garden of Olives.

---

[188] John 13:2 and 12.

[189] Cf. P. Browe, "Die Kommunion an den drei letzten Kartagen," *Jahrbuch für Liturgiewissenschaft,* 10 (1930), 70.

[190] Cf. The Gelasian Sacramentary (edit. Wilson), p. 72; the eighth century *Ord. Rom.* XXIII from Einsiedeln, n. 8. M. Andrieu, *Les Ordines Romani,* III, 270; and *Ord. Rom.* XXX, n. 25, Andrieu, III, 470.

[191] "Ipsae hostiae . . . cum processione, scilicet cum cereis et incenso, super quoddam altare honorifice deportentur . . ." *De eccl. off.,* 27. MPL, 147: 50.

[192] Cf. J. Kettel, "Zur Liturgie des Gründonnerstags," *Liturgisches Jahrbuch,* 3 (1953), 65-74.

[193] Cf. J. A. Jungmann, "Die Andacht der 40 Stunden und das heilige Grab," *Liturgisches Jahrbuch,* 2 (1952), 184-198.

[194] *Ibid.,* 197.

The ceremonies on Holy Thursday are concluded with the stripping of the altars. Although the special ceremony used for this purpose is very expressive of the stripping off of Christ's clothing for the flagellation and crucifixion, it is very probable that it takes its true origin from the simple and regular practice of the early Church of removing the altar cloths after each Mass.

In certain Rites within the Church today, e.g., the Rite of Lyons, all priests are permitted to celebrate Mass on this day, not privately, but all together at the same altar and at the same time by means of a true sacramental concelebration. In the Roman Rite, however, even though such a concelebration was provided for on certain more solemn occasions in the liturgical year, Holy Thursday was not one of them.[195] The Roman Rite has never shown itself preoccupied with a special celebration of the priesthood on this day. Rather it would seem that it wants to bring out symbolically the fact that at the Last Supper Christ alone offered the Holy Sacrifice. Nevertheless, it is hoped by some [196] that, in the future, permission might be granted for a genuinely sacramental concelebration.

Good Friday

In the liturgical books of the Roman Rite this day is called *Parasceve*, or preparation, for it coincides with the Parasceve of the Jews, the day of preparation for the great Sabbath. This is a day of great sorrow, *dies amaritudinis*, as Ambrose calls it.[197] And this sorrow was expressed by fasting; this indeed was a universal custom.[198] As another expression of this sentiment there existed a universal custom of not celebrating Mass on this day.[199] In the seventh century some even went so far as to keep their churches closed, a practice which the above-mentioned Council of Toledo dubbed as an abuse.[200] In time a discussion arose as to why no Mass was celebrated, since the days on which the saints died were kept as festivals. Helperich, a monk of the Monastery of St. Gall at the end of the ninth century, replied that Christ, unlike the saints, achieved no greater degree of glory through His death, for He died, not for His own sake, but for ours. The Jews, he went on to say, rejoiced over His death, while the Apostles lamented it.[201]

Once it had become traditional to hold some sort of liturgical service in public, it was always held in the afternoon hours. Our

---

[195] Cf. *Ord. Rom.* III, n. 1. Andrieu, *Les Ordines,* II, 131.
[196] H. Schmidt, "Geist und Geschichte des Gründonnerstags," pp. 249-250.
[197] *Epist.* 23, 12. *MPL,* 16: 1073.
[198] *Ibid.; The Apostolic Constitutions,* V, 18. *MPG,* 1: 890; IV Council of Toledo of 633, c. 8. *MPL,* 84: 369.
[199] Innocent I, *Epist.* 25, 4. *MPL,* 20: 555. And there is no trace of any sacramental celebration before or after this document.
[200] Can. 7. *MPL,* 84: 368.
[201] Cf. Pseudo-Alcuin, *De div. off., MPL,* 101: 1211.

earliest document tells us that the pope descended from his apartments at two o'clock.[202] And this arrangement continued up to and including the first part of the fifteenth century.[203] Just after that the ceremony was held in the morning, according to Burchard's Ceremonial, compiled in 1488.[204] The restoration of this service to its appropriate hours in the afternoon is due to Pius XII.

Three parts make up the Liturgy of Good Friday: (a) a reading service similar to our Mass of the Catechumens, (b) the veneration of the cross, and (c) a communion service.

The entire first part is composed of reading, chants, and prayers. And this is nothing else than the ancient type of service held on days which were a-liturgical, that is, days on which the Eucharistic Sacrifice was not offered. It is the Service of the Word, originally taken over from the Jewish Sabbath synagogue service and united, no later than the second century, to the Eucharistic Sacrifice as the part known today as the Mass of the Catechumens.[205] Etheria tells us that such a reading service was customary on this day in Palestine. From noon till three o'clock the people of Jerusalem listened to the readings from the psalms, apostles and prophets of whatever concerned our Lord's Passion. In between the various readings appropriate prayers were said. And the service ended with the reading of St. John's account of our Redeemer's dying moments.[206] The thought of the Passion, then, dominated their service just as it does ours today and did throughout the Middle Ages. The long list of orations which terminate this first part is nothing else than the ancient conclusion to the Mass of the Catechumens spoken of by Justin and which, though dropped from the ordinary Mass from the time of Pope St. Gelasius on, has been retained in the Liturgy of this one day of the year, in accordance with the law formulated by Anton Baumstark concerning [207] the survival of what is ancient in a liturgical season of high value. Apparently, to judge from the Paduan Codex of the Gregorian Sacramentary,[208] this Service of the Word was the only function held on this day in the early Church.

Upon completing the lengthy solemn orations, we turn to the unveiling and veneration of the cross, a feature which originated in Jerusalem itself in the fourth century after the discovery of the relics

---

[202] The eighth century *Ord. Rom.* XXIII, n. 9. Andrieu, *Les Ordines,* III, 270.

[203] "Sero" we read in the *Ord. Rom.* XV, n. 75. *MPL,* 78: 1315.

[204] Cf. B. Capelle, "Problèmes de pastorale liturgique: le Vendredi Saint," *Questions Liturgiques et Paroissiales,* 34 (1953), 262.

[205] Justin Martyr clearly describes it in his first *Apology*: the reading of the commentaries of the Apostles and the writings of the Prophets, a sermon, then the prayers of the assembled congregation, 67. J. Quasten, p. 19; see also Tertullian, *De anima,* 9. *MPL,* 2: 701.

[206] *Op. cit.,* n. 37, pp. 236-238.

[207] "Das Gesetz der Erhaltung des Alten in liturgisch hochwertiger Zeit," *Jahrbuch für Liturgiewissenschaft,* 7 (1927), 1, 23.

[208] K. Mohlberg, p. 24.

of the true cross by the Empress Helena. There, however, the veneration of the cross took place in the morning hours, according to
Etheria.[209]

The ceremony was quite simple. It took place at Golgotha, where
the bishop had his throne erected. The relic of the true cross was
placed upon a white bedecked table immediately before him, and, as
he held his hand upon the relic, the clergy and faithful passed before
him to venerate it. As for Rome—our first evidence for the service there
comes from the eighth century—a procession started out from St. John
Lateran at two o'clock in the afternoon and headed toward the Basilica
of the Holy Cross. The psalm *Beati immaculati in via* was sung as all
walked barefoot, the pope swinging a censer before the relic of the
cross all the while. Upon arriving at Holy Cross, the pope placed the
relic on the altar, prostrated himself before it and then kissed it. After
him, the clergy did the same. Thereupon it was carried out to the
faithful for them to venerate it.[210] The antiphon *Ecce lignum crucis*
originally was probably interspersed among the verses of Psalm 118
during the opening procession.[211] The Byzantine *Hagios o Theos* and
the *Improperia* appear for the first time in the so-called Romano-Germanic Pontifical of the tenth century which was composed at Mainz.[212]
Thence these hymns went to Rome and are witnessed to by the papal
Pontifical of the twelfth century, in which the unveiling ceremony also
appears for the first time.[213]

A Communion service, once called the Mass of the Presanctified,
forms the third part of this day's Liturgy. The early Roman Rite evidently knew nothing of Communion on Good Friday: no mention is
made of it in documents prior to the eighth century. Of course, the
mere silence of the earlier Roman texts does not of itself necessarily
disprove the existence of such a practice. Nevertheless, the story
which the eighth century service books tell seems to be that the
reception of Communion on this day had just recently been introduced in the environs of Rome but was not accepted as part of the
papal service. The pope did not receive, neither did his ministers.
But once they had returned to the Lateran, the people could receive
Communion, if they liked, at Holy Cross, or could go to some other
church in the city.[214]

---

[209] *Op. cit.*, n. 37, p. 232. The first Roman Ordo which affords us a clear-
cut description of pure Roman usage places the veneration of the cross before the
reading service too — but in the afternoon: see following footnote.

[210] *Ord. Rom.* XXIII, nn. 12-17. Andrieu, III, 270-271.

[211] However, it does not figure in the above-mentioned papal procession, but
it is spoken of for the first time in a contemporary document composed apparently
for the churches in the environs of Rome: *Ord. Rom.* XXIV, n. 35. Andrieu,
III, 294.

[212] B. Cappelle, *art. cit.*, pp. 257-258. Cf. also Andrieu, *Le Pontifical Romain*,
I, p. 236, n. 9, line 36.

[213] Andrieu (as in note 212), p. 236, n. 8.

[214] *Ord. Rom.* XXIII, nn. 21-22. Andrieu, *Les Ordines Romani*, III, 272.

This accords with what Amalar reports. When he had asked a Roman archdeacon about the practice of receiving Communion on Good Friday, he was told that no one communicated at the papal service.[215] On the other hand, the Church was evidently anxious to give in to popular piety in this matter and, while not according it an official place in the more prominent papal service, allowed Communion to be distributed to the faithful in their parish churches. Thus we find another document of this same eighth century which describes the rites in the titular churches of Rome. In it we find that after the veneration of the cross, or rather, while the people were still venerating it, the hosts consecrated the day before were brought unobtrusively to the main altar. After the recitation of the Pater together with its embolism, a particle of the large host was mixed with unconsecrated wine and water. Then all communicated in silence.[216]

In the early documents there is no mention of a "mass" of the presanctified. Communion was simply distributed after the traditional Communion prayer, the Pater. The first time elements of a Dry Mass are found in the papal Liturgy for this day is in the Roman Pontifical of the twelfth century.[217] After the transfer of the consecrated host, rubrics indicate that the altar is to be incensed, the prayer *In spiritu humilitatis* recited, the Pater and its embolism said, the host broken into three pieces, one of which is to be dropped into the unconsecrated wine. This action was unquestionably imported from the Oriental Rites, through Gallican hands,[218] to give this part of the service added solemnity and the appearance of a real Mass. This Eastern usage, in turn, is based on the decree of the Council of Laodicea of 365,[219] repeated by the Council *In Trullo* of 692,[220] according to which the Eucharistic Sacrifice was not to be celebrated on ferial days of Lent. Instead use was to be made of the Mass of the Presanctified.

Once it had become customary to distribute Communion on Good Friday, the practice was fervently adhered to for centuries. True, in the Roman Pontifical of the thirteenth century we find the first indication of a change of spirit: *communicat solus pontifex*. Capelle finds the explanation for this rubric in the fact that at the time reception of Communion in Rome was very rare.[221] It was at the same period that the Fourth Lateran Council (1215) was forced to make the reception of Communion at least once a year during the Paschal season obligatory. The rubric we have just mentioned simply faced up to the situ-

---

[215] *De eccl. off.*, I, 15. *MPL*, 105: 1032.
[216] *Ord. Rom.* XXIV, nn. 36-38. Andrieu, III, 294. Hence, the presence of this well developed Communion service in the Gelasian Sacramentary (ed. Wilson, 77) must be a Gallican interpolation.
[217] Cf. M. Andrieu, *Le Pontifical Romain*, I, 237, nn. 10-11.
[218] It is present *in toto* in the Romano-Germanic Pontifical of the tenth century: see references in Andrieu as in note 217.
[219] Can. 49. Hefele-Leclercq, *op. cit.*, I, 1022.
[220] Can. 52. Hefele-Leclercq, *op. cit.*, III, 569.
[221] *Art. cit.*, p. 260.

ation: people did not want to receive. Outside of Rome, however, reception of Communion on this day continued in full vigor even after it was officially forbidden. In fact, in the seventeenth century Rome had to repeat the prohibition several times. Again we must thank Pius XII for restoring to the faithful the opportunity of uniting themselves to their Savior on the day He gave Himself for their salvation. As history shows, the Holy See, in re-instating general Communion on this day, was not guided by antiquarianism (if she had been, she would not have revived this practice, for the early Roman Liturgy knew nothing of it), but rather by genuine pastoral solicitude. At the same time, Pius XII's Holy Week Ritual restored this service to its primitive simplicity, removing all the dry-mass accretions of the late Middle Ages.

Holy Saturday

Even more so than Friday, this day is completely a-liturgical and traditionally so. Innocent I gives as the reason for no Eucharistic celebration on this day the tradition that the Apostles spent the day in grief over the loss of Christ.[222] The Church keeps the day in quiet mourning, for her Bridegroom has been taken away from her and lies in the tomb. This is the theme of Matins for Holy Saturday: Christ's death and burial, His lying in the tomb, the descent into Limbo.

It is with the Easter Vigil that the real Easter Liturgy begins, and in which the entire liturgical year and Holy Week reach their climax.[223] Let us take a rapid look at the preceding days of Holy Week and see how they actually lead up to and find their fulfillment in the Easter Vigil.

On the very first day, Palm Sunday, we hear re-echoed the prophecies of the Messianic King and His glorification through the Resurrection. As He approached the Holy City on the donkey the people acclaim Him to be the promised King. Upon arriving in Jerusalem our Lord went into the Temple and seeing the terrible commercial traffic that went on there overturned the tables of the money-changers and the sellers of doves. When asked by what authority He did this, He answered, "Destroy this temple and in three days I will raise it up again." [224] This, of course, He said in reference to His death and Resurrection. The Epistle of the Mass echoes this same idea in the words of St. Paul: "He humbled Himself, becoming obedient unto death, even to the death of the cross. For which reason God has

[222] *Epist.* 25, 4. *MPL,* 20: 555.
[223] For a fuller explanation of this last assertion see J. Miller, "The Easter Vigil: Climax of the Week and the Year." *People's Participation and Holy Week* (Proceedings of the North American Liturgical Week of 1956, Elsberry, Missouri, 1957), 132-145.
[224] John 2:19. The other evangelists make this incident coincide with Christ's

exalted Him and given Him a name which is above all names."[225]
And in the Collect we pray that we may learn the lessons of His Passion and thus share in the glory of His Resurrection.

On Monday we read the Gospel account of Christ raising Lazarus from the dead, and in the prayer over the people we beg God to let "us come with joy to the celebration of the great deeds whereby He has made us anew." The Introit of Tuesday speaks of the cross of Christ as our "salvation, life and resurrection," while again the prayer over the people speaks of our being cleansed from the weaknesses of sinful nature in order to take part in the divine renewal. In the second Collect for Wednesday we ask for the grace of the Resurrection as the fruit of Christ's Passion, and the Collect and Postcommunion on Holy Thursday indicate too that resurrection and immortality come to us through the cross. Finally, Good Friday itself, though dedicated specifically to the remembrance of the Passion, begins with two readings, the first of which describes the mercy of God striking us in order to heal us, quickening us after two days and raising us up on the third to a new life in His eyes; and the second is the account of the Passover meal in Exodus, eaten in preparation for the Passage of the Lord, for the deliverance of His Chosen People—a figure of the Resurrection.

But all these days reach their climax, not on Easter Sunday so much as in the Easter Vigil itself. It is obvious that the readings and ceremonies of the Vigil have as their theme our incorporation into Christ through His work of redemption. In the procession with the lighted Paschal Candle we follow Christ in pilgrimage from darkness to light, from death to life, just as the Chosen People followed the column of fire in their passage from slavery to freedom.[226] The magnificent Exsultet hymn is a monument to the "night which became radiant as day . . . the truly happy night which alone deserved to know the time and the hour in which Christ arose from the world below . . . the night which frees from the vices of the world and the dark haze of sin all those who believe in Christ, the night which restores us to grace and the fellowship of the saints." And before the great sacrament of resurrection, Baptism, is conferred, or at least before we renew ourselves in the spirit of our baptismal innocence, we meditate on the Old Testament prophecies which foretold this new life in Christ.[227] And finally we usher in the day of salvation with the sacramental re-enactment and re-offering of the great deed of redemption, the Holy Sacrifice of the Mass.

But why is the year's climax reached only at night?

---

triumphal entry into Jerusalem: Matt. 21:12-17; Mark 11:15-17; Luke 19:45-46.
[225] Phil. 2: 8-9.
[226] Cf. Origen, *Contra Celsum,* 8, 22. *MPG,* 11: 1151.
[227] Cf. Jean Daniélou's three chapters on the Old Testament types of Baptism: *The Bible and the Liturgy,* 70-113.

According to the mind of the ancients, an important feast always began at the Vespers of the preceding evening. But on this evening the Church is not satisfied to rejoice simply with first Vespers; she spends the whole night in prayer, meditation, and exultation. She keeps vigil; she stays awake. As St. Augustine says of this "mother of all Christian vigils," [228] "we observe the night in which our Lord arose by watching; we contemplate the life in which there is no sleep nor death, and which Christ began for us in His own flesh by raising it up from the dead. . . . Nor is it incongruous for us thus to stay awake in vigil: for He slept that we might remain awake, He died that we might live." [229]

But this holy night is not simply commemorative of the past. In Baptism we have not arisen to a purely earthly life; the grace which is the principle of our new life in Christ is also the seed of glory. We are called to live in the presence of God in heaven for all eternity. Although we have arisen with Christ to a new life of grace, we still await our ascension into heaven, the consummation of our hope. The Church has traditionally expected in this night the second coming of Christ, the *Parousia*, in which together with her Spouse she is to begin the eternal day of the nuptial feast. "This is the night," observes Lactantius, "which we celebrate with a night-long vigil because of the coming of our King and God. This night has a twofold significance: in it Christ received life after dying, and in the future He will come into possession of the kingdom of the whole world." [230] And St. Jerome, after him, relates this holy expectation to that of the Jews, who believed that the Messias would come to deliver them during their celebration of the Pasch. For this reason the Christians "held fast to a tradition of apostolic origin that during the Easter Vigil no one was to leave before midnight, for all awaited the coming of Christ. But after the middle of the night, when they felt He would not come, they were then to celebrate the feast." [231] Jerome writes this by way of commentary on that passage of the Gospel: "And at midnight the cry arose: 'Behold, the Bridegroom cometh. Go ye forth to meet him!'"

For several centuries the Church has known the incongruity of celebrating the Easter Vigil—a service whose texts and symbolism obviously call for the night hours—at a very early hour on the morning of Holy Saturday, when Christ certainly had not yet risen. That this was not always done is proven beyond doubt by historical documents. The *Epistula Apostolorum*, an apocryphal writing coming from Asia Minor or Egypt and dating from 140 to 160, indicates that the Vigil was held during the night until after midnight.[232] The term *ab-*

[228] *Sermo* 219. *MPL*, 38: 1088.
[229] *Sermo* 221. *MPL*, 38: 1090.
[230] *De div. instit.*, 7, 19. *MPL*, 6: 797.
[231] *Comm. in evang. sec. Matt.*, lib. IV, c. 25, 6. *MPL*, 21: 192.
[232] J. Quasten, 336-337.

noctantem used by Tertullian in reference to this vigil seems to indicate the same thing.[233] We also have trustworthy witnesses to such an horarium in Jerome, as cited above, in Augustine [234] and Paulinus of Nola.[235] According to the *Apostolic Constitutions*,[236] the faithful gathered at Vespers of Saturday and continued the Vigil until the dawn of Sunday, whence the name for such vigils—*pannuchis*.[237] In the ninth century Rabanus Maurus indicates that the Vigil began towards the Vesper hour, about five o'clock in the evening.[238] And in the tenth century Pontifical of Poitiers we are told that the Vigil should begin at such a time so that the people will not be dismissed before midnight, the reason being the apostolic tradition that the Lord would come during this Vigil.[239]

This reason is also, probably, behind the insistence of Rupert of Deutz that the Alleluia should not be sung before midnight and therefore the ceremony should be protracted by some means such as a sermon.[240] *Circa initium noctis* is still the time indicated for beginning the Vigil in the twelfth century *Decretum Gratiani*,[241] but thereafter the tendency of placing the Vigil earlier and earlier in the day shows itself. Mabillon's *Ordo Romanus* X of the twelfth century has the function begin at noon,[242] while the twelfth century Roman Pontifical allows it to begin at eleven o'clock in the morning.[243] From this point it was only a small step to the early morning hours,[244] which finally became obligatory with the *Missale Romanum* of Pius V in 1570. Fortunately Pius XII, in 1951, restored the Easter Vigil to its proper time.

The ceremonies of the Vigil may be divided into the following sections: (1) the blessing of new fire, (2) the blessing of the Paschal Candle with the procession and Preconium, (3) the reading service, (4) the blessing of baptismal water, conferring of Baptism and renewal of baptismal vows, (5) Mass and Lauds.

A blessing of new fire appears for the first time in the papal Liturgy, for this night only, in the twelfth century.[245] Though the

---

[233] *Ad uxorem*, 2, 4. *MPL*, 1: 1294.
[234] *Sermo* 219 and 228. *MPL*, 38: 1088, 1101.
[235] *Vita s. Ambrosii*, n. 48. *MPL*, 14: 43.
[236] V, 19. *MPG*, 1: 891-894.
[237] Athanasius, *Apol. ad Constantinum*, 25; *Apolog. pro fuga*, 24. *MPG*, 25: 625, 673.
[238] *De cleric. instit.*, 2, 38. *MPL*, 107: 350.
[239] Cf. M. Righetti, *Manuale di Storia Liturgica*, II (Milan: Ancora, 1946), p. 167, note 220.
[240] *De div. off.*, 7, 11. *MPL*, 170: 190.
[241] III, 1, 50. *MPL*, 187: 1722.
[242] N. 16. *MPL*, 78: 1014.
[243] M. Andrieu, *Le Pontifical Romain*, I, p. 238, n. 1.
[244] Jungmann has published a thorough history of this whole question: "Die Vorverlegung der Ostervigil seit dem christlichen Altertum," *Liturgisches Jahrbuch*, 1 (1951), 48-54.
[245] *Ord. Rom.* X, n. 16. *MPL*, 78: 1014; and M. Andrieu, *Le Pontifical Romain*, I, p. 238, nn. 2-4.

formula seems to have originated in Germany in the tenth century,[246] the actual practice of either enkindling a new fire or at least of bringing it out of "hiding" can be found in both Rome and Germany in the eighth century.[247] While it is conjectured [248] that the German practice was originally intended to supplant the pagan custom of enkindling fires during the Spring in honor of Wotan and other pagan deities, the Roman practice seems to have been simply a question of keeping a lamp burning elsewhere than in the church, which was supposed to be kept dark on Good Friday, and then using the lamp on Saturday for the normal illumination needed for reading.[249] Amalar, however, considers this whole procedure symbolic of the Resurrection of Christ.[250] And indeed this certainly seems to have been behind the insistence of the twelfth century Ordos that the fire be enkindled anew on Holy Saturday before the Vigil.[251] In fact, this new fire was so precious in the eyes of the faithful, that after the blessing of the Candle they lighted their own candles from it and brought a share of the new fire home.[252]

The use of a special Paschal Candle was originally foreign to the Roman Rite. However, that one was used in the north of Italy in the fourth century is attested to by a letter of St. Jerome, written in 384, in which he teases the deacon Presidius for presuming to vaunt his pride by blessing the candle in the presence of the bishop and his priests.[253] An indication that such a custom existed in Africa is the fact that Augustine quotes a few lines from such a Preconium.[254] The Fourth Council of Toledo in 633 energetically recommends adoption of the custom by other churches.[255] But the papal Ordos are silent on the matter, even though the titular churches and those in the suburbicarian dioceses followed this almost universal custom.[256] However, the practice must have been introduced into the papal Liturgy before the twelfth century, for by that time it appears in official documents.[257]

The most probable origin of the Paschal Candle is the ancient daily practice of lighting and blessing a lamp towards the evening

---

[246] Lechner-Eisenhofer, *Liturgik des römischen Ritus* (Freiburg: Herder, 6th edit., 1953), p. 156; cf. also the data from the Romano-Germanic Pontifical of the tenth century reported by Andrieu, *Le Pontifical Romain*, I, p. 238, nn. 2-4.

[247] Pope Zachary, *Epist. 13 ad Bonifacium. MPL*, 89: 951.

[248] Cf. A. Franz, *Die kirchlichen Benediktionen im Mittelalter* (Freiburg, 1909), I, 517.

[249] Cf. the above-cited letter of Pope Zachary in note 247, and *Ord. Rom.* XXIII, n. 24. Andrieu, *Les Ordines Romani*, III, 272.

[250] *De ordine antiphonarii*, 44. *MPL*, 105: 1293.

[251] As in note 245.

[252] *Ord. Rom.* XXVIII, n. 63. Andrieu, III, 404.

[253] *Epist. 28 ad Presidium*, 1. *MPL*, 30: 188.

[254] *De civitate Dei*, 15, 22. *MPL*, 41: 467.

[255] Can. 9. Hefele-Leclercq, *op. cit.*, III, 269.

[256] Cf. *Liber Pontificalis* (ed. L. Duchesne), I, 225; *Ord. Rom.* XXIII, n. 24; *Ord. Rom.* XXVI, nn. 6, 9, 10, 14. Andrieu, III, 272, 326-329.

[257] *Ord. Rom.* X, n. 17. *MPL*, 78: 1014; the twelfth century Roman Pontifical. Andrieu, *Le Pontifical Romain*, I, p. 240, n. 8.

hours to dispel the darkness of the night. This was a simple and necessary daily occurrence, but one which was elaborated and given a special ritual with psalms, chants, and orations. The ceremony was called the *Lucernarium*,[258] or service of light, and came to form a part of Vespers. The fact that the Easter Vigil originally began at the Vesper hour supports the claim that in the Paschal Candle and its Preconium we have the survival of this primitive daily custom. This further explains how it came to pass that it is the deacon who sings the *Preconium Paschale*,[259] for the blessing of the evening light in the church was a duty especially entrusted to him.

Our Paschal Candle today is decorated with five grains of incense. This rite takes its origin from a mistranslation of the formula intended as a blessing of the Candle itself. In the Gelasian Sacramentary [260] it reads as follows: "Veniat ergo, omnipotens Deus, super hunc incensum larga tuae benedictionis infusio. . . ." The word "incensum" as modified by "hunc" is masculine and obviously refers to the Candle, "cereus," meaning "this lighted Candle." But in service books from the tenth century on [261] the masculine "hunc" is replaced by the neuter "hoc," thus making "incensum" mean incense. While in the Holy Week Ordo of Pius XII the grains of incense are retained—they are symbolic of the five wounds of Christ, trophies of His victory over sin and death— the oration is returned to its original meaning, this time the word "cereum" being added to obviate any misunderstanding. The oration also returns to its original purpose: a blessing of the Candle.

The various inscriptions to be made upon the Candle—the cross, the Alpha and Omega, as well as the number of the current year— may seem novel. However, a cross with an Alpha and Omega are found already in the seventh century Mozarabic liturgical books.[262] And the Venerable Bede attests to the inscribing of the year on the candle in the eighth century.[263] For a while all these items figured in the Roman Rite, at least from the twelfth century on.[264]

As the deacon goes up the aisle of the church with the lighted Paschal Candle, he stops three times and sings, "Lumen Christi!" And all the faithful reply, "Deo gratias!" The forerunner of this greeting of light is also to be found in the fourth century Lucernarium rite.[265]

258 See footnotes 190, 191, 192 in Chapter 7: "The Divine Office." Anton Baumstark has shown that this is another carry-over from the Jewish Sabbath service: cf. *Liturgie Comparée*, 148-149, 160-163.
259 Gregory the Great, however, reports that in Ravenna it was the bishop who did so: *Epist. lib.* XI, 33. *MPL*, 77: 1146.
260 Edit. H. Wilson, p. 81.
261 B. Capelle, "Le rite des cinq grains d'encens," *Questions Liturgiques et paroissiales*, 17 (1932), 8; cf. also A. Franz, *Die kirchlichen Benediktionen im Mittelalter*, I, 529-530.
262 M. Férotin, *Le Liber Ordinum*, 209.
263 *De ratione temporum*, 47. *MPL*, 90: 494-495.
264 M. Andrieu, *Le Pontifical Romain*, I, 241, n. 10.
265 Cf. F-J. Dölger, "Lumen Christi," *Antike und Christentum*, V (1936), 1-43.

But the exclamation was used quite frequently apart from liturgical services. For instance, in an eighth century document [266] which describes the conduct of a group of Frankish monks in their refectory, we are told that whenever it became necessary to add more light because of the fall of night, the monk who lighted the lamp cried out, "Lumen Christi!" "Deo gratias!" was the quick reply of the others. It took quite a while for this greeting to become part of the Roman Liturgy for this night, though; we find no trace of it until the twelfth century.[267]

During the course of the Middle Ages many versions of the Paschal Preconium were composed. This appears quite natural if we remember that up until the sixth century the officiants at liturgical services were left the liberty of employing their own talents in fashioning the liturgical texts. Thus Ennodius (d. 521) offers us examples of two such hymns,[268] and Jerome, as we have seen,[269] was requested to compose one for the deacon Presidius of Piacenza. The text of our present *Laus cerei* is contained already in the Old Gallican Missal and the Gothic-Gallican Missal of the late seventh century.[270] The author of our Exsultet was in all probability St. Ambrose.[271]

With the reading of the prophecies begins the traditional Roman Easter Vigil properly so-called.[272] The original number of lessons was undoubtedly six, if we understand that this number also included the two non-Gospel readings of the Mass.[273] Nor was this anything special for the Easter Vigil, for we see the same number used for the Ember Saturday Masses, which were originally vigil-Masses. As mentioned before, the number twelve was reached in the Roman practice because all the lessons were read in both Latin and Greek. In many regions the number of lessons oscillated from anywhere between

[266] *Ord. Rom.* XIX, n. 22. Andrieu, *Les Ordines Romani,* III, p. 220.

[267] M. Andrieu, *Le Pontifical Romain,* I, 239-240, n. 7.

[268] *Opuscula* 9 and 10. *MPL,* 63: 258-262.

[269] As in note 253.

[270] *MPL,* 72: 364 f., 268 f.

[271] Cf. B. Capelle, "L'Exsultet pascal oeuvre de saint Ambroise," *Miscellanea Giovanni Mercati* (Vatican City, 1946), I, 219-246.

[272] If we prescind from the mere *bringing* of the fire out of "hiding" that is true of *Ord. Rom.* XXIII, all Roman documents up until the eleventh century have the service begin with the lessons, e.g., the Paduan Codex of the Gregorian Sacramentary, ed. K. Mohlberg, p. 25; *Ord. Rom.* XXIII, n. 27. Andrieu, III, 272.

[273] Despite Baumstark's contention that there were actually twelve different lessons (*Nocturna Laus,* Münster, 1957, pp. 45-54), A. Chavasse, by studying not only the content and object of the Roman lessons but also the origin of Rome's orations for this night, conclusively shows that the Easter Vigil proper, excluding the lessons of the Mass, possessed but four (or at most five) readings: "Lecons et oraisons des vigiles de pâques et de la pentecôte dans le sacramentaire gélasien," *Eph. Lit.,* 69 (1955), 209-226. In fact, the Paduan Codex of the Gregorian Sacramentary contains only four lessons for the vigil: K. Möhlberg, pp. 25-26.

four [274] to six [275] to ten.[276] Some localities even had as many as twenty-four, but this was due to the custom of reading each lesson in Greek as well as Latin.[277] The number twelve, that is twelve distinct lessons, finally succeeded in predominating and wound its way to Rome around the twelfth century; [278] but the reform of Pius XII reverts to the more ancient practice of Rome.

Upon the completion of these readings, which were obviously intended to be a preparation for Baptism, the blessing of baptismal water and the conferring of the sacrament itself follow. Our present day formula for blessing the water is found in the Gelasian [279] and Hadrian Sacramentaries.[280] However, the practice of blessing the water before it is used for Baptism goes back to primitive times; both Tertullian [281] and Cyprian [282] insist on the practice. In order to help the people who remained in church while Baptism was being administered spend the time in a holy manner, the Litany of the Saints was chanted. With the new Ordo of Pius XII another ceremony—the renewal of baptismal vows—is added to this ritual which greatly aids in bringing home to the faithful the full import of these rites. In this way the significance of Easter as the cause of baptismal grace is made clear, and the annual spiritual renovation of Lent culminates in a symbolic resurrection together with Christ to a more intense life of grace.

Newly baptized or at least renewed in the spirit of their Baptism, the faithful then take part in the celebration of the Easter Mass. Every text in it speaks of the joy and newness of life and light that is ours through the resurrection of Christ. And since the ancient Vigil used to end in the early morning hours, it concluded with the singing of Lauds, this Hour itself having the Resurrection as its theme. This too has been restored in the Ordo of Pius XII.

Thus in the Easter Vigil the Church is at least once in the course of the year *visibly* and *tangibly* what she always is invisibly: the Bride eagerly awaiting the return of her Bridegroom. She expresses this through her long night-watch, demonstrating her yearning for the dawn of that eternal day of Spring when she will inaugurate with Her Spouse the everlasting nuptials of the Lamb, the full blossoming of what was begun on the first Easter morn.

[274] Appendix to *Ord. Rom.* XXVIII. Andrieu, III, pp. 412-413.
[275] Cf. A. Wilmart, "Le Lectionnaire d'Alcuin," *Eph. Lit.*, 51 (1937), 156.
[276] *The Gelasian Sacramentary* (ed. H. Wilson), pp. 82-83.
[277] *Ord. Rom* XXXb, n. 41. Andrieu, III, 472; cf. Joannes Beleth, *Divinorum off. explicatio,* 106. *MPL*, 202: 110.
[278] In the Roman Pontifical of the twelfth century, although there are twelve distinct lessons, they are still read in both Greek and Latin: M. Andrieu, *Le Pontifical Romain*, I, 241, n. 12.
[279] Ed H. Wilson, pp. 84-86.
[280] Ed H. Lietzmann, *Das Sacramentarium Gregorianum*, n. 85, pp. 52-53.
[281] *De baptismo*, 4. *MPL*, 1: 1311.
[282] *Epist. Synodalis*, (70), 1. *MPL*, 3: 1077.

Easter Sunday

Our present Mass for Easter Sunday is, of course, not primitive, since, as we said, the solemn Easter Vigil ended towards the break of day with the celebration of Mass. With the progressive anticipation of the Vigil on Saturday another Mass had to be formulated for Sunday. Also, some provision had to be made for those many Christians who simply could not go to the Vigil. And so rather early—in the sixth century—we find a special Mass formulary. Ours today is substantially the same as the one which appears in the earliest forms of the Gregorian Sacramentary.[283] And just as the same Gospels were repeated on the fourth Sunday of Advent and the second Sunday of Lent as on the preceding Ember Saturdays, so we see that many of the texts used on Easter Sunday are taken from the Easter Vigil. The Gospels, for instance, are accounts of the same episode from different Evangelists: The holy women come to the tomb to anoint the body of Jesus, but find He is risen; in the Vigil, St. Matthew's Gospel is used, in the Sunday Mass St. Mark's.

To bring out the exceptional rank of Easter, the Church continues its celebration throughout a whole week. Every day of this week is provided with its own Mass formulary, each commemorating one of our Lord's many apparitions after His resurrection. At the same time each contains many allusions to Baptism. The latter phenomenon again is explained by the fact that in the early Church those who had received Baptism at the Easter Vigil attended Mass and received Communion daily during the octave, wearing all the while their white baptismal robes. These robes were finally put aside on the following Sunday, the octave day of Easter. This is why the Sunday was given the name *Dominica in albis* (*deponendis*), the Sunday for taking off the white. But once the Easter Vigil, and with it the accompanying administration of Baptism, was anticipated, the Easter octave ended on the following Saturday, and therefore it was on this day that the newly-baptized laid aside their white clothing. The following Sunday then changed names; thereafter it has been called *Dominica post albas*.[284]

3. Preparation for Easter

The desire to celebrate fittingly the chief festival of the Church Year has called forth even in earliest times a special period of preparation. Far from being dedicated to the memory of our Lord's sufferings, mention of which appears only in the last two weeks of this season, Lent rather concentrates its attention on the means of spiritual renovation, on penance, fasting, almsgiving, prayer, meditation, and serious self-examination. It is, therefore, a halt in the spiritual

---

[283] K. Mohlberg, p. 26.
[284] *Ibid.*, p. 28.

life during which we take stock of our resources, a spiritual retreat
by means of which the soul purifies itself of all its evil inclinations
and propensities in order to rise with Christ on Easter to a higher
level of spiritual life; it begins again, regains its youth by more intimately attaching itself to the source of supernatural grace, the Risen
Christ. Indeed, this is the native meaning of the word Lent. It comes
from the Anglo-Saxon root *lencten,* used even in poetic German as
Lenz, both of which mean Spring. Lent does in reality bring about
a spiritual Spring in our lives, for our fervor is reborn as it rejuvenates
itself in the spirit of the baptismal innocence in which it first arose
from the death of sin together with Christ.

With great seriousness Pope St. Leo urged the faithful not to lose
this opportunity of growing closer to Christ by purifying themselves
of evil attraction through fasting, prayer, and penance and thus preparing themselves for a genuine renewal of the spiritual life as the
proper grace of the Easter celebration.[285] Models for this fast of forty
days were found in Moses,[286] Elias,[287] and our Lord Himself.[288] Just
as our Lord fasted for forty days and nights to prepare Himself for
His public ministry, so the faithful, following His example, were to
go through this same period of spiritual fortification to equip themselves with the spiritual energy necessary to make a new start in their
combat with the devil.

These scriptural precedents, however, did not become a real
determining influence in the institution of the forty-day fast until the
fourth century. Until that time our sources have nothing to say of such
a fast; rather they indicate fasts of varying lengths. Tertullian speaks
only of the fast on the *Biduum*: Good Friday and Holy Saturday.[289]
Irenaeus, about the year 190 in his famous letter to Pope Victor regarding the Quartodeciman question, describes just about as much
diversity in the matter of fasting as in the celebration of Easter: in
some places the faithful fasted only on one day, in others two days,
and still in others for forty consecutive hours.[290] And even in Rome
of the third century a fast of only two days is prescribed by the *Apostolic Tradition*.[291] On the other hand, Dionysius of Alexandria attests
to the practice of fasting during the entire week before Easter.[292]

In the fourth century, however, things seem to change. In his
Festal Letters, St. Athanasius often alludes to the forty-day fast preceding Easter.[293] The Council of Laodicea in 360 explicitly com-

---

[285] *Sermones* 39-50 *in Quadragesima. MPL,* 54: 263-308.
[286] Exodus 34:28.
[287] 3 Kings 19:8.
[288] Matt. 4:2.
[289] *De jejuniis,* 2. *MPL,* 2: 1006.
[290] Eusebius, *Historia ecclesiastica,* V, 24, 12. *GCS,* 9 (1), p. 495.
[291] Edit. B. Botte, n. 29, pp. 64-65.
[292] *Epistola Canonica ad Basilidem episc. MPG,* 10: 1275-1278.
[293] E.g., *Epist. Fest.* XIX, 9. *MPG,* 26: 1429.

mands it.[294] St. Ambrose speaks of it,[295] as also, of course, Pope St. Leo I.[296] And Etheria says that, while in her home country (probably Spain) the faithful fast for forty consecutive days, in Jerusalem this is parcelled out over a period of eight weeks.[297]

Though by the fourth century a Lenten fast of forty days was practically universal, it was not calculated everywhere in the same manner, as Etheria remarks. The above custom of Jerusalem of spreading it out over eight weeks was due to the fact that in the East Saturdays and Sundays were not included in the fast. Thus with only a five-day fast week, if the East had followed the Roman system of the six-week fast, ten days would have been lacking to the scriptural forty. By adding two more weeks they completed the prescribed number; Lent officially began for them then with Sexagesima Sunday. In Syria still another factor had to be taken into consideration—the clear-cut distinction there between the Lenten fast and the one proper to Holy Week.[298] In this case three additional weeks of five days each were required in order to attain the usual forty. Thus Lent began with Septuagesima Sunday.

Finally, Rome itself realized that by exempting Sundays from the fast its own six-week period lacked four days. This was eventually corrected by beginning Lent on the Wednesday previous to the first Sunday of the six-week period. Thus we have the week of Quinquagesima.[299] But this could not have been instituted before the time of Gregory the Great, for, in one of his homilies,[300] he is at pains to explain how there can be a fast of forty days beginning with Quadragesima Sunday. Yet, the custom of beginning the fast on Quinquagesima Sunday was already known in the region of the Italian Alps in 450, according to St. Maximus of Turin, but he dismisses it as a show of vanity on the part of his people.[301] In France there was a further step; the First Council of Orleans, held in 511, forbade the observance of Sexagesima and Quinquagesima Sundays.[302]

Thus during the fifth and sixth centuries it would seem that attempts at imitating the oriental practice of anticipating the regular forty-day Lenten fast were being made. Outside of Rome such efforts met with disapproval. In Rome it was otherwise. The Mass formularies for these three Sundays before Lent and the Wednesday, Friday, and Saturday of Quinquagesima make their appearance for the

[294] Can. 5. Hefele-Leclercq, op. cit., I, 1022-1023.
[295] De Elia et jejunio, X, 34. MPL, 14: 709.
[296] Sermo 44, 2; 48, 1. MPL, 54: 286, 298.
[297] Journal de Voyage (Editions du Cerf), n. 27, pp. 206-208.
[298] Apostolic Constitutions, V, 13. MPG, 1: 859-866.
[299] Cf. F. Cabrol, "Caput jejunii," DACL, II, 2134-2137.
[300] Homil. XVI in evangelia, n. 5. MPL, 76: 1137.
[301] Sermo XXVI, MPL, 57: 583.
[302] Can. 24. Hefele-Leclercq, op. cit., II, 1014.

first time about the end of the sixth century or during the course of the seventh.[303]

We may say that the function of the three Sundays before Lent is to give us every reason for entering eagerly into the spiritual exercises of this period as the means of achieving the goal offered us by our much needed Redeemer. After the joyous period of Christmas and the Sundays subsequent to it, we are immediately confronted with fallen man (readings from Genesis on Septuagesima Sunday) and the lamentable results of Original Sin (the malice of men occasioning the deluge [Sexagesima Sunday] and the consequent need for sacrificial atonement [story of Abraham on Quinquagesima Sunday].) Christ is proposed on each of these Sundays as the effective antidote to human tragedy and incompetence: on Septuagesima Sunday Christ as the new head of the human race calls all men to salvation; on Sexagesima Sunday, as another Noah, He repopulates the earth with the seed of faith; on Quinquagesima, as the Savior promised to men of faith like Abraham, He saves the believing blind man on the way to Jericho.

The special severity and sobriety of the Lenten fast is foreshadowed by the quieting of the joyful Alleluia cry. Just as the grief-stricken Hebrews could not sing the joyful chants of Sion as long as they were held captive in exile, so the Church suppresses her hymns of gladness, conscious of the weight and gravity of the alienation from God caused by the sins of mankind.[304] To make this temporary cessation of the Alleluia more solemn and impressive, the entire night office of Septuagesima Sunday was filled with its repetition.[305] During

---

[303] Though they figure in the Gelasian Sacramentary, E. Bourque argues that they are an interpolation: *Etude sur les sacramentaires romains. Les textes primitifs* (Rome, 1949), pp. 233-234. However, J. Froger tries to maintain that these three Sundays existed before the time of Gregory the Great: "Les anticipations du jeûne quadragésimal," *Mélanges de science religieuse*, 3 (1946), p. 218 But Froger's principal argument, the assignment of one of Gregory's homilies for Septuagesima Sunday, is extremely weak. In fact, A. Chavasse has shown that the homily really belongs to a feast in August, very likely that of St. Lawrence, August 10, and, further, that, though it is possible for Sexagesima and Quinquagesima to have existed before Gregory, Septuagesima must have been instituted during the seventh century: "Temps de préparation à la Pâque," *Recherches de science religieuse*, 37 (1950), 143-144; "Le calendrier dominical au vi siècle," *ibid.*, 38 (1952), 241. The three Sundays appear both in the Paduan Codex of the Gregorian Sacramentary (ed. Mohlberg, pp. 11-12) as well as in the Würzburg Lectionary (G. Godu, "Epitres," *DACL*, V, col. 312, nn. 34-41; *idem*, "Evangiles," *DACL*, V, col. 902 nn. 53-55). It should be noted, however, that in these early books there is always some confusion about Septuagesima; e.g. the Gospel list of Würzburg lacks the name Septuagesima, having only *Die dominica*; Alcuin's lectionary lacks the station for this Sunday (Godu, "Epitres," col. 302, n. 29). Hence, we notice a good deal of hesitation in all these documents well towards the end of the seventh century.

[304] Cf. Amalar, *De eccl. off.*, I, 1. *MPL*, 105: 993.

[305] *Idem, De ordine antiphonarii*, 30. *MPL*, 105: 1282.

the late Middle Ages all sorts of pedagogical customs developed, even the "burial" of the Alleluia.[306]

The day before the beginning of Lent is called Shrove Tuesday. This means Confession Tuesday. The reason for the title is not difficult to discover. According to the ancient penitential practice of Rome—continued for a longer time in Gallican lands—Confessions were to be made just before Lent, at least by public sinners, in order that the proper Lenten penance might be imposed.[307] Even though in some places confessions were heard on Wednesday,[308] it was nevertheless the general practice for the faithful to begin their sacramental penance on Ash Wednesday, continue it during Lent, and receive reconciliation on Holy Thursday. For the devout, of course, this confession was accompanied by absolution, so that they were able to receive Communion daily during the Lenten season.[309]

It is also in the public penitential practice of the Church that we find the origin of placing ashes on the heads of the faithful. The sprinkling of oneself with ashes was considered a sign of penance even in the Old Testament. After the Prophet Jonas had announced to the men of Ninive that their city was to be destroyed after forty days, "they proclaimed a fast and put on sackcloth and sat in ashes."[310] In the Christian era we find Tertullian mentioning the same practice.[311] Later Isidore of Seville unequivocally speaks of the penitents as being sprinkled with ashes to remind them that they are dust and ashes.[312] This same system of public penance lasted until the tenth century.[313] By the end of the next century, however, public penance seems to have fallen into complete disuse; but the devout still continue to receive ashes on their heads out of a spirit of humility and penance.[314] It would seem that the tenth century Romano-Germanic Pontifical is the first to provide a blessing for the ashes on Ash Wednesday,[315] though some of these orations can be found in the eighth century Pontifical of Egbert, Bishop of York, for the blessing of ashes during the consecration of a church.[316]

From what has already been said, we can see that Lent is indeed a season of special importance in the life of the Church. This is further borne out by the fact that, unlike any other season, it is provided, not

---

[306] Cf. L. Gougaud, "Les adieux à l'Alleluia," *Ephemerides Liturgicae,* 41 (1927), 566-571.

[307] Cf. H. Thurston, *Lent and Holy Week,* 67-69.

[308] Regino of Prüm, *De eccl. disciplina,* I, 288; *Admonitio synodalis. MPL,* 132:245; 136:562.

[309] Nicholas I, *Epist.* 97 *ad Bulgaros,* n. 9. *MPL,* 119: 983-984.

[310] Jonas 3:5-6; for the sprinkling of ashes see Jeremias 6:26; 25:34.

[311] *De poenitentia,* 11. *MPL,* 1: 357.

[312] *De off. eccl.,* II, 17, 4-5. *MPL,* 83: 802.

[313] Regino of Prüm, *op. cit.* (note 308), I, 291. *MPL,* 132: 245.

[314] Thus we find Pope Urban II in 1091 at the Synod of Benevento recommending the practice to both clerics and laity alike: can. 4. *MPL,* 151: 81.

[315] Andrieu, *Le Pontifical Romain,* I, 209, line 41-45.

[316] Thurston, *op. cit.,* 95.

only with special Mass formularies for the six Sundays, but also with special Masses and stational churches for each weekday. It is a season characterized by the great antiquity of its Mass formularies: all of these go back at least to the time of Gregory the Great,[317] Thursdays alone being excepted, since they were first inserted into the Lenten Liturgy by Gregory II between 715-731.[318] Another sign of their antiquity is the presence of the *Oratio super populum* each day after the Postcommunion. This prayer was the original final blessing of the Mass up until the end of the sixth century. At that time Gregory the Great dropped this form of blessing for the rest of the year and composed entirely new formulas for the Lenten season, pointing them directly at the penitents.[319] A third peculiarity of the Lenten season, again of great antiquity, is the oft-recurring special tract for Mondays, Wednesdays, and Fridays: *Domine non secundum peccata nostra.* In the fifth-century Gallican church there was a fast three times a week, from September to Easter, which was an importation from the Orient; [320] the Tract is what remains of this ancient practice.[321] Finally, to emphasize the special importance and character of the Lenten ferias, the 1955 Decree simplifying the rubrics directs that both the Office (in private recitation) and the Mass of the feria may be said in preference to all feasts under the rank of double of the first or second class, should they occur.[322] In practice this means that only the feasts of St. Joseph (March 19), of the Annunciation (March 25), and of St. Matthias (February 24) must be celebrated.

Besides the penitential practices, two other factors influenced the selection of themes for the various Lenten Masses; namely, the ancient scrutinies leading up to the conferring of Baptism, and the cultus of the saints in the stational churches.

Although one could, in the early Church, become a catechumen and receive instruction in the faith any time during the year, when one finally wanted to receive Baptism he had to make this desire known to the authorities at the beginning of Lent.[323] Such catechumens were then called *electi* or *competentes,* and they had to observe the Lenten fast and submit to a series of exorcisms and special instructions. After their enrollment on the list of the *baptizandi,* they had to assist at three special public ceremonies called *scrutinia,* or scrutinies. Though the word scrutiny brings to mind the thought of an

---

[317] They all appear in the Paduan Codex and the *Comes* of Würzburg.
[318] *Liber Pontificalis* (ed. L. Duchesne), I, 402.
[319] Cf. C. Callewaert, "Qu'est-ce que l'oratio super populum?" *Eph. Lit.,* 51 (1937), 310-318; J. A. Jungmann, "Oratio super populum und altchristliche Büssersegnung," *Eph. Lit.,* 52 (1938), 76-96.
[320] Gregory of Tours, *Historia Francorum,* X, 31; Caesarius of Arles, *Regula ad Monachos,* n. XXII. MPL, 71:566; 67:1102.
[321] Cf. Th. Michels, "Montag, Mittwoch, und Freitag als Fasttagssystem in kirchlicher und monasticher Überlieferung," *JLW,* 3 (1923), 102.
[322] Tit. II, n. 22.
[323] Pope Siricius (385), *Epist. ad Himerium,* 2. MPL, 13: 1135.

examination—and later it was explained as such—as far as can be ascertained most of the scrutinies had nothing to do with teaching or examination; they were concerned with exorcisms.[324] However, during the second scrutiny, called *In aurium apertione,* the *competentes* are taught about the four Gospels, the Creed and the Pater. It is possible that these three instructions were given on three different occasions. And, of course, such instruction would account for the connection between the word scrutiny and teaching-examination. Formerly these scrutinies were held on the third, fourth and fifth Sundays of Lent, but by the beginning of the seventh century they had been moved to the Friday of the third week, Wednesday and Friday of the fourth week.[325] And today the Masses for these last mentioned days contain several clear-cut references to Baptism, a remnant of the special ceremonies held on these days for the catechumens.

The second influence felt in the choice of texts for the Masses of Lent was the institution of the stational churches. We have already seen how the word *statio,* originally a military term meaning to stand guard or keep watch, was gradually taken over by the Church to designate her liturgical assemblies. And let us recall, too, that in the early centuries great stress was laid on the community character of the Mass. In Rome, especially, this led to the custom whereby the pope's celebration of feastdays was regarded as the official service— certainly not the only service. With the increase of the Christian population of Rome, the pope was led to celebrate at various times in different parish churches of the city, so that all the faithful would be permitted at one time or other to participate in his "official" service.[326] Since not all days brought with them a stational or official celebration, right after the *Pax Domini sit semper vobiscum* in the Mass, the Archdeacon or some other minister would announce to the faithful the date and the locality of the next station.[327] If a procession were to precede the station, as for instance on a penitential day, the *ecclesia collecta,* or the church where the people would gather for the proces-

[324] Dom Cyrille Lambot, after examining the works of Ambrose and Leo, remarked that the word *scrutinium* was a liturgical term for *exorcism: Recueil d'ordines du xi siècle* (London, 1931), pp. xxx-xxxii.

[325] At the same time as these scrutinies were moved their number was increased to seven (perhaps including the enrollment and the *redditio symboli,* at the beginning and on Holy Saturday respectively), the reason being a purely symbolic one: to make the number parallel the seven gifts of the Holy Spirit (*Ord. Rom.* XI, n. 81. Andrieu, *Les Ordines Romani,* II, p. 442.). This change was probably due to St. Gregory the Great (cf. C. Callewaert, "S. Grégoire, les scrutins et quelques messes quadragésimales," *Eph. Lit.,* 53 [1939], p. 203).

[326] We should not think that this practice was peculiar to Rome; many other bishops throughout Christendom shared the same idea that the chief shepherd should go about the various churches of his diocese and celebrate Mass with his flock. For references about this custom outside of Rome see M. Righetti, *op. cit.,* II, 107-108.

[327] H. Wilson, *The Gelasian Sacramentary,* p. 236; *Ord. Rom.* I, n. 108; *Ord. Rom.* XV, n. 56. Andrieu, *Les Ordines,* II, p. 102; III, p. 107; *Liber Pontificalis* (ed. Duchesne), II, 4.

sion to the stational church, would also be announced. Because Lent was a season of such sacredness to the Church, eventually all of its ferias were fitted out, so to speak, with both *ecclesiae collectae* and *stationales*—once the choice of the churches was no longer made on the spur of the moment but set down for good. C. Callewaert attributes to Pope Hilary (461-468) the first systematic organization of these stational churches.[328] With good reason we can suspect that Gregory the Great also lent his hand to further this development. And Gregory II (715-731) instituted the stational services for Thursdays of Lent.[329]

Once the celebration of these Masses came to be bound up with particular churches in Rome, it was only natural to expect that the saints after whom they were named or whose relics were venerated therein would affect the choice of the Mass texts to some degree. Cardinal Schuster tells us that:

> The Mass on the Thursday following Ash Wednesday at the church of St. George in *Velabro*, by its Gospel narrative of the centurion at Capharnaum, calls to mind St. George, whom tradition presents to us as the pattern of a valiant soldier. The next day the stational Mass is at the church of Sts. John and Paul (built by the generous Pammachius, who distributed his substance for the welfare of the poor); and the scriptural lessons there read teach us that alms are of no value unless given with a pure conscience and a single intention. The following Monday the station is at the Basilica of St. Peter *ad Vincula* on the Esquiline, and the remembrance of the *Pastor Ecclesiae* inspires the choice of the classic description of the Good Shepherd taken from the book of Ezechiel. On the next Wednesday the stational festival is at the Liberian Basilica (St. Mary Major), and the Liturgy finds in the Gospel lesson a delicate way of conveying to our minds the praises of the Blessed Virgin.[330]

Such an effect can also be seen in the Mass for the Thursday of the third week of Lent, which was offered in the church of Sts. Cosmas and Damian, who were self-sacrificing physicians; the Gospel speaks of our Lord's curing the sick. And many other examples could be given.

With Passion Sunday, the fifth of Lent, the theme of the season changes; it turns directly now to the Passion of our Lord. And in the Gospel for this Sunday we read that Jesus went out of the Temple and hid Himself. Because of this, since the seventeenth century it has been

[328] *La durée et le caractère du carême ancien* (Bruges, 1920), 86-96; regarding Hilary's contributions to the stational services see *Liber Pontificalis* (ed. Duchesne), I, 244, note 24.

[329] *Liber Pontificalis*, I, 402.

[330] *The Sacramentary*, II, pp. 7-8.

customary to veil all the sacred images of the church. Before this time, perhaps as early as the ninth century,[331] a veil was drawn across the entire sanctuary, separating the altar from the people at the very beginning of Lent, and was finally removed only on Wednesday of Holy Week when the words were read in the Passion: "Velum templi scissum est." In most places this veil was called the *velum quad-ragesimale*, or Lenten Veil, while in Germany it was called the *Hungertuch*, or Hunger Veil. Thurston understands the practice as an outgrowth of the practice of public penance whereby, originally, public penitents were actually excluded from the church during Lent. Once this died out, the veil was drawn between sanctuary and nave to represent symbolically the same idea of exclusion from church which sin merits.[332]

4. Paschal Time

By the second century the joy of the Easter celebration had impelled the Church to extend it for fifty days. This festive season we call Paschal Time, but early writers called it simply the fifty days: *Pentecostes* or *Quinquagesima*.[333] Even in pre-Christian times this period of the year was called "Pentecost" or "the days of Pentecost."[334] Whence our name Pentecost for the concluding day. Since these weeks were, so to speak, one continual feast of Easter, one was supposed to pray standing; there was to be no kneeling or fasting.[335] And today, in order to bring out this festive joy even more, we use white vestments on ferias as well as on Sundays.

Sundays after Easter

Since the general theme of Paschaltide is the divine life which penetrates and transfigures the humanity of Christ and, through His Resurrection, our own lives, quite fittingly the Church has chosen her Gospel texts from St. John's Gospel. The effects of Christ's redemptive work are constantly brought to mind. We hear Christ speak of the plans for His Church, of Himself as the Good Shepherd. And the last three Sundays are taken from our Lord's discourse, as reported by St. John, at the Last Supper, the theme of which is, "though I go to the Father, I will not leave you orphans; where I am you shall be; I am the Vine, you the branches, etc."

[331] Cf. M. Righetti, *op. cit.*, II, p. 128.
[332] *Lent and Holy Week*, p. 100; see also J. A. Jungmann, *Der gottesdienst der Kirche* (Innsbruck: Tyrolia-Verlag, 1955), p. 206, footnote 5.
[333] Tertullian, *De baptismo*, 19. *MPL*, 1: 1331; Maximus of Turin, *Homil.* 61 *in fest. Pent. MPL*, 57: 371.
[334] Acts 2:1, the Jewish festival of weeks as indicated in Exodus 34:22; Deut. 16:10.
[335] Tertullian, *De oratione*, 23. *MPL*, 1: 1298-1299; *De corona militis*, 3. *MPL*, 2:99; Maximus of Turin, *Homil.* 61. *MPL*, 57:371; Augustine, *Epist.* 55, c. 15. *MPL*, 33:218.

Rogation Days

The joyful character of Paschaltide is momentarily interrupted by the Rogation Days, upon which processions of supplication are held. One of these processional days is called *Litaniae majores*, the original Roman institution, to distinguish it from the *Litaniae minores* of Gallican origin. The Roman procession was begun to christianize an already existing pagan custom called the *Robigalia*.³³⁶ At this time of the year the crops were just starting to grow. To protect them from the blight caused by rust (*robigo*), the pagan Romans went in procession down the Via Flaminia as far as the Milvian Bridge and there offered the god *Robigus* the entrails of a dog and a sheep. When the Christians of Rome became strong enough in number the same procession was held, but to beg the true God to grant a good crop. The name *Litaniae majores* for this procession appears for the first time during the pontificate of Gregory the Great.³³⁷ The procession is held on the feast of St. Mark.

The Minor Litanies were instituted by Mamertus, Bishop of Vienne, around 470.³³⁸ It seems that in 469 a terrible earthquake wrought havoc on the city of Vienne. To beg God to protect the city against a recurrence of such a terrible thing, the good bishop ordained that every year three days of fast and procession should precede the feast of the Ascension. This was soon imitated in other localities. Finally even Rome accepted the new Rogation days under Leo III, who reigned from 795 to 816.³³⁹

The Ascension

A special feast to commemorate our Lord's Ascension into heaven does not appear in any of the earliest lists of festivals available. We find the first references to it in documents dating from the beginning of the fourth century.³⁴⁰ By the beginning of the fifth century it was observed by everyone.³⁴¹ Before this time the Ascension was commemorated in different ways: in Jerusalem it was observed on the same day as the descent of the Holy Spirit;³⁴² in the first century Pseudo-Barnabas seems to say that it was celebrated as one feast with Easter.³⁴³

³³⁶ Ovid, *Fastes*, IV, 901 ff.
³³⁷ *Charta de litaniis majoribus*. MPL, 77: 1329.
³³⁸ Sidonius Apollinaris, *Epist*. 5, 14; 7, 1. MPL. 58: 514, 563.
³³⁹ *Liber Pontificalis* (ed. Duchesne), II, 12.
³⁴⁰ We find mention made of it in some variants of can. 43 of the Council of Elvira in 300 (Hefele-Leclercq, *op. cit.*, I, 245, note 2), but the first certain trace of the feast is found in the work of Eusebius written for the Council of Nicea in 325, *De solemnitate Paschali*, 5. MPG, 24: 699.
³⁴¹ Augustine, *Epist*. 54 *ad Januarium*, 1. MPL, 33: 200.
³⁴² Etheria, *Journal de Voyage* (Edit. du Cerf), n. 43, pp. 248-250.
³⁴³ *Letter of Barnabas*, 15, 9. *The Fathers of the Church*, I (New York, 1947), 216.

During the reading of the Gospel account of our Lord's ascent into heaven the rubrics direct that the Paschal Candle be extinguished. Entering the Roman Liturgy through the Missal of Pius V, this brief gesture is a picturesque way of representing to us our Lord's departure for celestial regions; the Light of the world is now gone—we must continue to radiate Him before men. During the Middle Ages various other dramatic actions were employed towards this same end. Among these we ought to single out the Ascension Day procession, reported by Rupert of Deutz,[344] which was intended to be a figure of Christ's triumphant entrance into heaven.

The theme of the Ascension is beautifully enshrined in the words of Psalm 67, *Ascendens in altum, captivam duxit captivitatem,* sung in the Alleluia verse of the Mass. Indeed, Christ has led our nature captive into heaven as He took His place at the right hand of the Father. He has opened to us our true home, and He awaits the day when we can join Him. As Pope St. Leo says so aptly in the second nocturn of Matins, "The ascension of Christ is our own exaltation, and whither the glory of the Head has preceded, thither the hope of the body is also called. Let us, therefore, rejoice, dearly beloved, with due gladness. For today, not only have we been confirmed as possessors of paradise, but in Christ have we even penetrated the heights of heaven, having gained far more through the ineffable grace of Christ than we had lost through the malice of the devil. For those whom the virulent enemy cast down from the happiness of their first estate, these the Son of God has placed as one body with Himself at the right hand of the Father." [345]

Pentecost

This day was already of great importance in the liturgical life of the Old Testament, for it was the conclusion of the "feast of weeks," the harvest period. "You shall count, therefore, from the morrow of the Sabbath [the Passover], wherein you offered the sheaf of the first-fruits, seven full weeks, even unto the morrow after the seventh week be expired, that is to say, fifty days, and so you shall offer a new sacrifice to the Lord."[346] This feast had even been given the name Pentecost in pre-Christian times,[347] for the term means nothing else than the fiftieth day. The fact that on this day, too, the Holy Spirit descended upon the Apostles and thus inaugurated the newly-founded Church's activity among men was a parallel which the Fathers exploited from the beginning: Here were offered to God the first-fruits of the new creation in Christ.[348]

[344] *De div. off.,* IX, 9. *MPL,* 170: 259.
[345] *Sermo* 73, 4. *MPL,* 54: 396.
[346] Leviticus 23:15-16.
[347] 2 Machabees 12:32.
[348] See, for example, Leo I, *Sermo* 75 *in Pentecosten. MPL,* 54: 401 ff.

It is generally believed that this feast, along with Easter, dates back to apostolic institutions. But it must be admitted that the passage in 1 Cor. 16:8, which makes reference to Pentecost, can be understood as the Jewish feast just as well as the Christian. Our first unequivocal evidence to the feast of Pentecost, as something well established, is in Tertullian.[349]

Just as on Easter, so on Pentecost it was customary, at least in some churches, to administer Baptism,[350] whence came the similar construction of the Pentecost Vigil. But it would seem that this second date for receiving Baptism was really meant for those invalid catechumens and others who for some reason could not receive Baptism during the Easter Vigil.[351]

It is difficult to say when the fast on the Vigil of Pentecost first appeared. Etheria states categorically that no one fasted in Jerusalem from Easter till *after* Pentecost.[352] And St. Leo does not seem to know of any such practice yet in Rome.[353] Since no such indications are to be found in the Gregorian Sacramentary, the orations in which a fast is mentioned in the Leonine and Gelasian Sacramentaries are considered a Gallican interpolation.[354]

Originally Pentecost enjoyed no octave celebration; it was the conclusion of the great fifty days of Easter. The regular weekly fasts began the very next day as well as the regularly recurring Ember Days. In Etheria's journal, for instance, we are told that on Monday the people fasted.[355] St. Leo also speaks of the fast in the week after Pentecost.[356] However, the *Apostolic Constitutions* [357] prescribe a week's celebration of Pentecost and a fast the *following* week. The practice could not have been too widespread, however, judging from the above evidence. And finally with St. Gregory the Great we come upon a well-developed octave within which fall the summer Ember Days.[358]

E. The Christmas Cycle

Apart from the fact that the major feasts belonging to the season dedicated to the mystery of the Incarnation fall on fixed days of the month, the Christmas cycle shows many signs of attempts to imitate

---

[349] *De baptismo* 19. MPL, 1:1331; *De corona militis*, 3. MPL, 2:99; see also Origen, *Contra Celsum*, 8, 22. MPG, 11:1550.
[350] Jerome, *In Zachariam*, 14, 8. MPL, 25:1528; Augustine, *Sermo* 272. MPL, 38:1246; Leo I, *Epist.* 16 *ad episcopos Siciliae*, 3. MPL, 54: 698.
[351] This seems indicated in the formulas and directions of the Gelasian Sacramentary (ed. Wilson), pp. 110-114.
[352] *Journal*, n. 41, p. 244.
[353] *Sermo* 78, 1. MPL, 54:416.
[354] Cf. M. Righetti, *op. cit.*, II, 212.
[355] N. 44, p. 252.
[356] *Sermo* 78, 1. MPL, 54: 416.
[357] V, 20. MPG, 1: 902.
[358] Cf. the Paduan Codex of his Sacramentary (ed. K. Mohlberg), pp. 38-39.

the arrangement of the principal cycle of the year, that of Easter. The season opens with a period of preparation called Advent, which at present consists of four weeks, each with a Sunday having its special Office and Mass formulary. At times an even more complete imitation of Lent was evident, in that this preparation was observed for a full six weeks in some places—forty days in round figures. The climax of the cycle enjoys a night celebration of Mass, has an octave day, and finds its theme echoed for some forty days until February 2. The cycle, however, is of much later introduction into the liturgical life of the Church than the Easter cycle; there is no uncontroverted documentary evidence for the existence of its principal feast, Christmas, until the middle of the fourth century, and of its period of preparation, Advent, until even later.

1. Christmas

It might seem strange that a liturgical celebration of the mystery of the Incarnation, so important today to popular piety, found such a late acceptance on the part of the Church. But if we understand the mentality of the early Church, this will appear to be less of an anomaly. Christians of the early centuries were filled with awe at the thought of the suffering and glorified Messias, the divine and kingly High Priest, who through His sacrifice and resurrection wrought the redemption of mankind. Basking in the sunshine of their newly-acquired share in divine life, their thoughts were naturally attracted to the goal and objective of the earthly life of the Messias, toward their divine sonship under Christ their Head. Enthralled with the heavenly terminus of that life, they were little inclined to concentrate on the human terminus of the Incarnation. And presumably the apologetic endeavors of the primitive Church had a great deal to do with this attitude; it exploited, so to speak, the potentialities of the Resurrection and held it out as a herald of hope to a decadent and dying world. A like process eventually started to draw attention to the Incarnation, but this time as a defense against the heresy of Arius and his followers, who denied the divinity of Christ. After the Council of Nicea, which in 325 condemned this error, greater emphasis was laid on the Incarnation of the divine Logos, in order to stress the divine personality of the Redeemer. And within from ten to twenty years later we witness the introduction of a liturgical celebration of Christ's birth.

The sixth century author of the *Liber Pontificalis* states that Pope Telesphorus (127-136) introduced the practice of a midnight Mass on Christmas.[359] But no one today admits the authenticity of this attribution. Neither Tertullian nor Origen make any mention of such a feast in their lists. Furthermore, in the East Christ's birthday was

[359] Edit. L. Duchesne, I, 129.

celebrated on January 6 until the end of the fourth century.[360] In most localities of the Eastern Church Christmas was introduced only in the last decade or so of the fourth century. In fact, if we understand St. John Chrysostom correctly, he seems to say, in a sermon dated 386, that the celebration of Christmas had begun in Antioch only ten years previous.[361]

Everything points to Rome as the place of origin of Christmas. In the Philocalian Calendar, which was completed by 354, we find the birthday of Christ indicated on December 25, thus giving testimony to the existence of the feast.[362] According to St. Ambrose, his sister Marcellina received the veil from Pope Liberius, who reigned from 352 to 356, on Christmas Day.[363] Neither of these two witnesses indicates that the feast was a new one; the whole tenor of their statements warrant, instead, our belief that it had been firmly established for some time. This gives credence to another source, John of Nicea, unfortunately not always a reliable author, when he says that Christmas was first celebrated in Rome under Pope Julius I, whose pontificate extended from 337 to 352.[364] Actually most authors are of the opinion that this feast was instituted early in the pontificate of this pope.

But we must ask how this date was decided upon as the birthday of the Savior. The Evangelists say nothing regarding the exact day or month. There is in fact no way of precisely ascertaining it. This, however, did not prevent early Church writers from making all sorts of calculations and guesses. As Clement of Alexandria indicates, some held January 6 to be the Savior's birthday, others April 20, others May 20 and still others November 17.[365] And the anonymous author of the treatise De Pascha Computus states that Christ was born on March 28 simply because on this day the sun was created! [366]

Since the actual date of Christ's birth is unknown, liturgiologists propose three theories to explain the choice of December 25. L. Duchesne sees the choice of this day as a consequence of the presumed date of Christ's death, March 25.[367] H. Engberding makes the date of Christmas depend immediately on that of the Annunciation and

[360] Cf. Cassian, Collationes, 10, 2. MPL, 49: 820; Epiphanius, Adv. Haer., 51, 16. MPG, 41:919; Etheria, op. cit., nn. 25, 26, 49, pp. 202, 206, 264. In fact, Christmas was not celebrated in Armenia until the fourteenth century: Hefele-Leclercq, op. cit., VI, 850, note 15.
[361] Homil. in diem natalem Jesu Christi, 1. MPG, 49: 351. And for Constantinople we have St. Gregory of Nazianzen giving on Dec. 25, 379 or 380: Homil. 38 in Theophania, 3 and 4. MPG, 36: 314-315.
[362] Kellner, op. cit., 138.
[363] De virginitate, 3,1. MPL, 16: 231.
[364] Kellner, op. cit., 135.
[365] Stromata, I, 21. MPG, 8:887.
[366] MPL, 4: 1044.
[367] Christian Worship, 261-262. The idea was that Christ must have died on the same day on which He was conceived, and that would be March 25, the day the Angel announced God's choice to Mary.

our Lord's conception, which are celebrated on March 25.[368] However, it is questionable whether or not March 25 was really the point of departure in this calculation; it would rather seem that the choice of March 25 depends on the already presupposed date of our Lord's birth, December 25. For the institution of Christmas antedates by far that of the Annunciation; we find no mention of the latter until the reign of Pope Sergius I, between 687 and 701.[369] A third hypothesis which has gained wide acceptance sees in the fixing of Christ's birth on December 25 an attempt on the part of the Church to counteract the influence and attraction of the pagan feast of the Sol Invictus, Mithras, whose cult was given such impetus by the Emperor Aurelian in 274.[370]

The chief peculiarity of the Christmas celebration is that of three Masses. This threefold celebration was definitely a custom in the time of Gregory the Great, for he explicitly alludes to it,[371] but very likely it existed already before him, for several Masses are provided for in the Gelasian Sacramentary.[372] Originally, it seems, there were only two Masses: one at midnight, the other in the morning. The source of this practice is probably to be found in the twofold celebration obtaining in Jerusalem, where at midnight a Mass was celebrated at the grotto in Bethlehem and another in the morning in the principal church of Jerusalem—this, of course, happening on the feast of the Epiphany.[373] In imitation of this Palestinian custom, at Rome the pope celebrated the midnight Mass at the relics of the crib in the Basilica of St. Mary Major and in the morning at the stational church, the Basilica of St. Peter. The introduction of a third Mass, the second in our series of three, was due to the presence in Rome of a Byzantine colony which observed on this day the anniversary of the martyr of Sirmium, St. Anastasia, whose body was buried in Rome. With the passing of this colony the cult of St. Anastasia also waned. Thus, from the practice of celebrating the second Mass in her honor with a mere

[368] "Der 25 Dezember als Tag der Feier der Geburt des Herrn," Archiv für Liturgiewissenschaft, 2 (1951), 25-43.

[369] Liber Pontificalis (ed. L Duchesne), I, 381. Thus the presence of the four major feasts of the Blessed Virgin (Annunciation, Assumption, Purification and Nativity) in the Gelasian and Gregorian Sacramentaries must be the work of a later hand: cf. E. Bourque, Etude sur les sacramentaires romains. Les Textes Primitifs (Rome, 1949), 252; see Register 2. Heortologisches: Marienfeste, for a discussion of the Marian feasts in A. Baumstark's "Untersuchungen" appended to K. Mohlberg's Die älteste erreichbare Gestalt des Liber Sacramentorum anni circuli der römischen Kirche, 192.

[370] Cf. B. Botte, Les origines de la Noël et de l'Epiphanie (Paris-Louvain, 1932), p. 14; H. Frank, "Frühgeschichte und Ursprung des römischen Weihnachtsfestes im Lichte neurer Forschung," Archiv für Liturgiewissenschaft, 2 (1951), 1-24; I. Schuster, The Sacramentary, I, 362.

[371] Homil. 8 in evang. MPL, 76: 1103.

[372] Edit. H. Wilson, pp. 2-4; cf. also E. Bourque, ut supra (note 369), pp. 247-248.

[373] Etheria, op. cit., n. 25. pp. 202-204.

commemoration of Christmas—as evidenced by the formulary for the second Mass in the Gregorian Sacramentary [374]—we find the Church later celebrating a second Mass in the church of the martyr, but a Mass devoted to the theme of Christmas and allowing only a commemoration of the saint. A further change took place in the twelfth century, when, though the main stational church was the Basilica of St. Peter, the pope, because of fatigue and the long journey necessary to go all the way to St. Peter's, decided to return to the Marian Basilica to celebrate the main station.[375] This resulted in a change of the stational church for the third Mass to St. Mary Major's, as is apparent in our modern Missal.

From what we have said, then, the occasion for this trination on Christmas was the necessity of celebrating three different stations: at the crib, at St. Anastasia's, and at the official public station of St. Peter's. We have already seen how a similar bination or trination was observed on the feasts of certain martyrs, with a Mass at the saint's tomb and another in a public church. But in both cases this custom was peculiar to Rome, with the pope himself celebrating all the Masses. It was only in the tenth century that this Christmas polyliturgy became common throughout the Church—and even then it was three different priests who celebrated. The permission for the same priest to celebrate all the Masses was granted only in the twelfth century.[376]

During the late Middle Ages liturgical authors who were oblivious of the true historical origins of the three Masses sought out the "mystical," actually the allegorical reasons for this practice. Durand, for instance, states that the first Mass symbolizes the eternal generation of the Word by the father without a mother, the second the temporal generation by a mother without a father, and the third both the eternal and temporal.[377] But before him Amalar—only two Masses existed in his time and place—says the reason for the midnight Mass was to commemorate the song of the angels, the Gloria in excelsis Deo, while the second Mass symbolized the fact that Christ was already both God and man in the womb of the Virgin.[378] How he arrives at this latter symbolism is truly a mystery.

With Innocent III we come upon a different slant: while the first and second Masses represent the eternal and earthly generation of the Word, the third Mass symbolizes His birth in the hearts of men through the gift of faith.[379] But when we consider the texts of the Masses and see that elements of all three "generations" are present in each, we must conclude that the above explanations are pure allegories.

[374] Edit. K. Mohlberg, p. 2.
[375] *Ord. Rom.* XI, n. 17. *MPL*, 78: 1032.
[376] Cf. M. Righetti, II, 58.
[377] *Rationale div. off.*, VI, 13, n. 24. M. Righetti, II, 58.
[378] *De eccl. off.*, III, 41. *MPL*, 105: 1159.
[379] *Sermo 3 in nativitate Domini. MPL*, 217: 459-461.

Though the Introit and Gradual and Communion of the midnight Mass do speak of the eternal generation of the Word, the Gospel is exclusively concerned with His earthly birth. On the other hand, the texts of the second Mass lend themselves beautifully to a portrayal of His birth in our hearts. It is to the Gospel of the third Mass—St. John's prologue—that we must go for the clearest allusion to both His eternal and temporal birth, but it is also in this Gospel that we hear of His illuminating the minds of men.

Though representations of the Nativity scene in Bethlehem have a history extending back to the early Middle Ages,[380] our modern practice of erecting cribs for the celebration of Christmas goes back to St. Francis of Assisi. Once he had conceived the idea, he presented it in 1223 to Pope Honorius III, who gave his approval. That same year St. Francis arranged figures around a representation of the Christ Child in the manger upon arriving in the little town of Greccio on Christmas eve. Thence the practice spread rapidly.[381]

2. Epiphany

The feast of the Epiphany has been called variously *Theophania*,[382] *festivitas declarationis*,[383] *apparitio*,[384] and *manifestatio*.[385] But it would seem that the different churches of Christendom were not in agreement as to which manifestation was being commemorated on this day, because of the differences in mentality and the introduction of the feast of Christmas.

The feast is definitely of Eastern origin and is spoken of for the first time by St. Clement of Alexandria in the beginning of the third century. The Gnostic sect of the Basilidians, he says, celebrated the birth and baptism of Christ on the sixth of January.[386] And in the beginning of the next century, the Passion of St. Philip, from Thrace, speaks of the Epiphany as a *dies sanctus*.[387] As for its acceptance in the West, our earliest references go back to the latter part of the fourth century. The Council of Saragossa in 380, for example, says that the feast of the Epiphany was preceded by a three-week fast.[388] St. Ambrose is a witness for Milan,[389] St. Augustine for Africa,[390] and St. Leo I for Rome.[391]

---

[380] Cf. H. Leclercq, "Crèche," *DACL*, III, 3021-3029.
[381] Cf. S. Donovan, "Crib," *The Catholic Encyclopedia*, IV, 489.
[382] While the Gelasian Sacramentary (edit. H. Wilson, p. 11) calls it *Theophania*, the Gregorian (edit. K. Mohlberg, p. 6) gives it the title *Epiphania*.
[383] Leo I, *Sermo 32 de Epiphania*, 1. *MPL*, 54: 238.
[384] Ambrose, *Sermo* 8, 2-3. *MPL*, 17: 640.
[385] Fulgentius, *Sermo* 4, 1. *MPL*, 65: 733.
[386] *Stromata*, I, 21. *MPG*, 8: 887.
[387] Cf. Cabrol-Leclercq, *Monumenta Ecclesiae Liturgica*, I, n. 3812.
[388] Can. 4. Hefele-Leclercq, *op. cit.*, I, 387.
[389] *Sermones* 8-12. *MPL*, 17: 639-649.
[390] *Sermones* 199-204. *MPL*, 38: 1026-1039.
[391] *Sermones* 31-38. *MPL*, 54: 234-263.

It would seem that in the East the feast of the Epiphany was originally intended as a celebration of the very first manifestation of Christ, namely, His birth.[392] But once the Roman feast of Christmas was introduced into the East, the baptism of Christ became the object of the oriental Epiphany feast. As the *Apostolic Constitutions* state, "On the feast of the Epiphany work ceases, for on this day the divinity of Christ was made manifest when at His baptism the Father gave His testimony and the Paraclete descended upon Him in the form of a dove."[393]

For the West, however, the feast of the Epiphany was from the beginning a commemoration of the visit of the Magi, a manifestation of Christ to the Gentile world.[394] Gradually the churches of the West tended to combine all the different manifestations of Christ's divinity into this one feast. Thus we find that, together with the visit of the Magi, our Lord's baptism in the Jordan and the changing of water into wine at the marriage feast of Cana were commemorated.[395] The multiplication of loaves was even added to these in a sermon of an unknown author usually attributed to St. Augustine.[396] While Rome, at first, limited its own celebration to the coming of the Magi, it eventually accepted a few extracts for the Office from Milan or other Gallican churches which combined both Eastern and Western ideas. This state of affairs is reflected in the Benedictus and Magnificat antiphons for the feast:

Benedictus

Hodie caelesti Sponso juncta est
Ecclesia, quoniam in Jordane lavit
Christus eius crimina; currunt cum
muneribus Magi ad regales nuptias,
et ex aqua facto vino laetantur
convivae, alleluia.

Magnificat

Tribus miraculis ornatum diem sanctum colimus:
hodie stella Magos duxit ad praesepium;

[392] Cf. Etheria, *op. cit.*, n. 25, p. 202; Epiphanius, *Adv. Haer.*, 51, 16. *MPG*, 41: 919; and Cassian, *Collationes*, 10, 2. *MPL*, 49: 820.

[393] VIII, 33. *MPG*, 1:1135. See also in this connection Gregory of Nazianzen, *Homil.* 39 *in Theophania*, 1. *MPG*, 36:335; and John Chrysostom, *Homil. de baptismo Christi*, 2. *MPG*, 49:365.

[394] Leo I, Augustine and Fulgentius: see notes 391, 390 and 385. See also the formulas in the Gelasian Sacramentary (edit. H. Wilson, pp. 11-12); and the Gregorian Sacramentary (edit. K. Mohlberg, pp. 6-7).

[395] Cf. Paulinus of Nola, *Poema* 27, v. 47 ff. *MPL*, 61:649; The Calendar of Polemius Silvius in *MPL*, 13:676; Sedatius, bishop of Beziers, *Homil. de Epiphania. MPL*, 72:771; Maximus of Turin, *Homil.* 23 *de Epiphania. MPL*, 57: 271-276.

[396] *Serm. supposit.* 136, 1. *MPL*, 39:2013.

hodie vinum ex aqua factum est ad nuptias;
hodie in Jordane a Joanne Christus baptizari
voluit, ut salvaret nos, alleluia.

According to K. Holl, the special attention given to the baptism
of Christ in the East was due, as in Rome for the feast of Christmas,
to the desire of the Church to withdraw the faithful from the influence
of a popular pagan festival, which fell in this case on January 6. At
this time the mystery cults celebrated the virginal birth of Eos, the
god-patron of Alexandria. During the night between January 5 and 6
the waters of the Nile were supposed to acquire a special power, and
the Egyptians were accustomed to go there and carry some of its
water away to their homes. The Eastern Church, to emphasize Christ's
baptism and the power imparted to the waters of the world through
contact with His pure body, blessed baptismal water and conferred
the sacrament on this day.[397] The mention of the marriage feast of
Cana was brought in to express a profound religious idea, namely, that
of the mystical nuptials of Christ with His Church, through which
in the waters of Baptism, she is able to give birth to "new sons
of God." [398]

3. Advent

Louis Bouyer claims that the view in which the formal object of
the Christmas and Epiphany cycle is the temporal birth of our Lord
is in reality a recent one.[399] The Advent texts themselves, taken in
their most obvious sense, express an expectation of the second coming,
the *Parousia*, of our Lord. It is true that our modern Missal and Breviary contain many expressions which explicitly speak of the coming of
Christ as Judge. And we have St. Gregory the Great's homily [400] for
the first Sunday of Advent which so emphatically interprets Luke
21:25 (itself an explicit prediction of the last things) in this way.
Must we not say, then, that the theme of Advent is the second coming
of Christ at the end of time, as the glorious Judge of all men?

We must be cautious here. Certainly there are formulas of the
Advent Liturgy which do very explicitly point to the *Parousia*. But to
say that this is the more ancient view would be mistaken. We cannot
be satisfied merely with a textual interpretation of our present-day
Liturgy; rather we must go back and examine all available sources to

---

[397] "Der Ursprung des Epiphaniefestes," *Sitzungsberichte der Preussischen
Akademie der Wissenschaften* (1917), 402-438.
[398] See A. Baumstark, *Liturgie Comparée*, 175; O. Casel, "Die Taufe als
Brautbad der Kirche," *Jahrbuch für Liturgiewissenschaft*, 5 (1925), 144-147; H.
Frank, "Hodie caelesti Sponso juncta est Ecclesiae. Ein Beitrag zur Geschichte
und Idee des Epiphaniefestes," *Vom Christlichen Mysterium*. Gesammelte Arbeiten
zum Gedächtnis von Odo Casel (Düsseldorf, 1951), 192-226.
[399] *Liturgical Piety*, 202.
[400] *Homiliarum*, lib. I, n. 1. *MPL*, 76: 1081.

see which of our Advent formulas are truly of Roman origin and belong to the original Roman sources—for we have already seen what a tremendous influence Gallican hands played in the definitive formation of our Roman Liturgy.

Fortunately, Walter Croce has done just this. He has shown, by a painstaking comparison of the orations in all early documents, both Roman and Gallican, that the orations which speak of the coming of the Judge are not Roman, but Gallican.[401] As for the homily of St. Gregory the Great on Luke 21:25, we must first remember that the titles for these homilies were added by compilers. The homily itself gives no indication that it was given on the First Sunday of Advent. Rather, if we examine it, we see that it was a sermon preached on the occasion of a great disaster in Rome, and in it, in order to give hope to his hearers, Gregory chose Luke 21:25, the prediction of the last things, as his text. Furthermore, this Gospel selection does not appear in any of the early Gospel lists for Rome; it is first found in books of the Gallican Rite which were produced under the influence of St. Columbanus, who, as we know, used every means to lift the minds of his charges to the things of the future world.[402]

Thus, it would seem, we are forced to admit that the more ancient idea behind Advent is the preparation for a commemoration of our Savior's birth. To this, of course, we must add the purpose of all liturgical commemoration—to prepare for the future coming of Christ—but we must remember that this was not the specific theme of Advent.

Of course, we can only speak of the existence of this preparatory period of Advent once the feasts of Christmas and Epiphany had been introduced in the West. And even then for several centuries there was a great deal of diversity both as to the number of weeks that constituted the period and the manner in which they were observed. We first hear of such a period of preparation in conjunction with the feast of the Epiphany. The Council of Saragossa in 380 commands that the feast be preceded by a three-week fast.[403] On the other hand, some time before 491 the diocese of Tours practiced a fast three times a week, beginning with the feast of St. Martin on November 11, until Christmas.[404] A century later this fast was extended to all the dioceses in France by the First Council of Macon in 581.[405] Thus it is easy to see how such a practice came to be called *Quadragesima Sancti Martini*. And it was observed even in England in the time of Cuthbert

---

[401] "Die Adventmessen des römischen Missale in ihrer geschichtlichen Entwicklung," *Zeitschrift für katholische Theologie*, 74 (1952), 279-295.

[402] See the scholarly article of W. Croce, "Die Adventsliturgie im Licht ihrer geschichtlichen Entwicklung," *Zeitschrift für katholische Theologie*, 76 (1954), 258-296.

[403] Can. 4. Hefele-Leclercq, *op. cit.*, I, 387. Probably this was intended by way of preparation for the reception of Baptism on the feast.

[404] Gregory of Tours, *Historia Francorum*, 10, 31. MPL, 71: 566.

[405] Can. 9. Hefele-Leclercq, *op. cit.*, III, 203.

(d. 687) and Egbert (d. 729).[406] Lastly, we also have evidence of a pre-Christmas fast in the north of Italy towards the end of the fourth century.[407]

For Rome things were otherwise. We find no uncontroverted evidence for the existence of Advent there until the latter part of the sixth century. True, Berno of Reichenau claims that Pope Hilary I (d. 468) commanded a three-week fast before the Epiphany,[408] but Berno wrote in the eleventh century, and little credence is given to his statement. The Gelasian Sacramentary, however, contains a number of orations for Advent which are of truly Roman origin.[409] Also the Würzburg Epistle list and the Gregorian Sacramentary provide formulas for the Sundays of Advent. On the other hand, St. Benedict makes no mention of this institution in his Regula, which otherwise shows such an ardent attempt at adopting the Roman cursus. Thus we must conclude that the period of Advent was introduced in Rome sometime between 547, the death of St. Benedict, and approximately 560, the earliest date possible for the compilation of the Gelasian Sacramentary.

Today in our Advent Liturgy we notice a certain atmosphere of sorrow and penance. This was not always so. Originally, the Roman Liturgy knew nothing of an Advent fast, but by the thirteenth century we find Innocent III informing the Bishop of Braga that it was then the custom in Rome.[410] Furthermore, today we drop the singing of the Allelulia on ferias, and the Gloria and Te Deum are silenced. We also use violet vestments. But none of these things were true of the early Roman Rite. At least the Gloria and Te Deum were sung as late as the twelfth century.[411] These traits of penitential sorrow come from the same source as the eschatological ideas contained in the Advent formulas: the Gallican Liturgy imbued with the spirit of St. Columbanus and his disciples.[412]

A consideration of the primitive Roman orations, antiphons, and responses shows that the Roman Liturgy was thoroughly taken up with a holy enthusiasm and profoundly joyful expectation of the coming of our Savior. Any trace of sorrow or penance is completely external to the real core of the Advent Liturgy. This whole period is imbued with the exultant happiness occasioned by the announcement

[406] Bede, *Hist. angl.*, III, 27; IV, 30. MPL, 95: 167, 226.
[407] Cf. S. *Filastrii Episcopi Brixiensis Diversarum Hereseon Liber*, 149. CSEL, 38: 121.
[408] *De officio Missae*, IV. MPL, 142: 1066.
[409] Croce's claim that originally there were two, then three, Sundays of Advent, according to the data revealed in the Gelasian Sacramentary, seems true: "Die Adventmessen des römischen Missale," 295-301; "Die Adventsliturgie," 271, note 69.
[410] *Corpus iuris canonici*, decret. lib. III, tit. 46, cap. 2 (edit. A. Freidberg, Leipzig, 1881), vol. II, col. 651.
[411] *Ord. Rom.* XI, nn. 3, 4. MPL, 78: 1027.
[412] Cf. W. Croce, "Die Adventmessen des römischen Missale in ihrer geschichtlichen Entwicklung," 279, note 11, 315-316; "Die Adventsliturgie im Licht ihrer geschichtlichen Entwicklung," 292.

of the *gaudium magnum*, the tidings of great joy brought to Mary and the shepherds. And it is really this joy, a joy springing from the certainty of fulfillment, that gives meaning to the longing, yearning, the holy desire for the Savior and for the freedom of deliverance which so many of the texts of Advent instill in us. Perhaps one of the most beautiful expressions of this sentiment is the O-Antiphons proper to the last week of Advent, but also Gaudete Sunday, the Introit for the Second Sunday of Advent as well as the Communion verse for the same day.

F. The Sanctoral Cycle [413]

The celebration of festivals in honor of the saints certainly needs no justification for a Catholic. From the very beginning the holiness of those who had followed Christ with total dedication was emphasized, out of a twofold motive: The way of salvation is rendered much easier when we have models to lead, guide, and encourage us along that way; and these very models, we know, because of their holy lives, have gained heaven and everlasting friendship with God by reason of which they can intercede for us and gain for us the graces we need in our own personal combat with the powers of darkness. The New Testament writers already set an example in this matter when they hand on the memory of those who suffered for Christ—the Holy Innocents [414] and St. Stephen [415]—but above all when they describe the glory enjoyed by these martyrs in heaven, as, for example, the Apocalypse does.[416]

The saints, then, are feted because of their fidelity to Christ, because of their likeness to Him: for "holiness begins from Christ; by Christ it is effected." [417] Their liturgical festivals will, accordingly, reveal the marked characteristics which relate them either to Christ's Passion and Resurrection, or to His Incarnation.

1. Feasts with an *Easter* theme

Cult of the martyrs

The feasts of the martyrs[418] are intimately connected with Easter.

[413] As we have already said, the feasts of the saints do not really constitute an independent cycle within the Church year. Rather the separation of their feasts from those of the Christological cycle is but a mechanical device for dividing up our Missals and Breviaries — a practice definitively accepted around the eighth century. The compiler of the Gelasian Sacramentary had once before attempted such a repartition: one section for the Easter-Christmas cycle, another for the saints, and still a third for the Votive Masses. The Gregorian Sacramentary, however, established a system of feasts completely interwoven of temporal and sanctoral material.

[414] Matt. 2:16-18.

[415] Acts 7:54-60.

[416] 6:9-11; 7:9-12; 14:12-13.

[417] Pius XII, *Mystici Corporis*, 63.

[418] For the meaning of this term see H. Delehaye, *Sanctus. Essai sur le culte des saints dans l'antiquité* (Bruxelles: Société des Bollandistes, 1927), 74-108.

These feasts find in Easter their cause as well as their climax. They are meant as shining examples of how the grace of the paschal mysteries became operative for our forebears in the Mystical Body, and they are thus an encouragement for us to fight the good fight in union with the Passion of our Head, that we too may complete the transformation begun in Baptism with the hoped for birth into celestial regions.

As St. Ambrose says: "We celebrate the birthdays of the martyrs to announce the glory of the Lord's resurrection to those who were companions to His passion. . . . We announce the paschal grace to the holy martyrs: while their bodies are laid in the tomb and grow cold, their spirit is already warmed by the heat of immortality." [419] By the same token these *natalitia martyrum* lead us back to the feast of Easter, for they impel us to seek more consciously and devoutly for this same paschal grace.

Our first documentary proof for the celebration of a martyr's anniversary comes from the second century. In the famous letter of the Smyrnians narrating the beautiful martyrdom of their bishop Polycarp, we find a chapter in which the faithful express the hope of being able to celebrate the anniversary of their shepherd at his tomb: "There the Lord will permit us to meet together in gladness and joy to celebrate the birthday of his martyrdom both in memory of those who fought the fight and for the training and preparation of those who still must do so." [420]

During this same period we run across evidence of a like devotion to these heroes of the faith in other places. In Rome, for instance, St. Clement I reportedly divided the city into regions and appointed a notary in each to gather carefully all the facts relating to the martyrdoms which took place in his locality.[421] Pope Anteros (d. 236) collected these reports and preserved them,[422] and after him Pope Fabian charged seven subdeacons with the supervision of the work of the notaries.[423] That such activities were not simply those of historical-minded popes, but rather of leaders of their communities who were anxious to render to the martyrs all the honor belonging to them and especially to keep the day of their martyrdom as a holy memorial, is provided by a letter of St. Cyprian, Bishop of the sister-church of Rome, Carthage. He expressly orders the priests and deacons, not only to take care of those in prison, but also to note down the day on which they undergo martyrdom, so that their memory might be celebrated along with that of the other martyrs.[424] Cyprian

[419] *De natali martyrum sermo* 61. *MPL,* 17: 728.
[420] *The Fathers of the Church,* I (New York, 1947), 160.
[421] *Liber Pontificalis* (ed L. Duchesne), I, 52 and 123.
[422] *Ibid.,* I, xcv, 62-65 and 147.
[423] *Ibid.,* I, 65 and 148.
[424] "Dies eorum quibus excedunt adnotate, ut commemorationes eorum inter memorias martyrum celebrare possimus," *Epist.* 37, 2. *MPL,* 4:337.

was no innovator, for Tertullian, before him, wrote of such memorials.[425] And after him, we are told, Gregory the Wonder-Worker collected information about the martyrs and encouraged the faithful to celebrate their anniversaries.[426] And in the fourth century the Palestinian towns of Gaza and Constantia possessed their own lists of martyrs and observed their festivals.[427] It was from such lists of martyrologies that Philocalus composed his *Depositio martyrum*, which was completed by 354.

Unlike our modern civil practice of celebrating as a feast the day on which great men were born into this world, the Church has always observed the day of death of her martyrs and saints. This day she calls their *dies natalis*, their birthday into eternal life. We came upon this term in the above-cited letter of the Smyrnians concerning the birthday of their bishop Polycarp. Although the expression was not unknown in pre-Christian pagan literature,[428] it was left to the Church to bring to it its truly profound supernatural significance. Because of the fact that everyone is born into this world with Original Sin on his soul, early Christian writers were led to look with disdain on the human birthday.[429] They clearly saw that man was fully freed from this taint only by means of death. Therefore, through a holy death, the saints have been born in the highest sense of the word, for they have definitely received the full grace of Christ's resurrection, as they have arisen with Him to eternal life.

This cult of the martyrs was at first a strictly local affair. Rome observed the feasts only of Roman martyrs, while Alexandria was concerned only with Alexandrian martyrs, etc. A striking proof of this policy is seen in the fact that, even though St. Ignatius of Antioch met his death in Rome, his feast was not entered either in the Gelasian or Gregorian Sacramentaries. On the other hand, the fact that certain martyrs of Carthage do find a place therein is explained by the special relationship of that see with Rome, that of a daughter to a mother.[430] The reasons behind such limitation is brought out by St. Maximus of Turin in one of his sermons. In his own words: "As we must celebrate the general commemoration of all the holy martyrs, so, my brethren, ought we to celebrate with special devotion the feasts of those who shed their blood in our own locality. For while all the saints, wherever they may be, assist us all, yet those who suffered for us intercede for us in a special manner. For the martyr suffers, not for himself alone, but for his fellow citizens also. By his sufferings he

---

[425] *De corona militis*, 3. *MPL*, 2:99.
[426] Gregory of Nyssa, *Vita Gregorii Thaumaturgii*. *MPG*, 46:954.
[427] Sozomen, *Hist. eccl.*, 5, 3. *MPG*, 67: 1222.
[428] E.g., *dies aeterni natalis* in Seneca, *Epist.* 102.
[429] For Patristic references see F-J. Dölger, *Sol Salutis*, 144-145, note 2; A. Rush, *Death and Burial in Christian Antiquity* (Washington: The Catholic University Press, 1941), 72-87.
[430] Cf. H. Kellner, *op. cit.*, 212.

obtains for himself a reward in heaven, and gives good example to his fellow citizens. He gains rest for himself and salvation for them." [431]

A change in this restrictive attitude was brought about by the conversion of the northern peoples of Europe. Once they accepted the faith, having no saints of their own, they adopted, along with the Roman ritual, its calendar of saints. Rome, on the other hand, did not allow any Frankish or Anglo-Saxon saints into her Calendar. It was only with the sixteenth century revision of her liturgical books that Rome manifested a certain degree of universality in her lists. About the only exceptions to the local character of martyr-cult were Sts. John the Baptist and Stephen the proto-martyr, both of whom were venerated universally. [432] Even the Apostles, though they had a special claim as martyrs and as propagators of the faith to the veneration of all Christians were not exempt from this rule and found no earlier acceptance either in the Calendar of Rome or that of other places than ordinary martyrs and saints.

Cult of confessors and virgins

Up until the fourth century it was only those who died for the faith who enjoyed an official *cultus* within the Church. Once the persecutions had ceased, the prodigies and strenuous aceticism of the anchorites drew the attention of the Christian world, and men began to realize that the holiness of the many virgins, ascetics, and other saintly men put them on a level with the martyrs. Though the *cultus* of such confessors and virgins began to flourish only in this century, the motivation behind it can be traced back to St. Clement of Alexandria (d. 215), who called the holy man a martyr, since his life, which leads him to observe the commandments faithfully and renounce the pleasures of this world, is the equivalent of martyrdom. [433] Jerome expresses this same idea as he tries to console Eustochium on the loss of her mother, Paula, who, he says, "was crowned with a long martyrdom. Not only is the shedding of blood considered a confession (of faith), but the obedience of a devout mind and heart is also a daily martyrdom." [434] And a fifth-century writer, Sulpicius Severus, says that Martin of Tours did not lack the glory of the martyrs, even though by reason of his time he had not the opportunity to suffer in this way. His reason for saying this: "Both because of his virtue and strong desire Martin could have been and wanted to be a martyr." [435] These texts [436] prove beyond a shadow of a doubt that the cult rendered the

[431] *Homil.* 81. *MPL*, 57: 427.
[432] Cf. H. Kellner, *op. cit.*, 217-218, 223-225.
[433] *Stromata*, IV, 4; VII, 3. *MPG*, 8:1227; 9:415.
[434] *Epist.* 108 *ad Eustochium virginem*, 31. *MPL*, 22: 905.
[435] Epist. II, 9, 12. *MPL*, 20: 179-180.
[436] For many other texts see H. Delehaye, *op cit.*, 109-112.

confessors and virgins was, in its theme, a prolongation of the veneration of the martyrs.[437]

In the East it seems that St. Gregory the Wonder-Worker was among the earliest, if not the very first (d. 270), confessors to be so honored.[438] And so great was the veneration for the holy ascetics, that Anthony himself (d. 358) had to command his brethren to bury him in an unknown place, lest Pergamius, a very rich man of the neighborhood, construct a *martyrium*, or memorial chapel, over his grave.[439] As for Hilarion (d. 372), as soon as they transported his body back to his own monastery, they began the celebration of a solemn feast in his honor.[440] And Gregory of Nyssa lists St. Basil among the saints honored with a special feast.[441]

As for the West, Sts. Silvester and Martin seem to vie with one another for the honor of being the first confessor to receive liturgical cult. Gregory of Tours tells us that Bricius, one of the early successors of Martin as Bishop of Tours, had a small basilica built over the tomb of Martin,[442] who died in 397. But in the *Liber Pontificalis* we read that Pope Symmachus (498-514) built a church in honor of St. Martin near the Church of St. Silvester on the Palatine.[443] It is not certain, however, how far back this church in honor of St. Silvester dates.

With the ever increasing number of saints, it became quite impossible to allow each his special feast day. There soon sprang up a common commemoration of all saints, martyrs especially, in the beginning, so that no one would be neglected. The first instance of such a feast of all martyrs is to be found in Antioch in the fourth century, where St. John Chrysostom preached several sermons on this feast.[444] The day chosen for this commemoration was the first Sunday after Pentecost. In the West, we have seen, Maximus of Turin made mention of such a general feast in the fifth century. Greater impetus was given to the idea, when, after the Emperor Phocas (d. 610) gave the Pantheon to Pope Boniface IV, the latter cleansed it from its former pagan use and made it a church in honor of Mary and all the martyrs; the dedication of the church *Sancta Maria ad Martyres* was thereafter observed annually on the thirteenth of May.[445] A further step was taken when Pope Gregory III (731-741) dedicated one of the chapels in St. Peter's to all the apostles, martyrs, confessors, and all the just and perfect who were at rest throughout the world.[446] Finally, so John Beleth informs us, Gregory IV (827-844) decided to transfer the

[437] *Ibid.*, 114.
[438] Cf. Gregory of Nyssa, *Vita S. Gregorii Thaumaturgii. MPG,* 46: 893.
[439] Jerome, *Vita S. Hilarionis,* 31. *MPL,* 23:46.
[440] Sozomen, *Hist. eccl.,* III, 14, 16. *MPG,* 67: 1078.
[441] *Eulogy on St. Basil. MPG,* 46: 788.
[442] *Historia Francorum,* X, 31. *MPL,* 71: 565.
[443] Edit. L. Duchesne, I, 267-268, note 35.
[444] Cf. *MPG,* 50: 706-712.
[445] *Liber Pontificalis,* I, 317, note 2.
[446] *Ibid.,* I, 417.

feast of all martyrs from May 13 to November 1, because the food supply was insufficient in May for the great multiude of pilgrims who came to Rome for this feast.[447] And other writers tell us that this same pope urged Louis the Pious to have this festival in honor of all saints introduced in his kingdom, which he did in 835.[448]

Cult of the dead

While honoring all her saints, the Church does not forget those who have died whose present condition cannot be absolutely ascertained. The day after the feast of All Saints the Church dedicates in suffrage for the souls of the departed not declared saints. Religious Orders were the first to observe this custom. Isidore of Seville, for instance, set aside the day after Pentecost for this purpose.[449] While it was Amalar who chose November 2 for this commemoration of the dead,[450] the real moving power behind the spread of the practice was Odilo, Abbot of Cluny, who introduced it in his monastery about 998.[451] It was only natural that all other monasteries coming under his jurisdiction followed suit. And the Carthusians adopted the custom in the following century.[452] As for Rome, the observance is first recorded in official documents of the thirteenth century.[453]

2. Feasts with a *Christmas* theme

Feasts of Mary

The feasts of Mary—with the exception of the Seven Dolors [454]—are especially connected with the Incarnational cycle of the liturgical year because of Mary's role in the plan of redemption. Her divine maternity is the source of all her glory and preferred rank in the kingdom of God, for this was her precise part in the redemption of the world: to provide the God-Man with flesh of her flesh and nurture Him until, in God's time, He should enter upon His public ministry.

While devotion to Mary flourished from the very beginning of the Church—witness John's care of her, the eulogies paid her by the earli-

---

[447] *Rationale divinorum officiorum*, 127. *MPL*, 202: 133.
[448] Cf. Ado, *Martyrologium*. *MPL*, 123:387; Sigebert of Gembloux, *Chron. ad annum* 835. *MPL*, 160: 159.
[449] *Regula monachorum*, 24, 2. *MPL*, 83: 894.
[450] *De ordine antiphonarii*, 65. *MPL*, 105: 306.
[451] *Statutum pro defunctis*. *MPL*, 142: 1038.
[452] Guido, *Consuet. Carth.*, 11. *MPL*, 153: 655.
[453] *Ord. Rom.* XIV, n. 98. *MPL*, 78: 1224.
[454] It stands in obvious relation to the passion of Christ. The first traces of this feast are found in the twelfth century: Bernard, *De passione Christi et doloribus et planctibus Matris eius*. *MPL*, 182: 1134-1142; Amadeus, *De mentis dolore et martyrio beatae virginis Mariae*. *MPL*, 188: 1325-1331. The feast was treated in detail by the Servites in the following century, and Innocent IX in 1688 granted permission for a second feast under the same title on the third Sunday of September.

est Fathers of the Church, and the devout frescoes and other artistic representations of her, dating from primitive times—the development of her liturgical cult does not seem to begin until her divine maternity is championed at the Council of Ephesus in 431 against the heresy of Nestorius. The very church in which this council held its meetings was dedicated to her. And in Rome, in order to celebrate the definition of her divine maternity, Pope Sixtus III (432-440) rededicated to the Mother of God the basilica built by Pope Liberius (352-366).[455] It seems too that her name was inserted in the Communicantes sometime in the fifth century.[456]

Evidence for Mary's liturgical feasts that is both sufficient and uncontroverted is of rather late date. In the fifth century definite proof can be found for the existence of the feast of the Annunciation. While two of the sermons of Proclus, Patriarch of Constantinople (d. 447), certainly center around this theme but do not really speak of it as a feast,[457] Antipater, Bishop of Bosra, considers one of the Sundays before Christmas as dedicated to the Annunciation.[458] At the beginning of the sixth century a "Commemoration of the holy Mother of God and Virgin Mary" is attested to in Antioch in the homilies of Severus; [459] it was celebrated during January. A similar festival was kept in Gaul on January 18, as Gregory of Tours in the sixth century indicates.[460] At the turn of the century we find the same feast, but now on August 15, commanded to be observed in all churches of the empire by the Emperor Maurice (d. 602).[461] On the other hand, there is a probability that a *Natale S. Mariae* was celebrated in Rome as the octave of Christmas by the end of the sixth century.[462] The first definitive clue to the existence of the four major Marian feasts in Rome— Annunciation, Assumption, Nativity, and Purification—is a statement in the *Liber Pontificalis* that Pope Sergius I (687-701) had started the custom of having processions on these feasts.[463] Therefore they must have been introduced in Rome sometime in the seventh century.

The feast of the Purification was originally called *Hypapante*, or *Occursus Domini*, the meeting of the Lord, and was not, strictly speaking, a feast of Mary. Even today, it is only in the Divine Office (and possibly the Offertory of the Mass) that we find any texts which may be interpreted as referring to Mary. Our earliest evidence for

---

[455] *Liber Pontificalis,* I, 232 and 235, note 2.
[456] See V. Kennedy, *The Saints of the Canon of the Mass* (Vatican City, 1938), 92-93.
[457] *Oratio* I and II. MPG, 65: 679.
[458] *In sanctissimae Deiparae Annunciatione.* MPG, 85: 1775.
[459] Cf. A. Baumstark, *Liturgie Comparée*, 207.
[460] *De gloria martyrum,* 1, 9. MPL, 71: 713.
[461] Nicephorus Callistus, *Hist. eccl.*, 17, 28. MPG, 147: 292.
[462] Cf. B. Botte, "La première fête mariale de la liturgie romaine," *Ephemerides Liturgicae*, 47 (1933), 425-430.
[463] I, 376. It is noteworthy that Sonnatius, Bishop of Rheims from 614-631, included three of these, the Annunciation, Assumption, and the Nativity, in his calendar: *Statuta*, 20. MPL. 80: 446.

the existence of the *Hypapante* dates from the end of the fourth century. Etheria reports that the Palestinian Christians celebrated the Presentation of the Child Jesus in the Temple forty days after the Epiphany.[464] Nicephorus tells us, further, that in 527 the Emperor Justinian decreed universal observance of this feast after a terrible pestilence had caused great suffering among the people.[465] In the same century we hear of a procession with candles on this day in the East.[466] The blessing for these candles found its way into the Roman Rite in the twelfth century because of the influence of the tenth century Romano-Germanic Pontifical.[467]

Even the Annunciation was apparently, in the beginning, a feast of our Lord, for its title in the older books was *Annuntiatio Domini* [468] or even *Conceptio Christi*.[469] Nevertheless, being so replete with references to Mary, it easily became one of her most important feasts. We have already seen above that Proclus and Antipater give evidence that the feast was celebrated in the East before Christmas as early as the fifth century. Other regions observed it on different dates. The Tenth Council of Toledo, held in 656, took notice of this diversity and decided in favor of December 18.[470] Probably the reason for this was that it had been the regular practice to avoid celebrating feasts during Lent. However, the Council *In Trullo* of 692 evidently had no qualms on this point, for it explicitly mentions March 25 as the date for this feast.[471] It was, of course, this latter date which Rome followed when it introduced the feast in the course of the seventh century. It is noteworthy, though, that Rome in the eighteenth century introduced another feast on December 18 very similar to the feast of the Annunciation formerly held on this day; it is the *In Exspectatione Partus Beatae Mariae Virginis*.

We have already seen that it was through the efforts of the Emperor Maurice at the end of the sixth century that the feast of the Assumption, called then the *Dormitio*, spread throughout the empire. It is not certain whether the feast existed before with this precise title, but from this moment on it was clearly devoted to a commemoration of Mary's "home-going" and celebrated on August 15. Under Byzantine influence Rome accepted it during the middle of the seventh century, and thence it spread throughout western Europe. We have already noted the existence in Rome before this time of a *Natale S. Mariae* on January 1 and in the East and other places in the West a similar

---

[464] *Journal de Voyage*, n. 26, p. 206. But again there is no mention made of its Marian character.

[465] *Hist. eccl.*, 17, 28. *MPG*, 147: 292.

[466] Cyril of Scitopolis mentions it in his life of St. Theodosius written before 565: cf. *Kyrillos von Skytopolis*, ed. Eduard Schwartz (Leipzig, 1939), p. 236, 24.

[467] Cf. M. Andrieu, *Le Pontifical Romain*, I, 206-209.

[468] *Liber Pontificalis* (ed. L. Duchesne), I, 376.

[469] Cf. H. Kellner, *op. cit.* 231.

[470] Can. 1. Hefele-Leclercq, *op. cit.*, III, 294.

[471] Can. 52. *Ibid.*, III, 569.

feast in the middle of January. This feast, it would seem, by reason of its title, *Natale*, was dedicated to Mary's death, just as the Church always observed a saint's feast on the day of his death. It is not without probability that, once the doctrine of the corporeal assumption of Mary gained in fervor, the former festival celebrated in January disappeared.[472]

Another ancient feast of the Blessed Virgin is that of her birth, celebrated on September 8. Certainly of oriental origin just as all the others, it is first attested to in a hymn composed by the famous Greek hymnographer, St. Romanus, who died in 556.[473] Our first witness for it in the West is Sonnatius, Bishop of Rheims.[474] And, as we saw, Rome began to observe it during the course of the seventh century.

The feast of the Immaculate Conception is of later origin than the others so far mentioned. John, Bishop of Eubea around 740, states explicitly that the feast is not recognized by all,[475] which would indicate that it was of recent institution at that time. From the Orient this feast spread to the Greek monasteries in Italy during the tenth and eleventh centuries. Thence it was brought to England during the eleventh century,[476] and from there it passed to the rest of Europe. But Rome was extremely hesitant in accepting it. In the thirteenth century St. Thomas could say that, while Rome allows other churches to celebrate the feast, she herself does not do so.[477] But in the next century, in 1330 to be exact, according to John Bacon, Pope John XXII began to observe the feast at Avignon.[478] And in 1476 Pope Sixtus IV approved a special Office and Mass for the feast.[479]

Other feasts of the Blessed Mother are of still later introduction. The Holy Name of Mary was approved by Julius II in 1513 for Spain and, in thanksgiving for deliverance from the Turks, was extended to the entire Church by Innocent XI in 1683. The Presentation appears for the first time, officially, in the constitution of Manuel Comnenus in 1166; it was authorized by Gregory XI in 1371 for certain places, introduced in Rome by Sixtus IV, suppressed by Pius V because of a lack of serious historical evidence for such an event in the life of Mary,

[472] Cf. B. Capelle, "La fête de l'Assomption dans l'histoire liturgique," *Ephemerides Theologicae Lovaniensis*, 3 (1926), 33-45.

[473] Cf. M. Righetti, *op. cit.*, II, 263.

[474] *Statuta*, 20. *MPL*, 80: 446.

[475] *MPG*, 117: 1305.

[476] See the excellent treatment of its history in "On the Origins of the Feast of the Immaculate Conception of the Blessed Virgin Mary," a chapter in Edmund Bishop's *Liturgica Historica*, pp. 238-259.

[477] *Summa Theol.*, III, 27, 2, ad 3.

[478] Cf. M. Righetti, *op. cit.*, II, 259.

[479] See the very good treatment of the feast by Cornelius Bouman, "The Immaculate Conception in the Liturgy," Chapter IV in *The Dogma of the Immaculate Conception. History and Significance*. Edited by E. O'Connor (Notre Dame, Indiana: University of Notre Dame Press, 1958), pp. 113-159.

and finally re-introduced and extended to the entire Church by Sixtus V in 1585. The feast of the Visitation was first celebrated by the Franciscans in the thirteenth century and was officially recognized by Boniface IX in 1389, during the Great Schism, and by the Council of Basel in 1441. Victory over the Turks at Lepanto on October 7, 1571 moved Pius V to institute a feast of Our Lady of Victory, while two years later his successor, Gregory XIII, permitted the celebration of the feast of the Holy Rosary on this day in every church or chapel having an altar consecrated under this title; Clement XI extended this feast to the entire Church and Leo XIII provided it with a new proper Office. Already observed in some dioceses, the feast of the Maternity of Mary was extended to the universal Church by Pius XI in 1931 to commemorate the fifteenth centenary of the Council of Ephesus. After World War II Pius XII instituted the feast of the Immaculate Heart of Mary in 1945, to be celebrated on the octave day of the Assumption.

Other saints

While St. John the Baptist was from early times commemorated as a martyr,[480] he nevertheless has a direct connection with the Incarnation of our Lord and played an important role in pointing Him out as the promised Messias. Furthermore, he is the only other saint besides the Blessed Virgin whose earthly birthday is observed as a feastday, because it has been traditionally believed that he was already sanctified in his mother's womb by Mary's visit, after she had conceived the Son of God.

The feast of St. Gabriel the Archangel certainly belongs to the Christmas cycle, for he was the bearer of the "good tidings" to Mary at the Annunciation. His liturgical *cultus* came rather late into the worship of the Church, and then only in isolated places in the tenth and eleventh centuries. It was only in 1921 that his feast was inserted into the universal Church calendar.

The earliest trace of a liturgical veneration of St. Joseph is met with in the eighth century Coptic calendars on July 20.[481] In the West his feast appears in isolated spots in the tenth century but remains strictly local throughout the entire Middle Ages. The final universal recognition given to his feast was due to the private devotion of saints like Bernard, Gertrude, Bernardine of Siena, etc. Sixtus IV introduced the feast in the Roman Liturgy and fixed it on March 19, while Gregory XV in 1621 made it a holyday of obligation.

As parents of our Lady, Sts. Anne and Joachim enjoyed a feast in the Liturgy of the Eastern Church at a relatively early date. Justinian in the sixth century ordered a church built in honor of St.

---

[480] Since the fourth century, according to H. Kellner, *op cit.*, 218.
[481] *Ibid.*, 273.

Anne in Constantinople, [482] while both saints had their commemoration in the menology of Constantinople. In the West, however, we do not find universal liturgical honors paid them until the Renaissance period. Though Urban VI had authorized a feast of St. Anne for the English in 1378, it was prescribed for the entire Church only in 1584 by Gregory XIII. The feast of St. Joachim, on the other hand, was first approved by Julius II before 1513.

[482] *Ibid.,* 275.

CHAPTER NINE

The Sacraments and Sacramentals

A. Introduction

A study of sacramental ritual is important for the priest, indeed useful for the layman as well, for without it understanding of the sacraments is really incomplete, and consequently in practice their use will leave something to be desired and will not achieve the fullest possible effect. Admittedly, dogmatic sacramental theology rarely has the time to go into the history of the evolution of these rites or even an explanation of the significance of the surrounding ceremonials; it must ordinarily be content with a discussion of their nature and essence, proving their institution by Christ, indicating their special effects and, in general, determining the rules for a valid and licit administration and reception of them. Unfortunately, this understandable limitation often occasions an undesirable attitude in priests and seminarians toward the ceremonies which surround the sacraments.

Sacramental theology teaches that, though grace is offered *ex opere operato*, the amount of grace received will depend on the dispositions of the recipient. These dispositions, in turn, are enlarged, deepened, and made more fervent by means of an earnest and intelligent preparation. This is the precise function of the ceremonies which surround the "matter and form" of the sacraments. The Church has instituted such ceremonies in order to remove the obstacles to grace, to instill within the heart and soul of the recipient proper attitudes of respect, reverence, faith, humility, and charity—all of which are necessary if the grace of the sacraments is really going to make the soul grow in the spiritual life. Furthermore, these very ceremonies enlighten the mind as to the true meaning of the sacrament about to be received; they are a living catechetics aimed at bringing about a reasonable and reasoning participation in the sacramental action. But what is of utmost importance in this whole question is that the so-called "externals" are not mere whimsical ornaments to the central action; they themselves are *sacramentals* backed up by the all-powerful prayer of the Church and they produce their effects *ex opere operantis Ecclesiae*. When they are performed reverently and with meaning by the priest and recipient, they form the best possible preparation for the reception of sacramental grace. Since it is the duty of the priest thus to prepare and instruct the faithful, he must know the history and spirit of these ceremonies.

Our study of the sacraments will show, among other things, that in their secondary ceremonial they have been in evolution over the centuries. The basic reason for this evolution has been the Church's attempt to speak to the people in their own language. This language, however, is essentially a *sign* language, a symbolism, and its importance in the sacramental ritual cannot be overestimated. The sacraments are *signs*, theology teaches; this principle underlies even the last and most minute ceremony used in their confection. A second principle is that the *sacraments effect what they signify.* And again the application of this axiom is just as extensive as that of the first. It was precisely in order to be able to speak to men of all ages and places, that the Church has allowed her sacramental rites to enjoy such a wide diversity and evolution. If we are to understand what the sacraments are meant to do for us, we have to understand this sign language. If we lose sight of this principle, we will hardly appreciate the history of the sacramental ritual of the Catholic Church, for here, perhaps more than in any other phase of her liturgical life, has she been extraordinarily *catholic.*

1. The word *sacramentum*

Originally the word *sacramentum* belonged to Roman legal parlance and meant agreement, obligation of a contract and, in particular, the oath which one took to bind himself to such an agreement or contract. It is specifically from the final part of such an oath, the *sacratio*, or the making holy and inviolable of the foregoing terms of the agreement by swearing oneself to its observance, that our word *sacramentum* comes. It was also used to designate the oath which one took upon entering the military service, the oath of allegiance. Finally, it was used as the equivalent of the Greek word *mysterion*, found in pagan literature. We find the word used for the first time in Christian literature by Tertullian (and after him by Cyprian and Arnobius) in the sense of oath of allegiance, inasmuch as entrance into the Christian religion through Baptism enrolled one in the *militia Christi*. But in the course of use Tertullian evolved its meaning, giving it the sense of a ritual-mystery, an efficacious symbolic action. It was this sense which succeeded in becoming preponderant both in Tertullian himself and in Christian writers after him.[1]

[1] Cf. the interesting work of J. De Ghellinck, E. De Backer, J. Poukens, G. Lebacqz, *Pour l'histoire du mot sacramentum.* Louvain: Spicilegium Sacrum Lovaniense, 1924.

2. Relationship between the sacraments and the Mass

In this last sense of a mystery, or an efficacious symbolic action, Cyprian calls the Eucharist the "sacrament of the Lord's passion and our redemption." [2] The Holy Sacrifice of the Mass is "the sacrament" in the strictest sense of the word, for in it the redemptive work of Christ and Christ Himself are made truly present; the other sacraments contain and pass on to us the power of both Christ and His redemptive work. In this connection St. Thomas says:

> The Eucharist is the greatest of the sacraments for a threefold reason. First, because in it is contained substantially Christ Himself, while in the other sacraments there is a certain instrumental power communicated to them by Christ [and specifically by His passion [3]]. But whatever is had by *essence* is always greater than that which is *shared*.
>
> Secondly, because of the order of the sacraments to each other, for all the sacraments seem to be ordered to the Eucharist as to their end. It is obvious that the sacrament of Holy Orders is ordained to the consecration of the Eucharist. The sacrament of Baptism is ordered to the reception of the Eucharist, and for this reception a person is perfected or strengthened through Confirmation in that he will not through fear withdraw from such a great sacrament. Likewise through Penance and Extreme Unction one is prepared to receive the Body of Christ more worthily. And at least in its significance, Matrimony has a bearing on this sacrament inasmuch as it signifies the union of Christ and His Church which unity is symbolized through the sacrament of the Eucharist, whence the words of the Apostle: 'This is a great sacrament, but I speak of Christ and His Church' (Eph. 5:32).
>
> And thirdly, because of the ritual of the sacraments, for most of them are completed by the reception of the Eucharist. [4]

The other sacraments, then, bring to us the grace of redemption signified and represented by the Holy Sacrifice of the Mass. Many of them have as their specific purpose to prepare us to take part in this Sacrifice and receive Holy Communion. And, in the ideal, many of them are confected during the Mass and imply the reception of Communion as their ultimate perfection.

3. The sacramentals

It seems that Peter Lombard, who died in 1160, was the first to use the term "sacramental" in reference to the non-essential ceremonies

---

[2] *Epist.* 63, 14. *MPL,* 4: 397.
[3] *Summa Theol.,* III, 62, 5.
[4] *Ibid.,* 65, 3. Emphasis added.

of Baptism.[5] Before him, Hugh of St. Victor (d. 1141) distinguished between sacraments which are necessary for salvation and sacraments which are not. The latter, he says, though they are not necessary for salvation, nevertheless aid towards the sanctification of the soul, because, through them, virtue is exercised and a greater degree of grace can be acquired. As examples, he mentions aspersion with water and reception of ashes.[6] At the same time Peter Abelard, among many others, simply speaks of major and minor sacraments.[7] And as late as 1179 the third Council of the Lateran gave the generic name sacrament to such ceremonies as the installation of bishops and abbots, funerals, and the nuptial blessing.[8]

St. Thomas makes a clear distinction between sacraments and sacramentals. In general, he says the latter prepare us for the reception of grace; in themselves they do not confer grace. They either remove the obstacles to the divine operation, as holy water is directed against the snares of the devil, or by reason of the pious movements caused in the soul against Satan and towards God they remit venial sin.[9] Or again they may simply confer a worthiness in a material thing for the confection of a sacrament, as in the consecration of the altar, a church, the holy oils, and thus cause devotion and reverence in the soul and prepare it for the divine operation.[10] And they are able to cause these spiritual effects in us by reason of the impetratory power and merits of the Church's prayer;[11] they operate *ex opere operantis Ecclesiae,* not simply because of our own personal merits.

As we have seen, the medieval theologians, even when making the distinction between sacraments and sacramentals, did not exclude from this latter notion the non-essential ceremonies of the sacraments. In fact, Peter Lombard explicitly mentioned them. But today there is a tendency among canonists and theologians [12] to reserve the concept of sacramental to those rites instituted by the Church which are not part of the sacrifice of the Mass, the administration of the sacraments, or the canonical Hours of the Office. This trend seems to have begun with St. Robert Bellarmine.

Yet when we consider the recent pronouncements of the Magisterium of the Church we can find no justification for such a trend. The Code of Canon Law, for instance, defines sacramentals as "things or actions which the Church is accustomed to use, in imitation of the sacraments, in order to obtain through her impetration certain effects, especially spiritual ones." [13] And when Pius XII speaks of the efficacy

---

[5] *Sententiarum,* lib, IV, d. 6, c. 8. *MPL,* 192: 855.
[6] *De sacramentis,* lib. I, 9, 7. *MPL,* 176: 327.
[7] *Epitome theol. christ.,* 28. *MPL,* 178: 1738.
[8] Can. 2. Hefele-Leclercq, *Histoire des Conciles,* V, 725.
[9] *Summa Theol.,* III, 65, 1 ad 6 and 8; 71, 3 ad 2; 87, 3.
[10] *Ibid.,* III, 65, 1 ad 6; 83, 3 ad 3.
[11] *Ibid.,* III, 64, 1 ad 2.
[12] See A. Michel, "Sacramentaux," *DTC,* XIV, 465-482.
[13] Can. 1144.

of the Liturgy, he makes the sole distinction of the *ex opere operato* effect of the Mass and the sacraments, and the *ex opere operantis Ecclesiae* quality of the prayers and ceremonies with which the Church has embellished the Mass and sacraments—the "sacramentals" and other rites of Church institution.[14] Even though he uses the term "sacramentals" as a special category—it seems most probable he means sacramental objects—he insists that all those prayers and actions which the Church has instituted produce their effect by reason of the impetratory power of the Spouse of Christ.

From these two statements, therefore, it would seem that whatever action or prayer enjoys the following characteristics fulfills the requirements of and should be called a sacramental: (1) it must imitate the sacraments and be, therefore, a *sensible sign*; (2) it must be instituted by the Church, specifically by the Holy See; [15] (3) it must be intended to produce principally spiritual effects; (4) it must bring this effect about through the impetratory power of the Church— *ex opere operantis Ecclesiae*, which is superior to the simple power of an individual's prayer, which works *ex opere operantis*, but inferior to the efficacy of the sacraments, which work *ex opere operato*. Therefore, since the surrounding ceremonial of the sacraments—prayers, exorcisms, blessings, gestures—meet these requirements, they should be understood as sacramentals. And this holds true also of the Divine Office.

Another problem is occasioned by the Code's use of the words "things or actions." Are both sacred actions and blessed objects sacramentals in the same sense? Are both liturgical in the same sense? We may be permitted here to understand the word sacramental in an analogical sense, especially when we take into consideration two other canons. Canon 1146 says that the legitimate minister of the sacramentals is a cleric to whom power has been granted for it by competent ecclesiastical authority and who is not prevented for any reason from exercising such power. Canon 1150, on the other hand, when speaking of the things that have been consecrated or blessed, makes no mention of a minister but only indicates that such things should be treated reverently and not used for profane purposes. In the first case the sacramental is the actual prayer or blessing of the Church performed by a deputed minister; in the second we have the product of a sacramental, the blessed object.

Therefore, sacramentals consist immediately and primarily in the Church's prayer of impetration, and only in second place and mediately (through this impetratory prayer) in the sanctification of an object. In the most proper sense, a sacramental would be the immediate objective of the Church's impetratory power, namely, the *blessing* or similar *action* actively using the Church's prayer; the thing blessed,

---

[14] *Mediator Dei*, 27.
[15] CIC., can. 1145.

because of this blessing, increases our reverence for divine worship or helps to elevate the tenor of our daily lives. The private use of such blessed objects is not, therefore, liturgical in the strict sense of the word, but rather brings to us and our lives the aid of the Church's liturgical prayer.[16]

The sacramentals produce a variety of effects. First of all, they prepare us for the reception of grace by removing obstacles to it and, in general, by exciting within us proper dispositions conducive to such a reception. Furthermore, certain sacramentals, e.g., constitutive blessings, confer a spiritual deputation; in other words, they set a person aside, place him in a new state, dedicate him to the performance of certain ritual actions. Obvious examples of sacramentals which produce such effects would be clerical tonsure,[17] the blessing of abbots and abbesses, the consecration of virgins, and religious profession—if and when the ceremonies of the latter are recognized as sacramentals by the Holy See. Although the principal effect of sacramentals is spiritual, they may also produce material benefits either by obtaining temporal goods or by removing temporal evils; namely: the blessings against insects harmful to crops, blessing of seed, blessing of a sick person, and all the other blessings for good weather, ships, automobiles, etc.

As regards the administration of the sacramentals, canon 1148 directs that the rites approved by the Church be accurately observed, and, in the case of consecrations or constitutive blessings, states that unless the prescribed form is employed such blessings are invalid. In general, the minister of sacramentals is any cleric who has been given such power by legitimate ecclesiastical authority and is not forbidden to use it.[18] Only a bishop, unless an apostolic indult permits otherwise, can validly perform consecrations. On the other hand, any priest can confer blessings which are not reserved, and even should a priest confer such a reserved blessing, it is valid but his action is illicit—unless otherwise determined.[19] There is one important restriction regarding exorcisms. Apart from those exorcisms forming part of the ritual of the sacraments, the power to exorcize possessed persons cannot be exercised except by special and explicit permission of the local Ordinary.[20]

The subject of the Church's blessings is, in the first place, a Catholic. They may, however, be given to catechumens and even, unless the Church explicitly forbids it, to non-Catholics in order to obtain

16 Cf. C. Vagaggini, who argues in this same vein: *Il Senso Teologico della Liturgia* (Rome: Edizioni Paoline, 1957), 76-77.
17 While some theologians would maintain that minor orders and the subdiaconate are participations of the sacrament of Holy Orders, others consider them to be only sacramentals.
18 Can. 1146.
19 Can. 1147.
20 Can. 1151.

for them the light of faith and together with it bodily health.[21] Cate-chumens, non-Catholics, and even excommunicated persons may re-ceive the exorcisms against diabolical possession.[22] Non-Catholics may also receive blessed ashes and palms.[23] In general, however, sacra-mentals must be refused to the following persons: (a) those under pain of excommunication or interdict after the declaratory or condem-natory sentence,[24] (b) those who because of the gravity of their of-fenses have been deprived of the sacramentals,[25] (c) Catholics who have contracted a mixed marriage, regardless whether or not it is valid, without the Church's dispensation.[26]

According to the Code of Canon Law, sacramentals may be di-vided into (1) consecrations or constitutive blessings which make the person or thing thus blessed sacred to God in a permanent manner, (2) invocative blessings which call down upon the recipient the favor of Almighty God, (3) exorcisms which ward off the devil and his evil influence. Since, in the definition given by the Code, sacramentals are imitations of the sacraments, the latter provide another basis of divi-sion which will bring out the dependence and relationship of the sac-ramentals to the sacraments. To give but a few examples, (a) with Baptism are related—apart from the exorcisms and anointings per-formed during the administration of this sacrament—the exorcism of possessed persons, the blessing of water, the blessing of baptismal water on Holy Saturday, the blessing of the Oil of Catechumens, the Asperges, religious profession, and the consecration of virgins; (b) with Penance are related the imposition of blessed ashes and the public confession of faults—the Confiteor, etc.; (c) many sacramentals are di-rectly related with the Holy Eucharist—practically the entire Mass, and indirectly all sacramentals are connected with the Eucharist; (d) with Confirmation and Holy Orders are related the consecration of Chrism, various impositions of hands which impart a power or strength (some-times, of course, they imply exorcism and therefore belong to Bap-tism), the blessing of abbots and abbesses, the anointing of kings, the consecration of places of cult, the blessing of objects used in divine worship; (e) with Matrimony are related the rites of espousal, blessing of the home, blessing of a mother before and after childbirth, blessing of the ring, and the nuptial blessing; (f) with Extreme Unction are re-lated the blessing of the Oil of the Infirm, the commendation of the dying, and the burial of the dead.[27]

[21] Can. 1149.
[22] Can. 1152.
[23] SCR, March 9, 1919. A. Michel, *art. cit.*, 481.
[24] Cc. 2260, 1; 2275, 2.
[25] Can. 2291, 6.
[26] Can. 2375.
[27] For a more lengthy treatment of sacramentals see G. Lefebvre, "Sacra-mentaux," ch. 21 of *Liturgia* (Paris: Bloud et Gay, 1935), pp. 749-792.

4. The role of sacraments and sacramentals in the spiritual life

The sacraments—and in an intermediary way also the sacramentals—are prolongations of the Incarnation, inasmuch as they continue Christ. They are extensions of the Passion and Resurrection, since they carry out the work of redemption and bring to us the saving virtue of grace and life obtained for us through Christ's redemptive act. Genuine actions of Christ Himself, they allow Him to remain among us and sanctify each step of our human lives. Indeed, they are channels of divine life, which little by little will succeed, if we place no obstacle in the way of their operation and truly cooperate with them, in divinizing us, in transforming us into the likeness of Christ, our Head.

As Pius XII remarks in his encyclical *Mystici Corporis,* "we see how the human body is given its own means to provide for its own life, health and growth and for the same of all its members. Similarly the Savior of mankind, out of His infinite goodness, has provided in a marvelous way for His Mystical Body, endowing it with the sacraments; so that by so many consecutive, gradated graces, as it were, its members should be supported from the cradle to life's last breath, and that the social needs of the Church also be generously provided for." [28] The sacraments, therefore, bring to the members of the Mystical Body the divine life of their Head and thus permit them really to grow up into one body with Him.

But the sacraments are not only channels of life, they are also *signs* of life.[29] They symbolize and teach us about the hidden action taking place in our souls. As signs they must have a relationship to our natural life in order to be able to signify the type of supernatural effect produced unseen by our eyes. Signifying washing, Baptism cleanses the soul and, like a rebirth, enables the soul to live the new supernatural life. The Eucharist is the food of this supernatural life upon which the organism of the soul feeds and grows to maturity. Penance, like medicine for the physical body, repairs the damage done to the soul by sin, the spiritual sickness. Just as boys grow into men and then begin to take their place in society independent of their parents, so in Confirmation we have the sacrament of spiritual maturity through which the Christian soul, going beyond its previous self-centered life of personal nourishment, growth, and learning, now widens its horizons and begins to live more consciously with and for others in the Mystical Body. The anointing with oil symbolizes the new strength and courage given the Christian to do just this. Christ also blesses the marital union with a special sacrament to enable the souls concerned to sacrifice themselves for one another and, most especially, to dedicate their common life for the spiritual and material

[28] Par. 24.
[29] See the remarkable book of F. Louvel and L. Putz, *Signs of Life.* Chicago: Fides, 1953.

good of their offspring. Another sacrament, Holy Orders, provides the supernatural community with its rulers and official teachers as well as with men endowed with special powers of sanctification, just as the natural community is furnished its leaders through election and deputation to government. Finally, as all men must pass through the gateway of death to eternal life, Christ, through His Church, strengthens the soul for this ordeal by means of the invigorating spiritual "massage" with Holy Oil, just as the trainer will prepare the muscles of his athlete for his combat on the field of sport. Thus fortified for this final bout with the devil, the Christian soul looks forward with confidence towards a happy victory and the reward of everlasting life in the heavenly home of his Father.

With the authority given her by Christ, the Church extends the reign of God and the effects of Calvary by enlarging the field of action of the Holy Sacrifice of the Mass and the sacraments. She institutes the sacramentals which, more than simply preparing the soul for the reception of the sacraments, continue and prolong their action so that they embrace all the activity of human life, sanctify it, elevate it, and consecrate it to God by bringing to it all the value of the Church's prayer as the Spouse of Christ. And by using material things for her sacramentals, she carries the redemptive work of Christ even into the realm of inanimate nature, liberating it too from slavery to the devil and dedicating it to the service of God and the sanctification of souls, thus making it an image and symbol of the world transfigured and divinized by Christ.

B. Baptism

1. Theological summary

The word baptism comes from the Greek βαπτιζω meaning to dip repeatedly, to bathe. It is often used in Greek texts in a metaphorical sense as when one is said to be immersed in calamities, baptized in difficulties. Finally, it is used in Christian literature to specify that sacred washing through which one is cleansed of Original Sin and born into the kingdom of God. In the New Testament we find the term used in all three of these senses: [30] an ordinary washing of hands or vessels,[31] the ritual ablutions of the Jews; [32] overwhelming trials and sufferings; [33] the penitential washing recommended by John the Baptist,[34] and the sacrament instituted by Jesus.[35]

St. Paul speaks of Baptism as a mystical association with the death and resurrection of Christ by means of which the soul dies to sin and

[30] Cf. J. Bellamy, "Baptême dans la sainte Ecriture," *DTC*, II, 167-177.
[31] Mark 7:4, 8.
[32] Hebr. 9:10.
[33] Mark 10:38-39; Luke 12:50.
[34] Matt. 3:7; Acts 1:22.
[35] Matt. 29:19; Acts 2:38, 41.

rises with Him to a new life of grace.[36] He also calls it the bath of regeneration.[37] And St. Peter, though he does not mention the word Baptism, certainly refers to its effects when he says that "we have been begotten, through the resurrection of Jesus Christ from the dead, unto a living hope, unto an incorruptible inheritance—undefiled and unfading—reserved for us in heaven." [38] "You have been reborn, not from corruptible seed but from the incorruptible, through the word of God who lives and abides forever. . . . As newborn babes, crave the spiritual milk that by it you may grow to salvation. . . . Be yourselves as living stones, built thereon [on Christ] into a spiritual house, a holy priesthood, to offer spiritual sacrifices acceptable to God through Jesus Christ. . . . You are a chosen race, a kingly priesthood, a holy nation, a purchased people; that you may proclaim the virtues of Him who has called you out of darkness into his marvellous light, you who in times past were not a people but are now the people of God, who had not obtained mercy but now have obtained mercy." [39]

And so, through Baptism the soul dies to its former life of sin and enslavement to the power of the devil. It rises with Christ to the supernatural life; God's grace and greatness are infused and the soul now lives the life of Christ. Baptism brings about such a faithful reproduction of Christ in the soul that we say the soul is refashioned to His likeness; it is another Christ. In the words of St. Paul, "I live, no longer I, but Christ lives in me." [40] The soul is now begotten as a child of God through a spiritual adoption in the Son; it belongs to the family of the Holy Trinity. For this reason Baptism is our initiation into the society of the redeemed. Because we are members of Christ, we are members of one another, fellow-citizens of the saints, forming the one Mystical Body of Christ. And to enable us to take part in the life of this supernatural organism, Baptism imprints an indelible mark on our souls, branding us to the likeness of Christ the Priest, empowering us to be Christ's mouthpiece in that glorious chorus of praise and prayer which enjoys the extraordinary value and efficacy of Christ's virtue of religion, the virtue of Him who is always acceptable to the Father. The sacramental character of Baptism also opens and conditions the soul to receive the flow of grace coming from the other sacraments. And lastly, it marks us out for heaven; it is the pledge of our inheritance of heaven which, as children of God, brothers of Christ, we have been promised and shall receive, if we generously allow the work of transformation into Christ begun in Baptism to be so fully completed that the Eternal Father shall be able to recognize us as other Christs when He sits in judgment over us.

[36] Rom. 6:3-11.
[37] Titus 3:5.
[38] 1 Peter 1:3-4.
[39] *Ibid.*, 1:23; 2:2, 5, 9-10.
[40] Gal. 2:20.

2. Pagan and Jewish precedents

Given the fact that Baptism is the initiation rite, properly speaking, through which the soul begins its participation in the divine life of the dead and risen Christ, students of comparative religion thought that they had here the most obvious point to prove that Christianity was simply an evolution of earlier pagan, and of course the Jewish, religions.[41] In this view, Christianity, under the impulse of the Hellenistic hopes of divinization, took the Jewish purification rite and transformed it into the "syncretistic mystery of baptism." [42] That baptisms, lustral purifications, and other rites of initiation were used in the mystery-religions with the idea of bringing about salvation through regeneration—explicit mention was made of resurrection in the cult of Mithras, according to Tertullian [43]—cannot be denied.

One of these rites, the *Taurobolium*, which formed part of the Cybele-Attis cult and also, later, that of Mithras, was especially expressive of the concept of redemption and bore an underlying affinity to the sacrifice of Calvary—which was why it was so detested by Christians. A trench was dug, and over it were placed several planks with perforations. The initiate stood in the trench, while a bull was slaughtered upon the planks. As the blood of the bull dripped down into the trench, the initiate allowed it to trickle upon his face and garments; he even moistened his tongue with it and drank it as a "sacramental" act. He emerged believing himself purified from sin and "born again *in aeternum*." [44]

But the lustral purifications seem to have been by far the most widespread; such washings were known to the Eleusinian and Sabaist cults, while a baptismal bath was frequent in the mysteries of Isis and Dionysus.[45] Some of these cults even possessed a sort of catechumenate, or period of trial and preparation, which involved a progressive revelation of the mystery, a solemn obligation to secrecy, confession, and practices of mortification such as fasting, absolute continence, pilgrimages, etc. There were *symbola*, pass-words to distinguish the prospective members from curiosity seekers, instruction periods in which a *traditio sacrorum*, or a teaching of the religious doctrines and practices of the cult, took place, and, finally, examinations prior to the formal admittance of new members.[46]

[41] Cf. e.g., R. Reitzenstein, *Die Vorgeschichte der christlichen Taufe*. Berlin-Leipzig, 1929; P. Gennrich, *Die Lehre von der Wiedergeburt in dogmengeschichtlicher und religionsgeschichtlicher Beleuchtung*. Berlin, 1907; J. Leipoldt, *Die urchristliche Taufe im Licht der Religionsgeschichte*. Leipzig, 1928.

[42] A. Oepke, "Die Taufe als synkretistisches Mysterium," in G. Kittel, *Theologisches Wörterbuch zum Neuen Testament*, I (Stuttgart, 1933), 541-543.

[43] *Liber de praescriptionibus*, 40, MPL, 2:66.

[44] S. Angus, *The Mystery-Religions and Christianity* (London, 1928), 94-95.

[45] H. Rahner, *Griechische Mythen in christlicher Deutung* (Zürich, 1945), 102; see a complete summary of such rituals in A. Oepke, *art. cit.*, 528-532.

[46] Cf. S. Angus, *op. cit.*, 77-93.

No one can deny that there exists a great similarity between our Christian Baptism and such rites of initiation from the mystery religions. But the attempt to prove from this that Christianity, and specifically Baptism, directly evolved from these pagan institutions is indeed far-fetched. Leaving aside a strict apologetical refutation [47]— Tertullian had already undertaken one in his day [48]—let it suffice to say here that a real dependence of Christianity on these mystery religions can in no way be proved; our adversaries are merely content to point out the similarities and draw from them unwarranted conclusions. Furthermore, even granted for the sake of argument that our Lord and His Church did consciously adopt and adapt certain elements of ceremonial from these earlier religions, the kernel of our sacrament remains specifically Christian; the reality and its effects are strictly new and of divine origin. It certainly may be allowed that God will use the symbolism and imagery already developed by man and infuse into them a real divine efficacy—substitute the substance for the shadow. In fact, we may say that such a procedure on His part would be most benign and all-wise, inasmuch as He would then treat man with a superior and enlightened pedagogy, using man's natural religious instincts to lead him along the way already prepared for by them to the realm of specifically supernatural occurrence. But, for all that, the Christian sacrament of Baptism would still owe nothing of its essence to the pagan mysteries. [49]

It is, of course, the unequivocal teaching of Sts. Peter and Paul, the Fathers, and of the Liturgy that certain events and ceremonies of the Old Testament prefigure Baptism. The so-called prophecies of the Easter Vigil are clear enough in this regard. The above-mentioned Apostles are no less emphatic. St. Peter, for instance, sees such a figure in Noah's ark. While sinful man was destroyed through water and a few elect souls saved by means of the ark, Baptism washes away the wretchedness of the "old man" and makes him an heir of eternal life. [50] For St. Paul the miraculous cloud which guided the Israelites through the desert is a symbol of the illuminating guidance offered in Baptism, the passing through the Red Sea figurative of the liberation of the soul from sin and slavery to the devil, [51] circumcision a sign of the spiritual circumcision wrought by Christ in Baptism, [52] the baptism of John an immediate preparation for the sacrament, and finally

[47] For this see V. Iacono, *Il Battesimo nella dottrina di S. Paolo.* Rome, 1935; J. Coppens, "Baptême et mystères paiens," *Dictionnaire de la Bible,* Supplément (1928), 903-924; and see the latter's bibliography.

[48] *De Baptismo,* 5. *MPL,* 1:1312-1314.

[49] Odo Casel, *Le mystère du culte dans le Christianisme* (Paris: Editions du Cerf, 1946), 66-70.

[50] 1 Peter 3:20-22.

[51] 1 Cor. 10:2. The same is true of the spiritual drink coming from the rock smitten by the rod of Moses: v. 4.

[52] Col. 2:11-12.

the death of Christ [53] is both the sign and cause of our death to sin and resurrection to grace.

3. Historical development of the baptismal ritual

Pre-baptismal rites of the catechumenate

For an adult to receive Baptism worthily it is obvious that some preparation must precede it. This seems to have been the purpose behind the first six chapters in the *Didache* concerning the "two ways," for at the head of the chapter following them stand the words: "after all these things have been said, baptize. . . ." [54] Justin Martyr is more emphatic and explicit. Only after a person is taught the Christian faith, believes what he is taught, and promises that he can live accordingly, can he be admitted to Baptism. A more immediate preparation for Baptism consists, for Justin, in prayer, fasting, and the confession of sins.[55] This period of instruction and moral build-up was in time called the catechumenate (from the Greek, meaning to instruct).

In Africa, by the time of Tertullian, the catechumenate had greatly developed. He calls the candidates "novices," for they are beginning to learn divine knowledge.[56] He also uses the technical term "catechumen," clearly distinguishes such a person from the rest of the faithful, and indicates that this period of preparation lasted much longer than that of certain heretical sects whose catechumens became "perfect" or were initiated before they knew what they were about.[57] In fact, it was because of his insistence on a good intellectual and moral training before the reception of Baptism that he disapproved of infants receiving this sacrament.[58] Among the duties of candidates for Baptism, he lists, in addition to instruction, various spiritual exercises: prayer, fasting, vigils, confession of faults,[59] and reports that a catechumen has to renounce Satan and all his works at least twice: sometime before the day of Baptism and during the rite itself.[60]

For Rome of the third century, Hippolytus has left us a detailed account of the catechumenate. When a person wished to become a

[53] Rom. 6:3-11.

[54] J. Quasten, *Monumenta*, p. 9; see also his note 5.

[55] I *Apology* 61. J. Quasten, op. cit., p. 14. A preliminary fast of two days is also enjoined on the candidate by the author of the *Didache*, 7, 4. Quasten. p. 10.

[56] *De poenitentia*, 6. MPL, 1: 1346.

[57] "Ante sunt perfecti catechumeni, quam edocti," *Liber de praescriptionibus*, 41. MPL, 2:68.

[58] *De Baptismo*, 18. MPL, 1:1330.

[59] *Ibid.*, 20. MPL, 1:1332.

[60] *De spectaculis*, 4 and 13; *De corona*, 3. MPL, 1:709, 720; 2:98.

Christian, he had to present himself to the "doctors," [61] or teachers of catechumens, before the hours of worship. There were "sponsors" already in those days, for the prospective convert had to have with him this very first time one who was already a Christian and could give acceptable testimony in his favor. The convert was then interrogated by the catechists on the kind of life he lived, and for this Hippolytus lists a whole set of questions.[62]

The convert then began his course of instructions on the requirements of the Christian life, the moral aspect of which he had to live up to even before receiving Baptism in order to give proof of his sincerity and promise for the future. In general, these instructions lasted for three years. However, if he were especially zealous and persevering in learning the faith and showed marked signs of good conduct, he might be admitted to Baptism before the three years had elapsed.[63] While the catechumens were allowed to attend the public instructions which were part of the Mass (the part we now call the Mass of the Catechumens), they were not permitted to pray with the faithful, nor were they admitted to the kiss of peace, for they were not as yet purified.[64] After they had finished praying as a conclusion to their "class" in Christian doctrine, they received an imposition of hands from their teacher, who prayed over them; this was presumably an exorcism.[65]

A special group of catechumens appears in Hippolytus. They are called *electi*,[66] for, after an examination regarding their moral conduct, an examination supported by those who know them, they are set aside from the other catechumens and will be admitted to Baptism on the next occasion for its administration (the Easter Vigil). These selected candidates are now taught the Gospels and receive a daily exorcism from clerics. When the day of Baptism approaches, it is the bishop himself who exorcizes them, and apparently some sort of examination is attached to this exorcism, for Hippolytus states that if anyone is found impure he should be put aside. On Holy Thursday

[61] These were either clerics or laymen, according to Hippolytus (*La Tradition Apostolique*, ed. B. Botte, p. 47, n. 19). Cyprian, on the other hand, gives the impression that the catechists, *doctores audientium*, were ordained lectors, and the prerequisites for such a position were stringent (*Epist.* 24. *MPL*, 4:294).

[62] *La Tradition Apostolique* (ed. B. Botte), n. 16, pp. 44-46.

[63] *Ibid.*, n. 17, p. 46.

[64] *Ibid.*, n. 18, pp. 46-47.

[65] *Ibid.*, n. 19. p. 47.

[66] The term *electi* seems to have been quite current in Rome; Leo I also uses it: *Epist.* 16, 7. *MPL*, 54:702. But other names were used elsewhere. Augustine in Africa speaks of the *competentes* as those seeking Baptism: "cum fontis sacramenta peteremus," *De fide et operibus*, VI, 9. *MPL*, 40:202. And in the East we usually meet the term *illuminandi* for those about to be baptized (*Apostolic Constitutions*, VIII, 6: 3-14; 8:1-6. *MPG*, 1:1078, 1082), for Baptism was the sacrament of illumination: Justin, I *Apology* 61. J. Quasten, 15; Pseudo-Dionysius, *De eccl. hier.*, II, 1 and 2. Quasten, 276-278.

they are urged to bathe.[67] After fasting on Good Friday, they are gathered together by the bishop on Holy Saturday (morning?) for another session of prayer and exorcism at which the bishop traces the sign of the cross on their forehead, nose, and ears. Finally, after having spent the entire night of Holy Saturday listening to the appointed readings of the Easter Vigil and thus receiving their last instruction, they are admitted to Baptism.[68]

With Hippolytus the discipline of the catechumenate seems to have reached an almost definitive form; later authors simply add more specific details. For instance, in 492, John, a Roman deacon, gives a good description of the rite of making a person a catechumen. The person was first exsufflated, that is, the minister blew upon him to drive out the devil and make way for the coming of Christ. To this was joined a formal exorcism commanding the devil to depart and not to return. The soul was then claimed for God by means of an imposition of hands and a blessing (perhaps the sign of the cross) upon the head of the convert. Salt was placed on his tongue, signifying that by the wisdom of God and the hearing of His word he would be preserved from the corruption of the world, just as salt is used to preserve meat.[69] And while Hippolytus does speak of the *electi*, or those being immediately prepared for Baptism on Easter, he does not indicate when exactly they are chosen and placed in this new category of catechumens. At the end of the fourth century Pope Siricius (d. 399) supplies this information. This last stage began at the opening of Lent: the names of the *electi* were listed and they were told that thereafter they had to give themselves up to frequent prayer, observance of the regular Lenten fast, and daily exorcisms.[70] Whether the testimony of the candidates' sponsors was sought again in Rome, Siricius does not say, but this certainly was done in Jerusalem towards the end of the fourth century. Etheria reports that the bishop interrogated the sponsors the day before Lent began on how well the catechumen was doing. On this same day, if the catechumens were

[67] For a discussion of this custom, followed even by many of those already baptized, see A. Chavasse, *Le sacramentaire Gélasien* (Tournai: Desclée, 1958), 130 ff.

[68] *La Tradition Apostolique*, n. 20, pp. 47-49; n. 21, pp. 49-51.

[69] *Epist. ad Senarium*, 3. *MPL*, 59: 401-402. This same ceremony is contained in the Gelasian Sacramentary: ed. H. Wilson, 113-114. At this same period Africa seems to be in accord with Rome, for Augustine mentions several of these rites of introduction into the catechumenate: imposition of hands and the sign of the cross (*De pecc. mer. et rem.*, 2, 26. *MPL*, 44:176); he also speaks of the convert receiving an exsufflation (*Contra Cresconium*, II, 5, 7; *De symbolo ad catechumenos*, 1; *Contra Iulianum op. imperf.*, V, 64. *MPL*, 43:471; 40:628; 45:1504).

[70] *Epist. ad Himerium Tarrac.*, 2. *MPL*. 13:1135; see also Leo I, *Epist.* 16, 7. *MPL*, 54:702. For Africa Ferrandus of Carthage (d. 531) notes that, in addition to what was already mentioned by Pope Siricius, more intense instructions were given, exorcisms and renunciations of Satan took place during the scrutinies, and the candidate had to learn the Creed and Our Father by heart and repeat them before the assembly of the faithful: *Epist. ad Fulgentium. MPL*, 65: 378.

enrolled in the ranks of the *competentes*, they began holding three-hour instruction periods every day until Holy Week.[71]

We have come across the word scrutiny many times now; let us see exactly what it involved. The word *scrutinium* (from *scrutor*, to investigate) certainly means some sort of examination, but it did not always mean an intellectual examination. We first come across the term in Ambrose,[72] who explains it as an attempt to search deep into the soul and body to drive out the devil and sanctify the candidate. A contemporary of St. Augustine, Quodvultdeus, speaks of proving or examining the hearts of the candidates by letting God's fear touch them, His power putting the devil to rout and delivering the soul from the latter's servitude.[73] In like manner Pope St. Leo I states that the candidates are to be scrutinized or proved by exorcisms.[74] The conclusion that scrutiny, at least in the beginning, was used as the equivalent of exorcism seems inescapable. But towards the end of the fifth century the concept changes meaning, for the Roman deacon John indicates that the scrutinies have as their object to verify whether the candidate has faithfully retained the teaching given him.[75] And after him most writers repeat the same explanation.

There was also a variation in the number of scrutinies. At first there were three. John again is our witness for this,[76] but he does not say exactly when they occurred. We find, however, from the Gelasian Sacramentary that these three scrutinies were held on the third, fourth, and fifth Sundays of Lent.[77] In addition to these three, the Gelasian book also contains a description of a final reunion in the morning hours of Holy Saturday as an immediate preparation for the Baptism to be administered during the night vigil. Here the candidates had to recite the Creed, were exorcized by means of the "Effeta" ceremony, and renounced Satan.[78]

Sometime between the middle of the sixth to the middle of the seventh century the use of the scrutinies was revised, as is seen in the *Ordo Romanus* XI.[79] Now the scrutinies are seven in number because of symbolic reasons: the seven gifts of the Holy Spirit.[80] They con-

---

[71] *Journal de Voyage*, nn. 45, 46, pp. 254-256.

[72] *Scrutaminum: Expl. symboli*, prolog. *MPL*, 17:1155.

[73] *Sermo ad catech. de symbolo*, 1. *MPL*, 40:637.

[74] "Secundum apostolicam regulam et exorcismis scrutandi et ieiuniis sanctificandi et frequentibus sunt praedicationibus imbuendi," *Epist.* 16 *ad episcop. Siciliae*, 7. *MPL*, 54:702.

[75] *Epist. ad Senarium*, 4. *MPL*, 59:402.

[76] *Ibid.*, 2. *MPL*, 59:401.

[77] Ed. H. Wilson, pp. 34, 38-39, 42.

[78] *Ibid.*, pp. 78-79. The "Effeta" ceremony might already be implied in the ceremonies mentioned for this morning by Hippolytus. It was certainly a primitive element of the original Gelasian book: cf. M. Andrieu, *Les Ordines Romani du haut moyen-âge*, II, 400, ff.

[79] The presence of similar ceremonies in the Gelasian Sacramentary is explained by Andrieu as a later addition depending completely on this *Ord. Rom* XI: cf. *Les Ordines*, II, 380-396.

[80] N. 81. Andrieu, II, 442.

cern now, not adults, but infants, as their rites continually show, and
hence these ceremonies, for the most part, are no longer functional
but symbolic, reminiscent of the times when catechumens really had
to be examined as to their motives for joining the Church, to be
instructed in the truths of the faith, taught the Creed and the Our
Father, and examined on what they had successfully learned. Furthermore, these scrutinies are no longer held on the before-mentioned
Sundays of Lent, but during the week, a change brought about by
Gregory the Great.[81] For now, since the recipients of Baptism are
infants, the presence and cooperation of the whole Christian community are not really necessary for passing judgment on the worthiness of the candidates for admission into the Christian fold. What we
find, first of all, is a formal announcement, to be made on Monday of
the third week of Lent, of the first scrutiny, which is to be held on
Wednesday of the same week, and at which the new-born infants are
to be made catechumens.[82] A second scrutiny is to be held on the following Saturday,[83] a third—the most solemn one—during the fourth
week,[84] a fourth and fifth during Passion Week,[85] a sixth during Holy
Week,[86] and the last one on the morning of Holy Saturday.[87]

While the second, fourth, fifth, and sixth scrutinies consisted in a
series of exorcisms involving signs of the cross traced over the catechumens, first by their sponsors and then by acolytes, and the imposition of hands, with the exorcisms being pronounced first by acolytes
then by a priest, the third scrutiny dealt principally with the handing
over or teaching of the Gospels, Creed, and the Lord's prayer, as well
as with their explanation. Whence the title of the scrutiny: *In aurium
apertione*. While in Rome all these elements were "handed on" at the
same session,[88] in Africa and other places they were handed on at
three different sessions, the candidates being expected to recite publicly at the next scrutiny what they had learned.[89]

And the last scrutiny was something special too; originally, it
seems, it was designed to give the candidates a last opportunity before receiving Baptism during the Easter Vigil to protest their faith in
Christ by reciting, or repeating, the Creed they had been taught. This
is how the scrutiny opens in the Gelasian Sacramentary; even the

---

[81] Cf. C. Callewaert, "S. Grégoire, les scrutins et quelques messes quadragésimales," *EL*, 53 (1939), 203.
[82] *Ord. Rom.* XI, Title and n. 1. Andrieu, II, 417.
[83] *Ibid.*, n. 37. Andrieu, II, 426.
[84] *Ibid.*, nn. 39-75. Andrieu, II, 426-441.
[85] *Ibid.*, nn. 76 and 78. Andrieu, II, 441-442.
[86] *Ibid.*, n. 80. Andrieu, II, 442.
[87] *Ibid.*, n. 82. Andrieu, II, 443.
[88] However, Leo I seems to suppose a separation of them in his day as well
as a repetition of the Creed by the candidate at some later date: *Epist.* 124, 8.
MPL, 54:1068.
[89] Thus: Rufinus, *Comm. in Symbol. Apost.*, 3. *MPL*, 21:339; Augustine,
Sermones, 212, 2; 213, 1; 214, 1; 215, 1; 57, 1; 58, 1 and 11; Confessiones,
VIII, 2, 5. *MPL*, 38:1060, 1061, 1065-1066, 1072, 387, 393, 399; 32:751.

later Paduan codex of the Gregorian Sacramentary retained the title, *Orationes in Sabbato Paschae ad Reddentes*.[90] The very first rubric in the Gelasian book for this scrutiny says that in the morning the "infants recite the Creed;" later another rubric for the same service has the minister recite the Creed before each as he places his hand on the head of the person.[91] Evidently this second rubric is a later insertion made for catechumens who were not adults and were therefore unable to recite the Creed themselves.[92]

This scrutiny also contains a long verbal exorcism commanding the devil to release once and for all his hold on the soul. After this, the age-old custom of opening the ears and nose of the candidate follows: "Effeta, quod est adaperire, in ordorem suavitatis!" This is also to be understood in an exorcistic sense, for immediately thereupon follows: "Tu autem effugare, diabole, appropinquavit enim iudicium Dei!" First the ears of the candidate are opened to divine truth as the minister touches them with sputum, then the nostrils are opened to the good odor of eternal life obtained through the sacraments.[93] (Even though this ceremony was sometimes called *Apertio aurium*,[94] it is not to be confused with the ceremonies of the third scrutiny. While the former had a symbolic and exorcistic intent, the latter had a practical one: instruction.)

An anointing with oil on the chest and back then follows, after which comes a last renunciation of Satan by the candidate. And with this the morning preliminaries are over, according to the Gelasian book.[95] This anointing has also, as the above *Effeta* ceremony, an exorcistic effect of preparation for the fight against the devil, the first effect of which is a strong and courageous renunciation of him and his pomps. It is interesting to note that Pseudo-Dionysius has his candidate look to the West (which symbolizes the darkness of Satan) and, after three exsufflations against the devil, emphasized by gestures of the hands, renounce him and his works; then turning toward the East (the symbol of Christ and His light), he protests his allegiance to the Son of God.[96]

By way of general conclusion, we can see from all the documentary sources that the catechumenate was once a very vital thing in the life of the Church. But once Rome and its environs were con-

[90] Ed. K. Mohlberg, p. 25.
[91] Ed. H. Wilson, pp. 78-79.
[92] For the *Ord. Rom.* XI has the minister follow the same method as prescribed by the second Gelasian rubric: n. 86. Andrieu, II, 443.
[93] See explanation in Ambrose, *De mysteriis*, I, 3. J. Quasten, 114.
[94] Ambrose, *De sacramentis*, I, 1. J. Quasten, 139.
[95] Ed. H. Wilson, p. 79. These last two ceremonies are omitted in the *Ord. Rom.* XI, but in the *Apostolic Tradition* of Hippolytus (ed. B. Botte, n. 21, p. 50) and the *De Sacramentis* of Ambrose (I, 2, 4-5. J. Quasten, 140) they take place at the font during the actual ceremony of Baptism.
[96] *De eccl. hier.*, II, 2, 6. J. Quasten, 281; see also Ambrose, *De mysteriis*, II, 7. J. Quasten, 116.

verted and a tradition had been established, the rites proper to such an institution gradually lost their practical purpose; for infant [97] Baptism these ceremonies were retained because of their symbolic value. Nevertheless, in northern lands, with the conversion of the various tribes still in progress, a functional use of these rites and a clear distinction among classes of catechumens were maintained for a longer time.[98] Despite the fact that northern bishops so freely added to and subtracted from the ritual of the other sacraments, Baptism comes to us substantially as it was developed by the Romans.

Matter and form of the sacrament

Though the references to Baptism in the New Testament are not explicit as to how the sacrament was conferred,[99] the primitive and medieval Church preferred immersion and allowed infusion and aspersion only by way of exception. The first piece of post-apostolic evidence we have is in the *Didache*, where the author prescribes Baptism in "living water," undoubtedly meaning running water. This has justly been interpreted as Baptism by immersion, for the author goes on to say that, when such water is lacking, water may be poured over the head of the candidate three times.[100] Tertullian likewise speaks only of immersion: *homo in aquam demissus.*[101] This same manner of administering Baptism is attested to in the third century by Hippolytus,[102] in the fourth and fifth centuries by Ambrose [103] and Jerome,[104] and in the sixth century by Gregory the Great.[105] The practice continued even as late as the thirteenth century, for St. Thomas claimed that, even though infusion was allowed, immersion was the *usus communior.*[106] A little later, however, infusion and aspersion seem to have gained a place of honor, for in 1311 the Synod of Ravenna allowed the administration of Baptism by either immersion or aspersion without giving preference to either.[107] One last remark is in order. Even though early authors use the word immersion consistently, we cannot always be sure that the sacrament was conferred by means of

[97] Though infant Baptism was almost the exclusive form of this sacrament in Rome from the sixth century on, we find it mentioned as early as 420 by Pope Celestine I: *Epist.* 21 *ad. episc. Galliarum*, 12. *MPL*, 50:536.

[98] Cf., among others, Leidradus of Lyons, *De sacramento Baptismatis*, 1. *MPL*, 99: 857.

[99] With the possible exception of Acts 8:38, where Philip and the Ethiopian eunuch "went down into the water," and St. Paul's way of speaking in Romans 6:3-11, in which he likens Baptism to being buried.

[100] C. 7. J. Quasten, 9-10.

[101] *De baptismo*, 2. *MPL*, 1:1309; see also his use of the word *mergitamur*, *De corona*, 3. *MPL*, 2:98; etc.

[102] *La Tradition Apostolique* (ed. B. Botte), n. 21, p. 50.

[103] *De sacramentis*, II, 6, 16. J. Quasten, 148.

[104] *Adv. Luciferianos*, 8. *MPL*, 23:172.

[105] *Epistolarum* lib. I, n. 43. *MPL*, 77:498.

[106] *Summa Theol.*, III, 66, 7.

[107] Can. 11. Hefele-Leclercq, *Histoire des Conciles*, VI, 638.

total immersion, for there is evidence from the frescoes in the catacombs that, though the candidate stood knee-deep in water, the minister baptized him by pouring water on his head.[108]

In the Acts of the Apostles there is frequent mention of Baptism
or of being baptized "in the name of Jesus." [109] This expression has
received a variety of explanations at the hands of theologians. Peter
Lombard and Cajetan, for instance, claim that Baptism was truly conferred with this phrase, it being the form of the sacrament,[110] and
that Baptism could still be thus conferred if the Church were to so
permit. By this time, St. Thomas restricts valid Baptism to the use of
the Trinitarian formula, but he admits that the Apostles used the
formula "in nomine Jesu" because of a special dispensation and in
order to make the name of Jesus more honored before Jew and Gentile.[111] The more common opinion today is that this formula was never
used by the Apostles as the form of Baptism, but rather as its name—
Christ's Baptism—to set it off from John's Baptism and to indicate its
specifically Christian character. This is certainly the sense of Acts
19:5 where Paul asks the Ephesians what Baptism they had received.
They answer: John's. After Paul explained the difference between
John's and Jesus' Baptism, the people were baptized in the name of
Jesus.

Following our Lord's command "to baptize all nations in the
name of the Father, the Son and the Holy Spirit," the whole of tradition consistently testifies to the use of this Trinitarian formula. There
is, however, a slight variation in the way it is put to use. While the
Didache [112] states that the formula was spoken all at once as the water
was thrice poured upon the head of the candidate, most writers, Tertullian among them,[113] and Roman documents thereafter, show that
the Trinitarian formula was spoken in three parts by way of a confession of faith in the Three Persons. Let us take the evidence of the
Apostolic Tradition:

> He who is to be baptized descends into the water, and
> he who baptizes imposes his hand upon the former's head,
> asking, 'Do you believe in God the Father Almighty?' He
> answers, 'I believe.' The minister then baptizes him, all the
> while keeping his hand on the other's head. He then asks the
> candidate, 'Do you believe in Jesus Christ, the Son of God,
> who was born of the Holy Spirit and of the Virgin Mary,
> died and was buried and arose living from the dead on the
> third day, ascended into heaven, is seated at the right hand of
> the Father, and will come to judge the living and the dead?'

[108] Cf. P. De Puniet, "Baptême," *DACL,* II, 300.
[109] E.g.: 2:38; 8:16; 10:48; 19:5.
[110] Cf. J. Bellamy, "Baptême dans la sainte écriture," *DTC,* II, 172.
[111] *Summa Theol.,* III, 66, 6 ad 1.
[112] C. 7. J. Quasten, 9.
[113] *De corona,* 3. *MPL,* 2:98.

He answers, 'I believe.' He is baptized a second time. Finally, the minister asks him, 'Do you believe in the Holy Spirit, in the Holy Church and in the resurrection of the body?' He answers, 'I do believe.' And a third time he is baptized.[114]

The introduction of a single Trinitarian formula seems to have taken place first in the East; [115] in the West, it can be attested to in Spain as early as the sixth century.[116] And in Spain such a practice seems to have had as its immediate foundation faith in the unity of the Trinity.[117] The first liturgical book in which we find a trace of this is the Bobbio Missal,[118] a Gallican service book of the seventh century, where the interrogations are separated from the actual baptismal act by a final question: "Vis baptizari?" Alcuin included this arrangement in the supplement to the Hadrian Sacramentary,[119] and, from this time on, the single Trinitarian formula united with a single immersion (later a triple infusion) passed into all the service books of the West.

Post-baptismal rites

Immediately after the baptismal act the minister anoints the newly baptized person on the very top of the head with chrism. Tertullian already speaks of such an anointing: "The flesh is washed that the soul might be cleansed; the flesh is anointed that the soul might be consecrated." This anointing is not to be confused with Confirmation, for he adds: "The flesh is signed that it might be made secure [or sealed]; the flesh is overshadowed by means of the imposition of hands that the soul might be illuminated by the Spirit." [120] This baptismal anointing and its distinction from Confirmation is brought out even more clearly in the *Apostolic Tradition*. After the newly baptized person comes out of the baptismal pool, we are told, a priest anoints him with *oleum sanctificatum*—Chrism—and says: "I anoint thee with holy oil in the name of Jesus Christ." Once the neophyte has put on his clothes, he is presented to the bishop, who, imposing his hands, performs the *consignatio* with Chrism; this latter is Confirmation.[121]

114 Ed. B. Botte, n. 21, pp. 50-51. Other writers and documents offer testimony of the same ritual: Ambrose, *De sacramentis*, II, 7. J. Quasten, 149; H. Wilson, *The Gelasian Sacramentary*, p. 86; Augustine says that where the candidate is an infant the sponsors make the response: *credit, Epist*, 98, 7. *MPL*, 33:363; Gregory the Great, *Epist.*, lib. I, n. 43. *MPL*, 77:498.
115 Cf. P. DePuniet, *art. cit.*, *DACL*, II, 282.
116 *Ibid.*, 333; cf. also Gregory's letter to the Spanish bishop Leander cited in note 114.
117 Cf. Gregory's letter as in note 114.
118 *MPL*, 72:502.
119 H. Wilson, *The Gregorian Sacramentary*, p. 163. For more particulars about the general development of this format see M. Andrieu, *Les Ordines Romani*, III, 85-90.
120 "Caro abluitur ut anima immaculetur; caro ungitur ut anima consecretur. Caro signatur ut et muniatur; caro manus impositione adumbratur ut et anima Spiritu illuminetur." *De resurrectione carnis*, 8. *MPL*, 2:852.
121 *La Tradition Apostolique* (Ed. B. Botte), nn. 21-22, pp. 51-52.

Anointing has traditionally been accepted as symbolic of the virtue and gifts of the Holy Spirit, as in Isaías (61:1): "The Spirit of the Lord is upon me, because the Lord has anointed me." St. Ambrose says that the neophyte receives this anointing on the crown of the head, for "the eyes of the wiseman are in his head; the fool walketh in darkness."[122] He therefore understands this rite to symbolize wisdom. But wisdom has always been specially attributed to the Holy Spirit. It seems inescapable, then, that this rite intends to bring out symbolically the sanctity that is now inherent in the newly baptized person because of his being possessed by the Holy Spirit. We may also see in it our own configuration to Christ, the Anointed One, our participation in His priesthood that St. Peter speaks of: "You are a chosen race, a royal priesthood, a holy nation, a purchased people."[123]

The white garment given to the neophyte is mentioned as early as the time of St. Ambrose. He says: "After these things, you have received white garments, that it may be manifest that you have put off the trappings of sin and put on the chaste veils of innocence, of which the prophet spoke, 'Sprinkle me with hyssop, and I shall be cleansed; wash me, and I shall be made whiter than snow.'"[124] The Roman deacon John likewise attests to the custom of dressing the neophytes with white garments and also of placing a *chrismale* upon their heads after the anointing.[125] Note well the distinction between these two white cloths. In our present Roman Ritual only one cloth is given to the newly baptized infant and it is placed on his head;[126] in adult Baptism this same cloth is placed on the head of the neophyte, but, in addition, he is given a white garment. The first cloth is the *chrismale*, a cloth placed over anointed areas of the body out of reverence;[127] the second is the traditional white garment which is symbolic of spiritual innocence. Unfortunately, confusion can arise, since the same formula is used as both are given to the neophyte.

As today, so in former times the newly baptized was given a lighted candle. Pseudo-Ambrose speaks of the "resplendent candles of the neophytes."[128] For Gaul, Amalar reports that the neophytes carried

[122] *De sacramentis,* III, 1, 1. J. Quasten, 151. He thus quotes Ecclesiastes 2:14.

[123] 1 Peter 2:9.

[124] *De mysteriis,* VII, J. Quasten, 129.

[125] *Epist. ad Senarium,* 6. *MPL,* 59:403. St. Gregory the Great's generosity in donating money to the poor for these garments is well known: *Epist.* lib. VIII, 1 and 23. *MPL,* 77: 904, 925. And the formulas used for giving these two garments to the neophytes are already to be found in the Bobbio Missal, *MPL,* 72: 502.

[126] While the Roman Ritual says that a white cloth is placed on the child's head instead of a white garment, our American *Collectio Rituum* reads: "imponit baptizato vestem candidam vel loco vestis candidae capiti eius linteolum . . ."

[127] This is reported by several sources: the letter of John the Deacon in note 125; Ambrose in note 124; Trojanus, *Epistola, MPL,* 67:995; Augustine, *Sermo* 376, 2. *MPL,* 39:1069.

[128] "lumina neophytorum splendida," *De lapsu virg. consecr.,* 5, 19. *MPL,* 16:388.

candles which were lighted at the end of the litanies during the Easter Vigil.[129] The formula presently spoken as the candle is presented indicates that the flame is symbolic of the purity of this baptized soul and is inspired by the Gospel narrative of the five wise virgins who had well provided themselves with light in order to greet the Bridegroom.[130]

Another ancient ceremony, now fallen into disuse, was the giving of a mixture of milk and honey to the newly baptized. We find that Tertullian,[131] Hippolytus,[132] Jerome,[133] and John the Roman deacon [134] all mention the rite. Tertullian indicates its meaning when he speaks of the "mixture of milk and honey by which God gives birth to His own."[135] But besides being a symbol of the spiritual rebirth and youth of the newly baptized Christian, it was also meant to hark back to the promised land flowing with milk and honey (Exod. 13:5), which itself was a figure of the Church.

4. Modern ritual

Most of the ancient institutions described above have been preserved till our own time. Many modifications, of course, have been introduced—especially because of the predominance today of infant Baptism. At present we have in the Roman Ritual two distinct forms for administering the sacrament, one for infants, the other for adults. Because of frequently granted Apostolic rescripts, however, even adults may be baptized according to the rite prescribed for infants, so that the rite proper to adult Baptism is rarely used.

The ceremonies in the ritual for infant Baptism can be divided into three main parts: (a) initiation into the catechumenate (Tit. I, c. 2, nn. 1-7); (b) all the ancient Lenten scrutinies, including the last one formerly held on Holy Saturday morning, combined into one group of exorcisms, confession of faith, and renunciation of the devil (n. 7 from *Exorcizo te, immunde spiritus* to n. 15); (c) the actual baptismal act with the rites symbolic of its effects (nn. 17-26).

The ritual for adult Baptism, on the other hand, preserves more completely the ancient institution of the catechumenate. Instead of telescoping all the scrutinies into one, it indicates each of the seven by a repetition of the same fundamental exorcisms and prayer. These ceremonies may be divided thus: (a) introductory psalm and prayer (Tit. I, c. 4, nn. 2-4); (b) initiation into the catechumenate (nn. 5-15); (c) rites proper to the *competentes*: the first six scrutinies (nn. 16-28)

[129] *De ordine antiphonarii*, 44. *MPL*, 105:1295; cf. also Pseudo-Alcuin, *De div. off.*, 19. *MPL*, 101:1221.
[130] Matt. 25:1-13.
[131] *De Corona*, 3. *MPL*, 2:99.
[132] *La Tradition Apostolique* (ed. B. Botte), n. 23, p. 54.
[133] *Adv. Luciferianos*, 8. *MPL*, 23:172.
[134] *Epist. ad Senarium*, 12. *MPL*, 59:405.
[135] *Adv. Marcionem*, I, 14. *MPL*, 2:287.

and the last scrutiny, formerly of Holy Saturday morning (nn. 29-37);
(d) interrogations on faith, the baptismal act, and the concluding rites
symbolic of Baptism's effects (nn. 38-50).

5. Sacramentals flowing from Baptism

Religious profession

Just as the Christian life itself possesses a rite of initiation, the
religious life, which is the summit of the Christian life, knows a ceremony by which a Christian enters this new state of religious profession. The Church has always taught that, so far as the infusion of
sanctifying grace is concerned, martyrdom is the equivalent of Baptism of water. We have seen, in discussing the introduction of the
feasts of martyrs, that the ascetical life was looked upon as a living
martyrdom, and hence gradually the act by which a person bound
himself to this type of life came to be regarded as a second Baptism
capable of forgiving sins.[136]

Pseudo-Dionysius, for one, calls religious profession a *mysterion*
and places it on a par with Baptism and the Eucharist.[137] Certainly it
is not a sacrament, yet many modern theologians claim for it the
power of satisfying for and forgiving sin. St. Thomas certainly favored
this view. If a man, he says, can satisfy for his sins by almsgiving, "so
much the more will it be sufficient for the satisfaction for sins if a
man totally dedicate himself to divine service by entering religion, for
this exceeds every kind of satisfaction, even that of public penance,
just as holocaust is superior to sacrifice. Hence we read in the lives of
the Fathers that those who entered religion received the same grace
as those who were baptized." [138]

Whether the ceremonies of profession proper to modern religious
communities may be called sacramentals will depend on whether they
have been specifically raised to the dignity of a liturgical act by the
Congregation of Rites or directly by the pope. The regular monastic
profession most certainly is sacramental, for it has been so spoken of
from earliest times, was contained in many pontificals, and today
forms part of the blessing for an abbot-elect, should the person chosen
for this office not yet have made his profession.

Just as Baptism was prefaced by a period of trial and examination, so also the religious life had its novitiate even in early centur-

---

[136] Cf. Odo Casel, "Die Mönchsweihe," *Jahrbuch für Liturgiewissenschaft,* 5
(1925), 5.

[137] *De eccl. hier.,* 6, 3. *MPG,* 3:533.

[138] ". . . multo magis in satisfactionem pro omnibus peccatis sufficit quod
aliquis se totaliter divinis obsequiis mancipet per religionis ingressum, quae excedit
omne genus satisfactionis, etiam publicae poenitentiae, sicut holocaustum excedit
sacrificium. Unde legitur in Vitis Patrum quod eandem gratiam consequuntur
religionem ingredientes quam consequuntur baptizati." *Summa Theol.,* II-II, 189,
3 ad 3.

ies.[139] Thus in the time of Pachomius we find that certain interrogations were made, trials imposed, and instructions given to those who presented themselves to him as prospects for the religious life.[140] This period of trial came in time to be more clearly defined,[141] and in St. Benedict's day scrutinies were held at regular intervals—at least three times before profession.[142] While formerly official service books retained something of this "catechumenate" in the very rite of profession,[143] at present the Roman Pontifical has omitted such interrogations and scrutinies. Yet they are still used by the Benedictines and other religious Orders. In some monastic rituals a clear-cut renunciation of the world and Satan is called for, just as in Baptism the catechumen is expected to renounce the devil and his pomps. The catechumen protested his loyalty, faith, and allegiance to Christ, and in religious profession the pronouncing of the vows holds a similar place. The baptismal garment finds a parallel in the religious habit with which the newly professed is finally clothed.[144] In fact, for some earlier writers the vesting of the candidate with the habit seems to have been the essential act of profession; [145] it is certainly symbolic of the fact that with religious profession a person has begun a new type of life.[146] Finally, just as in the early Church the newly baptized was received into the brotherhood of Christians by means of the kiss of peace,[147] so the newly professed religious is welcomed into the community with it.

Consecration of Virgins

We find the expression *velatio virginum* and *consecratio virginum* as early as the second half of the fourth century, when the monastic life for women had become an established and flourishing institution.[148] In 393 a Synod held at Hippo reserved this ceremony to the

[139] The term "novice" was already used by Tertullian in reference to the catechumens: *De poenitentia,* 6. *MPL,* 1:1346.

[140] *Vita Pachomii,* 7 and 22. *MPL,* 73: 233, 343.

[141] Cf. Cassian, *De coenobiorum institutione,* IV, 3, 7. *MPL,* 49: 154-156, 160.

[142] *Regula,* 58. Holstenius, II, 53, ff.

[143] E.g. the tenth century Romano-Germanic Pontifical: cf. P. De Puniet, *Le Pontifical Romain,* II (Paris: Desclée, 1931), 71 ff.

[144] Cf. R. Reitzenstein, *Historia Monachorum und Historia Lausiaca. Eine Studie zur Geschichte des Mönchtums und der frühchristlichen Begriffe Gnostiker und Pneumatiker* (Göttingen, 1916), 107. E. Malone, "Martyrdom and Monastic Profession as a Second Baptism," in Mayer, Quasten, Neunheuser, *Vom christlichen Mysterium* (Düsseldorf: Patmos, 1951), 124.

[145] Cf. *Vita Pachomii,* 7. *MPL,* 73:233; see also Cassian's words on the significance of changing from the clothes of the world to the religious habit: *De coenob. instit.,* IV, 5. *MPL,* 49: 158-159.

[146] Cf. Odo Casel, *art. cit.,* 7; also P. Oppenheim, "Mönchsweihe und Taufritus," in *Miscellanea K. Mohlberg* (Rome, 1948), I, 274-276.

[147] *La Tradition Apostolique* (Ed. B. Botte), n. 22, p. 53; cf. also F-J. Dölger, "Der Kuss im Tauf-und Firmungsritual nach Cyprian von Karthago und Hippolyt von Rom," *Antike und Christentum,* 1 (1929), 189.

[148] Council of Carthage of 390, can. 3. Hefele-Leclercq, *op. cit.,* II, 77.

bishop and limited its celebration to the great feasts of the Church Year: Easter, Christmas, and Epiphany.[149] Rome, too, made a clear distinction between women who proposed to keep their virginity intact and those who, in addition, had made public profession of such an intention and had received the veil together with the Church's special blessing.[150] Unfortunately, the custom of giving an official blessing to virgins in the name of the Church almost died out, except in a few rare examples. The Carthusian Order has piously maintained it together with some Benedictine convents. St. Charles Borromeo tried to revive it in the sixteenth century, but his example was not followed by other bishops.[151] But there have been sporadic attempts by the popes to encourage its adoption: Benedict XIII conferred the consecration upon nearly two hundred nuns in Rome, and Benedict XIV spoke of its observance in many Benedictine convents. It has also been revived in some convents in the United States.

The consecration of a virgin takes the form of a Preface which, except for a few clauses added in the Gelasian Sacramentary [152] and reproduced in all subsequent versions, goes back to the Leonine book.[153] Its basic theme, of course, is virginity, the objective of which is union with Christ in the eternal nuptials of the Lamb. The mention of the call of the Gentiles through the "innumerable stars" shows that this formula was first intended for use on the feast of the Epiphany, a feast dedicated to the espousals which took place between Christ and His Church at the time of His Baptism.

Other ceremonies carry out further the symbolism of the mystical marriage between Christ and the newly consecrated virgins. They receive a veil as spouses of Christ. Later in the Middle Ages the practice was begun of also giving the virgins a ring and a crown, both of which are traditional symbols of marriage. Thus the soul, already consecrated, spiritually espoused, to Christ in Baptism, is again consecrated to His service and a way of life of mystical marriage—the completion and perfection of Baptism. And just as the soul receives a spiritual deputation to divine worship in Baptism by means of the character received, so now this character is enlarged, given fuller scope, as it were, so that in the ceremony in which the virgin is given a Breviary, she becomes an official minister for the praying of the Divine Office in the name of the Mystical Body.

Blessing of water—the Asperges

We have seen how both pagan and Jewish religion laid great stress on lustral purifications, and how in Tertullian's day Christians

---

[149] Can. 38. Hefele-Leclercq, *op. cit.*, II, 89.
[150] *Canones ad Gallos*, 1 and 2. Hefele-Leclercq, *op. cit.*, II, 136.
[151] *Acta Synodica Mediol.*, I, 159. P. De Puniet, *op. cit.*, II, 157.
[152] Ed. H. Wilson, 156-157.
[153] K. Mohlberg, *Sacramentarium Veronense*, n. 1104, pp. 138-139.

washed their hands each time before they prayed.[154] After the time of Constantine a fountain was placed in the atrium before the church building for this precise purpose.[155] As the Christians washed their hands here, their thoughts were of spiritual interior purification. Gradually the Church was led to confer a special blessing on water to be used for such spiritual ablutions. The first authentic blessing of water that has come down to us appears in the fourth century *Euchologion* of Serapion of Thmuis,[156] and a similar formula is found in the *Apostolic Constitutions*.[157] In both cases reference is made to the curative effects of the water. A letter of Pope Vigilius in 538 indicates that an aspersion of water was used in the consecration of a church.[158]

The taking of blessed water upon entering a church should remind us of our Baptism and help us bring about within us a renewal of the purity and innocence that flooded our souls when they were washed for the first time of Original Sin. This is especially brought home to us on Sundays, when before the Sung Mass the priest walks through the church and sprinkles us with blessed water and prays that we may be purified and protected thereby. It was precisely to remind us of our Baptism and to imitate in this way the Great Easter Vigil, says Rupert of Deutz,[159] that the Asperges was instituted. Everything points to the ninth century as the time when this custom began.[160]

C. Confirmation

1. Theological summary

In Baptism the soul is reborn to the supernatural life, the life of Christ begins to develop within it; in Confirmation this new life is perfected, strengthened, protected, and sealed off from anything that might harm or hinder it. In this sacrament the Holy Spirit is given to the soul, so that He might bring to fruition the seed of divine life planted in it, just as on Pentecost the Holy Spirit descended upon the Apostles to continue the work of redemption which Christ had begun through His teaching, death, and resurrection. His work in their souls was, as Christ intimated at the Last Supper,[161] to achieve the complete development of what He had initiated, to inspire them to interpret faithfully His mind, to impel them towards an ever more fervent union with Him, to attune them to God's operation within their souls

---

[154] *De oratione*, 13. *MPL*, 1:1271.
[155] Paulinus of Nola, *Epist.* 32, 15. *MPL*, 61: 337.
[156] N. XVII. J. Quasten, 66.
[157] VIII, 29. *MPG*, 1:1126.
[158] He says that such a ceremony is not necessary when a church is reconstructed: *Epist.* I, 4. MPL, 69:18.
[159] *De div. off.*, VII, 20. *MPL*, 170: 200.
[160] Baluze, *Capitularia reg. franc.*, I, 903. M. Righetti, IV, 398.
[161] "But the Advocate, the Holy Spirit, whom the Father will send in my name, will teach you all things and bring to your mind whatever I have said to you" John 14:26.

so that they might be perfect instruments in God's hands for the salvation of the world. They were to become perfect reproductions of Christ on earth.

As St. Paul says, "It is God who has secured us and you in Christ, who has anointed us, who has also stamped us with His seal and given us the Spirit as a pledge in our hearts." [162] And so the Holy Spirit is given to us in Confirmation, sealing Christ's life within us, nurturing it, making it grow, perfecting it with divine inspiration and grace to the point where we will have "attained . . . to perfect manhood, to the mature measure of the fullness of Christ." [163] And thus too the presence of the Holy Spirit within our souls is "a pledge of our inheritance," [164] eternal life.

Confirmation also imprints another character on the soul. Theologians are not at all agreed upon the precise meaning of this new participation in the priesthood of Christ. To look upon it as a quasi-ordination for the apostolate of Catholic Action is an exaggerated view. The Christian already accepts the obligation of the lay apostolate in Baptism, since through it he becomes a member of the Mystical Body [165] with the concomitant duty of maintaining a unity of interest and a mutual exchange of life with the other members. Confirmation does add something here; it reinforces and extends the baptismal character. This much is brought out by the symbolism of the sacramental rite, for in Confirmation a person is anointed with perfumed oil: he is thus invited to spread the good odor of Jesus Christ and he receives the anointing of prophets and martyrs [166] to proclaim the truth of the Gospel as a quasi-official witness.[167]

Although St. Thomas speaks of the character of Confirmation as a passive power,[168] it is, as he himself explains it, more active than that of Baptism, for it empowers a Christian to engage in worship, no longer as one newly-born seeking only self-development, but as a grown-up in the community of the faithful able to fight against the enemies of the faith.[169] Thus the character of Confirmation enables a

[162] 2 Cor. 1:21-22.
[163] Ephesians 4:13. St. Ambrose, too, calls Confirmation a *spiritale signaculum*, or simply *perfectio: De sacramentis*, III, 2, 8; *De mysteriis*, VII, 42. J. Quasten, 153, 131. See also: J. Crehan "The Sealing at Confirmation," *Theological Studies*, 14 (1953), 273-279; "Ten Years' Work on Baptism and Confirmation," *Theological Studies*, 17 (1956), 494-515; Th. Camelot, "Sur la théologie de la confirmation," *Revue des sciences philosophiques et théologiques*, 38 (1954), 637-657.
[164] Eph. 1:14.
[165] Pius XI, *Letter to the Patriarch of Lisbon on Catholic Action*, Nov. 10, 1933, 13-14. J. Loeffler, *Directives for Catholic Action Expounded by Pope Pius XI* (St. Louis: Central Bureau Press, 1943), p. 32. Cf. also the excellent work of T. Hesburgh, *The Theology of Catholic Action*. Notre Dame, Indiana, 1946.
[166] Cf. A-G. Martimort, "La confirmation," *Communion solennelle et profession de foi.* Lex Orandi, 14 (Paris, 1952), 159-201. Th. Camelot, *art. cit.*, 648.
[167] St. Thomas, *Summa Theol.*, III, 72, 5 ad 2.
[168] *Ibid.*, III, 63, 6.
[169] *Ibid.*, III, 72, 5.

Christian to offer the Mass through the ordained minister and to receive the other sacraments with an eye towards the Christian com-, bat, towards an apostolic application of these graces to the conversion and redemption of the world about him.[170] The strength given the newly confirmed is not so much against the interior enemies of the soul as it is for his struggle with the enemies without; yet he is not so much to treat them as enemies as to convert them to friendship with Christ. To indicate that he must be brave in this respect, the bishop lightly slaps on the cheek the candidate for Confirmation.

2. History of the rite

Our first witness to the sacrament of Confirmation is the author of the Acts of the Apostles. After the conversions wrought by the grace of God through Philip in Samaria, the Apostles Peter and John were sent there to confer this second sacrament upon the newly baptized. The ritual was very simple. "They [Peter and John] prayed for them that they might receive the Holy Spirit . . . then they laid their hands on them, and they received the Holy Spirit." [171] As we see, there is no mention of an anointing.[172] Also, from the context, we see there is a clear distinction between Baptism and Confirmation.

With Tertullian we go a step further. The imposition of hands and some formula are indicated as the essence of the sacrament: "the hand is imposed in blessing, calling and inviting the Holy Spirit." [173] This "blessing" might well be the same as the prayer which the Acts of the Apostles report. And as we have seen,[174] Tertullian also clearly shows a difference between Baptism and Confirmation.

We find similar testimony coming a few years later from Cyprian, in the same locality, Carthage. Confirmation is clearly set off from Baptism, for "one is not regenerated by the rite of imposition of hands which confers the Holy Spirit, but rather by Baptism, as the Holy Spirit is not received until after a person has been regenerated." [175] In another place Cyprian describes the rite of Confirmation. "The newly baptized person is presented to the head of the Church; he receives the Holy Spirit through our prayer and the imposition of our hand and is perfected by means of the Lord's sign [the sign of the cross]." [176] Though the rite ends with the sign of the cross, there is still no indication of the use of oil.

---

[170] Cf. the resumé of recent theological discussions on the character of Confirmation in Th. Camelot, *art. cit.*, 652-657.

[171] 8:14-17; also 19:6.

[172] Though Paul speaks of our being anointed in 2 Cor. 1:21, exegetes feel that this must be taken in a purely metaphorical sense: as the equivalent of the Holy Spirit Himself.

[173] *De baptismo*, 8. *MPL*, 1:1316.

[174] Note 120.

[175] *Epist.* 74, 7. *MPL*, 3:1178.

[176] *Epist.* 73, 9. *MPL*, 3: 1160.

With the *Apostolic Tradition* of Hippolytus we come across the exact words which were used in the sacrament and, for the first time, an explicit mention of the use of chrism. Placing his hand on the recipients' head, the bishop prays: "Lord, God, who has made them worthy to merit the remission of sins by means of the bath of regeneration of the Holy Spirit, send into them thy grace, that they may serve thee according to thy will, for thine is the glory, Father, Son and Holy Spirit, in the Holy Church, now and forever. Amen." The only difference between this formula and our present one is that the former lacks an explicit mention of the sending of the Holy Spirit and of His specific gifts. After this first imposition and prayer, the bishop pours chrism into his hand and, placing it upon the head of the recipient, anoints him saying, "I anoint thee with holy oil in the Lord, Father almighty, Christ Jesus and the Holy Spirit." He then traces the sign of the cross on the recipient's forehead and gives him the kiss of peace.[177]

From this time on these rites formed part of the Roman tradition on Confirmation. The anointing, however, was definitely not considered the real matter of the sacrament. Even though Innocent I, in 416, speaks only of the anointing performed by the bishop,[178] he is speaking here of the distinction between the baptismal anointing and that of Confirmation, the latter being in the power of the bishop alone. Furthermore, Leo I, who wrote after him, states categorically that Christians "are to be confirmed only by means of an invocation of the Holy Spirit and the imposition of hands." [179]

A change in the matter and form of this sacrament was very probably brought about because of the clearer symbolism of the anointing with chrism. It expressed more exactly the effects of Confirmation, that is, a strengthening by reception of the Holy Spirit. Add to this the fact that it was often called "consignatio"; it was also conferred in a special place called the "consignatorium." And great emphasis was laid on the expressions like "signaculum" and "seal" by men like Ambrose.[180]

The Gelasian Sacramentary presents a particularly curious example of transition. In the Ordo for Holy Saturday night for the conferring of Baptism and Confirmation, it says that for the latter sacrament the bishop, to confirm (*ad consignandum*), imposes his hand as he speaks the formula similar to that already seen in the *Apostolic Tradition* but now containing explicit mention of the infusion of the Holy Spirit and His seven gifts. Only after this imposition of hands does the bishop trace the cross on the foreheads of the recipients with chrism. Later, in another Ordo inserted before the lessons of the

---

177 *La Tradition Apostolique* (ed. B. Botte), n. 22, pp. 52-53.
178 *Epist.* 25 *ad Decentium*, 6. *MPL,* 20:554.
179 *Epist.* 159, 7. *MPL,* 54:1139.
180 *De mysteriis,* VII, 42; *De sacramentis,* III, 2, 8. J. Quasten, 131, 153.

Pentecost vigil there is no mention whatsoever of the imposition of hands.[181] The rubric for this imposition must have been added at a time when the emphasis had shifted to the anointing as the matter of the sacrament.

Nevertheless, the *Ordo Romanus* XI, a Roman document of the seventh century, gives the impression that the bishop confirmed by means of an invocation of the sevenfold gifts of the Holy Spirit and *after* that traced a cross on the forehead of the recipient with chrism. Still there is no explicit mention of an imposition of his hand, unless this is implied in the wording of the rubric "dat orationem pontifex super eos." [182] However, we do find explicit mention in later Ordos of the imposition of the bishop's hand upon the head of each recipient.[183]

The case was definitively decided in favor of anointing when the scholastics in their discussion concerning this sacrament saw in chrism the true matter. This was the opinion of St. Thomas,[184] and in it he allowed no room for the imposition of the bishop's hand. And Pope Eugene IV, in his *Decretum pro Armenis* of 1439, states that the matter of Confirmation is chrism blessed by the bishop, while its form is "Signo te signo crucis, et confirmo te chrismate salutis, in nomine Patris, et Filii et Spiritus Sancti." And although he admits that the Apostles conferred this sacrament by means of an imposition of hands, he says the Church does so through Confirmation, evidently taking the word confirmation as synonymous with anointing.[185] Finally, in 1840, the Congregation of Propaganda declared that those who were not present during the first imposition of hands were not to be disquieted regarding the validity of their Confirmation.[186] Today, however, it is the express wish of the Church that those to be confirmed be present for the entire rite.[187]

The historical evidence which we have reviewed makes inescapable the conclusion that the Church has changed the matter and form of this sacrament.[188] It is true that some theologians regard the manner in which the bishop anoints the forehead of the recipient, that is, by placing most of his right hand on the top of the head, while with the thumb he traces the cross on the forehead, as an imposition

---

[181] Ed. Wilson, 86-87, 117.

[182] Nn. 100-101. Andrieu, *Les Ordines Romani*, II, 446.

[183]*Ord. Rom.* XXXb, nn. 55-56. Andrieu, III, 473; *Ord. Rom.* X (Mabillon's numeration), n. 24. *MPL*, 78:1017. A different tradition was handed on in the mixed Gregorian Sacramentary. The imposition of the bishop's hand is no longer done individually but collectively: *MPL*, 78:90.

[184] *Summa Theol.*, III, 72, 2.

[185] Denz., 697.

[186] Cf. M. Righetti, IV, 94, note 40.

[187] CIC, can. 789.

[188] P. De Puniet, *Le Pontifical Romain*, I (Paris, 1930), 85; M. Righetti, IV, 95; Th. Camelot, "Sur la théologie de la confirmation," *Revue des sciences philosophiques et théologiques*, 38 (1954), 637-639.

of his hand. And in this they seem to be supported by canon law.[189] Historically speaking, however, all the evidence points to the first imposition of hands as the original matter of the sacrament.

3. Modern ritual

The ceremonies of Confirmation are extremely simple; they may be divided into three parts: (a) an initial laying on of hands, (b) anointing with chrism and a slap on the cheek, (c) concluding antiphon, oration, and blessing.

With hands joined before him, the bishop begins with the brief prayer: "May the Holy Spirit come upon you, and may the power of the All High preserve you from sin. Amen." This is followed by versicles and responses. Then the bishop extends both hands over those to be confirmed and recites the following prayer:

> Almighty and eternal God, who didst deign to regenerate these thy servants by water and the Holy Spirit, and didst give them the remission of all their sins; send into them thy sevenfold Spirit, the Holy Paraclete from heaven. Amen.
> The Spirit of Wisdom and Understanding. Amen.
> The Spirit of Counsel and Fortitude. Amen.
> The Spirit of Knowledge and Piety. Amen.
> Fill them with the Spirit of thy fear, and mark them with the sign of the cross of Christ in mercy unto life eternal. Through the same Lord, etc. Amen.

Seated on the faldstool, the bishop then traces the cross on the forehead of each person as he speaks the words: "I sign you with the sign of the cross, and I confirm you with the chrism of salvation. In the name of the Father, the Son and the Holy Spirit. Amen." While he traces the cross with his thumb, the fingers of his right hand are supposed to be placed on the head of the person.[190]

After anointing the person, the bishop lightly slaps him on the cheek to remind him that the life of an apostle guided by the maxims of Christ's Gospel may likely involve suffering for Christ. Such an action appears for the first time in the Pontifical of Durandus of Mende;[191] however, he does not claim it to be one of his own innovations.

[189] "Sacramentum confirmationis conferri debet per manus impositionem cum unctione chrismatis in fronte et per verba in pontificalibus libris ab Ecclesia probatis praescripta." Can. 780.

[190] "Unctio autem ne fiat aliquo instrumento, sed ipsa manu capiti confirmandi rite imposita." Can. 781, #2.

[191] See his *Rationale divinorum officiorum*, VI, 84, 6; and his Pontifical in M. Andrieu, *Le Pontifical Romain au Moyen-Age*, III (Vatican City, 1940), 334, n. 4.

The ceremonies are concluded with the antiphon *Confirma hoc Deus,* followed by versicles and responses and an oration begging God that the coming of the Holy Spirit upon these newly confirmed will fashion their hearts into a temple for His glory. Finally, the bishop blesses the newly confirmed: "Thus will be blessed every man who fears the Lord. May the Lord bless thee out of Sion, that you may see the good things of Jerusalem all the days of your life and have life eternal. Amen."

It is interesting to note that the hierarchy in some lands is making an effort to return to the more ancient, and theologically more fitting, practice of conferring Confirmation on children before they receive their first Holy Communion. As the French Directory for the Administration of the Sacraments says, "Confirmation gives, through its character, the strength necessary to render an authentic witness by the profession of the faith both in actions of worship as well as during one's life. Confirmation should, therefore, be received before the Holy Eucharist—especially in our age when children themselves are called to give their witness before a dechristianized world." [192] In 1932 the Congregation of the Sacraments in Rome stated that "it is very opportune that children should not approach the sacred table for the first time, unless after the reception of the sacrament of Confirmation, which is, as it were, the complement of Baptism and in which is given the fullness of the Holy Spirit."[193]

D. Penance

1. Theological summary

That the Church has power to forgive sins is clear from the Gospel. Our Lord said to His Apostles, after breathing upon them, "Receive the Holy Spirit; whose sins you shall forgive, they are forgiven them; and whose sins you shall retain, they are retained." [194] This special power given to the Church was to be a continuation of Christ's mission summed up in His own words, "I have come to call, not the just, but sinners." [195]

Having been given the power of the keys, the Church was left to decide which sins would be forgiven and how they would be forgiven. If, therefore, she exercised this power with a certain rigorism at times, refusing to grant pardon for this or that sin, or at least the repeated commission of certain sins, this was due to the circumstances of the time and was ultimately meant for the good of souls, just

---

[192] *Directoire pour la pastorale des Sacrements,* adopté par l'Assemblée plénière de l'Episcopat pour tous les diocèses de France, Avril 3, 1951 (Paris: Maison de la Bonne Presse, 1951), n. 33, p. 53.

[193] *AAS,* 24 (1932), 272.

[194] John 20:22-23. Cf. P. Galtier, *Aux Origines du Sacrement de Pénitence* (Rome, 1951), 51 ff. for the exact sense of these words.

[195] Matt. 9:13; "to penance" some codices add.

as was the eventual change in her rigoristic attitude. A refusal to remit sins at one particular epoch, in one given set of historical circumstances or in regard to individual persons, can in no way be taken to mean that the Church does not possess the power to remit them. This was Tertullian's oversight. Since the Church in the second century manifested an almost terrible divine anger towards specified sins —adultery, fornication, apostasy, homicide—some traditionalists, like Tertullian and his followers, reproached the Church for later wanting to relax her discipline.[196] Just as it was the right and duty of the Church to demand extraordinary signs of repentance before reconciling the inveterate enemies of justice to the body of the faithful, in order to protect the latter from bad example and check the spread of corruption, so likewise it belongs to her prudence and power to lessen the severity of her penitential practice in order to make her sacraments more available to the weak and thus allow grace to triumph over vice.

In the following pages it will also become apparent how the Church has changed the manner in which Penance was administered. From public satisfaction (sometimes confession) she turns to private, secret satisfaction; from difficult and lengthy exercises of penance which had to be performed after confession but before absolution, she turns to a benign attitude which grants the pardon of sins even before satisfaction is performed. Finally, the very formula of absolution has known a variety of expressions over the centuries, some long, some short, some optative, some declarative—but always expressive of the Church's conviction that she is the keeper of the keys.

2. History of penitential discipline

While in the apostolic period we have many references to Penance, none of them indicates the manner in which the sacrament was administered. At the turn of the first century all we find in the *Didache* is the general prescription to confess one's sins before prayer as well as before the Eucharistic Sacrifice.[197]

Pope St. Clement is more explicit when he writes to the Corinthians, urging the rebellious elements in the community to confess their sins and submit to the penance imposed by the Church. "It is better for a man to confess his sins than to harden his heart. . . .[198]

[196] Cf. Tertullian's work, *De pudicitia*, esp. cc. 3, 5 and 7. *MPL*, 2: 1037-1038, 1039-1041, 1045.

[197] 4, 14; 14, 1. J. Quasten, 13, note 1. Quasten claims that this refers to some non-sacramental confession of sins similar to our Confiteor: *Patrology*, I (Westminster, Maryland, 1951), 33. E. Vacandard holds the same opinion: "Confession du I au XII siècle," *DTC*, III, 840. While the *Didache* may be referring to some private "act of contrition," it is hard to see here any indication of a public apology, since such apologies do not make their appearance until the seventh century.

[198] *Epist. ad Cor.*, 51. *MPG*, 1:314.

Be obedient to the presbyters; accept their reprimands in penance, bending the knees of your heart. . . .[199] Let us cast ourselves down before the feet of the Lord and, crying, let us beg Him to be merciful towards us . . . and restore us to the fellowship [of the Church]." [200] We have in these quotations three phases of the sacrament of Penance indicated: a *confession* of sin (it is not certain from these texts whether it is public or private); a period of *satisfaction* for the sin, public it would seem, for Clement speaks of the humiliation involved in doing penance; finally, *reconciliation* to the Church and the sacraments.

With the end of the second century and the beginning of the third the penitential practice of the Church receives more attention from Christian writers. The first thing to notice is that it had been the practice of the Church to grant pardon only once for serious sins committed after Baptism.[201] If one sinned grievously afterwards, he could only live a life of penance and depend on God's mercy, but he could no longer receive sacramental absolution, or reconciliation, as it was called in those days. Furthermore, while lesser sins were forgiven immediately upon confession,[202] other more grievous ones were not absolved until after a long and hard penance. And there were even other sins, according to Tertullian's way of thinking, which not only were not *de facto* forgiven, but could not *de iure* be forgiven: adultery, along with other serious sins of the flesh, apostasy, and murder.[203] So severe and humiliating were the penances meted out, that most sinners refused to submit to the sacrament.[204]

That such rigorism actually existed in the early Church is borne out by the testimony of Pope Innocent I, who says that in former times some bishops followed a more severe observance in that they imposed a heavy penance for the three sins mentioned above but would not grant absolution after the penance had been performed.[205] As late as 300 the Council of Elvira sanctioned such extreme measures against molesters of children and also for bishops, priests, or deacons who had committed adultery.[206] Cyprian bitterly complained about such rigorism: "Cry and moan day and night, work hard at expiating your sin, but after all this effort you will die outside the Church." [207] What was worse, he accuses some bishops of inequality in this matter: one bishop would not hesitate to absolve from these serious sins, while another never would.[208] Though he had urged stringent penances,

---

[199] *Ibid.*, 57. *MPG*, 1:323.
[200] *Ibid.*, 48. *MPG*, 1:307.
[201] Tertullian, *De poenitentia*, 7. *MPL*, 1:1352.
[202] Tertullian, *De pudicitia*, 7. *MPL*, 2:1046.
[203] *Ibid.*, 1, 3, 5, 7 and 22. *MPL*, 2: 1033, 1037-1038, 1039-1041, 1045, 1082.
[204] Tertullian, *De poenitentia*, 10. *MPL*, 1:1355.
[205] *Epist.* 6, 2. *MPL*, 20:498.
[206] Canons 71 and 18. Hefele-Leclercq, I, 259, 232.
[207] *Epist.* 52, 28. *MPL*, 3:818.
[208] *Ibid.*, 21. *MPL*, 3:811.

lasting even till the end of life, for those who had lapsed into idolatry, he insisted that they be reconciled to the Church on the point of death, if, of course, they had performed the penance imposed.[209]

It was to settle the unrest caused by such severity and inequality that Pope Callistus declared that the Church should forgive sins of the flesh when due penance had been performed.[210] This gave Tertullian the occasion to write his *De Pudicitia*, in which he takes a strong—and heretical—stand against such untraditional and lax behavior on the part of authorities. In this way his sympathies with the rigorist heretic Montanus manifested themselves and brought him, eventually, into open and definite schism.

There can be no doubt that confession was necessary. Cyprian urges his Christians to confess their sins while there is yet time.[211] And he relates how the bishop Basilides confessed his blasphemy and then laid aside his episcopal dignity to do penance.[212] Origen, too, says that the sinner must tell his sin to the priest and seek medicine.[213] Although both he [214] and Tertullian [215] speak of a "publication" of the penitent's sins, it is not certain that we must take such statements as clearly indicating the confession itself was public, since the statements could very well refer to the publicity attendant upon the performance of the satisfaction enjoined for the sins.

Satisfaction after confession of sin first of all implied, at least for mortal sins, a temporary excommunication from the sacraments and from participation within the confines of the church proper at the public prayers.[216] Such expulsion would certainly be evident to those entering the church. Furthermore, other physical penances were imposed which also betrayed the fact that serious sin had been committed. Besides being made to fast and to observe long vigils, penitents had to change their dress radically, had to put on sackcloth and ashes, and had to kneel at the entrance of the church and beg the

---

[209] *Epist.* 54. *MPL*, 3:880-888.

[210] "Ego et moechiae et fornicationis delicta, poenitentia functis, dimitto." This is reported by Tertullian, not without sarcasm, in his *De pudicitia*, 1. *MPL*, 1:1033. Callistus is not named as the author of this edict by Tertullian, but the fact that Hippolytus hurled similar charges against this pope has inclined historians to see him as the true author. Quasten, however, opposes this view: *Patrology*, II (Westminster, Maryland, 1953), 234-235.

[211] *Liber de lapsis*, 29. *MPL*, 4:503.

[212] *Epist.* 68, 6. *MPL*, 3:1066.

[213] *Homil.* 2 *in Levit.*, 4. *MPG*, 12:418.

[214] ". . . proferenda in publicum." *Homil.* 3 *in Levit.*, 4. *MPG*, 12:429.

[215] Speaking of sinners who attempt to escape "publicationem sui." *De poenitentia*, 10. *MPL*, 1:1355.

[216] Cf. Origen, *In Jesu Nave homil.* 21, 1. *MPG*, 12:929; Tertullian: "Si quis ita deliquerit, ut a communicatione orationis et conventus et omnis sancti commercii relegetur," *Liber apologeticus adv. Gentes*, 39. *MPL*, 1:532; cf. his other works: *De pudicitia*, cc. 3, 5, and 7; *De poenitentia*, 7. *MPL*, 2; 1038, 1039, 1045; 1:1352. Cyprian says that the penitents could assist *ad limen* of the church: *Epist.* 31, 6. *MPL*, 4:321.

faithful for their prayers.[217] Then too, very often the entire local Church gathered to pass judgment on a sinner, to determine what penance should be imposed on him—even whether he should be finally admitted to sacramental reconciliation.[218]

The period of penance (and, practically speaking, of excommunication) imposed on the sinner varied with the gravity of the sin and the scandal it caused. As we have already mentioned, it pertained to the bishop to decide on the amount of time to be spent in penance; sometimes he imposed a whole lifetime of mortification and plainly let the penitent know that even then he had no hope of reconciliation: he was left to the mercy of God. Irenaeus tells the story of a certain Mark, who, after being converted from his sinful ways, had to spend the remainder of his life in penance but was finally absolved.[219] And Cyprian indicates that those who had lapsed into idolatry, especially priests, should be made to do penance for the rest of their lives, but that, in general, other sinners, after having performed penance for a suitable period (*iusto tempore*), are to be reconciled.[220] In 300 the Council of Elvira determined specific periods of satisfaction for certain sins. Thus, for example, five years penance had to be performed by a person who had committed adultery once, but ten years were imposed upon the person who had lived in adultery for over a long period.[221]

Reconciliation at this time was commonly called *pax* or *pacem dare*.[222] In contrast to the initial excommunication imposed after confession, reconciliation was also called a giving of communion: *communionem praestare*,[223] or simply a giving of the *right* of communion: *ius communicationis*.[224] This reconciliation or communion was granted to a penitent once he had performed the penance imposed, and it was given through a symbolic gesture: the imposition of hands, not only by the bishop himself, but by the whole clergy.[225]

Regarding the minister of Penance, all the writers and documents of Christian antiquity are in accord in saying that this role was the right of the bishop. In cases of necessity or whenever the required permission was obtained from the bishop, a priest could absolve from sin. What is extraordinary is the evidence of certain documents that, in certain very urgent cases when neither bishop nor priest was avail-

---

[217] Tertullian, *De poenitentia*, cc. 7 and 9. *MPL*, 1:1352, 1354; *De pudicitia*, 13. *MPL*, 2: 1056.

[218] Cf. Tertullian, *Liber apologeticus adv. Gentes*, 39. *MPL*, 1:532.

[219] *Adv. haer.* I, 13. *MPG*, 7: 587.

[220] *Epist.* 9, 2; *Epist.* 11, 2. *MPL*, 4: 257, 263.

[221] Cc. 69 and 64. Hefele-Leclercq, *op. cit.*, I, 259, 256-257.

[222] Cf. Cyprian, *Epist.* 52, 13; *Epist.* 10, 2. *MPL*, 3:804 ff; 4:261.

[223] Cf. Council of Elvira, can. 32. Hefele-Leclercq, *op. cit.*, I, 238.

[224] Cyprian, *Epist.* 9, 2. *MPL*, 4: 257-258.

[225] ". . . ad exomologesim veniant, et per manus impositionem episcopi et cleri ius communicationis accipiant." Cyprian, *Epist.* 9, 2; *Epist.* 11, 2. *MPL*, 4: 257-258, 263.

able, deacons were delegated to act as the minister of Penance. Cyprian is clear on this, though it might be argued that he was in error here, as he was in regard to the necessity of re-baptizing lapsed Catholics. "If they [the *lapsi*] labor under some inconvenience or danger from illness, and, not waiting for my visit, they may make their confession to any available priest, or, if one cannot be found and death is imminent, to a deacon also, and thus, having received the imposition of hands, go to the Lord in peace." [226] This might seem strange indeed were it not for the fact that this same extraordinary delegation is explicitly mentioned later by a Council, by several compilers of ecclesiastical decrees, and by two official service books for the administration of the sacrament of Penance.

In the year 300 the Council of Elvira, while insisting that excommunicated persons must present themselves to the bishop for absolution, states that should the penitent fall gravely ill, the priest must give him absolution, even a deacon, if he has permission of the bishop.[227] While Binterim and Frank refuse to see in this text any references to a sacramental absolution on the part of the deacon,[228] Jean Morin (Morinus) by means of an exacting exegesis of the text and with the support of other authorities feels compelled to acknowledge a delegation of sacramental power here.[229] Later Pseudo-Alcuin repeats the same prescription.[230] And both the *Poenitentiale* of Egbert of York and the *Ordo Romanus Antiquus*, today called the tenth century Romano-Germanic Pontifical, contain the same disposition.[231] It is again repeated in the Decretals of Ives and Burchard.[232] Even the Councils of York in 1194 and London in 1200 grant this permission in extreme urgency.[233]

Theologians today, however, deny that deacons really had or exercised a true sacramental power. While ignoring the later testimony, they concern themselves with an interpretation of the above text from Cyprian, an interpretation which usually does violence to

---

[226] ". . . si incommodo aliquo et infirmitatis periculo occupati fuerint, non expectata praesentia nostra, apud presbyterum quemcumque praesentem, vel, si presbyter repertus non fuerit, et urgere exitus coeperit, apud diaconum quoque, exomologesim facere delicti sui possint, ut manu eis in poenitentiam imposita, veniant ad Dominum cum pace." *Epist.* 12, 1. *MPL,* 4:265.

[227] ". . . cogente tamen infirmitate necesse est presbyterum communionem praestare debere, et diaconum si ei iusserit sacerdos." Can. 32. Hefele-Leclercq, *op. cit.,* I, 238. "Sacerdos" here means bishop because of the constant contrast between the words "presbyter" and "sacerdos."

[228] *Ibid.*

[229] *Commentarius Historicus de Disciplina in administratione sacramenti Poenitentiae* (Paris, 1651), lib. VIII, cap. XXIII, 11, p. 591.

[230] "Si autem necessitas evenerit et presbyter non fuerit praesens, diaconus suscipiat poenitentem, ac det sanctam communionem." *De divinis officiis,* 13. *MPL,* 101: 1196.

[231] Cf. Morin, n. 12, p. 591.

[232] *Decreta,* 15, cc. 161 and 162. *MPL,* 161: 893; *Decreta,* 19, cc. 153 and 154. *MPL,* 140: 1013.

[233] Cf. Morin, n. 14, p. 591.

the text.[234] As we said above, it is perfectly possible that we have here later compilers of ecclesiastical decrees simply copying an erroneous position of Cyprian. But if these texts mean what they seem to say, and if all these different sources arrived at their decisions independently of Cyprian—which does not seem to have been proved—then we would have here a case analogous to that of Confirmation, wherein, although the bishop is the ordinary minister, it has come to pass that the Holy See has granted permission to simple priests to act as extraordinary ministers. In Penance, again if we are to take these texts seriously, although the bishop and priests were the ordinary ministers, past ages seem to have known extreme circumstances in which deacons were allowed to exercise the power to forgive sins.

From the fourth to the sixth century the Church became more lenient in her penitential discipline. Though authors still insist that the bishop alone enjoys the role of minister of this sacrament,[235] there are instances in which priests are allowed to act as the ordinary minister. Socrates tells us that priest-penitentiaries were instituted in the East because of the persecutions, although this institution was later abolished because of scandal.[236] In Rome the administration of this sacrament was regularly entrusted to the priests.[237]

The same three phases of Penance are to be noted in this period also: confession, satisfaction, and reconciliation. And just as in the time of Tertullian and Cyprian, so at this time there is no uncontroverted evidence for two types of Penance: one public, the other private. True, confession of one's sins was probably made in private to the bishop or priest,[238] but the satisfaction to be performed was obvious and public enough. That there was a type of excommunication is apparent from the writings of Augustine.[239] Of course, this often entailed nothing more than being put in the ranks of the penitents.[240] Sackcloth and ashes were still the hallmark of the penitents,[241] and they had to receive the imposition of hands frequently.[242] Al-

---

[234] Cf. E. Amann, "Pénitence-sacrement," DTC, XII, 779; E. Vacandard, "Absolution de péchés au temps des pères," DTC, I, 154-156.

[235] Augustine, Sermo 351, 4, 9. MPL, 39:1545; Jerome, Comm. in Matt., 16, 19. MPL, 26:122; Council of Hippo in 393, can. 34. Hefele-Leclercq, II, 88; cf. also A. Chavasse, Le Sacramentaire Gélasien, p. 141.

[236] Hist. eccl., V, 19. MPG, 67: 614-618.

[237] Liber Pontificalis (ed L. Duchesne), I, 164, 249; Leo, Epist. 108 ad Theod., 3 and 5; Epist. 167 ad Rusticum, inquis. ix. MPL, 54: 1012, 1013-1014, 1206; Innocent I, Epist. 25, 7. MPL, 20:559; Gregory I, Homil. in Ezech. lib. II, X, n. 13-14. MPL, 76: 1065-1066.

[238] Augustine, Sermo, 351, 4, 9. MPL, 39: 1545; Paulinus, Vita s. Ambrosii, 39. MPL, 14:40; Leo I, Epist. 168, 2. MPL, 54:1211.

[239] Epist. 153, 3, 6; Sermo, 232, 7. MPL, 33:655; 38:1111.

[240] Who were often located on the left side of the church: Eligius of Noyon, Sermo 8. MPL, 87:620.

[241] Sackcloth: the Council of Agde in 506, can. 15. Hefele-Leclercq, op. cit., II, 987; ashes: Gregory I, Moral., 35, 6. MPL, 76:753.

[242] Council of Agde, can. 15. Hefele-Leclercq, op. cit., II, 987; Felix III, Epist. 7, 3. MPL, 58:926; possibly also Augustine, Sermo 232, 7. MPL, 38:1111; and Hilary of Arles, Vita, 13. MPL, 50:1233.

though several councils and synods still leave to the discretion of
the bishop the amount of time to be spent in penance (that is, satisfaction for sin),[243] the trend becomes more pronounced at this time
to consider Lent as the most ideal time of the year for the performance
of public satisfaction.[244]

The final step in the reception of the sacrament of Penance was,
of course, the rite of reconciliation received after the penance enjoined had been performed. We have seen how in the primitive Church
the imposition of hands formed an important element in this rite.
The same remains true of this fourth to sixth century period, and we
are told explicitly that the ceremony took place before the altar.[245]
The sacrament, of course, was not conferred merely by an imposition
of hands. This action appears to have been what theologians would
call the "matter" of the sacrament. It was accompanied by a "form,"
that is, a formula specifying the significance of the symbolic action.
Of this formula many Fathers speak; it was usually called *sacerdotalis
supplicatio*.[246]

St. Jerome describes the rite. The priest, he says, offers his
oblation for the penitent, imposes his hand on him, invokes the return
of the Holy Spirit, and having invited the people to pray, reconciles
him to the altar.[247] And by this time the reconciliation ceremony regularly took place on Holy Thursday.[248] For this occasion the Gelasian
Sacramentary provides an *Ordo agentibus publicam poenitentiam*
which substantially represents the Roman practice of the sixth century.[249] According to it, after the penitents have left their special section of the church and have prostrated themselves in the middle of
the church, the deacon presents them to the bishop (or to the priest),
requesting the remission of their sins with the formula *Adest, o ven-
erabile pontifex. . . .* The bishop then admonishes the penitents to
avoid in the future the sins for which they have just completed a
long satisfaction. There follow several orations of absolution, and,
judging from the rubric, "dicit orationes sacerdos super eos," an imposition of hands accompanied them, though there is no explicit mention of
such an action. The ceremony finished, the newly reconciled penitents
are allowed to take part in the Mass once again and receive Holy Communion.

During the sixth century we notice a decided change in peniten-

---

[243] Council of Hippo of 393, for example, can. 34. Hefele-Leclercq, II, 88.
[244] Ambrose, *Epist.* 20, 26. *MPL*, 16:1044; Innocent I, *Epist.* 25, 7. *MPL*,
20:559; Leo I, *Sermo* 49, 3. *MPL*, 54:303.
[245] *Ante absidem*: Council of Hippo of 393, can. 34. Hefele-Leclercq, II, 88.
[246] Leo I, *Epist.* 108, 2; 167, 2. *MPL*, 54:1011, 1203; Paulinus calls it an
intercessio: *Vita s. Ambrosii*, 39. *MPL*, 14:40.
[247] *Altario* could mean *to* the altar or *at* the altar: *Adv. Luciferianos*, 5. *MPL*,
23:167.
[248] Innocent I, *Epist.* 25, 7. *MPL*, 20:559; Eligius of Noyon, *Sermo* 8. *MPL*,
87:622.
[249] Ed H. Wilson, pp. 63-66.

tial discipline. From insistence on a strictly public satisfaction and reconciliation the Church gradually changes to a purely private practice. Furthermore, while up until this time the long period of satisfaction had to be gone through before a person was reconciled, now we notice the trend to absolve from sin immediately after confession and the imposing of the penance—except, always, in the case of notorious sinners. This transformation is usually ascribed to the influence of the Irish missionaries, especially the work of St. Columbanus.[250] In the Penitential attributed to Theodore of Canterbury (d. 690) we find that there was no public reconcilation because there was no public satisfaction.[251] Nevertheless, the same book makes provision for certain cases of public penance which very likely had to do with notorious sinners.[252] This, apparently, was the type of penitential discipline with which Columbanus and his disciples were familiar, and it was only to be expected that they would propagate their own practices when they arrived on the Continent, especially since, as Jonas of Orleans reports,[253] the use of this sacrament was a rare thing in his country.

In 589 the practice of private penance must have been already a widespread thing, for it called forth a rebuke from the Third Council of Toledo,[254] which insisted that the older discipline be reinstated. Nevertheless, the development went on, and in the eighth century it had become an established practice for a person to have his own confessor.[255] In one of his disciplinary decrees, St. Boniface (d. 755) recognized that current need militated against the former discipline and let priests know that they now enjoyed the role of ordinary ministers of the sacrament and should grant absolution immediately after confession.[256] By 813 the Council of Chalon could say that in most places the use of public penance had fallen away.[257] It was precisely to provide guidance in this period of varying discipline that such a plethora of penitential books called *Poenitentialia* cropped up, indicating when public or private penances were to be given, and what each penance should consist in.[258]

[250] Cf. M. Righetti, *op. cit.*, IV, 177.
[251] Caput XII, *MPL*, 99:936.
[252] Capitulum XI ff. *MPL*, 99:940.
[253] *Vita Colombani*, 11, *MPL*, 87: 1018.
[254] Can. 11. Hefele-Leclercq, III, 226.
[255] Egbert, *De institutione catholicae dialogus*, XVI, 4. *MPL*, 89:442.
[256] *Conc. Liptinense*, c. 31. *MPL*, 89:823.
[257] Can. 25. Hefele-Leclercq, III, 1144. We still find, however, traces of the older practice, for in the same century Rabanus Maurus lays down certain rules whereby a public penance was to be imposed for notorious sins, while a private penance was to be given for occult sins: *De cleric. institutione*, II, 30. *MPL*, 107: 342-343; cf. also can. 31 of the council of Rheims in 813. Hefele-Leclercq, III, 1137; and the synodal decrees of Hincmar of Rheims, dating about 852, can. 13. *MPL*, 125:776.
[258] See the history and description of these books in H. Leclercq, "Pénitentiels," *DACL*, XIV, 215-251.

By now the term "confession"[259] had become synonymous with
the sacrament of Penance, both because of the frequency and the
great importance attached to confession as well as because of the
growing tendency to make the whole sacrament consist in it, especially
since absolution was usually granted right after the confession of
sins. Many pastors of souls urged frequent confession. St. Boniface
exhorted his people to run to confession as soon as they fell into any
sin whatever,[260] and Alcuin recommends the same practice, especially
to youth.[261] People did not take easily to these ideas, for we also find
church authorities feeling the need to command confession after long
intervals. For instance, Chrodegang of Metz (d. 760) prescribes that
his clerics confess before their bishop at least twice a year,[262] while
Theodulf of Orleans insists that people go to confession just before
Lent, at least.[263] Still, by the end of the twelfth century, even though
the Church prescribed confession three times a year—before Christmas,
Easter and Pentecost—Alan of Lille complains that many hardly confess once a year, and even then only for the sake of form.[264] And so,
in the beginning of the thirteenth century, the Fourth Lateran Council
found it necessary to impose a solemn obligation on all to confess
their mortal sins at least once a year.[265]

The ritual for the imposition of public penance, when it was
used, remained substantially the same during the Middle Ages.[266]
Regino of Prüm[267] and the papal Pontifical of the thirteenth century[268] are in essential accord for the ceremonies used on this occasion. The penitents present themselves to the bishop on Ash Wednesday at the doors of the church, wearing sackcloth, going barefoot and
with heads bowed.[269] Leading them into the church, the bishop pros-
trates himself and sings the seven penitential psalms along with all
the clergy. Rising, he imposes his hand on the penitents, sprinkles
them with blessed water, saying the Asperges. As he places blessed
ashes on their heads, he recites the formula: *Recordare quia cinis es
et in cinerem reverteris.* He then places sackcloth on their heads and
recites the antiphon: "Apud Dominum misericordia est et copiosa

[259] E.g., St. Columbanus, *Regula coenobialis,* c. X. *MPL,* 80:216.
[260] *Sermo* 3, 4. *MPL,* 89: 849.
[261] *Opusc.* 7 *de confess. pecc.,* 1 and 7. *MPL,* 101:651-656.
[262] *Reg. canonic.,* c. 14. *MPL,* 89:1104.
[263] *Capitulare,* I, 36. *MPL,* 105:203.
[264] ". . . vix laicus vel clericus!" *Summa de arte praedicatoria,* c. 31. *MPL,*
210: 172-173.
[265] Denz. 437.
[266] The same as the ritual contained in the Gelasian Sacramentary, except
that the latter makes no mention of the bishop sprinkling the penitents with
ashes: ed. H. Wilson, pp. 14-15.
[267] *De eccl. discipl.,* I, 291. *MPL,* 132: 245-246; reproduced also by
Burchard of Worms, *Decretum* XIX, 26. *MPL,* 140: 984.
[268] M. Andrieu, *Le Pontifical Romain* (Vatican City, 1940), II, 578.
[269] At this point Regino indicates that the pastors of the various parishes
are present at the cathedral for this ceremony, and they are the ones who impose
a fitting penance on the sinners from their own parishes.

apud eum redemptio. Ita enim lapsis hominibus subvenit, ut non solum per baptismi et confirmationis gratiam, sed etiam per penitentiae medicinam spiritus humanus vitae reparetur eternae." The penitents reply, "Deo gratias!" The bishop then announces to them that they will be cast out of the church as Adam was cast out of paradise. After he commands the clergy to expell them, the clergy accompany them to the church door singing or reciting the responsory, *In sudore vultus tui.* . . . And the church doors are closed behind them.

The Gelasian ritual for reconciliation of the penitents on Holy Thursday is also found in the papal Pontifical of the thirteenth century but in greatly reduced form. From this Pontifical through that of Durandus of Mende it entered our present Pontifical. But now this ritual is but a record of the past, since a reconciliation of a public penitent is a rare thing indeed.

During this same medieval period there was a concomitant evolution of the formulas used for private penance. From the optative or deprecatory orations so evident in the ceremonies we have just described, the Church gradually changed to more formally juridical orations, namely, those employing declaratory phrases. Thus, for example, in Regino of Prüm we find a formula of absolution that is an obvious fusion of optative and declarative forms:

> Exsurge qui dormis, exsurge a mortuis et illuminabit te Christus.
> Frater, Dominus Jesus Christus, qui dixit discipulis suis: Quaecumque ligaveritis super terram, erunt ligata et in coelo; et quaecumque solveritis super terram, erunt soluta et in coelo; de quorum numero quamvis indignos nos esse voluit, ipse te absolvat per ministerium nostrum ab omnibus peccatis tuis, quaecumque cogitatione, locutione, atque operatione negligenter egisti, ut a nexibus peccatorum absolutum perducere te dignetur ad regna coelestia. Amen.
> Nos etiam, frater charissime, secundum auctoritatem nobis indignis a Domino commissam absolvimus te ab omni vinculo delictorum, ut merearis habere vitam aeternam per eum qui vivit, etc. . . .[270]

3. Modern ritual

Under the influence of the scholastic theologians, notably St. Thomas Aquinas,[271] the declarative formula finally won out as the strict form of sacramental absolution. However, even before his time, as with Regino, but especially afterwards, the trend became to begin with an optative formula and end with a declarative one. It is from this period that we receive our present formulas.

[270] *De eccl. discipl.*, I, 295. *MPL*, 132: 246-247.
[271] *Summa Theol.*, III, 84, 3.

After the priest has given an admonition and imposed a penance on the sinner, he says:

"Misereatur tui omnipotens Deus, et, dismissis peccatis tuis, perducat te ad vitam aeternam. Amen."

Then stretching forth his hand towards the penitent (a remnant of the former imposition of hands), he continues:

"Indulgentiam, absolutionem, et remissionem peccatorum tuorum tribuat tibi omnipotens et misericors Dominus. Amen." The next prayer appears for the first time in the Ritual of Cardinal Sanctorius in 1584:

"Dominus noster Jesus Christus te absolvat; et ego auctoritate ipsius te absolvo ab omni vinculo excommunicationis ["suspensionis," for clerics], et interdicti, in quantum possum et tu indiges."

Then the strict form of absolution follows:

"Deinde ego te absolvo a peccatis tuis, in nomine Patris, et Filii, et Spiritus Sancti. Amen."

The final oration, "Passio Domini nostri Jesu Christi, merita beatae Mariae Virginis, etc.," appears in the *Agenda* of the fifteenth century,[272] and it was inserted in the *Sacerdotale* of Castellani in 1567.[273] From there it found its way into our Ritual.

E. Extreme Unction

1. Theological summary

Our only clear-cut witness in the New Testament to an anointing of the infirm is to be found in the Epistle of St. James. There the apostle writes: "Is anyone among you sick? Let him bring in the presbyters of the Church, and let them pray over him, anointing him with oil in the name of the Lord, And the prayer of faith will save the sick man, and the Lord will raise him up; and if he be in sins, they will be forgiven him."[274] Tradition has always interpreted this passage as the promulgation of the sacrament of Extreme Unction.[275] The Council of Trent says that this sacrament was also implied in Mark 6:13, where it is reported that the disciples, during their preaching mission, anointed the sick and thus cured them.

The symbolism of this sacrament is obvious enough. It is borrowed from the ancient medical practice of rubbing the sick with oil. This anointing together with the prayer of the priest have always been the core of this sacrament; the only thing that has varied is the number of anointings and the various members of the body which received the anointings.

[272] Cf. Righetti, IV, 205.
[273] Cf. A. Villien, *The History and Liturgy of the Sacraments* (London: Burns, Oates, 1932), 199.
[274] 5:14-15.
[275] Council of Trent, Sess. 14, cap. I *de institut. sacr. extr. unct.* Denz. 908.

2. Evolution of the rite

It is not clear from the early writings of Christianity whether the frequent mention there of the use of Holy Oil for the sick should always be understood as the sacrament of Extreme Unction. In the *Apostolic Tradition* of Hippolytus there is reproduced within the framework of the Mass-Canon a blessing of oil which asks God, who sanctifies those who use and receive it, to give comfort and health to all who taste of it or otherwise use it.[276] Though it is clear from this last phrase that the oil was intended for the sick,[277] it does not tell us who is to apply it. But a few centuries later Pope Innocent I writes that the Epistle of James is without a doubt to be understood to refer to the sick members of the faithful who may be anointed with this oil blessed by the bishop. But he goes on to say that not only priests may use this oil, but also the faithful—except the penitents, who just as with the other sacraments, have this one denied to them.[278] The Gelasian Sacramentary also contains a blessing for oil which calls down God's blessing upon everyone who anoints with it, tastes it, or touches it. And it specifies the result of this blessing: protection or defense of body, mind, and spirit, the expelling of all pain, infirmity, all illness of mind and body.[279]

While Caesarius of Arles in one letter speaks of calling in the priests to anoint the sick,[280] in another he urges the people to anoint themselves and their relatives with this Holy Oil according to the words of St. James.[281] Venerable Bede explicitly states that not only priests may use this oil, but that whoever does must invoke the name of the Lord while anointing.[282] And he too describes its healing effects both in the physical order and in the spiritual—at least as regards the *peccata leviora*. A blessing appearing in the Bobbio Missal sums up the effects as *salutaris gratiam et peccatorum veniam et sanitatem coelestem*.[283] Finally, an eighth century *Ordo Romanus* confirms what we have already seen regarding the direct use made of this Holy Oil by the faithful, when it speaks of the vases of oil brought forward by various people.[284] It is a valid supposition that such oil was intended for the use of the donors.

Beginning with the Carolingian epoch, the first thing to be noticed is the fact that the administration of this sacrament becomes

---

[276] *La Tradition Apostolique* (ed. B. Botte), n. 5, p. 34.
[277] See a similar blessing in Serapion of Thmuis, *Euchologion*, 17. J. Quasten, 66.
[278] *Epist.* 25, 8. MPL, 20: 560.
[279] Ed. H. Wilson, 70. This same prayer, with a slight rearrangement of parts, is contained in the Hadrian form of the Gregorian Sacramentary: Lietzmann, *Das Sacramentarium Gregorianum*, p. 45.
[280] *Supposit. epist.* 265, 2 of Augustine. MPL, 39: 2238.
[281] *Supposit. epist.* 279, 5 of Augustine. MPL, 39: 2273.
[282] *Expos. super Epist. Jacobi*, 5. MPL, 93: 39.
[283] MPL, 72: 574.
[284] XXXb, n. 11. Andrieu, *Les Ordines*, III, p. 468.

limited to priests; no longer do we find any mention of the faithful performing the anointing. Furthermore, because of ignorance [285] or lack of interest, Extreme Unction had fallen into disuse. There were even some who felt that when a person had led a good life, he had no need of this sacrament.[286] To combat this attitude, several decrees insisted on the importance of affording this help to the dying.[287] In particular the Council of Pavia in 850 instructed priests to teach the faithful the importance of the help which this sacrament offered to the person undergoing the trials and sufferings of death. It said that the effects of the sacrament are the remission of sin and the restoration of health.[288]

It is also apparent at this time that from a remedy for all sorts of bodily infirmities this sacrament was becoming more and more limited to a sacrament for the dying. By the time of St. Bonaventure, theologians generally held that it was to be conferred only towards the very end of life.[289] This is also the view of St. Thomas; it is to be given only when the sickness is serious enough to cause death.[290] And so by this time the proper name for the sacrament had become *extreme* anointing.

The earliest ritual that has come down to us for this sacrament is that of Theodulf of Orleans.[291] When compared to the various Ordos for administering the sacrament during the ninth and tenth centuries, this ritual is seen to be a type basic to all of them.[292] In these documents the number of anointings varied anywhere from five to twenty-four. Included therein were not only the five senses, but also the temples, the chest, the heart, between the shoulder blades, the places of greatest pain, the joints of the body, the loins, inside and outside the ears, on top and underneath the eyelids, at the top and at the very end of the nose.

The order of the ceremonies varied somewhat from document to document, yet substantially they followed this arrangement: (1) greeting, aspersion of the room with blessed water, (2) confession, (3) recitation of the seven penitential psalms and the Litany of the Saints, (4) profession of faith and the recitation of the Pater (5) anointing of the sick person, (6) the Kiss of Peace and Holy Viaticum.

[285] Cf. Jonas of Orleans, *De institut. laicali*, 3, 14. *MPL*, 106: 261.

[286] For instance, the monks of Corbie hesitated to give the sacrament to their abbot, Adalard, because they were certain that no sins would detain his soul: cf. Paschasius Radbertus, *Vita s. Adalardi*, 80. *MPL*, 120: 1547.

[287] *Capitulare*, 10 and 21. *MPL*, 97: 124, 220; Boniface, *Statuta*, IV, 29. *MPL*, 89: 823.

[288] Can. 8. Hefele-Leclercq, IV, 187. Trent adds: "when necessary for salvation," Denz. 909.

[289] *Comm. in Sent.*, IV, d. 23, a. 11: "numquam nisi in extremo adhibenda est."

[290] *Summa Theol.*, suppl., 32, 2.

[291] *Capitulare. MPL*, 105: 220-222.

[292] Cf. C. DeClercq, "Ordines unctionis infirmi des IXe et Xe siècles," *Ephemerides Liturgicae*, 44 (1930), 100-122.

When possible the sick person was carried to the church after his confession, and ashes as well as sackcloth were placed on him. During these ceremonies other priests or clerics recited the seven penitential psalms and the Litany of the Saints, as they stood around the body. Some Ordos have these prayers recited as one of the priests performs the anointings. According to some Ordos several priests performed the anointings, but it is not clear whether they took turns in repeating the same anointings or simply divided them according to their own number. The Creed and the Our Father were to be recited or sung by the sick person, when possible; when not, the priest did so for him.

The formulas used during the anointings in this epoch varied from long orations, brief optative (*indulgeat tibi Dominus*) and declarative (*Ungo te . . .*) forms to mixed ones. While many of the formulas explicitly invoke the three Persons of the Blessed Trinity, some of them are satisfied with a very general mention; still others are directed toward one or the other Person.

The order of the three sacraments, as seen in most of these documents, is the more ancient and traditional one, namely, Penance, Extreme Unction and Holy Viaticum. The true sacrament of the dying was the Viaticum, the food, so to speak, for the journey to eternity. It was only due to the theological speculation of the twelfth and thirteenth centuries, insisting on the administration of Extreme Unction at the very end of life, that there resulted an inversion of the traditional order. Thus the present Roman Ritual contains the unfortunate rubric: *postquam infirmus Viaticum sumpserit, inungatur a sacerdote.*[293] Modern national Rituals, however, are going back to the original disposition once again.

3. Modern ritual

According to the Ritual approved by Rome in 1954 for the United States, a special continuous rite is prescribed for cases when such a procedure is feasible. The ceremonies may be divided thus:

a) Greeting and aspersion of the sick person, by-standers, and room, followed by three orations. The first, *Introeat, Domine Jesu Christe, domum hanc . . . aeterna felicitas . . .*, is to be found in a ninth century Ordo.[294] The second, *Oremus et deprecamur*, is reported by *Ordo Romanus X*,[295] and the third, *Exaudi nos, Domine, sancte Pater, omnipotens aeterne Deus . . .*, forms part of an oration for the blessing of water in the Gelasian Sacramentary.[296]

b) Then follows the confession of the dying person, if he can and wants to make it. This, in turn, is followed by the Confiteor, Miserea-

[293] Tit. VI, cap. 1, n. 14.
[294] Cf. Righetti, IV, 241.
[295] N. 31. *MPL*, 78: 1020.
[296] Ed. H. Wilson, 286.

tur, Indulgentiam. If a person does make his confession at this point, the repetition of the Confiteor is a needless duplication. It is to be hoped that in future editions the recitation of it will either serve as a framework for the sick person's confession or be omitted when a sacramental confession takes place.

c) The Gospel concerning our Lord's curing the Centurion's son is read, in order to increase the faith of the sick person. And this is followed by a short litanic prayer begging God's grace and help for the dying person.

d) Here begins the ceremony of the anointing. First the priest places his right hand on the head of the person and pronounces an exorcism. Then, with the thumb of his right hand, he anoints, in the form of a cross, first the eyes, then the ears, nose, lips, hands and feet. When a priest is the recipient, the anointing is given on the back of his hands, since he has already been anointed on the palms at ordination. The formula used is the optative one: *"Per istam sanctam unctionem et suam piissimam misericordiam indulgeat tibi Dominus quidquid per visum [auditum, odoratum, gustum, tactum, gressum] deliquisti. Amen."* In case of imminent death or a great number of persons to be anointed immediately, the above form is to be pronounced without reference to particular senses, as the anointing is made on the forehead only. After each anointing the priest is to wipe with cotton the spot just anointed. After the last he is to wipe his thumb with salt or bread and then wash his hands.

e) The rite of Extreme Unction is concluded with a group of versicles and responses and three orations, the first of which is found for the first time in the Gregorian Sacramentary of the mixed type,[297] the second in the Hadrian book,[298] and the third in the Gelasian Sacramentary.[299]

4. Sacramentals connected with Extreme Unction

Commendation of the departing soul

Once the soul has been fortified with the three last sacraments, the Church does not leave the Christian to die alone. She stands by his side, in the person of the priest, and helps him to make even his very last moments in the Church Militant holy and sacred. Even as the choirs of angels accompany the soul to Paradise, so the Mystical Body gathers about the bed of the dying Christian and with her prayer affords him a steadfast means of support and encouragement in this most sacred event of life. Death is no small happening, neither is it a matter of purely individual concern. The Christian is a member of the Church in his dying moment just as much as he was in the full

[297] *MPL*, 78: 234.
[298] H. Wilson, *The Gregorian Sacramentary*, pp. 138 and 206.
[299] Ed. H. Wilson, 282.

bloom of life. Everything the Church has done for him in the past was meant to prepare him for the awe-inspiring day on which Christ, the Bridegroom of his soul, comes to take him up into eternal regions. Like a genuine mother, she helps him yield up his soul to God with joyful resignation, with a confidence based on faith, with a happiness sparked by the glorious hope of fulfillment. And the Church herself, with the satisfaction of a mother proud of her achievement, offers to God another product of her careful sanctifying hand. Though it is fraught with danger, this is truly the happiest moment of earthly life!

These ideas are brought out beautifully in many of the prayers of the *Commendatio animae*. The whole ritual, with very few exceptions, originated in the Gallican Rite. Though a group of prayers for this occasion figures in the Gelasian Sacramentary,[300] only the *Commendamus tibi, Domine* is of Roman origin. Of the rest, the litany for the dying seems to be the oldest component part of the Frankish material. It is often spoken of as customary in monasteries when one of the brethren lies dying.[301] The saints, then, are called to aid the dying person, to welcome him into their company as he leaves the Church Militant. Many of the other prayers date from Ordos of the eighth century.[302] But there are some of more recent origin. The oration *Commendo te omnipotenti Deo* is formed from the text of a letter of St. Peter Damian (d. 1072) written to a certain sick person.[303] The prayer *Delicta iuventutis* is not to be found in any of the medieval Ordos but appears in 1512 in the Benedictional of Meissen. The prayers to Mary and Joseph appear for the first time in the Roman Rituals of 1913 and 1922. Though the American Ritual omits a reading of the Passion according to St. John, it is part of the Roman Ritual and can be traced back as far as the ninth century *Ordo Romanus* XLIX.[303a] The three *Piae orationes* to our Lord figure in the Ritual of Paul V, while the Subvenite and the final oration, *Tibi, Domine, commendamus*, prescribed for the moment of death, appear in many Ordos of the ninth and tenth centuries.[304] Finally, Pope Benedict XIV in 1747 ordered that at the moment of death the Apostolic Blessing with a plenary indulgence be granted the dying person. Thus, more explicitly, the pope, as Vicar of Christ and visible Head of the Mystical Body, wants to assist at the death bed of each and everyone of his children.

[300] *Ibid.*, 299.

[301] We are told that in 704, when S. Austreberta, Abbess of Padilly, died, her sisters stood about her bed chanting various psalms and invoking the saints in litanic fashion: cf. L. Gougaud, "Etude sur les Ordines commendationis animae," *Eph. Lit.*, 49 (1935), 11.

[302] *Ibid.*, 12-15.

[303] *Epist.* 15. *MPL*, 144: 497-498.

[303a] N. 2. Andrieu, *Les Ordines*, IV, 529.

[304] For a full history of these prayers see L. Gougaud, *art. cit.*

Burial of the dead

Even after the soul has departed from the body, the Church demands that we treat the mortal remains with reverence, using this
as another occasion for asking God to deliver the soul from whatever
pains of punishment it may yet have to undergo for its entrance into
heaven and for the ultimate resurrection of the body. This ceremony,
too, be it noted, is fundamentally a joyous one. From St. Jerome we
learn that it was customary to sing Alleluias at funerals.[305] And this
was done in the same spirit as the above Commendation of the soul:
the glory of the resurrection was already being celebrated. The
Requiem Mass is filled with joyful thoughts of our immortal hope.
And the funeral service in the church is concluded with the singing of
the In Paradisum, calling upon the angels and martyrs to lead the
soul into the bosom of Abraham, the heavenly Jerusalem. The idea
immediately comes to mind that the soul, in its approach to heaven,
is re-living Christ's Ascension, at which the angelic hosts met Him and
led Him triumphantly into His Father's house.

From earliest times it has been the practice of the Church to
offer Mass for the departed soul. Thus Cyprian speaks of this as
an established practice, for in one of his letters the question is raised
of denying a Mass *pro dormitione* to certain persons.[306] Victor of
Vitensis also speaks of the Christian practice of burying the dead
amid the singing of hymns,[307] while the *Apostolic Constitutions* indicate that psalms were also sung as the body was carried to the cemetery, Mass being offered for the dead both in the churches and
cemeteries.[308]

We must wait until the tenth century, in the Missal of Rathold,
before we come upon anything closely resembling our present rites for
burial.[309] There, after the body is washed (certain prayers were even
prescribed for this), it is carried to the church as the responsory
Subvenite is sung. Upon entering the church, the funeral cortege
sings the Miserere with the antiphon *Requiem*. Mass is then offered
for the departed soul.[310] After Mass the celebrant approaches the
coffin and begins the oration *Non intres*. The responsory Subvenite is
again sung. Kyrie eleison, Christe eleison, Kyrie eleison follow with
the oration *Deus cui omnia vivunt*. Another responsory is sung: *Ante-
quam nascerer novisti me*, and it is followed by the Kyrie and oration
Fac quaesumus. After this come the Pater, Requiem aeternam, *A
porta inferi* and the oration *Inclina, Domine, aurem tuam*. As the
corpse is removed from the church, the antiphon *Aperite illi portas*

[305] *Epist.* 77, 11. *MPL*, 22: 697.
[306] *Epist.* 66, 2. *MPL*, 4:411.
[307] *De persec. Vandalica*, I, 5; II, 11. *MPL*, 58: 187, 212.
[308] VI, 30. *MPG*, 1: 987-990.
[309] *MPL*, 78:469-470.
[310] Note that the Preface for the Requiem Mass used in Rathold's Missal
is almost the same as ours.

iustitiae is sung together with Psalm 117. At the grave three series of antiphon-psalm-oration are sung. Finally, a capitulum, the Miserere, Requiem aeternam, the oration *Absolve, Domine* and *Requiescat in pace* conclude the service.[311]

As can be seen, this ritual described by Rathold is basically the same procedure followed today; we need mention only the differences. Instead of repeating the responsory, Subvenite, today we sing another, the Libera, which is to be found in the tenth century Antiphonary of Hartker.[312] While Rathold mentions no incensation of the corpse, the ritual for burial contained in the Roman Pontifical of the twelfth century places such an incensation at the very beginning of the service of absolution after Mass, but there the celebrant incenses the altar first.[313] Today, as the body is borne out of the church, the antiphon In Paradisum is sung. The first part of this antiphon very probably comes from the acts of the martyr S. Euplus, not later than the fifth century,[314] while the second part, *Chorus angelorum*, certainly depends on a similar antiphon found in Rathold.[315] The canticle Benedictus with the antiphon *Ego sum resurrectio* is sung on the way to the cemetery. This, according to Righetti, comes from an older custom of singing Lauds of the Office of the Dead separately from Matins and after the Requiem Mass.[316]

F. Holy Orders

1. Theological summary

The word "ordo" can be taken in a general sense as meaning "class." Thus we have two general classes within the Church: clerics and laymen. In fact, we find Tertullian occasionally using the word in this sense, for he speaks of the ecclesiastical or sacerdotal order [317] as contrasted with the order of the laity. "Ordo" can also be understood as the ritual by which a person attains a different station and power within the Church. For this sense, however, Latins have traditionally employed the term *ordinatio*.[318]

Though we do not propose to go into the theology of the sacrament of Holy Orders, a simple résumé of the conclusions of theology will help to explain the historical evolution of both the number of Orders as well as the ritual by which they are conferred. Holy Orders is a true sacrament instituted by Christ Himself by which the

---

[311] Cf. also the eleventh century papal burial service in *Ord. Rom.* X, nn. 36-40. *MPL,* 78: 1023-1026.
[312] See cut in F. Cabrol, "Absoute," *DACL,* I, between col. 204-205.
[313] N. 16. M. Andrieu, *Le Pontifical Romain,* I, 282.
[314] Cf. M. Righetti, IV, 342.
[315] *MPL,* 78: 169.
[316] *Op. cit.,* IV, 342; cf. the Roman Pontifical of the thirteenth century: Andrieu, *Le Pontifical Romain,* II, 510, n. 21.
[317] *De exhortatione ad castit.,* 7. *MPL,* 2:971; *De idololatria,* 7. *MPL,* 1:745.
[318] Cf. Tertullian, *De praescriptione haer.,* 41. *MPL,* 2:68.

character or spiritual power to confect the Eucharist and other sacraments is conferred.[319] It is also defined that by divine ordination there exists in the Church a sacred hierarchy which consists of bishops, priests, and ministers.[320] It is certain that bishops (Apostles), priests, and deacons already existed in apostolic times,[321] but that the subdiaconate and minor orders are of ecclesiastical origin. While some deny that the subdiaconate and minor orders possess the nature of a sacrament, others hold that in their fount, the diaconate, they enjoy this quality; that the Church, in other words, was given the power to divide the diaconate into various inferior grades.[322] These are to be considered as potential parts of the sacrament of Orders.

It is to be noted that the Council of Trent does not number the episcopate among the seven orders.[323] Similarly the Council of Benevento in 1091 speaks only of the priesthood and diaconate as belonging to the *sacros ordines—sacros* here understood as major orders.[324] This gives rise to a discussion among theologians as to whether the episcopate is to be called an order or a sacrament, whether, in other words, it is distinct from the priesthood, whether espiscopal consecration confers a special and distinct character. St. Thomas[325] makes a distinction between order as a sacrament and an office. Since order as a sacrament specifically has to do with the confection of the Eucharist, he does not consider the episcopate a sacrament, because the bishop has no power over the Eucharist superior to that of a priest. It is, however, an order in the sense that the bishop receives added and superior powers over the Mystical Body.[326] Therefore, just as the subdiaconate and minor orders are potential parts, or participations in the diaconate, so the episcopate is the complement, the extension of the priesthood. Tonsure, on the other hand, is considered by no one as an order; it is simply an ecclesiastical ceremony of initiation into the ranks of the clergy.

2. Origin of the various grades of the Hierarchy

As we have already seen, the episcopate, priesthood, and diaconate existed in apostolic times. Admittedly it took time for the distinction between presbyters and bishops to be clearly expressed. At first various local churches were governed by a presbyteral college, and it is not always very explicitly set down in the ancient documents whether

[319] Council of Trent, Sess. xxiii, cap. 3, and canons 1 and 3. Denz. 959, 961, 963.

[320] *Ibid.*, can. 6. Denz. 966.

[321] Acts 6:1-6; 15:6. Timothy seems to have been a bishop: cf. 1 Tim. 5:22.

[322] St. Thomas, *Summa Theol.*, suppl., 37, 2 ad 2; R. Garrigou-Lagrange, *Eucharistia* (Rome: Marietti, 1946), Tract. de Ordine, pp. 410-411.

[323] Denz. 958.

[324] Can. 1. Denz. 356.

[325] *Summa Theol.*, suppl., 40, 5.

[326] Cf. R. Garrigou-Lagrange, *op. cit.*, 411-412.

this college as such governed or whether the presbyters were more or less like an advisory board for the bishop. But from the second century on,[327] the monarchical type of government is very clearly attested to, one wherein the bishop presides in the place of God, the priests in the likeness of the apostolic college, and the deacons as servants or ministers of Jesus Christ.[328]

In the third century we find clear-cut evidence in the writings of Cyprian for the subdiaconate,[329] and for the orders of exorcist [330] and lector.[331] Later, between 251 and 253, Pope Cornelius writes to Fabius about a locality in which there were one bishop, forty-six priests, seven deacons, seven subdeacons, forty-two acolytes, and fifty-two exorcists, lectors, and porters.[332] These various orders were truly functional. They originated for the precise purpose of having specially suited men available to perform the various duties connected with the administration of the sacraments and the good of the Church. And it was customary for each church, so far as possible, to possess its own group of clerics of various grades. This is certainly to be inferred from Gregory the Great's anxiety that churches have a priest and at least a deacon.[333] And this practice was still in force, or at least urged, in the ninth and tenth centuries, for the Admonitio Synodalis prescribes that every priest have a cleric, or at least a school boy, to assist him at the celebration of Mass,[334] and Remigius of Auxerre complains that a priest without a deacon is a priest in name only.[335] In fact, young men remained in a given order for long periods of time; some had no intention of going higher in the ecclesiastical hierarchy. With the establishment of seminaries in conformity with the decrees of the Council of Trent, these minor orders became nothing more than remnants of the past and were considered as so many steps on the way to the priesthood. Today, canon law lays it down as a requirement for anyone receiving tonsure to have the intention of ascending to the priesthood.[336]

3. Dates for ordinations

Present Church law specifies the days of the year on which ordinations may take place.[337] Episcopal consecrations are to be conferred on Sundays and feast days of the Apostles. Ordination to major orders

---

[327] Cf. Ignatius of Antioch, Epist. ad Magnes., VI. MPG, 5: 667.
[328] See the excellent work of William Moran, The Government of the Church in the First Century. New York: Benziger Bros., circa 1905.
[329] Epist. 3, 1; Epist. 24. MPL, 4: 234, 293.
[330] Epist. 16. MPL, 4: 276.
[331] Epist. 16; Epist. 24. MPL, 4: 276, 293.
[332] Eusebius, Hist. eccl., VI, 43, 11-12. GCS, 9 (2), p. 619.
[333] Epist. lib. I, 15; 78; Epist. lib. II, 43. MPL, 77: 461, 532, 581.
[334] MPL, 132: 456.
[335] De div. off., 40. MPL, 101: 1247.
[336] Can. 973, #1.
[337] Can. 1006.

must take place on the Saturdays of the four Ember Weeks, the Saturday before Passion Sunday, and during the Easter Vigil. However, for any sufficiently grave reason a bishop may ordain on any Sunday or holyday of obligation. Minor orders may be conferred on Sundays and feasts that are doubles. Tonsure may be given on any day and at any hour.

Actually Sunday was the original day for ordinations, as far as can be determined. Hippolytus, in the third century, specifies this day for the consecration of bishops.[338] In the fifth century St. Leo insists that priestly and episcopal (as well as diaconal) ordinations be conferred during the weekly vigils starting on the eve of Sundays. In effect, the ordinations were held on Sundays: *mane ipso die dominico*.[339] Since such vigils were regularly held throughout the year on Ember Saturday evenings, Pope Gelasius I determined that ordinations should take place on these occasions and also on the median week-end of Lent, the eve of Passion Sunday.[340] Several popes followed this same disposition.[341] The reason for placing the ordinations during the Ember Saturday Vigils was because the faithful assisted at them in great number, and, as the author of the *Liber Pontificalis* reports, the Church wanted promotion to sacred orders to be a public thing, something in which the community as a whole could take part and, as the party very much concerned and affected, approve.[342]

It has always been the custom to confer major and minor orders during the celebration of Mass. The tradition has not been equally constant as to when during the Mass the various orders should be given. Our first witness in this matter is an eighth century Roman Ordo, written in Rome but, it seems, for use in Gaul.[343] The ordination of priests and deacons took place after the Gradual of the Mass,[344] while that of the subdeacon and minor orders occurred before Communion.[345] When we come to the tenth century Romano-Germanic Pontifical we notice that all the ordination rites for minor orders and the subdiaconate are grouped together *before* those of the diaconate and priesthood. From this the custom grew up of conferring all orders one after the other, before the Alleluia verse or the last verse of the Tract.[346] The Pontifical of Durand, however, has the various orders con-

---

[338] *La Tradition Apostolique* (ed. B. Botte), n. 2, p. 27.
[339] *Epist.* 9 *ad Dioscorum*, 1; *Epist.* 10 *ad episc. Vienne*, 6; *Epist.* 6 *ad Anastasium*, 6; *Epist.* 111 *ad Marcion. Aug.*, 2. MPL, 54: 625, 634, 620, 1021.
[340] *Epist.* 9 *ad episc. Lucaniae*, 11. MPL, 59: 52.
[341] Pelagius I, *Epist. ad Laurentium.* MPL, 69:416; Gregory II, *Epist.* IV. MPL, 89:502; Zachary, *Epist.* 13 *ad Bonifacium.* MPL, 89:952; *Liber Diurnus Romanorum Pontificum*, tit. IX, 6. MPL, 105: 75-76.
[342] Ed. L. Duchesne, I, 139.
[343] *Ord. Rom.* XXXIV. Andrieu, *Les Ordines*, III, 594-595.
[344] N. 5, 11, pp. 605, 606.
[345] N. 2, 3, pp. 603, 604.
[346] Cf. the thirteenth century Roman Pontifical, n. IV. Andrieu, *Le Pontifical Romain*, II, 329.

ferred with a lesson, responsory, or oration intervening.[347] Of course, on Ember Saturdays, according to our present Pontifical, the various orders are to be given after the reading of the appropriate lesson of the Mass.

4. Evolution of the ritual

Tonsure

The wearing of the hair short or completely cut off is not a specifically Christian practice, nor one specially indicative of the clerical state. In antiquity it was customary to mark slaves in this way, and in some Hellenic cities and among Jews adolescents offered their hair to the deity of their choice as a sign of dedication.[348] The same idea, basically, is implied in Acts 18:18, where it is stated that Paul had his head shaved because of a vow. Later it was considered a mark of religious devotion among Christians in the East.[349] Although St. Jerome discourages the practice of completely shaving the head because it smacked too much of a custom in vogue among heathen priests, he says that clerics ought not wear their hair too long, as the rich do.[350] Also from him, we learn that virgins cut their hair too, but he seems to say that this was mainly a question of corporal cleanliness.[351]

The *Liber Pontificalis* informs us that Pope Benedict II (d. 685) received locks of hair from the Emperor Constantine Pogonatus' sons, Justinian and Heraclius.[352] The Emperor did this as a sign of submission; by accepting them the pope was understood to have figuratively adopted the Emperor's sons. A century later—again our informant is the *Liber Pontificalis*[353]—the people of Spoleto went to Rome and were tonsured according to Roman custom in token of their dependence on the pope. As early as the fifth century, however, we have evidence that a special tonsure was worn by clerics.[354] And in 633 the Fourth Council of Toledo made the wearing of the tonsure obligatory on all clerics.[355]

Up until the eighth and ninth centuries there were three types of tonsure. The crown tonsure, called the tonsure of St. Peter,[356] con-

---

[347] *Ibid.*, III, p. 339-340. De Puniet claims that this procedure is already to be found in the Gallican Church of the ninth century: *Le Pontifical Romain*, I (Paris: Desclée, 1930), 137; cf. The mixed Gregorian annotated by H. Ménard in *MPL*, 78: 475, note 685.

[348] Cf. H. Lesêtre "Nazaréat," *Dictionnaire de la Bible*, IV, 1516; Numbers 6:18.

[349] Socrates, *Hist. eccl.*, III, 1. *MPG*, 67: 371.

[350] *Comm. in Ezechielem*, 44, 20. *MPL*, 25: 437.

[351] *Epist.* 147, 5. *MPL*, 22: 1199.

[352] Ed. L. Duchesne, I, 363, 364 note 5.

[353] *Ibid.*, I, 495; cf. 420.

[354] Gregory of Tours, *De vitis patrum*, 17, 1. *MPL*, 71: 1078.

[355] Can. 41. Hefele-Leclercq, III, 272.

[356] Gregory of Tours, *De gloria martyrum*, 28. *MPL*, 71: 728.

sisted in shaving the entire head except for a small ring or *corona* of hair that was left encircling the head. A second type seems to have been prevalent among monks, especially the Greeks, according to which the hair was simply cut close all over the head.[357] And this was called the tonsure of St. Paul. Lastly there was the Gallican and Celtic practice of shaving only the front part of the head, from ear to ear, and letting the hair on the remainder of the head grow long.[358] However, in the decrees of the above-mentioned Council of Toledo an abuse is already singled out whereby certain Gallican clerics shaved only a small circle atop the head. It was this, in the long run, which won out and is still worn in countries where the rules of tonsure are observed. Members of the older religious Orders, however, remain faithful to the tonsure of St. Peter.

There is no evidence for a *ceremony* of tonsure until the eighth century. Apparently up until that time a person was simply enrolled as a member of the clergy and began to wear the tonsure. But in the eighth century Gelasian manuscripts—all Gallican—a well developed rite appears.[359] This same rite was subsequently appended to the Gregorian Sacramentary by Alcuin in the ninth century.[360] It opens with an invitation to the faithful to pray that the Holy Spirit will descend upon the new cleric who offers up his hair out of love and accepts the habit of religion. As the prelate cuts the hair of the candidate, the antiphon, *Tu es, Domine, qui restitues haereditatem meam mihi*, together with the response, *Hic accipiet benedictionem*, etc., and another antiphon, *Haec est generatio*, with the same response, are sung. After the person has been tonsured, the prelate concludes the ceremony with the oration, *Praesta omnipotens Deus*. These few formulas have been handed on till our own day with a slight change in order. The giving of the surplice to the newly tonsured cleric appears for the first time in the Pontifical of Durand at the end of the thirteenth century.[361]

The symbolism of the whole ceremony of tonsure, prayers and actions combined, shows admirably the parallel between the cleric and the religious. Just as the religious at his profession renounces the world and promises to follow Christ, so the cleric is taught that he must renounce the world, symbolized by the cutting of hair, and look to Christ as his true inheritance, *Dominus pars hereditatis meae*. This is the very meaning of the word *clerus*: part, share, or lot. The cleric is one whose part in the life of the Church is apostolic and liturgical service, one whose lot is God Himself. Though we find no trace

---

[357] Bede, *Historia eccl. angl.*, IV, 1. *MPL*, 95: 172.

[358] Cf. Smith, *De tonsura clericorum*, *MPL*, 95: 327-332; L. Gougaud, "Celtiques," *DACL*, II, 2997.

[359] For complete texts see P. De Puniet, *Le Pontifical Romain*, I, *Appendix* I, pp. 282-283.

[360] Cf. H. Wilson, *The Gregorian Sacramentary*, n. LV, pp. 182-183.

[361] M. Andrieu, *Le Pontifical Romain*, III, 337.

of the tonsure ceremony in the fourth century, nevertheless, St. Jerome, commenting on the fifth verse of Psalm 15—"The Lord is the portion of my inheritance and of my cup; it is thou who holdest my lot"—says that from the moment he enlists in the ranks of the clergy, renunciation is the daily lot of the cleric and he must possess nothing outside of God.[362]

Minor Orders

The ritual for each of the Minor Orders: porter, lector, exorcist and acolyte, is very simple and comprises three parts: (1) an admonition concerning the duties of the order, (2) the handing over of the instruments proper to it together with a formula indicating the instruments' proper powers, (3) concluding prayers asking the blessing of God on the newly-ordained.

As it stands today this ritual can be traced back to the Pontifical of Durand at the end of the thirteenth century.[363] In the development of these ceremonies, however, the only role that Durand played was to enlarge the admonition opening each ordination. The basic one-sentence statement of the duties of each order was handed down through the service books of centuries and is found in its most primitive form, at least for the ordination of porters,[364] in the *Statuta Ecclesiae Antiqua* composed about 500.

Our present matter and form—the handing over of the instruments with the accompanying formula—are found for the first time in the same *Statuta*.[365] The only early Roman witness to the ordination of lectors is found in a Coptic version of Hippolytus' *Apostolic Tradition*,[366] where it is stated that the bishop simply gives the book of lessons to the lector. Later, in an eighth century Ordo for lectors, the pope gives a book to the young candidate, hears him sing and, if pleased, gives him a blessing which places him among the Church's lectors.[367] There is also another Roman Ordo,[368] dating from the same period, which contains, among other things, a rite for ordaining acolytes in Rome. According to it, the candidate is given a sack (in which particles of the Sacred Host intended for distribution at Communion time were carried), and the pope recites practically the same formula as for lectors.

[362] *Epist.* 52 *ad Nepotianum, de vita clericorum,* 5. *MPL,* 22: 531.
[363] M. Andrieu, *Le Pontifical Romain,* III, 340-347.
[364] See the rubric regarding this order, n. 9. Andrieu, *Les Ordines,* III, 618. The admonition for the order of Acolyte is called for, but the text is not given: n. 6. *Ibid.* That for the Lector has been taken from the *Praefatio* preceding the final oration for this order contained in the eighth century Gelasian: see H. Wilson, p. 147, and comments on the origin of these formulas by A. Chavasse, *Le sacramentaire Gélasien,* p. 12.
[365] Nn. 6-9. Andrieu, *Les Ordines,* III, 618.
[366] Ed. B. Botte, n. 12, p. 43.
[367] See text in *Ord. Rom.* XXXV, n. 4. Andrieu, *Les Ordines,* IV, 33-34.
[368] XXXIV, n. 2. Andrieu, *Les Ordines,* III, 603.

Apart from these three documents, two for lectors, one for aco-lytes, we have no idea how Minor Orders were conferred in Rome; the rites we possess today have all passed through non-Roman hands, and the suspicion is justified that the non-Roman areas either already had their own rites or substituted new ones for the Roman. It is not altogether impossible that the pure Roman genius was quite content with a simple nomination of young men to these posts.[369]

The ordination to each Order today is concluded by means of a series of prayers. Rubrics in our present Pontifical indicate that these prayers are to be used as blessings, for crosses appear in the text—they are found there as early as the twelfth century.[370] Actually the first so-called blessing is simply an invitation to the faithful to pray for the newly-ordained. This is followed by *Oremus, flectamus genua, Levate*, and a formal oration, or blessing. As a matter of fact, this so-called first blessing was called "praefatio" in all documents from the Gelasian Sacramentary [371] to the Pontifical of Durand.[372] It is not known exactly when the Preface came to be used as a blessing too. However, even in the Gelasian Sacramentary an oration can be seen in it, for it ends with *Per Dominum*, etc. If the entire arrangement were used according to its true spirit, both the *Per Dominum* and the sign of the cross would be dropped from the invitatory Preface. In other words, this Preface would be used as an exhortation to the by-standers to pray for the newly-ordained, just as with the Preface con-tained in the long list of Solemn Orations on Good Friday. The very meaning and sentence structure of this first part demands such a treatment. The following, taken from the ordination of lectors, will illustrate what we mean:

> Oremus, fratres charissimi, Deum Patrem omnipotentum, ut super hunc famulum suum, quem in ordinem Lectorum dignatur assumere, benedictionem [our present text has a cross indicated here] suam clementer effundat; quatenus **legat** distincte quae in Ecclesia Dei legenda sunt, et eadem operibus impleat. [Present text has Per Dominum, etc. at this point.] Oremus; Flectamus genua ! Levate !
>
> Domine, sancte Pater, omnipotens aeterne Deus, bene-dicere [cross indicated here] dignare hunc famulum tuum in officium Lectoris: ut assiduitate Lectionum instructus sit atque ordinatus, et agenda dicat, et dicta opere impleat, ut in utroque sanctae Ecclesiae exemplo sanctitatis suae con-sultat. Per Dominum.

[369] For this whole matter see M. Andrieu, "Les ordres mineurs dans l'ancien rit romain," *Revue des Sciences ecclésiastiques*, V (Strasbourg, 1925), 232-274.

[370] Cf. Andrieu, *Le Pontifical Romain*, I, 125-127.

[371] Ed. H. Wilson, 147.

[372] Andrieu, *Le Pontifical Romain*, III, 341-347.

It is to be noted again that these orations, even though they appear in the Gelasian Sacramentary, do not belong to the purely Roman ritual for ordination. They were part of the ritual only in Gallican lands. This seems to be the significance of a rubric contained in the *Ord. Rom.* XXXV [373] for the ordination of a lector. According to it, the pope uses the commonplace formula already referred to, while bishops in other provinces were to use formulas identical or similar to the one in use today in our Pontifical.

The Subdiaconate

The present ritual for ordaining subdeacons consists of the following: (1) calling them forth and indicating the canonical title of their ordination, (2) a preliminary admonition regarding the obligation of celibacy about to be contracted, (3) the Litany of the Saints, (4) an admonition concerning their liturgical duties, (5) the tradition, or handing over, of the instruments—an empty chalice with paten (accompanied by a formula spoken by the bishop), after which the archdeacon has the candidates touch cruets filled with water and wine, (6) a blessing, (7) the dressing with their proper vestments—amice, maniple and tunic, (8) the giving of the book of Epistles.

This involved ceremony is of late origin. Until the latter part of the twelfth century the ritual for the ordination of subdeacons was almost like that for Minor Orders. The change that occurred had as its obvious purpose to give more dignity to the subdiaconate by having the ceremonial imitate that for the diaconate, for only during this period did the subdiaconate come to be considered a major order. As late as 1091 the Council of Benevento counted only the diaconate and priesthood as *ordines sacros.*[374] A century later, however, Peter the Chanter said that the subdiaconate had only recently been placed among the major orders.[375]

It is not difficult to trace the evolution of the rites pertaining to this order. The documents containing the rites can be roughly divided into (1) early Roman, (2) Gallican, (3) later Gallican-Roman.

1. *Early Roman.* According to the *Apostolic Tradition* of Hippolytus, the subdeacon "received no imposition of hands; he was simply *nominated* to assist the deacon." [376] In the sixth century the Roman deacon John testifies to a ritual consisting of the delivery of the empty chalice.[377] Lastly, the eighth century *Ordo Romanus* XXXIV states that after the candidate had taken an oath that he had not committed any of the four crimes which would prohibit his ordination,[378] the

---

[373] N. 6. Andrieu, *Les Ordines,* IV, 34.
[374] Denz. 356.
[375] *Verbum abbreviatum,* 60, MPL, 205: 184.
[376] Ed. B. Botte, n. 14, p. 43.
[377] *Epist. ad Senarium,* 10. MPL, 59: 405.
[378] Sodomy, attempt against the virtue of a consecrated virgin, bestiality, or adultery: n. 16. Andrieu, *Les Ordines,* III, 607.

chalice was then handed to him and he received the same blessing as the acolytes.[379]

2. *Gallican.* With the sixth century *Statuta Ecclesiae Antiqua*, in addition to the delivery of the empty chalice and paten, we come upon the delivery of the cruet with water and towel, the last items given by the archdeacon.[380] The formula spoken by the bishop as he hands the subdeacon the chalice and paten is first attested to in the *Missale Francorum*, which dates from the beginning of the eighth century.[381] But there it appears in a much enlarged state, the central portion of which was later to become the main part of the admonition concerning the subdeacon's liturgical duties, composed by Durand in the last part of the thirteenth century. It also, for the first time, provides the blessing with its Preface. In the tenth century Romano-Germanic Pontifical we find the rite somewhat evolved.[382] There is, first of all, the one-sentence statement of the subdeacon's liturgical duties. Thereupon follow the delivery of the chalice and paten with our present formula. The other piece figuring as the central portion of the formula of the *Missale Francorum* now appears separated from the formula for the delivery of the chalice. The rite concludes with the invitatory Preface and blessing.

3. *Gallican-Roman.* It was mainly through the tenth century Romano-Germanic Pontifical that most of the above described Gallican rites found their way to Rome. They were first taken up by the twelfth century papal Pontifical. In this latter document all the rites are the same as in the Romano-Germanic Pontifical, except that the longer formula for the delivery of the chalice reappears from the *Missale Francorum*.[383] While all of the above rites remain in the thirteenth century papal Pontifical, the formula for the delivery of the chalice is abbreviated. In some of the late thirteenth century manuscripts of this service book we also find the investiture with the insignia proper to the subdeacon.[384] This fact establishes the supposition that it was really Durand who introduced this rite into the ordination of subdeacons, for in his own Pontifical these ceremonies appear exactly as they are today.[385] Later scribes simply inserted parts of Durand's rite within the framework of the earlier Pontificals. We have just said that Durand's rite is the same as ours. This is true with one singular exception: the preliminary admonition regarding the obligation of celibacy is lacking. This, then, is posterior to Durand's work. The elements of the ordination to the subdiaconate which we owe specifically to Durand are the following: he composed our present instruc-

[379] N. 3. *Ibid.*, III, 604.
[380] N. 5. *Ibid.*, III, 618.
[381] K. Mohlberg, *Missale Francorum* (Rome, Herder, 1957), n. 6, p. 5.
[382] Andrieu, *Le Pontifical Romain*, I, 128-129, footnotes.
[383] *Ibid.*, I, 129, n. 3.
[384] *Ibid.*, II, 335-336.
[385] *Ibid.*, III, 349-358.

tion concerning the Subdeacon's liturgical duties; it was he who either invented or popularized the investiture ceremony, that is, the giving of the amice, maniple, and tunic; it was also he who advanced the chanting of the Litany of the Saints so as to include the candidates for the subdiaconate (it was already in existence for deacons and priests) and invented the delivery of the Epistolary.[386]

The Diaconate

While the matter and form of the preceding Orders consisted in the delivery of the instruments proper to the office and the accompanying words, the essential rite of the diaconate and priesthood has always been the imposition of hands with the qualifying words. This was the simple rite handed down by the Apostles; all other ceremonies were added in time by the Church. From the ninth century on, it became customary to hand the candidate for the priesthood a chalice with water and wine together with the paten upon which lay a host; and to the candidate for the diaconate the book of the Gospels. Subsequent theologians began to discuss whether such a ceremony was necessary for the validity of the ordination. There were some who claimed that the delivery of the instruments proper to the priesthood and diaconate constituted the essential matter of the sacrament; e.g.: St. Thomas,[387] Capreolus, Dominicus Soto, Vasquez, Gonet, etc.[388] But an ever increasing number of theologians who were acquainted with the historical origins of the *traditio instrumentorum* saw a great difficulty in this position. Finally, in 1947 Pope Pius XII, in his apostolic constitution, *Sacramentum Ordinis*,[389] authoritatively declared that only the imposition of hands together with the consecratory Preface (specifically the words: "Emitte in eum, quaesumus, Domine, Spiritum Sanctum quo in opus ministerii . . ." for the diaconate) constituted the essential matter and form of ordination.

The present rite for the ordination of deacons comprises the following ceremonies: (1) presentation of candidates by the archdeacon and their election by the bishop, (2) instruction concerning the liturgical duties of deacons, (3) Litany of the Saints, if it has not already been sung during the previous ordination of subdeacons, 4) two short invitatory Prefaces: *Commune votum* and *Oremus, fratres charissimi*, (5) the consecratory Preface with the imposition of the right hand of the bishop on the heads of the candidates (the sacramental form being only spoken, not sung), (6) investiture with diaconal stole

---

[386] It is true that this last ceremony appears in some of the later manuscripts of the thirteenth century papal Pontifical, but they seem to depend on Durand's book for this.

[387] *Summa Theol.*, suppl., 37, 5.

[388] Cf. R. Garrigou-Lagrange, *Eucharistia* (Rome: Marietti, 1946), "De Ordine," p. 413.

[389] *AAS*, 40 (1948), 5-7.

and dalmatic, (7) delivery of the Gospel book, (8) *Oremus; flectamus genua*, and two orations that conclude the rite.

1. The first allusion to the public election of the deacon is to be found in the Gelasian Sacramentary,[390] but this is definitely a Gallican interpolation.[391] It was formerly the custom that the people of the locality actually chose their clergy. In the announcement made by the bishop, as contained in this service book, the people are still given a voice in this election, albeit a negative one: they are asked if they have anything against the persons nominated by the bishop. The *Missale Francorum* contains a similar formula, announcing the bishop's choice but inviting the people's consent, though the wording is much different.[392] In the mixed forms of the Gregorian Sacramentary coming from the ninth century the candidates are first presented by the archdeacon, who then testifies to their character. The bishop then elects them but invites the people's consent.[393] It is this procedure that was followed by all subsequent Pontificals, including our own.

2. Just as the instructions for the Minor Orders and the subdiaconate, so the one attached to the ordination of deacons was composed by Durand.[394] In it the bishop unfolds once again for the candidate all the duties which will be his as a deacon. In first place comes his role of assisting the celebrant at Mass. As the Pontifical says, it is the deacon's duty to minister at the altar, to baptize, and to preach. As his model the deacon is given the tribe of Levi and Stephen the Protomartyr.

3. The Litany of the Saints is called for in the rubrics of an Ordo that was inserted into the Gelasian book [395] by Gallican hands. Litanic prayer is a very easy and popular style of communal devotion. Thus it is an apt instrument to emphasize the truly public character of the ordination of the Church's higher ministers. All are able to join in and beg heaven's grace for those who are empowered to dispense the sacraments to the faithful.

4. The first of the two invitatory Prefaces immediately following the Litany of the Saints can be found in the Gelasian Sacramentary,[396] but there its role is that of the final conclusion to the whole ordination ceremony for deacons. We find it in this position only there and in the *Missale Francorum*.[397] Hence, Andrieu's suspicion that its appearance in the Gelasian book is due to a Gallican interpolation certainly seems valid.[398] Its present position in the Roman Pontifical really serves

---

[390] Ed. H. Wilson, p. 22, n. XX.
[391] Cf. A. Chavasse, *Le sacramentaire Gélasien*, pp. 22-27.
[392] Ed. K. Mohlberg, n. 7, p. 6.
[393] E.g., *MPL*, 78: 221.
[394] Andrieu, *Le Pontifical Romain*, III, 359-361.
[395] Ed. H. Wilson, p. 22, n. XX.
[396] *Ibid.*, 28, n. XXIII.
[397] Ed. K. Mohlberg, n. 7, p. 7.
[398] *Les Ordines*, III, 558, note 4. A. Chavasse also shares this view: *Le sacramentaire Gélasien*, p. 12.

no purpose, since it is a duplication of the traditional invitatory form, *Oremus, fratres charissimi*, which, in this case, actually follows it. The more traditional invitatory is found already in the so-called Leonine Sacramentary.[399] The present formulation of this invitatory combines the original formula of the Leonine with an oration which precedes it in the same Sacramentary; later, in the Gelasian, this oration serves as the conclusion to the invitatory.[400] It is first found in this combined form in the *Missale Francorum*.[401]

5. The consecratory Preface has been a constant in all the liturgical books of the West. It is first reported in the Leonine book.[402] Though the *Apostolic Tradition* of Hippolytus does not employ this long Preface type of consecratory prayer, the prayer actually contained therein bears exactly the same sense as the essential words of our present formula.[403] It would seem that Durand was the first to give this formula the usual Preface introduction, and it was he who called for the singing of the formula in the Preface tone. It was also he who introduced within this Preface the words *Accipe Spiritum Sanctum*. This phrase, he indicated, was to be spoken, not sung.[404] Recently the Congregation of Rites added the rubric that the essential words, *Emitte in eum, quaesumus, Domine*, etc., were simply to be spoken, in order to bring out their character as the sacramental form.[405]

6. No special ceremony of investiture with the diaconal stole is found until the ninth century.[406] We find the investiture with the dalmatic for the first time in the tenth century *Ordo Romanus* XXXV.[407]

7. Delivery of the Gospel book appears in the tenth century Romano-Germanic Pontifical.[408] However, De Puniet claims that there is evidence for this rite in England in the ninth century.[409]

8. Our present ritual concludes with two orations. The first is really the blessing which, for all other Orders, follows immediately upon the invitatory Preface. The prayer in its present form is found in the Hadrian Sacramentary,[410] but it is only a re-formulation of an oration already appearing in this role in the Leonine Sacramentary.[411] This unusual separation from its proper invitatory is found for the

[399] K. Mohlberg, *Sacramentarium Veronense*, n. 949, p. 120.
[400] Ed. H. Wilson, n. XXII, p. 26.
[401] Ed. K. Mohlberg, n. 7, p. 6.
[402] *Sacramentarium Veronense*, n. 951, pp. 120-121.
[403] Ed. B. Botte, n. 9, pp. 39-41.
[404] M. Andrieu, *Le Pontifical Romain*, III, 361, n. 9 (and notes), n. 10.
[405] Feb. 20, 1950. *Eph. Lit.*, 64 (1950), 284.
[406] Amalar, *De eccl. off.*, II, 20. MPL, 105: 1096; see also the tenth century Romano-Germanic Pontifical: Andrieu, *Le Pontifical Romain*, I, 133 note.
[407] N. 26. Andrieu, *Les Ordines*, IV, 38.
[408] Andrieu, *Le Pontifical Romain*, I, 133.
[409] *Le Pontifical Romain*, I, 188.
[410] H. Lietzmann, *Das Sacramentarium Gregorianum*, p. 7; M. Andrieu, *Les Ordines*, III, 559.
[411] *Sacramentarium Veronense*, n. 950, p. 120.

first time in the twelfth century papal Pontifical.[412] And the final prayer, *Domine, sancte Pater, fidei spei et gratiae,* is found in the Gelasian
in this very same position [413] but is really a Gallican interpolation.
Through it the Church begs Almighty God once again that the same
grace and virtues which moved the very first deacons will fill the
life of these newly-ordained members of the same order.

The Priesthood

The primitive rite for the transmission of the priestly power is
spoken of by St. Paul when he tells Timothy not to neglect "the grace
that is in thee, granted to thee by reason of prophecy with the *laying
on of hands* of the presbyterate." [414] It is this same simple rite that is
described by Hippolytus in his *Apostolic Tradition:* "When one or-
dains a priest, the bishop lays his hand on the candidate, and all the
priests present do the same; the bishop pronounces a formula like to
that for deacons" [415] (but here it contains specific references to the
role of the priest in the life of the Church).

Today a person is ordained a priest with this same essential rite.
However, since the first and third centuries a great number of ceremonies and formulas have been added to bring out more clearly the
sublime functions of the priesthood. The immense evolution during
these seventeen centuries will be more strikingly seen if we outline
briefly our modern rite. It includes the following elements: (1) presentation and election of candidates, (2) instruction on the liturgical
duties of the priest followed by the Litany of the Saints, if it has not
already been sung for the ordination of subdeacons and deacons, (3)
imposition, in silence, of both hands by the bishop and the attending
clergy, (4) invitatory Preface with blessing, (5) consecratory Preface,
(6) investiture with priestly stole and chasuble, (7) oration calling
down upon the newly-ordained all the graces necessary for a right exercise of the priesthood, (8) anointing of the new priest's hands with
the Oil of Catechumens, during which the Veni Creator is sung, (9)
delivery of the chalice filled with wine and water and the paten holding an unconsecrated host, (10) offering of lighted candles to the
bishop by the newly-ordained at the beginning of the Offertory, (11)
recitation of the Apostles' Creed by the newly-ordained, (12) be-
stowal of power to absolve from sin, (13) promise of obedience to
the bishop, (14) special blessing for the newly-ordained, (15) imposition of a penance.

1. The formulas used for the presentation and testimonial in
favor of the candidates given by the archdeacon are the same as those
spoken at the ordination of deacons. We find these formulas recorded

---

[412] Andrieu, *Le Pontifical Romain,* I, 132-133.
[413] Ed. H. Wilson, n. XXIII, p. 28-29.
[414] 1 Tim. 4:14.
[415] Ed. B. Botte, n. 8, pp. 37-38.

for the first time for the ordination of priests in the mixed form of the Gregorian Sacramentary.[416] They were taken up by the tenth century Romano-Germanic Pontifical [417] and thence were received in Rome and maintained till our own day. The formulas used for the election, however, varied. While the mixed Gregorian book retained the same formula as that used for deacons, the *Missale Francorum* is the first to record the one we actually use today.[418] Though dropped in some intermediate books, it was again taken up by Durand.[419]

2. Although our present instruction concerning the liturgical duties of the priest comes from Durand,[420] a one-sentence admonition is already presented in some manuscripts of the twelfth century papal Pontifical [421] and in all the manuscripts of the thirteenth century Pontifical: [422] "Sacerdotem oportet offerre, benedicere, preesse, predicare et baptizare."

3. Unlike the ordination of deacons, the ritual for the ordination of priests has the candidates receive the imposition of hands, not during the consecratory Preface, but before the invitatory Preface and its blessing. The first time an explicit rubric appears prescribing this procedure is in the tenth century Romano-Germanic Pontifical.[423] Before this, manuscripts simply stated that the bishop held his hands over the candidate and blessed (consecrated) him. This procedure was feasible as long as only one was being ordained, but when there was more than one, the bishop found it necessary to impose his hands and then pronounce the consecratory formula.

However, this does not explain how the matter of this sacrament came to be separated from the form by the invitatory Preface and blessing. Perhaps when sections of different Ordinals were simply placed side by side without discrimination, later users followed them slavishly, not knowing their disparate origins, and thus in time it came to be customary to perform the ceremonial the way we do it today. This is unfortunate; perhaps in some future reform the laying on of hands will once again be directly attached to the consecratory Preface, and all, bishop and priests, will keep their hands, not simply extended as for orations, but far outstretched during the whole sacramental form.

Another impropriety of the present situation is that after the invitatory Preface and its blessing, all the priests return to their places while the bishop is actually chanting the consecratory Preface. This, after all, is the highly symbolic rite spoken of by St. Paul wherein the

---

[416] *MPL*, 78: 221.
[417] Andrieu, *Le Pontifical Romain*, I, 131, n. 6.
[418] Ed K. Mohlberg, n. 8, p. 8.
[419] Andrieu, *Le Pontifical Romain*, III, 365.
[420] *Ibid.*, III, 366.
[421] *Ibid.*, I, 134, line 28.
[422] *Ibid.*, II, 341, 343.
[423] *Ibid.*, I, 134, line 41.

whole presbyterate lays hands on the candidates for the priesthood. What is the nature of such an imposition of hands made by the assisting priests? Today, without doubt, the imposition performed by the bishop is the only one truly productive of the priestly character in the candidates. Nevertheless, the action of the assisting priests, while not productive of the character, is indicative that they are cooperators with the bishop. Here they help him choose candidates and ordain, transmitting their priestly power to another member of the priestly rank. This is a type of concelebration, not genuinely sacramental, but rather ceremonial.

However, there may be more to this symbolic gesture than meets the eye. It may be a remnant of the time (the first and second centuries) when all priests seem to have possessed the fullness of the priesthood and were, from the point of view of sacramental power, completely equivalent to bishops. Perhaps the words of St. Paul imply that the sacramental power to ordain could not be exercised by these priest-bishops except when they acted together as the *presbyterate*. As a matter of fact, there have been respected ecclesiastical writers of the past who maintained that the reservation to bishops of the power of ordaining was simply a matter of Church discipline, done in order to avoid discord and scandal.[424] And today there are competent theologians who are of the opinion that simple priests could ordain other priests validly if given the proper jurisdictional delegation by the pope.[425] And it is noteworthy that one manuscript of the twelfth century papal Pontifical even has all the assisting priests pronounce the formulas in a lower voice with the bishop.[426]

4, 5. Our present invitatory Preface with its blessing is reported in the Leonine Sacramentary.[427] The same is true of the consecratory Preface, and it remains universally accepted and unchanged until we arrive at the tenth century Romano-Germanic Pontifical, which uses the same opening phrase as for the ordination of deacons: *Adesto quaesumus, omnipotent Deus.*[428] It did not receive the usual introduction for Prefaces until the twelfth century,[429] and it was Durand who prescribed that it be sung on the regular Preface tone.[430]

6, 7. Though we find explicit mention of the candidate putting on the *planeta* during the ceremony (in this case, before the consecratory Preface) as early as the eighth century,[431] the first sign of a real

[424] Cf., e.g., Isidore of Seville, *De eccl. off.*, II, 7, 2. *MPL*, 83: 787; Rabanus Maurus, *De cleric. instit.*, I, 6. *MPL*, 107: 302; Ivo of Chartres, *Sermo de excell. ordinum. MPL*, 162: 518.

[425] Cf. H. Bouëssé, *Le Sacerdoce Chrétien* (Paris: Desclée de Brouwer, 1957), 122-123; see other authors mentioned on p. 194, note 25.

[426] M. Andrieu, *Le Pontifical Romain*, I, n. 17, p. 135, recension L.

[427] K. Mohlberg, *Sacramentarium Veronense*, p. 121, nn. 952-953.

[428] M. Andrieu, *Le Pontifical Romain*, I, 135, line 42.

[429] *Ibid.*, line 20.

[430] *Ibid.*, III, 368, n. 9.

[431] *Ord. Rom.* XXXIV, n. 11. Andrieu, *Les Ordines*, III, 606.

investiture comes from the ninth century *Ordo Romanus* XXXV:[432] the archdeacon takes the candidate outside the sanctuary and vests him with the *planeta*; after the consecratory Preface the bishop places the stole about his neck. The Romano-Germanic Pontifical seems to have been the first to provide formulas for this investiture; while the one for the giving of the stole is like ours, the one for the chasuble is different.[433] Our present formula for giving the chasuble appears in the thirteenth century papal Pontifical.[434] The oration concluding the investiture ceremony figures for the first time in the *Missale Francorum*.[435]

8. The ceremony of anointing the hand of the newly-ordained, according to the documents that have come to light, is not at all a Roman element. It appears for the first time in the eighth century *Missale Francorum*.[436] The fact that Irish influence was predominant in Poitiers, where the Missal came into existence,[437] leads to the suspicion that such a rite already existed in Ireland. This book contains two formulas, the first of which has been retained for our present use, the second of which, containing a reference to the use of chrism, was dropped.[438]

The road which the first formula took on its way into the official Roman Rite seems to have been the following: it was added, first of all, to the mixed form of the Gregorian Sacramentary,[439] and passed into all subsequent Roman books through the Romano-Germanic Pontifical.[440] It would seem that the consecration of the bishop's hands with chrism, a rite apparently initiated in the ninth century by the *False Decretals*,[441] led bishops to allow only Oil of Catechumens to be used for the anointing of the priest's hands. There is no longer any mention of the use of chrism for priestly ordination until, in passing, the compiler of the thirteenth century papal Pontifical alludes to its use in some places.[442] Towards the end of the same century Durand explicitly excludes its use,[443] and thus present practice was established. The singing of the Veni Creator Spiritus during the anointing appears only from the thirteenth century on.[444]

9. The delivery to the newly-ordained of a chalice filled with water and wine together with the paten holding an unconsecrated host,

---

[432] Nn. 27, 31. *ibid.*, IV, 38-39.
[433] M. Andrieu, *Le Pontifical Romain*, I, 136, nn. 21-22, line 45.
[434] *Ibid.*, II, 346.
[435] Ed. K. Mohlberg, n. 8, p. 9.
[436] *Ibid.*, n. 8, p. 10.
[437] Cf. G. Ellard, *Ordination Anointings in the Western Church before 1000 A. D.* (Cambridge, Mass.: The Medieval Academy of America, 1933), 19.
[438] Cf. Ellard, *ibid.*, 21, for the origin of this second formula.
[439] *MPL*, 78: 223.
[440] Andrieu, *Le Pontifical Romain*, I, 136, n. 24, line 45.
[441] Cf. Ellard, *op. cit.*, 51-61.
[442] Not in Rome however: Andrieu, *Le Pontifical Romain*, II, 347.
[443] *Ibid.*, III, 369.
[444] In the thirteenth century papal Pontifical: *ibid.*, II, 346.

a rite which has occasioned much discussion among theologians, was not originally introduced by the authority of either pope or council, but rather through the inventive genius of local bishops sometime during the ninth century—and at that sporadically.[445] It was accepted by the compilers of the tenth century Romano-Germanic Pontifical,[446] whence it passed into all subsequent Roman books. Unknown to the Oriental Rites, this element is entirely peculiar to the Western Church. Though this ceremony is certainly unessential to the conferring of priestly power, it is nevertheless useful to bring out emphatically the genuine Catholic notion of a sacrificial priesthood: *Accipe potestatem offerre sacrificium Deo. . . .*

10. While today the newly-ordained bring lighted candles and present them to the consecrating prelate at the beginning of the Offertory, we read in the Romano-Germanic Pontifical that they were to offer the bishop a particle to be consecrated during the Canon of the Mass. [447] After this, however, the Roman books speak of an offering of candles, loaves of bread, and even wine.[448] Our present practice, then, is what remains of this Offertory procession, which itself was a survival of the regular oblation made by the people. Our present custom of having the newly-ordained sacramentally concelebrate the Mass with the consecrating prelate comes from the thirteenth century. Both the papal Pontifical of that century and St. Thomas attest to it.[449]

11-15. All the concluding ceremonies—the giving of the power to forgive sins, receiving the promise of obedience from the newly-ordained, and the giving of a penance—apparently spring from Durand's initiative.[450] The special blessing for the newly-ordained appears in the mixed Gregorian Sacramentary,[451] but there is no indication given as to exactly when, during the Mass, it was to be imparted. Durand, however, has it given right after the imposition of the penance. The giving of the power to absolve from sin, just like that of offering Mass, is a purely symbolic gesture here, making more explicit another aspect of the Catholic priesthood that was given earlier, at the first imposition of hands.

The Episcopate

The consecration of a bishop consists of the following elements: (1) presentation of the candidate, reading of Apostolic mandate, taking the oath, examination of the bishop-elect's faith, (2) one-sentence

---

[445] It is called the *matter* of the sacrament only in the Council of Florence's *Decretum pro Armenis* of Nov. 22, 1439: Denz. 701.
[446] Andrieu, *Le Pontifical Romain*, I, 136, line 45 for n. 25, p. 137.
[447] *Ibid.*, 137, n. 28, line 35.
[448] *Ibid.*, II, 249, 33.
[449] *Ibid.*, II, 349; *Summa Theol.*, III, 82, 2.
[450] Andrieu, *Le Pontifical Romain*, III, 371-373.
[451] *MPL*, 78: 223.

liturgical instruction, (3) invitatory Preface, Litany of the Saints, (4) imposition of Gospel book on the neck of the bishop-elect and imposition of the hands of consecrator and co-consecrators on the head of the bishop-elect with the formula: *Accipe Spiritum Sanctum,* (5) blessing: *Propitiare,* (6) consecratory Preface, in the middle of which is inserted the anointing of the bishop's head with chrism during the singing of the Veni Creator, (7) anointing of the bishop's hands, (8) blessing and delivery of crosier and ring, delivery of Gospel book, (9) presentation made by new bishop to consecrator of two candles, two loaves of bread, and two barrels of wine at the Offertory, (10) concelebration of the Mass, (11) blessing and imposition of mitre and gloves, enthronement of new bishop, (12) new bishop's blessing to the faithful as the Te Deum is sung, (13) antiphon *Firmetur manus tua* and oration *Deus omnium fidelium pastor* for new bishop, (14) final blessing given by new bishop, (15) *ad multos annos.*

1. Though the sixth century *Statuta Ecclesiae Antiqua* gives directions for a thorough examination of the faith and morals of the bishop-elect, no formulas are provided.[452] Our present formulas for this examination are seen for the first time in the twelfth century papal Pontifical.[453] And today the reading of the Apostolic mandate takes the place of the election of the bishop; the people have no part in it. Formerly either the local cathedral chapter or the people all together chose their bishop.[454] The requirement that the bishop must take an oath of allegiance to the pope and his legitimate successors is not found in any Pontifical before our present one.

2. The one-sentence liturgical instruction seems strange here, since all the other Major Orders are furnished with an extensive and beautifully worded admonition on the duties proper to the new office. This instruction appears for the first time in the thirteenth century papal Pontifical.[455]

3-6. Here again, as in the case of ordination to the priesthood, we find the matter of the sacrament—imposition of hands—separated from the sacramental form—the words of the consecratory Preface— by means of the formula *Accipe Spiritum Sanctum* and the blessing which normally belongs with the invitatory Preface. The formula *Accipe Spiritum Sanctum* has no essential sacramental value; it is found for the first time in Durand's Pontifical.[456] In the *Ordo Romanus* XLb, which probably dates from around the ninth century, the connection between the invitatory Preface and its blessing is not yet disturbed, for the Litany is chanted first, and only after the blessing are the Gospel book and the hands of the consecrators imposed on the head

[452] N. 1. Andrieu, *Les Ordines,* III, 616.
[453] M. Andrieu, *Le Pontifical Romain,* I, 142-144.
[454] Cf. *Ord. Rom.* XXXIV, n. 14. Andrieu, *Les Ordines,* III, 606; *Missale Francorum* (ed. K. Mohlberg), n. 9, pp. 10-11.
[455] M. Andrieu, *Le Pontifical Romain,* II, 356, 358.
[456] *Ibid.* III, 382.

of the bishop-elect.[457] The separation seems to have taken place for the first time in the tenth century Romano-Germanic Pontifical.[458] However, the separation of the sacramental imposition of hands from the consecratory Preface was already effected in the mixed form of the Gregorian Sacramentary.[459] The insistence that more than one bishop consecrate a new bishop was mentioned in the *Apostolic Tradition* [460] and was made obligatory by the Council of Nicea in 325.[461] The imposition of hands itself, of course, comes from Apostolic times [462] and was universally followed throughout the Church. The formulas for the invitatory Preface are found in the Gelasian Sacramentary,[463] those for the blessing and consecratory Preface in the Leonine book.[464] Up until the ninth century no anointings are found in the consecration of bishops. This rite was first promoted by the *False Decretals.*[465] It appears also in the mixed Gregorian book,[466] and, by way of the Romano-Germanic Pontifical, it entered the official Roman Liturgy.[467] Durand added the singing of the Veni Sancte Spiritus, while other books of the same period prescribed the singing of the Veni Creator Spiritus.[468]

7. The anointing of the new bishop's hands seems to have begun during the tenth century [469] and, again, entered the Roman Rite through the Romano-Germanic Pontifical.[470] But it seems to have been Durand who introduced the antiphon *Unguentum in capite* and the psalm *Ecce quam bonum* for this anointing.[471] In our present rite two formulas are actually employed for the anointing of the bishop's hands. The first, *Ungantur manus istae,* unused by the late medieval Pontificals, came from the *Missale Francorum,*[472] where, as a matter of fact, it was used as the second formula for the consecration of the *priest's* hands. And our present second formula, *Deus et Pater Domini,* is found in the tenth century Pontificals such as the Romano-Germanic one [473] and that of Troyes.[474]

8. As early as the seventh century Isidore of Seville attests to the practice of giving the newly-consecrated bishop a crosier and ring

[457] Nn. 2, 3, 4, 5. Andrieu, *Les Ordines,* IV, 307.
[458] M. Andrieu, *Le Pontifical Romain,* I, 146, line 38.
[459] *MPL,* 78: 223.
[460] Ed. B. Botte, n. 2, p. 27.
[461] Can. 4. Hefele-Leclercq, I, 539.
[462] Acts 13:3; 2 Tim. 1:6.
[463] Ed. H. Wilson, 151.
[464] Nn. 946, 947, p. 119.
[465] Cf. G. Ellard, *op. cit.,* 51-54.
[466] *MPL,* 78: 224.
[467] M. Andrieu, *Le Pontifical Romain,* I, 146, line 38 for n. 24, p. 148.
[468] *Ibid.,* III, 383, n. 33, and line 30.
[469] Cf. G. Ellard, *op. cit.,* pp. 69, 87.
[470] M. Andrieu, *Le Pontifical Romain,* I, 149.
[471] *Ibid.,* III, 384.
[472] N. 8, p. 10 in Mohlberg's edition.
[473] Ellard, p. 95.
[474] *Ibid.,* p. 87.

during the ceremony,[475] and we find the two formulas that are spoken as these objects are presented to the new bishop in the tenth century Romano-Germanic Pontifical.[476] But we must wait until Durand's time before a blessing of them is introduced.[477] On the other hand, the delivery of the Gospel book appears for the first time in the twelfth century papal Pontifical.[478]

9. Though there is mention in one late manuscript of the twelfth century papal Pontifical [479] of the Offertory procession in which the new bishop presents to his consecrator the bread, wine, and candles, this practice does not take hold until the thirteenth century.[480]

10. The practice of having the new bishop concelebrate the Mass with the consecrating prelate also finds some support in certain manuscripts of the twelfth century Pontificals.[481] In Durand's book it is an established custom.[482]

11-15. Most of these rites were introduced for the first time through Durand's Pontifical.[483] Of these, however, the greeting *Ad multos annos* appears for the first time in the thirteenth century papal Pontifical.[484] We may possibly see in this an attempt to imitate an earlier, purely papal, practice of the ninth century.[485]

5. Sacramentals related to Holy Orders

Consecration of Oils

A blessing of oils may possibly be inferred from what Tertullian says in his treatment of Baptism: when the candidate comes forth from the baptismal font, he is anointed with a blessed anointing, *perungitur benedicta unctione*.[486] But by the third century it was definitely an established custom to bless three kinds of oil: Oil of Catechumens, Chrism, and Oil for the Infirm.[487] While Oil for the Infirm might be blessed during the Canon of any Mass, the other two were blessed immediately before the administration of Baptism. Since we know it was a long established custom to confer Baptism during the Easter Vigil—and the Saturday and early hour of Sunday of which Hippolytus speaks in the *Apostolic Tradition* must indeed be the Easter Vigil—we must conclude that the more primitive usage was to consecrate the Holy Oils during that Vigil. This custom was maintained in Arles by

---

[475] *De eccl. off.*, II, V, 12. MPL, 83: 783-784.
[476] M. Andrieu, *Le Pontifical Romain*, I, 149.
[477] *Ibid.*, III, 385.
[478] *Ibid.*, I, 150.
[479] *Ibid.*
[480] *Ibid.*, II, 369.
[481] *Ibid.*, II, 365.
[482] *Ibid.*, III, 387.
[483] *Ibid.*, III, 389-391.
[484] *Ibid.*, II, 367.
[485] *Ord. Rom.* IX, n. 6. MPL, 78: 1007.
[486] *De Baptismo*, 7. MPL, 1: 1315.
[487] *La Tradition Apostolique* (ed. B. Botte), n. 5, pp. 33-34; n. 21, p. 49.

St. Caesarius,[488] even though in Rome, by the sixth century, the consecration had been advanced to Holy Thursday.[489] This more recent
Roman practice spread throughout the West;[490] even the Orientals
conformed to the Roman usage. It seems reasonable to infer from
what Rupert of Deutz says that the blessing of Oils was moved to
Holy Thursday to lighten the ceremonies of the Easter Vigil.[491]

Though John the Deacon remarks that in some circumstances
simple priests were allowed to bless the Oils [492]—and this was certainly the regular practice in Rome, except for Chrism, which was reserved
to the pope [493]—it was insisted upon that bishops normally perform
these blessings. Thus from the Council of Carthage in 390 comes
legislation in this matter,[494] and it is maintained through Popes Innocent I [495] and Gelasius I.[496] Again in the sixth century, Montanus, then
Archbishop of Toledo, protested against the presumption of certain
priests who took it upon themselves to bless the Oils.[497] And the requirement for the bishop to bless the Oils remains the law of the
Church even till our own day.

It was an old Roman custom for the blessing of Oils to take the
form of concelebration, whereby the priests who assisted the bishop
actually blessed the Oils together with him: *et benedicit tam domnus
papa quam omnes presbyteri*, says the Gregorian Sacramentary.[498]
Amalar, too, attests to the practice as a *mos Romana*.[499] The last document to require strict concelebration is the twelfth century papal
Pontifical.[500] Later Pontificals simply refer to the assisting clergy as
witnesses to what is done and as helpers of the bishop: "tamquam
eius testes, et ministerii sacri chrismatis cooperatores." [501] The former
concelebration is now excluded for the blessing of the Oil of the
Infirm and, in the case of the Oil of Catechumens and Chrism, reduced
to the inhalations and greetings of the newly-blessed Oils.

The blessing of Oil for the Infirm has remained in its primitive
place in the course of the Mass, that is, immediately before the words
"Per quem haec omnia," towards the end of the Canon. Our actual
formula of blessing, "Emitte, quaesumus, Domine, Spiritum Sanctum

---

[488] Cf. G. Morin, "Une particularité arlésienne de la liturgie du samedi saint,"
Eph. Lit., 49 (1935), 146-149.
[489] H. Wilson, *The Gelasian Sacramentary*, pp. 69-72.
[490] Eligius of Noyon claims that by the seventh century "all the world"
blessed oils on this day: *Homil. X in Caena Domini. MPL, 87:* 629.
[491] *De div off.*, V, 17. *MPL, 170:* 141.
[492] *Epist. ad Senarium*, 7, 8. *MPL, 59:* 403.
[493] Cf. A. Chavasse, *Le Sacramentaire Gélasien*, 138.
[494] Can. 3. Hefele-Leclercq, II, 77.
[495] *Epist. 25 ad Decentium*, 3. *MPL, 20;* 554.
[496] *Epist. ad episc. Lucaniae*, 6. *MPL, 59:* 50.
[497] *Epist. ad clerum Palentinum*, 2. *MPL, 65:* 52.
[498] Ed. H. Lietzmann, 45.
[499] *De eccl. off.*, I, 12. *MPL, 105,* 1016.
[500] M. Andrieu, *Le Pontifical Romain*, I, n. 37, p. 221.
[501] Durand's Pontifical: M. Andrieu, *ibid.*, III, 576, n. 70; see also the
thirteenth century papal Pontifical: *ibid.*, II, p. 223, n. 48.

tuum Paraclitum de coelis in hanc pinguedinem olivae . . .," is found, as far as its latter half is concerned, in the *Apostolic Tradition*.[502] It is found fully formed but with the word "tasting" in the Gelasian Sacramentary,[503] and this is finally omitted in the Gregorian book.[504] The exorcism which precedes this blessing in our modern Pontifical appears in the Romano-Germanic Pontifical.[505]

Unfortunately, the *Apostolic Tradition* records no formulas for the confection of Chrism and the Oil of Catechumens. It does, however, refer to the Chrism as the *oil of thanksgiving*, indicating that it was blessed by means of a consecratory Preface, and to the Oil of Catechumens as the *oil of exorcism*, implying that it was mainly through an exorcism that the oil was removed from the dominion of Satan to be used against him.[506] Thus we find that in the Gelasian Sacramentary Chrism was blessed with a consecratory Preface; the form given is the same as we have today.[507] And the Oil of Catechumens was confected by means of an exorcism.[508] According to our present Roman Pontifical a formula of exorcism is made to precede the consecratory Preface for the blessing of Chrism. This was actually the original Roman formula for blessing the Oil of Catechumens.[509]

The rubrics for the blessing of the Oil of Catechumens and Chrism call for what the Pontifical terms an *halatio* performed by the bishop and the assisting priests before the actual blessing. Since this is obviously meant to be an exorcistic action, a better term would be *exsufflatio* or *exhalatio*, for *halatio* signifies a breathing of life or spirit into something. As the unblessed oils are brought to the sanctuary in procession, the hymn O Redemptor is sung. Composed by Venantius Fortunatus, it was inserted into this ritual by the compiler of the Romano-Germanic Pontifical.[510] Though a greeting of the newly-consecrated Chrism is called for in the eighth century *Ordo Romanus* XXIV,[511] the actual formula *Ave sanctum Chrisma* appears for the first time in the thirteenth century papal Pontifical.[512] As for the place in the Mass at which Chrism and the Oil for Catechumens are blessed, in the primitive Church their blessing normally took place immediately before their use. When it was decided to bless them on Holy Thursday, this ritual was simply added on to the Mass; their blessing occurs after Communion. The Gelasian Sacramentary places these

[502] Ed. B. Botte, n. 5, p. 34.
[503] Ed. H. Wilson, 70.
[504] Ed H. Lietzmann, 45.
[505] M. Andrieu, *Le Pontifical Romain*, I, 221.
[506] Ed. B. Botte, n. 21, p. 49.
[507] Ed. H. Wilson, p. 71.
[508] Again our present formula is already recorded, *ibid*, 72. But this is a Gallican revision based on the original Roman formula as contained in the Ordo for Baptism, p. 118.
[509] *Ibid.*, p. 118.
[510] M. Andrieu, *Le Pontifical Romain*, I, 222.
[511] N. 20. Andrieu, *Les Ordines*, III, 291.
[512] M. Andrieu, *Le Pontifical Romain*, II, 462.

blessings between the breaking of the host and Communion.[513] This was apparently the Gallican practice (Amalar attests to it[514]), but the older Roman Ordinals describe the true Roman tradition in placing the blessings after the Communion.[515]

Blessing of Abbots

St. Benedict, in the sixth century, seems to intend such a ceremonial installation of the newly-elected abbot.[516] Pope St. Gregory certainly acknowledged the utility of the practice of blessing new abbots,[517] for he accorded the ceremony a place in his Sacramentary. At that time this blessing consisted in a simple oration: "Concede, quaesumus, omnipotens Deus, et hunc famulum tuum quem ad regimen animarum eligimus, gratiae tuae dona prosequere, ut te largiente, cum ipsa tibi nostra electione placeamus." [518] Another rite which seems to be a part of the original ceremony is the delivery of the crosier to the newly-blessed abbot, for Theodore of Canterbury speaks of it in the seventh century.[519]

With the growth of the local abbot's power in the Middle Ages— in many places the abbot was also the bishop—this blessing came to resemble more and more the consecration of bishops. In the ninth century Sacramentary of Gellone there appears a consecratory Preface (though the prologue is of later introduction) in which mention is made of an imposition of hands.[520] Although the formula itself speaks of such an imposition, Ivo of Chartres states that actually no imposition took place.[521] Perhaps he was only protesting against its use as an innovation, for service books do contain it. And the phrase of the Preface, "ut qui per nostrae manus impositionem hodie abbas constituitur . . . permaneat," suggests a real laying on of hands. With the exception of the introductory interrogation, the penitential psalms, delivery of the ring and mitre, and the concluding rites—all of which date from Durand's Pontifical[522]—everything else is already at hand in the Romano-Germanic Pontifical of the tenth century.[523]

Dedication of Churches

In the Old Testament there were celebrations similar, at least in idea, to our dedication of churches. After Solomon had built the

---

[513] Ed. H. Wilson, 70.
[514] *De eccl. off.*, I, 12. *MPL*, 105: 1014.
[515] XXIII, n. 7; XXIV, n. 13. Andrieu, *Les Ordines*, III, 270, 290.
[516] *Regula*, cap. 64 "De ordinando Abbate." Holstenius, *Codex Regularum* (Rome, 1661), II, 58.
[517] Cf. P. De Puniet, *Le Pontifical Romain*, II, 96.
[518] Ed. H. Lietzmann, 128; Ed. H. Wilson, 140.
[519] *MPL*, 99: 929.
[520] Cf. De Puniet, II, 116.
[521] *Epist. 73 ad Bernardem abbatem. MPL*, 162; 94.
[522] M. Andrieu, *Le Pontifical Romain*, III, 401 ff.
[523] *Ibid.*, I, 170-173.

Temple, he gathered together all the people of Israel, placed the Ark of the Covenant in the Holy of Holies and had sacrifices offered, he himself pronouncing a long prayer.[524] And again, after Judas Machabeus regained the Holy City from the hands of Antiochus IV, he set about cleansing the Temple and altar and determining once again the various liturgical services. The Temple worship itself was re-inaugurated with a sacrifice offered with great solemnity.[525] It is to be noted, however, that on both these occasions the dedication of the Temple consisted, not in a blessing or consecration of the building and altar, but rather in an inaugural use. In the case of Solomon, the Ark was placed in the Holy of Holies and sacrifice offered; for Judas Machabeus, the cleansing of the Temple simply meant ridding it of idols and offering sacrifice once again.

The Christian Church followed the same principle of simplicity. Although Gratian has Pope Clement I declare that churches must be consecrated with divine prayers,[526] it is generally recognized that this is an incorrect attribution. The oldest and surest record of a dedication of a church is that contained in Eusebius' *Ecclesiastical History* wherein he describes the inauguration of the cathedral of Tyre around 314.[527] And here the whole rite consisted in the celebration of Mass; in other words, in using the cathedral for the first time. In the sixth century, Pope Vigilius writes to Profuturus of Braga and tells him expressly that a church is considered to be consecrated once Mass has been celebrated in it. He does mention sprinkling it with Blessed Water but only to exclude the action.[528] In the same letter he refers to the practice of depositing the relics of saints in the church. He would have us believe, however, that the deposition of relics was not really an essential part of the service. Ambrose was one who laid much importance on the relics, for upon being asked to consecrate a newly-built church, he said he would do so if he were to find some relics. Having found them, miraculously at that, he began the dedicatory service with an all-night vigil.[529] In England, if relics could not be obtained, it was the custom to deposit consecrated hosts within the altar table.[530]

It is easy to see how a rite, formerly of secondary importance, such as the translation and redeposition of a martyr's relics, came to occupy the limelight simply because it was a rarer occurrence. To these customs of Roman origin there were joined, in time, other rites of distinctly Gallican origin stemming from the *Missale Francorum*

---

[524] 2 Paralip. 5-7.
[525] 1 Mach. 4:36-59; 2 Mach. 10:1-5.
[526] *De consec.* I, xiii. *MPL*, 187: 1710.
[527] X, 3ff. *GCS*, 9(2), 860-862.
[528] IV. *MPL*, 69:18.
[529] *Epist. 22 ad sororem*, 1, 2. *MPL*, 16:1019, 1020.
[530] Cf. the 816 Council of Chelsea, can. 2. L. Duchesne, *Christian Worship*, 403, note 1.

and the Sacramentary of Angoulême.[531] The essential part of the dedicatory ritual in these two books is the consecration of the altar.[532]
The ceremony of anointing the altar is particularly detailed. The
church itself is blessed and anointed with Chrism without any prayer
formulas.[533] These Gallican ceremonies were later inserted into the
Gelasian book and combined with the formulas already present there
to give the following arrangement: two orations to bless the building,
a blessing pronounced over the mixture of water and wine to be used
for the lustral purifications (nine different ones), the Preface for
consecrating the altar, an offering of incense upon it, and finally the
blessing of the altar cloths, paten, chalice, etc.[534]

Other rites were added in time, of course; all of them found their
way into the official Roman Rite through the Romano-Germanic Pontifical,[535] with still other additions coming from Durand.[536]

G. Matrimony

1. Theological summary

As St. Paul clearly teaches, Christian marriage is supposed to
mirror the union between Christ and His Church. Just as Christ is the
Head of the Church, which He saved and sanctified in love, so the
husband is the head of the wife, whom he must cherish and love, for
whom he must make every sacrifice. And just as the Church is subject
to Christ, looks to Him for support and nourishment, for a new Name
and a new home, for sanctity and glory, so ought the wife to respect
and love her husband, make his life hers, accepting his name as a
symbol of their new life together. Thus both parties make a sacrifice
of themselves, just as Christ gave Himself, emptied Himself, taking
upon Himself the form of a slave, in order that His Spouse, the
Church, might be reborn to His divine life. In this way Matrimony
reflects the reality and the effects of Christ's sacrifice, for through
marriage the contracting parties give themselves to one another, so
that in and through one another they might complement each other's
efforts for salvation. "This is a great mystery—I mean in reference to
Christ and His Church." [537] Little wonder, then, that Christ elevated
this marvelous institution to the dignity of a sacrament, making human
love productive of divine love with all its effects of life and grace.

531 For a description of the ritual for consecrating churches contained in these
documents see A. Chavasse, Le sacramentaire Gélasien, 40-42.
532 In fact the whole ritual bears the title "Consecratio altaris" in the
Missale Francorum (ed. K. Mohlberg), n. 12, p. 17.
533 See the text of the ancient Ordo contained in the Angoulême book: A.
Chavasse, op. cit., 41-42.
534 H. Wilson, The Gelasian Sacramentary, 133-136; see also comparative
tables in Chavasse, 43-44.
535 M. Andrieu, Le Pontifical Romain, I, 177-190.
536 Ibid., III, 458 ff.
537 Ephesians 5:32.

afterwards, out of sorrow, they no longer did. Those who attended the marriage were to throw handfuls of wheat upon the couple, especially the bride, and shout "Increase and multiply!" Upon this followed seven days of feasting and rejoicing.[540]

3. History of Christian rites

While lay people can be the extraordinary ministers of Baptism, that is, in case of necessity, for Matrimony they are the ordinary and sole ministers. As Pius XII says, "the contracting parties are ministers of grace to each other." [541] Although the presence of the priest having proper delegation is necessary for the validity of the sacrament—except in case of necessity (see can. 1098), when the exchange of consent before two witnesses is sufficient—he is there only as the official witness of the Church to bless the union in her name; he is not the minister.

The essential rite of the sacrament is the exchange of consent between the contracting parties. Some theologians have thought that the nuptial blessing was the form of the sacrament.[542] While it is true that prior to the ninth century no official declaration can be found as to what constituted the strict form of the sacrament, nonetheless, an exchange of consent was either implicit or explicit in the ceremonies from the very beginning. But in the ninth century Pope Nicholas I, in reply to the Bulgarians, said that exchange of consent alone was essential to Matrimony, and even though all the other ceremonies had been performed, if the consent were left out, the marriage would be invalid.[543]

In the second century, in order to safeguard the sanctity of Matrimony, St. Ignatius of Antioch insisted that the faithful contract marriage with the approval of the bishop so that their marriage might be according to God and not concupiscence.[544] A little more specific in his description of the nuptial rites of his time, Tertullian speaks of the intervention of the Church to confirm the marriage with the Eucharistic Sacrifice and the nuptial blessing.[545] Pope Siricius also mentions the priestly blessing,[546] and Ambrose speaks of the veil which the priest placed over the bride.[547] In addition to these ceremonies, Isidore of Seville records the placing of a ring on the left hand of the

[540] Cf. Calmet's *Dictionary of the Holy Bible*, II (London, 1823), article "Marriage."
[541] *Mystici Corporis* (America Press Edition), 27.
[542] Cf. e.g.: Melchior Cano, *De locis theologicis*, VIII, 5; Sylvius, *In Suppl.*, 42, a. 1, quaeritur II; Tournely, *De matri.*, q. 7 ff. J. M. Hervé, *Manuale Theologiae Dogmaticae* (Paris, 1926), IV, 487.
[543] Cap. 3. MPL, 119: 980.
[544] *Epist. ad Polycarpum*, V. MPG, 5: 723.
[545] *Ad uxorem*, II, 9. MPL, 1: 1415-1416.
[546] *Epist. 1 ad Himerium*, 4. MPL, 13: 1136.
[547] *Epist. 9 ad Virgilium*, 7. MPL, 16: 984.

2. Pagan and Jewish ritual

Since marriage is as old as history and instituted
self, its sacred meaning has generally—not always, due
tion by men—shone forth in the variety of ceremoni
men have surrounded it. And the Church has always be
maintaining the honorable nuptial ceremonies of vari
order to enhance the dignity of marriage with the forr
have developed within different cultures.[538] Hence, it w
briefly the ceremonies of marriage in pre-Christian tin

In the Roman Empire a couple contracted marriag
the *confarreatio*, or eating wheat or corn together,
sharing of a common life; the *coemptio*, the purchasin
by means of a dowry of gifts to her parents, syn
superiority over woman; the *usus*, or cohabitation, wh
sufficient from a legal point of view. Before marriag
the pledge of their fidelity, the betrothed would excl
the man would place upon the hand of his intend
custom saw in the ring a sign of the woman's obligat
the man and of her subjection to him.

A nuptial crown of flowers worn by the bride w
pagan times, as well as the *flammeum*, a veil that co
head. It was also customary in some places for th
couple to offer some sort of sacrifice to the deity of t
least a prayer, in order to gain his favor for their ne
The joining of the right hands was a universal custo
in which the bride was led to the home of her husba

The Jews were also familiar with many of th
petition for the hand of a man's daughter (someti
whole family), the payment of the dowry and
maiden's family, a betrothal accomplished by giv
piece of silver or a written document promising ma
nuptial ceremony began as the couple were place
each wearing a black veil. Another square veil wa
of them, and the Rabbi, or synagogue chanter, or r
a cup of wine and, having pronounced a blessing o
to the bridegroom and then to the bride to drin
then placed a golden ring upon the bride's finger ir
union. The contract of marriage was read, after
of wine was brought forth and, after several bless
by the couple. What remained of the wine was ca
as a sign of cheerfulness, and then the bridegr
against the wall in memory of the destruction of
the destruction of the Temple, both parties wore

---

538 Cf. Council of Trent, sess. xxiv, *Decretum de ref*
539 Cf. M. Righetti, IV, 334-336.

bride.[548] In the above-mentioned letter to the Bulgarians, Pope Nicholas I sums up all these ceremonies: the betrothal, in which the couple promise to wed; placing the ring on the left hand of the bride-to-be; the giving of the dowery; the actual wedding, consisting of the offering of Mass, the nuptial blessing and reception of the nuptial veil. He adds that after the ceremony both parties wear crowns.[549] Another element, the joining of the right hands, is mentioned by Gregory of Nazianzen.[550]

The formula of the nuptial blessing given after the Pater Noster during the nuptial Mass comes from two sources. The short oration springs substantially from the Leonine Sacramentary.[551] The blessing proper is composed of two parts, the oldest being the latter part from the words *fidelis et casta nubat in Christo . . .;* [552] the first part was made to replace an older formulation and is found for the first time in the Gregorian Sacramentary.[553] This, then, is the *benedictio sacerdotalis* spoken of in so many of the early references to the matrimonial ritual.

The modern ritual for marriage opens with a brief exhortation by the assisting priest. He may either read the one printed in the American Ritual, or prepare a short talk of his own. Following upon this is the formal exchange of consent. The Roman Ritual requires that one question be put to each spouse and that each answer affirmatively. Our American Ritual, however, in addition to the question: "Do you N . . . take N . . ., here present, for your lawful wife (husband)," has the couple join their right hands and repeat after the priest, each separately and individually, the words: "I N . . ., take you, N . . ., for my lawful wife (husband), to have and to hold, from this day forward, for better, for worse, for richer, for poorer, in sickness and in health, until death do us part."

Instead of these declaratory expressions of consent, the Roman Ritual, immediately after the previous questions and the answers to them, proceeds to the confirmation of the marriage (having the couple join their right hands) just as the American Ritual does at this point. The formula which the priest speaks: "Ego coniungo vos in matrimonium: In nomine Patris, et Filii, et Spiritus Sancti. Amen," might give the wrong impression, unless explained. The priest does not join the couple in marriage. He is simply attesting officially to their having united themselves. At this point the American Ritual calls upon all present as witnesses to this union and quotes the Gospel text:

[548] *De eccl. off.,* II, 20, 8. *MPL,* 83: 811-812; cf. also Tertullian, *Liber Apologeticus,* 6. *MPL,* 1: 353; Gregory of Tours, *Vitae Patrum,* 20, 1. *MPL,* 71: 1093.
[549] Cap. 3. *MPL,* 119: 979-980.
[550] *Epist.* 193. *MPG,* 37: 315-316.
[551] K. Mohlberg, *Sacramentarium Veronense,* p. 140.
[552] *Ibid.,* n. 1110, p. 140, line 22.
[553] Ed. H. Lietzmann, 111.

"What God has joined together, let no man put asunder," thus reminding all of Christ's prohibition of divorce.

Now comes the blessing of the ring or rings, the formula for which appears for the first time in one manuscript of the twelfth century papal Pontifical.[554] While the Roman Ritual at this point simply has the husband place the ring on the left hand of the bride without saying anything, our American Ritual has him (and her, too, if she gives a ring) speak the following: "In the name of the Father, and of the Son, and of the Holy Spirit. Take and wear this ring as a pledge of my fidelity!" In this new ritual, therefore, the ring worn by one person symbolizes the obligations of the other. While the Roman Ritual concludes with the antiphon, *Confirma hoc Deus*, and an oration coming from the Leonine Sacramentary,[555] our American Ritual adds Psalm 127 and several orations calling down upon the newly-married couple the graces needed for the various aspects of their new life together.

In the Nuptial Mass, which ought normally to follow, all the orations come from the Leonine Sacramentary,[556] the antiphonal chants are the same that appear in the eighth to ninth century Gregorian Antiphonary,[557] and the Gospel is one already used for this purpose in the Roman Evangeliary of the seventh century.[558] The Epistle is found in some manuscripts of the twelfth century papal Pontifical.[559] The same holds true for the brief blessing at the end of Mass: *Deus Abraham, Deus Isaac. . . .*[560]

4. Sacramentals related to Matrimony

Blessing of the home

One of the things the Church has retained from the old pagan nuptial practice of leading the bride to her new home in a processional manner is the so-called enthronement of the bride in the home. This is what we see in the blessing of the nuptial chamber. The first time such a blessing appears is in the Bobbio Missal [561] with the title "Benedictio Thalami super nubentes." This was in the seventh century. Since that time many such blessings have sprung up. Our present one comes from a late manuscript belonging to the family of the twelfth century papal Pontifical.[562] It reads: "Bless, O Lord, this marriage bed,

---

[554] M. Andrieu, *Le Pontifical Romain*, I, 301.
[555] K. Mohlberg, *Sacramentarium Veronense*, n. 1109, p. 140.
[556] *Ibid.*, 139-140.
[557] Cf. Tommasi, *Opera*, V (Rome, 1750), 228-229.
[558] Cf. T. Klauser, *Das römische Capitulare Evangeliorum* (Münster, 1935), 45.
[559] M. Andrieu, *Le Pontifical Romain*, I, 261, line 27.
[560] *Ibid.*, 301.
[561] *MPL*, 72: 570.
[562] M. Andrieu, *Le Pontifical Romain*, I, 302.

that all those dwelling here may remain in Thy peace, and continuing in Thy Will may grow old in length of days and arrive in Thy heavenly kingdom. Through Christ our Lord. Amen."

The Roman Ritual also provides an ordinary blessing for the homes of Catholics. One of these is found in the Gelasian Sacramentary.[563] But ours comes from the tenth century Romano-Germanic Pontifical.[564] It asks of God an abundance of natural goods, His protection, the indwelling of His angels, and the granting of the desires of those who live in the home.

Blessing of women

The Ritual also provides a blessing for a woman before and after the birth of her child. The first blessing given her recalls the miraculous intervention of God in the pre-natal period of Mary and Elizabeth and begs Him now to protect the foetus that it may see rebirth in Baptism. It comes from the Pontifical of Durand.[565] For the blessing after childbirth the Middle Ages offered a variety of formulas.[566] The ancient Church considered this blessing of the mother after childbirth very much as the Old Testament did, and insisted on it as a ceremony of purification; the mother could not enter the church until after forty days from the time of parturition. This was, of course, widely misunderstood to mean that women contracted moral impurity through childbirth. Even though explained over and over again that it was simply a question of legal impurity, an idea inherited from the Old Testament, the practice was never popular.[567] Today these ideas have no part in the Church's blessing; it is entirely devoted to expressing the joys of motherhood, likens them to those of Mary, and asks God to bless this woman and her child with final entrance into heaven together.

[563] Ed. H. Wilson, 286.
[564] M. Andrieu, *Le Pontifical Romain,* II, 454.
[565] *Ibid.,* III, 679-680.
[566] Cf. Ad. Franz, *Die kirchlichen Benediktionen im Mittelalter* (Freiburg, 1909), II, 210 ff.
[567] Cf. M. Righetti, IV, 349-350.

BIBLIOGRAPHY

Listed here are major works which have been consulted. They are arranged so as to be helpful for the reader who may wish to further his own knowledge of the Liturgy. After listing the works which serve either as basic background reading or as reference works for the whole of liturgiology, we have divided other works according to the chapter titles of this present text. We have not bothered to reproduce in this listing the myriad references to the older Patristic collections or the many articles cited; these may be found in the footnotes of the various chapters.

GENERAL WORKS

Aigrain, R. *Liturgia*. Paris, 1935.

Andrieu, M. *Les Ordines Romani du haut Moyen-Age*. 4 vols. Louvain, 1931, 1949, 1951, 1956.

————. *Le Pontifical Romain au Moyen-Age*. 4 vols.: I. *Le Pontifical Romain au XIIe siècle;* II. *Le Pontifical de la Curie Romaine au XIIIe siècle;* III. *Le Pontifical de Guillaume Durand;* IV. *Tables.* Series Studi e Testi: 86, 87, 88, 99. Vatican City, 1938, 1940, 1940, 1941.

Beauduin, L., O. S. B. *Liturgy the Life of the Church*. Collegeville, 1929.

————. *Mélanges Liturgiques*, Louvain, 1954.

Bishop, E. *Liturgica Historica*. Oxford, 1918.

Baumstark, A. *Liturgie Comparée*. Chevetogne, 1940; translated into English by F. L. Cross: *Comparative Liturgy*. London, 1958.

Borgmann, K. *Volksliturgie und Seelsorge*. Kolmar im Elsass, 1942.

Botte, B., O. S. B. *La Tradition Apostolique d'Hippolyte*. Texte Latin, Introduction, Traduction et Notes. Collection Sources Chrétiennes. Paris, 1946.

Bouyer, L. *Liturgical Piety*. Notre Dame, Indiana, 1955.

Bugnini, A., C. M. *Documenta Pontificia ad Instaurationem Liturgicam Spectantia* (1903-1953). Rome, 1953.

Cabrol, F., O. S. B. *Les Origines Liturgiques*. Paris, 1906.

————. *Liturgical Prayer*. Westminster, Maryland, 1950.

Callewaert, C. *Liturgicae Institutiones*. 3 vols.: I. *De S. Liturgia Universim;* II. *De Breviarii Romani Liturgia;* III. *De Missalis Romani Liturgia.* Bruges, 1933,[3] 1931, 1937.

————. *Sacris Erudiri. Fragmenta liturgica collecta a monachis S. Petri de Aldenburgo in Steenbrugge, ne pereant.* Steenbrugge, 1940.

Capelle, B., O. S. B. *Travaux Liturgiques*. I. *Doctrine.* Louvain, 1955.

Daniélou, J., S. J. *The Bible and the Liturgy*. Notre Dame, Indiana, 1956.

Dictionnaire d'archéologie Chrétienne et de Liturgie. F. Cabrol—H. Leclercq. 15 vols. Paris, 1907-1953.

Dix, G., O.S.B. *The Shape of the Liturgy*. Westminster, England, 1945.

Dolger, F-J. *Sol Salutis. Gebet und Gesang im christlichen Altertum*. Liturgiegeschichtliche Forschungen, 4-5. 2nd edition. Münster, 1925.

Duchesne, L. *Christian Worship. Its Origin and Evolution*. 5th edition. London, 1949.

————. *Liber Pontificalis*. 3 vols. 2nd revised edition by Jean Bayet. Paris, 1955, 1957.

Ellard, G., S. J. *Christian Life and Worship*. Milwaukee, 1935.

————. *Men at Work and Worship*. New York, 1940.

Guardini, R. *The Spirit of the Liturgy*. New York, 1954.

Howell, C., S. J. *Of Sacraments and Sacrifice*. Collegeville, 1952.

Jungmann, J., S. J. *Die Frohbotschaft und unsere Glaubensverkündigung*. Regensburg, 1936.

————. *Liturgical Worship*. New York, 1941.

————. *Gewordene Liturgie*. Innsbruck, 1941.

————. *Der Gottesdienst der Kirche*. Innsbruck, 1955. Translated into English by C. Howell, S. J.: *Public Worship—A Survey*. Collegeville, 1957.

————. *Die Stellung Christi im liturgischen Gebet*. Liturgiegeschichtliche Forschungen, 7-8. Münster, 1925.

Lefèbvre, G., O. S. B. *Catholic Liturgy*. St. Louis, 1954.

Lechner, J.—Eisenhofer, L. *Liturgik des romischen Ritus*. 6th edition. Freiburg, 1953.

Lietzmann, H. *Das Sacramentarium Gregorianum nach dem Aachener Urexemplar*. Liturgiegeschichtliche Quellen, 3. Münster, 1921.

Michel, V., O. S. B. *The Liturgy of the Church*. New York, 1937.

Miller, J., C.S.C. *The Relationship between Liturgical and Private Prayer*. Trier, 1955.

Mohlberg, K., O. S. B. *Sacramentarium Veronense*. Rerum Ecclesiasticarum Documenta, I. Rome, 1956.

————. *Missale Francorum*, RED, II. Rome, 1957.

————. *Missale Gallicanum Vetus*. RED, III. Rome, 1958.

————. *Miscellanea Liturgica in honorem L. Cuniberti Mohlberg*. 2 vols. Bibliotheca "Ephemerides Liturgicae," 22, 22. Rome, 1948-1949.

————. in collaboration with A. Baumstark. *Die älteste erreichbare Gestalt des Liber Sacramentorum anni circuli der romischen Kirche*. Liturgiegeschichtliche Quellen, 11-12. Münster, 1927.

Oppenheim, P., O. S. B. *Institutiones Systematico-Historicae in Sacram Liturgiam*. 10 vols.: I. *Introductio Historica in Litteras Liturgicas*. Rome, 1945; II-IV. *Tractatus de iure Liturgico*, 1939-1940; V. *Introductio in Scientiam Liturgicam*, 1940; VI. *Notiones Liturgiae Fundamentales*, 1941; VII. *Principia Theologiae Liturgicae*, 1947; Liturgia Specialis: I. *De Fontibus et Historia Ritus Baptismalis*, 1943; II. *Ius Liturgiae Baptismalis*, 1943; III. *Commentationes ad Ritum Baptismalem*, 1943.

O'Shea, W., S. S. *The Worship of the Church*. Westminster, Maryland, 1957.

Panfoeder, C., O. S. B. *Christus unserer Liturge*. Liturgia, I. Mainz, 1924. *Die Kirche als Liturgische Gemeinschaft*. Liturgia, II. Mainz, 1924.

Parsch, P. *Volksliturgie. Ihr Sinn und Umfang*. 2nd edition, Klosterneuburg, 1952.

Pascher, J. *L'Evolution des Rites Sacramentels.* Paris, 1952.

Perkins, M. *The Sacramental Way.* New York, 1948.

Pétré, H. *Ethérie, Journal de Voyage.* Texte Latin, Introduction et Traduction. Collection Sources Chrétiennes. Paris, 1948.

Quasten, J. *Monumenta eucharistica et liturgica vetustissima.* Florilegium Patristicum, VII. Bonn, 1935.

————. *Patrology.* 2 vols. Westminster, Maryland, 1951, 1953.

Righetti, M. *Manuale di Storia Liturgica.* 4 vols.: I. *Introduzione Generale.* 2nd edition. Milan, 1950; II. *L'Anno Liturgico e il Breviario,* 1946; III. *L'Eucarestia,* 1949. IV. *I Sacramenti — I Sacramentali,* 1953.

Rousseau, O., O. S. B. *The Progress of the Liturgy.* Westminster, Maryland, 1951.

Trapp, W. *Vorgeschichte und Ursprung der liturgischen Bewegung.* Regensburg, 1940.

Vagaggini, C., O. S. B. *Il Senso Teologico della Liturgia.* Rome, 1957.

Von Hildebrand, D. *Liturgy and Personality.* New York, 1946.

Wesseling, T., O. S. B. *Liturgy and Life.* New York, 1941.

Wilson, H. *The Gelasian Sacramentary.* Oxford, 1894.

————. *The Gregorian Sacramentary under Charles the Great.* Henry Bradshaw Society, 57. London, 1920.

CHAPTER TWO: Liturgical Families of Christendom

Attwater, D. *Eastern Catholic Worship.* New York, 1945.

Baumstark, A. *Liturgie Comparée.* Chevetogne, 1940. Translated into English by F. L. Cross: *Comparative Liturgy.* London, 1958.

Brightman, E. *Liturgies Eastern and Western.* I. *Eastern Liturgies,* Oxford, 1896.

King, A. *The Rites of Eastern Christendom.* 2 vols. Rome, 1947, 1948. *Liturgies of the Primatial Sees.* London, 1957.

Raes, A., S. J. *Introductio in Liturgiam Orientalem.* Rome, 1947.

Salaville, S., A. A. *An Introduction to the Study of Eastern Liturgies.* London, 1938.

CHAPTER THREE: Liturgical Books of the Roman Rite

Bourque, E. *Etude sur les Sacramentaires Romains.* 2 vols.: I. *Les Textes Primitifs.* Studi di Antichità Cristiana, XX. Rome, 1949. II. *Les Textes Remaniés.* Québec, 1952.

Chavasse, A. *Le Sacramentaire Gélasien.* Tournai, 1958.

Frere, W. H. *Studies in Early Roman Liturgy.* II. *The Roman Gospel-Lectionary;* III. *The Roman Epistle-Lectionary.* Alcuin Club Collections, XXX, XXXII. London, 1934, 1935.

Klauser, T. *Das römische capitulare Evangeliorum. Texte und untersuchungen zu seiner ältesten Geschichte.* Liturgiegeschichtliche Quellen und Forschungen, 28. Münster, 1935.

Oppenheim, P., O. S. B. *Institutiones Systematico-Historicae in Sacram Liturgiam.* IV. *De Libris Liturgicis deque iure ex eis manante.* Rome, 1940.

CHAPTER FOUR: Liturgical Places

Anson, P. *Churches: Their Plan and Furnishing.* Milwaukee, 1948.

Braun, J., S. J. *Der christliche Altar in seiner geschichtlichen Entwicklung.* Munich, 1924.

―――. *Die liturgische Gewandung im Occident und Ortent.* Freiburg, 1907.

―――. *Die liturgischen Paramente in Gegenwart und Vergangenheit.* Freiburg, 1924.

Fletcher, B. *A History of Architecture.* London, 1928.

Greene, T. *The Arts and the Art of Criticism.* Princeton, 1947.

Grisar, H. *History of Rome and the Popes in the Middle Ages.* 2 vols. St. Louis, 1912.

Grossi Gondi, F., S. J. *I Monumenti Cristiani.* Rome, 1923.

Henze, A.―Filthaut, T. *Contemporary Church Art.* New York, 1956.

Hertling, L.―Kirschbaum, E., S. J. *The Roman Catacombs and their Martyrs.* Milwaukee, 1956.

Kirsch, J. *Die römischen Titelkirchen im Altertum.* Paderborn, 1918.

Klauser, T. *Der Ursprung der bischoflichen Insignien und Ehrenrechte.* Krefeld, 1953.

O'Connell, J. B. *Church Building and Furnishing.* Notre Dame, Indiana, 1955.

Reinhold, H. A. *Speaking of Liturgical Architecture.* Notre Dame, Indiana, 1952.

Roulin, E. *Nos Eglises.* Paris, 1938.

―――. *Vestments and Vesture.* St. Louis, 1933.

Watkin, E. I. *Catholic Art and Culture.* New York, 1944.

Wölfflin, H. *Principles of Art History.* New York, 1932.

CHAPTER FIVE: Structural Elements of Liturgy

Bardy, G. *La Question des Langues dans l'Eglise ancienne.* Paris, 1948.

Fischer, Balt. *Die Psalmenfrömmigkeit der Märtyrerkirche.* Freiburg, 1949.

Guardini, R. *Sacred Signs.* St. Louis, 1956.

―――. *The Spirit of the Liturgy.* New York, 1954.

Hughes, A. *Early Medieval Music up to 1300.* Vol. II of The New Oxford History of Music. London, 1954.

Klauser, T. *Die Cathedra im Totenkult der heidnischen und christlichen Antike.* Liturgiegeschichtliche Quellen und Forschungen, 21. Münster, 1927.

―――. *The Western Liturgy and Its History. Some Reflections on Recent Studies.* Translated into English by F. L. Cross. London, 1952.

Korolevsky, C. *Living Languages in Catholic Worship.* Westminster, Maryland, 1957.

Mohrmann, C. *Liturgical Latin. Its Origins and Character.* Washington, 1957.

Ohm, T., O. S. B. *Die Gebetsgebärden der Volker und das Christentum.* Leiden, 1948.

Oppenheim, P., O. S. B. *Tractatus de Textibus Liturgicis.* Rome. 1945.

Quasten, J. *Musik und Gesang in den Kulten der heidnischen und christ-lichen Frühzeit.* Liturgiegeschichtliche Quellen und Forschungen, 25. Münster, 1930.

Reese, G. *Music in the Middle Ages.* New York, 1940.

Rush, A., C. Ss. R. *Death and Burial in Christian Antiquity.* Washington, 1941.

Schmidt, H., S. J. *Liturgie et Langue Vulgaire.* Rome, 1950.

Sunol, G., O. S. B. *Introduction à la paléographie musicale grégorienne.* Paris, 1935.

Wellesz, E. *Eastern Elements in Western Chant.* Boston, 1947.

CHAPTER SIX: The Mass

Botte, B., O. S. B. *Le Canon de la Messe Romaine.* Edition critique, Intro-duction et Notes. Collection Textes et Etudes Liturgiques, 2. Louvain, 1935.

—————, in collaboration with C. Mohrmann. *L'Ordinaire de la Messe.* Texte critique, Traduction et Etudes. Collection Etudes Liturgiques, 2. Louvain-Paris, 1953.

Bussard, P. *The Meaning of the Mass.* New York, 1942.

Casel, O., O. S. B. *Le Mémorial du Seigneur.* Paris, 1945.

Dix, G., O. S. B. *The Shape of the Liturgy.* Westminster, England, 1945.

Dumoutet, E. *Le Désir de voir l'hostie et les origines de la dévotion au Saint Sacrement.* Paris, 1926.

Ellard, G., S. J. *The Mass of the Future.* Milwaukee, 1948.

Fischer, Balt.—Arnold, F. X. *Die Messe in der Glaubensverkündigung.* Freiburg, 1953.

Guardini, R. *Meditations before Mass.* Westminster, Maryland, 1956.

Jungmann, J., S. J. *The Mass of the Roman Rite.* 2 vols. Translated by F. Brunner, C. Ss. R. New York, 1951, 1955.

—————. *Missarum Sollemnia.* 2 vols. 4th enlarged German edition. Frei-burg, 1958.

—————. *The Eucharistic Prayer. A study of the Canon Missae.* Chicago, 1956.

—————. *The Sacrifice of the Church.* Collegeville, 1955.

Kennedy, V., C. S. B. *The Saints of the Canon of the Mass.* Studi di Anti-chità Cristiana, XIV. Vatican City, 1938.

Masure, E. *The Christian Sacrifice.* London, 1944.

—————. *The Sacrifice of the Mystical Body.* London, 1954.

Nielen, J. *The Earliest Christian Liturgy.* St. Louis, 1941.

Oesterley, W. *Jewish Background of the Christian Liturgy.* Oxford, 1925.

Parsch, P. *The Liturgy of the Mass.* St. Louis, 1936.

Pascher, J. *Eucharistia. Gestalt und Vollzug.* Münster, 1953.

Righetti, M. *Manuale di Storia Liturgica.* III. *l'Eucarestia.* Milan, 1949.

Srawley, J. H. *The Early History of the Liturgy.* Cambridge, England, 1947.

Vonier, A., O. S. B. *Key to the Doctrine of the Eucharist.* Westminster, Maryland, 1946.

CHAPTER SEVEN: The Divine Office

Battifol, P. *History of the Roman Breviary.* London, 1898.

Baudot, J., O.S.B. *The Breviary. Its History and Contents.* St. Louis, 1929.
Baumstark, A. *Nocturna Laus. Typen frühchristlicher Vigilienfeier und ihr Fortleben vor allem im römischen und monastischen Ritus.* Liturgiegeschichtliche Quellen und Forschungen, 32. Münster, 1957.
Bäumer, S., O. S. B. *Histoire du Bréviaire.* 2 vols. Translated and revised by R. Biron, O. S. B. Paris, 1905.
Britt, M., O. S. B. *The Hymns of the Breviary and Missal.* New York, 1948.
Callewaert, C. *Liturgicae Institutiones.* II. *De Breviarii Romani Liturgia.* Bruges, 1931.
Hanssens, J., S. J. *Nature et Genèse de l'Office des Matines.* Analecta Gregoriana, LVII. Rome, 1952.
Hoornaert, R. *The Breviary and the Laity.* Collegeville, 1946.
Lauda Jerusalem Dominum. Special issue of *La Vie Spirituelle.* vol. 76. January, 1947.
Maison-Dieu, La. n. 21 (1950): *Le Trésor de l'Office Divin.;* n. 33 (1953): *Les psaumes, prière de l'Assemblée Chrétienne.*
Marmion, C., O. S. B. *Christ the Ideal of the Monk.* St. Louis, 1926.
Parsch, P. *The Breviary Explained.* St. Louis, 1952.
Pascher, J. *Das Stundengebet der römischen Kirche.* Munich, 1954.
Pourrat, P. *Christian Spirituality.* I. Westminster, Maryland, 1953.
Righetti, M. *Manuale di Storia Liturgica.* II. *Il Breviario.* Milan, 1946.

CHAPTER EIGHT: The Liturgical Year

Botte, B., O. S. B. *Les Origines de la Noël et de l'Epiphanie.* Louvain, 1932.
Bouyer, L. *The Paschal Mystery.* Chicago, 1950.
Casel, O., O. S. B. *Le Mystère du Culte dans le Christianisme.* Paris, 1946.
Daniélou, J., S. J. *The Bible and the Liturgy.* Notre Dame, Indiana, 1956.
Delehaye, H. *Sanctus. Essai sur le culte des saints dans l'antiquité.* Bruxelles, 1927.
————. *Les Origines du culte des martyrs.* Bruxelles, 1933.
Filthaut, T. *Die Kontroverse über die Mysterienlehre.* Warendorf im Westf., 1947. Translated into French: *La Théologie des Mystères. Exposé de la Controverse.* Paris, 1955.
Gaillard, J., O. S. B. *Holy Week and Easter.* Collegeville, 1954.
Guéranger, P., O. S. B. *The Liturgical Year.* 14 vols. New York, 1900-1910.
Kellner, H. *Heortology. A History of the Christian Festivals.* London, 1908.
Le Huitième Jour. Cahiers de la Vie Spirituelle. Paris, 1947.
Loehr, A., O. S. B. *The Year of our Lord.* New York, 1937.
————. *The Great Week.* Westminster, Maryland, 1958.
Maison-Dieu, La. n. 9 (1947): *Dimanche et Célébration Chrétienne;* n. 30 (1952): *L'Economie du Salut et le Cycle Liturgique;* n. 31 (1952): *Le Carême;* n. 37 (1954): *Les réformes de la Semaine Sainte et la pastorale liturgique;* n. 41 (1955): *La Semaine Sainte.*
Marmion, C., O. S. B. *Christ in His Mysteries.* St. Louis, 1939.
McGarry, W., S. J. *He Cometh.* New York, 1942.
Parsch, P. *The Church's Year of Grace.* 5 vols. Collegeville, 1953-1958.
Peus, F.—Kompmann, T. *Mysterium und Gestalt des Kirchenjahres.* Paderborn, 1952.

Righetti, M. *Manuale di Storia Liturgica.* II. *l'Anno Liturgico.* Milan, 1946.
Schuster, I., O. S. B. *The Sacramentary.* 5 vols. New York, 1924-1930.
Thurston, H., S. J. *Lent and Holy Week.* London, 1904.

CHAPTER NINE: The Sacraments and Sacramentals

Coppens, I. *L'imposition des Mains.* Paris, 1925.
De Ghellinck, J.–De Backer, E.–Poukens, J.–Lebacqz, G. *Pour l'Histoire du Mot Sacramentum.* Spicilegium Sacrum Lovaniense, III. Louvain, 1924.
De Puniet, P., O. S. B. *Le Pontifical Romain. Histoire et Commentaire.* 2 vols. Louvain, 1930.
Ellard, G., S. J. *Ordination Anointings in the Western Church before 1000 A. D.* Monographs of the Medieval Society of America, 8. Cambridge, Mass., 1933.
Franz, A. *Die kirchlichen Benediktionen im Mittelalter.* 2 vols. Freiburg, 1909.
Galtier, P., S. J. *De Poenitentia.* Paris, 1923.
————. *Aux Origines du sacrement de Pénitence.* Analecta Gregoriana, LIV. Rome, 1951.
Herbin, P. *Maladie et Mort du Chrétien.* Paris, 1955.
Kelly, B., C. S. Sp. *The Sacraments of Daily Life.* New York, 1943.
Louvel, F., O. P.–Putz, J., C. S. C. *Signs of Life.* Chicago, 1953.
Maison-Dieu, La. n. 6 (1946): *Le Baptême, Sacrement Pascal;* n. 15 (1948): *La Liturgie des Malades;* n. 32 (1952): *Le Baptême, entrée dans le Peuple de Dieu.*
Pascher, J. *Die Liturgie der Sakramente.* Münster, 1951.
————. *l'Evolution des Rites Sacramentels.* Paris, 1952.
Philipon, M., O. P. *The Sacraments in the Christian Life.* Westminster, Maryland, 1954.
Righetti, M. *Manuale di Storia Liturgica.* IV. *I Sacramenti – I Sacramentali.* Milan, 1953.
Villien, A. *The History and Liturgy of the Sacraments.* London, 1932.

PERIODICALS

Archiv für Liturgiewissenschaft (ALW), continuation of *Jahrbuch für Liturgiewissenschaft (JLW).* The former, Regensburg, 1950 ———; the latter, Münster, 1921-1950.
Ephemerides Liturgicae (EL). Rome, 1887 ———.
Liturgisches Jahrbuch (LJ). Münster, 1951 ———.
Maison-Dieu, La. Paris. 1945 ———.
Orate Fratres (OF). Collegeville, Minn., 1926-1952. Continued by *Worship.* Collegeville, 1952 ———.
Questions Liturgiques et Paroissiales (QLP). Louvain, 1911 ———.
Proceedings of the National (later called *North American) Liturgical Weeks.* Elsberry, Mo., 1940 ———.

INDEX